# WITTGENSTEIN AND JUSTICE

# WITTGENSTEIN
# AND JUSTICE

*On the Significance of Ludwig Wittgenstein*
*for Social and Political Thought*

## Hanna Fenichel Pitkin

*University of California Press*
Berkeley, Los Angeles, and London

University of California Press
Berkeley and Los Angeles, California
University of California Press, Ltd.
London, England
Copyright © 1972, by
The Regents of the University of California
First Paperback Edition, 1973

ISBN: 0-520-02329-3
Library of Congress Catalog Card Number: 76-138508
Printed in the United States of America

3 4 5 6 7 8 9 0

"Speech too, and windswept thought
   He has taught himself,
And the spirit that governs cities . . . "
                    —SOPHOCLES

# PREFACE

THIS IS both a very personal and a very impersonal book, and each of these peculiarities requires some accounting. The book is impersonal in the sense that it contains little that is original, and that it makes unusually heavy use of direct quotations. It is intended to introduce a body of literature—the later philosophy of Ludwig Wittgenstein and some related developments in contemporary philosophy—and to survey its potential significance for our thinking about political and social life. Two features of that literature necessitate the extensive use of quotations. First, this kind of philosophy relies centrally on examples, especially on examples of linguistic usage or of what we say under various circumstances. The discovery and elucidation of such examples—of examples that succeed in making the philosophical point—is enormously difficult. It is an art, not a technique, and it requires talent. Philosophers like Wittgenstein, J. L. Austin, Stanley Cavell, Paul Ziff, have that talent to remarkable degrees; so I have leaned again and again on the specific examples they adduce.

In addition, the literature being introduced here is difficult to summarize or restate or paraphrase because of certain characteristic obscurities of style, particularly in Wittgenstein himself. Not that Wittgenstein's language, his writing style, is obscure. He writes elegant, lucid German. And while there are some problems about its translation, they are not major obstacles (as is sometimes the case with Hegel or Heidegger). What is obscure and difficult is Wittgenstein's style of thought, his philosophical style. Erich Heller has said "there are philosophies which, however difficult they may be, are in principle easy to teach and to learn. Of course, not everyone can teach or learn philosophy—any more than higher mathematics; but the philosophies of certain philosophers have this in common with higher mathematics: they present the simple alternative of being either understood or not understood. It is, in the last analysis, impossible to *mis*understand them. This is true of Aristotle, or St. Thomas Aquinas, or Descartes, or Locke, or Kant. Such philosophies are like mountains: you climb to their tops or you give up; or like weights: you lift them or they are too heavy for you. In either case you will know what has happened and 'where you are.' But this is not so with the thought of Plato, or St. Augustine, or Pascal, or Kierkegaard, or Nietzsche. Their philosophies are like human faces on the features of which are inscribed, disquietingly, the destinies of souls; or like cities rich in history. 'Do you understand Kant?' is like asking 'Have you been to the summit of Mount Blanc?' The answer is *yes* or *no*. 'Do you understand Nietzsche?' is like asking 'Do you know Rome?' The answer is simple only if you have never been there."[1]

Wittgenstein is, as Heller says, a philosopher of the second kind. He does not develop a systematic doctrine, or write discursive essays. His books are not divided into chapters, but into numbered paragraphs. Sometimes a paragraph contains a complete thought: an epigram, an aphorism, a riddle, an example. Sometimes an argument is developed through several successive numbered sections. Often one has a general sense of continuing themes, but of six or eight themes being developed simultaneously: appearing, disappearing, reappearing unexpectedly. The effect is that of an elaborate mosaic, or perhaps of an intricately woven tapestry. Thus, what Wittgenstein says is bound very intimately to the way in which he says it, as is often true of poetry. To some extent, Cavell's philosophizing presents similar difficulties. So, where I found doctrine uniquely embodied in the original text I have quoted shamelessly. I suppose it is unusual, also, to make as extensive use as this book does of an unpublished doctoral dissertation, not the author's own. About that I can say only that I use Cavell's dissertation because it is indispensable; and that many of us think it should have been published, and honored, long ago.

But this is also a very personal book, because in a sense it is a record of my own intellectual development, the topics that concerned me. It was written because of the significance that Wittgenstein had for my thinking, in an attempt to make that significance available to others. While writing, I often thought of it in images like this one: It was as if I had been for some years on an intellectual journey through territory which, though it might be familiar to some, was totally strange to me. After the beginning, I was accompanied by no guide, but followed trails suggested by certain books. Those trails led me further and further from the familiar ground where my colleagues did their work, and I felt increasingly isolated intellectually. So I hastily sketched an account of my travels, sealed it into a bottle, and threw it into the nearby seas, in hopes that it would be found by someone in the area from which I had come, that he would become intrigued and follow me to the place where I now am.

I first became acquainted with language philosophy while I was a grad-

[1] Erich Heller, *The Artist's Journey into the Interior* (New York: Random House, 1959), pp. 202–203.

uate student in Berkeley, through Stanley Cavell. What I encountered at that time was primarily Oxford ordinary-language analysis, particularly Austin's. Though my own field was political science and not philosophy, I decided to write my doctoral dissertation using language-philosophical techniques like Austin's to clarify a troublesome concept in political theory, the concept of representation. Only after that dissertation was essentially completed did I encounter, in rapid succession, Paul Ziff's book, Wittgenstein's later writings, and the manuscript of Cavell's dissertation.[2] Their impact on me was immediate and intense. I felt that for the first time I understood the real significance of the painstaking, grinding work I had been doing on representation. For the first time I became genuinely interested and involved in my work. And all that I had learned about politics, society, and human thought seemed reorganized, enriched, by my new understanding. It was, in short, a transforming experience. No doubt I had been prepared for it by my earlier studies in philosophy, my conversations with Cavell, and my struggles with my own dissertation.

Full of enthusiasm and continuing to read avidly, I began to try to talk about these new discoveries with my colleagues, and to teach courses about them. The results were severely disappointing. People were unfamiliar with the literature that interested me, Wittgenstein's later writings having been published only shortly before and Cavell's manuscript remaining unpublished. As I continued to explore, the gap between me and those I wanted to address widened. When I tried to suggest readings, it quickly became clear how extensive and inaccessible the literature was. Moreover, to political scientists the literature seemed remote in content as well, and irrelevant to their own interests; what few studies did purport to apply the new philosophy directly to politics struck me as almost perverse misrepresentations. Even my teaching was unsatisfactory. Some students left quickly, bored; others were interested, even enthusiastic, but often emerged with ideas I found embarrassingly bizarre. And, worst of all, I was unable to articulate my own ideas. At that point, I began what was to be a short article about ordinary-language philosophy and politics; it became this book.

The book, then, is liable to all the obvious dangers of such an account. In the areas of philosophy with which it deals, I am largely an autodidact and an amateur; no doubt I have made many blunders as a result, failed to see conections to existing work and to give credit where credit seems due. Moreover, there is danger that what was a transforming intellectual experience for me, discovered gradually at just the right time, may be of only minor interest when served up in predigested form for others. Indeed, one explanation of my colleagues' and students' failure to find in Wittgen-

<hr />

[2] Paul Ziff, *Semantic Analysis* (Ithaca: Cornell University Press, 1960); Ludwig Wittgenstein, *Philosophical Investigations*, tr. by G. E. M. Anscombe, third edition (New York: Macmillan, 1968); Stanley Louis Cavell, "The Claim to Rationality" (unpublished dissertation, Harvard University).

stein what I found there might be that it was not there to be found, that mine was an idiosyncratic and disproportionate response to an objectively uninteresting philosophical doctrine.

But these are relatively superficial dangers, involving as they do at most my personal embarrassment upon the publication of this book. There is a deeper and, to me, more serious danger inherent in the nature of the material to be treated here. For the peculiar difficulties of Wittgenstein's own style, to which I have already alluded, raise the gravest doubts about whether such a book could possibly succeed, whether it is not bound to betray its own cause. Briefly, Wittgenstein's style is obscure, so I have attempted to make clear and lucid and accessible what I think he was trying to say. Though presumptuous, that is a worthy undertaking if Wittgenstein's obscurity betokens a failure on his part, an inability to express his teachings more clearly. But it becomes a disaster if Wittgenstein's obscurity is intentional, in some way necessary to his teaching, if what he has to say can be said and learned only by indirection. Then any attempt to state the message clearly and systematically would be bound to betray it; and any such attempt to introduce readers to Wittgenstein would become a mechanism preventing their genuine encounter with his ideas.

Wittgenstein himself comments on the peculiarities of his style in the introduction to his most important work, suggesting that it was both a failure and an essential element of his way of philosophizing. At first, he says, he had intended to organize his thoughts into a book proceeding "from one subject to another in a natural order and without breaks."[3] But "after several unsuccessful attempts," he realized that he would be unable to do so. And he apologizes: "I should have liked to produce a good book. This has not come about, but the time is past in which I could improve it."[4] But Wittgenstein also says that his disjointed and obscure philosophical style results from the very nature of philosophy as he understands it; that it is "of course, connected with the very nature" of his "investigation."[5]

Before Heller, Wittgenstein himself used the analogy of getting to know a city, as a way to illuminate his work in philosophy. He chose not Rome, but London, a city that he in fact had to learn to know slowly. Two of his students tell us that he said, "In teaching you philosophy I'm like a guide showing you how to find your way around London. I have to take you through the city from north to south, from east to west, from Euston to the Embankment and from Piccadilly to the Marble Arch. After I have taken you many journeys through the city, in all sorts of directions, we shall have pased through any given street a number of times—each time

---

[3] Wittgenstein, *Philosophical Investigations*, p. ix.
[4] *Ibid.*, p. x.
[5] *Ibid.*, p. ix.

traversing the street as part of a different journey. At the end of this you will know London; you will be able to find your way about like a born Londoner."[6] Significantly, the aim is that the student should become capable of moving about on his own, a notion very different from mastering a doctrine.

For Wittgenstein, philosophy was a highly personal thing—both his own philosophizing and philosophy as a traditional enterprise. Heller suggests that this is why understanding his philosophy "on its own level is as much a matter of imagination and character as it is one of 'thinking.' "[7] Wittgenstein's own philosophizing was, as Heller says, "a consuming passion; and not just 'a' passion, but the only possible form of his existence: the thought of losing his gift for philosophy made him feel suicidal. He could not but have contempt for philosophers who 'did' philosophy and, having done it, thought of other things," who did philosophy "for a living" and, to score debater's points, argued various positions they did not really hold.[8] Above all else, Wittgenstein cherished what the existentialists came to call "authenticity"—the willingness and ability to say what you really mean and to live by what you say.

But in a more general sense, also, Wittgenstein saw all philosophizing as a highly personal activity, as an expression of self, even as symptomatic. The philosopher is a man in the grip of an idea, an obsession; he is his own prisoner "held captive" by "a picture" that haunts him. Wittgenstein knew this from his own experience, and believed that he had found a philosophical method to provide for the prisoners' liberation—his own and that of other philosophers. Cavell has suggested parallels between Wittgenstein and Freud, that for Wittgenstein the primary goal of philosophy is self-knowledge; and that he writes indirectly and obscurely because, like Freudian therapy, he "wishes to prevent understanding which is unaccompanied by inner change." Both Freud and Wittgenstein "are intent upon unmasking the defeat of our real need in the face of self-impositions which we have not assessed, . . . or fantasies ('pictures') which we cannot escape."[9]

Such therapy, always personal, always must address itself to the particular individual self and to a particular philosophical position. Thus, Wittgenstein's philosophy was always, in an important way, what philosophy had been for Socrates: a dialogue between guide and seeker, between teacher and student, between two philosophizing individuals. Such

[6] D. A. T. Gasking and A. C. Jackson, "Wittgenstein as a Teacher," in *Ludwig Wittgenstein: The Man and His Philosophy*, ed. by K. T. Fann (New York: Dell, 1967), p. 51.

[7] Heller, *The Artist's Journey into the Interior*, p. 203.

[8] *Ibid.*, p. 204.

[9] Stanley Cavell, *Must We Mean What We Say?* (New York: Charles Scribner's Sons, 1969), p. 72. Wittgenstein himself was aware of the parallels, but also stressed a difference: "They are different techniques." See Norman Malcolm, *Ludwig Wittgenstein, A Memoir* (London: Oxford University Press, 1962), p. 57.

philosophy is not easily put into discursive form and published in books.[10] For what is appropriate to say to one man, what might lead him to self-knowledge or philosophical insight, is trivial or useless for another. One can easily apply to Wittgenstein what Philip Rieff says of Freud: that he "has no message, in the old sense of something positive and constructive to offer," and yet "his doctrine contains intellectual and moral implications that, when drawn, constitute a message. . . . His is a very intimate wisdom, tailored to this patient and that occasion."[11] That, too, can help to explain Wittgenstein's style. For if things are said only indirectly, if the reader is allowed—or forced—to find for himself the truths relevant to him, then a book of philosophy may after all be able to accomplish something. Wittgenstein says, "in philosophizing we may not *terminate* a disease of thought. It must run its natural course, and *slow* cure is all important."[12] Again one might draw the parallel to interpretation in psychoanalysis. Timing is essential, and questions or indirect statements can often penetrate where direct assertions cannot, allowing the reader or patient to assimilate as much of an insight as he is ready for. "In philosophy it is always good to put a *question* instead of an answer to a question. For an answer to a philosophical question may easily be unfair; disposing of it by means of another question is not."[13]

The putting of questions instead of answers, the use of indirection and suggestion, also have something to do with the fact that philosophical disease and philosophical cure must both be expressed in the same medium. If, as Wittgenstein maintains, philosophical problems somehow grow out of the vagaries of human language, it is most unfortunate that we have no other medium but language available for solving them, or explaining their nature, or suggesting new methods for dealing with them. "The difficulty in philosophy," as Wittgenstein points out, "is to say no more than we know."[14] We are constantly making new messes in the process of trying to clean up the old. With the very words we use to clarify or resolve one philosophical problem, we seem inadvertently but inevitably to create others. Thus, "in the end when one is doing philosophy one gets to the point where one would like just to emit an inarticulate

---

[10] No doubt that is why the Platonic dialogues sometimes give us pictures of Socrates that seem so inconsistent. But Plato himself was aware of the problem; see his "Seventh Letter."

[11] Philip Rieff, *Freud, The Mind of the Moralist* (New York: Viking Press, 1959), p. x. Compare Stanley Cavell, "Existentialism and Analytic Philosophy," *Daedalus*; 93 (Summer 1964), 970, 972.

[12] Ludwig Wittgenstein, *Zettel*, tr. by G. E. M. Anscombe, ed. by G. E. M. Anscombe and G. H. von Wright (Berkeley and Los Angeles: University of California Press, 1967), par. 382.

[13] Ludwig Wittgenstein, *Remarks on the Foundations of Mathematics*, tr. by G. E. M. Anscombe, ed. by G. H. von Wright, R. Rhees, and G. E. M. Anscombe (Oxford: Basil Blackwell, 1964), p. 68.

[14] Ludwig Wittgenstein, *Preliminary Studies for the "Philosophical Investigations," Generally Known as The Blue and Brown Books* (New York and Evanston: Harper & Row, 1964), p. 45.

sound."[15] Wittgenstein's style is to some extent an elegant compromise with that desire.

Consequently, there is a very real danger that, in trying to make his ideas accessible, lucid, and systematic, I may make their real content and significance inaccessible. In particular, in our impatient and technical age, there is danger of trivializing ordinary-language philosophy into just one more technique. Since method often dictates to content, as Cavell has said, it may well happen that "an intellectual commitment to analytic philosophy trains concern away from the wider, traditional problems of human culture which may have brought one to philosophy in the first place."[16] That this has already happened widely in contemporary philosophy is no secret to anyone who reads the professional journals. Yet I find that Wittgensteinian philosophy need not be trivialized or trivializing; it can do full honor to both the problems of traditional philosophy and our own. Moreover, this book is not itself a work of philosophy, but explores the implications of some philosophical themes for our understanding of politics and society. Perhaps those implications, at least, can be examined systematically without being distorted in the process. In any case, the book is intended only as an introduction. It is not a full account of Wittgenstein's philosophy or ordinary-language philosophy, nor are any of the suggested applications fully worked out. The reader is urged to study Wittgenstein for himself, and make his own applications.

The book proceeds gradually from explication to application. After an introduction, it sets forth certain basic themes in Wittgenstein's philosophy, in Chapters II, III, and IV, but also VI. This broadens into a consideration of some of the general implications of these themes, in Chapters V to VII; then the book is directed more specifically at various continuing concerns of social science and political theory, in Chapters VIII to XIV.

My intellectual debt to Stanley Cavell has already been mentioned and should be evident throughout the book; I am grateful to him in addition for having read the manuscript and given me more useful suggestions in an afternoon than I had dreamed possible. I am grateful also to my friends and former colleagues, John H. Schaar and Sheldon S. Wolin, for reading and commenting on the manuscript; but even more, for having created an enclave in Berkeley where serious work in political theory could be done with pleasure. And I am deeply grateful to the students in my 1969 Wittgenstein seminar, particularly to Harold Sarf and Jon Schiller, whose patient interest and unfailing critical sense forced me, again and again, closer to what I really meant to say.

[15] Wittgenstein, *Philosophical Investigations*, par. 261.
[16] Cavell, *Must We Mean What We Say?* p. 74. Wittgenstein himself anticipated that "The seed I am most likely to sow is a certain jargon." See K. T. Fann, *Wittgenstein's Conception of Philosophy* (Berkeley and Los Angeles: University of California Press, 1969), p. 111.

The writing of this book has had much financial assistance. I was given a free summer to begin it by a Faculty Research Grant from the University of Wisconsin, a free year to write it by a fellowship from the American Council of Learned Societies, and assistance in the final tidying up from the Committee on Research of the University of California at Berkeley.

For all of this generous help, I am most grateful.

# CONTENTS

# I

## Introduction

IT IS BY no means obvious that someone interested in politics and society needs to concern himself with philosophy; nor that, in particular, he has anything to learn from an obscure, misanthropic, enigmatic philosopher like Ludwig Wittgenstein, who never wrote about such topics at all. Wittgenstein's interests were philosophy itself, language, and the relationship between the two. Yet his investigations can yield insights of the most fundamental significance for social science or political theory. In a way, there is no shortcut to these insights or their significance; the rest of this book is an attempt to make them evident. Yet something must be said at the outset to hint at where we are going, if only to suggest why the effort is worth-while.

What Wittgenstein has to offer a student of human collective life is clearly not any kind of new data. No more than any other philosopher does he adduce information of which we had previously been ignorant. Nor does he, as some philosophers have, claim to develop any new theory for interpreting familiar facts. What he has to offer is something like a new perspective, a new way of seeing what has always been visible, what has gone unnoticed precisely because of its familiarity. Wittgenstein says that he provides "remarks on the natural history of human beings," but not on the bizarre customs of strange tribes. Rather, he makes observations about *us*, "observations which no one has doubted, but which have escaped remark only because they are always before our eyes."[1] Sometimes it is not easy to see the obvious; sometimes we have to learn to see, and the learning can be a slow and difficult process. It is almost a matter of forming new habits of thought, and at one point Wittgenstein himself speaks of his contribution as "a new style of thinking."[2] He also asks

---

[1] Ludwig Wittgenstein, *Philosophical Investigations*, tr. by G. E. M. Anscombe, third edition (New York: Macmillan, 1968), par. 415; compare p. 56.

[2] Ludwig Wittgenstein, *Lectures and Conversations on Aesthetics, Psychology and Religious Belief*, ed. by Cyril Barrett (Berkeley and Los Angeles: University of California Press, 1967), p. 28.

whether his ideas constitute a *Weltanschauung*.[3] Characteristically, Wittgenstein only poses the question and does not answer. But Cavell suggests that the answer can be neither flatly affirmative nor flatly negative: not affirmative, "because it is not a *special*, or competing way of looking at things." Yet not negative, because if it succeeds, "the world will seem—be—different."[4]

The key to the elusive Wittgensteinian perspective is language: the fact of human language and how it operates; new ways of studying it; a new conception of its significance for philosophy, and by extension for any intellectual enterprise; and ultimately an awareness of our language as a new approach to what philosophy has always undertaken—questioning, examining, and coming to terms with our own assumptions and commitments.

At the broadest and most general level, Wittgenstein simply calls attention to the centrality and significance of language in human life, thought, activity. In this regard, he is far from unique, but simply part of a very wide contemporary confluence of interests. Of course, philosophers and social theorists have always had an interest in human speech and conceptualization. But concern with these topics has surely increased sharply in our own time, and there seems to be a widespread sense that the study of language may reveal solutions to outstanding problems in the most diverse fields. We have seen not merely the growth of an autonomous science of linguistics, and of communications and information theory and cybernetics; but also a new concern with language in fields ranging from philosophy, semantics, and literature, through anthropology, psychology, and history. Even rigorously behavioral studies of man have increasingly had recourse to symbolic systems, if only as intervening variables between stimulus and response. To some extent the new interest has furthered the specialization and fragmentation of fields of study. Yet an increasing number of writers appear to regard language as holding possibilities for a new synthesis in the study of man, for once again understanding man as an integral whole.[5] In short, Wittgenstein may be seen as part of a very broad modern tendency to seek, in the study of language, progress on issues of the greatest significance.[6]

"We—mankind—are a conversation," says Martin Heidegger explicat-

---

[3] Wittgenstein, *Philosophical Investigations*, par. 122.

[4] Stanley Cavell, *Must We Mean What We Say?* (New York: Charles Scribner's Sons, 1969), p. 86.

[5] See particularly the works of Maurice Merleau-Ponty; but also Georges Gusdorf, *Speaking*, tr. with an introduction by Paul T. Brockelman (Evanston: Northwestern University Press, 1965); Paul Henle, ed., *Language, Thought and Culture* (Ann Arbor: University of Michigan Press, 1965); Noam Chomsky, *Language and Mind* (New York: Harcourt, Brace & World, 1968), and *Cartesian Linguistics* (New York and London: Harper & Row, 1966); and Susanne Öhman, *Wortinhalt und Weltbild* (Stockholm: Kungl. Boktryckeriet P. A. Norstedt & Söner, 1951).

[6] Öhman, *Wortinhalt und Weltbild* p. 9.

ing his favorite poet, "The being of man is found in language."[7] That may well strike us as an extravagant claim, one more attempt to define man and confine his nature. After all, from a social-scientific perspective, language is just another part of human behavior, governed by causal laws and susceptible of objective study. And so it is. Yet it is also something more, something unique and profoundly fundamental to human life. Only men have language, though of course many species communicate in various ways.[8] And language is the carrier of human culture, by which mankind continually produces and contemplates itself, a reflection of our species-being. Language, one might say, is the medium of mind, the element in which our minds dwell as our bodies dwell on earth and in air. In mastering a language, we take on a culture; our native language becomes a part of ourselves, of the very structure of the self. Thus language has dual aspects: it is our means for self-expression, for articulating our unique individuality; yet at the same time it is what we have in common with other members of our community, what makes us like them and binds us to them. As a consequence, language lies at the heart of the problem of membership—in a group, in a culture, in a society, in a polity —central to almost every theoretical issue in social and political study. Moreover, language changes in systematic, predictable ways, yet obviously these changes result from the free choices of many individuals. Thus it can illuminate the nature of innovation and continuity in human affairs. Wittgenstein offers us new ways of conceptualizing and investigating such topics.

In particular, he is interested in the way a person is initiated into his native language and culture. For how we learn language tells us much about what language is, what concepts are, how our minds operate. Through language learning, Wittgenstein investigates freedom in a context of rules, and what it means to say that language is an open system. As a result, also, he is continually occupied with the topics of education, the nature of authority, creativity, individual growth.

Wittgenstein's stress, as we shall see, is on language as speech, as something human beings do, as a form of action. This view allows him to challenge an older and almost ubiquitous view of language, which stresses reference, correspondence, representation. In the older view, the meaning of a word is what in the world it stands for, and the function of language is primarily to express assertions about the world. Wittgenstein shows that this view of meaning cannot be correct, and that this view of language is correspondingly inadequate and misleading. The significance of this shift

---

[7] Martin Heidegger, *Existence and Being* (Chicago: Henry Regnery, 1968), p. 277.

[8] Animal communication is itself a field in which much fascinating progress has been made in recent years. See for instance Karl von Frisch's work on bees, John C. Lilly's work with dolphins, Konrad Lorenz's *King Solomon's Ring*, and recent successes by R. A. and B. T. Gardner in teaching deaf-and-dumb language to a chimpanzee.

is impossible to convey in summary form, but we can list a few of the topics on which it bears.

If language is seen as human activity rather than as a collection of labels for categories of phenomena, then we will no longer be surprised to find systematic inconsistencies in it—not as a fault or liability, but as essential to its functions. And that will provide new ways of working on problems that arise in any abstract, conceptual thinking, problems that have been central in traditional philosophy but that occur as often in political or social theory and other fields. Further, if language is seen as human activity, that activity may be carried on in quite different ways, depending on what the talking human beings are up to. We can investigate various kinds of discourse, and how language is used in them. And that, in turn, tells us things about what is talked about in those regions of language. Thus, for example, Wittgenstein allows us to investigate the nature of political discourse, and of the political.

Further, if words need not be used for referring and their meaning is not their reference, and if concepts may be internally inconsistent, then many of our traditional and common-sense assumptions about the relationship between language and reality are called into question. That, too, is a very old philosophical issue, whether in the form of how mind is related to matter or in the form of how theory is related to action. Yet the problem is also central in contemporary thought, and has received new impetus from developments in linguistics, anthropology, and experimental psychology. While Wittgenstein cannot be said to present a doctrine about the relationship between language or thought and the world, there is a remarkable convergence between his investigations and the theories of ethnologists like Edward Sapir and Benjamin Lee Whorf. And he gives us new ways of investigating the issues with respect to our own language, where they matter most. In particular, this topic is of central concern for social science, where language and conceptualization themselves enter into, form a part of, the subject matter to be studied, shape and direct the human activities to be examined. Thus Wittgenstein is of central importance for recent controversies over the nature and feasibility of the scientific study of man, and for recent attempts to counterpose behavioral and phenomenological ways of studying psychology, sociology, politics.

CONCEPTUAL PROBLEMS AND ORDINARY-LANGUAGE PHILOSOPHY

But language is not merely a basic feature of human nature to be investigated, not merely part of the subject matter the social scientist studies. To say that it is the medium in which mind operates is to suggest that language is as much a feature of the investigator as of the investigated, as much a tool as a datum of social science, as much the substance as the problem of political theory. In this respect, too, the work of Wittgenstein and certain other contemporary philosophers has important implications for social and political thought. Here what they have to offer is new insights about the nature and the pitfalls of what we do when we think conceptually, and new ways of coping with some of those pitfalls. It is in this area that Wittgenstein's work is both most accessible and most easily misunderstood. For it is here that his contribution may easily look like a matter of methodology, of technique; so we must take care to forestall such a misunderstanding.

The broad contemporary fascination with language has had particular impact in philosophy itself, so that today almost all Anglo-Saxon philosophers are "language philosophers" of some kind.[9] But one can distinguish two major conflicting approaches within this general orientation. The one approach regards the way that people ordinarily talk as careless, deficient, and misleading. It assigns to philosophy the task of correcting or of wholly replacing ordinary speech, as science corrects or replaces our common-sense understanding of the world. This approach either seeks to construct ideal languages, free of the logical imperfections of everyday talk, or else it seeks to translate ordinary, ambiguous utterances into clear, unambiguous "logical form," separating what is meaningful in them from what is nonsense. This was, on the whole, the orientation of Wittgenstein's early work, the *Tractatus Logico-Philosophicus*.

The other approach to the philosophical importance of language takes the way that people ordinarily talk to be "in order as it is." This approach maintains that ordinary speech does not stand in need of general correction, translation, or replacement. (Of course, these philosophers acknowledge that we sometimes speak ambiguously, carelessly, mistakenly.) This orientation takes our ordinary ways of speaking as themselves appropriate data for philosophical study, as needing to be examined rather than superseded. This is the approach of Wittgenstein's later writings, in conscious rejection of the *Tractatus*. But there are also significant subdivisions within this approach. Besides Wittgenstein himself, a number of his followers pursue it in various directions—philosophers like G. E. M. Anscombe, Norman Malcolm, John Wisdom, and Stanley Cavell. While Wittgenstein was at Cambridge and afterward, a quite separate and parallel philosophical movement developed at Oxford. It is often spoken of as "ordinary-language philosophy," and probably its most famous practitioners are J. L. Austin and Gilbert Ryle. In addition, a branch of this general approach has been developing in the United States under the impetus of scientific linguistics; this branch, stressing the scientific and systematic study of natural language, includes such figures as Noam Chomsky, Paul Ziff, Jerry A. Fodor, and Jerrold J. Katz.

Although there are important differences among the three branches of the approach accepting ordinary speech as it is, and although the

[9] See for example, V. C. Chappell, ed., *Ordinary Language* (Englewood Cliffs: Prentice-Hall, 1964), p. 1; Robert R. Ammerman, ed., *Classics of Analytic Philosophy* (New York: McGraw-Hill, 1965), p. 12.

members are often critical of each other's work, I have found many of their ideas mutually complementary, and have borrowed from them all. What they share is an awareness of a certain, characteristic kind of problem or question or puzzlement that has been central to traditional philosophical disputes, and that arises from language and is resolvable through the study of ordinary language. Most of these writers, including Wittgenstein, call this kind of problem simply "philosophy"; call the man who is preoccupied with it, "the philosopher" or "the traditional philosopher," and call the activity of investigating it, "philosophizing." But for two reasons I shall call these problems "conceptual" instead. First, Wittgenstein's attitude to traditional philosophy is complex and highly problematic, and should be investigated rather than assumed. Following his own way of speaking here is likely to prejudice our eventual examination of the topic, because so much of what he says sounds like an unwarranted criticism of "philosophy." The second reason for calling such problems "conceptual" is to stress that they are not confined to philosophy proper nor to professional philosophers. They occur almost as readily in political theory, in social-scientific theory, or indeed in any form of abstract, general, conceptual thought.

In a preliminary way, conceptual problems or puzzlements may be characterized by two recurrent features they display. They arise in the course of abstract contemplation, not in the course of activity or as the result of some new factual discovery, and they have a peculiar, paradoxical quality, often signaled by expressions like "really" or "strictly speaking." Someone in the grip of conceptual puzzlement of this kind may say, for instance, "Really, strictly speaking, you can never know what someone else is feeling." Or, "Really, strictly speaking, every action is self-interested." Or, "Really, strictly speaking, there is no such thing as causation, but only statistical correlation of events." Such "insights" are always in apparent conflict with "what we all ordinarily take for granted"; they present themselves as discoveries. Yet they are also somehow parasitic on and unable to divorce themselves from our ordinary ways of talking about knowledge and feelings, or self-interest and actions, or causation. Some philosophers are aware of the paradoxicality in such conceptual insights and acknowledge it. With others, it becomes manifest only in the history of philosophy, as the conceptual problem gives rise to an endless dispute that is never resolved. Such disputes can go on over generations of theorists or philosophers; new writers choose a position on one or the other side, but the two sides talk past each other and their arguments do not seem to meet. One may feel that somehow they are both right, though the logical incompatibility of the two sides is quite evident.

Within philosophy, the distinctive contribution of ordinary-language philosophers is generally taken to be their provision of new methods for dealing with such problems. They argue that the central problems of traditional philosophy have originated in ordinary language, and that an investigation of language will at least illuminate them, if not resolve or eliminate them altogether. These men are perfectly aware that philosophers have not traditionally thought of their concerns as linguistic; such problems present themselves as ontological. Traditional investigations have been about the nature of, say, freedom, not about the word "freedom." But ordinary-language philosophers and Wittgenstein nevertheless insist that these investigations have also been about the word at issue, and can be treated at the linguistic level. They recommend that we back off from the ontological question and concentrate on the semantic one instead; that we ask, not "What is freedom?" but "What does 'freedom' mean?" or, better still, "How do we use the word, 'freedom'?" And they teach the techniques of that sort of inquiry.

Both the validity of such inquiry and the kind of relevance it has for traditional problems of philosophy are frequently misunderstood, and some of the most severe criticism leveled against ordinary-language philosophy is based on misunderstandings of this kind. Too often even ordinary-language philosophers themselves are not as clear as one might wish about what they are doing. One fundamental kind of criticism comes from the side of scientific linguistics and challenges the ordinary-language philosopher's methods of investigation.[10] If he is to show that a traditional philosopher, or any thinker, has deviated from our ordinary ways of talking, has misused language or distorted meanings, then he must be prepared to justify his own account of meanings. Yet his study of language is not scientific, and he seems to make no special effort to observe the speech of ordinary men empirically. Indeed, his method does not seem to differ much from that of traditional philosophers, whose conclusions he rejects.

A second kind of criticism is more frequently leveled from the side of traditional philosophy.[11] These critics ask: Even assuming that we can get reliable knowledge of ordinary speech, why should it be binding on the philosopher? The ordinary man, after all, is of only mediocre intelligence and likely to be thoroughly conventional. Why should his habits be taken as normative, used as mandatory standard for the man of genius? Respect for ordinary men may be laudably democratic, but surely in intellectual matters we should foster the extraordinary, the creative, the unique. It seems perverse to attempt to limit a Plato or a Kant to the common sense of shopkeepers and farmers. Moreover, it seems profoundly

[10] For example, Paul Ziff, *Semantic Analysis* (Ithaca: Cornell University Press, 1960); Jerry A. Fodor and Jerrold J. Katz, "The Availability of What We Say," *Philosophical Review*, LXXII (January 1963), 57–71, and *The Structure of Language* (Englewood Cliffs: Prentice-Hall, 1964); Benson Mates, "On the Verification of Statements About Ordinary Language," in Chappell, ed., *Ordinary Language*.

[11] For example, Mates, *op. cit.*; Ernest Gellner, *Words and Things* (London: Victor Gollancz, 1959); Herbert Marcuse, *One-Dimensional Man* (Boston: Beacon Press, 1968), especially Chapter 7; and Michael Polanyi, *Personal Knowledge* (New York and Evanston: Harper & Row, 1964), pp. 113–116.

conservative in intent, a charge that takes on special importance if ordinary-language philosophy is to be applied in political or social thought. And, indeed, there are passages in the writings of some ordinary-language philosophers that sound almost Burkean in their glorification of "the distinctions men have found it worth drawing, and the connexions they have found worth making, in the lifetimes of many generations," distinctions and connections which "have stood up to the long test of survival of the fittest."[12] Further, the critics argue, the whole ordinary-language orientation tends to trivialize and demean philosophy. For it seems to reduce the great philosophical inquiries and systems of the past to a series of mistakes, and mistakes about mere words at that. And philosophers have always been concerned not with mere words, but with the most profound realities: the true nature of man, of the world, of God. Are we really to reduce the role of philosophy to the correction of linguistic errors? Then philosophy would indeed seem to become, as Bertrand Russell once charged, "at best, a slight help to lexicographers, and at worst an idle, tea-table amusement."[13]

Though these criticisms are not without foundation, they do fundamentally misconceive ordinary-language philosophy and Wittgenstein. In seeing how this is so, let us begin with the criticisms, raised from the side of linguistics, about the ordinary-language philosopher's methods, his evidence for the claims he makes about what we ordinarily say. He proceeds, after all, much as traditional philosophers did: he thinks. He contemplates, perhaps reads some books, perhaps talks to a few other thinkers, and then makes a "discovery." He does not conduct controlled experiments, or anthropological field studies, or sample surveys of public opinion. He offers no statistics, and his work has none of the trappings of science.

The ordinary-language philosopher may respond that he does not need to do scientific research, because we all already have the requisite information, simply by being native speakers of our own language. But that knowledge is largely implicit and inarticulate; and when the traditional philosopher tries, in the course of his investigations, to make it articulate, he gets it wrong, partly because he is not aware that his questions are about language. Wittgenstein and the ordinary-language philosophers stress the role of inarticulate, implicit knowledge in mastering a language, that we all know how to use our language, but have difficulty explicating the rules according to which we do so, Wittgenstein says: "Compare *knowing* and *saying*: how many feet high Mont Blanc is—how the word 'game' is used—how a clarinet sounds. If you are surprised that one can

[12] J. L. Austin, *Philosophical Papers* (Oxford: Clarendon Press, 1961), p. 130; but compare pp. 133, 137, where we are told that ordinary language can be improved upon after all.

[13] Bertrand Russell, *My Philosophical Development*, quoted in Erich Heller, *The Artist's Journey into the Interior* (New York: Random House, 1959), p. 210.

know something and not be able to say it, you are perhaps thinking of a case like the first. Certainly not of one like the third."[14] And Ryle distinguishes between "knowing that" something is so, and "knowing how" to do something, the latter often being quite inarticulate.[15]

No doubt the ordinary-language philosopher has the advantage of being aware that it is language he wants to examine. But that does not seem sufficient to establish his claim to tell us what we ordinarily say. We should like to understand the nature of evidence and proof here. But for that we must look more closely at the way in which an ordinary-language philosopher actually proceeds. Austin says that he collects terms related to the one that he is studying, and he suggests starting with the dictionary. "Quite a concise one will do, but the use must be *thorough*. Two methods suggest themselves, both a little tedious but repaying. One is to read the book through, listing all the words that seem relevant; this does not take as long as many suppose. The other is to start with a widish selection of obviously relevant terms, and to consult the dictionary under each: it will be found that, in the explanations of the various meanings of each, a surprising number of the terms occur, which are germane, though of course not often synonymous. We then look up *these*, bringing in more for our bag from the 'definitions' given in each case; and when we have continued for a little, it will generally be found that the family circle begins to close, until ultimately it is complete and we come only upon repetitions."[16]

Austin is not, apparently, suggesting that we consult the dictionary for definitions of the term we are studying; for the sort of problems at issue here, dictionary definitions are no help. The ordinary-language philosopher is interested in the borderlines of concepts, in fine distinctions in meaning, in the minutiae of our language. For this purpose, dictionary definitions are too gross; indeed, a dictionary will define a word in terms of its near synonyms, from which an ordinary-language philosopher wants to distinguish it. For example, the dictionary will define (one sense of) "authority" as "The power to influence action, opinion or belief." But the ordinary-language philosopher will be concerned with the way "authority" differs from "power" or "influence."

While Austin explicitly mentions synonyms, he is equally interested in antonyms, and in other words in the same family as the one he is studying. A concept like "nature," for instance, has few synonyms, but much can be learned from the differing ways in which it contrasts with "unnatural," "artificial," "conventional," "civilized," "improved," "perverted," and

[14] Wittgenstein, *Philosophical Investigations*, par. 78.

[15] Gilbert Ryle, *The Concept of Mind* (New York: Barnes and Noble, 1949), Ch. II; Roderick M. Chisholm, *Perceiving* (Ithaca: Cornell University Press, 1957), p. 15. Compare also Polanyi, *op. cit.*, pp. 89–90; and R. M. Hare *et al.*, "Symposium on the Nature of Analysis," *Journal of Philosophy*, 54 (November 1957), 741.

[16] Austin, *Philosophical Papers*, pp. 134–135.

so on.[17] Or, to study the concept of "representation," he will not rest content with that word and its synonyms and antonyms, but will look also at the noun "representative," at the adjective "representative," at the verbs "to represent" and "to misrepresent," at "representational" and "nonrepresentational," and so on. For the distinctions he needs may be hidden in some members of the word family, but evident in others. Thus he may be at a loss to say how "being sure" differs from "being certain" until he notices the difference between "assure" and "ascertain."

The ordinary-language philosopher will also be interested in idioms and other characteristic phrases in which a word commonly occurs. He will notice, for example, that one can be "free from" some restraint or danger, but also "free to" do something; or that one can have "power over" someone, but also "power to" do something.[18] He will also be concerned with the etymological history of the word he is studying: first, because a word's former meanings are the root sources of its present ones. Austin says, "A word never—well, hardly ever—shakes off its etymology and its formation. In spite of all changes in and extensions of and additions to its meanings, and indeed rather pervading and governing these, there will still persist the old idea."[19] Each time a word's meaning was extended in a new direction that extension must have "made sense" in terms of the older meaning; there must have been a reason why that particular word was selected for that particular new task. So the older meaning is in a way still present in the newer one. Though a series of such changes may take a word very far from its origins, it will still be accompanied, as Austin says, by "trailing clouds of etymology."[20] Thus, even in modern English, "in an *accident* something befalls: by *mistake* you take the wrong one: in *error* you stray: when you act *deliberately* you act after weighing it up (*not* after thinking out ways and means.)."[21]

Etymology is also sometimes helpful in a more direct way: information about the historical circumstances in which a word originated may tell us something important about its meaning. Ziff points out that one can be helped to understand the fine distinction in meaning between "freedom" and "liberty" by noting their historical origins. " 'Liberty' is a word of Latin origin introduced into English via Old French and introduced alongside a perfectly good Anglo-Saxon equivalent, viz. 'frēo'. So one at once suspects that 'liberty' will be connected with more formal matters than

[17] Roland Hall, "Excluders," in Charles E. Caton, ed., *Philosophy and Ordinary Language* (Urbana: University of Illinois Press, 1963), pp. 67–73.

[18] Of course, nonlinguistic philosophers and theorists also come upon and make good use of such insights from time to time. The distinction between "freedom to" and "freedom from," for example, is utilized to good advantage by Sir Isaiah Berlin, *Two Concepts of Liberty* (Oxford: Claredon Press, 1958), though I think even this remarkable essay could be improved by more sophisticated attention to linguistic usage.

[19] Austin, *Philosophical Papers*, p. 149. Compare Ziff, *Semantic Analysis*, p. 190.

[20] Austin, *Philosophical Papers*, p. 149.

[21] *Ibid.*, pp. 149–150.

its Anglo-Saxon equivalent."[22] That this is indeed the case can then be demonstrated by noting, for example, that one says, with respect to a ship, "They freed the lines," but not "They liberated the lines." There are analogous differences in meaning, for similar historical reasons, between "commence" and "begin," "initiate" and "start," "justice" and "fairness," and many other pairs.

Having collected the relevant words and expressions, the ordinary-language philosopher proceeds to look for differences in the ways in which closely related words are normally used, expressions in which the one sounds quite normal but the other sounds peculiar or odd or deviant. Thus, if one were concerned with delineating the meaning of "knowledge," one might distinguish it from "belief" by noticing that we ask "How do you know?" or "Why do you believe?" but it would sound distinctly odd to ask "How do you believe?" or "Why do you know?" Ziff explains: "One proceeds first by considering and examining deviant uses of the words in question. Secondly, one must formulate some sort of hypothesis to account for the fact that the utterances in question are or seem to be deviant. Thirdly, one determines whether or not it is possible to generate deviant utterances on the basis of the hypothesis."[23]

Ziff maintains that this technique has a scientific basis in linguistics. Language, he explains, is a coherent system, and what determines the meaning of a word is its position in that system, its relationship to other words. Meaning is determined by the word's "distribution" in language, the "linguistic environment" in which it occurs.[24] In particular, the meaning of a word depends on two sets of other expressions: the set of expressions in which it occurs normally, and the set of other words that can also normally occur in its position in those expressions. Thus, if we are studying the meaning of the word "good," the first set will include expressions like "That is good," "What good is that?" "She is good to me." The second set will consist of expressions like "That is fine," "That is pleasant," "That is mine," "What use is that?" "What man is that?" "She is mean to me."[25]

In common-sense terms, a word will not have a different meaning in every expression in which it appears; in at least some of the expressions its meaning will be the same. So we study all of the expressions in which it appears (or even all of the expressions in which words on the same etymological root appear). And, second, the meaning of an expression is delimited by what might have been said instead, but wasn't. Green leaves off where yellow and blue begin, so the meaning of "green" is delimited by the meanings of "yellow" and "blue." Ziff explains: "The significance of what is said depends on what is not said. The utterance

22 Ziff, *Semantic Analysis*, p. 190.
23 *Ibid.*, p. 195.
24 *Ibid.*, p. 49.
25 *Ibid.*, p. 147.

actually uttered stands in contrast with and takes its shape from what is not but could without deviation be uttered. The fact that 'excellent', 'splendid' and the like are available and yet not employed serves to determine the significance of 'That is a good painting.' . . . Again, consider: 'Answer: is she beautiful or ugly?'. Neither alternative need do yet if one has a forced option one can (on occasion) choose. Yet you must understand that if I say 'beautiful' under such conditions she need not rival Helen. So one might say that every natural language forces the option for any natural language has a limited lexicon and it imposes these limits on its speakers."[26]

Each word, then, has its own unique place in the system, determining

[26] *Ibid.* It is not always true, but only usually, that the meaning of a word depends on the contrast with close synonyms. It is not true, for instance, of the word "hello." See Garth Hallett, S. J., *Wittgenstein's Definition of Meaning as Use* (New York: Fordham University Press, 1967), pp. 82–83.

As Ziff points out (*Semantic Analysis*, pp. 176–181), difference in meaning is a matter of degree. At one extreme we have simple homonyms—words that sound alike, perhaps even are spelled alike, but have no connection in meaning or etymology. Thus the "bear" in "I can't bear it" differs totally from the one in "That is a bear." Their distributions in English will virtually never overlap; there will be virtually no English sentences containing the word "bear" that leave us in doubt as to whether the noun or the verb is meant. Here we have, simply, two words. Consider, however, the difference between "The division is incorrect" and "The division is marching." Here we have only a single word, yet two quite different meanings. That this is so is shown by the fact that in some verbal contexts, like the examples just given, it is obvious which kind of "division" is meant; but other verbal contexts are ambiguous. Thus, "The division is incomplete," "Which division?" "Lieutenant George's division," and so on. In a good dictionary, "bear" would call for two entries, but "division" for one entry with two headings.

Next, Ziff examines the difference between "brother" in "He is not literally my brother" and in "She has been a brother to me." These, he suggests, do *differ in meaning*, but not so much that it would be correct to say they *have different meanings*. Rather, they have different *senses*. This can be shown by the fact that some verbal contexts are not merely ambiguous as to which sense is meant, but really involve both simultaneously. Someone saying "I wish I had a brother" might well be wishing both for a male sibling and for a comrade who will behave in a brotherly fashion. Someone saying "I want to see Lieutenant George's division" on the other hand, is not likely to want simultaneously an army group and a bit of arithmetic.

"To talk of the sense of a word is, as it were, to talk of the word branching off in a certain direction. The etymological forebear of 'sense', viz. the French word 'sens', is suggestive, and so is the current use of 'sens' in 'Sens obligatoire!', 'Sens unique!'. To say that 'brother' has (at least) two different senses in English is, as it were, to say that (at least) two main branches can be found in connection with 'brother' in English. If the word 'brother' were a tree, it would have a single trunk with (at least) two main branches, but if 'division' were a tree, it would have two trunks joined at the roots, whereas the pair of 'bear'-s would be a pair of trees."

That is why a word's meaning can be studied by attention to different words on the same etymological root. Neither of the pair of "bear"s would tell us anything useful about the meaning of the other. But, different though army groups be from arithmetic problems, it is intuitively clear enough that the two "division"s have a common core (or trunk) of meaning, probably related by way of the verb: the activity of dividing something (an army group or a number). And if we define "brother" simply as "male sibling" we are likely to overlook important adjuncts about the characteristic (or at least culturally expected or culturally idealized) relationship between male siblings that forms part of the word's meaning. For some purposes it won't matter; in philosophy it might.

its meaning, and it can be demonstrated by ordinary-language philosophy. At first we are inclined to doubt that the fine distinctions really exist, or that they matter. We may want to claim that we, at any rate, use terms like "sure" and "certain" interchangeably. But it is quite amazing what a sufficiently talented ordinary-language philosopher can show us in this regard, how richly variegated our vocabulary turns out to be.[27] Ziff, for example, distinguishes between a statement and an utterance, and then continues: "But, neither are statements to be identified with assertions, nor assertions with contentions, nor contentions with descriptions, nor descriptions with remarks, nor remarks with comments, and so on. If in glancing at a painting in a gallery one says, 'That has lovely pigmentation.', one is making a comment, not a statement. If while walking through the gallery one glances out of a window and says 'It's a lovely day.', one is remarking on the weather, not commenting, not stating, not asserting, not describing. In uttering 'I suppose things have gotten a bit out of hand.' the speaker may be making a statement but hardly an assertion. One says 'He should retract his statement.' but not 'He should retract his assertion.'. To say 'The president made a statement to the press.' is not to say 'The president made an assertion to the press.'. Statements or descriptions may be inaccurate but not assertions."[28]

Do these fine distinctions matter? Sometimes they do. Austin points out, for instance, how often, in philosophizing or theorizing, we think in terms of broad, simple dichotomies, often labeling them with the first pair of terms that come to mind.[29] Thus, we think in terms of good and bad, or good and evil, beautiful and ugly, descriptive and normative, voluntary and involuntary, free and caused, and so on. Yet each of these terms is drawn from an intricate array of near synonyms with which it normally contrasts, and we do peculiar things to our own minds when we ignore the fine shadings of meaning involved. For instance, we are led to assume that if a thing is "excellent" or "magnificent" or "fine" it must be "good" (for surely it cannot be "bad"); or that if you "know" something you must certainly "believe" it (for you cannot "doubt" it). And we are led to assume that we can sensibly ask about *any* object "Is it beautiful or ugly?" or about *any* action "Was it voluntary or involuntary?" or about *any* utterance "Was it descriptive or normative?"

But each of these terms can be shown to have a quite limited range of applicability. "Good" means something different from "excellent" or "magnificent" or "fine." "Belief" is not merely a lesser degree of "knowledge," but a wholly different kind of concept. Many utterances are neither "descriptive" of, nor "normative" for, anything. The supposed dichoto-

---

[27] This leads Ziff to the conclusion that there are no true synonyms, really—a conceptual paradox and not a scientific discovery. *Ibid.*, pp. viii, 172.

[28] *Ibid.*, p. 120.

[29] Austin, *Philosophical Papers*, pp. 131, 138–143. Compare Cavell, *Must We Mean What We Say?* p. 36.

mous pairs do not exhaust the universe between them, nor are they really opposites. Austin says this about the dichotomy between "voluntary" and "involuntary." Our various adverbial expressions have each quite "limited ranges of application"; each makes sense only with certain verbs in certain contexts. "Voluntary" and "involuntary," far from both being applicable to every conceivable action, are normally used with quite different, and limited classes of verbs. Thus, "we may join the army or make a gift voluntarily, we may hiccough or make a small gesture involuntarily, and the more we consider further actions which we might naturally be said to do in either of these ways, the more circumscribed and unlike each other the two classes become, until we even doubt whether there is *any* verb with which both adverbs are equally in place. . . . I can perhaps 'break a cup' voluntarily, *if* that is done as an act of self-impoverishment; and I can perhaps break another involuntarily, *if*, say, I make an involuntary movement which breaks it. Here, plainly, the two acts described each as 'breaking a cup' are really very different and the one is similar to acts typical of the 'voluntary' class, the other to acts typical of the 'involuntary' class."[30] "Voluntary" and "involuntary" evidently are not opposites at all, nor do they divide all actions into two classes. The terms with which "voluntary" might naturally contrast are "under constraint," "under duress"; those with which "involuntary" might contrast are "deliberately" and "on purpose." So when we dichotomize all actions as either voluntary or involuntary, we are suggesting to ourselves and others that all actions are either done under constraint or else done on purpose, but never both. We should not be surprised if confusion results.

When Ziff speaks of formulating hypotheses, and of meaning being determined by a word's "distribution" in the language, he evidently intends to pursue a scientific method like those used in linguistics; and he means to criticize those ordinary-language philosophers whose methods are unscientific or intuitive. That, I take it, is the intention of the epigraph to his book: *Miracula sine doctrina nihil valent.* Yet it seems to me that his own procedures and Austin's are very much alike, and both depend ultimately on the same sort of proof.[31] Both proceed by the production of examples. Ziff more frequently uses examples of verbal expressions in which one of a pair of terms sounds natural and the other sounds odd. Austin more frequently uses examples of worldly situations in which one expression would sound normal and another odd. He says that though two expressions may often appear alike, and even be used together, one has only to tell a story—the *right* story—and "everybody will not merely agree that they are completely different, but even discover for himself

---

[30] Austin, *Philosophical Papers*, pp. 138–139. Compare Ziff, *Semantic Analysis*, pp. 210 ff.

[31] "But everything I have ever read in the philosophy of language, even work by the most behavioristic and empirical of authors, relies similarly on the intuitions of the speaker." John R. Searle, *Speech Acts* (Cambridge: Cambridge University Press, 1969), p. 15.

what the difference is and what each means." Suppose the problem is the difference between doing something "by accident" and "by mistake." Austin spins a tale: "You have a donkey, so have I, and they graze in the same field. The day comes when I conceive a dislike for mine. I go to shoot it, draw a bead on it, fire: the brute falls in its tracks. I inspect the victim, and find to my horror that it is *your* donkey. I appear on your doorstep with the remains and say—what? "I say, old sport, I'm awfully sorry, &c., I've shot your donkey '*by accident*'? Or '*by mistake*'? Then again, I go to shoot my donkey as before, draw a bead on it, fire—but as I do so, the beasts move, and to my horror yours falls. Again the scene on the doorstep —what do I say? 'By mistake'? Or 'by accident'?"[32]

Neither Ziff nor Austin finds it necessary to support his observations about what we ordinarily say with any sort of study of other ordinary men, or with public-opinion surveys. And Ziff denies explicitly that any such survey is necessary or even possible with respect to the kind of information about language in which both he and Austin are interested. For whether an utterance does or does not conform to the regularities in our language is not determined by how frequently it has been uttered; it may never have been uttered before, and yet be in every relevant way normal and ordinary. Ziff invents several such utterances ("Communication theoretical models of a natural language are wonderfully illuminating," "There is a purple gila monster sitting on my lap and smiling at me"). What is significant about such sentences is that any of us can invent them, and each of us can understand them without any difficulty, though we have never heard them before. Conversely, we can recognize that there is something odd about "an apple good" or "why do you know?" even after we have repeatedly heard them used as examples in a philosophical discussion. Even if a great many people ordinarily use "by accident" interchangeably with "by mistake," the patterns in our linguistic system— in those same people's linguistic system—continue to distinguish the two terms. To obliterate that distinction one would have also to talk of "traffic mistakes" as readily as of "traffic accidents," to talk of "making an accident" as readily as of "having an accident." The distinction in meaning is there, in the language, whether or not we are educated and attentive enough to make use of it.[33]

For *some* purposes, of course, statistical information about language can be very useful. If, for example, we are concerned whether "ain't" is (has yet become) correct or proper English, or if we are trying to delineate

---

[32] Austin, *Philosophical Papers*, pp. 132–133.

[33] Some words and some linguistic patterns are much more isolated than others, and thus more susceptible to becoming blurred. Consider a word like "behalf," which now is used exclusively in the twin expressions "in behalf" and "on behalf." Originally the meanings of these two expressions were quite distinct, the dictionary tells us, but the distinction is gradually disappearing. About the distinction itself we could also say that it remains in the language even if few people use it, yet it might disappear completely. This is possible because it is not reinforced by any other related patterns.

*15*

the geographic distribution of dialects, then surveys may be necessary. But if our problem is the meaning of some ordinary term, or what we would or would not naturally say under certain circumstances, any native speaker can tell us. That is why, as Cavell says, "If I lived in Munich and knew German fairly well, I might try to intuit or guess what the German expression for a particular phenomenon is. Or I might ask my landlady; and that would probably be the extent of the laborious questioning the problem demanded."[34]

Moreover, if we take the idea of a statistical survey seriously and examine it in detail, its weaknesses become evident. How might we proceed with such a survey? We might ask people how they use, say, "by mistake" or "by accident." But if, as the ordinary-language philosopher argues, our knowledge of the patterns in our language is largely implicit, a "knowing how" rather than a "knowing that," then we cannot trust their answers. Alternatively, we could tell each of them Austin's story about the two donkeys in the field and ask if it is convincing. But if it is not, that might be merely because the example is a weak one. And if it is, that might be merely because they have failed to examine it critically. Still another alternative would be some kind of participant observation, in which we ask no questions but merely observe actual instances of people using words like "mistake" and "accident." But if we wait for these expressions to occur naturally, our research will be slow indeed. So we might experimentally put people into an Austinian situation, with a gun, two donkeys, and the rest. But they might say anything, or nothing. And even if they used the word "mistake" in the experiment we had designed to exemplify "accident," that might be because they understood the situation in a way different from the one we had intended. Perhaps they called it a mistake because they (mistakenly) thought that it *was* a mistake.[35] In both participant observation and experimentally designed situations, our conclusions will depend not merely on what we hear said but also on the interpretation of what in the world is being talked about. Again, such studies may be useful for some purposes, but they will not suffice for answering the kind of question Austin, and Wittgenstein, want to raise.

For Ziff as much as for Austin, for Wittgenstein as much as for anyone doing ordinary-language philosophy, proof depends ultimately on the production or discovery of convincing examples, and in that sense on the consent of the reader. Of course that does not mean that an ordinary-language philosopher is wrong whenever a reader disagrees with him, nor that he is right just because readers are convinced. What it does mean is that in principle no other kind of proof is available here, beyond the convincing example. But any judgment of whether that kind of proof is sufficient, or is scientifically or otherwise inadequate, will depend on the

[34] Cavell, *Must We Mean What We Say?* p. 5.
[35] *Ibid.*, p. 35; and Austin, *Philosophical Papers*, pp. 131–132.

question of what sort of knowledge the philosopher, or anyone who is conceptually puzzled, lacks and needs.

By now we are also in a better position to consider the second group of criticisms commonly leveled against ordinary-language philosophy, those questioning why the ordinary man's speech should be binding on the philosopher. It should be clear by now that the appeal is never to the ordinary *man* at all, to the language and thought of the storekeeper and the farmer. The ordinary man may well be ignorant of or careless about the distinctions to be found in the language; that does not matter. He may confuse "by accident" with "by mistake," as we intellectuals may confuse a spade and a shovel. That does not prove that no difference exists. The appeal is not to the ordinary man, but to the regularities in our language, to the ordinary contexts in which a word or expression is at home, where it occurs naturally. That means both the verbal contexts in which the word is at home, as "know" is at home, and "believe" is not, in the context "How do you————?"; and the worldly context in which an expression might naturally be used, as in Austin's little stories.

So far we have not yet stressed the significance of the latter kind of context, and much of what has been said has been about relationships among words, within language. But contrary to what the critics believe, the intent of ordinary-language philosophy is never merely verbal. The ultimate intent is as much ontological as traditional philosophy ever was. To be sure, ordinary-language philosophers are sometimes misleading in this respect. For example, Austin anticipated the eventual absorption of his kind of work into an expanded science of linguistics; and Ziff construes the whole of his elaborate, elegant investigation into the meaning of "good" as if it were directed toward producing a more adequate dictionary definition.[36] Yet both Ziff and Austin insist that they are concerned not merely with words, but also with the world. In seeking to determine meaning, Ziff says, "we look at the language and we look at the world and we look back and forth."[37] And Austin studies excuses by looking not merely at what our terms of excuse and apology are, but also at when, in what circumstances, they are used.[38] He says that in studying "what we should say when, what words we should use in what situations, we are looking again not *merely* at words (or 'meanings', whatever they may be) but also at the realities we use the words to talk about."[39] Of course, these philosophers' saying so does not make it so; but it should at least warn us to be skeptical of critical claims that ordinary-language philosophy ignores reality in favor of language.

We come, then, to the question of why ordinary language should be in

[36] Chappell, ed., *Ordinary Language*, p. 3; Ziff, *Semantic Analysis*, p. 89.
[37] Ziff, *Semantic Analysis*, p. 54; compare pp. 74–75.
[38] Austin, *Philosophical Papers*, p. 123; that is why he compares his own work to Aristotle's, p. 128.
[39] *Ibid.*, p. 130. Compare Cavell, *Must We Mean What We Say?* pp. 97–114.

any way binding on, or mandatory for, the philosopher or any other thinker with new ideas. This question and the corresponding criticism rest, I am convinced, on a fundamental misunderstanding of what ordinary-language and Wittgensteinian philosophy are all about, though again these philosophers have themselves helped to contribute to that misunderstanding. Concentrating to this point on techniques of studying language, we have not yet really made clear how the resulting information is to be applied to traditional philosophy or theory. It is unfortunately all too easy to assume that the point is the *refutation* of some philosophical position or theoretical doctrine, on the basis of evidence from ordinary usage. It is all too easy to assume that, by showing a philosopher or theorist has deviated from our ordinary usage, we have shown his argument to be wrong, his position invalid. Austin himself speaks of the "wile of the metaphysician" in seducing us away from ordinary usage; and even Wittgenstein, as late as the *Blue and Brown Books*, refers to the traditional philosopher's "misuse" of certain terms, to his using words "wrongly."[40]

Such expressions clearly imply rules whose violation is wrongful.[41] Yet Ziff points out that meaning is not a matter of rules at all, but of language regularities. Of course there are "rules of grammar" that we are taught in school; but, as Ziff points out, generally they are "laid down to inhibit the speakers of the language from speaking in a way they in fact speak."[42] The regularities of language, which govern the meanings of words and the way we talk, are different from such rules. Unlike rules, "they are not sources of constraint," but simply reflect our linguistic habits.[43] It is possible to deviate from these regularities, but that is not to violate any rules. Yet Ziff immediately goes on to call such deviation a "misuse" of words, in the same way as one can misuse a screwdriver though there are no rules for using screwdrivers.[44] But that seems to dodge the real problem by focusing on the relatively trivial distinction between "rules" and "regularities." The real problem would seem to be: How can there be "misuses" in the absence of rules?

Indeed, there are books on the use of various tools, as there are books on correct English usage, and they contain instructions that certainly look like rules ("Never use a screwdriver to check an electric circuit"). Are these rules designed, like the grammar taught in school, to inhibit us from proceeding as we normally do, or are they descriptive generalizations abstracted from what we normally do? John Rawls has suggested that we

---

40 Austin, *Philosophical Papers*, p. 55; Ludwig Wittgenstein, *Preliminary Studies for the "Philosophical Investigations," Generally Known as The Blue and Brown Books* (New York and Evanston: Harper & Row, 1964), pp. 46–47, 57; compare *Philosophical Investigations*, pars. 402, 403.
41 Gilbert Ryle, "Ordinary Language," in Chappell, ed., *Ordinary Language*, p. 35; and "The Theory of Meaning," in Caton, ed., *Philosophy and Ordinary Language*, p. 143.
42 Ziff, *Semantic Analysis*, p. 36.
43 *Ibid.*, p. 35.
44 *Ibid.*

can think of such rules either way—either as descriptive generalizations of what we in fact do when engaging in a certain practice, or as defining the practice, telling us what we must do in order to pursue that practice.[45] We shall say more about this "complementarity between statement and rule," as Cavell calls it, in a later chapter. For now the point is only that though we are dealing with mere regularities of usage, we do sometimes cite these regularities as standards of what you "can't say," of what is a "misuse" or "mistake." Thus, we might, for example, correct a child: "You aren't supposed to say that you *know* when you merely think so. You have to be in a position to know . . ."

But this is not the sort of misuse or violation of which traditional philosophers are being accused; indeed, the point is that they are not being accused of anything. The ordinary-language philosopher, and Wittgenstein, are not hunting for misuses or deviations from ordinary usage with a view toward refuting a philosophical position, but with a view toward understanding it better.[46] A deviation is not a sin but a clue, which can help us to see what the philosopher or theorist is up to, what he is assuming or presupposing. The point is not to forbid deviations from ordinary usage (implying that we could deviate if only we were permitted); but understanding the ways in which we cannot deviate from it without implying certain things or assuming certain things. Nor does the appeal to ordinary speech constitute a conservative defense of ordinary beliefs or common sense.[47] The same ordinary language that allows the expression of various common-sense beliefs also allows their negation, their questioning, their doubting. What is binding is not ordinary beliefs, but the ordinary language in which they are expressed; and it is not binding because the common man is normative for the theorist, but because the ordinary language is also the theorist's own. Nor is the ordinary-language philosopher opposed to the introduction of new technical terms or new definitions. He is interested only in a certain characteristic kind of deviation from ordinary usage that does not involve any technical terms or redefinitions, and that is paradoxically unable really to leave ordinary usage behind.

The attempt to refute a philosophical position with evidence from ordinary usage is always a vulgarization of the ordinary-language philosophical enterprise. Wittgenstein is not concerned with refuting metaphysics or ending philosophy, but with understanding it. As he clearly recognizes, "there is no common sense answer to philosophical problems," because someone who has a conceptual "insight" is perfectly well aware that his "discovery" conflicts with what we ordinarily say.[48] The man investigating a conceptual problem is not out of his senses, Wittgenstein says, nor does

[45] John Rawls, "Two Concepts of Rules," *Philosophical Review*, LXIV (January 1955), 9–11, and *passim*.

[46] K. T. Fann, *Wittgenstein's Conception of Philosophy* (Berkeley and Los Angeles: University of California Press, 1969), p. 86.

[47] Cavell, *Must We Mean What We Say?* p. 240.

[48] Wittgenstein, *Blue and Brown Books*, p. 58.

he disagree with common sense as a scientist might. "That is, his disagreement is not founded on a more subtle knowledge of fact. We therefore have to look round for the *source* of his puzzlement."[49] That is what interests Wittgenstein. Thus he, and I think the best of ordinary-language philosophy as well, never studies language regularities as such, for their own sake, but only where they lead us into conceptual puzzles.[50]

The full implications of these ideas for philosophy and political theory can be discussed only late in this work. But it clearly has more immediate and more limited utility for any kind of theorizing or general thought that is hampered by conceptual problems. If such problems can arise in any field, and if they interfere with work on some substantive problem or issue, then language-philosophical techniques may be useful for resolving them. We can pursue the Wittgensteinian course of backing off from the ontological question to the question of meaning, and from that to the question of use; and there we may find release from what is confusing us. Of course, political and social theory are not constantly enmeshed in such obstructive, conceptual problems; and the intention is not to substitute the study of language for the study of politics or society. Ordinary-language investigations are in order where conceptual puzzlement obtrudes itself and distracts us from our work.

Thus, for example, in studying representative government we may come upon a long-standing and seemingly endless controversy, in which both sides seem to talk past each other, about whether the representative is supposed to do what he thinks best or what his constituents want. Then we may suspect that a conceptual paradox is involved, and examine the meaning of "representative" as a way of resolving that controversy into more manageable terms. Or, we may find ourselves puzzled or in conflict about the limits, the fundamental nature of our field, as when political scientists are troubled about the limits and nature of political phenomena. No doubt we can sometimes save time with a stipulative definition, but it cannot tell us what we want to know: what we ourselves consider political. Or again, we may find that both theoretical and empirical work on some particular topic encounters persistent difficulty and confusion, as has been

[49] *Ibid.*, pp. 58–59; compare Wittgenstein's "Bemerkungen über Frazers *The Golden Bough*," *Synthese*, 17 (1967), 234: "Man muss beim Irrtum ansetzen und ihm die Wahrheit überführen. D.h., man muss die Quelle des Irrtums aufdecken, sonst nützt uns das Hören der Wahrheit nichts. . . . man muss den *Weg* von Irrtum zur Wahrheit finden."

[50] G. E. Moore, "Wittgenstein's Lectures in 1930–1933," in Ammerman, ed., *Classics of Analytic Philosophy*, p. 284. I believe that Wittgenstein was much more explicitly aware of this than, say, Austin or Ziff, which may be why his philosophy strikes us as "deeper" or "more serious" than most ordinary-language philosophy. One student of Wittgenstein's who later did philosophy at Oxford said that the latter seemed by comparison "to lack any philosophical mainspring: it was like a nursery clock-face, equipped with all the necesary hands and figures, except that one was free to move the hands around just as one pleased." Stephen Toulmin, "Ludwig Wittgenstein," *Encounter*, XXXII (January 1969), 59, 62. Compare *Ludwig Wittgenstein: The Man and His Philosophy*, ed. by K. T. Fann (New York: Dell, 1967), p. 45.

the case for instance in political science on the topic of power. Here again the investigators' concepts may require some attention; we may profitably stop looking at power phenomena in the world for a time, and back up to an examination of how we talk about "power."

## THE REEXAMINATION OF FUNDAMENTALS

But these examples, and our treatment of them, may suggest that Wittgenstein's advice to those concerned with society and politics would be: Avoid philosophy if you can; but where your work is stymied by conceptual problems, use ordinary-language philosophical techniques. There is undoubtedly some value in that message; and these techniques are a part of Wittgenstein's contribution, though he must share credit with the ordinary-language philosophers. But if we stop here, we profoundly impoverish our understanding of Wittgenstein's potential contribution, and we miss altogether what he has to offer that is truly unique. Here we are most in danger of trivializing a radically new perspective on the world into just one more technique of methodology. For instead of advising that we avoid philosophy if we can, and use its techniques when we must, Wittgenstein might instead tell us: You already *are* using philosophy, but in blind, fragmented, distorted forms of which you are only dimly aware. These forms control your thought more than you know, impose themselves on you, and prevent rather than promote the accurate perception of reality.

If philosophy has to do with fundamentals, with underlying assumptions and ultimate commitments, with the basic necessities of how things are, then we all bring a kind of philosophy to our work, whether or not we have ever philosophized. But unless we have philosophized, what we bring will be what we have inherited, unexamined. No doubt there have been times in human history when the inherited and unexamined assumptions men held were attuned to their world and their lives, so that they sufficed, without self-consciousness or reassessment. Before philosophy there was tribal, mythological society. But in a time as fragmented as ours, evolving as rapidly as ours, what we inherit are at best unclear and fragmented pieces of philosophy, and they do not serve us well in our lives or our work. So we need, as we must in modern times in so many fields other than political and social science, to reexamine our own fundamental presuppositions, to philosophize, so that those presuppositions, having been made explicit, can be measured against our perceptions of outer and inner reality.

Karl Mannheim observed that "an ontology handed down through tradition obstructs new developments, especially in the basic mode of thinking, and as long as the particularity of the conventional theoretical framework remains unquestioned we will remain in the toils of a static mode of thought which is inadequate to our present stage of historical and intellectual development." He recommended "a clear and explicit avowal

*21*

of the implicit metaphysical presuppositions" we hold, rather than "a verbal denial of the existence of these presuppositions accompanied by their surreptitious admission through the back door."[51] But in our time we can see that the willingness to make "a clear and explicit avowal" is not enough. It is not a matter of honesty and good intentions; the problem is becoming aware what our presuppositions are, permitting them to make contact with each other and with the rest of our ideas, perceptions, and knowledge.

For most of us who work in political or social studies, the inherited, unexamined fragments of philosophy we bring to our work derive from some form of positivism, and thus from a model of the physical sciences developed by philosophers in the 1920s. These fragments are likely to include certain assumptions about what constitutes "the real world," such as that it is "out there" rather than "in here." They are likely to include the assumption that the world consists exclusively of facts, about which we make descriptive statements, and of values, about which we make normative statements. They are likely to favor the abstract and general over the concrete and specific; objectivity over the self; rationality over affect. In any case, they are likely to include the assumption that these categories are mutually exclusive, so that one must choose between them.

Wittgenstein himself once held many of these assumptions, and in his later philosophizing tried to bring them to awareness and understand their sources. But the significance of his contribution for us is not so much that he opposed the conventional positivism, that he can be cited as an authority against it. These conventional assumptions are in fact under severe attack today from an emerging younger generation. But not every form of attack against unexamined assumptions is fruitful, not every form is philosophical. It is becoming fashionable now to favor the concrete over the general, subjectivity over science, feeling and action over rational comprehension. But that fashion merely accepts the old polarities and reinforces them, choosing the opposite pole. No real reassessment of fundamentals, no increase in awareness takes place. What Wittgenstein has to offer here is not a new doctrine but a new invitation to philosophize for ourselves, and a new way of going about it that may be the only possible one for our time and condition.

In his attempt to renew philosophy and make it accessible for our needs, Wittgenstein seems less akin to ordinary-language philosophers in the Anglo-Saxon tradition than to Continental ones: to existentialism and phenomenology, to Nietzsche or Marx, or even to Zen. One might say that Wittgenstein makes it possible for us once again to think dialectically, to break through the ossified forms of inherited impositions and forge, for ourselves and in terms of our realities, new syntheses.[52] Substantively,

[51] Karl Mannheim, *Ideology and Utopia*, tr. by Louis Wirth and Edward Shils (New York: Harcourt, Brace, 1936), pp. 89–90.
[52] Compare Fann, *Wittgenstein's Conception*, p. xiii.

Wittgenstein promotes dialectical thought because he allows us to examine and do justice to our own conflicting commitments. For example, he provides new ways of seeing that, and investigating how, man is both an animal shaped by his environment, and a free, responsible actor. Thus, he allows us renewed access to the fundamental problems of social and political study: free will and scientific objectivity, the nature and validity of judgment, the relationship between thought and action. And he offers hope of a new reconciliation of rational objectivity—that precious and hard-won human capacity—with authenticity and affect and commitment, those qualities without which rational objectivity means death. Wittgenstein promotes dialectical thought also in the sense in which dialectic is related to dialogue. He allows us to take opposing voices—outer or inner —seriously, to make opposing arguments genuinely meet. And thereby he shows us how to put the investigating self back into the investigation, and into assertion and judgment and choice, without sacrificing objectivity. But at this stage, such pronouncements as these must necessarily seem both vague and propagandistic. It is time to go to work.

# II

## *Wittgenstein's Two Visions of Language*

WITTGENSTEIN was a philosopher twice-born. His philosophical work was accomplished in two distinct periods of his life, separated by a decade, and characterized among other things by radically different conceptions of the nature of language. Wittgenstein's early work may be seen as the culmination of an ancient and well-established tradition which conceives of language as reference, as our way of referring to things in the world. That tradition still predominates, and is deeply ingrained in our unexamined assumptions. In his later writings, Wittgenstein develops a powerful and original version of a different view, also with some antecedents in the tradition but much less influential. It conceives of language as speech, as an activity. In this chapter we shall examine the two views, and how Wittgenstein came to make the transition from the one to the other.

Wittgenstein is not a man easy to characterize, except by saying that he was extraordinary, "a man of the rarest genius."[1] In addition to his philosophical achievements, he was a master of literary style, a promising engineer, the architect of a modern mansion and the builder of a mountain cabin, a gifted sculptor, a talented musician who might have made his career as a conductor, several times a hermit by choice, a rich man who gave up his wealth, a Cambridge professor who loathed the academic life (he called it a "philosophical desert," considered the "absurd job" of being a professor of philosophy "a kind of living death"). He taught classes not by lecturing, nor yet by what we usually think of as discussion. Wittgenstein *thought* aloud before his class. "The impression was of a tremendous concentration.... There were frequent and prolonged periods of silence, with only an occasional mutter from Wittgenstein, and the stillest attention from the others. During these silences, Wittgenstein was extremely tense and active. His gaze was concentrated; his face was alive;

[1] Erich Heller, *The Artist's Journey into the Interior* (New York: Random House, 1959), p. 201.

his hands made arresting movements; his expression was stern. One knew that one was in the presence of extreme seriousness, absorption, and force of intellect." Wittgenstein was always exhausted by his teaching, and often revolted by it. Sometimes he would stop, put his head in his hands, and exclaim something like "I'm a fool!" or "You have a dreadful teacher!"[2] After class, he would flee to a movie, where he would sit in the front row, struggling to lose himself and his thoughts in the screen.

Ludwig Josef Johann Wittgenstein was born in Vienna in 1889, but came to study in England, first at the University of Manchester and later at Cambridge. Moving from engineering into mathematics, and from mathematics into philosophy, he finally became a student of Bertrand Russell's at Cambridge. In 1921 he published a slim volume of philosophy called *Tractatus Logico-Philosophicus*, for the English edition of which Russell wrote an introduction.[3]

Wittgenstein said at the time that he regarded the *Tractatus* as having solved all philosophical problems—as essentially putting an end to philosophy.[4] Of course the book did not do that; instead, it became the inspiration for a whole new school of philosophy that began in a group known as the Vienna Circle, and is now generally called logical positivism.[5] But the book did put an end to philosophy for Wittgenstein himself. He was unhappy with Russell's introduction, and they quarreled over the work. Earlier, in 1912, Wittgenstein's father had died, leaving him a considerable fortune. Now Wittgenstein gave this money away, abandoned philosophy, and became a village grammar-school teacher in rural lower Austria. Later, for a time, he was a gardener's assistant in a monastery, and himself considered becoming a monk. Then he returned to Vienna to design a mansion for his sister. In all this time, and indeed for the rest of his life, he lived in the simplest and most frugal style. "His dress was unconventional; it is impossible to imagine him with necktie or hat. A bed, a table, and a few deck-chairs were all of his furniture. Ornamental objects of whatever kind were banished from his surroundings."[6]

In 1929, at the age of forty, Wittgenstein returned to Cambridge and to philosophy, saying he felt that now he could do creative work again.[7]

[2] Norman Malcolm, *Ludwig Wittgenstein, A Memoir* (London: Oxford University Press, 1962), pp. 16, 26; *Ludwig Wittgenstein: The Man and His Philosophy*, ed. by K. T. Fann (New York: Dell, 1967), pp. 52, 57, 60.

[3] Malcolm, *Ludwig Wittgenstein*, pp. 11–12.

[4] *Ibid.*, p. 11; K. T. Fann, *Wittgenstein's Conception of Philosophy* (Berkeley and Los Angeles: University of California Press, 1969), p. 4n, and *Ludwig Wittgenstein*, p. 66.

[5] For an introduction to Wittgenstein's influence on the Vienna Circle, see Justus Hartnack, *Wittgenstein and Modern Philosophy*, tr. by Maurice Cranston (Garden City: Doubleday, 1965), Ch. III. For more detail, see Friedrich Waismann, *Wittgenstein und der Wiener Kreis*, ed. by B. F. McGuinness (London: Basil Blackwell, 1967).

[6] Malcolm, *Ludwig Wittgenstein*, p. 10; Hartnack, *Wittgenstein and Modern Philosophy*, p. 7.

[7] Malcolm, *Ludwig Wittgenstein*, p. 12.

In June of that year he was awarded a D. Phil., submitting the *Tractatus* for a dissertation. The following month he was scheduled to read a paper on logical form, clearly related to the ideas of the *Tractatus*, before an annual meeting of British philosophers. But at the last moment he refused to read it, explaining years later to G. E. Moore "something to the effect that, when he wrote [the paper] he was getting new ideas about which he was still confused, and that he did not think it deserved any attention."[8]

Then Wittgenstein began to teach about these new ideas at Cambridge, and he dictated and wrote several interrelated manuscripts about them. But none of this material was published during his lifetime; he died in 1951 with the *Tractatus* his only published work.[9] Only then did his later writings begin to appear, the most significant ones being the *Philosophical Investigations* (1953), *Remarks on the Foundations of Mathematics* (1958), and *The Blue and Brown Books* (1958). This last work originated as transcriptions of Wittgenstein's Cambridge lectures in 1933–34 and 1934–35, taken down by students and circulated as mimeographed manuscripts in blue and brown covers, respectively. Its full title begins *Preliminary Studies for the 'Philosophical Investigations.'*[10]

Because his later writings were not publicly available until very recently, Wittgenstein was known almost exclusively for the *Tractatus*, and many people still think of him as a logical positivist. But that is a serious misunderstanding. For the incident of the canceled lecture in 1929 really did mark a turning point in Wittgenstein's thought, at which he had begun "getting new ideas." He himself construed the entire body of his later writing and teaching as a sustained and radical *criticism* of the *Tractatus* and of his own earlier views. And so one must distinguish between the "early" and the "later" Wittgenstein. Perhaps we need not accept Wittgenstein's own judgment on this matter as definitive. Certainly there are also some profound continuities in his work. But on the subject of language and the relationship between language and philosophy, the later works really are a rejection of the *Tractatus*. And since language is the subject with which we will begin here, we must respect Wittgenstein's own im-

[8] Stanley Cavell, *Must We Mean What We Say?* (New York: Charles Scribner's Sons, 1969), p. 44; compare Fann, *Ludwig Wittgenstein*, p. 58.

[9] Toulmin suggests that Wittgenstein's later reluctance to publish grew out of the traumatic experience of his quarrels with Russell over Russell's unsatisfactory introduction to the *Tractatus*: Stephen Toulmin, "Ludwig Wittgenstein," *Encounter*, *XXXII* (January 1969), 58.

[10] Other posthumous publications include: *Notebooks 1914–1916*, tr. by G. E. M. Anscombe (Oxford: Basil Blackwell, 1961); *Philosophische Bemerkungen*, ed. by Rush Rhees (Oxford: Basil Blackwell, 1964); *Zettel*, tr. by G. E. M. Anscombe, ed. by G. E. M. Anscombe and G. H. von Wright (Berkeley and Los Angeles: University of California Press, 1967); *Lectures and Conversations on Aesthetics, Psychology and Religious Belief*, ed. by Cyril Barrett (Berkeley and Los Angeles: University of California Press, 1967); Paul Engelmann, *Letters from Ludwig Wittgenstein, with a Memoir*, tr. by L. Furtmüller, ed. by B. F. McGuinness (New York: Horizon Press, 1968); and *On Certainty*, tr. by Denis Paul and G. E. M. Anscombe, ed. by G. E. M. Anscombe and G. H. von Wright (New York and Evanston: Harper & Row, 1969).

pulse that the *Investigations* and the *Tractatus* ought really to be read together, because the former can "be seen in the right light only by contrast with and against the background of my old way of thinking."[11] We shall therefore begin with a review of Wittgenstein's early ideas on language and meaning.

The fundamental assumption of the *Tractatus* is that language is a picture of reality; its function is to represent the world to us. Wittgenstein told one of his students how this idea came to him.[12] It was during the First World War, in the trenches, while he was serving in the Austrian army. He was reading a magazine that contained a schematic drawing showing the possible sequence of events in an automobile accident. Looking at the drawing, Wittgenstein was struck by the way it resembled a statement or proposition—an allegation—about what happened. It depicted or described a possible state of affairs. And it was able to do so because the various parts of the picture corresponded to various things in the world. Wittgenstein said that this gave him the idea of the inverse relationship: that a proposition is like a picture, by virtue of similar correspondence between its parts and things in the world. The parts of a sentence or proposition are, of course, words. Each of these words stands for an object, and the way the proposition relates them to each other is supposed to correspond to the way the objects are related in the world. "I hit John" is one state of affairs; "John hit me" is a different state of affairs.

In the *Tractatus*, Wittgenstein calls a proposition "a picture of reality," and "a model of reality as we imagine it."[13] And he says, "we picture facts to ourselves."[14] Such a picture can be accurate or inaccurate, true or false, depending on whether it "agrees with reality," and that agreement is essentially a matter of correspondence of parts.[15] A proposition has "exactly as many distinguishable parts as . . . the situation that it represents," and these parts are essentially the *names* of the objects in the world that are combined in the particular situation.[16] Each word is the name of a thing, and the proposition relates them to each other in a certain pattern, thereby purporting to say something true about reality. "The fact that the elements of a picture are related to one another in a determinate way represents that things are related to one another in the same way."[17] The proposition is a kind of blueprint or map, where real relationships are represented by corresponding relationships in a different medium.[18]

Clearly Wittgenstein's model of a typical proposition is a declarative

[11] Wittgenstein, *Philosophical Investigations*, p. x.
[12] Malcolm, *Ludwig Wittgenstein*, p. 8.
[13] Ludwig Wittgenstein, *Tractatus Logico-Philosophicus*, tr. by D. F. Pears and B. F. McGuinness (New York: Humanities Press, 1961), par. 4.01.
[14] *Ibid.*, par. 2.1.
[15] *Ibid.*, par. 2.21.
[16] *Ibid.*, pars. 4.04, 4.22, 4.221.
[17] *Ibid.*, par. 2.15.
[18] *Ibid.*, pars. 2.13, 4.014, 4.0312, 5.5423.

sentence, used to say something true or false about the world, "the existence of a state of affairs."[19] Truth and falsity are the only relevant modes. "A proposition must restrict reality to two alternatives: yes or no."[20] And what the proposition asserts truly or falsely is its meaning or sense, the thing one grasps when one understands the proposition. "The sense of a proposition is its agreement and disagreement with possibilities of existence and non-existence of states of affairs."[21] Hence, understanding a proposition means knowing "the situation that it represents," knowing "what is the case if it is true," what would count as verification or falsification of it.[22] "A proposition is the expression of its truth-conditions."[23]

Of course there are also other forms of expression in language, but either they can be translated into such basic propositions or else they are meaningless. A complex sentence, for instance, could be taken apart into the "elementary propositions" of which it is composed. "A proposition is a truth-function of elementary propositions."[24] Or a question, though not itself an assertion or a picture of reality purporting to tell us something, nevertheless is related to and can be translated into a corresponding simple proposition about reality—roughly, the proposition that would *answer* the question. The question is, as it were, just a different form of that proposition. And a negative proposition is just a different form of its positive counterpart. In other words, "I hit John" and "I did not hit John" and "Did I hit John?" are like different modes or different forms of the same picture of reality; they share a single core of meaning, except that one asserts, one negates, and one questions.[25] To understand their meaning one must understand the meaning of the basic core assertion into which they can be analyzed, must know what would have to be the case in the world for it to be true. Understanding "Did I hit John?" requires knowing what would count as my having hit John. Thus the meaning, the thought in language, is often "disguised," and must be laid bare by analysis, translating complex sentences into their elementary propositions, each of which consists of "names in immediate combination."[26]

This kind of analysis is the task of philosophy, properly understood. "Philosophy aims at the logical clarification of thoughts." Rather than generate original propositions of its own, philosophy should "clarify" propositions. For, "without philosophy thoughts are, as it were, cloudy

[19] *Ibid.*, par. 4.21; compare par. 4.5: "The general form of a proposition is: This is how things stand."
[20] *Ibid.*, par. 4.023.
[21] *Ibid.*, par. 4.2.
[22] *Ibid.*, pars. 4.021, 4.024.
[23] *Ibid.*, par. 4.431.
[24] *Ibid.*, par. 5.
[25] There is an interesting parallel here to Freud's theory that unconscious thought, for instance as expressed in dreams, merely pictures states of affairs; so that the psychoanalyst must figure out whether they are being affirmed, denied, wished for, feared, questioned, supposed, and so on. Sigmund Freud, *The Interpretation of Dreams*, tr. by James Strachey (New York: Basic Books, 1961), pp. 310–338.
[26] Wittgenstein, *Tractatus*, pars. 4.002, 4.221.

and indistinct: its task is to make them clear and to give them sharp boundaries."[27] Each proposition has one and only one correct, complete analysis, in accord with the logic of the language.[28] "What a proposition expresses it expresses in a determinate manner, which can be set out clearly."[29] Language, in short, is a kind of logical calculus operating according to strict, definite rules, and the job of philosophy is to study these rules and make them explicit.[30]

Whatever in language cannot be analyzed into elementary propositions is either lacking in sense or nonsensical. Wittgenstein does recognize a special category of propositions which cannot be verified or falsified even in principle but which are not nonsensical. This category consists of tautologies, which are true a priori, by definition, and contradictions, which are false a priori, by definition. Tautologies include the rules of logic and the propositions of mathematics. Tautologies and contradictions "say nothing," tell us nothing about the world. "For example, I know nothing about the weather when I know that it is either raining or not raining." Though they are not nonsensical, they "lack sense." They are simply part of our system of symbols, its "limiting cases."[31]

If a proposition cannot be analyzed into testable elementary propositions and is neither a tautology nor a contradiction, then it is simply senseless or nonsensical. It may look as if it makes sense, but in fact it means nothing because it represents no alleged state of affairs in the world. Nothing could prove it true or false; it is just a lot of words strung together. Wittgenstein argues in the *Tractatus* that unfortunately much of what we try to do with language—including the bulk of traditional philosophy—falls into this category. For example, any proposition about good or bad, right or wrong, beauty or ugliness—any proposition about "value" —falls into this category. For the meaning of a proposition is the worldly state of affairs that would exist if it were true. But the world, in and of itself, contains no value. In the real, factual world, "everything happens as it does happen: *in* it no value exists."[32] Consequently, value propositions cannot be meaningful. "It is clear that ethics cannot be put into words. Ethics is transcendental."[33] And the same is true of esthetics and metaphysics. Thus, "most of the propositions and questions to be found in philosophical works are not false but nonsensical."[34] Philosophical propositions are "not irrefutable, but evidently nonsensical"; for they try "to raise doubt where no question can be asked." A question can exist

[27] *Ibid.*, par. 4.112. But compare par. 5.5563: "In fact, all the propositions of our everyday language, just as they stand, are in perfect logical order."
[28] *Ibid.*, par. 3.25.
[29] *Ibid.*, par. 3.251.
[30] Compare Wittgenstein's own later summation of his early views: *Philosophical Investigations*, par. 81.
[31] Wittgenstein, *Tractatus*, pars. 4.461, 4.466.
[32] *Ibid.*, par. 6.41.
[33] *Ibid.*, par. 6.421.
[34] *Ibid.*, par. 4.003.

only where an answer can exist, and "an answer only where something can be said."[35]

These ideas have obvious affinities with logical positivism. But unlike many of the logical positivists, Wittgenstein—even in his early work—cherishes ethics and esthetics and religion and question of value. Such matters are not worthless or unimportant to him; only they cannot be *talked* about in a meaningful, sensible way. Meaningful talk consists only of propositions, and "propositions can express nothing of what is higher."[36] That which is "higher"—the beautiful and the good—"cannot be put into words"; such things "*make themselves manifest. They are what is mystical.*"[37] Thus the meaningful sector of language is confined within narrow limits and governed by clear, unequivocal rules; the task of philosophy is to separate the meaningless from the meaningful use of language by clarifying the latter in accord with the rules, showing "what cannot be said, by presenting clearly what can be said."[38] And though what lies outside the narrow boundaries may be of the greatest importance, it cannot be expressed verbally. "What can be said at all can be said clearly, and what we cannot talk about we must consign to silence."[39]

## THE LATER PHILOSOPHY

These, then, are Wittgenstein's views in the *Tractatus*. They embody a conception of language in which words stand for, or refer to, (classes of) phenomena in the world; and sentences make true or false assertions about combinations of such phenomena. It is a conception traditional at least since Plato and Aristotle, and almost universally accepted today, if only for lack of an accessible alternative.[40] It has, as we shall see, the most profound implications for basic questions such as how men understand each other and what the world is like. In his later writings, Wittgenstein rejects almost every feature of this view of language. He denies that the essential function of language is to picture reality, that the basic model of a meaningful sentence is a true or false proposition about things in the world, that language is a logical calculus operating according to strict rules, that propositions about value or metaphysics are meaningless, and that the job of philosophy is to correct our messy, careless, ordinary ways

[35] *Ibid.*, par. 6.51. "Evidently" is my translation for "*offenbar,*" where Pears and McGuinness have "obviously."

[36] *Ibid.*, par. 6.42. The German text is "*können nichts Höheres ausdrücken.*" On the extent to which Wittgenstein's attitude toward higher things was "not a mocking, but a respectful silence," unlike that of the logical positivists, see Toulmin, "Ludwig Wittgenstein," and Fann, *Wittgenstein's Conception*, p. 25.

[37] Wittgenstein, *Tractatus*, par. 6.522; compare par. 5.62: "What the solipsist *means* is quite correct; only it cannot be *said.*"

[38] *Ibid.*, par. 4.115.

[39] *Ibid.*, p. 3; compare par. 7.

[40] Karl-Otto Apel, *Analytic Philosophy of Language and the Geisteswissenschaften*, tr. by Harald Holstelilie (Dordrecht: D. Reidel, 1967), p. 37.

of talking. Wittgenstein's major later work, the *Philosophical Investigations*, begins with a quotation from Saint Augustine's *Confessions*, which is then examined and criticized. The passage is an account of how Augustine first learned to talk; and it soon becomes clear that in criticizing Augustine, Wittgenstein is really criticizing his own earlier views. Augustine says:

When they (my elders) named some object, and accordingly moved toward something, I saw this and I grasped that the thing was called by the sound they uttered when they meant to point it out. Their intention was shewn by their bodily movements, as it were the natural language of all peoples: the expression of the face, the play of the eyes, the movement of other parts of the body, and the tone of voice which expresses our state of mind in seeking, having, rejecting or avoiding something. Thus, as I heard words repeatedly used in their proper places in various sentences, I gradually learnt to understand what objects they signified; and after I had trained my mouth to form these signs, I used them to express my own desires.[41]

As an introspective, imaginative account of what language-learning "must have been like," this passage is perhaps familiar and innocent enough. But Wittgenstein proceeds to show that it rests on a number of unwarranted and false assumptions, assumptions which he himself once shared.

Wittgenstein's first direct comment is that the passage from Augustine presents us with a "picture of language," in which words are essentially the names of objects in the world, so that each word could be attached to the appropriate object like a label.[42] "The individual words in language name objects . . . Every word has a meaning. This meaning is correlated with the word. It is the object for which the word stands."[43] The basic function of a word is to signify or refer, to stand for an object. Such assumptions are, again, familiar enough and not unreasonable. They remind us of some of the ways in which we do teach children the names of certain kinds of objects, or colors, or the numbers from one to ten. We point to the object, or a picture, or a color, or a group of objects, and say the appropriate word, and the child repeats it. After a while the child can name the object correctly without the adult's example. Because this is a common procedure when an adult consciously sets out to teach a child a certain word or vocabulary set, it springs readily to mind as a good example of the nature of language-learning.

But, to begin with, certain words cannot be taught that way, by ostensive definition. No adult can point out a "the" or a "today" or a "whether"; yet children do somehow acquire these words as well.[44] Nor is the problem

[41] Augustine, *Confessions*, I. 8., cited in Wittgenstein, *Philosophical Investigations*, par. 1.
[42] Wittgenstein, *Philosophical Investigations*, par. 15; compare Waismann, *Wittgenstein*, p. 169.
[43] Wittgenstein, *Philosophical Investigations*, par. 1.
[44] Compare Wittgenstein, *Blue and Brown Books* (New York and Evanston: Harper & Row, 1964), p. 77; and Paul Ziff, *Semantic Analysis* (Ithaca: Cornell University Press, 1960), p. 82: "Owing to their unduly narrow focus philosophers

confined to prepositions, articles, and conjunctions. Though one can point to a bachelor, one cannot teach the meaning of "bachelor" by pointing, nor that of "divorce" or "challenge" or "interlude." Captivated by the "Augustinian" picture, one is likely to brush such words aside, as being somehow acquired later in other ways. Wittgenstein says, "If you describe the learning of language in this way you are, I believe, thinking primarily of nouns like 'table', 'chair', 'bread', and of people's names, and only secondarily of the names of certain actions and properties; and of the remaining kinds of word as something that will take care of itself."[45] But of course the remaining kinds of word will not "take care of itself," and until one has an account of language-learning that explains how children learn those words, any explanation of how they learn "chair" or "bread" should be highly suspect. A common philosophical assumption at this juncture is that other words can somehow be explained or learned out of various combinations of the ones learned ostensively. But even a moment's serious reflection shows the total inadequacy of that assumption. Just try to construct the meaning of, say, "when" out of simple nouns that we teach by pointing to objects.

Moreover, Augustine takes a great deal for granted about what goes on when we point and speak and the child speaks after us. What, Wittgenstein asks, if the child just "naturally reacted to the gesture of pointing with the hand by looking in the direction of the line from finger-tip to wrist, not from wrist to finger-tip"?[46] Or, as Ziff puts it even more strikingly, "I throw a cat a piece of meat. It does not see where the meat fell. I point to the meat: the cat smells my finger."[47] As a matter of fact, *both* Wittgenstein and Augustine make the mistake of assuming that children just naturally follow the pointing finger in the right direction, whereas in reality even this simple reaction has to be learned. But it can be learned by the child, and it must be mastered before ostensive definitions can work.

But this is still a relatively minor point. Much more vital is the problem of the child's capacity to figure out *what* the adult is pointing *at*. After all, an adult standing in the kitchen with his child, facing toward the stove, might point forward and downward and teach the child the meaning of "stove," or "oven," or "hot," or "white," or "enamel," or "scratch," or "dirt," or "baking," or "cooking," or "dinner," or "object," or "thing," and so on. How does the child know what he is pointing to, what he intends? "One can ostensively define a proper name, the name of a colour, the name of a material, a numeral, the name of a point of the compass and so on. The definition of the number two, 'That is called "two" '—pointing to two nuts—is perfectly exact. —But how can two be

have failed to realize that what is fundamental here are conditions, not referents and not truth conditions and not even the satisfaction of conditions but simply conditions. 'Hello' has no referent. It cannot be associated with truth conditions."

[45] Wittgenstein, *Philosophical Investigations*, par. 1.
[46] *Ibid.*, par. 185.
[47] Ziff, *Semantic Analysis*, pp. 92–93.

defined like that? The person one gives the definition to doesn't know what one wants to call 'two'; he will suppose that 'two' is the name given to *this* group of nuts! —He *may* suppose this; but perhaps he does not. . . . An ostensive definition can be variously interpreted in *every* case."[48]

It is not that one cannot teach a child some words by pointing, but rather that the process cannot be as Augustine imagines it; we need a better understanding of what actually goes on. It helps to consider, with Cavell, a real example of the way a child, as we say, "learns a new word."[49] Consider the little girl whose parents can tell you that she already "knows" two dozen words, including the word "kitty." What does it mean to say that she has learned it? One day, after her father said "kitty" and pointed to the kitten, she repeated the word and also pointed to the kitten. But what does "repeating the word" mean here, and what was she pointing at? All we know is that she made a sound her father *"accepted, responded to* (with smiles, hugs, words of encouragement, etc.)" as a repetition of what he had said, and that she made a gesture he took as pointing to what he had pointed at. Then, "the next time a cat came by, on the prowl or in a picture book she did it again." We conclude she knows, has learned a new word.

But one day, some weeks later, the child smiles at a fur piece, strokes it, and says "kitty." Her parents' first reaction is one of surprise, and perhaps disappointment: the child hasn't mastered the word after all. But the second reaction is happier: "she means by 'kitty' what I mean by 'fur.' Or was it what I mean by 'soft,' or perhaps 'nice to stroke'?" She has learned to say the *word* right enough, but has not understood the idea of a kitten. Grasping our concept of "kitty," understanding what a kitty is, is another matter. But the parents' happier second reaction still runs as if the child had a certain number of concepts ready, in mind, and made the wrong guess from among them. Instead of choosing the concept of a kitty to correspond to the English word "kitty," she mistakenly picked the concept of fur or of softness or of niceness-to-stroke. Alternatively, a philosopher might want to say that she has formulated the wrong inductive generalization: her use of "kitty" refers not merely to kittens but also to fur pieces and perhaps other small, soft, furry things. It is too broad. But if we correct her, she will gradually narrow it down by a process of further induction until she is clear on what does and what does not count as a "kitty."

But why should one suppose that she means "kitty" to be the name of a certain class of objects at all? Cavell continues: "Perhaps she didn't mean at all what in my syntax would be recorded as 'That is an X.' After all, when she sees a real kitten she not only utters her allophonic version

[48] Wittgenstein, *Philosophical Investigations*, par. 28; compare Waismann, *Wittgenstein*, p. 51.
[49] Stanley Cavell, "The Claim to Rationality" (unpublished dissertation, Harvard University), pp. 205–207.

of 'kitty,' she usually squeals the word over and over, squats down near it, stretches out her arm towards it and opens and closes her fingers (an allomorphic version of 'petting the kitten'?), purses her lips and squints with pleasure. All she did with the fur piece was, smiling, to say 'kitty' once and stroke it. Perhaps, the syntax of that performance should be transcribed as 'This is like a kitty,' or 'Look at the funny kitty' or 'Aren't soft things nice?', or 'See, I remember how pleased you are when I say "kitty",' or 'I like to be petted.' Can we decide this? Is it a *choice* between these definite alternatives?"[50]

The example still tempts us into the wrong interpretation, because a word like "kitty" *can* function as a label. But children's early vocabulary need not consist of such nouns. Consider the child that has "learned," has begun to use, " 'bye" together with a hand-wave when we encourage it to "wave bye-bye" as we depart. Or consider the child that has begun to say "up," lifting its arms in a characteristic way to be picked up. Here there is much less temptation to suppose that the child has made a correct "inductive generalization" as to what objects count as a " 'bye" or as an "up." Instead, we are inclined to say that the child "associates" the sound with a certain situation, as it associates certain gestures with that situation. Neither the sound nor the gesture need be (taken as) the name of anything. The situation recurs; the gestures and sound, or perhaps just the one or the other, are repeated. That is a kind of induction, if you like, but not an induction about recurrent characteristics of an object to which the sound refers; rather, it is an induction about features of the total situation that make it reminiscent of an earlier situation in which the sound was made.[51] Does the child at this stage know what " 'bye" or "up" means? There can be no clear-cut answer, either affirmative or negative. But the question quickly resolves itself in another, more useful one: What can the child do with the words at this point, and what can it (does it) not yet do?

Cavell means to show us, among other things, that the difference between learning and maturation is not nearly as clear as we suppose, that the question of *what* a child has learned when it repeats or volunteers a word must be taken as problematic. A child beginning to master language needs to learn not merely the right label for an object, but also what *counts* as the object to be labeled; not merely the word, but the concept. He needs to learn, as Ernst Cassirer has said, "to come to terms with the

---

50 *Ibid.*, p. 206.

51 Compare Wittgenstein, *On Certainty*, par. 538: "The child, I should like to say, learns to react in such-and-such a way; and in so reacting it doesn't so far know anything. Knowing only begins at a later level." I find quite amazing the ubiquity and tenacity of the label-and-object view of language learning in the literature of experimental psychology. Rare exceptions include Z. P. Dienes, *Concept Formation and Personality* (Leicester: Leicester University Press, 1959); the literature in which a child is observed while actually learning a natural language is much more perceptive.

objective world."[52] Being adults and competent speakers ourselves, we tend to think of the child as a small adult with communication trouble. An adult coming into a strange country, Wittgenstein says, "will sometimes learn the language of the inhabitants from ostensive definitions that they give him; and he will often have to *guess* the meaning of these definitions," guess the corresponding word or words in his own language. In this respect, "Augustine describes the learning of human language as if the child came into a strange country and did not understand the language of the country; that is, as if it already had a language, only not this one."[53] But a child in the process of acquiring its first, its native, language is at the same time becoming acquainted with the world, what kinds of objects and entities it contains, what counts as an entity in it.

The child learns simultaneously both what "kitty" means and what a kitty is; and neither process happens all at once, in a flash of insight that might be based on a lucky guess.[54] When we say to the little girl, "kitty," and point to the cat, we are not really, fully, telling her either what "kitty" means or what a kitty is. We cannot yet tell her what "kitty" means because, as Cavell puts it, "It takes two to *tell* something; you can't give someone a piece of information unless he knows how to *ask* for that (or comparable) information. . . . You can't *tell* a child what a word means when the child has yet to learn what 'asking for a meaning' is (i. e., how to ask for a meaning), in the way you can't *lend* a rattle to a child who has yet to learn what 'being lent (or borrowing) something' means."[55] (Just try to get the child to "return" the rattle that an older child has "lent" her!) Even if we get the child to repeat "kitty" after us, she has at most mastered a new activity, a new game; she has not yet learned the "meaning" of a "word."

Similarly, when we point to the "kitty," we are not yet telling the child what a kitty is. For to know what a kitty is requires knowing that it is a kind of animal, that it is alive, can feel pain, will grow into a cat, will die, is related in one way to lions and in another to dogs, that it can be comforted and punished and teased, and so on. "Kittens—what we call kittens—don't exist in her world yet."[56] Of an older child, "one ignorant of, but ripe for" the concept of, say, a lion, in the sense that she knows what an animal is, how to ask for a name, and so on, one can comfortably say that when we tell her "that is a 'lion,' " she learns both what a lion is and what "lion" means. Even then the process will not be instantaneous or exhaustive. The child may still have some special ideas about lions different from ours—perhaps that they bear some unknown intimate

[52] Ernst Cassirer, *An Essay on Man* (Garden City: Doubleday, 1953), p. 171.
[53] Wittgenstein, *Philosophical Investigations*, par. 32.
[54] Lev Semenovich Vygotsky, *Thought and Language,* ed. and tr. by Eugenia Haufmann and Gertrude Vakar (Cambridge: M.I.T. Press, 1966), p. 27.
[55] Cavell, "Claim to Rationality," p. 204.
[56] *Ibid.*, p. 207.

relation to lies or lying. "But," Cavell says, "that probably won't lead to trouble and one day the person who was this child may, for some reason, remember that she believed these things, made these associations, when she was a child."[57] "Although I didn't tell her, and she didn't learn, either what the word 'kitty' means or what a kitty is," Cavell says, if things continue normally, eventually "she will learn both."[58]

## LANGUAGE AS ACTIVITY

What Wittgenstein offers as a substitute for the misleading picture of language he finds in Augustine, or at least as a first step toward a different and better view, is a conception of language as activity. In a variety of ways and on many levels, he explores the idea that language is founded on speaking and responding to speech, and that these are things we *do*. Language is first of all speech, and "the *speaking* of language is part of an activity, or of a form of life."[59] In this sense, "words are also deeds."[60] Thus, understanding a language is not a matter of grasping some inner essence of meaning, but rather of knowing how to do certain things. "To understand a language means to be master of a technique."[61] In this activity, this technique, words are put to use, so that "language is an instrument. Its concepts are instruments."[62] Wittgenstein advises us, "Ask yourself: On what occasion, for what purpose, do we say this? What kind of actions accompany these words? (Think of a greeting.) In what scenes will they be used; and what for?"[63] Specifically, he embodies and explores this pragmatic understanding of language in two great analogies: the comparison between words and tools, and that between words and pieces or counters or signals in a game.

"Think of the tools in a tool box," he says; "there is a hammer, pliers, a saw, a screw-driver, a rule, a glue-pot, glue, nails and screws. —The functions of words are as diverse as the functions of these objects."[64] The emphasis is now on the "functions" of words, rather than their "meanings"; and not every one can be used for every purpose, though many can be used for a variety of purposes. At the same time, they also have certain features in common, by virtue of the fact that they are tools, things designed for human beings to work with. But that similarity can also deceive us about their great variety of function. "It is like looking into the cabin of a locomotive. We see handles all looking more or less alike. (Nat-

[57] *Ibid.*, p. 214.
[58] *Ibid.*, p. 206.
[59] Wittgenstein, *Philosophical Investigations*, par. 23. The view Wittgenstein develops has antecedents, to be sure, such as Saussure's stress on *parole*, and the later Croce.
[60] *Ibid.*, par. 546.
[61] *Ibid.*, par. 199.
[62] *Ibid.*, par. 569.
[63] *Ibid.*, par. 489.
[64] *Ibid.*, par. 11.

urally, since they are all supposed to be handled.) But one is the handle of a crank which can be moved continuously (it regulates the opening of a valve); another is the handle of a switch, which has only two effective positions, it is either off or on; a third is the handle of a brake-lever, the harder one pulls on it, the harder it brakes; a fourth, the handle of a pump: it has an effect only so long as it is moved to and fro."[65]

Different words, like different tools, are used in very different ways. What this means becomes clearer when one turns to the second analogy, much more fully developed in the *Investigations*: the analogy between language and games, between words and the pieces or signals we use in playing games. "Words are a signal; and they have a *function*."[66] One may think of words used as signals in competitive games, like "check" in chess or "double" in bridge. Or better still, one may think of the ritual use of words in children's games, like the cry "olly-olly-oxen free, free, free!" which was used, at least in my childhood, as a ritual expression in hide-and-go-seek, allowing all players to return safely to home base without being tagged. Uttering such an expression in the course of play is obviously not making a true or false assertion about facts. Rather, it changes the status, the relationships, of the players. Uttering such an expression is like making a move in the game, and the expression is just a device by means of which the move is made.

The significance of such expressions in our language can perhaps be made more accessible by means of Austin's notion of "performatives."[67] Austin calls our attention to an apparent peculiarity of certain verbs: in their first person singular active form, they are used not for making true or false statements, but for taking an action. They are a way of "*doing* something rather than merely *saying* something."[68] Specifically, the first person use of these verbs is the performing of the very action which the verb "names." So Austin calls these verbs "performatives." The characteristic example is that of promising. When we say "I promise," we are not describing our activity or our state of mind, not saying anything true or false, but performing the action named—promising. Similarly, if at the appropriate moment "in the course of a marriage ceremony I say, as people will, 'I do,' " then "I am not reporting on a marriage, I am indulging in it." Or again, if I say "I bet you sixpence it will rain tomorrow," I am not making a factual prediction but a bet. Or suppose that in the appropriate circumstances "I have the bottle of champagne in my hand and say

[65] *Ibid.*, par. 12.

[66] Wittgenstein, *Zettel*, par. 601; compare *Philosophical Investigations*, par. 7; and Waismann, *Wittgenstein*, pp. 105, 150, 169.

[67] J. L. Austin, *Philosophical Papers* (Oxford: Clarendon Press, 1961), pp. 66–67, 220–239; see also his posthumously published *How to Do Things with Words*, ed. by J. O. Urmson (New York: Oxford University Press, 1965). Something like Austin's notion of performatives is developed also by H. L. A. Hart in "The Ascription of Responsibility and Rights," in Antony Flew, ed., *Logic and Language* (*First and Second Series*) (Garden City: Doubleday, 1965).

[68] Austin, *Philosophical Papers*, p. 222.

'I name this ship the *Queen Elizabeth.*' " Then I am not describing a christening ceremony, but performing the christening.[69]

Performative verbs, Austin points out, display a "typical asymmetry" between their first person singular present active form, and other persons and tenses. "For example, when we say 'I promise that . . .', the case is very different from when we say 'He promises that . . .', or in the past tense 'I promised that . . .'."[70] The latter utterances may be descriptions or assertions or reports of what was said; uttering them is not promising. But uttering "I promise" *can*, on occasion, itself *be* promising. Of course, the right words have to be said in the right circumstances. Any of the above utterances said while reading aloud, while reporting on someone else's saying them, while rehearsing a play, as a joke, and so on, will not "perform" the action. The circumstances must be right, the procedure must accord with the appropriate conventions, the speaker must be in a position to perform the action.

Having once discovered performatives, Austin was increasingly struck by the difficulties his concept entailed, and devoted much energy to trying to preserve it despite them. He was forced to acknowledge that the contrast between performatives and words used to make descriptive statements about the world, statements which can be true or false, was not as sharp as he had supposed. Even performative utterances have factual implications, and these may be true and false. For example, when we promise we imply that we think we are able to perform what we promise, and that we intend to perform, and these implications may be true or false. If they are false, we might say that the act of promising was insincere. And with some performatives one can feel the fragility of the distinction between their performative and descriptive use, in examples of such insincerity. Thus, if I say "I condemn you," in a way I am thereby condemning you, no matter how I feel or what I think. That is the performative aspect of the utterance. Yet the utterance also seems to have a descriptive aspect; and if I do not sincerely condemn you in my mind, then as a descriptive utterance it is, in a way, false. Though officially, by pronouncing the words I am condemning you, nevertheless I do not really condemn you.

Moreover, Austin soon noticed that performative utterances can equally well be cast with the verb in the passive voice and in the second or third person. One need not literally say "I warn" in order to warn someone; one can say "Passengers are warned to . . ." One can even warn without using that verb at all, for instance by posting a sign that says "Dangerous Bull." Similarly, in suitable circumstances one can promise simply by saying "you can count on it," or "yes," or any number of other things. So the sharp dividing line between performative and descriptive utterances blurs.

---

[69] *Ibid.*

[70] *Ibid.*, p. 229; compare p. 66n.

38

Performatives can (almost) be true or false, and even nonperformatives can be used to perform actions. Eventually Austin conceded that "perhaps indeed there is no great distinction between statements and performative utterances."[71]

It remains true that certain verbs have the peculiarity that, in uttering them in the first person singular present active, we are performing the action they name. But the existence of these verbs is relatively uninteresting compared to the far greater discovery implicit in Austin but made explicit by Wittgenstein: that much or perhaps all of language is performative in a looser sense, is what we might call quasi-performative. Though speaking may not always be performing the action named in the speech, it is always performing an action, for whose consequences the speaker is responsible.

To develop this way of looking at language, Wittgenstein introduces what he calls "language games." On one level, a language game is literally a game, the sort of informal but ritualized interaction between a child and an adult by means of which a child is trained in certain features of his native language. For example, the adult points and says a word, and the child repeats it, as in Cavell's example of teaching the child to say "kitty." The adult and the child engage in a kind of game involving both action and speech; but the use of speech in it is still very much like the use of gesture.

More commonly, Wittgenstein means by a language game a kind of drastically simplified version or model of how language works, a sort of primitive instance of language.[72] Though these models are usually invented by Wittgenstein, they are often based on some small part of our actual language. Both the language games from which children learn and the language games which are primitive or reduced parts of a complete language always involve, in Wittgenstein's examples, both speech and other activity linked with that speech. The language game is "the whole, consisting of language and the actions into which it is woven."[73]

The first language games that Wittgenstein invents are meant to illuminate Augustine's account of how he learned to talk. Though the assumptions involved in that account are false about our (or any natural) language, they could be considered "correct for a simpler language than ours."[74] Augustine's "concept of meaning has its place in a primitive idea of the way language functions. But one can also say that it is the idea of a language more primitive than ours."[75] Wittgenstein proceeds to sketch an imaginary primitive version of a "language" for which Augustine's account would be accurate:

[71] Austin, *How to Do Things*, p. 52.
[72] But not the language of a "primitive" people!
[73] Wittgenstein, *Philosophical Investigations*, par. 7.
[74] Wittgenstein, *Blue and Brown Books*, p. 77.
[75] Wittgenstein, *Philosophical Investigations*, par. 2.

The language is meant to serve for communication between a builder A and an assistant B. A is building with buildingstones: there are blocks, pillars, slabs and beams. B has to pass the stones, and that in the order in which A needs them. For this purpose they use a language consisting of the words "block", "pillar", "slab", "beam". A calls them out;—B brings the stone which he has learnt to bring at such-and-such a call.

Wittgenstein invites us to conceive of this as "a complete primitive language," and to imagine a society that has no more language than this.[76] Children would learn the language from adults by "being trained in its use," as an animal is trained, by "example, reward, punishment, and suchlike."[77] Indeed, an animal could easily be trained to perform the role of the assistant in this game.

A somewhat more complex language game can be generated by extending this one to include the "names" of the cardinal numbers, one through ten.[78] The assistant would memorize the series of words, "one", "two," and so on through "ten," in order. When the builder called out, say, "Five slabs!" the assistant would go to the slabs and say the series of number words to himself until he reached five, picking up one slab at each word. Then he would bring the slabs to the builder. But the extension is really a quite different game from the original. For instance, the training for it would be quite different. It would involve memorizing a list of words in order. And though the *use* of the number words would be taught through the same sort of training as the use of the names of the stones, the way gestures like pointing are used is different in the two processes. In the ostensive teaching of numbers, "the same word, e.g. 'three', will be taught by pointing either to slabs or to bricks, or to columns, etc. And on the other hand, different numerals will be taught by pointing to groups of stones of the same shape."[79] When the training was over, the assistant would also be expected to respond to the number words in a very different way from the way he is expected to respond to the names of the stones. These differences show clearly that the number words are "an entirely different *kind* of instrument" in the language.[80]

We may be tempted to ask: "But how does the assistant know what to bring when he hears the word 'slab,' and what to do with the word 'five'? Doesn't he need first of all to grasp their meaning?" Wittgenstein responds: "Well, I assume that he *acts* as I have described. Explanations come to an end somewhere."[81] No such thing as the meaning of the word "five" is in question here, only how the word "five" is used. In this language game, the question of meaning is reduced to either of two extremely simple alternatives. We might say that the assistant understands the

[76] *Ibid.*
[77] Wittgenstein, *Blue and Brown Books*, p. 77.
[78] Wittgenstein, *Philosophical Investigations*, par. 8; *Blue and Brown Books*, p. 79.
[79] Wittgenstein, *Blue and Brown Books*, p. 79.
[80] *Ibid.*; compare *Philosophical Investigations*, par. 17.
[81] Wittgenstein, *Philosophical Investigations*, par. 1.

meaning of "slab," "block," and so on; but then "understanding the meaning" implies no more and no less than performing certain actions upon hearing the words. A dog could do it. Alternatively, we might want to say that he need not "understand the meaning" of the words at all, that there is no such thing as "meaning" or "understanding the meaning" involved in this language game; there is only how the words are used by A and responded to by B.

In this language, as it is defined, there can be no discourse as we know it, no science or literature or philosophy. There cannot even be so simple an action as "asking the name of" an object, even of one of the blocks.[82] There are no words for asking "what is that?" or "what is that called?" Within the language, it is not even possible to *wonder* what a certain building stone is called, for the speakers would not have the vocabulary (or syntax) to ask themselves that question. There can be no asking for the meaning of a word, or explaining the meaning of a word, or giving a synonym. And are there even concepts in this language? "It is not in every language-game that there occurs something that one would call a concept."[83]

Asking the name of an object "is, we might say, a language-game on its own. That is really to say: we are brought up, trained, to ask: 'What is that called?'—upon which the name is given. And there is also a language-game of *inventing* a name for something."[84] Asking for and explaining the names of things or the meanings of words are themselves language games; and we can expect them to be as different from the builders' game and from each other as the game played with number words was from the game played with the names of the building stones. Thus there emerges still a third aspect of what Wittgenstein means by a language game: besides games by which children are taught language, and imaginary primitive combinations of speech and action, language games also include our many verbal activities, the things we actually do by or with the use of language. "Review the multiplicity of language-games in the following examples, and in others:

Giving orders, and obeying them—
Describing the appearance of an object, or giving its measurements—
Constructing an object from a description (a drawing)—
Reporting an event—
Speculating about an event—
Forming and testing a hypothesis—
Presenting the results of an experiment in tables and diagrams—
Making up a story; and reading it—
Play-acting—
Singing catches—
Guessing riddles—

[82] *Ibid.*, par. 27.
[83] Wittgenstein, *Foundations of Mathematics*, p. 195.
[84] Wittgenstein, *Philosophical Investigations*, par. 27; my italics.

Making a joke; telling it—
Solving a problem in practical arithmetic—
Translating from one language into another—
Asking, thanking, cursing, greeting, praying."[85]

Any of these could be considered as a separate language game, and we could imagine a language consisting only of the words and actions necessary for that game. "It is easy to imagine a language consisting only of orders and reports in battle. —Or a language consisting only of questions and expressions for answering yes and no. And innumerable others."[86] In imagining such languages we need to think not only of the necessary vocabulary, but even more of what the speakers of the language *do,* as they talk. In each case "the speaking of language is part of an activity," and, consequently, "to imagine a language means to imagine a form of life."[87]

One reason Wittgenstein stresses the diversity of language games we play is to show what is wrong with the traditional assumption, formerly shared by him and implicit in the passage from Augustine, that the essential function of language is to make assertions about matters of fact. He says, "It is interesting to compare the multiplicity of tools in language and of the ways they are used, the multiplicity of kinds of word and sentence, with what logicians have said about the structure of language. (Including the author of the *Tractatus Logico-Philosophicus.*)"[88] Confronted with this multiplicity of language uses, we are less likely to suppose that one or two of them must be privileged cases which define the essence of language, and that the others need to be translated into these privileged cases before they can be fully understood. Referring, describing, asserting, stating, appear as just some more language games, no more exemplary than the rest. Wittgenstein no longer feels the need of translating or analyzing ordinary utterances into their true "logical form," the form of a simple assertion. Of course, sometimes in specific cases for specific purposes analysis is useful; it is useful to learn that "when he said X, he really meant Y." But we must not therefore suppose that there exists "something like a final analysis of our forms of language, and so a *single* completely resolved form of every expression."[89] Calling one sentence an analyzed version of another "readily seduces us into thinking that the former is the more fundamental form; that it alone shews what is meant by the other, and so on. For example, we think: If you have only the unanalysed form you miss the analysis; but if you know the analysed form that gives you everything. —But can I not say that an aspect of the matter is lost on you in the *latter* case as well as the former?"[90]

[85] *Ibid.,* par. 23.
[86] *Ibid.,* par. 19.
[87] *Ibid.*
[88] *Ibid.,* par. 23.
[89] *Ibid.,* par. 91.
[90] *Ibid.,* par. 63.

It is not that we never refer or describe, never make true or false assertions, never use words as labels. But these functions are not privileged or definitive. Just so, one can think of a label as a kind of tool, and we might keep some labels in our tool box; but anyone trying to generalize about tools, using only labels as his example, would be badly misled. Taking ostensive definitions as a model, one cannot understand how children learn language. Taking reference as a model, one cannot understand how words have meanings. As Cavell says, the point is not *"merely* that 'language has many functions' besides naming things; it is also that the way philosophers account for naming makes it incomprehensible how language can so much as perform *that* function."[91]

In this respect, the builders' game is meant to show us how different the learning of a natural language must be from that model. In the game, meaning is really indistinguishable from the appropriate action-response. Each word is associated with only a single language game, and when the assistant has mastered this game he knows all there is to know about the word. His training is a training for repetition: to do the same whenever he hears the same command. But a child has barely begun to learn its native language when it has learned to repeat a sound after us as we point. This pointing-and-naming is itself one language game, and mastering it is not mastering any others. Learning the meaning of a word in a natural language means becoming able to use it in all, or most, of its appropriate language games, not merely to repeat it after someone else. Thus, one might summarize Wittgenstein's critique of the passage from Augustine this way: Augustine describes the learning of language as if the child had only to learn new words, in connection with language games which it has already mastered. But the language games in which the word is to be used must also, somehow, be learned. "The ostensive definition," says Wittgenstein, "explains the use—the meaning—of the word [only] when the overall role of the word in the language is clear. Thus if I know that someone means to explain a colour-word to me the ostensive definition 'That is called "sepia"' will help me to understand the word."[92] Only if I know what a color is, am I fully ready for the meaning of "sepia." Here again, knowing what a color is means being able to do something, knowing how color terms are used.

## LEARNING LANGUAGE GAMES

Words are relatively easy to teach, but how does the child learn concepts, or come to master language games? Wittgenstein answers that the child learns them not by explanation, but by training. "How do I explain the meaning of 'regular', 'uniform', 'same' to anyone? —I shall explain

[91] Cavell, "Claim to Rationality," p. 208.
[92] Wittgenstein, *Philosophical Investigations*, par. 30; compare *On Certainty*, par. 548.

these words to someone who, say, only speaks French by means of the corresponding French words. But if a person has not yet got the *concepts*, I shall teach him to use the words by means of *examples* and by *practice*."[93] Training differs from explanation in at least these two ways: it is relatively nonverbal, relying on gestures, facial expressions, and the like; and it aims primarily at producing certain actions from the learner, quite apart from what goes on in his head. Dogs can be trained, but they cannot "understand explanations." One might teach a child the expression "the same," in such ways: "In the course of this teaching I shall shew him the same colours, the same lengths, the same shapes, I shall make him find them and produce them, and so on. I shall, for instance, get him to continue an ornamental pattern uniformly when told to do so. And also to continue progressions. . . . I do it, he does it after me; and I influence him by expressions of agreement, rejection, expectation, encouragement. I let him go his way, or hold him back; and so on."[94]

Nor would the kind of training given the assistant in the builders' game be sufficient for training a child in the language games of a natural language. For, as Noam Chomsky has recently pointed out, the most striking feature of a natural language is its "creative aspect." We can understand sentences we have never heard before if the words are familiar, and any competent speaker can use familiar words in contexts he has never before encountered. "A mature speaker can produce a new sentence of his language on the appropriate occasion, and other speakers can understand it immediately, though it is equally new to them. Most of our linguistic experience, both as speakers and hearers, is with new sentences; once we have mastered a language, the class of sentences with which we can operate fluently and without difficulty or hesitation is so vast that for all practical purposes (and, obviously, for all theoretical purposes), we can regard it as infinite."[95] The creative openness of language is even more striking when we look beyond changing sentences to changing correlations between speech and world. "The normal use of language is not only innovative and potentially infinite in scope, but also free from the control of detectable stimuli, either external or internal. It is because of this freedom from stimulus control that language can serve as an instrument of thought and self-expression, as it does not only for the exceptionally gifted and talented, but also, in fact, for every normal human."[96]

In short, to master a natural language it is not enough to be trained to do the same thing whenever the same situation occurs. The child does

[93] Wittgenstein, *Philosophical Investigations*, par. 208.
[94] *Ibid.*
[95] Noam Chomsky, "Current Issues in Linguistic Theory," in Jerry A. Fodor and Jerrold J. Katz, eds., *The Structure of Language* (Englewood Cliffs: Prentice-Hall, 1964), pp. 51, 50; compare Eric Lenneberg, "The Capacity for Language Acquisition," *ibid.*; and Wittgenstein, *Blue and Brown Books*, p. 21.
[96] Noam Chomsky, *Language and Mind* (New York: Harcourt, Brace & World, 1968); p. 11; compare Ziff's excellent discussion in *Semantic Analysis*, pp. 64–66.

not merely learn to construct new combinations of familiar pieces; it learns to *speak*, to tell us what it sees and thinks and feels.[97] The question is: How is that kind of learning possible? That question has a familiar traditional answer, closely correlated with the traditional view of language as a means of referring to phenomena: The child must somehow be brought to figure out, or intuit, or guess, the "universal" behind the particular examples or instances he is given, the "essence" of a concept, the meaning of a word. This traditional account Wittgenstein wants to challenge in two ways. First, he seeks to show that this explanation is not adequate, that the grasping of definitions or essences or universals cannot explain what needs to be explained. And, second, he tries to show that even the mastery of definitions, principles, generalities, depends ultimately on our natural human capacities and inclinations, which do not themselves have any further explanation.

The kind of training that is necessary to the acquisition of a natural language, Wittgenstein says, requires "inducing the child to go on" in the same *way*, in new and different cases. This is different from training for repetition, which "is not meant to apply to anything but the examples given"; this teaching "points beyond" the examples given.[98] Wittgenstein investigates this kind of training by means of language games that center on expanding a mathematical series. "A writes down a row of numbers. B watches him and tries to find a system in the sequence of these numbers."[99] At some point, B may say, "Now I can go on," and proceed to continue the series. Wittgenstein imagines these games as a kind of training, rather than explanation, the teacher "inducing" the child to go on in such ways as this: "he stops short in his enumeration with a facial expression and a raised tone of voice which we should call one of expectancy."[100] The training here is clearly different from that in the builders' game, for here the child must ultimately do more than repeat the same action on command. He will be expected to write down new numbers in accord with the teacher's system. He will be expected not to do the same thing, but to go on in the same way.

Though we might assume that, to continue the series, the learner must think of the correct mathematical formula for it, Wittgenstein argues that grasping the formula is neither necessary nor sufficient. When the learner says he can go on and proceeds to do so, he *may* just have thought of the formula. But he need not have; he might merely think, "Yes, I know *that* series," or have a sensation roughly parallel to the thought,

[97] Ziff, *Semantic Analysis*, p. 61; Fann, *Ludwig Wittgenstein*, p. 260; Paul Henle, ed., *Language, Thought and Culture* (Ann Arbor: University of Michigan Press, 1965), Ch. III.

[98] Wittgenstein, *Philosophical Investigations*, par. 208; compare Gilbert Ryle, *The Concept of Mind* (New York: Barnes & Noble, 1949), pp. 42–43.

[99] Wittgenstein, *Blue and Brown Books*, p. 112; compare p. 13; *Philosophical Investigations*, pars. 143, 151, 179–190; and Waismann, *Wittgenstein*, p. 153.

[100] Wittgenstein, *Blue and Brown Books*, p. 105.

"That's easy!"—a slight, quick intake of breath.[101] The significance of this point will become clear only later, when we turn to the nature of understanding. More important for present purposes is that even if the learner does think of the formula, even if it "comes to mind," he might nevertheless be unable to continue the series correctly. For even an algebraic formula needs to be applied, and that always means that it may be applied incorrectly. Giving the formula to a child that does not yet understand anything about mathematical series would not enable it to continue the series; the formula is helpful only to someone who correctly understands the technique of its application. It seems as though one would need a rule for the application of the formula. But that rule would itself require interpretation and application; so one would need another rule for its correct use. And so on, indefinitely. "A rule stands there like a sign-post. —Does the sign-post leave no doubt open about the way I have to go?"[102] Not only might someone read the arrow as pointing toward its butt rather than toward its head, but he might not even understand that it is meant to point at all, or that he is to follow it, or that he is to proceed in that direction on the path rather than setting out cross-country.

It may seem unfortunate that Wittgenstein uses analogies like games and mathematical series, for they are likely to mislead. They may suggest that Wittgenstein takes language, like games and mathematics, to be a matter of strict rules—rules that the child must learn, that the adult knows, that clearly define the meanings of words and sharply separate correct from incorrect usage.[103] But, of course, that was Wittgenstein's view when he wrote the *Tractatus*, a view that he says occurs often in philosophizing and that he is concerned to reject in his later writings. Characteristically he does so, as it were, on its own home grounds: by exploring the way rules actually work even in games and mathematical series, by showing that *even here* rules cannot account for what needs to be explained. Thus, he shows that while some games have formal, explicit rules, there are also informal children's games of which this is not true at all, and games in which one makes up rules as one goes along.[104] Moreover, while learning a game may entail explicitly learning its rules, it need not; one might learn it simply by observation and practice.[105] And even a game governed by definite, formal rules is not "everywhere circumscribed by rules"; there are no "rules for how high one throws the ball in tennis, or how hard; yet tennis is a game for all that and has rules too."[106] And above all, again,

[101] Wittgenstein, *Philosophical Investigations*, par. 151; compare *Blue and Brown Books*, pp. 112–113.

[102] Wittgenstein, *Philosophical Investigations*, par. 85; compare Waismann, *Wittgenstein*, pp. 154–155.

[103] Thus, for example, David Pole, *The Later Philosophy of Wittgenstein* (London: Athlone Press, 1963). My discussion is based on Cavell's criticism of Pole on this point: *Must We Mean What We Say?* pp. 47–52.

[104] Wittgenstein, *Philosophical Investigations*, par. 83.

[105] *Ibid.*, par. 31.

[106] *Ibid.*, par. 68; compare par. 84.

even the strictest rule or system of rules ultimately requires application.

The rule, the algebraic formula for generating a mathematical series, are analogies for the meaning of a word, in the sense of its dictionary definition. As formulas and rules require application, words in the language need to be *used*. And just as no rule dictates its own application, the dictionary definition of a word does not tell us how to use that word. It does not tell us, that is, unless we already know a great deal about that word, have the place for it already prepared in our system of concepts, know the language games in which it belongs. That is why, as we noted earlier, a dictionary definition is not much help in philosophy. And that is why language-learning cannot be understood as a matter of "grasping universals" or "essences" or "meanings."

We are almost irresistibly tempted to suppose that the numbers the teacher writes down, the examples he gives, are like clues from which the child is to guess the real message. But Wittgenstein suggests that the teacher's examples, and the child's own attempts, are not merely all that the child has to go on to guess the hidden essence. They are all there is; there is no hidden essence beyond them to guess. "We are tempted," Wittgenstein says, "to think that our examples are *indirect* means for producing a certain image or idea in a person's mind,—that they *hint* at something which they cannot show."[107] It seems as though "the instructor *imparted* the meaning to the pupil—without telling him it directly; but in the end the pupil is brought to the point of giving himself the correct ostensive definition. And this is where our illusion is."[108] We are tempted to exclaim, "Don't you get him to *guess* the essential thing? You give him examples,—but he has to guess their drift, to guess your intention."[109] But that implies, as we have seen before, that the child already has a language, a conceptual system, among whose elements he then selects one, guessing the meaning we intended or the response we wanted. "There is a queer misunderstanding we are most liable to fall into, which consists in regarding the 'outward means' the teacher uses to induce the child to go on as what we might call an indirect means of making himself understood to the child. We regard the case as though the child already possessed a language in which it thought and that the teacher's job is to induce it to guess his meaning in the realm of meanings before the child's mind, as though the child could in his own private language ask himself such a question as, 'Does he want me to continue, or repeat what he said, or something else?' "[110]

But, to put it baldly, there is no further knowledge that the teacher has at which his examples only hint. The examples constitute his knowledge, too. When I teach someone a new concept (as distinct from a new name to

---

[107] Wittgenstein, *Blue and Brown Books*, p. 125.
[108] Wittgenstein, *Philosophical Investigations*, par. 362.
[109] *Ibid.*, par. 210.
[110] Wittgenstein, *Blue and Brown Books*, p. 105.

fit into a system of concepts, a language game he has already mastered) by example and practice, "I do not communicate less to him than I know myself."[111] Of course the teacher knows the formula, the rule, the definition; but that can be *explained* to the pupil who has the necessary concepts, has mastered the relevant language games. For such a pupil, it does not need to be *hinted at*. The place where explanation fails and training is called for is where the pupil lacks the knowledge of how to *use* the word. And that kind of knowledge is completely contained in the examples; about how to use the words, the teacher himself knows only from the examples he has mastered. The knowledge of language games is a "knowing how" rather than a "knowing that."

"One gives examples and intends them to be taken in a particular way. —I do not, however, mean by this that he is supposed to see in those examples that common thing which I—for some reason—was unable to express; but that he is now to *employ* those examples in a particular way. Here giving examples is not an *indirect* means of explaining—in default of a better. For any general definition can be misunderstood too."[112] The child is to do certain things and not other things on the basis of the examples; what he is to do is reflected in the teacher's response. The correct, or intended, action by the child will win encouragement or praise. If the child is thereby induced to do the right thing again, and repeatedly, he has "learned" what there is to learn.

But, of course, everything depends on the child responding correctly to the "training methods" we have available and being able to do the things we are trying to train him to do—pronounce our sounds and notice what we notice in the world. Only if the child is encouraged by encouraging gestures, deterred by movements to hold him back, pleased by our signs of agreement, can it be trained at all. And only its natural capacity to perceive and speak as we do enables it to learn. Wittgenstein says, "If a lion could talk, we could not understand him."[113] Characteristically, he does not explain; but Ziff does: "To be able to speak and to understand English one must have (either natural or artificial) sensory organs capable of making contrasts between 'bin', 'fin', 'gin', 'kin', etc., and between a bin, a din, a fin, gin, kin, etc."[114] That much is simply natural; that much must simply be accepted as given.

In teaching the mathematical series language games, what the teacher does by way of encouragement or correction must depend on what specific mistakes the learner makes, where he goes wrong. Perhaps "first of all, series of numbers will be written down for him and he will be required to copy them. . . . And here already there is a normal and abnormal learner's reaction. —At first perhaps we guide his hand in writing out the

[111] Wittgenstein, *Philosophical Investigations*, par. 208.

[112] *Ibid.*, par. 71.

[113] *Ibid.*, p. 223.

[114] Ziff, *op. cit.*, p. 75; compare Willard van Orman Quine, *Word and Object* (Cambridge: M.I.T. Press, 1960), p. 83.

series . . . ; but then the *possibility of getting him to understand* will depend on his going on to write it down independently. —And here we can imagine, e.g., that he does copy the figures independently, but not in the right order: he writes sometimes one sometimes another at random. And then communication stops at *that* point. —Or again, he makes '*mistakes*' in the order."[115] At each step, "the effect of any further *explanation* depends on his *reaction*."[116]

Suppose, for example, that we have gotten our pupil to write the series 2, 4, 6, 8, . . . and tested him on it up to 1,000. Now we get him to continue it beyond 1,000 and he writes 1,000, 1,004, 1,008, 1,012. "We say to him: 'Look what you've done!'—He doesn't understand. We say: 'You were meant to add *two*: look how you began the series!' —He answers: 'Yes, isn't it right? I thought that was how I was *meant* to do it.'——Or suppose he pointed to the series and said: 'But I went on in the same way.' . . . In such a case we might say, perhaps: It comes natural to this person to understand our order with our explanations as *we* should understand the order 'Add 2 up to 1,000, 4 up to 2,000, 6 up to 3,000, and so on.' "[117] Such training must have a foundation in natural, prelinguistic, human reactions.

In his later writings, then, Wittgenstein develops a radically different view of the nature of language-learning, meaning, and language itself. In the traditional view, words stand for things, and the child must somehow form a correct induction about the class of things for which a particular words stands. In Wittgenstein's later view, words are used to do things, and the child must master how they are used. Such learning is necessarily a matter of training rather than explanation since it precedes the possibility of explanation. And it rests ultimately on our natural capacities. Cavell sums up the view this way: "We learn and teach words in *certain* contexts, and then we are expected, and expect others, to be able to project them into further contexts. Nothing *insures* that this projection will take place (in particular, not the grasping of universals nor the grasping of books of rules), just as nothing insures that we will make, and understand, the same projections. That on the whole we do is a matter of our sharing routes of interest and feeling, modes of response, senses of humor and of significance and of fulfillment, of what is outrageous, of what is similar to what else, what a rebuke, what forgiveness, of when an utterance is an assertion, when an appeal, when an explanation—all the whirl of organism Wittgenstein calls 'forms of life.' Human speech and activity, sanity and community, rest upon nothing more, but nothing less, than this."[118]

[115] Wittgenstein, *Philosophical Investigations*, par. 143.
[116] *Ibid.*, par. 145.
[117] *Ibid.*, par. 185.
[118] Cavell, *Must We Mean What We Say?* p. 52.

# III

## *Language Learning and Meaning*

THE PROBLEM of language-learning, of how we come to master our native language, is a continuing central concern in Wittgenstein's later work. Again and again he inquires "How did we *learn* the meaning of this word . . . ? From what sort of examples? In what language-games?" But he is not interested in these matters for their own sake; he uses them to investigate the nature of what the child learns: language, concepts, meaning. And these, in turn, illuminate human life and thought, and our world. In this chapter we shall explore one of the most fundamental features of language-learning and meaning that Wittgenstein stresses: their piecemeal, conglomerate quality. Like the training by examples which "point beyond" themselves, learning one's native language is what I shall call a "learning from cases." And the concepts and meanings one learns are consequently also composite, assembled out of cases. The significance of these ideas may be approximated (though also in each case somewhat distorted) by looking at three nonlinguistic examples: the contrast between common-law and Roman-law systems; Michael Oakeshott's contrast between habitual, inarticulate morality and didactic morality based on explicit principles; and Thomas Kuhn's contrast between science seen as the activity of scientists and science seen as a body of achieved knowledge.

The contrast between common-law and Roman-law systems is perhaps the most familiar. Legal systems which originated under Roman domination derive from a single, authoritative, systematic legal code, drafted for and promulgated by a ruler and altered only by legislation. Roman-law judges are supposed to decide cases with reference to this code, supplemented where necessary by the commentaries and opinions of legal experts as to what the code means. They need not read or consult each others' decisions. Common law, by contrast, is not derived from any compre-

---

[1] Ludwig Wittgenstein, *Philosophical Investigations*, tr. by G. E. M. Anscombe (New York: Macmillan, 1968), par. 77.

hensive legal code; and though it may be altered by legislation, the great bulk of it does not originate in legislation. It originates in judicial cases, in particular decisions of particular judges, in accord with the principle of *stare decisis* which requires consistency and continuity, so that earlier decisions become binding precedent for later cases. The elaboration of principles in the common law is accomplished less by the commentaries of legal scholars than by the actual decisions rendered by judges in particular disputes.

Common-law courts do not normally give advisory opinions, considering principles in the abstract; their decisions are always reached in the context of some specific, real dispute. As a consequence, in studying the common law, it is often difficult to be sure just which features of a case were the decisive ones. Unlike hypothetical examples we invent, real legal cases have an infinite complexity of "features" that might be relevant. Participants, judges, students, have to determine what the relevant features are. The characteristic reasoning of common-law courts is what one commentator has called "reasoning by example."[2] Of course, common-law courts do write opinions and are expected to be consistent; so principles of common law do exist also. But the way those principles are articulated, and used, and learned, is different from the way the precepts of Roman law are articulated, used, and learned. The articulation of principles by a common-law court, like the court's statement about which features of a case were decisive, is always subject to further articulation and revision in later cases, in ways that could not have been foreseen. Facts in a case that were never explicitly mentioned in the decision settling it may turn out in retrospect, in the light of a later case, to be quite crucial. An articulation of principle that seemed fully adequate at the time may turn out, in the light of later, unanticipated cases, to be an improper formulation. Sometimes we get the disturbing impression that, as one commentator has said, in the common law "the rules change from case to case and are remade with each case."[3] One might say that the principles always remain in some sense derivative, dependent on the particular cases from which they are abstracted. That is why the common law is so often taught by the "case method," so that students learn not merely the principles but also the concrete content of the particular decisions in which these principles were fashioned. The abstract principles are given their full meaning and content, are fleshed out, by the details of the cases in which they arose; and only someone who can go back to the cases in all their original richness and complexity will know how to apply the principles consistently in new cases.

The distinction between Roman-law and common-law systems is paralleled by the distinction Michael Oakeshott draws between two forms,

[2] Edgar Bodenheimer, "A Neglected Theory of Legal Reasoning," *Journal of Legal Education*, 21 (1969), 373.
[3] Edward H. Levi, *Introduction to Legal Reasoning* (1949), p. 2, cited *ibid*.

as he calls them, of the moral life, each with its characteristic way of being learned.[4] The one form of moral life, he says, is reflective, rationalistic, principled, and articulate; its practitioners can say what they are doing and why, state the principles on which they act. The child is instructed in its principles systematically. In its other form, "the moral life is *a habit of affection and behavior,* not a habit of reflective *thought* but a habit of *affection* and *conduct.* . . . There is on the occasion, nothing more than the unreflective following of a tradition of conduct in which we have been brought up."[5] This being brought up in a tradition is very different than learning from explicit, systematic principles or rules; and Oakeshott himself compares it to the way a child learns language. "We acquire habits of conduct, not by constructing a way of living upon rules or precepts learned by heart and subsequently practiced, but by living with people who habitually behave in a certain manner: we acquire habits of conduct in the same way as we acquire our native language. . . . What we learn here is what may be learned without the formulation of its rules."[6]

Focusing on the first, the explicitly principled form of morality, we are likely to say that morality is the system of rules we teach our children; focusing on the second, the inarticulate form, we are likely to say that morality is an activity or a way of conducting oneself. For it is not merely that the one form is taught by means of rules and the other by means of practice; the two forms are *constituted* in correspondingly different ways. The first kind of morality is deductive; its principles exist prior to its practice, and define that practice. The second kind is built up out of the practice itself. It is one of those activities which "emerge naively, like games that children invent for themselves." It appears, "not in response to a premeditated achievement, but as a direction of attention pursued without premonition of what it will lead to. . . . For a direction of attention, as it is pursued, may hollow out a character for itself and become specified in a 'practice.' "[7]

This kind of activity also has principles or rules, but they are abstracted from the practice and emerge out of it. As in language, Oakeshott says, so in inarticulate habitual morality: "what is learnt (or some of it) can be formulated in rules and precepts"; but the rules "are mere abridgements of the activity itself; they do not exist in advance of the activity."[8] This means, first, that the rules get their real content and meaning from the activity, are fleshed out by it. In a similar way, a constitutional or ideological principle is meaningful in the political life of a nation only to the extent that it is lived and practiced; and *what* it means, its content, is defined precisely by *how* it is lived and practiced. In that sense, "the

4 Michael Oakeshott, *Rationalism in Politics* (New York: Basic Books, 1962), esp. "The Tower of Babel" and "Political Education."
5 *Ibid.,* p. 61.
6 *Ibid.,* p. 62.
7 *Ibid.,* p. 135.
8 *Ibid.,* pp. 62, 101.

freedom of an Englishman is not something exemplified in the procedure of *habeas corpus*, it *is*, at that point, the availability of that procedure."[9] And this means, second, that learning the rules or principles intellectually is not equivalent to mastering the practice; for *that* would require knowing how to use and apply them in all the inarticulate detail of the practice. Thus, for example, a cookbook is of use only to someone who already knows how to cook. "It is the stepchild not the parent of the activity" of cooking.[10]

A third parallel to Oakeshott's discussion of morality and the difference between Roman-law and common-law systems may be found in Kuhn's influential study, *The Structure of Scientific Revolutions*.[11] Though we often, and justifiably, think of science as a systematic body of acquired knowledge, Kuhn argues that to the practicing scientist it looks much more like an activity; and so the historian of science does well to regard it as an activity, too. Though school children are taught science in terms of its accumulated, systematic principles, scientists themselves learn their profession primarily through studying what Kuhn calls "paradigms" of scientific achievement. By paradigms, Kuhn says he means "universally recognized scientific achievements that for a time provide model problems and solutions to a community of practitioners."[12] They are concrete achievements in actual scientific practice, serving as "models from which spring particular coherent traditions of scientific research."[13] They are not articulated explications of principles or rules or theory, but unanalyzed bundles of scientific practice, including "law, theory, application, and instrumentation together."[14]

Studying paradigms "is what mainly prepares the student for membership in the particular scientific community with which he will later practice. Because he there joins men who learned the bases of their field from the same concrete models, his subsequent practice will seldom evoke overt disagreement over fundamentals. Men whose research is based on shared paradigms are committed to the same rules and standards for scientific practice."[15]

Kuhn recognized that the term "paradigm" is in at least one way misleading. "In its established usage, a paradigm is an accepted model or pattern. . . . In grammar, for example, '*amo, amas, amat*' is a paradigm because it displays the pattern to be used in conjugating a large number of other Latin verbs, e.g., in producing '*laudo, laudas, laudat*.' In this

[9] *Ibid.*, p. 121.
[10] *Ibid.*, p. 119; compare also p.101.
[11] Thomas S. Kuhn, *The Structure of Scientific Revolutions* in *International Encyclopedia of Unified Science*, Second Edition, (Chicago: University of Chicago Press, 1970). Compare Oakeshott, *op. cit.*, pp. 119, 213, 215.
[12] Kuhn, *op. cit.*, p. x.
[13] *Ibid.*, p. 10; compare "Postscript—1969," pp. 174–210.
[14] *Ibid.*
[15] *Ibid.*, p. 11. Kuhn is ambivalent on this last point, as subsequent quoted passages indicate.

standard application, the paradigm functions by permitting the replication of examples any one of which could in principle serve to replace it. In a science, on the other hand, a paradigm is rarely an object for replication. Instead, like an accepted judicial decision in the common law, it is an object for further articulation and specification under new or more stringent conditions."[16] It is an example, in short, that "points beyond itself," that needs to be applied to always new and different problems. For instance, a paradigm developed in studying one set of phenomena may be "ambiguous in its application to other closely related ones. Then experiments are necessary to choose among the alternative ways of applying the paradigm to the new area of interest."[17]

Like Oakeshott, Kuhn is anxious to make the point that learning from paradigms (in this open-ended sense) has different effects than learning from explicit rules or principles which someone else has abstracted for you. He, too, says that "rules . . . derive from paradigms, but paradigms can guide research even in the absence of rules."[18] It is relatively easy to determine what the shared paradigms of a mature scientific community are, but that is not yet a determination of the community's shared *rules*. The latter "demands a second step and one of a somewhat different kind. When undertaking it, the historian must compare the community's paradigms with each other and with its current research reports. In doing so, his object is to discover what isolable elements, explicit or implicit, the members of that community may have *abstracted* from their more global paradigms and deployed as rules in their research."[19] The scientists themselves apparently can "agree in their *identification* of a paradigm without agreeing on, or even attempting to produce, a full *interpretation* or *rationalization* of it. Lack of a standard interpretation or of an agreed reduction to rules will not prevent a paradigm from guiding research. . . . Indeed, the existence of a paradigm need not even imply that any full set of rules exists."[20]

Finally, as in our earlier examples, the principles or rules abstracted gain their significance and content only from the cases, the activity, on which they are based. The very concepts in which the principles are formulated derive their meaning from the paradigms in which they originate. The verbal definitions of such concepts, as Kuhn says, "have little scientific content when considered by themselves. . . . The scientific concepts to which they point gain full significance only when related, within a text or other systematic presentation, to other scientific concepts, to manipulative procedures, and to paradigm applications."[21]

[16] *Ibid.*, p. 23.
[17] *Ibid.*, p. 29.
[18] *Ibid.*, p. 42.
[19] *Ibid.*, p. 43.
[20] *Ibid.*, p. 44.
[21] *Ibid.*, p. 142; compare p. 47.

Common law, habitual morality, science as an activity, all display important features illuminating how we learn our native language, and what it is we learn. They are all activities which do have principles, rules, general theories; but either the principles remain completely inarticulate and implicit, or they are abstracted *ad hoc* when they are needed and remain always secondary to the concrete instances from which they are drawn. In none of our examples are the principles laid down in a systematic, deductive way at the outset, by some authority or in accord with some conscious plan; rather they accrue gradually through practice, subject to the exigencies of practice. Thus, their real meaning and full significance is completed only by the concrete cases from which they derive, and is accessible only to someone familiar with those cases, with the practice. These principles, and the corresponding practice, are both *learned from* and *constituted by* particular cases.

All this is equally true of the way a child learns its native language. But our examples are also likely to be misleading in certain respects. For they suggest that there is an alternative way of learning and constituting those activities: the didactic morality of articulated principles, the systematic code of Roman law. But in learning to speak no such alternative is available. No natural language is or could be didactically laid down by a legislator, nor could any child be taught its native language as a body of articulated rules. The child must grow and learn simultaneously, and what it learns neither needs to be nor can be fully articulated. At least until it is mature enough to ask for and understand definitions, the child simply encounters words. Mostly, it encounters them in situations where no one is trying to teach it anything; in this respect our whole discussion in the previous chapter was misleading. The child simply lives among persons who talk. For the most part, as Ziff says, "one is not taught one's native language, one learns it."[22]

Most of the time, the child does not encounter words in isolation either; here, too, the previous chapter misleads. Perhaps we tend to think of learning language as a matter of learning isolated words, because children speak isolated words long before they combine them into more complex utterances; or perhaps we are misled by thinking only of those occasions when we deliberately try to teach a word to the child.[23] But the child

[22] Paul Ziff, *Semantic Analysis* (Ithaca: Cornell University Press, 1960), p. 35.
[23] Eric Lenneberg, "The Capacity for Language Acquisition," in Jerry A. Fodor and Jerrold J. Katz, eds., *The Structure of Language* (Englewood Cliffs: Prentice-Hall, 1964), pp. 593–4: "All children go through identical phases in the process of acquiring speech. First, they have a few words or phrases, never longer than three syllables, that refer [sic] to objects, persons, or complex situations. At this stage they may have a repertoire of fifty short utterances that are somewhat stereotyped

normally encounters not isolated words but whole utterances, in complex verbal contexts and worldly situations. What it learns about language, it learns from these contexts, verbal and worldly, and not from rules or principles or formulae. No two situations a child experiences are exactly alike; each has an unlimited number of possible "features" which might be singled out as semantically relevant. No one tells the child what is relevant, because no one is able to do so. The child may or may not notice any or all of the objects and people present, feelings (its own and other people's), actions (before, during, and after speech), relationships, and, of course, the spoken words. Wittgenstein says the child learns a word "under certain circumstances, which, however, [it] does not learn to describe," for "a description of those circumstances is not needed." In order to be able to use a word correctly, one "would *not* have to be able to describe its use."[24] And if an adult were asked to describe a word's use explicitly, he might well "give a quite inadequate description. (Like most people, if they tried to describe the use of money correctly). (They are not prepared for such a task)."[25]

Of course, we must not construe the child's learning as a matter of intentional inductive inquiry, as if the child were a small adult doing research on the "code" that is our language. The child need not formulate a hypothesis in order to speak, nor can it yet formulate a hypothesis. It is simply moved to do something that feels appropriate to the situation, because something about the situation seems familiar. Placed in the chair where yesterday we played pat-a-cake, the child claps its hands. Standing before the bathroom mirror, it begins to "shave" like father. In a certain situation, it makes a sound that was made there before.[26] First of all children imitate us, try to be like us and do what we do. Thus, they often repeat our utterances with a startlingly accurate imitation of our intonation and gestures. No doubt the word must already "mean something to" the child, or it would not be repeated in this situation, but the child need not think about its reasons, and need not "know what the word means."

and are never combined one with the other. All attempts to make the child string up the words that he is known to use singly will fail until he reaches a certain stage of maturation. When this is attained, the combining of words seems to be quite automatic, that is, he will surprise the parents by suddenly putting two words together that may not have been given him for repetition, in fact, that may often sound queer enough to make it quite unlikely that anyone in the child's environment has ever spoken these words in just that sequence. 'Eat cup' may mean [sic?] 'the dog is eating out of the cup' or 'is the dog eating the cup?' and so on. Whatever was meant by this utterance (which was actually heard), it is a sequence of words that nobody had used in the particular situation in which the words were spoken. As the child grows older, longer phrases are composed of individual vocabulary items which had been in the child's repertoire for many months, sometimes years."

[24] Ludwig Wittgenstein, *Zettel*, tr. by G. E. M. Anscombe, ed. by G. E. M. Anscombe and G. H. von Wright (Berkeley and Los Angeles: University of California Press, 1967), pars. 114–115.

[25] *Ibid.*, par. 525.

[26] See particularly Torgny T. Segerstedt, *Die Macht des Wortes* (Zürich: Pan-Verlag, 1947), pp. 35–60.

Consider another example of actual language-learning, in this case involving a three-and-a-half-year-old friend of mine. It is quite characteristic for children about that age to startle us from time to time by suddenly saying something far beyond their usual vocabulary, sounding incongruously grown-up. My friend came into her parents' bedroom in the morning, dragging her blanket. Told to take the blanket back and put it on her bed, she said, "I simply can't function in the morning without my blanket." At first her parents were astonished; they had no idea that a word like "function" was in the child's vocabulary. But then they recognized the expression as one the mother characteristically uses about her morning coffee, and everything seemed clear: the child had merely "picked up" the expression. Moreover, she "picked it up" well enough to use it correctly on this (almost?) appropriate occasion. Or should we say rather that something in the configuration of the situation reminded her of those other situations, involving mother and coffee, and she just found herself saying the words? Does the child at this moment know what a function is, what "function" means? The question has no clear answer; one wants to say yes and no. The child clearly knows something about the word, knows how to do at least one thing with it competently. But she cannot yet use it in other linguistic environments than "simply can't . . . without"; and if we asked her what it means she could not tell us.

With this example, we are no longer tempted at all to say that the child learned whatever it learned about the meaning of "function" from an adult's pointing out a function to it. Clearly it was the child itself that "looked at language and looked at the world and looked back and forth," as Ziff puts it, without deliberate adult inducement. And the language it looked at was not a word in isolation but a whole phrase, learned to some extent as a unit.[27] And the "world" it looked at was not just a collection of objects, one of which was being labeled or referred to. The world included people, and their feelings and actions, and consequences. What recurred was a context somehow familiar because a person (mother, child) was about to be deprived of something (coffee, blanket) and said something which altered the situation so that the person was not deprived after all. But if we say that the child recognizes recurrent factors in speech situations, that again is liable to be misunderstood to mean that the word is the name of the situation, rather than of an object. Thus we think of "bye-bye" as the child's label for situations of departure, and "no-no" as its term for referring to forbidden objects (we even join in, telling the child, "That's a 'no-no' "). But words need not be labels here at all, but like signals in a game, the appropriate thing to do under these circum-

<hr/>

[27] Clearly, much depends on the phrase "to some extent." For the phrase "simply can't_____without my . . ." forms a relatively fixed verbal environment for "function" at this point, but the child easily substituted "blanket" for "coffee" as the occasion required. Compare Lev Vygotsky, *Thought and Language*, ed. and tr. by Eugenia Haufmann and Gertrude Vakar (Cambridge: M.I.T. Press, 1966), pp. 87, 127–128; and Wittgenstein, *Zettel*, par. 150.

stances. "I simply can't function without . . ." is not the name of a situation, but an appropriate utterance to be said in that situation. If the child has learned the meaning of words by induction here, the induction was not about "what counts as an x" but about "when one says x."

To be sure, this is an account only of the early stages in language-learning. Once the child has begun to speak, its mastery of language is furthered by its own efforts and our responses. But our responses, too, can be misunderstood; no one tells the child what counts as a response, what as encouragement, what as correction. The child simply moves from cases in which it hears the word used to cases in which it utters the word. If there are authorities in this process, it is because the child takes them as authorities. "If what can be said in a language is not determined by rules, nor its understanding secured through universals, and if there are always new contexts to be met, new needs, new relationships, objects, perceptions to be recorded and shared," as Cavell says, then "though 'in a sense' we learn the meaning of words and what objects are, the learning is never over, and we keep finding new potencies in words and new ways in which objects are conceptualized."[28]

As the child begins to master considerable portions of its native language, the systematic nature of language becomes a powerful aid to learning. New cases encountered can be assimilated to and fit into familiar patterns, and the accumulated store of familiar cases grows larger. (Chomsky has argued persuasively that at least some linguistic transformation patterns are inborn and occur in every human language, so that they need not be learned at all. For our purposes, it does not matter whether he is right in this interesting hypothesis.) Even if the child encounters a wholly new concept, the verbal context may be familiar enough to convey some idea of the meaning. Ziff speaks in this connection of "the principle of composition," roughly, a rule of economy or simplicity in trying to pair an utterance with those aspects of the circumstances in which it is uttered that are relevant to its meaning.[29] This again sounds more like scientific research than like a child learning to talk, but Ziff's basic point is valid.

We have said that the child learns the meanings of words from encountering these words in use, in verbal and worldly contexts. But not all of these examples it encounters will be suitable for learning: not every context is one in which a word can be correctly learned.[30] The child hears "the cat is on the mat," but in fact no animal is sitting on any small rug nearby; rather, a logico-grammatical discussion is under way. Or perhaps the speaker makes a mistake, pointing to a plastic cup and saying "that

[28] Stanley Cavell, "The Claim to Rationality" (unpublished dissertation, Harvard University), p. 219.

[29] Ziff, *Semantic Analysis*, pp. 61–66.

[30] Cavell, "Claim to Rationality," p. 201. The entire controversy in the philosophical literature over the validity of arguments from "paradigm cases" is founded on this problem about learning our native language. See, for example, the debate between A. G. N. Flew and J. W. N. Watkins in *Analysis* 18 (December 1957), 25–42.

is a glass." Or perhaps he tells the child a lie, or speaks in metaphor, or makes a joke, or reads a quotation, or speaks ironically. Adults can usually recognize "standard" deviations like quotation, poetry, irony, from certain characteristic and largely conventional "markers" by which they are distinguished.[31] But the child has yet to master those markers. How does it distinguish "valid" examples? (Child)

The simple answer is that the child has no way of separating the "valid" from the "invalid" examples that it encounters, but the principle of composition is of significant help in eliminating deviations. Though there may be no cat on any mat when the child hears "the cat is on the mat," that sentence is structurally much like countless others encountered in other environments ("the dog is on the rug," "the cat is on the bed," "the cat is on the prowl," and so on). Moreover, though the environmental conditions for saying "the glass is half full" may be exactly the same as those for saying "the glass is half empty," those for saying "keep pouring until it is half full" are significantly different from those for saying "keep pouring until it is half empty"; and though we may say "fill it half full," we are not likely to say "fill it half empty."[32] Such problems of learning seem puzzling only as long as we think of each word or expression as a label for some visible phenomenon that should (ideally) be present to be named. But the child can learn a great deal about, say, rain, even if we make a mistake and say "it's raining" when in fact it is not raining. It can, for example, learn that rain requires the wearing of slickers and boots, will be good for the crops, means cancellation of the picnic. And perhaps if a mistake has been made, the child will later learn that "it isn't raining after all."[33]

Of course, sometimes the child will in fact learn wrong, draw the wrong conclusions about a word and make spurious connections among patterns. Each of us has at least one treasured example of such a mistake he once made as a child. Mine concerned the word "nebbach," a Yiddish word which had found its way into my parents' otherwise almost completely German vocabulary. "Nebbach" in fact means something like "unfortunately," and functions as an interjection ("I saw George and, nebbach, he's looking terrible"). Somehow I developed the idea that it was connected with the German words "neben" and "nebenbei," which mean "next to" or "beside," and I concluded that "nebbach" meant something like "by the way," "by the bye" or "incidentally" ("I saw George and, incidentally, he's looking terrible"). And I understood and used the word that way until well into my adolescence, when one day I used it in a particularly incongruous context, on an occasion when my mother happened to have the time to listen and to question me. Then, of course, she corrected me and I found out what "nebbach" really means. The point is,

[31] Ziff, Semantic Analysis, pp. 72–74.
[32] Ibid., p. 154.
[33] Ibid., pp. 138–139.

first, that children can mislearn; second, that such mislearning is likely to be reinforced by some spurious correlation or pattern of exactly the same sort that helps them to learn correctly in other instances; and third, that children can sometimes get along nicely for years with their incorrect understanding.

Eventually we become able to ask for and understand explanations, and to look up definitions in a dictionary. We become able to abstract rules, principles, definitions, explicitly for ourselves when we need them. Wittgenstein says, "we talk, we utter words, and only *later* get a picture of their life."[34] And the picture, the principle, the definitions, we abstract is always in a way tentative, subject to revision or replacement after further experience, as is true in all learning from cases.

MEANING

All that has been said about how we learn our native language is intended primarily to clarify the nature of language itself, of meaning, and of conceptual thought. For what we learn from cases is all we know, and we do eventually know meanings and concepts. As with the common law, habitual morality, science as activity, not just the learning, but the very substance of the enterprise is constituted of cases, conglomerate. The meanings of words are not merely learned from cases of their use; they are generated by, changed by, fleshed out and given content by, their use in various cases. The child learns the meaning of "function" from hearing it used, or using it, in expressions like "I simply can't function without . . ." on appropriate occasions. And the adults, who know what "function" means, do not know anything different in kind from what the child knows; they have only encountered more cases. We may be inclined to suppose that you cannot understand an expression like "I simply can't function without . . ." until you know what "function" means. But Wittgenstein suggests that, quite the other way around, the meaning is built up out of such expressions.

"What 'determining the length' means is not learned by learning what *length* and *determining* are; the meaning of the word 'length' is learnt by learning, among other things, what it is to determine length."[35] And, one might add, learning this in various contexts; for, of course, "determining length" is a very different activity for the length of a life, the length of a term paper, and the length of a room. Wittgenstein says that we are inclined to think of "measuring the distance to the sun" as if it *could* also

---

[34] Wittgenstein, *Philosophical Investigations*, p. 209; compare Michael Polanyi, *Personal Knowledge* (New York and Evanston: Harper and Row, 1964), p. 250: "The formalization of meaning relies therefore *from the start* on the practice of unformalized meaning."

[35] Wittgenstein, *Philosophical Investigations*, p. 225.

be measured by a ruler.[36] For many purposes this does no harm. It does harm if the analogy leads us into contradictions, confusions, paradoxes; if we begin to feel that distance (length) is the sort of thing which can *in principle* be measured by a ruler wherever it occurs. But why should we suppose that? Is the length of a room (or the distance from wall to wall) a more definitive, more privileged instance of "length" than other instances? We learn the meaning of length from a great variety—a whole family—of cases. The question "How do we measure length," with its family of instances, helps us to understand what length *is*. What length is may be *abstracted* from the uses of "measuring length" together with the uses of "being longer than," together with the uses of "having changed in length," and so on. And each of these expressions will have a variety of uses, differing for lives, term papers, or rooms.

This does not mean that the word "length" is vague or loose, lacks meaning, or cannot be defined. We can define it, and, of course, as Cavell points out, "for some sorts of precision, for some purposes, we will need definitions."[37] But the definitions are based on, and secondary to, cases; and they do not interfere with the creative openness of natural language. We *can* give one of our concepts rigid limits, use one of our words for a rigidly limited concept, but Wittgenstein says we can also use it "so that the extension of the concept is *not* closed by a frontier."[38] And that is how we ordinarily use the concepts in our natural language, as distinct, say, from the concepts of mathematics. It is difficult to find and tell the boundary of an ordinary concept because it has none. "We do not know the boundaries because none have been drawn . . . we can *draw* a boundary—for a special purpose."[39] But when we do that, though we "are free" to draw the boundary as we like, it "will never entirely coincide with the actual usage, as this usage has no sharp boundary."[40] If someone else tried to draw a sharp boundary, "I could not acknowledge it as the one that I too always wanted to draw, or had drawn in my mind. For I did not want to draw one at all."[41]

Cavell says, "We learn the use of 'feed the kitty,' 'feed the lion,' 'feed the swans,' and one day one of us says 'feed the meter,' or 'feed in the film,' or 'feed the machine,' or 'feed his pride,' or 'feed wire,' and we understand, we are not troubled."[42] The passage can serve equally well to show how language is learned, or what language is like: how meanings

---

[36] Wittgenstein, *Foundations of Mathematics*, tr. by G. E. M. Anscombe, ed. by G. H. von Wright, R. Rhees, and G. E. M. Anscombe (Oxford: Basil Blackwell, 1964), p. 67.

[37] Cavell, "Claim to Rationality," p. 219.

[38] Wittgenstein, *Philosophical Investigations*, par. 68.

[39] *Ibid.*, par. 69; my italics.

[40] Ludwig Wittgenstein, *Blue and Brown Books* (New York and Evanston: Harper and Row, 1964), p. 19.

[41] Wittgenstein, *Philosophical Investigations*, par. 76.

[42] Cavell, "Claim to Rationality," p. 220.

are composed, how adults operate with language, how language grows and changes.[43] Each involves a kind of projection from a series of familiar, paradigmatic cases into new and unprecedented ones; yet, in each, not just any projection will be acceptable, and the permissible routes of projection are deeply controlled.

It is tempting to say that this is the whole point about natural language, what natural language is *for*. Why do we not confine words to the precise context in which they originate, or in which we first encounter them? Why do we not use a new and different word each time we encounter a new context? But each context is new. The result would not be a language at all; for how could one "learn" the "meanings" of "words" which were used once only and then discarded, like paper tissues? Surely the point in talking is precisely to connect new, unfamiliar situations to old, familiar ones, whether it be to aid our own understanding or to inform someone else or to further some activity or to express some feeling. And language can make such connections for us only if concepts are projectible, but projectible in regularized ways, ways that really do make relevant connections. Cavell says, "what Wittgenstein ultimately wishes to show is that it *makes no sense* at all to give a general explanation for the generality of language, because it makes no sense at all to suppose words in general might *not* recur, that we might possess a name for a thing (say 'chair' or 'feeding') and yet be willing to call *nothing* (else) 'the same thing.' "[44] As Wittgenstein says, "concepts are not for use on a single occasion" only.[45]

The individual must draw his own conclusions, abstract his own definitions from the cases he encounters; it is all up to him. And yet it is not all up to him, for there is such a thing as making a mistake, learning wrong. Children do that, and then we correct them. But even as adults we sometimes find out that we do not know the meaning of a word we thought we knew. Actually, one must distinguish at least three levels here, since it is always conceivable that the adult "correcting" a child could himself be mistaken about correct usage or the meaning of a word. We must distinguish the child (or, more broadly, any speaker), the adult (or, more broadly, any hearer) who might potentially correct him, and what we generally call "the English language." The language has regularities or rules, so that it makes sense to call some usages correct or normal or ordinary, others odd or incorrect. Yet English, like any natural language, is not a closed, finished system, "everywhere circumscribed by rules." We are always able to say new things, to project old concepts into new situations; at the same time, not just any projection will do. Projections are controlled at all three of the levels mentioned: not just any will occur to us, will be understood or accepted by the person we address, will be in accord with the regularities of the English language.

---

[43] Polanyi, *op. cit.*, p. 105.
[44] Cavell, "Claim to Rationality," p. 233; compare p. 228.
[45] Wittgenstein, *Zettel*, par. 568.

Cavell says that language "is tolerant in the way steel is; its concepts are tempered. While it is true that we must use the same word in, project a word into, various contexts (must be willing to call some contexts the same), it is equally true that what will *count* as a legitimate projection is deeply controlled. You can 'feed peanuts to the monkey' and 'feed pennies to a meter,' but you cannot feed a monkey by stuffing pennies in its mouth, and if you mash peanuts into a coin slot you won't *be* feeding the meter. Would you be feeding a lion if you put a bushel of carrots in his cage? That he in fact does not eat them would not be enough to show that you weren't; he *may* not eat his *meat*. But in the *latter* case 'may not eat' means 'isn't hungry then' or 'refuses to eat it.' And not every case of 'not eating' is 'refusing food.' The swan who glides past the Easter egg on the shore, or over a school of minnows, or under the pitch-fork of meat the keeper is carrying for the lion cage, is not refusing to eat the egg, the fish or the meat. What will be, or count as, 'being fed' is related to what will count as 'refusing to eat,' and thence related to 'refusing to mate,' 'refusing to obey,' etc."[46]

All this is most directly applied to the meaning of a word when Wittgenstein turns to what he calls "the great question that lies behind all these considerations." That is the question of "the nature of language," and he explores it by again making use of his analogy between language and games. Wittgenstein imagines a critic complaining that he has "nowhere said what the essence of a language-game, and hence of language is: what is common to all these activities, and what makes them into language or parts of language." The early Wittgenstein of the *Tractatus* might have accepted the critic's question as perfectly legitimate, and answered that the essence of language is its capacity to picture the world. But in the *Investigations* he rejects the idea that language has that kind of an essence: "I am saying that these phenomena have no one thing in common which makes us use the same word for all,—but that they are *related* to one another in many different ways. And it is because of this relationship, or these relationships, that we call them all 'language.' "[47]

To explain this idea, Wittgenstein turns to the question of what the word "game" means, trying to show that the meaning is not some single, characteristic feature that all games have in common: "Don't say: 'There *must* be something common, or they would not be called "games" '—but *look and see* whether there is anything common to all. —For if you look at them you will not see something that is common to *all*, but similarities, relationships, and a whole series of them at that . . . Look for example at board-games, with their multifarious relationships. Now pass to card-games; here you find many correspondences with the first group, but many common features drop out, and others appear. When we pass next to ball-games much that is common is retained, but much is lost. —Are they all

[46] Cavell, "Claim to Rationality," p. 223.
[47] Wittgenstein, *Philosophical Investigations*, par. 65.

'amusing'? Compare chess with naughts and crosses. Or is there always winning and losing, or competition between players? Think of patience. In ball games there is winning and losing; but when a child throws his ball at the wall and catches it again, this feature has disappeared. Look at the parts played by skill and luck; and at the difference between skill in chess and skill in tennis. Think now of games like ring-a-ring-a-roses; here is the element of amusement, but how many other characteristic features have disappeared! And we can go through the many, many other groups of games in the same way; can see how similarities crop up and disappear."[48]

Thus, we might explain to someone what a game is by describing various games to him, and then we might add (inducing him to go on) "This *and similar things* are called 'games.' "[49] And in teaching him by the presentation of examples this way, we would not be telling him less than we know ourselves, for there *is* no essential characteristic of game-ness. What we find when we examine examples of games is not a shared essence, but "a complicated network of similarities overlapping and criss-crossing: sometimes overall similarities, sometimes similarities of detail."[50] One might say, the relationship among the cases is nontransitive: case A resembles case B this way, case B resembles case C a different way, case C resembles case D in yet a third way, case E is like cases A and D, but not like B and C, and so on. "We extend our concept . . . as in spinning a thread we twist fibre on fibre. And the strength of the thread does not reside in the fact that some one fibre runs through its whole length, but in the overlapping of many fibres."[51]

Wittgenstein calls this kind of network of partially overlapping similarities "family resemblances," for they overlap and crisscross in the same way as "the various resemblances between members of a family: build, features, colour of eyes, gait, temperament, etc."[52] Games, he says, "form a family." And instances of what we would call "language," or the use of language, form a family. Perhaps no member of the family will have all of the family characteristics; perhaps some of the characteristics are even mutually inconsistent, so that no one member *can* have them all. To recognize a member of the family as a relative, one need not be able to *say* just how he resembles, reminds us of, the others, though one might be able to say if one tried. Cavell puts it this way: "There is a Karamazov essence, but you won't find it if you look for *a* quality (look, that is, with the wrong 'picture' of a quality in mind)." You find it by learning to recognize instances, "that *that* is what 'an intellectual Karamazov' is, and *that* is what 'a spiritual Karamazov' is, and *that* is what 'Karamazov authority' is."[53]

[48] *Ibid.*, par. 66.
[49] *Ibid.*, par. 69.
[50] *Ibid.*, par. 66; compare par. 75.
[51] *Ibid.*, par. 67.
[52] *Ibid.*
[53] Cavell, "Claim to Rationality," p. 233.

This notion of "family resemblance" has been perhaps as widely adopted and hailed as any other insight in Wittgenstein's work; yet I think its point is almost always partly misunderstood, because Wittgenstein's analogies are deceptive. First, they falsely suggest a physical objectivity to the relevant features that does not in fact exist. One can see each separate fiber in a rope, see where one leaves off and another begins. One can establish the biological basis for family membership and family resemblance; characteristic features are controlled by chromosome patterns, and so on. But in language it is seldom so clear which features count, and a concept must always be projectible into new situations. Second, the analogies still suggest, or at least allow, a label-and-object interpretation. They allow us to think that if all games do not share a single common feature, at least groups of games share partly overlapping clusters of features.[54] But the real point is not features of games at all, but features of the situations in which we talk about games—not how to recognize a game, but when to say "game."

MENTAL ACTIVITIES

This becomes much clearer in those long sections of the *Investigations* where Wittgenstein explores concepts like "understanding," "intending," "meaning," "expecting," "reading"—verbals which we might want to say refer to mental activities. His treatment of these concepts is extraordinarily dense and complex, and he constantly shifts from one to another. Still, the basic pattern of the argument is discernible. If words were simply labels for phenomena, then verbs would be labels for actions or states of being. Some would refer to physical activities or states, which one might be able to depict in an illustration. But others, like "understand" or "expect," could not be illustrated that way. If we are nevertheless convinced that these verbs must refer to something, we will postulate or assume an invisible, mental, inner, private activity or state, accessible only to introspection.[55] (We may feel reinforced in this assumption by the facts of brain physiology. Surely, we may feel, whenever we read or understand or mean we are using our brains, which must mean that some physiological process is going on there. So we think vaguely that that process must be what the word refers to.) Wittgenstein endeavors again and again, to wean

---

[54] See, for example, Renford Bambrough, "Universals and Family Resemblances," in George Pitcher, ed., *Wittgenstein: The Philosophical Investigations* (Garden City: Doubleday, 1966), pp. 186–204. Perhaps this temptation would have been slightly lessened if the English "game" were as intimately tied to a significant and wide-ranging verb ("gaming," after all, is quite restricted) as the German "*Spiel*" is to "*spielen*." The passage quoted at n. 48, above, more accurately reflects ordinary usage in German than in English for the same reason.

[55] Wittgenstein, *Blue and Brown Books*, p. 125. The point forms the main theme of Gilbert Ryle's *The Concept of Mind*, (New York: Barnes and Noble, 1949), where he calls it "the dogma of the Ghost in the Machine" (pp. 15–16). Though Ryle's treatment is much easier to understand, Wittgenstein's ranges further.

us from this habit of thought. He shows us that the inner or mental process is a postulate and not an observed fact; though a characteristic inner process or feeling may be present in *some* instances of understanding, reading, expecting, it is not present in *all* instances. Part of the difficulty turns out to arise from the fact that these words are not (or not merely) labels for referring to *anything*. They are used in other language games as well, and those uses also help to shape their meaning. In addition, as we shall see in the next chapter, their meaning is dependent on the context of their use.

Take "understanding": what happens when someone suddenly understands? Wittgenstein again has recourse here to the language games in which one person writes down a series of numbers and the other is supposed to continue the series correctly. At one moment the man is watching, puzzled; at the next moment he says "Now I understand," or "Now I can go on," and proceeds to continue the series. What changed? Certainly his saying those words or his physical movements cannot constitute his understanding; so we try to "get hold of the mental process of understanding which seems to be hidden behind the coarser and therefore more visible accompaniments."[56] But when we look "inward," at what goes on in our minds as we suddenly understand something, we may find any number of different thoughts or feelings, or none at all. "For example, while A was slowly putting one number after another, B was occupied with trying various algebraic formulae on the numbers which had been written down. After A had written the number 19 B tried the formula $a_n = n^2 + n - 1$; and the next number confirmed his hypothesis. Or again, B does not think of formulae. He watches A writing his numbers down with a certain feeling of tension, and all sorts of vague thoughts go through his head. Finally he asks himself: 'What is the series of differences?' He finds the series 4, 6, 8, 10 and says: Now I can go on. Or he watches and says 'Yes, I know *that* series'—and continues it, just as he would have done if A had written down the series 1, 3, 5, 7, 9. —Or he says nothing at all and simply continues the series. Perhaps he had what might be called the sensation 'that's easy!'. (Such a sensation is, for example, that of a light quick intake of breath, as when one is mildly startled.)"[57] It might even be that "nothing at all occurred in B's mind except that he suddenly said 'Now I know how to go on'—perhaps with a feeling of relief; and that he did in fact go on working out the series without using the formula."[58]

Now, which of these phenomena is the activity or state of understanding? But he might think or say any of these things without having understood. "For it is perfectly imaginable that the formula should occur

---

[56] Wittgenstein, *Philosophical Investigations*, par. 153.
[57] *Ibid.*, par. 151.
[58] *Ibid.*, par. 179.

to him and that he should nevertheless not understand. 'He understands' must have more in it than: the formula occurs to him. And equally, more than any of those more or less characteristic *accompaniments* or manifestations of understanding."[59] None of them, we want to say, is the understanding itself. But perhaps we are wrong to assume that the understanding is any single phenomenon, always present when someone truly understands. We need not assume that, when a man tells us "Now I understand," he is giving a descriptive report of an event or process he has just observed within himself. "It would be quite misleading . . . to call the words a 'description of a mental state'. —One might rather call them a 'signal'; and we judge whether it was rightly employed by what he goes on to do."[60] Understanding is not merely a state or activity to be labeled, but a commitment about performance to come.

Or consider the example of "meaning." We say something, and mean it or don't mean it; or we say something and mean something else by it. Or we speak with or without meaning. But how do we do those things? "What is going on in us when we *mean* (and don't merely say) words"?[61] What, for instance, "is it to *mean* the words '*That* is blue' at one time as a statement about the object one is pointing to—at another as an explanation of the word 'blue'?"[62] Certainly we needn't look any different when we mean it one way than when we mean it the other way. So we conclude that the difference must be inner—an intention, a directing of our attention. And sometimes the intention will be there and apparent; but not always. The word "meaning" is used in language games far more complex than we at first suppose.

Recall the example of what might happen in the number-series game if a pupil correctly wrote the series of even numbers up to 1,000, but then continued 1,004, 1,008, 1,012 . . . The teacher stops him, and the pupil says in surprise, "Yes; isn't this how I was meant to do it?" The answer, of course, is no. The teacher meant for him to write 1,002 after 1,000, and 1,004 after 1,002. Yet the teacher did not think about 1,000 or 1,002 or 1,004 until after the pupil made his mistake. Indeed, since the series is infinite, he cannot have thought about all the terms the pupil is to write; yet he meant for them to appear in their proper sequence. The teacher knows what he meant the pupil to do in a case like this one, without having to cast his mind back to his own thoughts and feelings at the time he set the task. "The language-game 'I mean (or meant) *this*' (subsequent explanation of a word) is quite different from this one: 'I thought of . . . as I said it.' "[63] Meaning is not an activity, with duration, that takes place while we speak. "If we say to someone 'I should be delighted to see

[59] *Ibid.*, par. 152.
[60] *Ibid.*, par. 180.
[61] *Ibid.*, par. 507.
[62] *Ibid.*, p. 18; compare par. 666.
[63] *Ibid.*, p. 217; the example is from par. 185.

you' and mean it, does a conscious process run alongside these words
. . . ? This will hardly ever be the case."[64] Nor is it helpful to postulate an
unconscious process. "The process which we might call 'speaking and
meaning what you speak' is not necessarily distinguished from that of
speaking thoughtlessly by what happens *at the time when you speak*."[65]

Sometimes, asked what you meant, you will need to cast your mind
back and try to recall your thoughts as you spoke; but at other times this
will be pointless. Compare saying "I shall be delighted to see you" with
saying "The train leaves at 3:30." Asked whether you meant the first of
these utterances, "you would then probably think of the feelings, the experiences, which you had while you said it." But about the second utterance, the question whether you meant it really would not make much
sense. You would not know what you were being asked, and would be at
a loss to answer. You might answer, "Why shouldn't I have meant it?
What are you suggesting?" At any rate, you would not try to remember
what went on in your mind at the time you spoke. "In the first case we
shall be inclined to speak about a feeling characteristic of meaning what
we said, but not in the second."[66]

In still other cases, our answer about "what we meant" will look much
more like a decision made retrospectively, at the time when we are asked,
than like a recollection of our thoughts at the time we originally spoke.
We can even have meant things of which we were ignorant at the time.
Consider this conversation:

> "Napoleon really was very bourgeois."
> "You mean the man who won the Battle of Austerlitz?"
> "I don't know about any battles; was there more than one Napoleon?"
> "Well, yes. There was Napoleon I after the French Revolution, who won
> the Battle of Austerlitz; and then there was Louis Napoleon in the mid-
> nineteenth century. I thought you might mean him because he really *was* very
> bourgeois."
> "No, no. I meant the one who won the Battle of Austerlitz."

He meant that one, though he did not even know there was such a battle.
Again, "I meant" here seems to have the quality of a quasi-performative;
it is difficult to decide whether saying it describes an existing connection
or makes a new one. We use expressions like "So you meant . . ." or "So
you really wanted to say . . ." in order, Wittgenstein says, "to lead someone from one form of expression to another," from what he first said to
what he is now willing to accept as an interpretation of it.[67]

The reason we suppose that the "meaning" must have been an activity

[64] Wittgenstein, *Blue and Brown Books*, p. 34.
[65] *Ibid.*, p. 43.
[66] *Ibid.*, p. 146.
[67] Wittgenstein, *Philosophical Investigations*, par. 334. Of course there will be
other times when we will feel unable to decide whether we meant the man who
won the Battle of Austerlitz or not (if, for example, we have been reading about
Napoleon but didn't know that there were two, and so don't know which one we
were reading about).

going on at the same time as the speech is, first of all, because we use the past tense. We ask *"Did you mean . . .?"* and answer that we *meant* for him to write 1,002 after 1,000. "The past tense in the word 'to mean' suggests that a particular act of meaning had been performed when the rule was given, though as a matter of fact this expression alludes to no such act."[68] And, of course, that fact of usage goes with a whole set of "rules" of the grammar of "what you meant" that prevent it from being merely an *arbitrary* decision made later, when you are asked. "What is there in favour of saying that my words describe an existing connection," a meaning that was already there before I was asked about it? "Well, they relate to various things which didn't simply make their appearance with the [later] words. They say, for example, that I *should have* given a particular answer then, if I had been asked."[69] What I meant is not the same thing as what I mean now, or what I now wish I had meant, or what I would mean if I uttered the same words now. The question of what I meant "refers to a definite time . . . but not to an *experience* during that time."[70]

Sometimes, in order to answer it, I will have to remember my thoughts at the time. But at other times that won't be necessary at all, or won't be helpful. The grammar of the verb "mean"—the way we have learned to operate with it—pulls us in opposite directions here. On the one hand it tells us that the act of meaning took place with the original speech; on the other hand, when we look for that act, nothing we perceive satisfies us as being the act itself. In short, a verb like "to mean" is not simply a label for some recognizable inner process; it is a complex, composite tool put together out of a variety of heterogeneous parts—the various contexts and language games in which the word is used. These include feelings and actions and circumstances, phenomena to which the word can refer, but also phenomena which characterize the occasions for its use as a signal. Similarly, "neither the expression 'to intend the definition in such-and-such a way' nor the expression 'to interpret the definition in such-and-such a way' stands for a process which accompanies the giving and hearing of the definition."[71] The intention *with which* one acts does not "accompany" the action, nor does the meaning of what one says "accompany" speech. Meaning and intention are "neither 'articulated' nor 'non-articulated'; to be compared neither with a single note which sounds during the acting or speaking, nor with a tune."[72] These verbals do not stand for a process or activity that accompanies speech because they do not, in that sense, stand for anything at all.[73] Their grammar, the language

---

[68] Wittgenstein, *Blue and Brown Books*, p. 142; compare p. 39.

[69] Wittgenstein, *Philosophical Investigations*, par. 684.

[70] *Ibid.*, pp. 216–217.

[71] *Ibid.*, par. 34.

[72] *Ibid.*, p. 217.

[73] Karl-Otto Apel, *Analytical Philosophy of Language and the Geisteswissenschaften* (Dordrecht: D. Reidel, 1967), p. 36.

games in which they are used, is vastly more complex than the analogy with verbs like "eat" would suggest. That is why verbs like "know," "intend," "understand," and "mean" are peculiarly deficient in their participial forms. We do not say "I am knowing it," "He was understanding it," and the like. And a Wittgensteinian perspective makes the reason why we don't readily apparent: we have no use for such expressions, they are not among our language games for these concepts. Meaning, intending, knowing, are not (always) processes that have duration, like eating or running. "Suppose it were asked: *When* do you know how to play chess? All the time? or just while you are making a move? And the *whole* of chess during each move? —How queer that knowing how to play chess should take such a short time, and a game so much longer!"[74]

Our concepts, then, are compounds, assembled out of the variety of cases in which they are characteristically used. We learn their use and their meaning from such cases, and the meaning itself is merely a distillate of what we have learned. These cases may be extremely heterogeneous, not just in the sense that there are a lot of different kinds of, say, "games," but in the sense that a lot of different language games may be played with a single word. And even if the word is a noun, many of these language games need not be label-and-object kinds of games, but may involve quasi-performative signaling. So the meaning of a word may be a conglomerate of very diverse kinds of parts indeed. That turns out to be a fact of profound significance, as we shall see shortly; but first we need to examine one more element in the configuration of language: the significance of context.

[74] Wittgenstein, *Philosophical Investigations*, p. 59. Compare Ryle, *Concept of Mind*, p. 116; also Jean-Paul Sartre on the inner mental state we call "love": "I am not constantly thinking about the people I love, but I claim to love them even when I am not thinking about them." "An Explication of *The Stranger*," in Germaine Brée, ed., *Camus* (Englewood Cliffs: Prentice-Hall, 1962), p. 113.

# IV

## *Context, Sense, and Concepts*

MEANING is compounded out of cases of a word's use, and what characterizes those cases is often the speech situation, not the presence of something being referred to. As a consequence, the significance for meaning of situation, of circumstances, of context, is much greater than one might suppose. We commonly assume, and with good reason, that the meaning of a word remains fixed no matter in which context it is used. We think of the word as a constant, inserted into a variety of different verbal expressions on various occasions. In the first half of this chapter, we shall see what is wrong with that assumption, how meaning is context-dependent and needs to be completed by context. We shall then be ready, in the second half of the chapter, to sum up the significance of what has been said so far for conceptual thought.

We may begin where we left off, with the vocabulary of "mental activity," specifically "meaning" and "understanding." It was suggested that these will strike us as mysterious inner processes only as long as we insist that the words must be simply labels for classes of phenomena; instead, we need to recognize their function in other language games as well. But that is not sufficient for solving the problems about these verbals. One way of explaining why not would be to say that, after all, the words *can sometimes* be used as labels, can be used for referring to meaning or understanding. And surely what they are then used to refer to *is* a mental activity (what else might it be?). Only we began with the wrong notion, the wrong picture, of what a mental activity is, and how one is recognized.

A more accessible way of explaining why the distinction between labeling and signaling functions is not enough to solve the problems about these verbs might be to show what remains unsolved. A word like "meaning" may sometimes be a true performative, so that in saying "I mean" we *make* a connection rather than describe one. But "understanding" is at most quasi-performative; saying "I understand" is by no means equivalent to understanding. We may say we understand and then discover that we

71

were wrong; "I understand" can be false in a way that "I promise" cannot. So there remains the question: How do we tell when we ourselves understand? How do we know when to say "I understand" and not have it turn out false? And the old answer will still tempt us: We know by introspecting the characteristic process or feeling of understanding. Moreover, the explanatory power of the idea of signaling or quasi-performative functions is much less with respect to other verbals of "mental activity" that Wittgenstein discusses—verbs like "expecting," "reading," or "pointing to." What does help in solving these problems is precisely the significance of context.

We have said that sometimes the pupil in the number-series games says "Now I understand" because he has had a characteristic experience, such as the formula occurring to him. But we said that such an experience is neither necessary nor sufficient to his understanding, and thus cannot be the understanding itself. Wittgenstein says that the "particular circumstances" are what justifies someone in saying he understands when the formula occurs to him: "it is *the circumstances* under which he had such an experience that justify him in saying in such a case that he understands."[1] What sort of circumstances? Well, for instance, "such circumstances as that he had learnt algebra, had used such formulae before."[2] Only in the appropriate surrounding circumstances will the experience or feelings characteristic of sudden understanding *be* understanding. As Cavell says, a man can understand "in the absence of any particular feeling, and in the absence of any particular behavior. The *question* is: *what* particular behaviors and what particular feelings will *count as*" understanding in various circumstances. The point is "that 'in themselves' *no* particular feeling or particular behavior" will be understanding.[3]

What it comes to is something like this: we learn such a word in a variety of contexts, learn to use it in a variety of contexts. Sometimes what makes a context suitable for its use will be a characteristic feeling we experience, sometimes certain behavior on someone else's part, sometimes a commitment we are willing to undertake, but always against a background of suitable surrounding circumstances. We learn to say "I understand," for instance, when the formula occurs to us, under certain circumstances; but we also learn to say "he understands" when he smiles, takes that chalk from us, and moves to the blackboard, under certain circumstances. We further learn from the way the word is used that neither the experience of thinking of the formula nor his smiling and moving themselves are the understanding. For either might occur without our (or his) being able to continue the series correctly. And even being

[1] Ludwig Wittgenstein, *Philosophical Investigations*, tr. by G. E. M. Anscombe (New York: Macmillan, 1968), pars. 154, 155; compare his "Bemerkungen über Frazers *The Golden Bough*," *Synthese*, 17 (1961), p. 247.

[2] *Ibid.*, par. 179; compare pars. 181, 323.

[3] Stanley Cavell, "Claim to Rationality," (unpublished dissertation, Harvard University), p. 54.

able to continue the series is not the understanding itself, for we can imagine circumstances in which we would say that he understood but was nevertheless unable to continue the series correctly. Our concept of understanding is a conglomerate of these various occasions for its use, including their appropriate surrounding circumstances. Wittgenstein says, "these kinds of use of 'understanding' make up its meaning, make up my *concept* of understanding. For I *want* to apply the word 'understanding' to all this."[4] We have, as Wittgenstein says, a whole series of props in readiness to support our concept; yet each of them is dependent on circumstances, each is corrigible, none is the understanding itself. (That they should be grouped together in a single concept may now strike us as quite arbitrary, but we must postpone that question.)

We may still be tempted to conclude that the understanding must be the sum total of the characteristic experiences plus all the necessary surrounding circumstances. But Wittgenstein responds that the surrounding circumstances merely "constitute the scene for our language-game," are not themselves part of the game.[5] In some circumstances, thinking of the formula justifies us in saying we understand; then, "I understand" is equivalent to "I know the formula." But that does not mean that these expressions are equivalent everywhere, synonymous. As Wittgenstein puts it, "we do say: 'Now I can go on, I mean I know the formula', as we say 'I can walk, I mean I have time'; but also 'I can walk, I mean I am already strong enough'; or: 'I can walk, as far as the state of my legs is concerned', that is, when we are contrasting *this* condition for walking with others." But Wittgenstein warns against supposing "that there is some *totality* of conditions corresponding to the nature of each case (e.g. for a person's walking)," that "I can walk" is a label for the totality of these conditions.[6] Different concepts, different expressions, may "touch here and coincide over a stretch. But you need not think that all lines are *circles*," that if they coincide over a stretch they must coincide everywhere.[7]

One could say of understanding or meaning what Wittgenstein says of intending: that it is "embedded in its situation, in human customs and institutions. If the technique of the game of chess did not exist, I could not intend to play a game of chess."[8] That is why a speaker can "mean" something of which he is ignorant at the time (the Napoleon who won the Battle of Austerlitz); our language and our culture make the connections between what he says and what he means (can mean). And that is why the teacher can mean, or intend, for the pupil to write 1,002 after 1,000, even if he did not think about those numbers. He "meant" for the

[4] Wittgenstein, *Philosophical Investigations*, par. 532; compare Gilbert Ryle, *The Concept of Mind* (New York: Barnes and Noble, 1949), p. 96.
[5] Wittgenstein, *Philosophical Investigations*, par. 179.
[6] *Ibid.*, par. 183; compare Ludwig Wittgenstein, *Blue and Brown Books* (New York and Evanston: Harper and Row, 1964), p. 114.
[7] Wittgenstein, *Philosophical Investigations*, p. 192.
[8] *Ibid.*, par. 337.

pupil to write 1,002 in the sense that he had "mastered a particular technique in arithmetic and algebra, and that he taught someone else the expansion of a series in the usual way."[9] The circumstances make possible the intention.

Consider another mental activity, "expecting." It, too, lacks definitive physical markers; we can't always tell from a man's behavior whether he is expecting anything, or what he is expecting. It, too, is associated with certain characteristic feelings or experiences, but they are neither necessary nor sufficient to constitute expectation. Thus we may be "expecting N. to tea on Thursday" without having any particular inner experience or feeling, without even thinking about him. And, conversely, the feeling is not enough. Here, for instance, is a characteristic feeling Wittgenstein calls "certainly a case of expecting": "I watch a slow match burning, in high excitement follow the progress of the burning and its approach to the explosive."[10] Yet even this characteristic feeling is dependent on circumstances. "An expectation is imbedded in a situation, from which it arises. The expectation of an explosion may, for example, arise from a situation in which an explosion *is to be expected*."[11] But now suppose, as Cavell suggests, "that while you are shaving one morning you drop your razor into the basin and suddenly are overcome with this feeling characteristic of watching a flame approach an explosive." If someone notices your tenseness and asks what's wrong, you are not likely to say, "I'm waiting for the explosion," or even, "I'm expecting an explosion," but perhaps something like, "I have this queer feeling that something is about to explode." But, what makes the feeling *queer*? We were imagining it to be merely our ordinary, characteristic feeling of expecting an explosion. "Obviously, its queerness comes from its occurring *there*, where, though you are not in fact expecting anything (= there is nothing in those circumstances to be expected . . . ), you have this feeling of expecting something."[12]

So there is such a thing as a feeling characteristic of waiting for an explosion, and one might recognize that feeling even if it occurred in circumstances where no explosion is to be expected. But that feeling does not, itself, constitute "expecting an explosion." For that, appropriate surrounding circumstances are also necessary. And it is possible to expect without any particular characteristic feeling, in which case the expectation presumably consists only of the surrounding circumstances, including what precedes and follows. Nor is there a separate characteristic feeling for each of the different things one might expect.

Another method by which Wittgenstein demonstrates the significance of context in mental activities is by inventing experiments in which we

[9] *Ibid.*, par. 692.
[10] *Ibid.*, par. 576.
[11] *Ibid.*, par. 581.
[12] Cavell, "Claim to Rationality," p. 124.

are to perform these activities on command. He invites us, for instance, to say "It's cold in here" and *mean* "It's warm in here." Or to point to a piece of paper—and then to its color, and then to its shape. It is not that we flatly cannot point to the color or the shape, but that we feel embarrassingly unsure about whether we have succeeded in doing it or not. We experience a peculiar sense of strain; we concentrate, we "blink with effort" as we "try to parade the right meanings before" our minds.[13] Yet in the normal course of our lives we do not experience any extra strain in pointing to the color of an object or meaning something by our words; no special concentration is required.

We experience strain and effort in the experiments, not because meaning and pointing are particularly difficult activities, nor because they are involuntary, but because they are not simply activities at all—or not in the sense in which we had been thinking of activities. Sometimes meaning, or pointing to, is defined not by anything we do or that goes on in us, but by the surrounding circumstances. "There are, of course, what can be called 'characteristic experiences' of pointing to (e.g.) the shape. For example, following the outline with one's finger or with one's eyes as one points. —But *this* does not happen in all cases in which I 'mean the shape', and no more does any other one characteristic process occur in all these cases. —Besides, even if something of the sort did recur in all cases, it would still depend on the circumstances—that is, on what happened before and after the pointing—whether we should say 'He pointed to the shape and not to the colour'."[14] And for some cases of pointing, there will simply be no characteristic experience at all. We may think following the outline with our finger to be characteristic of pointing to the shape, but "do you also know of an experience characteristic of pointing to a piece in a game *as a piece in a game*? All the same one can say: 'I mean that this *piece* is called the "king", not this particular bit of wood I am pointing to'."[15]

The sense of strain and oddness we experience in trying to point to the color of a piece of paper and then to its shape disappears as soon as we realize that these expressions are simply out of their normal contexts. We are straining to perform a certain action or have a certain feeling when what is missing is not anything we do or feel at all, but a particular set of circumstances. We need to ask in what context the expression "point to the color" might normally, actually be used. For then, as Cavell indicates, we immediately realize that "point to the color" is normally used in circumstances where the object itself is not present. "If we look at the way 'point to the color of your car' is actually used, we realize that the context will normally be one in which we do not point to *that* object, but to something else which has that color, and whose color thereby serves as a

[13] Wittgenstein, *Philosophical Investigations*, pars. 510, 33, and p. 176.
[14] *Ibid.*, par. 35.
[15] *Ibid.*

*sample* of the original. And as soon as we put the request in its normal context, we find nothing could be easier."[16] What someone does when she "points to the color of his car" requires no special mental effort or strain on his part, to assure that he is not pointing, by mistake, to its shape or to the car itself. Pointing to the color rather than the shape is not a special mental activity, nor is it any way queer or difficult; it is simply a matter of different circumstances, a different context. So we are no longer tempted "to regard pointing to something, or meaning it, as requiring a peculiar inner effort . . . once we see that, and see how, the difficulty was of our own making."[17] We made the activity seem mysterious by imagining it in an inappropriate context, by depriving the expression of the normal context in which it is at home, in which it is used and learned, in which it has meaning. Such an ordinary expression "only seems queer when one imagines a different language-game for it from the one in which we actually use it."[18] The context of use supplements and completes the meaning in essential ways, and an inappropriate context can prevent an expression from making sense even though we know perfectly well what the words mean—indeed, just because we know what the words mean.

## MAKING SENSE

We are inclined to suppose that we can tell by inspection whether we know the meaning of a particular word, or whether a particular expression or sentence makes sense in English. "It is raining" and "How are you?" make perfectly good sense; "to why up red hurry" is patent nonsense; perhaps some poetic lines fall somewhere in between. And in a way that supposition is correct, but in a way it is false. For it is secure only as long as we consider the word or expression in the abstract, rather than in actual use. As soon as we imagine it actually spoken by someone, not as a philosophical example, the context begins to play an essential role in determining whether or not we can understand what was said, whether the utterance makes sense.

Consider a perfectly clear and familiar expression like "all of it," as it might appear in a question like "Did you . . . all of it?" where the blank is filled in by some verb. We know what "all of it" means, know how to ask such questions and how to answer them; they make perfect sense. Or do they? Cavell suggests that we imagine that question being asked in response to each of the following statements:

> I polished the table. (Did you polish all of it?)
> I scratched the table.

16 Cavell, "Claim to Rationality," p. 91a.

17 *Ibid.*, p. 91b; compare Ludwig Wittgenstein, *On Certainty*, tr. by Denis Paul and G. E. M. Anscombe, ed. by G. E. M. Anscombe and G. H. von Wright (New York and Evanston: Harper and Row, 1969), par. 622.

18 Wittgenstein, *Philosophical Investigations*, par. 195.

I played the Brahms concerto.
I played the violin.

I smoked the cigarette.

I ate the apple.
I bit the apple.

I swept out the room.
I decorated the room.
I entered the room.

I nicked the cup.
I broke the cup.
I dropped the cup.

I noticed the envelope.
I glanced at the envelope.[19]

For some of these cases the question "All of it?" makes clear sense; for others, it seems to make no sense at all, and for still others one might say that their sense is neither perfectly clear nor entirely unclear. Of these, Cavell says that they "have" or "make" *some* sense.

It is easy to pick out the clear-cut cases. The question "All of it?" makes perfectly good sense, for example, when asked of "I polished the table," "I played the Brahms concerto," "I smoked the cigarette," "I ate the apple." It makes no apparent sense when asked of "I entered the room," "I hit the target," "I noticed the envelope." But Cavell shows that there are borderline cases. "What might it mean to ask whether you played all of the violin, or how much of the table you scratched, or whether you dropped the whole cup? But there might be a point in these questions. Asking our questions about the violin might be explained as asking whether you played chromatic scales on each string to the top of the finger board, or it might be asking whether you used higher positions where they would have enhanced the tone or made the phrasing smoother; about scratching the table they might suggest that there was a purpose in scratching it—say, to determine what the undercoat of paint had been; asking whether you dropped the whole cup would make clear sense if, say, the cup in question was a magician's prop composed of two halves, one of which, when a gull from the audience is asked to drink from it, falls off when he tips the cup."[20] Even in contexts where the question seems to have no clear sense, the sense can sometimes be *made* clear by appropriate explanations; and, conversely, even in the contexts where it seems to make clear sense, we may nevertheless be surprised to discover that that clear sense is not what the questioner meant after all. Defending or showing the sense of what you say is a matter of making connections;

[19] Cavell, "Claim to Rationality," p. 240.
[20] *Ibid.*, p. 241.

sometimes the speaker can do this in acceptable ways, and sometimes not.

Some cases which at first seem to make no sense can nevertheless be shown to make sense once they are fitted into an appropriate context. "To make some sense" seems to mean "to make clear sense in some context." But that is all that "to make *clear* sense" can mean, for it surely cannot mean "to make clear sense in *all* contexts." So what is the difference between making some sense and making clear sense? With the examples that make clear sense, the context, the application, seems immediately obvious; with the examples that make only some sense, the context or application have to be found with some effort. Or perhaps one should say they have to be invented. Yet not just any invention will do; the context or application must be recognizable as fully natural, ordinary use. Cavell tries to explain this by contrasting the way one can make sense of, say, "Did you play all of the violin?" with a Wittgensteinian example of an expression whose "grammar needs to be explained": "The rose has teeth in the mouth of the beast." As one possible explication of this expression, Wittgenstein gives "The cow eats its food and then dungs the rose with it," so the rose's teeth are in the cow's jaw.[21] But that is clearly only one of many possible "perfectly good" explanations for the line, "because one has no notion in advance where to look for teeth in a rose."[22] With expressions like "Did you play all of the violin?" which, Cavell says, "have some sense—as it were, a sense that needs *completion* —we feel that there is a *right* context for its use, and that 'figuring out' its application is a matter of hitting upon *that* context."[23] With such expressions, "we haven't the same freedom" as with "The rose has teeth." It is as though we need only "exercise the very capacity for projection upon which language as a whole depends. We have freedom, but we are also subject to the same requirement of all projection, that its appropriateness be made out in terms of the 'invitation to projection' by the context; we have to show *how* the next context is an instance of this old concept."[24]

And sometimes that will turn out not to be possible. "If I ask 'Have you eaten all of the apple?' and you answer flatly, Yes, then what will your response be if I walk over and say, 'But you haven't eaten it all; you've left the core, and the stem and the seeds to waste'? You *may* tolerate that. Perhaps that is my form of life with apples; I 'eat apples' that way and that is not so bizarre but that you may be willing to accept my version of 'eating all the apple' and fit yours to it, conceding, 'I ate all of it except the core.' But this tolerance has its limits. If on another occasion someone objects, 'But you haven't smoked all of the cigarette, you have left the whole filter to waste,' then even if he normally drags on the filter until the ash gives out, and then chews and swallows the rest, we are not likely to

[21] Wittgenstein, *Philosophical Investigations*, p. 222.
[22] *Ibid.*, and *Blue and Brown Books*, p. 10.
[23] Cavell, "Claim to Rationality," p. 243.
[24] *Ibid.*

accede to his version of 'smoking the whole cigarette' and effect a reconciliation between his and our version of that activity, saying, 'Well, I
smoked it all except the filter': his way of 'smoking' is *too* bizarre; you
can't talk to everyone about everything. If someone objects to our claim
of having decorated the entire room on the ground that we have left spaces
between the bric-a-brac, or failed to place an object everywhere one
would fit (physically), we might feel, 'You have a very different conception of "decorating" than I have' or even, 'You don't know what *decorating*
is.' You can't share every pleasure with everyone. If someone says we
haven't played all of the Brahms concerto on the ground that we only
played the *violin* part, then we probably won't feel for a moment that he
has a *different* concept of 'playing a concerto,' but simply that he has no
concept of *that* at all."[25]

What is acceptable is a matter of how bizarre we find the rationale,
whether we can be brought to see the intention, the practical purpose of
the question, asked in that way. Sometimes "the question 'All of it?' makes
*some* sense, maybe enough for the purpose at hand, and maybe represents
the only, or best, way of finding out what you want to know, when it is
asked about 'I broke the cup' or 'I scratched the table.' There *may*, that
is, be point in asking whether you broke *all* of the cup: e.g., on one side
there is a gold monogram which you want to preserve if possible."[26] In that
case, we can again see what the questioner meant by his question: "He
has got concepts, our concepts, of 'breaking something' and of 'breaking
all of something,' and he has shown *how* the concept projects into this
context in a way we can all understand."[27] But what would be his point
in asking if we broke all of the cup if what he turned out to mean was
"that there may be *some fragment or other* which could be broken into
smaller fragments? To be told 'But you haven't broken it all; here is a
part (fragment) which isn't broken,' might strike us as a joke," and that
might be his point in saying it, too.[28]

The meaning of the expression "all of it," though in a way quite constant, is in another way different in each context, depending on the
speaker's point in saying it. Thus, we might say "I played all of the violin;
*I mean*, I played chromatic scales on each string to the top of the finger
board," or "I played all of the violin; *I mean*, I used higher positions where
they would have enhanced the tone or made the phrasing smoother." It
is not easy to find a satisfactory way of expressing this duality, how the
meaning both stays fixed, and fluctuates with the speaker's point; how it
is both independent of and dependent on context.

One reason we have trouble here is relatively accessible: our terminology of meaning, point, and so on works differently with respect to isolated

[25] *Ibid.*, pp. 243–244.
[26] *Ibid.*, p. 244.
[27] *Ibid.*, p. 245.
[28] *Ibid.*, pp. 244–245.

words than with respect to sentences, and we become tangled up in our own vocabulary.[29] We can speak of "meaning" in connection with both words and sentences, but the meaning of a word is not the same as meaning in relation to a sentence. The meaning of a word is something like its dictionary definition, a synonym or synonymous phrase that can be substituted for it. Sentences do not have meanings in this sense; there are no dictionaries of sentences. When we ask about meaning in connection with a sentence (unless it is a short sentence in a foreign language), we are usually asking not what the sentence means but what some speaker means by saying it. The answer will be a restatement of his thought, valid only for that particular context and others like it, not a generally valid definition. ("I can walk; I mean, I have the time"; "I can walk; I mean, I am strong enough now.") But though sentences do not have meanings, they do have, or make, *sense*. Words do not make sense, though they may have, or be used in, various senses.

But terminological difficulties are not the only ones in trying to understand what it is about meaning or sense that stays fixed and what it is that varies with context. Evidently the difference is similar to that between the meaning of a word and its use, or between learning a new word in a familiar language game and learning a new language game. Meaning, or whatever stays fixed regardless of context, is by no means all of what is regular or regulated about language, nor all that we learn when we learn language. Besides the meaning or sense, there is something else which makes a phrase like "all of it" sound peculiar in some contexts and lack all sense in others. There is something which makes "pointing to the color" of an object seem difficult. There is something which characterizes certain situations as being such that an explosion "is to be expected." These regularities in language Wittgenstein calls "grammar," and they go far beyond the element of meaning or sense that stays fixed regardless of context. Grammar is what a child learns through experience and training, not explanation; it is what we all know but cannot say. Grammar includes all the patterns or regularities or rules in language, permitting new projections and yet controlling what projections will be acceptable. (Obviously the notion is quite different from what we ordinarily call "grammar," which is learned in school. We shall discuss it in the next chapter.)

Contemporary philosophers usually distinguish here among semantics, syntactics, and pragmatics. Semantics is roughly equivalent to the meanings of words; syntactics is the additional element of significance contributed by word order, by syntax. Thus "the man bit the dog" means something different from "the dog bit the man," because of the way the words are arranged. "Pragmatics," as that term is usually used, deals with

[29] The discussion in this paragraph is based on Paul Ziff, *Semantic Analysis* (Ithaca: Cornell University Press, 1960), pp. 149–151; and Gilbert Ryle, "Ordinary Language," in V. C. Chappell, ed., *Ordinary Language* (Englewood Cliffs: Prentice-Hall, 1964).

the circumstances of a word or an expression's use in speech. It concerns "the origin, uses and effects of signs within the behavior in which they occur."[30] Sometimes semantics and syntactics are grouped together under the term "semantics" and contrasted with pragmatics.

That contrast may at first seem to correspond to the difference we have been pursuing, semantics (including syntax) being what stays fixed apart from context, and pragmatics being what varies. But that way of putting it is likely to reinforce the assumption we are trying to dispute in this discussion: that meaning is wholly separable from context. The discussion of pragmatics and semantics by contemporary philosophers differs in several crucial ways from Wittgenstein's treatment of these matters. Benson Mates is a fairly representative spokesman for the non-Wittgensteinian approach here. He says, in criticizing ordinary-language philosophy, "We have all heard the wearying platitude that 'you can't separate' the meaning of a word from the entire context in which it occurs, including not only the actual linguistic context but also the aims, feelings, beliefs, and hopes of the speaker, the same for the listener and any bystanders, the social situation, the physical surroundings, the historical background, the rules of the game, and so on ad infinitum. There is no doubt some truth in this, but I fail to see how it helps one get started in an empirical investigation of language. At the very least provisional divisions of the subject have to be made somewhere."[31] Mates suggests that, as a provisional division, "there is much to be said for" the distinction between semantics and pragmatics. And he finds that the work of ordinary-language philosophers is flawed because many of the common factors they find "among the cases in which an expression is employed belong more to the pragmatics of the expression than to its semantics." Factors which "belong in the category of the pragmatics of the expression . . . should be avoided when 'eliciting' or 'seeing' the meaning."[32]

Mates, then, quite characteristically takes the pragmatics of an expression, its use in speech, to be both subjective and infinitely complex, and thus totally unsuitable for any systematic study. Anything and everything might be relevant to an expression's use, depending on the subjective feelings and motives of speakers and hearers. Wittgenstein, by contrast, shows that the use of an expression is as deeply and rigorously controlled as its semantics or its syntax or its inflection. To be sure, neither meaning nor use is "everywhere circumscribed by rules," and all rules require interpretation and application. But both meaning and use must be and are learned by the child from cases, from just that seemingly infinite, variable welter of experience Mates rejects as unmanageable. Pragmatics are as much, and in the same way, rule-governed as semantics.

[30] Charles Morris, *Signs, Language and Behavior* (New York: George Braziller, 1955), p. 219.
[31] Benson Mates, "On the Verification of Statements," in Chappell, *op. cit.*, p. 71.
[32] *Ibid.*, p. 72.

That is why, in addition to whatever our words, and their syntactical combination in an utterance, may mean, our saying them has further implications. Because these implications are not part of the meaning of the words, cannot be strictly deduced from them, the logician wants nothing to do with them; they seem to him arbitrary, subjective, infinitely complex. Yet they are as regulated and systematic as any other aspect of our natural language. "The actual use of language carries 'implications' which are of course not deductive, but which are nevertheless fully controlled in our understanding of one another: there is no reason in logic . . . why, if you say, 'Now I hear you,' you 'must' imply that before this moment there was something specific preventing your hearing me (and not that since hearing is a physiological or causal process always going on in the present moment, in a *now*, you can indifferently say 'I hear you' and 'I hear you now')."[33] It is not in every context that I can meaningfully say "Now I hear you" or ask "Did you . . . all of it?" It is not in every context that a perfectly ordinary, meaningful expression will make sense. Wittgenstein imagines someone saying, "At all costs I will get to that house," and then comments: "But if there is no difficulty about it —*can* I try at all costs to get to the house?"[34] Saying "at all costs" has implications, and only where those implications are appropriate does the expression make sense.

Austin makes a similar point in discussing what he calls "the natural economy of language." We examined earlier his demonstration that one cannot classify any and all actions as either voluntary or involuntary. Not only are the words "voluntary" and "involuntary" confined to different, and quite narrow, classes of verbs; but in addition, "in the great majority of cases of the use of the great majority of verbs," no modifier at all is appropriate. "For the *standard* case covered by any normal verb . . . no modifying expression is required or permissible." A modifier is in order "only if we do the action named in some *special* way or circumstances, different from those in which such an act is naturally done. . . . It is bedtime, I am alone, I yawn: but I do not yawn involuntarily (or voluntarily!), nor yet deliberately. To yawn in any such peculiar way is just not to just yawn."[35] It is not in every context that an action can be done voluntarily, that it makes sense to call an action "voluntary."

It is a fact of the utmost importance that we do not constantly say all that could be said. We do not talk all the time, do not utter everything that happens to be true, or everything we know, or everything we think. As a consequence, when we do speak, that action itself has significance; the context in which we speak and our act of speaking have implications for the meaning and sense of what is said.[36] Saying something is an action

---

[33] Cavell, "Claim to Rationality," p. 272.

[34] Wittgenstein, *Philosophical Investigations*, par. 623.

[35] J. L. Austin, *Philosophical Papers* (Oxford: Clarendon Press, 1961), pp. 137–138.

[36] Stephen Toulmin has said that language does not consist of "timeless propo-

with implications going beyond the implications of what is literally said, of the abstract meaning the utterance would have if no one said it. Thus, if in the ordinary course of events, someone asks you whether you dress the way you do voluntarily, then as Cavell points out, "you will not understand him to be curious merely about your psychological processes (whether your wearing [those clothes] 'proceeds from free choice . . .'); you will understand him to be implying or suggesting that your manner of dress is in some way peculiar. If it be replied to this that 'voluntary' does not *mean* 'peculiar' (or 'special' or 'fishy') and hence that the implication or suggestion is part merely of the pragmatics of the expression, not part of its *meaning* (semantics), my rejoinder is this: that reply is relevant to a different claim from the one urged here; it is worth saying *here* only if you are able to account for the *relation* between the pragmatics and the semantics of the expression."[37] While that relation clearly is not one of simple logical implication ("voluntary" does not mean or imply "peculiar"), it is nevertheless objectively obligatory in the grammar of the language. The man wouldn't ask if I dress that way voluntarily unless he thought that my way of dressing is somehow peculiar. "Call this implication of the utterance 'pragmatic'; the fact remains that he wouldn't (couldn't) say what he did without implying what he did: he MUST MEAN that my clothes are peculiar."[38] Though "voluntary" neither means nor implies "peculiar," his asking in these circumstances "Do you dress that way voluntarily?" does have implications. *"Learning what these implications are is part of learning the language*; no less a part than learning its syntax, or learning what it is to which terms apply: they are an essential part of what we communicate when we talk."[39]

This, then, is one respect in which the Wittgensteinian treatment of meaning and use differs sharply from the usual contemporary distinction between semantics and pragmatics. A second, closely related difference concerns the relationship between these two aspects of language. Mates

---

sitions, but of utterances dependent in all sorts of ways on the context or occasion on which they are uttered. Statements are made in particular situations, and the interpretation to be put upon them is bound up with their relation to these situations: they are in this respect like fireworks, signals or Very lights." *The Uses of Argument* (London and New York: Cambridge University Press, 1958), p. 180. Toulmin points out that medieval logic dealt with context-dependent utterances rather than timeless propositions, and speculates that the change might have followed the introduction of printing and widespread literacy: "in a largely pre-literate world the transient firework-like character of our utterances would remain overwhelmingly obvious. The conception of the proposition as outlasting the moment of its utterance —like a statue which stands unaltered after the death of the sculptor who fashioned it—would become plausible only after the permanent recorded word had come to play a much larger part in the lives of speculative men" (p. 181). But Toulmin concedes that the cause of the change is more likely the shift of interest from Aristotelian to Platonic thought toward the end of the Middle Ages.

[37] Stanley Cavell, *Must We Mean What We Say?* (New York: Charles Scribner's Sons, 1969), p. 9.

[38] *Ibid.*

[39] *Ibid.*, pp. 11–12.

clearly and characteristically takes semantics to be entirely independent of pragmatics, so that one can confine one's study to the former and avoid the infinite morass of the latter. Thus, the meaning of a word or an expression is essentially self-contained and fixed, no matter how or where that word or expression is used. But Wittgenstein argues that meaning and use are intimately, inextricably related, because use helps to determine meaning.[40] Meaning is learned from, and shaped in, instances of use; so both its learning and its configuration depend on pragmatics. One may call the signaling, performative aspects of "I promise" part of its pragmatics, but they contribute to the semantics, the meaning of "promise" just as much as "he promised" or "they might promise" or "that's a promise." Semantic meaning is compounded out of cases of a word's use, including all the many and varied language games that are played with it; so meaning is very much the product of pragmatics.

Wittgenstein is often believed to have taught that meaning and use are identical. But a careful reading shows that this is not a correct interpretation; he regards meaning and use as separate, but intimately related and interdependent. "We say 'behaviour flows from character' and that is how use flows from meaning."[41] As a man's character remains relatively fixed and manifests itself in his actions, so meaning is the relatively fixed element running through a word's many uses. But a man's character is also shaped by his actions, and we read his character from what he does. So, too, meaning is gradually shaped by use and can be learned from use. "Let the use *teach* you the meaning."[42]

Such passages clearly indicate that use and meaning are not identical for Wittgenstein. If he sometimes seems to write as if they were, this is partly because of problems of translation, but also because he is writing specifically for someone who is in the grip of conceptual puzzlement.[43] Such a person will feel that what he needs is meaning—the essence of the puzzling concept; what he in fact needs is an overview of the word's use. Thus, the heart of Wittgenstein's message, directed to such a person, is really: "Don't *ask for* the meaning; *ask for* the use."[44] But in that case,

[40] Compare Karl-Otto Apel, *Analytic Philosophy of Language and the Geisteswissenschaften* (Dordrecht: D. Reidel, 1967), pp. 40–41.

[41] Ludwig Wittgenstein, *Remarks on the Foundations of Mathematics*, tr. by G. E. M. Anscombe, ed. by G. H. von Wright, R. Rhees, and G. E. M. Anscombe (Oxford: Basil Blackwell, 1964), p. 7. Compare *Philosophical Investigations*, pars. 30, 43, 138, 197, 556, 557, 561; *On Certainty*, par 64; and Friedrich Waismann, *Wittgenstein und der Wiener Kreis*, ed. by B. F. McGuiness (London: Basil Blackwell, 1967), p. 167.

[42] Wittgenstein, *Philosophical Investigations*, p. 212; compare p. 220.

[43] In the most commonly cited passage, *ibid.*, par. 43, Anscombe's translation reads that the word "meaning" can be *defined* by the doctrine that the meaning is the use. The original German has *erklären*, that the word can be *explained* by that doctrine.

[44] Quoted by Gilbert Ryle in "Theory of Meaning," in C. E. Caton, ed., *Philosophy and Ordinary Language* (Urbana: University of Illinois Press, 1963), p. 143; my italics. Compare John Wisdom, "Ludwig Wittgenstein, 1934–1937" in Fann, ed., *Ludwig Wittgenstein* (New York: Dell, 1967), p. 46.

the preference of philosophers like Mates for "an empirical investigation of language" which "avoids" pragmatics seems positively perverse, a sure guarantee that the resulting study will remain irrelevant to conceptual puzzlement (which is centrally related to philosophy). That is the third, and most significant, way in which Wittgenstein's discussion of meaning and use differs from the contemporary philosophical distinction between semantics and pragmatics. For Wittgenstein, it is the pragmatics of an expression about which we are likely to be confused, and of which we need to be reminded.

### CONCEPTUAL PUZZLEMENT

Let us use an example to help us sum up the significance of what has been said so far about meaning and concepts; and thus approach Wittgenstein's discussion of conceptual puzzlement and paradox. We have elaborated three main theses: that words are not, or not merely, labels but often signals; that language is learned from instances of use, and consequently meaning is compounded out of instances of use; and that meaning is context-dependent, that meaning and sense need to be completed by context. These three theses further imply a simple but remarkably important conclusion: the various cases out of which the meaning of a word is compounded need not be mutually consistent; they may—perhaps must— have contradictory implications. These inconsistent or contradictory implications are what give rise to conceptual puzzlement and paradox.

Let us illustrate by reference to a concept that has in fact been a central philosophical concern, the concept of knowledge. At least since Socrates, philosophers have been interested in the nature of true knowledge, how it may be distinguished from mere opinion or belief. (Of course, Socrates was concerned not about knowledge but about *episteme*, but we must postpone the significance of that complication). In various dialogues, the Platonic Socrates gradually establishes a number of criteria by which to distinguish true knowledge.[45] It is eternal and must continue to abide and exist always; it is more firmly fixed in the mind than opinion; it is instilled by teaching rather than persuasion or propaganda; it is able to "give an account of itself"—that is, the man who knows can explain; and, finally, knowledge must be true.

We shall be occupied only with the last criterion, a criterion which many subsequent philosophers have also noted and puzzled over.[46] Knowledge must be true; a falsehood can never be part of knowledge; someone who

---

[45] Plato, *Republic*, V. 474B–480; *Cratylus*, 440; *Meno*, 97; *Gorgias*, 454; *Timaeus*, 28; *Theaetetus*, 202.
[46] For example, Thomas Hobbes: "There are two things necessarily implied in this word knowledge; the one is truth, the other evidence; for what is not true can never be known. For let a man say he knoweth a thing never so well, if the same shall afterwards appear to be false, he is driven to a confession, that it was not knowledge, but opinion." *Elements of Law*, I, 6, 2.

knows cannot be wrong. Of course, falsehoods are often mistaken for knowledge, and someone who claims to know may well be wrong. But that does not make the falsehoods knowledge. If we claim to know something —say, that Napoleon was born in 1765—and it subsequently turns out that Napoleon was in fact born in 1769, then we say in retrospect: "We *did not know* when Napoleon was born. We claimed to know. We thought we knew; but we did not know." For a proposition really to qualify as knowledge, it cannot turn out to be false. That is not the only requirement, but it is one requirement.[47]

This discovery easily leads onto an epistemological path something like the following: Since knowledge must be true, for anything really to be knowledge it must never throughout all eternity subsequently turn out to be false. But about the kinds of things we normally encounter in our human lives on earth, we cannot be absolutely sure that they will never throughout all eternity turn out to be false. Indeed, we can be fairly sure that some of what we now think we know *will* later turn out to be false. Therefore, strictly speaking, we ought not to claim to "know" any of the things we ordinarily claim to know. We should only have said that we *believed* Napoleon was born in 1765. For if someone says he believes that Napoleon was born in 1765 and it subsequently turns out that the correct date is 1769, we do not say in retrospect what we would say about a claim to know. We do not say, "He thought he believed that Napoleon was born in 1765, but he didn't really believe that." We continue to assert that he believed it, though we may add "but he was mistaken," or "but it turned out to be a false belief." There is such a thing as false belief, but no such thing as false knowledge. So it seems that about ordinary, fallible, human things we ought not, strictly speaking, to claim knowledge at all, but at most belief.

In philosophy, various epistemological and metaphysical schools of thought branch off at this point. Some maintain that there is no such thing as knowledge, really. Others argue that, really, we can only know our own sensations, or only tautological truths, or only transcendent Forms. We need not be concerned with them further here. The initial question: "Must knowledge be infallibly true?" and the initial insight: "If you know, you can't be wrong, so really, we ought not to claim to know . . ."— these are what interest us. For these are conceptual insights, conceptual puzzlement. One does not need to be a philosopher to discover them; anyone speculating abstractly about knowledge may happen upon them.

Now, consider one possible way of responding to these "discoveries" by referring to our ordinary usage. One might say: the kind of ordinary,

[47] The point is made by Wittgenstein, *On Certainty*, pars. 42, 90, 367; R. M. Chisholm, *Perceiving* (Ithaca: Cornell University Press, 1957), p. 16; Ryle, *Concept of Mind*, p. 152; Norman Malcolm, *Knowledge and Certainty* (Englewood Cliffs: Prentice-Hall, 1963), p. 60; and Austin, *Philosophical Papers*, pp. 65 ff. Additional requirements, as Austin and Wittgenstein point out, include "being in a position to know."

fallible, human situations in which we usually claim to know things are precisely the kind of situations from which each of us, in growing up, learned the word "knowledge." They are what we learned to call "knowing." They are paradigmatic for the concept; they define it. Wherever did this other, stricter concept of what knowledge "must" be like in order to qualify as knowledge come from? What makes the philosopher with his "discovery" think that what he calls "knowledge" is somehow more truly knowledge than what the rest of us call "knowledge"? The ordinary, fallible occasions on which we claim to know things define what knowledge is, so they cannot, in general, fail to be knowledge.

Hopefully, the reader can feel a certain power in the logic of both the initial "discovery" and the response. Together, they constitute a conceptual paradox, the two sides of a seemingly endless and insoluble dispute. The response is of a kind we characterized earlier as a vulgarization of ordinary-language philosophy: it attempts to refute a conceptual insight, a philosophical position, with evidence from ordinary language. But the "discovery" cannot be refuted that way, for of course we all know quite well that the "discovery" conflicts with ordinary usage. That is why we immediately conclude that "really, strictly speaking," we ought not to talk as we ordinarily do.

What is helpful here is to take seriously the question asked ironically in the refutation: Where *does* the "stricter" idea of knowledge, by which our ordinary claims to know seem inadequate, come from? The obvious but surprising answer is that it, too, comes from ordinary usage. It comes from such facts of ordinary usage as the one we cited in introducing it: that when what someone claims to know turns out to be false, we conclude that he did not know it. The "stricter" notion of knowledge involved in the "discovery" derives from ordinary usage just as surely as the "more ordinary" notion seeking to refute it. But they derive from different parts, different aspects of our ordinary use of the concept "knowledge." Our ordinary ways of operating with that family of words just do include both of these facts, contradictory as they may seem: that we claim to know only (or mostly?) in fallible, human situations, but that we say in retrospect someone didn't know if what he said turns out to be false. The concept of knowledge is compounded out of both what we are claiming when we claim to know, and when we are permitted, supposed, to make such claims. It is tempting to say that the facts are contradictory, but that is nonsense. The facts just are as they are. The contradiction arises only when we try to derive a general, abstract answer to the question of whether knowledge must be infallibly true. The grammar of the word pulls us inexorably in opposite directions here. It is perfectly possible to formulate some consistent generalizations about the concept of "knowledge," for example, a dictionary definition. But to other general questions about it, no consistent answer is possible.

So long as we suppose that a word like "knowledge" must be a label for some (class of) phenomena, we are blocked from seeing the duality of its grammar. For, of course, phenomena in the world are not supposed to have contradictory characteristics, to be both X and not X at the same time. But as soon as we shift our attention from the noun to the verb, and begin thinking of it as a signal instead of a label, the difficulty no longer blocks us but becomes accessible to investigation. We establish: yes, this *and* this is what we say, what we do. And that recognition can yield new perspective on the nature of knowledge.

Austin has pointed out that claiming to know is more like promising than one might suppose. The verb "to know" is not a performative; saying "I know" does not constitute knowing. But it is quasi-performative. When we claim to know we are not merely describing our state of mind; we are also making a certain kind of commitment. Saying we feel quite sure may describe our state of mind, but saying we know does more than that, does something different. It means issuing a certain kind of guarantee, taking a certain kind of responsibility for the truth of what we claim to know. Knowledge is not a stronger version of belief, Austin says, any more than promising is "something superior, in the same scale as hoping and intending, even to merely fully intending: for there *is* nothing in that scale superior to fully intending. When I say 'I know', *I give others my word*; *I give others my authority for saying* that [the thing I have claimed to know is true.] When I have said only that I am sure, and prove to have been mistaken, I am not liable to be rounded on by others in the same way as when I have said 'I know'. I am sure *for my part*, you can take it or leave it: accept it if you think I'm an acute and careful person, that's your responsibility. But I don't know 'for my part', and when I say 'I know' I don't mean you can take it or leave it (though of course you *can* take it or leave it)."[48]

What strikes us when we make the conceptual "discovery" that if you know you can't be wrong is the apparent gap or disparity between what we appear to offer in claiming to know and what is actually ours to give. We offer, or claim, infallibility, yet obviously we are not infallible, and no one supposes us to be. In the light of Austin's suggestion, we might now say: The apparent gap is bridged by our act of speaking, by our authority in speaking, by our commitment. When we claim to know or call something knowledge, we take on responsibility for guaranteeing that the thing will never turn out to be false. Of course both we and our listeners know that it might; but we give our word, our guarantee, all the same, and those to whom we speak normally accept it.

It is tempting to speculate about how enormously useful it is for human beings to have a concept that works in such a way, to play these language games. For it obviously enables some people to act on the strength of other people's responsibility, other people's information. In a world beset with unforeseeable and uncontrollable events, it makes action a little more

48 Austin, *Philosophical Papers*, pp. 67–68.

feasible and responsibility a little more bearable. But for the game to work as it does, for the concept to function as it does, the rules *must* include the "gap" between what we offer in speaking and what seems ours to give. Creatures that really could infallibly foresee the future, that really were omniscient, would have no need for such a concept. And if "I know" meant nothing different from "I believe" or "I am sure," it could not perform for us as it does, could not give us the kind of freedom to act on another's information that it does give. The inconsistency implicit in the grammar of knowledge is not a fault, flawing that concept; it is essential to the concept's function.

## WITTGENSTEIN'S DIAGNOSES

Wittgenstein offers two main accounts of what goes on in conceptual puzzlement, "insight," and paradox, though the accounts are evidently related. The one stresses the kind of inconsistency in grammar we have just been discussing; the other stresses the significance of context.

Wittgenstein's first diagnosis is that conceptual puzzlement arises from our desire for order, neatness, system, in our language. Obviously the ability to generalize, to abstract, to find and make patterns, is an essential feature of the human mind. It is what makes language possible; it enables us to understand instructions of the form "This, and things like it, are called 'games' " or "Continue this series in the same way" or "Like that, only more so." It allows us to extrapolate from what is familiar, and thus to master ideas like "permanence," "infinity," "God," without experiencing them directly in any empirical way. But this very capacity can also create problems as we seek order in our language. Wittgenstein suggests that the ability is paralleled by a kind of need, a "craving for generality," a "demand for absoluteness."[49] In the grip of this need, we think that we require a better definition, yet definitions do not satisfy us, "as in certain states of indigestion we feel a kind of hunger which cannot be removed by eating."[50] Wittgenstein says that we do not just happen to find "the crystalline purity of logic" when we are conceptually puzzled; it is a "requirement" that we bring to our investigations.[51] "The puzzles which we try to remove always spring from just this attitude towards language."[52]

But what is wrong with seeking clarity, generality, and order in language, with looking for rules? In the *Blue and Brown Books*, Wittgenstein still says that the desired rules, the desired order, simply do not exist. "We are unable clearly to circumscribe the concepts we use; not

---

[49] Wittgenstein, *Blue and Brown Books*, p. 17; Cavell, *Must We Mean What We Say?*, p. 77.

[50] Wittgenstein, *Blue and Brown Books*, p. 27.

[51] Wittgenstein, *Philosophical Investigations*, par. 107; compare pars. 108, 38.

[52] Wittgenstein, *Blue and Brown Books*, p. 26; compare *Philosophical Investigations*, par. 81. Wittgenstein says explicitly that he has in mind his own work in the *Tractatus*.

because we don't know their real definition, but because there is no real 'definition' to them. To suppose that there *must* be would be like supposing that whenever children play with a ball they play a game according to strict rules."[53] The kind of ideal calculus we are looking for does exist in mathematics, but "our ordinary use of language conforms to this standard of exactness only in rare cases."[54] But there are other passages which say what becomes his firm position in the *Investigations*: there are rules of a sort to be found, but we become "entangled" in them, and they do not yield the kind of clarity we were seeking. In conceptual puzzlement, one "sees a law in the way a word is used, and, trying to apply this law consistently, comes up against cases where it leads to paradoxical results."[55] It is we who "lay down rules, a technique, for a game," but "when we follow the rules, things do not turn out as we had assumed," and we are "entangled in our own rules."[56]

But now one might suppose that this is because we have laid down the wrong rules, made an incorrect generalization instead of the correct one. (That supposition would correspond to the vulgarization of ordinary-language philosophy which attempts to refute a conceptual "insight" by evidence from ordinary language, a "better rule.") Wittgenstein, however, is saying something profoundly different. It is neither that language has no rules, so that our quest for order is in that sense misguided; nor that we have simply come up with the wrong rules. Rather, the rules that can be abstracted from our ordinary use of an expression, from the cases in which that expression occurs, are in fact often mutually inconsistent or contradictory. The cases have contradictory implications. "It may seem

[53] Wittgenstein, *Blue and Brown Books*, p. 25.
[54] *Ibid.*
[55] *Ibid.*, p. 27. Toulmin points out the close parallel of such passages to Heinrich Hertz's discussion, familiar to Wittgenstein, of nineteenth-century debates about the nature of the "force of electricity": "Why is it that people never in this way ask what is the nature of gold, or what is the nature of velocity? Is the nature of gold better known to us than that of force? Can we by our conceptions, by our words, completely represent the nature of any thing? Certainly not. I fancy the difference must lie in this. With the terms 'velocity' and 'gold' we connect a large number of relations to other terms; and between all these relations we find no contradictions which offend us. We are therefore satisfied and ask no further questions. But we have accumulated around the terms 'force' and 'electricity' more relations than can be completely reconciled amongst themselves. We have an obscure feeling of this and want to have things cleared up. Our confused wish finds expression in the confused question as to the nature of force and electricity. But the answer which we want is not really an answer to this question. It is not by finding out more and fresh relations and connections that it can be answered; but by removing the contradictions existing between those already known, and thus perhaps by reducing their number. *When these painful contradictions are removed, the question as to the nature of force will not have been answered; but our minds, no longer vexed, will cease to ask illegitimate questions.*" Heinrich Hertz, *Principles of Mechanics*, introduction, cited in Toulmin, "Ludwig Wittgenstein," *Encounter*, XXXII (January 1969), 68.
[56] Wittgenstein, *Philosophical Investigations*, par. 125. Compare Cavell, *Must We Mean What We Say?*, p. 77.

queer to say that we may correctly use either of two forms of expression which seem to contradict each other; but such cases are very frequent."[57] If words were labels, this could not be; for the things labeled could not have contradictory characteristics. But if words are tools, each used in a variety of language games, then it is not surprising at all. "It is not to be expected of [a] word that it should have a unified employment; we should rather expect the opposite."[58]

In contemplating a concept abstractly, we generalize too hastily and in the wrong way. We think of an example—or rather, a picture springs to mind—and we extrapolate a generalization from it. We are convinced the generalization is correct, because we know that the example is correct. And this procedure would work well if all valid examples of a word's use had the same, or at least mutually consistent, implications. It never occurs to us that there might be other, equally correct and valid examples of usage inconsistent with the first. Wittgenstein says that conceptual puzzlement is like a disease, and its "main cause" is "a one-sided diet: one nourishes one's thinking with only one kind of example."[59] We have a mental picture, and believe that it forces a particular generalization on us; but that belief merely reflects "the fact that only the one case and no other occurred to us."[60] If we do notice other, conflicting cases, our conviction that there must be a single consistent rule leads us to dismiss them as confusing details. "A picture is conjured up which seems to fix the sense *unambiguously*. The actual use, compared with that suggested by the picture, seems like something muddied."[61] So we cling to the picture, and to our generalization based on it.

As a consequence, when we are conceptually puzzled, we need exactly what we do not want. We want to escape the confusing encumbrance of detailed cases and proceed directly to the essence, the central core, of the puzzling concept. But that desire only entangles us in the implicit grammatical contradictions; any rule that would satisfy the desire will conflict with other cases. It is as if "in the actual use of expressions we make detours, we go by side-roads." In conceptual puzzlement we believe that we see "the straight highway before us," but "we cannot use it, because it is permanently closed."[62] The very craving for generality and clarity cuts us off from what would resolve our puzzlement: the messy, confused plurality of other valid examples of the word's use. Instead of "craving for generality," Wittgenstein says, one could also speak here of our "con-

---

[57] Wittgenstein, *Blue and Brown Books*, p. 29; compare Waismann, *Wittgenstein*, p. 125.

[58] Ludwig Wittgenstein, *Zettel*, tr. by G. E. M. Anscombe, ed. by G. E. M. Anscombe and G. H. von Wright (Berkeley and Los Angeles: University of California Press, 1967), par. 112; compare par. 113.

[59] Wittgenstein, *Philosophical Investigations*, par. 593.

[60] *Ibid.*, par. 140.

[61] *Ibid.*, par. 426.

[62] *Ibid.*

temptuous attitude towards the particular case," or rather, toward all particular cases but the one, which we take to be general.[63] We want to consider the concept in general, in the abstract, so we dismiss "as irrelevant the concrete cases," which alone could have shown us what we need to understand.[64] "One might say: the axis of reference of our examination must be rotated, but about the fixed point of our real need."[65] That is why Wittgenstein insists that we should not just speculate abstractly but should "look and see" how a word is actually used. "But the difficulty is to remove the prejudice which stands in the way of doing this. It is not a *stupid* prejudice."[66] It is not stupid because in so many other situations our capacity to generalize, to make and find patterns, is our most powerful tool. "In numberless cases we exert ourselves to find a picture and once it is found the application as it were comes about of itself. In this case we already have a picture which forces itself on us at every turn,—but does not help us out of the difficulty, which only begins here."[67]

All this should make a little clearer the value of ordinary-language philosophy's painstaking attention to the details of usage. For Wittgenstein treats the disease of conceptual puzzlement by varying our diet, by reminding us of the richness and plurality of our actual ordinary speech.[68] In doing so, he does not really tell us anything new; he "assembles reminders" for us.[69] Here "the problems are solved, not by giving new information, but by arranging what we have always known."[70] What we really lack when we are conceptually puzzled is not a definition or rule, but a clear overview of the relevant cases. Wittgenstein says he is "*not* after *exactness*, but after a synoptic view."[71] The idea of perspicuity, of a "perspicuous representation," he says is of "fundamental importance" and "earmarks the form of account" he gives, his way of looking at things. A main cause of conceptual puzzlement is the fact "that we do not *command a clear view* of the use of our words. —Our grammar is lacking in this sort of perspicuity."[72] Thus the real task here is "not to resolve a contradiction . . . , but to make it possible for us to get a clear view" of the problem troubling us, of "the state of affairs *before* the contradiction is resolved."[73] Of course, a perspicuous overview of inconsistency is not the

[63] Wittgenstein, *Blue and Brown Books*, p. 18.
[64] *Ibid.*, pp. 19–20.
[65] Wittgenstein, *Philosophical Investigations*, par. 108.
[66] *Ibid.*, par. 340.
[67] *Ibid.*, par. 425.
[68] "The motto here is: Take a *wider* look round." Wittgenstein, *Foundations of Mathematics*, p. 54.
[69] Wittgenstein, *Philosophical Investigations*, par. 127.
[70] *Ibid.*, par. 109; compare "Bemerkungen über Frazers *The Golden Bough*," p. 235: ". . . weil man nur richtig zusammenstellen muss, was man *weiss*, und nichts dazusetzen, und die Befriedigung, die durch die Erklärung angestrebt wird, ergibt sich von selbst."
[71] Wittgenstein, *Zettel*, par. 464; compare par. 113.
[72] Wittgenstein, *Philosophical Investigations*, par. 122.
[73] *Ibid.*, par. 125.

same as a single, unifying, consistent rule that fits all the cases. But if no single, unifying, consistent rule *can* fit all the cases, then an overview of the chaotic facts may well be what is really needed.

## LANGUAGE IDLING

Wittgenstein's second diagnosis of conceptual puzzlement and paradox focuses on their characteristic speculative abstractness, their origin in contemplation rather than actual speech. In our craving for generality, we try to abstract from all the particular, concrete cases in which an expression might actually be used, to contemplate it in isolation, at rest. We try to consider it apart from any context; or, one might say, we create a new and special context of abstract contemplation. But this special context is not a context for speech; in it, language is not being used by one person to tell another something, but as an object for study. When we speculate this way about concepts, Wittgenstein says, "the language-game in which they are to be applied is missing."[74] Consequently, conceptual problems "arise when language *goes on holiday*"; they involve "confusions which occupy us . . . when language is like an engine idling, not when it is doing work."[75] Of course, we may feel that this is an advantage, not a fault. After all, in abstract contemplation we can often be more objective, detached, and perceptive than in the course of daily life; what we all normally take for granted is often wrong. But Wittgenstein maintains that the result of contemplating concepts in this particular abstract way is not new discovery, but puzzlement and paradox. For meaning and sense depend on context, are incomplete without it; so when we consider an expression apart from any context of speech, we deprive it of significant aspects of its meaning.

Let us return to the problem about the nature of knowledge. Traditional philosophers, developing the view that we don't really, strictly speaking, know the kinds of things we ordinarily claim to know, usually proceed in some such way as this: They begin from some simple, obvious fact—a fact so obvious that we will all agree it must surely be an example of knowledge if anything is. Descartes, for example, begins his meditation with a fact "too evident to be doubted; as, for instance, that I am in this place, seated by the fire, . . ."[76] Then these philosophers proceed to show that even such a fact can be doubted after all, might turn out to be false after all; so even *it* is not knowledge. But the kind of example chosen is, characteristically, an example of a piece of knowledge, not of a situation in which one person might actually be moved to *say* to another that he knows something. It is an example of "knowledge," not of "know"; it is a labeling rather than a signaling example.

[74] *Ibid.*, par. 96.
[75] *Ibid.*, pars. 38, 132.
[76] Norman Kemp Smith, ed. and tr., *Descartes Philosophical Writings* (New York: Random House, 1958), p. 177.

In his essay "Other Minds," Austin criticizes this way of proceeding and suggests that we analyze instead an imaginary case of someone actually claiming to know something and actually being challenged by a hearer.[77] Austin imagines someone announcing that there is a goldfinch at the bottom of the garden and being asked, "How do you know?" He proceeds to catalogue some of the possible kinds of answers that might be given, showing their great variety ("I saw it," "From its coloring," "I was brought up in the fens," and so on). The response given will, of course, depend on the facts of the case (whether the man saw the bird, where he was brought up), but also on what he thinks the questioner is doubting, what he thinks the point of the question was. If the context does not make clear what the questioner is doubting, he may even be asked, in turn, "How do you mean? What are you suggesting?"[78]

In conceptual puzzlement, in traditional philosophical speculation about knowledge like Descartes', no actual claim to know and no actual challenge to that claim are imagined, so we are at a loss to answer the doubt that is raised, or even to understand what kind of answer might be appropriate. In practice we can account for our knowledge only in relation to particular doubts; there is no answer to the generic question of how we ever know anything at all. Actual doubts about actual claims can (sometimes) be answered. But "the wile of the metaphysician," Austin says, consists in raising doubts about an imagined example of knowledge without "specifying or limiting what may be wrong with it," as context normally specifies and limits what may be wrong with ordinary claims to knowledge.[79] In the absence of such specifications or limits, we are at a loss to answer, and knowledge as a whole seems cast into doubt.

Austin attributes the choice of an unrealistic, abstract example to the traditional philosopher's "wile." But it should be obvious that Austin's kind of realistic example will not serve the purposes of conceptual puzzlement about knowledge; there is good reason why traditional philosophers have not used it. Examples of actual claims to knowledge can be doubted, but those doubts can also be answered; what we want to understand when we are conceptually puzzled is a broader doubt than that—the perpetual, abstract possibility of doubt. That is why we must choose an example of knowledge so obvious that no one can doubt it (in the ordinary way), and then show that it can, nevertheless, be doubted. We all know that it is grammatically wrong to claim to know when there is some particular

---

[77] Austin, *Philosophical Papers*, pp. 44–84.
[78] *Ibid.*, p. 55.
[79] *Ibid.* Compare Wittgenstein, *On Certainty*, par. 24: "The idealist's question would be something like: 'What right have I not to doubt the existence of my hands?' . . . But someone who asks such a question is overlooking the fact that a doubt about existence only works in a language-game. Hence, that we should first have to ask: what would such a doubt be like?, and don't understand this straight off."

reason to doubt. We do not say, "I know the answer, but I may be wrong," though of course we always may be. Austin says "It is naturally *always* possible ('humanly' possible) that I may be mistaken . . . but that by itself is no bar against using" the expression "I know" as we do in fact use it.[80] But why isn't it such a bar? If you have any particular reason to think you may be wrong, you should not claim to know; in conceptual puzzlement we come to think of generic human fallibility as one more such reason. That is not wile, but an extrapolation from the grammar of "knowledge," *part* of that grammar. Why shouldn't generic human fallibility be one more such reason?

We have arrived again at the apparent gap between what we seem to offer in claiming to know and what is ours to give. But we said before that that gap is bridged by the act of speaking. When we abstract from any such act, from any situation in which such an act might take place, the gap appears unbridgeable. In a similar way, if we speculate apart from any context about a concept like "permanence," we may easily persuade ourselves that nothing is ever permanent, that "really, strictly speaking," we should never call anything "permanent." Yet that word has normal uses, which define its meaning. And it is normally not used about things which are, as it were, absolutely permanent (for there are no such things on earth), but about things permanent by contrast with other specific things (a permanent rather than a temporary installation, a permanent rather than a temporary wave in the hair, and so on). The context specifies what might count as permanence in a given case; our act of speaking issues a guarantee that the thing is permanent in that sense. The grammar of "permanent" includes both these features, contradictory though they may seem: that "permanent" means "forever," and yet that it is used about things in this world which do not literally or absolutely last forever. (There is no way of talking about these matters without paradox, for, of course, "forever" has a similar grammar.)

Our concepts are fashioned in working use; they serve to differentiate some features of our world, our actions, our feelings, from others. They were not fashioned for speculating about the world as a whole, in general; for we would have no use for such concepts. In speculating abstractly about a concept apart from any context of speech, we use it without any of its usual contrasts; we, as it were, extrapolate the concept to infinity. But thereby we deprive it of the context, the contrasts, which normally complete its meaning. "What sometimes happens might always happen." Wittgenstein asks, "What kind of proposition is that? It is like the following: . . . 'If it is possible for someone to make a false move in some game, then it might be possible for everybody to make nothing but false moves in every game.' . . . Orders are sometimes not obeyed. But what would it

[80] Austin, *Philosophical Papers*, p. 66; compare Michael Polanyi, *Personal Knowledge* (New York and Evanston: Harper and Row, 1964), p. 303.

be like if no orders were *ever* obeyed? The concept 'order' would have lost its purpose."[81]

In speculating abstractly about knowledge, we seek an example that is better, stronger, than any ordinary, spoken claim to know something; because only if we can show that such an example, too, can be doubted, do we raise doubts about knowledge as a whole. But as a result, something most peculiar happens. We end up with an example *so* obvious that no one would need to *say* it, to claim to know it, and thereby we deprive "knowledge" of an essential part of its meaning. We take a really obvious example of knowledge, such as Descartes' "that I am in this place." But *is* that an example of *knowledge*? Certainly no one would claim that I *don't* know it. Yet neither I nor anyone else would have had occasion to claim to know it here and now, as Cavell says, "apart from some special reason which makes that 'description' of my 'knowledge' relevant to something I did or am doing or saying," apart from some reason for speaking about it at all.[82]

Cavell continues: "Perhaps one feels: 'What difference does it make that no one would have *said*, without a special reason for saying it, that you knew . . . ? You *did* know it; it's *true* to say that you knew it. Are you suggesting that one sometimes cannot say what is true?' What I am suggesting is that 'Because it is true' is not a *reason* or basis for saying anything, it does not constitute the *point* of your saying something; and I am suggesting that there must, in grammar, be reasons for what you say, or be point in your saying of something, if what you say is to be comprehensible. We can understand what the *words* mean apart from understanding *why* you say them; but apart from understanding the point of your saying them we cannot understand what *you* mean."[83]

Whether a fact so glaringly obvious that no one would say it, then and there, is an example of knowledge is a question that cannot be unequivocally answered yes or no. Some aspects of the grammar of "knowledge" incline us to say yes: after all, "you *did* know, or anyway you certainly didn't *fail* to know it," and so on. Other aspects of the grammar—less obvious ones—continue to suggest a negative answer. They suggest that "knowledge" exists only where someone (correctly) claims to know, because the meaning of "knowledge" is not merely descriptive. An important element in the meaning of "knowledge" is not referential, but quasi-performative; an important element of its meaning depends on the act of speaking, of claiming to know. That act, we have said, is what bridges the

---

[81] Wittgenstein, *Philosophical Investigations*, par. 345.

[82] Cavell, "Claim to Rationality," pp. 258–259. Compare Wittgenstein, *On Certainty*, par. 622; and par. 553: "It is queer: if I say, without any special occasion, 'I know'—for example, 'I know that I am now sitting in a chair', this statement seems to me unjustified and presumptuous. But if I make the same statement where there is some need for it, then, although I am not a jot more certain of its truth, it seems to me to be perfectly justified and everyday."

[83] Cavell, "Claim to Rationality," pp. 258–259.

apparent gap between what is meant or claimed by "I know" and what justifies us in saying it on particular occasions. Imagining examples of "knowledge" where no one would claim to know is inevitably imagining only part of the grammar, part of the meaning of the concept, and thus only part of what knowledge is. The conceptual problem arises in the first step, which "is the one that altogether escapes notice . . . (The decisive movement in the conjuring trick has been made, and it was the very one that we thought quite innocent.)"[84]

What it amounts to, startling though this proposition may seem, is that something too obviously true to be said does not fully make sense. In choosing the "most obvious" example, we choose one so obvious that we no longer are clear ourselves what it is an example of. Wittgenstein says it is like the question: "Has this room a length?"[85] The answer is so obviously yes that we do not know what the question means or what the answer should be (surely he *can't* mean . . . for he can't fail to know *that*). We are not even able to imagine the opposite: What would a room without a length be? But Wittgenstein asks, "Why do we say: 'I can't imagine the opposite'? Why not: 'I can't imagine the thing itself'?" Can I imagine every room having a length? Well, I simply imagine a room. "Only this picture, in connexion with this proposition, has a quite different role from one used in connexion with the proposition 'This table has the same length as that one over there'. For here I understand what it means to have a picture of the opposite."[86]

Passages like this one are what have led some commentators to the conclusion that Wittgenstein is a verificationist like the logical positivists, holding that the meaning of a proposition depends on the operations performed for its verification or falsification in reality.[87] But any number of utterances have clear meaning and make perfectly good sense, though they are not even assertions that could conceivably be true or false, let alone be operationally falsifiable. Wittgenstein says, "asking whether and how a proposition can be verified is only one particular way of asking 'How d'you mean?' The answer is one contribution to the grammar of the proposition."[88] Verification is only a small part of use, of grammar. And even where verification is relevant, the request for verification is not, as Cavell points out, "the only way in which an explanation of grammar can be requested; it is equally indicative of our failure to understand the grammar of an assertion if we cannot answer such questions as: 'How

84 Wittgenstein, *Philosophical Investigations*, par. 308.
85 Wittgenstein, *Blue and Brown Books*, p. 30.
86 Wittgenstein, *Philosophical Investigations*, par. 251.
87 See for example, C. S. Chihara and J. A. Fodor, "Operationalism and Ordinary Language: A Critique of Wittgenstein," in George Pitcher, ed., *Wittgenstein: The Philosophical Investigations* (Garden City: Doubleday, 1966), pp. 384–419.
88 Wittgenstein, *Philosophical Investigations*, par. 353; I have translated "*ein*" and "*eine*" as "one" rather than "a" to emphasize what I take to be the meaning of the passage. Compare Norman Malcolm, *Ludwig Wittgenstein* (London: Oxford University Press, 1962), pp. 65–66.

would you teach someone what that says?'; 'How would you hint at its truth?'; 'What is it like to wonder whether it is true?' "[89]

The meaning of a concept grows out of its use in actual human life. In conceptual speculation we want to think about that meaning entirely apart from its use, but it is only in use that an expression fully makes sense. Of course, "How do you know?" still has meaning when we ask it in general: "How does anyone ever know anything?" That is, the words have meaning, the sentence seems to make sense. Cavell says that we have not so much spoken nonsense or changed the meaning of the expression, as "deprived it of everything *but* meaning, *sc.*, deprived it of its normal application."[90] And what is wrong with that? "What is left out of an expression if it [is] used 'outside its ordinary language game'? Not what the *words* mean (they mean what they always aid, what a good dictionary says they mean), but what *we* mean in using them when and where we do. Their point, the point of *saying* them, is lost. . . . What we lose is not the meaning of our words—hence, definitions to secure or explain their meaning will not replace our loss. What we lose is a full realization of what we are saying; we no longer know what *we* mean."[91]

What puzzles us when we are conceptually puzzled is real enough; it is no mistake. There really are contradictory implications in the grammar of significant concepts like "knowledge," contradictory generalizations derivable from different parts of that grammar. The trouble with contemplating such a concept in the abstract, apart from any particular context in which it might actually be used, is that our puzzlement springs precisely from ignoring those features of its grammar we thereby exclude. It is not the definition that is troubling; the definition and the syntax are perfectly clear and consistent. The source of, and the solution to, our puzzlement lies in the rest of the grammar, in the complex jumble of cases of use, in the commitment made and responsibility taken when we speak, in the "surrounding circumstances" which set the context for speech.

[89] Cavell, *Must We Mean What We Say?* p. 56.
[90] Cavell, "Claim to Rationality," p. 64.
[91] *Ibid.*, pp. 261–262.

98

# V

## The Problem of Words
## and the World

WHAT HAS BEEN SAID so far about the Wittgensteinian vision of language evidently raises serious and difficult problems in an area central to traditional philosophy, but equally significant for the study of society and politics: the relationship between mind and reality, between language and the world. If one assumes that words are labels, and language primarily our means of referring to things in the world, then language and the world are obviously separate, though correlated. That assumption corresponds to the conventional wisdom of our time, with its positivistic roots. It teaches that things in the world are what they are no matter how we think about them, no matter what we call them. What we say may be accurate or inaccurate, true or false, depending on whether it corresponds well to the independently preexisting reality to which it refers. But if many words are wholly or partly signals rather than labels, if their grammar is often internally inconsistent in its implications, then the matter of "what they refer to" becomes seriously problematical. Similarly, if the meaning of what is said depends not just on corresponding facts but on the speaker and the situation, no simple notion of correlation between words and world will be acceptable. If the most obvious "truths" in any situation are too obvious to be said, and therefore too obvious to make sense, the nature of "the facts" at that point is no simple question. In this chapter we shall explore these problems and some of their implications.

Let us begin with a seemingly trivial example introduced, but not investigated, by Ziff. He notes that the words "corpse" and "cadaver" differ in meaning, the difference being of course the product of slightly different patterns of use. "Corpse" means a dead human body; "cadaver" means a dead body intended for dissection. Thus, a battlefield may be littered with corpses but not, normally, with cadavers. Ziff says "The words 'corpse' and 'cadaver' are very close synonyms, indeed almost exact synonyms. The only difference between them seems to be this: 'cadaver' is a word employed by persons who engage in the practice of medicine and it serves to characterize something answering to certain interests of those persons, viz. an interest in dissection."[1] But in the course of developing this point, Ziff also says, "There is no difference between a corpse and a cadaver, but there is a difference between 'corpse' and 'cadaver.' " He adds that despite the difference between the two words, "one points at a corpse if and only if one points at a cadaver: the class of corpses is identical with the class of cadavers."[2]

We may feel that Ziff's point is clear and obvious; yet what he says is literally false. A corpse is not the same thing as a cadaver, precisely because and to the extent that the two words differ in meaning.[3] And whether one "points at a corpse if and only if one points at a cadaver" depends on the activity of "pointing at" which, as we have seen, is thoroughly problematical. If what one points at sometimes depends not on one's physical movements or even one's intentions but on surrounding circumstances, then the same gesture may be pointing to a corpse in some circumstances and pointing to a cadaver in others. Sometimes it may, indeed, be both simultaneously, but not always. We can see what Ziff is trying to say, but apparently it is difficult to articulate without paradox. There is this *thing*, once a living human being but now dead, lying before us. In one context, we call it a corpse; in another context, a cadaver. But it doesn't change as a result of what we say; it is what it is, no matter what we call it. But then—what is it? If we say either "a corpse" or "a cadaver," we have already assumed a context; if we merely point silently, we have not answered the question. We would like to find some basic, neutral, context-free designation for the thing—say, "dead body"—but there is a nagging doubt: is "dead body" really any more neutral and free of context than the other terms, or it is just one more word with its own special, limited sphere of applicability, its own implications? If such terms were merely labels, obviously they would all refer to the same thing; since they are not, what they refer to in the world is problematical.

Wittgenstein discusses a closely related example in the second half of the *Investigations*: one of those picture puzzles which can be interpreted in more than one way, can be seen either as the head of a rabbit (those two loops are the ears) or as the head of a duck (those loops are the bill).[4] One person looks at the figure and says, "It's a duck," or "I see a duck," or possibly "I see a picture of a duck." Another person looks and

---

[1] Paul Ziff, *Semantic Analysis* (Ithaca: Cornell University Press, 1960), p. 211.
[2] *Ibid.*, pp. 211, 214.
[3] With respect to other concepts, Ziff himself sees this. When, for example, he distinguishes among the meanings of "statement," "assertion," "remark," etc., he does not hesitate to conclude that the phenomena associated with these words differ accordingly. "Statements and utterances need not be confused. . . . But neither are statements to be identified with assertions, nor assertions with contentions, nor contentions with descriptions, nor descriptions with remarks, nor remarks with comments, and so on." *Ibid.*, p. 120.
[4] Ludwig Wittgenstein, *Philosophical Investigations*, tr. by G. E. M. Anscombe (New York: Macmillan, 1968), p. 194.

says, "I see a rabbit." But the experimenter will call it a picture puzzle or, as Wittgenstein does, a duck-rabbit. And he will say about the subjects of the experiment, such things as, "The first man saw it as a duck, the second as a rabbit." Once the naive subjects become aware of the ambiguity, they can see the figure either way, and may say such things as "Now I see it as a rabbit" or "At first I saw it as a duck." Before becoming aware of the ambiguity, they would not have said such things; they were not then aware of seeing anything *as* something else, but simply of seeing it. It would have made as little sense for them to say that they were seeing one thing *as* another, "as to say at the sight of a knife and fork 'Now I am seeing this as a knife and fork'. This expression would not be understood.—Any more than: 'Now it's a fork' or 'It can be a fork too'. One doesn't '*take*' what one knows as the cutlery at a meal *for* cutlery."[5]

All that is familiar enough. "Seeing" is not the same as "seeing as"; each has its appropriate functions and implications. Seeing is not the same as seeing *as*, and each can be done only under appropriate circumstances. "I cannot try to see a conventional picture of a lion *as* a lion, any more than an F as that letter. (Though I may well try to see it as a gallows, for example.)"[6] Trying to see the picture of a lion as a lion gives a sense of incongruity of strain not unlike trying to point to the color of an object directly in front of you, and for the same reason. The necessary context is missing.

But now our problem is this: What are the objective facts of the world, as distinct from what particular people would or could say about them? Is the man who has not perceived the ambiguity in the duck-rabbit *seeing* a rabbit, or is he seeing a duck-rabbit picture puzzle *as* a rabbit? He would say the former; we might say the latter, and so would he in retrospect, after he had discovered the ambiguity. Is it obvious that one of these must be the real, objective truth? One might want to say: The experimenter's view is "truer" because he has some knowledge which the subject lacks— namely, that the picture is a trick picture. The real truth, which even the subject would acknowledge if he were well informed, is that he is seeing a duck-rabbit as a rabbit. But one might, alternatively, want to argue that truth is a matter of interpersonal, intersubjective agreement, what both men could agree on. In that case the subject's view is "truer." For the experimenter *could* say of the subject "he sees a rabbit" if he were trying to give a phenomenological account of the subject's experience. But the naive subject would not, no matter what he was trying to give an account of, say "I am seeing a duck-rabbit as a rabbit."

In any particular situation where men disagree about the facts, it is possible to look for alternative formulations of what was said and perhaps to reach agreement on one of them. If one man says "corpse" and another "cadaver," perhaps they will both settle for "dead body." If one man says

[5] *Ibid.*, p. 195.
[6] *Ibid.*, p. 206.

"seeing a rabbit" and the other "seeing as a rabbit," still they can converse until they agree on something. But is what they agree on then really the neutral, objective truth? Austin says that sometimes there is "no one right way of saying what is seen," because "there may be no one right way of seeing it."[7] But how can there sometimes be no one right way of seeing reality? Isn't the right way the one that corresponds to the facts?

### COMPARATIVE LINGUISTICS

Where Wittgensteinian and ordinary-language philosophy raise such problems, where they seem to challenge positivistic assumptions about a fixed, independent, preexisting world reflected more or less accurately in language, there are striking parallels with recent work in cultural anthropology and linguistics. From the earlier pioneering efforts of ethnographers like Wilhelm von Humboldt to the recent writings of Edward Sapir and Benjamin Lee Whorf, the anthropologists and linguists tell us that what a people considers as part of "the world" depends very much on that people's language.[8] Even some of the most obvious distinctions and correspondences that we take for granted as matters of fact are differently conceived in other cultures. Though he himself was bicultural, Wittgenstein's major works say remarkably little about such cultural and linguistic differences.[9] As a result, he often strikes us as ethnographically naive, seeming to postulate as parts of human nature what we know to be culturally determined. Yet the findings of comparative linguistics do complement and enrich his argument on words and the world.

To begin at the simplest level, different languages have radically different inventories of vocabulary; one is richly articulated where another is poor, presumably depending on what is significant in the corresponding culture. Thus, Eskimo languages have many different words for what we call "snow," depending on whether the snow is falling, packed, frozen,

[7] J. L. Austin, *Sense and Sensibilia*, ed. by G. J. Warnock (Oxford: Clarendon Press, 1962), p. 101.

[8] Edward Sapir, *Language* (New York: Harcourt, Brace & World, 1949); Benjamin Lee Whorf, *Language, Thought, and Reality*, ed. by John B. Carroll (Cambridge: M.I.T. Press, 1967); Wilhelm von Humboldt, *Über die Verschiedenheit des menschlichen Sprachbaues*, ed. by A. F. Pott (Berlin: S. Calvary, 1880); Leo Weisgerber, *Vom Weltbild der Deutschen Sprache* (Düsseldorf: Pädagogischer Verlag Schwann, 1950). See also Susanne Öhman, *Wortinhalt und Weltbild* (Stockholm: Kungl. Boktryckeriet P. A. Norstedt & Söner, 1951).

[9] Wittgenstein, *Philosophical Investigations*, p. 223; *Blue and Brown Books* (New York and Evanston: Harper and Row, 1964), pp. 102–103. But compare the extensive discussion in "Bemerkungen über Frazers *The Golden Bough*," *Synthese*, 17 (1961), where Wittgenstein is revealed as highly sensitive to differences in ethnic perspective. His comments on Frazer's naive ethnocentrism are scathing: "Welche Enge des seelischen Lebens bei Frazer! Daher: Welche Unmöglichkeit, ein anderes Leben zu begreifen, als das englische seiner Zeit! Fraser kann sich keinen Priester vorstellen, der nicht im Grunde ein englischer Parson unserer Zeit ist, mit seiner ganzen Dummheit und Flauheit. . . . Frazer ist viel mehr savage, als die meisten seiner savages." (pp. 237–238, 241).

slushy, and so on.[10] In Bulu, a language of the Cameroun, "there are at least twenty-five terms for different kinds of baskets but no specific generic which includes just baskets and nothing else."[11] In Anuak, which is spoken in the Sudan, a single word designates anything made of metal, from a needle to an airplane.[12] But such examples do not really shake our conventional assumptions about objectivity and fact. We feel that the Eskimo categories still add up to our snow, the Bulu categories to our basket, and that we could perceive the finer distinctions if we had some practical reason for doing so. The distinctions are objectively there, in the world.

Things are more challenging if we turn, for example, to the vocabulary of color. The Navaho have color terms corresponding roughly to our "white," "red," and "yellow," Henle says, but they have two terms corresponding to our "black," one for "the black of darkness, the other the black of such objects as coal. Our 'grey' and 'brown,' however, correspond to a single term in their language and likewise our 'blue' and 'green.' "[13] The German word for violet was introduced only in the nineteenth century, from French. Before that, the word that now means "brown" was used both for what we call "brown" and what we call "violet."[14] Nida says that in a high percentage of African languages there are only three color words. He adds, rather obscurely, that the words "correspond" to our "black," "white," and "red," but "nevertheless divide up the entire spectrum."[15] Of course, an eighteenth-century German could, when necessary, perceive the difference between brown and violet, as we can perceive the difference between the black of darkness and the black of coal. But how many, and which colors are there in the world?

Such differences become increasingly striking as we move from concrete to abstract, and as we move away from words that often function as labels to words involved in more complex language-games. We all know that there are certain words that can be translated only by lengthy, circumlocutory explanations, that really cannot be translated at all and therefore are often borrowed instead: words like the German "*Weltanschauung*," "*Gemütlichkeit*," or "*überhaupt*," or the French "*vis-à-vis*" or "*fait accompli*."[16] European languages lack a translation corresponding to the English "fair"; of course they do and can translate the word, but usually with the same word that also translates "just," so that the distinc-

[10] Whorf, *Language, Thought, and Reality*, p. 216.

[11] Eugene A. Nida, "Principles of Translation as Exemplified by Bible Translating," in *On Translation*, ed. by Reuben A. Brower (Cambridge: Harvard University Press, 1959), p. 26.

[12] Edward Sapir, "Language and Environment," *American Anthropologist*, n. s., 14 (1912), 228, quoted in Paul Henle, ed., *Language, Thought and Culture* (Ann Arbor: University of Michigan Press, 1965), p. 5. See also Öhman, *op. cit.*, pp. 44–45 and *passim*.

[13] Henle, *op. cit.*, p. 7.

[14] Öhman, *op. cit.*, p. 137.

[15] Nida, *op. cit.*, p. 13.

[16] Öhman, *op. cit.*, p. 68.

tion marked in English between "fair" and "just" is lost. Correspondingly, German has three words—*"vertreten," "darstellen,"* and *"repräsentieren,"* all of which must usually be translated by the English "represent." *"Darstellen"* means to depict or stand for, *"vertreten"* means to act for as an agent. *"Repräsentieren"* is quite close to *"vertreten"* and not easy to distinguish from it (it is more formal, more noble; German theorists sometimes argue that mere selfish interests can be *"vertreten"* but not *"repräsentiert"*), but it is conceptually quite unrelated to *"darstellen."* So for an English speaker, the way a painting or a painter or an actor "represents" is part of the same concept as the way an agent or a Congressman "represents." For a German speaker it is not. Here we are much less tempted to say flatly that what two men from different cultures see must be the same, even if their words for it are different. Here we are no longer tempted to say, as we did with respect to Eskimo words for snow, that a German speaker exposed to much painting and legislating would eventually notice the parallels between the two kinds of representing. It begins to seem that language can create objects, rather than just symbolize preexisting objects quite independent of our conceptualization.[17]

And such examples of differences in word meanings are still relatively rare and limited, compared to differences in the symbolization of relations, when we turn from vocabulary to grammar and syntax. Here some languages seem, as it were, to demand of their speakers kinds of information lacking, ambiguous, obscure, or merely implicit in other languages. Rabin illustrates a few cases: "A speaker of Turkish must express in a verbal sentence whether he experienced the event himself or is quite sure of it (*gitti* 'he went'), or knows of it by hearsay (*gitmish* 'he is alleged to have gone'). Of course *gitti* is not commensurate with *he went*, because it implies a certainty not present in the latter. The Russian equivalent to 'I speak' must mean either 'I speak habitually' or 'I am speaking at the moment'. H[ebrew] *halakhti* means indifferently 'I went', 'I have gone', 'I had gone', 'I was going': naturally it corresponds to none of these."[18] Hopi verbs, as Whorf points out, have no tenses, but must always indicate "what type of validity the speaker intends the statement to have": whether he is reporting an event, expecting an event, or making a generalization about events.[19] Chichewa, a language related to Zulu spoken in East Africa, "has two past tenses, one for past events with present result or influence, one for past without present influence. A past as recorded in external situations is distinguished from a past recorded only in the psyche or memory."[20] For translation into Navaho, Kluckhohn and Leighton point out, the English sentence "I drop it" is terribly vague.

[17] Torgny T. Segerstedt, *Die Macht des Wortes* (Zürich: Pan-Verlag, 1947), p. 98.
[18] L. Rabin, "Linguistics of Translation," in *Aspects of Translation* (Studies in Communication No. 2) (London: University College Communications Research Center, 1958), p. 128; compare Nida, *op. cit.*, pp. 22–23.
[19] Whorf, *op. cit.*, p. 217.
[20] *Ibid.*, p. 265.

"The Navaho must specify four particulars which the English leaves either unsettled or to inference from context."[21] The Navaho must make the "it" either definite or a general "something"; he must choose among verb stems depending upon whether the "it" is round, or long, or fluid, or animate; he must indicate whether the agent controls the object's fall; and he must specify rigorously "whether the act is in progress, or just about to start, or just about to stop or habitually carried on or repeatedly carried on."[22]

In English, Whorf points out, the sentences "I pull the branch aside" and "I have an extra toe on my foot" have little similarity; an English speaker presumably would not see these two "facts" as much alike.[23] But in Shawnee, for example, the two corresponding utterances are exactly alike except for the last two syllables (and the last part of a Shawnee linguistic construction is generally the least important and emphatic part).[24] Analyzing the parts of the Shawnee utterances, Whorf shows how the two "facts" appear so similar to a Shawnee speaker. Literal translations of both sentences run, roughly, "I – forked outline – branched or branchlike thing," and only then do they diverge, the former ending "by hand action – subject does this to appropriate object," the latter, "pertaining to the toes," with the absence of further suffix indicating that the subject manifests a condition in his own person. Shown this reasoning, Whorf suggests, even an English speaker can see the parallel. And where first he may have assumed that "sentences are unlike because they tell about unlike facts," he may now conclude that "facts are unlike to speakers whose language background provides for unlike formulations of them."[25]

Whorf's case for the influence of language on conceptions of the world is strongest where he demonstrates not merely one isolated linguistic peculiarity, but a pervasively different orientation reflected at a number of points in a language. Thus, he argues persuasively that Hopi is "a timeless language."[26] We have already noted that Hopi verbs lack tense, failing to distinguish among past, present, and future. The Hopi language "recognizes psychological time, which is much like Bergson's 'duration,' but this 'time' is quite unlike the mathematical time, $T$, used by our physicists. Among the peculiar properties of Hopi time are that it varies with each observer, does not permit of simultaneity, and has zero dimensions; i.e., it cannot be given a number greater than one. The Hopi do not say, 'I stayed five days,' but 'I left on the fifth day.' A word referring to this kind of time, like the word day, can have no plural." Hopi grammar makes it easy to distinguish among momentary, continued, and

[21] Clyde Kluckhohn and Dorothea Leighton, *The Navaho* (Cambridge: Harvard University Press, 1946), p. 204, quoted in Henle, *op. cit.*, p. 9.
[22] *Ibid.*, p. 10. Further such examples may be found in Rabin, *op. cit.*, p. 128.
[23] Whorf, *op. cit.*, p. 233.
[24] *Ibid.*, p. 234.
[25] *Ibid.*, p. 235.
[26] *Ibid.*, p. 216; compare pp. 134–159.

repeated events, and to indicated the actual sequence of reported events, so that "the universe can be described without recourse to a concept of dimensional time."[27]

Given such differences, one is no longer comfortable saying that time is whatever it is in the real world, objectively, quite independent of human beings' conceptualization of it. Indeed, the linguists and anthropologists who discuss such examples, and some philosophers commenting on them, conclude that our language shapes or even determines our world. Sapir says that "the 'real world' is to a large extent unconsciously built up on the language habits of the group."[28] Frantz Fanon agrees: "To speak a language is to take on a world, a culture," it means "to support the weight of a civilization. . . . A man who has a language consequently possesses the world expressed and implied by that language."[29] So, too, Peter Winch: "Our idea of what belongs to the realm of reality is given for us in the language that we use. The concepts we have settle for us the form of the experience we have of the world."[30]

In a way, the point is most poignantly made with respect to science, where our hopes for objectivity, independent of time and culture, are greatest. But science itself is part of a culture, and its language must be learned. "Something of the true situation verges on visibility," as Willard van Orman Quine has said, if we ask "who would undertake to translate 'Neutrinos lack mass' into the jungle language?"[31] Are neutrinos objectively there, in the world? As a layman is gradually trained to become a scientist, he is initiated into a new language, new ways of seeing, a new world, just as the jungle natives would have to be to understand about neutrinos. Kuhn says, "Looking at a contour map, the student sees lines on paper, the cartographer a picture of a terrain. Looking at a bubble-chamber photograph, the student sees confused and broken lines, the physicist a record of familiar subnuclear events. Only after a number of such transformations of vision does the student become an inhabitant of the scientist's world, seeing what the scientist sees and responding as the

[27] *Ibid.*, pp. 216–217.

[28] Quoted in Whorf, *op. cit.*, p. 134.

[29] Frantz Fanon, *Black Skin, White Masks*, tr. by Charles Lam Markmann (New York: Grove Press, 1967), pp. 38, 17–18.

[30] Peter Winch, *The Idea of a Social Science*, ed. by R. F. Holland (New York: Humanities Press, 1965), p. 15. Compare also Michael Polanyi, *Personal Knowledge* (New York and Evanston: Harper & Row, 1964), p. 112. Whorf says "every language is a vast pattern-system, different from others, in which are culturally ordained the forms and categories by which the personality not only communicates, but also analyzes nature, notices or neglects types of relationship and phenomena, channels his reasoning, and builds the house of his consciousness"; *op. cit.*, p. 252. Tullio de Mauro says that every language has "its own particular topography. . . . No language is merely the semantic clothing of a body of universal concepts and categories: on the contrary, each has the power to mould the thought of the communities adopting it"; *Ludwig Wittgenstein* (Dordrecht: D. Reidel, 1967), p. 11.

[31] Willard van Orman Quine, *Word and Object* (Cambridge: M.I.T. Press, 1960), p. 76; compare Peter Winch, "Understanding a Primitive Society," *American Philosophical Quarterly*, I (October 1964), 307–324, esp. p. 317.

scientist does."[32] But in such examples it may still seem obvious what the "objective truth" of the matter is; the student simply has not learned yet to see what is really there. That interpretation is no longer so easy to adopt if one examines the corresponding changes in vision that occur in what Kuhn calls scientific revolutions, when there is a shift in paradigms in the whole scientific community.

"Examining the record of past research from the vantage of contemporary historiography, the historian of science may be tempted to exclaim that when paradigms change, the world itself changes with them. Led by a new paradigm, scientists adopt new instruments and look in new places. Even more important, during revolutions scientists see new and different things with familiar instruments in places they have looked before. It is rather as if the professional community had been suddenly transported to another planet where familiar objects are seen in a different light and are joined by unfamiliar ones as well. . . . Paradigm changes . . . cause scientists to see the world of their research-engagement differently. In so far as their only recourse to that world is through what they see and do, we may want to say that after a revolution scientists are responding to a different world."[33]

Kuhn illustrates with an example from the work of Galileo: "Since remote antiquity most people have seen one or another heavy body swinging back and forth on a string or chain until it finally comes to rest. To the Aristotelians, who believed that a heavy body is moved by its own nature from a higher position to a state of natural rest at a lower one, the swinging body was simply falling with difficulty. Constrained by the chain, it could achieve rest at its low point only after a tortuous motion and a considerable time. Galileo, on the other hand, looking at the swinging body, saw a pendulum, a body that almost succeeded in repeating the same motion over and over again ad infinitum." The shift of vision occurred through Galileo's genius, but "that genius does not here manifest itself in more accurate or objective observation of the swinging body. Descriptively, the Aristotelian perception is just as accurate." Rather, Galileo was making use of a relatively new, late medieval theory of motion—the "impetus theory"—according to which the "continuing motion of a heavy body is due to an internal power implanted in it by the projector that initiates the motion." Until the impetus theory "was invented, there were no pendulums, but only swinging stones, for the scientist to see."[34]

What an Aristotelian or a scholastic saw, in turn governed what parameters it would occur to him to measure, and thus what laws of motion he could conceivably develop. "Contemplating a falling stone, Aristotle

[32] Thomas S. Kuhn, *The Structure of Scientific Revolutions* in *International Encyclopedia of Unified Science* (Chicago: University of Chicago Press, 1970), p. 111.

[33] *Ibid.*

[34] *Ibid.*, pp. 118–120.

saw a change of state rather than a process. For him the relevant measures of a motion were therefore total distance covered and total time elapsed, parameters which yield what we should now call not speed but average speed. Similarly, because the stone was impelled by its nature to reach its final resting point, Aristotle saw the relevant distance parameter at any instant during the motion as the distance *to* the final end point rather than as that *from* the origin of motion." Normal scientific research guided only by the conceptual categories of Aristotelian science "could not have produced the laws that Galileo discovered." Regularities which "could not have existed for an Aristotelian" were "consequences of immediate experience for the man who saw the swinging stone as Galileo did."[35] Thus one could say of Galileo what Kuhn in fact says about Lavoisier after his "discovery of" oxygen: that he "worked in a different world."[36]

If we are surprised that the constituents of the world should be so profoundly dependent on culture and language, that may be, as Cavell suggests, because we "forget that we learn language and learn the world *together*, that they become elaborated and distorted together, and in the same places."[37] We tend to forget how much more children learn from us adults than what we *tell* them—that we present ourselves as models to them, that we exercise authority, that we initiate children into significant portions of our world. As Cavell puts it, "when you say 'I love my love' the child may learn the meaning of the word 'love' and what *love* is. I.e., that (*what you do*) will *be* love in the child's world, and if it is mixed with resentment and intimidation, then love is a mixture of resentment and intimidation, and when love is sought *that* will be sought. When you say 'I'll take you tomorrow, I promise,' the child begins to learn what temporal durations are, and what trust is, and what you do will show what trust is worth. When you say 'Put on your sweater,' the child learns what commands are and what *authority* is, and if giving orders is something that creates anxiety for you, then authorities are anxious, authority itself uncertain. Of course, hopefully, the person, growing, will learn other things about these concepts and 'objects' also. They will grow gradually as the child's world grows."[38] But all the child knows about them is what it has learned, and all it has learned will be part of what they are.

We learn language and the world together, learn both about love and about the word "love," both about beauty and about the word "beauty." Our vocabulary and our worldliness expand gradually and together, and in some respects, as we have said, the process is never over. When we think about a child beginning to master its first words, beginning to learn what "kitty" means and what a kitten is, it may strike us that the child

[35] *Ibid.*, pp. 124, 123.
[36] *Ibid.*, p. 118.
[37] Stanley Cavell, *Must We Mean What We Say?* (New York: Charles Scribner's Sons, 1969), p. 19.
[38] Stanley Cavell, "The Claim to Rationality" (unpublished dissertation, Harvard University), p. 214.

really lives in a very different world from ours. "I have wanted to say: Kittens—what we call 'kittens'—don't exist in her world yet, she hasn't acquired the forms of life which contain them. They don't exist in something like the way cities and mayors won't exist in her world until long after . . . kittens do; or like the way God or love or responsibility or beauty don't exist in our world: we haven't mastered, or we have forgotten, or we have distorted, or learned through fragmented models, the forms of life which could make an utterance like 'God exists' or 'God is dead' or 'I love you' or 'I cannot do otherwise' or 'Beauty is but the first beginning of terror' bear all the weight it could carry, express all it could take from us. We don't know the meaning of the words."[39]

The idea is intriguing, but difficult. Evidently Cavell means to argue that confronted with words like "God" and "love" and "beauty" we today are like children, knowing a few uses of the terms and having some notion of their meaning, but an incompletely developed one. But when we say that a child has some idea of but does not fully know what a "function" is, we have an obvious standard of measurement: the child doesn't yet know what we know. What can it mean to say of all of us that we do not (fully) know what God or love or beauty is (means)? By what standard is our knowledge incomplete? By the experience of some earlier age or different culture, perhaps; as one might say that medieval Europe or the early Christians knew God in a way we do not, knew the concept in a way we do not. Or perhaps the standard of comparison is the exceptional individual of genius, like the poet. Thus, if we cannot give full weight or attach full meaning to a line like "Beauty is but the first beginning of terror," then Rilke is the "adult" to our immaturity in this area.

### THE OBJECTIVE WORLD

But there are more serious difficulties in Cavell's account, and in all that has been said on the side of Whorfian linguistic relativism; we have been developing only one half of a complex issue. Cavell said that language and the world are learned together, so that "to know how to use the word 'anger' is to know what anger is."[40] But surely that oversimplifies the correlation between language-learning and experiential learning of the world. In the first place, we *can* learn to *say* things about God or beauty which we ourselves do not fully appreciate, can learn to quote Rilke or Hegel without comprehending them. But then we will be like the child that has learned to say "I simply can't function without . . ." but does not really know what a function is and cannot do much else with the word. We can only repeat what we have learned from Rilke, cannot yet operate spontaneously and independently with his comprehension of beauty. Still, to the extent that this is possible, that it is even a way of gradually acquir-

[39] *Ibid.*, p. 207.
[40] *Ibid.*, p. 227.

ing an enlarged sensitivity and comprehension, the slogan "to know how to use the word 'anger' is to know what anger is" will not do.

Furthermore, if we look again at Cavell's examples of learning what love or trust or authority is, we notice that they are not in fact examples where language and the world are *directly* learned together, in a one-to-one correlation. For Cavell says the child learns what temporal durations are and what trust is from the adult's saying "I'll take you tomorrow, I promise," and from his subsequent actions. The words "trust" and "temporal duration" are not spoken at all. Or, again, Cavell illustrates the learning of what authority is by the adult's telling the child to put on its sweater; the word "authority" is not used by adult or child, but only by Cavell. So Cavell himself recognizes that the child *can* learn things about the world apart from the immediately relevant vocabulary, and vice-versa. When it later encounters the words "trust" and "authority" it will link them with the vocabulary it already has ("have to," "promise," "must," "for sure"), and that vocabulary will already be bound up with the experiences that we call (as the child cannot yet call them) "early encounters with authority" or "trust."

At one point Wittgenstein asks, "Could someone understand the word 'pain', who had *never* felt pain?"[41] As usual, he does not answer his own question, but I find that I want to say both yes and no. After all, we learn many words which refer to phenomena we have not experienced and cannot experience. And yet, experiential knowledge can add something more. Wittgenstein also asks, "Would this situation be conceivable: someone remembers for the first time in his life and says 'Yes, now I know what "remembering" is, what it *feels like* to remember'. —How does he know that this feeling is 'remembering'? Compare: 'Yes, now I know what "tingling" is'."[42]

As so often, what we are prepared to say here depends on the particular example that comes to mind. We do not even know how to imagine a man who, though he can talk, has never remembered anything in his life. A man who has never felt pain seems somewhat more possible, though by no means fully clear (physical pain, perhaps, but psychological pain?). Imagining a man who feels a tingling sensation for the first time in his life is not difficult at all. Similarly, we can all understand exclamations like "Now that I've experienced it, for the first time I understand what 'love' means!" (or "toothache" or "terror"). And it is important that the same insight could as easily be expressed by saying, "For the first time I understand what love is!" But what would we make of the exclamation, "Now that I've experienced it, for the first time I understand what 'twelve' means!"? Or "parallel"? Yet one would already have to know something about the meaning of "love" or "toothache" in order to be able to identify the experience when it occurs. And we can also imagine someone learning

[41] Wittgenstein, *Philosophical Investigations*, par. 315.
[42] *Ibid.*, p. 231.

the word "acrophobia," and saying to himself, "So *that's* what was happening to me that day on the church roof!"

Though it may seem strange, even the congenitally blind do learn to use and understand words like "see" and "green." And why not? Most of us learn to use and understand expressions like "trance" or "extra-sensory perception" or "religious ecstasy" without having those experiences. To suppose that one can learn the meaning of a word only from experiencing what it stands for is to remain captive to the label-and-object model of language. Does the congenitally blind person who has learned English know what green *is*? Well, as most of us know what a trance is, or religious ecstasy. Our conceptual system depends both on what we have learned to say and on what we have experienced; and both these dimensions expand as we learn and grow, though differently for different words, and not in any strict one-to-one correlation.

It is essential to notice how most of the writers cited in this chapter experience a certain difficulty in articulating their views, in finding vocabulary that allows them to say what they think without paradox. Kuhn, for example, tries to reserve the verbs "look at" and "contemplate" for things as they really, objectively, are in the world, using "see" for the scientist's phenomenological, subjective experience. ("When Aristotle and Galileo looked at swinging stones, the first saw constrained fall, the second a pendulum."[43]) But the attempt is not really successful in making clear Kuhn's ideas, for these verbs have ordinary uses which govern their meaning; and those uses and that meaning unfortunately do not correspond to Kuhn's distinction. It would be nice if "what he sees" were always equivalent to what he would *say* he sees. But the fact is that though the expression is used that way sometimes ("he sees a rabbit," said by the experimenter), it is also used at other times for what is really there for him to see ("he sees a duck-rabbit as a rabbit."). It would be nice if "look at" always corresponded to what *we* would say he looks at, or what is objectively there. But although it is used that way sometimes, it is also sometimes used for a phenomenological report of the speaker's experience. The fact is that we just do use these verbs in these seemingly ambiguous ways, now for what the viewer experiences, now for the source of his experience, normally for both at once. As Wittgenstein points out, we want to say both "But this isn't *seeing!*" and "But this is seeing!" and "it must be possible to give both remarks a conceptual justification."[44]

Moreover, Kuhn often wants to say that the distinction is invalid, that the objective facts change with a change in paradigm or concept, as when he says that before the impetus theory "there were no pendulums . . . for

[43] Kuhn, *op. cit.*, p. 121. That Kuhn is aware that his use of the verbs is in some way strained is shown by his nervous question (p. 120): "Did these men really *see* different things when *looking at* the same sorts of objects?"

[44] Wittgenstein, *Philosophical Investigations*, p. 203.

the scientist to see." Yet, in order to describe his example at all, he *must* find words for "the same thing" which is seen in one way by Aristotle, another way by Galileo. He uses "heavy body swinging back and forth on a chain," or "swinging body." Is that, then, an objective truth we can fall back on? The very statement of the problem introduces a bias in favor of the existence of a neutral, objective reality. We know what was really there because Kuhn tells us, has to tell us to make his point clear.

There are similarly difficult apparent ambiguities in the concept of "world" itself. Kuhn acknowledges, in his discussion of scientific revolutions, that "changes of this sort are never total. Whatever he may then see, the scientist after a revolution is still looking at the same world. Furthermore, though he may previously have employed them differently, much of his language and most of his laboratory instruments are still the same as they were before."[45] Kuhn himself is torn between ways of talking that suggest the world changes when concepts change and those that suggest it remains the same. He complains, "In a sense that I am unable to explicate further, the proponents of competing paradigms practice their trades in *different worlds*. One contains constrained bodies that fall slowly, the other pendulums that repeat their motions again and again. . . . Practicing in different worlds, the two groups of scientists see different things when they look from the same point in the same direction. Again, that is not to say that they can see anything they please. Both are looking at *the world*, and *what they look at has not changed*."[46] In the end, Kuhn is unable to relinquish the more conventional view of the matter: that the world is fixed and independent of our interpretations, and that only the interpretations change. He says that he is unable to relinquish it "in the absence of a developed alternative," even though it "no longer functions effectively."[47]

Cavell has similar difficulties, using expressions like "I have wanted to say that" to introduce the idea that the child lives in a different world from ours. And when Sapir says the real world is largely built up out of our language, he puts "real world" in quotation marks. One need not be profoundly Wittgensteinian to see that these writers' difficulties have the features of a conceptual paradox, and originate in the complex grammar of the word "world." As Wittgenstein remarks, "if the words 'language', 'experience', 'world', have a use, it must be as humble a one as that of the words 'table', 'lamp', 'door'."[48] The meaning of "world" is as much determined by the language games in which it is used as that of any other word; and if they have contradictory implications, then any general dis-

---

[45] Kuhn, *op. cit.*, pp. 129–130.

[46] *Ibid.*, p. 150; italics mine.

[47] *Ibid.*, p. 126.

[48] Wittgenstein, *Philosophical Investigations*, par. 97; compare "Bemerkungen über Frazers *The Golden Bough*," p. 234: "Denn, wenn ich damals anfing von der '*Welt*' zu reden (und nicht von diesem Baum oder Tisch), was wollte ich anderes als etwas Höheres in meine Worte bannen."

cussion of the nature of the world will be infected by the resulting ambiguities. The fact is that we talk about the world as being external to us and independent of our will, as remaining fixed while human interpretations of it change; we contrast "the real world" with our wishes, fantasies, and lies. But we *also* use expressions like "my world" or "the world of the ancient Greeks," or say that two people "live in totally different worlds." Nor is this latter, more subjective way of talking about world of recent origin, perhaps a response to the modern sense of relativity. As Ziff says, the word "world" derives etymologically from the Anglo-Saxon *weorold*, meaning the course of a man's life.[49] Thus, the world was always, in a way, my world. Moreover, a world is not a random or chaotic collection; the concept requires a certain coherence and consistency. A mere "heap of unrelated phenomena," as Arendt says, would be a "non-world," not a world at all.[50] And clearly it is our conceptual system that provides at least part, if not all, of this coherence. In this sense, human knowledge is, as Cavell says, "a positive, conventional structure which we 'bring to' the world . . . apart from which there is nothing we should call a 'world.' "[51] So the world is necessarily both objective and subjective, both independent of language and structured by language. One can say either "that is because of what the world is like," or "that is because of what we mean by 'world,' how we use the word." Both formulations are true, and their very duality illustrates what they are meant to express.

We could draw the conclusion that the word "world" is hopelessly flawed by ambiguity and should be abandoned. But we have seen that the ambiguity resides not merely in this particular word, but in many or perhaps all of the related concepts (for instance, "to see" and "to look at"). Nor is it easy to abandon a concept; at the minimum, as Kuhn discovers, we are unable to do so in the absence of a developed alternative. Perhaps we do need a new and better conceptualization here, but a new and better conceptualization *of what*? A new concept free of these ambiguities will not be a concept of the world at all, will not satisfy what troubles us. We cannot discuss *this* problem without encountering the inconsistent implications in our grammar in this region.

This much, however, seems clear: at least our *talk* about the world is conventionally delimited. Whether or not what we see is objectively there, whether or not there is any objective reality to see, what we say or think discursively about it must be said or thought in language. And that means that in saying it, we must introduce the assumptions and implications built into our language, we must take whatever position the act of speaking itself requires. "It is what it is no matter what we say about it," only as long as we do not undertake to say what "it" is. Our only ways of saying what something is do require language. "That" thing may be what it is

[49] Ziff, *Semantic Analysis*, p. 50.
[50] Hannah Arendt, *The Human Condition* (Garden City: Doubleday, 1958), p. 11.
[51] Cavell, "Claim to Rationality," p. 107.

whether we call it a corpse or a cadaver, but as soon as we try to say what it is we invoke a conceptual system with all that implies. Moreover, our conceptual system, which governs what we can say about reality, certainly also affects what we perceive. Our concepts affect what we are likely to notice or remember. As Wittgenstein says, they "lead us to make investigations"; they are not merely "the expression of our interest," but also "direct our interest."[52]

But that need not mean that our concepts wholly determine reality. Despite the illuminating parallels, Wittgenstein propounds no doctrine of linguistic determinism like that of Whorf, but attempts to hold a dialectical balance between the mutual influences of language and the world. The basic conceptual question about the relationship between words and the world allows of no single, consistent answer; but it can be replaced by a whole assortment of more specific questions which do have consistent answers and are enlightening. Thus, for example: we do experience reality before we learn language; what can and cannot be experienced that way? What is such experience like? In what ways is it modified when we learn language? Or again: we do sometimes notice distinctions which our language does not mark, or recognize a recurrent experience which we cannot identify; what are such occasions like? When and how do they occur? Or again: we do sometimes change our concepts because of something new and unexpected we have discovered about reality. Of course, such revisions always take place in the context of the rest of our conceptual system; but they do suggest that experience can modify concepts, and they should be investigated.

Above all, in exploring such questions we must expect different answers depending on which concepts we choose to investigate. As we already have seen, it makes sense with some, but not all, of our concepts to distinguish between having linguistic knowledge of the word and having experiential knowledge of the thing. Some concepts, some whole areas of our conceptual system, are relatively inaccessible to revision by experience, while about others it is relatively easy to make new discoveries which result in conceptual revision. If our example is a noun used primarily as a label for a simple physical object, we are most likely to find that what "it" is, is independent of what we call it. But if our example is a concept shaped in many complex language games, then we are more likely to feel that "it" is not "given" in the world but constructed or picked out by our conceptual scheme. We may feel that an elephant is obviously a "thing in the world," and that any people first coming upon elephants will give that species a distinctive name. But we will not feel the same security about stepsisters or trumps or mistakes. It is difficult seriously to imagine human beings lacking such concepts one day "happening upon" a stepsister or a mistake and giving the phenomenon a name. Accordingly, it is easy to imagine finding out new information

[52] Wittgenstein, *Philosophical Investigations*, par. 570.

about elephants that causes us to revise our notion of what elephants are (like); but if our concept of mistakes changes, it will not be because of new empirical discoveries we have made about mistakes.

This strongly suggests, finally, that the interdependence of words and the world, the determining and limiting role of concepts on what is perceived as reality, will generally be most intensive with respect to human, social, cultural, and political things. Here, even more than in our language for and conceptualization of the physical world, what we see and what is there for us to see will depend on the concepts we bring to our experience. For actions and relationships and feelings and practices and institutions do not walk up to us like elephants and stand there, gently flapping their ears, clearly distinct from their surroundings, waiting to be inspected and named. But a discussion of how and why the human world is special in this respect will have to wait for later chapters; first we must review Wittgenstein's treatment of the problems we have developed in this chapter, his treatment of the relationship between mind and reality.

# VI

## Grammar and Forms
of Life

THE PROBLEM about the relationship between words and the world arises, in a way, out of our concepts; yet it is not a "merely verbal" problem, and the nature of our concepts itself depends on our lives as animate creatures in the world. In this chapter we shall explore the way in which Wittgenstein tries to hold a dialectical balance between these two truths. In the process we shall examine his notions of "grammar," the unwritten rules governing our language and regulating our language games; "criteria," a constituent of grammar specifically intended to show how words are related to the world; and "forms of life," which underlie language games and grammatical regularities. "The relation between mind (language) and the world überhaupt is," Cavell suggests, "the central question" which these Wittgensteinian notions are meant to answer,[1]

Sometimes Wittgenstein seems to say that grammar concerns only relationships among words, the internal consistency of our language. This is often the case when he talks of two expressions being "grammatically related," or exposes false analogies between expressions as "grammatically misleading." Sometimes he even seems to stress the purely linguistic, non-empirical character of grammar, particularly when he is diagnosing conceptual puzzlement. He says that conceptual questions often strike us as being empirical but are really grammatical instead. He tells the person who is conceptually puzzled: "You interpret a grammatical movement made by yourself as a quasi-physical phenomenon which you are observing."[2] And he says that such puzzlement arises because "we predicate of the thing what lies in the method of representing it," which surely implies that language is a method of representation, and distinct from the world represented.[3]

[1] Stanley Cavell, "The Claim to Rationality" (unpublished dissertation, Harvard University), p. 129.
[2] Ludwig Wittgenstein, *Philosophical Investigations*, tr. by G. E. M. Anscombe (New York: Macmillan, 1968), par. 401; compare par. 251.
[3] *Ibid.*, par. 104.

But Wittgenstein also insists that his concern with grammar "does *not* mean that I want to talk only about words."[4] Wittgenstein does not really reject our desire, when we are conceptually puzzled, to get beyond mere words to the essence of the thing itself—to investigate knowledge, not merely the word "knowledge"; he redirects that desire. He says that he, too, is interested in essence, only, "*essence* is expressed by grammar."[5] We find out the answer to our questions about the essence of knowledge by studying the grammar of "knowledge." Wittgenstein also says "grammar tells what kind of object anything is."[6] And that certainly suggests that grammar is not merely about language but can be informative about objects in the world, can answer certain kinds of questions concerning objects in the world.

Conceptual puzzlement, Wittgenstein says, arises when we are confused about the grammar of an expression, entangled in the rules we see governing its use. The puzzlement ceases to be paradoxical and becomes amenable to investigation when we achieve a perspicuous overview of the grammar. Thus, if we are puzzled over whether knowledge must be true, infallible, Wittgenstein recommends that we proceed by investigating expressions in which that word, and related words, are used; for instance, by asking "what is the process of 'getting to know' like in this case?" Such a question may seem "only vaguely relevant, if relevant at all," to the essence of knowledge itself, but it is really "a question concerning the grammar of the word 'to know,' and this becomes clearer if we put it in the form: 'What do we *call* "getting to know"?' It is part of the grammar of the word 'chair' that *this* is what we call 'to sit on a chair', and it is part of the grammar of the word 'meaning' that *this* is what we call 'explanation of a meaning'."[7]

The grammar of a word, then, includes all the various verbal expressions in which that word is characteristically used. The grammar of "chair" includes not merely "to sit on a chair," but also "to mend a chair," "to lend a chair," "to match a chair," "to save someone a chair," "to chair a meeting," and so on. That much should be familiar from earlier chapters. But this passage tells us more than that; it begins to suggest the relationship between grammar and the world. We need to note carefully the words Wittgenstein italicizes in it. Grammar, he says, tells us what we would call anything in a particular case; for instance, what in a particular case we would *call* "getting to know." It tells us what would *count as* "getting to know." The italicized "*call*" is already a hint, but it might still conceivably be construed as concerning the relations among words: that grammar tells us what verbal account of phenomena would be called "getting to know," what groups of words would mean the same as the expres-

[4] *Ibid.*, par. 370; my italics.

[5] *Ibid.*, par. 371.

[6] *Ibid.*, par. 372.

[7] Ludwig Wittgenstein, *Blue and Brown Books* (New York and Evanston: Harper & Row, 1964), pp. 23–24.

sion "getting to know." But the italicized demonstrative "*this*" should preclude such an interpretation. Grammar tells us that *this*, a set of phenomena in the world, is what we call "getting to know." Thus Wittgensteinian grammar, as Cavell says, is very much a matter of "determining the relation between an expression and what in the world that expression is used *for*."[8] It specifies not merely the expressions in which a word is characteristically used, but also, crucially, "what counts as an application of" those expressions.[9]

Thus, the grammar of "chair" tells us not merely that a chair is the kind of thing one can "sit on," but what sort of worldly phenomena count as "sitting on a chair." It tells us not merely *that* one "sits on" a "chair," but *how* one sits on a chair. What makes it a chair is the *way* we use the object, that we sit on it in that characteristic way. As Cavell says, "You *can* sit on a cigarette, or on a thumb tack, or on a flag pole, but not in *that* way. Can you sit on a table or a tree stump in that (the 'grammatical') way? Almost; especially if they are placed against a wall. I.e., you can *use* a table or a stump *as* a chair (= a place to sit, a seat) in a way you cannot use a tack as a chair. But so can you use a screw-driver as a dagger; that won't make a screw-driver a dagger. What can *serve as a chair* is not a chair, and nothing would (be said to) serve as a chair if there were no (were nothing we called) (orthodox) chairs. We could say: It is part of the grammar of the word 'chair' that *this* is what we call 'to serve as a chair.' "[10]

But grammar does not tell us explicitly, in words, how one sits on a chair as distinct from a pin. It is crucial to Wittgenstein's position that the italicized "*this*" points not to a verbal description of circumstances, but to the (real or remembered or imagined) circumstances themselves. For it points to the kind of paradigmatic case of a word's use which we discussed in connection with "learning from cases"; it relies on connections already made between words and the world. The kinds of words whose grammar Wittgenstein investigates are not specialized, technical terms, like the names of species of songbirds, in connection with which there can be technical problems of identification. He investigates terms like "knowledge" and "meaning" and "pain," whose instances are not recognized by any characteristic markings, whose recognition is not a problem for special expertise or training. "There are no marks or characteristic features of sitting in a chair which could be listed or sketched on a page; that could be done for goldfinches, or for illustrating how West Point cadets are to sit. . . . There are technical handbooks on bird-recognition, but none which teach us the special marks for recognizing when someone is sitting, or intending to sit, or sitting uncomfortably," on a chair.[11]

[8] Cavell, "Claim to Rationality," p. 46.
[9] *Ibid.*, p. 131.
[10] *Ibid.*, pp. 82–83.
[11] *Ibid.*, p. 83.

Cavell says that when he italicizes the demonstrative "*this*," Wittgenstein means to "remind us of those very general facts of nature we all—all who can talk and act together—do (must) in fact be using as criteria; facts we *only* need reminding of, for we cannot fail to know them in the sense of having never *learned* them."[12] It is not that we know nothing about human sitting, but that we know too much; we cannot say what we know, cannot do justice to it. But then, we do not need to, either. If one persists in feeling that it should be easy to say how human beings sit on chairs, what counts as "sitting on a chair," perhaps that is because one is so easily captured by the first picture of sitting on a chair that comes to mind. But Wittgenstein might have said, as he did about "intending," that "there are a great many combinations of actions and circumstances that we should call 'sitting on a chair.'" Consider, with Cavell, the example of circumstances "in which someone was not now *on* the chair, but was (as we say, doing what we call) 'getting up for a moment to turn off the coffee,' *but she's sitting in that chair.*"[13]

Wittgensteinian grammar, then, does not relate a name to an object by teaching us the distinguishing features of that kind of object; it relates, "we might say, various concepts to the concept of that object. Here the test of your possession of a concept (e.g. of a chair, or a bird; of the meaning of a word; of what it is to know something) would be your ability to use the concept in conjunction with other concepts, your knowledge of which concepts are relevant to the one in question and which are not; your knowledge of how various relevant concepts, used in conjunction with the concepts of different kinds of objects, require different kinds of contexts for their competent employment."[14]

Grammar, one can say, establishes the place of a concept in our system of concepts, and thereby in our world. It controls what other concepts, what questions and observations, are *relevant* to a particular concept. That is the sense, I believe, in which "grammar tells us what kind of object anything is." Grammar relates the concept of "chair" to concepts like "sitting" and "mending" and "lending"; which is to say that for something to be a chair, it must be such that a human being can sit on it, and sit on it in *that* way. Unless, of course, it is "broken," which is something that can happen to chairs, but not in the same way that it can happen to clocks or homes or promises. And if it is broken then perhaps one can mend it, but mend it in *that* way, not as one mends a dress or one's ways. All this becomes easier to accept the more one moves away from nouns

[12] *Ibid.*; compare Ludwig Wittgenstein, *On Certainty*, tr. by Denis Paul and G. E. M. Anscombe, ed. by G. E. M. Anscombe and G. H. von Wright (New York and Evanston: Harper & Row, 1969), pars. 27–28: "We recognize normal circumstances but cannot precisely describe them. At most, we can describe a range of abnormal ones. What is 'learning a rule'?—*This*. What is 'making a mistake in applying it'?—*This*. And what is pointed to here is something indeterminate."
[13] Cavell, "Claim to Rationality," p. 86.
[14] *Ibid.*, p. 90; compare p. 93.

that tempt us to think of them as labels for simple physical objects. No one will be surprised to learn that knowing what "a mistake" is depends not on having mastered its distinguishing features or characteristics, but on having mastered what sorts of circumstances count as "making a mistake," "preventing a mistake," "excusing a mistake," and so on. And we will make no empirical discoveries about mistakes which our grammatical categories do not allow.

Grammar is learned, we have said, from cases, from the experiencing of words in certain verbal and worldly contexts. In that sense, it is dependent on experienced reality; in that sense, our experience of reality is prior to language, prior to grammar. (It is, one might say, roughly one and a half to two years prior. The child has a backlog of preverbal experience by the time it begins to talk.) But because in learning grammar we learn what will count as various circumstances, grammar is also prior to experience. Though not chronologically prior in learning, it is logically prior, once learned. It is prior not so much to what we can experience, but to what we can *say* (and therefore what we can think discursively) about our experience. That is why grammar can tell us what a thing is, and why Wittgenstein sometimes sounds like a philosophical Idealist who regards reality as a product of our conventions. In fact, the closest correct parallel is probably not Idealism, but Kant. Wittgenstein teaches what might be considered a sort of linguistic Kantianism; what Wittgenstein calls "grammatical knowledge" very much resembles Kant's "transcendental knowledge"; and the validity of grammar might well be said to be synthetic a priori.[15] It is useful to recall, also, that Austin said his approach might be called " 'linguistic phenomenology,' only that is rather a mouthful."[16]

The Idealist theme, the insistence that our language controls what can possibly occur in the world, seems to me one of the few deep threads of continuity between the *Tractatus* and Wittgenstein's later work. In the *Tractatus*, as we have seen, language is taken to picture reality, and certain aspects of our experience (religion, esthetics, ethics) are taken to transcend the reach of language altogether. So there would seem to be a reality independent of language. Yet there is a continuing stress at the same time on language as providing a framework which governs the possibilities of anything we can say about reality. "Logic is *prior* to every experience—that something *is so*."[17] The facts of reality can be formulated only in accord with that logic, for "to understand a proposition means to know what is the case if it is true. (One can understand it, therefore, without knowing whether it is true.)"[18] Consequently, "if I know an object I also know all its possible occurrences in states of affairs. (Every one of these possibilities must be part of the nature of the object.) A new possibility

[15] *Ibid.*, p. 175.
[16] J. L. Austin, *Philosophical Papers* (Oxford: Clarendon Press, 1961), p. 130.
[17] Ludwig Wittgenstein, *Tractatus Logico-Philosophicus*, tr. by D. F. Pears and B. F. McGuinness (New York: Humanities Press, 1961), par. 5.552.
[18] *Ibid.*, par. 4.024.

cannot be discovered later. . . . A speck in the visual field, though it need not be red, must have *some* colour: it is, so to speak, surrounded by colour-space. Tones must have *some* pitch, objects of the sense of touch *some* degree of hardness, and so on. Objects contain the possibilities of all situations."[19] In short, for each individual speaker of a language, "*the limits of my language* mean the limits of my world. Logic pervades the world: the limits of the world are also its limits."[20]

In the later philosophy, Wittgenstein no longer says that "objects" contain or govern the "possibilities of all situations," but that "grammar" does so. Knowing the grammar of a word, we know what kinds of things are—can be—said with it, what would count as appropriate occasions for saying them. A "tone" is the sort of thing that has a "pitch"—which is to say that our concepts of "tone" and "pitch" are grammatically related in certain ways. An "object" is the sort of thing that has some degree of "hardness" if we "touch" it—which is to say that these expressions are grammatically related in certain ways. Grammar governs "the '*possibilities*' of phenomena," by regulating "the *kind of statement* that we make about phenomena."[21]

In the later philosophy, Wittgenstein no longer says that "a new possibility cannot be discovered later"; for language is an open system, and even what is governed by rules need not be "everywhere circumscribed by rules." But the ways in which new instances can occur, what will count as a new instance, the avenues for conceptual growth and change, remain deeply controlled by grammar.

In his later writings, Wittgenstein no longer talks about the troublesome concept of "the world," but examines various particular ways in which our concepts and their grammar determine the possibilities of phenomena, by determining what would count as instances of various phenomena. For example, he asks "Can a machine have toothache?" If we say that it cannot, Wittgenstein asks what sort of a "cannot" that is: "Did you mean to say that all our past experience has shown that a machine never had toothache?"[22] No doubt our experience is consistent with this conclusion, but we do not arrive at the conclusion from experience; it is not an empirical generalization. It has to do with the meaning of terms like "machine" and "toothache," with their grammar. Grammar tells us that a "machine" is not the kind of thing that can "feel pain"; a "toothache" is not the kind of thing by which "machines" are afflicted. Nothing that we could experience or observe in connection with a machine would *be*, would count as, the machine's "having a toothache." When you say a machine cannot have a toothache, "the impossibility of which you speak is a logical one."[23]

[19] *Ibid.*, pars. 2.0123, 2.0131, 2.014.
[20] *Ibid.*, par. 5.6, 5.61; compare pars. 5.62, 6.43, 6.431.
[21] Wittgenstein, *Philosophical Investigations*, par. 90; compare par. 97.
[22] Wittgenstein, *Blue and Brown Books*, p. 16.
[23] *Ibid.*

Or again, "We say a dog is afraid his master will beat him; but not, he is afraid his master will beat him to-morrow. Why not?"[24] Clearly, "being afraid that his master will beat him to-morrow" is an expression which makes sense only against a certain background, in a certain context, like "point to the color." And in the instance of a dog, "the surroundings which are necessary for this behaviour to be" fear about tomorrow "are missing."[25] A dog cannot—logically, grammatically cannot—be afraid about something happening tomorrow. We are not willing, our language does not allow us, to ascribe that predicate to an animal. (Of course, we can do so, for instance, in the context of fiction; but then we also anthropomorphize the dog in other ways. For example, we imagine him as thinking in words.)

All this certainly sounds as though Wittgenstein were saying that the world's being the way it is, is determined simply by human convention. Because we attribute "fear about tomorrow" only to human beings, dogs cannot do it; nothing a dog could do would qualify. Grammar governs the possibilities of intelligible experience, and therefore it limits what the world could possibly turn out to contain. We can make only those empirical discoveries permitted by the concepts we already have. It is grammatically impossible to discover through empirical research a married bachelor, a four-sided triangle, a machine with a toothache.

But Wittgenstein also teaches a very different, conflicting theme about the relationship between concepts and world, a theme that sounds more like pragmatism or Nietzsche or even Marx than like ordinary-language philosophy. Wittgenstein's special genius lies in being able to hold these conflicting themes in balance, and teaching us ways of doing so for ourselves. This second theme concerns the way in which our concepts are dependent on the world, are the products not so much of the world directly, but of our lives conducted in that world. In crude summary, what Wittgenstein argues is that a concept is determined not by the "object" for which it is a "label" (since there may be none), but by the language games in which it is used; in that sense it is conventional. But our playing those language games rather than others is the result neither of accident nor of arbitrary free choice. It is the result of what the world in which we live is like, and what we are like, what we naturally feel and do. The "formation of concepts can be explained by . . . very general facts of nature. (Such facts as mostly do not strike us because of their generality.) . . . If anyone believes that certain concepts are absolutely the correct ones, and that having different ones would mean not realizing something that we realize—then let him imagine certain very general facts of nature to be different from what we are used to, and the formation of concepts different from the usual ones will become intelligible to him."[26]

[24] Wittgenstein, *Philosophical Investigations*, par. 650.
[25] *Ibid.*, par. 250.
[26] *Ibid.*, p. 230.

At one point Wittgenstein asks how it is that an arrow in a diagram *points*.[27] On the surface, this question is merely intended to remind us that the "pointing" of an arrow in a certain direction is a matter of human convention, that it has to be learned, that every rule still needs to be applied and can be misapplied. But there is also a deeper significance. For, where does our convention come from, that arrows in diagrams and on signposts "point" in the direction of the arrow tip? Arrows are something that human beings once used as instruments for hunting. They were made with a sharp tip at one end for this purpose, and to function they must be shot tip-first. So the convention about how an arrow points is not an arbitrary one. To be sure, if this planet's physics were very different, if what we call hunting had a totally different purpose than it now has, one might need very different "arrows" or might shoot arrows in some radically different way. So arrows that point are conventional; but that convention is not based on an arbitrary agreement that might just as well have been arranged some other way.

The argument is most easily apprehended where the conventionality of our concepts is obvious, and their foundation in nature therefore most surprising. Consider Wittgenstein's treatment of our systems for measuring, or for distinguishing colors. We have, for example, the convention that twelve inches equals one foot. "No one," Wittgenstein says, will ordinarily see it "as an empirical proposition. It expresses a convention. But measuring would entirely lose *its ordinary character* if, for example, putting twelve bits each one inch long end to end didn't ordinarily yield a length which can in its turn be preserved in a special way."[28] The conventional proposition has point only against the background of a certain constancy in the shape of what we call "objects," the human capacity to remember numbers of a certain size, the various uses the measuring of lengths has in our lives, and so on. The proposition "twelve inches equals one foot" presupposes all this background, but it does not, itself, assert or express the background truths that give measuring its present point. "The proposition *is grounded in* a technique. And, if you like, also in the physical and psychological facts that make the technique *possible*. But it doesn't follow that its sense is to express these conditions."[29] The proposition "twelve inches equals one foot" doesn't *mean* "objects do not generally change shape rapidly, human beings can remember numbers, etc."

"What we call 'measuring,' " Wittgenstein says, "is partly determined by a certain constancy in results of measurement."[30] Nothing that does not produce results with that kind of constancy would *be* (what we call) "measuring." The convention precludes our "suddenly discovering" a

[27] *Ibid.*, par. 454.
[28] Ludwig Wittgenstein, *Remarks on the Foundations of Mathematics*, tr. by G. E. M. Anscombe, ed. by G. H. von Wright, R. Rhees, and G. E. M. Anscombe (Oxford: Basil Blackwell, 1964), p. 159.
[29] *Ibid.*
[30] Wittgenstein, *Philosophical Investigations*, par. 242.

kind of measuring whose results are random. The convention about feet and inches is arbitrary. But our notion of measurement, which underlies it, is not arbitrary; it arises from the natural fact that, given our world and ourselves, when we *do* what is called "measuring" we *get* a certain constancy of results. "The procedure of putting a lump of cheese on a balance and fixing the price by the turn of the scale would lose its point if it frequently happened for such lumps suddenly to grow or shrink for no obvious reason."[31] If such a basic change took place in our world, the reading of the scale would not be "false," in our present sense of "true weight" and "false weight." Rather, the whole idea of weighing would have to be revised at least for "such lumps" of cheese, and our practices with cheese and scales would have to be changed as well. "*No* yardstick, it might be said, would be correct, if in general they did not agree. —But when I say that, I do not mean that then they would all be *false*."[32]

Much the same could be said about our system of colors. It, too, is an arbitrary convention we impose, different in different cultures.[33] But the kind of language games that are played with color words, the concept of a color, rests on a deeper convention not of our choosing, and presupposes those aspects of our nature and our world without which such language games would be impossible. What would it be like if men did not "generally agree in" their judgments of color? "One man would say a flower was red which another called blue, and so on. —But what right should we have to call these people's words 'red' and 'blue' *our* 'colour-words'? —How would they learn to use these words? And is the language-game which they learn still such as we call the use of 'names of colour'? There are evidently differences of degree here."[34] Wittgenstein summarizes: "We have a colour system as we have a number system. Do the systems reside in *our* nature or in the nature of things? How are we to put it? —*Not* in the nature of numbers or colours."[35] For, of course, the language games played with color words are the *source* of our concept of what a "color" is; they define "the nature of colors." And yet, if some fundamental aspects of the world and of ourselves *related to* what we call "colors" were different, our concept of color would have to be different as well.

"You say '*That* is red,' but how is it decided if you are right? Doesn't human agreement decide? —But do I appeal to this agreement in my judgments of colour? . . . Is it decided by appeal to the majority? Were

[31] *Ibid.*, par. 142.

[32] Wittgenstein, *Foundations of Mathematics*, p. 98.

[33] But the differences are often exaggerated. See Brent Berlin and Paul Kay, *Basic Color Terms* (Berkeley and Los Angeles: University of California Press, 1969).

[34] Wittgenstein, *Philosophical Investigations*, p. 226.

[35] Ludwig Wittgenstein, *Zettel*, tr. by G. E. M. Anscombe, ed. by G. E. M. Anscombe and G. H. von Wright (Berkeley and Los Angeles: University of California Press, 1967), par. 357.

we taught to determine colour in *that* way?"[36] One could imagine such a language game: "I get a number of people to look at an object; to each of them there occurs one of a certain group of words . . . ; if the word 'red' occurred to the majority of spectators . . . the predicate 'red' belongs to the object by rights." One can imagine such a game, and "such a technique might have its importance"; but it is *not* how we now, in fact, decide what color something is, or teach colors, or justify what we say about the colors of objects. Our present language game with color words "only works, of course, when a certain agreement prevails, but the concept of agreement does not *enter into* the language-game."[37] It is presupposed by, but it is not itself part of, the game or part of the *meaning* of "color."

But though Wittgenstein's point is most easily accessible through such examples, its real complexity and significance emerge only when he turns to concepts where the dividing line between arbitrary convention and underlying natural preconditions is unclear—concepts, therefore, which really raise problems about the relationship of thought to the world. The examples he discusses most extensively here are, again, foci of traditional philosophical speculation: the concepts of pain and anger. In particular, these concepts are associated with a tradition of speculation about our relations to other people's feelings. There is a striking difference between what we feel when we are angry or in pain, and how we find out that others are angry or in pain. So it is often said that we know of the feelings of others only indirectly, or that we cannot really know their feelings at all. Their behavior and their words seem like outward signs which do not give us access to the feelings themselves; about the feelings of others we can at best conjecture.

One might attempt to refute such arguments with evidence from our ordinary language. After all, we learned expressions like "my pain" or "I am in pain" in connection with certain inner feelings, but we learned expressions like "his pain" or "he is in pain" in connection with certain behavior displayed by others—wincing, moaning, complaining, and so on. Since that is how we learned those expressions, that must be what they mean. So his pain is whatever we learned to call "his pain," namely, such pain behavior. It is simply mistaken or perverse to demand that the phenomena defining "my pain" should show up in cases where "his pain" is at issue. But such an attempt at refutation, we have argued before, is a vulgarization of ordinary-language philosophy and cannot succeed. No one who is conceptually troubled about pain will find such a refutation satisfactory; he will respond that it misses the point. The point, he will say, is that there is something wholly arbitrary about combining such different phenomena as what I feel when I hurt and what he does after he hits his thumb with a hammer into a single concept called "pain."

[36] *Ibid.*, pars. 429, 431.
[37] *Ibid.*, par. 430; my italics.

Wittgenstein investigates the concepts of pain and anger with the aid of the notion of "criteria," explicitly defined only in the *Blue and Brown Books*, but used also in the later works. In my judgment, the notion of criteria never succeeds in resolving the problem about pain and anger, but only restates it, along the lines just sketched. Nevertheless, Wittgenstein is so much occupied with it, and it has received so much critical attention, that we must examine it briefly. Afterward, we shall see that Wittgenstein's more general ideas allow us to deal with the conceptual problem about pain without recourse to the notion of criteria.

Criteria are one part, or aspect, of grammar; and they come into play in the investigation or explanation of the grammar of an expression. For instance, "to understand the grammar" of various "states," like the state of expecting something, being of an opinion, knowing something, but also physical states like hardness, weight, fitting, "it is necessary to ask: 'What counts as a criterion for anyone's [or any thing's] being in such a state?' "[38] So Wittgenstein recommends as exercises for studying the grammar of "to fit," "to be able," and "to understand," questions such as these: "(1) When is a cylinder C said to fit into a hollow cylinder H? Only while C is stuck into H? (2) Sometimes we say that C ceases to fit into H at such-and-such a time. What criteria are used in such a case for its having happened at that time? (3) What does one regard as criteria for a body's having changed its weight at a particular time if it was not actually on the balance at that time? (4) Yesterday I knew the poem by heart; today I no longer know it. In what kind of case does it make sense to ask: 'When did I stop knowing it?' (5) Someone asks me 'Can you lift this weight?' I answer 'Yes'. Now he says 'Do it!' —and I can't. In what kind of circumstances would it count as a justification to say 'When I answered "yes" I *could* do it, only now I can't?"[39] Or again, one investigates the grammar of "having an opinion" by asking what counts as being in that sort of state. "What, in particular cases, do we regard as criteria for someone's being of such-and-such an opinion? When do we say: he reached this opinion at that time? When: he altered his opinion? And so on. The picture which the answers to these questions give us shews *what* gets treated grammatically as a *state* here."[40]

Criteria, then, are the things by which we tell whether or not something is the case, which give us occasion to say that something is so, which justify us in what we say. They are, as it were, potential answers to potential questions like "how do you know?" "how can you tell?" "what makes

[38] Wittgenstein, *Philosophical Investigations*, par. 572.
[39] *Ibid.*, par. 182.
[40] *Ibid.*, par. 573.

you think so?" "why do you say that?" But Wittgenstein also says two other things about criteria, which unfortunately seem to have contradictory implications for the concept of pain. On the one hand, criteria are supposed to be analytic; they *define* the thing that they are criteria of. Yet, on the other hand, criteria come into play only in certain cases, not all. And the only appropriate characterization of those cases seems to be: cases where the thing itself is not perceived directly, but only by means of criteria.

First, criteria are supposed to be definitive. Wittgenstein explicitly distinguishes them from what he calls "symptoms," which are merely empirically correlated with a concept. He says that if, for example, "angina" is medically defined by the presence of a particular bacillus, then we might justify the claim that someone has angina by saying that we have found the bacillus in his blood. That would be giving criteria. But we might instead justify the claim by citing his inflamed throat, which would be giving symptoms. A symptom is "a phenomenon of which experience has taught us that it coincided, in some way or other, with the phenomenon which is our defining criterion." The link between a concept and its symptoms is a "hypothesis," but the link between a concept and its criteria is a "tautology" or (part of) a definition.[41]

With respect to pain, Wittgenstein argues that the characteristic behavior and demeanor of someone who is hurt serve as criteria for his being in pain. They are not merely symptoms experientially correlated with something else, which is his pain itself. From these criteria we learned what "his pain" means, what his pain is. Thus, "when we learnt the use of the phrase 'so-and-so has toothache' we were pointed out certain kinds of behaviour of those who were said to have toothache," for instance, holding one's cheek.[42] We may correlate other phenomena with this criterion, for instance, the appearance of a red patch on his cheek; these are related to his having a toothache only by hypothesis. But his holding his cheek is not just empirically correlated with something else, which is his toothache; it defines his toothache. Wittgenstein might have said, it is part of the grammar of "toothache" that *this* is what we *call* "his having a toothache."

Since criteria define a concept, empirical evidence cannot violate the link between them and the concept. This sounds as though Wittgenstein were saying that a man's pain behavior *is* his pain, a position we have characterized as a vulgarization. Moreover, Wittgenstein says explicitly that the traditional conceptual puzzlement about pain is merely an objection against our grammatical convention: we "rebel" against using "*this* expression in connection with *these* criteria."[43] Wittgenstein says that

41 Wittgenstein, *Blue and Brown Books*, pp. 24–25.
42 *Ibid.*, p. 24.
43 *Ibid.*, p. 57.

"the proposition 'Sensations are private' is comparable to 'One plays patience by oneself'."[44] That is to say, it is a tautological proposition about our grammar, an arbitrary convention like those of games.

But Wittgenstein also says that criteria play a role only in certain cases, not all. And when one tries to specify in what cases criteria enter, the only possible conclusion seems to be: cases where something is not perceived or known directly, itself, but *only* by way of criteria.[45] Thus, in the passage quoted earlier, one asks for the criteria of a body's having changed its weight at a certain time "if it was not actually on the balance at that time." Or one asks for the criteria of my having been able to lift a weight when I said I could, if I did not try to lift it at that moment. About concepts like "pain," in particular, Wittgenstein has what may seem a most peculiar doctrine: with respect to my own pain, no criteria are normally involved at all. When we speak of our own pain, normally we proceed without the observation or knowledge of the presence of criteria. We do not identify our own sensations by criteria, for there *are* no criteria for our own being in pain or having a certain sensation.[46] We both look at a red object; can I be sure that you have the same mental image of it as I do, that we both see the same color? "What is the criterion for the redness of an image? For me, when it is someone else's image: what he says and does. For myself, *when it is my image: nothing.*"[47] But if I do not use or need criteria to tell when I am in pain, then surely (one feels) it must be because I perceive my own pain *directly.* By contrast it then seems clear that I have only indirect signs of someone else's pain, and that those signs can sometimes go wrong. Thus, those signs, his behavior, cannot be, or define, his pain itself. And, indeed, Wittgenstein explicitly denies that he is saying that pain behavior is pain, "that the word 'pain' really means crying."[48]

But then the whole notion of criteria has not improved our understanding of the problem of pain at all; at most it has restated the same dilemma in an equally insoluble way. Another man's pain behavior is all we ever experience of his pain; we never *have his* pain ourselves.[49] So that behavior must have been how we learned to use the expression "his pain," and it is not a mere symptom, correlated with *something else* we learned to call "his pain." Yet his behavior is not his pain itself; and

[44] Wittgenstein, *Philosophical Investigations*, par. 248.

[45] We have spoken of grammar as linking a word to expressions in which it is characteristically used, and to occasions when those expressions are characteristically used. But of course it also links a word with other, "related" words which need not appear with it in characteristic expressions. The latter links, I think, are what criteria are meant to provide. They link "knowledge" and "getting to know," for instance, to "finding out," "verifying," "forgetting"; they link "pain" to "wincing," "suffering," "comforting."

[46] *Ibid.*, par. 290; compare Cavell, "Claim to Rationality," p. 127.

[47] Wittgenstein, *Philosophical Investigations*, par. 377; my italics.

[48] *Ibid.*, par. 244; compare par. 304.

[49] Compare Austin, *Philosophical Papers*, p. 83; and Gilbert Ryle, *The Concept of Mind* (New York: Barnes and Noble, 1949), p. 209.

when we say of someone else that he is in pain, we are liable to be wrong in some ways in which we cannot be wrong about whether we ourselves are in pain. Fortunately, Wittgenstein's broader analysis of language and meaning supplies the perspective from which to untangle these difficulties.

Like our other concepts, "pain" is a conglomerate of cases, of various expressions in which these words are characteristically used, and various worldly occasions in which those expressions are characteristically used. Such a concept, as Austin points out about "anger," is a complex of diverse parts like "having mumps." It comprehends "a whole pattern of events, including occasions, symptoms, feeling and manifestation, and possibly other factors besides."[50] Yet together these make up our concept of anger, and we are right to want to call all of this diversity "anger." Austin argues that it is just "silly" to ask which of these elements really is the anger itself; and, in particular, that there is "no call to say that" what I characteristically feel when I am angry is the anger itself. I would suggest that Austin is wrong to consider conceptual puzzlement "silly," and that there is good reason why we want to say that what we feel when we are angry is the anger itself; there is also good reason for not saying so. The reason Wittgenstein has difficulties here, and the reason such concepts present a continuing problem in traditional philosophy, and the reason we ourselves are at a loss, is because the grammar of such concepts itself seems to have contradictory implications.

In the first place, that grammar displays a characteristic asymmetry between "first-," and "second-," and "third-person" expressions. If someone says about another man that he is in pain, it sometimes makes sense to ask him questions like "how do you know?" "how can you tell?" "how did you find out?" And it sometimes makes sense to say that one man "knows another is in pain," "has found out another is in pain," and so on. These questions and statements do *not* make sense concerning a man's saying of himself "I am in pain." The context of a conceptual discussion often gravely misleads us in this respect. For it invites the pursuit of analogies like this: "How do you know he is in pain?" "From his behavior." "Well, then how do you know you are in pain?" In a conceptual discussion, one gives an answer to the latter question as best one can, because it seems to make sense on analogy with the other. Perhaps one says "from my sensations." But if a man actually, in normal life, tells us that he has a toothache, we would never have occasion to respond "How do you know?" or "How can you tell?" What would such questions be designed to find out?

Thus, I never *know* that I myself am in pain, not because I am *ignorant* of my feelings, but because it makes no sense to say "I know I am in pain" (except as a forced answer to odd questions like "Are you sure you are in pain?"). "If we are using the word 'to know' as it is normally used (and how else are we to use it?), then other people very often know when

50 Austin, *Philosophical Papers*, p. 77.

129

I am in pain. . . . It can't be said of me at all (except perhaps as a joke) that I *know* I am in pain. What is it supposed to mean—except perhaps that I *am* in pain? Other people cannot be said to learn of my sensations *only* from my behaviour, —for *I* cannot be said to learn of them. I *have* them. The truth is: it makes sense to say about other people that they doubt whether I am in pain; but not to say it about myself."[51] With respect to my own pain, the "expression of doubt has no place in the language-game."[52] That is one basis for explaining why Wittgenstein says I do not need and cannot have criteria for my own pain. Criteria are potential answers to potential questions like "how can you tell?" But such questions do not make sense after just any utterance whatever; they make no sense after utterances like "I am in pain."

But though the grammar of such concepts contains this characteristic asymmetry, the asymmetry is not nearly as simple as we are inclined to suppose, or as our earlier argument suggested. Our discussion suggested that we learn to call this (feeling) "my pain," and that (behavior) "his pain." But thereby it singled out one aspect of an extremely complex set of language games, ignoring all the rest. We have "definitely learned a different and much more complicated use" of the word "pain."[53] We not only learn to speak of "my pain" when we hurt, but also that other people will utter words like "my pain" when they behave in certain ways in certain circumstances. We not only learn to speak of "his pain" when another person behaves that way, but also that he will use words like "his pain" when we experience hurt. So the feeling, the behavior, and the circumstances are interwoven in grammar in very complex ways to make up a single concept, and pain behavior and pain circumstances are as much a part of our concept of "pain" as pain feeling is. What, then, insistently makes us want to say otherwise? Well, still other aspects of the grammar of "pain." For example, that grammatically pain is something somebody "feels" or "has" or "suffers from" or "is in." And we do not "feel" or "have" or "suffer (from)," nor "are" we "in" pain behavior—wincing, groaning, screaming. Grammatically, one can "feign" or "pretend (to be in)" pain *by*, for instance, wincing, groaning, and the like. But one cannot "feign" or "pretend (to be in)" wincing or groaning.

Most of our difficulties here, as usual, arise from the label-and-object view of language, in this case unfortunately encouraged by Wittgenstein's treatment of criteria and his way of talking about "what we *call*" things. The question, "Is *that* what we call 'his pain'?" cannot be answered consistently; it is bound to lead to paradox. We do not learn to *call* this "his anger" and that "my anger." We learn when, under what linguistic and worldly circumstances, it is appropriate to *say* various things, to *speak of*

---

[51] Wittgenstein, *Philosophical Investigations*, par. 246.
[52] *Ibid.*, par. 288.
[53] Wittgenstein, *Blue and Brown Books*, p. 60.

various things.[54] It is sometimes appropriate for me to say "I am in pain" when I suffer, to say "he is in pain" when I see him behave in certain ways in certain circumstances, to say "he wasn't in pain after all" in other circumstances, and "I wasn't in pain after all" in still other, very different, circumstances. Only much later can we even ask ourselves such questions as whether pain is a "thing" and, if so, whether *that* (his behavior) is his pain. And when we say "I am in pain," it is often not as an assertion of empirical fact that may be true or false, but as a signal, like saying "Ouch!" We are trained (or anyway, we learn) as children to supplement and even replace our natural expressions of pain with verbal expressions of pain; and the latter need not function as empirical descriptions of our condition any more than the former do. As we grow up, "The verbal expression of pain replaces crying and does not describe it."[55] That is why questions like "how can you tell?" make no sense when asked after utterances like "I am in pain," just as they would make no sense after the utterance "Ouch!"

Yet there is such a thing as falsely claiming to be in pain; such expressions are not true performatives, whose mere uttering makes them so. Moreover, there are occasions when we really do learn of our own feelings from our behavior—particularly when we suddenly become aware of feelings of which we were not fully conscious. "I guess I must have been very angry," we say, "I've bitten my pipe stem completely in two!" In such contexts, a question like "how can you tell you were angry?" would make sense, and we do learn of our own anger from criteria. But such occasions are rare.[56] Indeed, while we can imagine them about anger, I am not sure that we can imagine them at all about pain. The best I can do is to recall a couple I know. The husband was present while his wife gave birth to their child. Afterward, he asked her, "Did it hurt a lot?" And she said, "No. It really didn't hurt at all; just hard work." And he asked, "So why did you scream like that?" She had no recollection of having screamed. Here it is not clear whether we should say that she was in pain but has forgotten, or that she was not in pain but nevertheless screamed (for some psychological or physiological reason).

So although there is a characteristic asymmetry between first and third person in the grammar of utterances about both pain and anger, and although both concepts have traditionally been used interchangeably in discussing our knowledge of the feelings of others, their grammar is also significantly different. Nor can one apply to them directly the conclusions we drew earlier concerning understanding and expecting. We concluded

[54] I believe that Wittgenstein uses this locution in connection with criteria only once, in par. 573 of the *Philosophical Investigations*.

[55] *Ibid.*, par. 244.

[56] Wittgenstein, *Zettel*, par. 539: "I infer that he needs to go to the doctor from observation of his behaviour; but I do *not* make this inference in my own case from observation of my behaviour. Or rather, I do this sometimes, but *not* in parallel cases."

that even the characteristic feeling of expecting will be expecting only in appropriate circumstances; otherwise it might be a "peculiar feeling that something is about to explode." But one cannot imagine a comparable case about pain, a situation in which we would be moved to say, "I have this peculiar painlike feeling even though there is no occasion for pain." And that is one reason why with pain we are particularly inclined to insist that what I feel when I am in pain is "the pain itself." As always, it is dangerous to generalize from any one example; we need to look and see in detail how our grammar functions.

But the basic initial puzzlement about pain still seems to remain. Even if "my pain" and "his pain" do not sort out neatly, the one corresponding to pain feeling and the other to pain behavior, still there seems to be something wholly arbitrary about blending such diverse phenomena into a single concept. A concept like pain, we have said, is a compound of diverse cases; it rests not on a single defining feature but on a multitude of props—feelings, circumstances, actions. Why should these be grouped together; what has our own suffering in common with someone else's holding his cheek? They seem to be linked by nothing beyond the arbitrary convention of our language. But Wittgenstein responds, "Is it arbitrary? —It is not every sentence-like formation that we know how to do something with, not every technique has application in our life."[57] That cryptic observation is meant, I believe, to suggest that the power of grammatical regularities is not arbitrary, because grammar itself is ultimately the product of our lives and thus of the nature of our selves and our world.

### FORMS OF LIFE

In the *Blue and Brown Books*, Wittgenstein calls the regularities of our grammar which bind diverse phenomena together into a single concept, "conventions." In the later writings, though he still considers grammar conventional, he has largely replaced this term with the expression "forms of life." That notion is never explicitly defined, and we should not try to force more precision from it than its rich suggestiveness will bear. But its general significance is clear enough: human life as we live and observe it is not just a random, continuous flow, but displays recurrent patterns, regularities, characteristic ways of doing and being, of feeling and acting, of speaking and interacting. Because they are patterns, regularities, configurations, Wittgenstein calls them *forms*; and because they are patterns in the fabric of human existence and activity on earth, he calls them forms *of life*. The idea is clearly related to the idea of a language game, and more generally to Wittgenstein's action-oriented view of language. "The *speaking* of language," he says, "is part of an activity, or of a form of life."[58] How we talk is just a part of, is imbedded in, what we do. "Commanding,

57 Wittgenstein, *Philosophical Investigations*, par. 520.
58 *Ibid.*, par. 23.

*132*

questioning, recounting, chatting, are as much a part of our natural history as walking, eating, drinking, playing."[59] We all know our shared forms of life, these basic, general, human ways of being and doing, though they have never been taught to us and we could not begin to be able to put into words what we know about them. Wittgenstein says that they are part of our "natural history," regularities "which no one has doubted, but which have escaped remark only because they are always before our eyes."[60]

The notion of forms of life should help us to understand the sense in which language may be said to be conventional. For calling it conventional is likely to make us feel that the foundations of language are extremely shaky, that at any time other people might abrogate the conventions which alone assure communication, coherence, and sanity. But that may be, as Cavell suggests, because as part of our liberal tradition we tend to "look upon our shared commitments and responses . . . as more like *agreements* than they are," to interpret convention as equivalent to contract, as if "whether our words will go on meaning what they do" depended on "whether other people find it worth their while to continue to understand us."[61]

Language might be said to be conventional in a number of different ways; not all of them are what Wittgenstein means by "forms of life." Sometimes we speak of conventions as contrived agreements, consciously and deliberately entered into by men. This kind of conventionality plays only a peripheral and occasional role in shaping language, as when specific language changes are imposed by legislation. Sometimes we speak of things as conventional which are not products of deliberate agreement or conscious choice, but have evolved as the indirect, inadvertent result of the continuing activity of many men. The great bulk of language, all the aspects which differ from one language to another, may be called conventional in this sense. But there is still a further sense in which one might speak of the conventionality of language—a sense which comes closest to the idea of "forms of life." We might speak here of "natural conventions," features of our lives and world which logically might well have been otherwise but which just happen to be this way among all men in all times and places. These conventions, as Cavell says, are "fixed" neither by custom nor by agreement but rather "by the nature of human life itself, the human fix itself. . . . That *that* should express understanding or boredom or anger . . . is not *necessary*: someone *may* have to be said to 'understand suddenly' and then always fail to manifest the understanding five minutes later, just as someone *may* be bored by an earthquake or by the death of his child or the declaration of martial law, or *may* be angry at a pin or a cloud or a fish, just as someone may quietly (but comfortably?) sit on a chair of nails. That human beings on the whole do not respond in these

[59] *Ibid.*, par. 25.
[60] *Ibid.*, par. 415.
[61] Cavell, "Claim to Rationality," p. 217.

ways is, therefore, seriously referred to as *conventional*; but now we are thinking of convention not as the arrangements a particular culture has found convenient. . . . Here the array of 'conventions' are not patterns of life which differentiate men from one another, but those exigencies of conduct which all men share."[62]

What the idea of "forms of life" implies about a concept like "pain" is, first of all, as with concepts of color and measurement, that the language games we play are only possible on the basis of underlying natural regularities. A concept linking pain behavior, pain feelings, and the occasions for pain is functional in our lives only because these phenomena really do occur together. Austin makes this point about the concept of anger: the feeling of being angry, he says "is related in a unique sort of way" to its characteristic behavioral expression. "When we are angry, we have an impulse, felt and/or acted on, to do actions of particular kinds, and, unless we suppress the anger, we do actually proceed to do them. There is a peculiar and intimate relationship between the emotion and the natural manner of venting it, with which, having been angry ourselves, we are acquainted. The ways in which anger is normally manifested are *natural* to anger just as there are tones *naturally* expressive of various emotions (indignation, etc.). There is not normally taken to be such a thing as 'being angry' apart from any impulse, however vague, to vent the anger in the natural way. Moreover, besides the natural expressions of anger, there are also the natural *occasions* of anger, of which we have also had experience, which are similarly connected in an intimate way with the 'being angry'."[63] It is possible to feign anger (or pain), and it is possible to suppress any expression of anger (or pain). But if there were no characteristic expressions of and situations for pain or anger, we could never be taught to use those words. We could not be taught what counts as our own pain, because no one would have any way of telling when we were in pain. And we could not be taught what counts as someone else's pain because there would be no way of telling when he is in pain. Without some characteristic expressions of pain, indeed, we could not have the concept of pain.

Of course, the fact that these phenomena normally and naturally occur together is proof neither against exceptions nor against miracles. The fact that we tend to express felt pain in pain behavior does not mean that a man's pain behavior is always and necessarily a guarantee that he is actually in pain. It is possible to feign pain, and it is possible to suppress all signs of pain. That is part of the point of the conceptual puzzlement about pain from which we began. But we treat such exceptional cases as they arise *within* our conceptual system. We sometimes conclude that someone was feigning or suppressing his pain, or was not in pain after all; but always on the basis of further information which is in principle no

[62] *Ibid.*, pp. 97–98.
[63] Austin, *Philosophical Papers*, pp. 76–77.

different from our initial information. Such situations do not call the concept of pain itself into question. What is not possible is that it should turn out on the basis of that kind of evidence that all people are always feigning when they display pain behavior, or suppressing pain when they do not display pain behavior ("What sometimes happens might always happen. . . .").

Nevertheless, the concept is not proof against miracles, either.[64] "I say, 'There is a chair'. What if I go up to it, meaning to fetch it, and it suddenly disappears from sight?—'So it wasn't a chair, but some kind of illusion'. —But in a few moments we see it again and are able to touch it and so on. —'So the chair was there after all and its disappearance was some kind of illusion'. —But suppose that after a time it disappears again —or seems to disappear. What are we to say now? Have you rules ready for such cases—rules saying whether one may use the word 'chair' to include this kind of thing?"[65] Our concepts of chairs, of material objects, of seeing and touching, are such that this kind of thing is not supposed to happen. Yet of course it could conceivably happen; our conceptual system cannot prevent it from happening. Here is not just a normal sort of deviation, like feigning, for which explanations are ready within our conceptual system, "a mistake for which, as it were, a place is prepared in the game." Here is "a complete irregularity," and if it occurs at all frequently our existing concepts will no longer be functional.[66]

Wittgenstein says, "We have here a *normal* case, and abnormal cases. It is only in normal cases that the use of a word is clearly prescribed; we know, are in no doubt, what to say in this or that case. The more abnormal the case, the more doubtful it becomes what we are to say."[67] At the extreme, as Austin puts it, "we don't know what to say. Words literally fail us."[68] But that is not an ordinary failure of perception or knowledge but a breakdown of the entire concept (as in Wittgenstein's example of cheese beginning to change weight arbitrarily, which makes scales not inaccurate but pointless). "If things were quite different from what they actually are—if there were for instance no characteristic expression of pain, of fear, of joy; if rule became exception and exception rule; or if both became phenomena of roughly equal frequency—this would make our normal language-games lose their point."[69] We would need new concepts, or would need to extend and project and modify our old ones, perhaps to the point of unrecognizability. The ordinary use of a concept "is what one might call a composite use suitable under the ordinary circumstances." If we assume circumstances different in fundamental ways, the

[64] *Ibid.*, p. 56.
[65] Wittgenstein, *Philosophical Investigations*, par. 80.
[66] Wittgenstein, *On Certainty*, par. 647.
[67] Wittgenstein, *Philosophical Investigations*, pars. 141–142; compare par. 385; *Blue and Brown Books*, pp. 150–151.
[68] Austin, *Philosophical Papers*, p. 56.
[69] Wittgenstein, *Philosophical Investigations*, par. 142.

old concept would have to be replaced, though we might be able to give the new concept a use analogous with the old. But there would be no fixed rule about this; we would have our choice among a number of possible projections or analogies. "One might say in such a case" that the old concept has more than one "legitimate heir."[70]

There is no general, fixed dividing line between what we mean by "chair" (or "pain") and the great welter of largely inarticulate knowledge we have about chairs (or pain). Normally we do not need to choose which elements of what we know are essential and definitive, for the accustomed features cluster together. When we need a decision, a definition, we can make one. No proposition is intrinsically a definition; what makes it one is the way we use it. "The same proposition may get treated at one time as something to test by experience, at another as a rule of testing."[71] Thus, for Wittgenstein the only difference between analytic and synthetic propositions is how we use them, and we may use them differently on different occasions. Even while he is explicating the distinction between criteria and symptoms, he immediately comments that "in practice, if you were asked which phenomenon is the defining criterion and which is a symptom, you would in most cases be unable to answer this question except by making an arbitrary decision *ad hoc*."[72] Nor should this surprise us, once we have understood how language is learned from and shaped by cases of its use. And this is another way of articulating why grammar is not merely about words but equally about the world, the one by way of the other.

Thus, if the world were different in fundamental ways, we might play different language games about the occasions for pain. Suppose that "the surfaces of the things around us (stones, plants, etc.) have patches and regions which produce pain in our skin when we touch them. (Perhaps through the chemical composition of these surfaces. But we need not know that.) In this case we should speak of pain-patches on the leaf of a particular plant just as at present we speak of red patches."[73] Or, as Strawson points out, if the world were such that all people in a given region or time felt pain at once, we might have expressions such as we now do for temperature, like "it's painful in here" or "it's painful today."[74]

So, when we talk of the way linguistic conventions limit the possibilities of what can happen in the world, what we will accept as instances of various phenomena, we must also recognize that those conventions are not merely arbitrary; they are part of a conceptual network which works,

[70] Wittgenstein, *Blue and Brown Books*, p. 62.

[71] Wittgenstein, *On Certainty*, par. 98; compare *Philosophical Investigations*, par. 79.

[72] Wittgenstein, *Blue and Brown Books*, p. 25.

[73] Wittgenstein, *Philosophical Investigations*, par. 312.

[74] P. F. Strawson, "Review of Wittgenstein's *Philosophical Investigations*," in George Pitcher, ed., *Wittgenstein: The Philosophical Investigations* (Garden City: Doubleday, 1966), pp. 47–48.

which functions for us. "Machines cannot feel pain." That is a part of grammar and a convention; nothing a machine could do would be, would count as, "feeling pain." And that convention seems arbitrary. Yet the matter is not so simple. For although "pain" is something one "feels," it can be recognized by, occurs in connection with, characteristic human and animal pain behavior in characteristic pain situations. That, we learn, is what pain *is like*, and subsequently we will attribute pain only to such creatures as behave that way in such situations. If an inanimate object behaved that way, we would (at least be tempted to) attribute pain to it; but we would also simultaneously be cast into doubt as to whether it really was an inanimate object. The convention is not flatly that only animate creatures feel pain, but that certain behavior is in certain circumstances a sign of someone's being in pain. And that convention is not arbitrary, but based on the natural human and animal expressions of and occasions for pain.

Wittgenstein asks himself whether this conception of criteria doesn't simply amount to the declaration that "there is no pain without *pain-behavior*." But instead of answering directly, he says, "It comes to this: only of a living human being and what resembles (behaves like) a living human being can one say: it has sensations; it sees; is blind; hears; is deaf; is conscious or unconscious. . . . Only of what behaves like a human being can one say that it *has* pains. . . . Look at a stone and imagine it having sensations. —One says to oneself: How could one so much as get the idea of ascribing a *sensation* to a *thing*? One might as well ascribe it to a number! —And now look at a wriggling fly and at once these difficulties vanish and pain seems able to get a foothold here, where before everything was, so to speak, too smooth for it."[75]

But why does Wittgenstein say we attribute pain only "to human beings and what resembles them," rather than "to animate creatures"? Clearly the latter is the truth, and his own first example is of a fly. But his reference to human beings here has a point, which shows still another sense in which grammatical conventions are not arbitrary. What it suggests is that the concept of pain did not originate in our detached observation of animal behavior, as a label for referring to what animate creatures sometimes are observed to do, but in our human need to communicate about our own pain or that of the person to whom we speak. It suggests that we don't talk about pain primarily out of scientific curiosity, just commenting on the passing scene, but in order to get someone to take some action. Talk about pain occurs *among* human beings who experience and express pain and respond to it, in contexts involving such activities as comforting, helping, apologizing, but also warning, threatening, punishing, gloating. Part of what we learn in learning what pain is, is that those in pain are (to be) comforted, gloated over, and the like, and that we ourselves can expect such responses to indications of our pain.

[75] Wittgenstein, *Philosophical Investigations*, pars. 281, 283, 284.

Both naturally and by cultural training, we respond to someone displaying pain behavior in a pain situation in appropriate ways (i.e., as if he were in pain), and we expect others to respond that way to our pain. If the link among occasion, feeling, and behavior here is conventional, that is not a convention subject to renegotiation at will. To change our conventions here, we would have to change what we do, how we live; we would have to change the links between pain and comforting, pain and threatening, pain and fear, pain and pity—not just between these words but between these ways of being and acting together. These patterns of action and response, too, are part of what Wittgenstein means by "forms of life."

At one point Wittgenstein asks whether all this means, in sum, "that human agreement decides what is true and what is false." But he responds: "It is what human beings *say* that is true and false; and they agree in the *language* they use. That is not agreement in opinions but in forms of life."[76] The conventionality of language is not contractual; and if it limits the empirical possibilities we can discover in our world, that limitation is not arbitrary. Thus, "the limit of the empirical—is concept-formation," but our concepts "are not assumptions unguaranteed, or intuitively known to be correct: they are ways in which we make comparisons and in which we act."[77] Our concepts rest ultimately not on "a kind of *seeing* on our part; it is our *acting* which lies at the bottom of the language-game."[78]

To the extent that our concepts and our language are shaped by human nature and the natural human condition, they cannot be justified, and must simply be accepted as given. We can explain the "essential nature" of freedom or knowledge by referring to the grammar of the words "freedom" or "knowledge"; we can explain their grammar by referring to the language games in which they are used; we can imagine a changed world or human beings changed so that those language games would lose their point or become unplayable, and thereby we can become aware of some of our human forms of life. But beyond that we cannot *explain* those forms of life, cannot give *reasons* for them. Wittgenstein says that explanations must have an end somewhere: "If I have exhausted the justifications I have reached bedrock, and my spade is turned. Then I am inclined to say: 'This is simply what I do.' "[79] Ultimately something has to be accepted as given—not the "truths" we predicate of the world, not the concepts in which we express them, but the language games that shape the grammar of those concepts and the conditions that produce those language games. "What has to be accepted, the given, is—so one could say—*forms of life*."[80] These views of Wittgenstein's have often been taken to indicate his cultural and political conservatism. In a later chapter

[76] *Ibid.*, par. 241.
[77] Wittgenstein, *Foundations of Mathematics*, pp. 121, 176.
[78] Wittgenstein, *On Certainty*, par. 204.
[79] Wittgenstein, *Philosophical Investigations*, par. 217.
[80] *Ibid.*, p. 226.

I shall try to show how this is a fundamental misunderstanding. But for now it is enough if the dual relationship between words and the world has been explored: on the one hand, the grammatical limitations on empirical discovery; on the other hand, the foundations of grammar in the reality of our language activity.

# VII

## Language Regions, Moral
## Discourse, and Action

WITTGENSTEIN'S DISCUSSION of language games and forms of life suggests that we might think of language as being subdivided into clusters of similar and related concepts, used in similar and related language games. Certain concepts will show similar grammatical peculiarities because they are at home in the same area of language, used in similar circumstances for similar purposes; other concepts will show quite different patterns because they originate in connection with quite different forms of life. Thus we have seen similar asymmetries between the first-person use and the second- and third-person use of several concepts in the region of mental activities or feelings. And we have found grammatical features in a concept like "world" related to those in concepts like "see" and "look at." Wittgenstein himself speaks at one point about "regions of language," and again invokes the analogy between language and an ancient city: "a maze of little streets and squares, of old and new houses, and of houses with additions from various periods; and this surrounded by a multitude of new boroughs with straight regular streets and uniform houses."[1] Some regions of the city are separate and clearly distinct. Wittgenstein suggests that we think of the specialized, technical subdivisions of language, such as the symbolism of chemistry or the notation of calculus, as "so to speak, suburbs of our language," neat, clearly laid out, unmistakably separate. But in the old city, regions will be more difficult to distinguish or delineate precisely.

Wittgenstein does not develop the theme further, but it is developed in various ways by his student, Friedrich Waismann, by the ordinary-language philosopher, Gilbert Ryle, and, from a different philosoph-

[1] Ludwig Wittgenstein, *Philosophical Investigations*, tr. by G. E. M. Anscombe (New York: Macmillan, 1968), pars. 90, 18; compare his *Blue and Brown Books* (New York and Evanston: Harper & Row, 1964), p. 81, and K. T. Fann, ed., *Ludwig Wittgenstein* (New York: Dell, 1967), p. 51.

ical stance, by Michael Oakeshott.[2] Each of them argues that there are significant subdivisions within language, differing in fundamental ways. Waismann calls the subdivisions "language strata"; Ryle calls them "categories"; Oakeshott calls them "voices in the conversation of mankind." All three agree that these subdivisions differ not merely in vocabulary or subject matter, but in the way in which language is used: in grammar, logic, structure—what counts as a statement, what as a justification, what as validity or truth, what constitutes agreement and what is the significance of disagreement. In this chapter we shall explore the idea of language regions, and one language region in particular.

To become aware of the variety of subregions in our language, Waismann suggests that we compare such kinds of utterances as "a sense-datum statement, a material object statement, a law of nature, description of something half forgotten, a statement of my own motives, a conjecture as to the motives by which someone else was actuated, quotation of the exact words so-and-so was using, brief summary of the tenor of a political speech, characterization of the *Zeitgeist* of a certain historical period, a proverb, a poetic metaphor, a mathematical proposition, and so on."[3] The concepts in some of these statements will be "absolutely precise and definable with mathematical rigour," but in others they may be "vague, or of an open texture."[4] Waismann explains the idea of open texture by saying that "empirical concepts," unlike mathematical ones, "are not delimited in all possible directions. Suppose I come across a being that looks like a man, speaks like a man, behaves like a man, and is only one span tall—shall I say it *is* a man? Or what about the case of a person who is so old as to remember King Darius? Would you say he is an immortal? Is there anything like an exhaustive definition that finally and once and for all sets our mind at rest?"[5]

Moreover, concepts will function in characteristically different ways in different regions of language. Oakeshott contrasts the way concepts are used in everyday practical discourse with the way they are used in science and with the way they are used in poetic discourse, in poetry. The concepts of science, he argues, are not merely different names for familiar objects, equivalent replacements for the concepts of our everyday discourse. "The word 'water' stands for a practical image; but the scientist does not first perceive 'water' and then resolve it into $H_2O$: *scientia* begins only when 'water' has been left behind. To speak of $H_2O$ as 'the chemical

[2] Friedrich Waismann, "Language Strata" and "Verifiability," in Antony Flew, ed., *Logic and Language* (Garden City: Doubleday, 1965); Gilbert Ryle, "Categories," *ibid.*, and *Dilemmas* (Cambridge: Cambridge University Press, 1966), and *The Concept of Mind* (New York: Barnes and Noble, 1949), Michael Oakeshott, *Rationalism in Politics* (New York: Basic Books, 1962), particularly "The Voice of Poetry in the Conversation of Mankind."
[3] Waismann, "Language Strata," p. 238–239.
[4] *Ibid.*, p. 236.
[5] Waismann, "Verifiability," p. 126.

formula for water' is to speak in a confused manner: $H_2O$ is a symbol the rules of whose behaviour are wholly different from those which govern the symbol 'water'."[6] If "water" and "$H_2O$" were merely labels, they would be used for referring to "the same thing"; but they are not merely labels. They are signals used in radically different language games, performing very different functions.

In poetic discourse, Oakeshott argues, concepts are used in ways differing sharply both from those of science and from those of our everyday practical discourse about what we do. First, the poet, unlike the scientist or our everyday selves, is always partly engaged in image-making, not just in image-using; he is always innovating on the store of available concepts.[7] And, secondly, poetic discourse is "contemplative," which is to say that its concepts and images are enjoyed for themselves, "neither as concretions of qualities any of which might appear elsewhere (as both coal and wood may be recognized for their combustibility or two men may be compared in respect of their mastery of a particular skill), nor as signs or symbols of something else."[8] Poetic discourse "appears when imagining is contemplative imagining; that is, when images are not recognized either as 'fact' or as 'non-fact', when they do not provoke either moral approval or disapproval, when they are not read as symbols, or as causes, effects, or means to ulterior ends, but are made, remade, observed, turned about, played with, meditated upon, and delighted in, and when they are composed into larger patterns which are themselves only more complex images and not conclusions."[9]

But quite apart from differences in the way concepts are used, Waismann argues that language regions differ in the way that propositions are formulated and related to each other; it is as if they were "constructed in a different *logical style*."[10] Propositions in different regions will "be *true* in different senses, *verifiable* in different senses, *meaningful* in different senses."[11] Some subdivisions of language, for instance, operate by the familiar Aristotelian logic, but others do not (though we often assume that they must). Take "the logic of half-faded memory pictures. Here the situation is such that we are often unable to call to mind one or the other point of detail, that is, that we are often unable to decide an alternative. What did that bathroom look like I saw the other day on a visit? Was it ivory, was it cream or pale biscuit or maize? . . . To insist, in these circumstances, on the law of excluded middle, without any means of de-

---

[6] Oakeshott, *Rationalism in Politics*, p. 222. From a Wittgensteinian perspective one might object that the word "water" does not "stand for an image" at all, practical or otherwise; that the relevant rules govern not its "behaviour" but our use of it; and that there need be nothing "confused" about calling "$H_2O$" the "chemical symbol for water." But Oakeshott's basic point is thoroughly valid.

[7] *Ibid.*, pp. 212, 216.

[8] *Ibid.*, p. 220; compare pp. 217 ff.

[9] *Ibid.*, p. 224.

[10] Waismann, "Language Strata," p. 235.

[11] *Ibid.*, p. 242.

ciding the issue, is paying lip service to the laws of logic."[12] Or take the logic of aphorisms. "A man who writes aphorisms may say a thing, and, on another occasion, the very opposite of it without being guilty of a contradiction. For each aphorism, as it stands, is quite complete in itself."[13] Wittgenstein suggests, similarly, that there need be no "law of the excluded middle" for commands; of course, it is inconvenient to have received contradictory commands, both of which are binding, but it can happen.[14]

Waismann argues that the very nature and meaning of truth is different in different language strata. Following Russell's notion of "systematic ambiguity," he distinguishes statements about an individual from those about a class of individuals, or a class of classes. "A statement such as 'Socrates is mortal' is true when there is a corresponding fact, and false when there is no corresponding fact." But the truth of a generalization like "all men are mortal" cannot be established in that way, "for there are indefinitely many facts such as 'Socrates is mortal', 'Plato is mortal', etc." So the notions of "truth" relevant to the two sorts of statements are different; "each type of statement has its own sort of truth."[15] Consequently, "a law of nature is never true in the same sense in which, say, 'There is a fire burning in this room' is, nor in the sense in which 'He is an amusing fellow' may be; and the two latter statements are not true in the same sense in which 'I've got a headache' is. . . . Again, in what sense is one to say of a proverb that it is true? Have you ever tried to put some rare and subtle experience, or some half-forgotten (but strong) impression into words? If you do, you will find that truth, in this case, is inseparably tied up with the literary quality of your writing: it needs no less than a poet to express fully and faithfully such fragile states of mind."[16]

The truths of mathematics, unlike those of science, poetry, everyday practical concerns, sensations, ethics, are strictly deductive, and entirely a matter of internal coherence. "Take for instance, a mathematical proposition, say a theorem of geometry. To say that it is true simply means that it can be deduced from such-and-such axioms." The axioms themselves are simply assumed; all the mathematician "is concerned with is that *if* these and these axioms apply, *then* the theorems apply too."[17] No recourse need be had to "observation" nor to "empirical evidence." There is no room here for productive "debate" among "various opinions," nor

[12] *Ibid.*, p. 237.

[13] *Ibid.*, p. 238.

[14] Ludwig Wittgenstein, *Remarks on the Foundations of Mathematics* tr. by G. E. M. Anscombe, ed. by G. H. von Wright, R. Rhees, and G. E. M. Anscombe (Oxford: Basil Blackwell, 1964), pp. 140–142; Waismann, *Wittgenstein*, pp. 119–131.

[15] Waismann, "Language Strata," p. 232; compare Friedrich Waismann, *Wittgenstein und der Wiener Kreis*, ed. by B. F. McGuinness (London: Basil Blackwell, 1967), p. 100.

[16] Waismann, "Language Strata," pp. 239–240.

[17] *Ibid.*, p. 239.

for the testimony of witnesses. Contrast, as Arendt suggests, the language of specific historical facts, like "Germany invaded Belgium in August 1914."[18] Yet such a factual truth, like the truths of mathematics, is "much less open to argument" than, say, a proposition of political theory, or art criticism, or political opinion. "It concerns events and circumstances in which many are involved, it is established by witnesses and depends upon testimony."[19] As a result, factual truth of this kind is characteristically subject to distortion by deliberate falsehood or lies, in a way that the truths of mathematics, science, poetry, and even political opinion are not.[20]

With respect to such factual historical truth, the witnesses form a kind of elite of experts; but, of course, there is a different elite for each event, depending on who happens to be a witness. Other realms of discourse are characterized by standing elites of experts, whose judgment of truth in that realm is normally decisive. Take science, whose truths "may not be merely personal but must instead be accepted . . . by many," as Kuhn observes. To be sure, this "many" is not the general public, but "the well-defined community of the scientist's professional compeers." Scientists, "by virtue of their shared training and experience, must be seen as the sole possessors of the rules of the game or of some equivalent basis for unequivocal judgments."[21] Much the same is true of mathematics, though the appropriate modes of resolution are different from scientific ones. Something similar, but also significantly different, is true about the language of poetry or of esthetic criticism. But are there experts on the truths of memory images, of expressions of sensation? And how does the expertise of an expert art critic differ from that of a mathematician?

As a corollary to differences of this kind, various language regions differ also in how judgments are supported in case of dispute, and more generally in the significance of dispute and the modes of its resolution. Wittgenstein points out that in arithmetic, for example, "there can be a dispute over the correct result of a calculation (say of a rather long addition). But such disputes are rare and of short duration. They can be decided, as we say, 'with certainty.' Mathematicians do not in general quarrel over the result of a calculation. (This is an important fact.) —If it were otherwise, . . . then our concept of 'mathematical certainty' would not exist."[22] The fact that we do normally agree in the results we obtain in calculation is no doubt partly the result of how we are *trained* in mathematics. We learn from the first that in this field there are "right answers" and "wrong

[18] Hannah Arendt, "Truth and Politics," in Peter Laslett and W. G. Runciman, eds., *Philosophy, Politics and Society* (Oxford: Basil Blackwell, 1967), p. 122.
[19] *Ibid.*, pp. 111, 112.
[20] *Ibid.*, p. 121.
[21] Thomas S. Kuhn, *The Structure of Scientific Revolutions* in *International Encyclopedia of Unified Science* (Chicago: University of Chicago Press, 1970), p. 168.
[22] Wittgenstein, *Philosophical Investigations*, p. 225; compare par. 240.

answers" (you can look them up in the back of the book).[23] Mastering arithmetic is a matter of becoming able to produce the answers that agree with those in the back of the book (and hence with those produced by every other person competent in arithmetic, except when he "makes a mistake"). "It would also be possible to imagine," Wittgenstein says, a different method of training for "a sort of arithmetic. Children could calculate, each in his own way—as long as they listened to their inner voice and obeyed it. Calculating in this way would be like a sort of composing."[24] But the resulting practice would be quite different from our arithmetic.

We are able to have an activity like arithmetic, and to teach it as we do, and to rely on that teaching to produce the results it produces, only because of what human beings are like and how their brains work. Mathematics, arithmetic, are based on human "forms of life." It is simply a fact about human beings that if you train them in *that* way, so that they calculate in *that* way, their answers will generally agree. "I have not said *why* mathematicians do not quarrel, but only *that* they do not. . . . If there were not complete agreement, then neither would human beings be learning the technique which we learn. It would be more or less different from ours up to the point of unrecognizability."[25] What we call "arithmetic" is partly determined by a certain constancy in results of calculation. " 'We all learn the same multiplication table.' This might, no doubt, be a remark about the teaching of arithmetic in our schools,—but also an observation about the concept of the multiplication table. ('In a horse-race the horses generally run as fast as they can.') There is such a thing as colour-blindness and there are ways of establishing it. There is in general complete agreement in the judgments of colours made by those who have been diagnosed normal. This characterizes the concept of a judgment of colour. There is in general no such agreement over the question whether an expression of feeling is genuine or not."[26]

In mathematics—or at any rate in arithmetic—disputes arise only when someone is in error; there is no such thing as "each man being entitled to his opinion." Truth is established deductively, by proof. Contrast this with, say, truths of specific historical fact, where "in case of dispute, only other witnesses but no third and higher instance can be invoked."[27] Where witnesses disagree, we are forced to adopt the majority account, or to estimate reliability, or to leave the conflict unresolved. Disagreement in political opinion, disagreement among literary critics, disagreement in

[23] Wittgenstein, *Foundations of Mathematics*, p. 190: "Our children are not only given practice in calculation but are also trained to adopt a particular attitude toward a mistake in calculating."
[24] Wittgenstein, *Philosophical Investigations*, par. 233.
[25] *Ibid.*, p. 226; compare par. 242 on "measuring," which has a different kind of "constancy of results" than arithmetical calculation does.
[26] *Ibid.*, p. 227.
[27] Arendt, "Truth and Politics," p. 116.

moral judgment—each will have different significance and possible modes of resolution. Each realm has its own "ways in which a judgment is supported," in which "conviction in" the judgment may be produced, as Cavell says. "It is only by virtue of these recurrent patterns of support that a remark will count as—will be—aesthetic, or a mere matter of taste, or moral, propagandistic, religious, magical, scientific, philosophical."[28]

Given Wittgenstein's suggestion that grammar tells us what kind of thing anything is, it is not surprising that Waismann urges the study of different language regions as a new way of investigating the ontology of different regions of the world. "If we carefully study the texture of the concepts which occur in a given stratum, the logic of its propositions, the meaning of truth, the web of verification, the senses in which a description may be complete or incomplete—if we consider all that, we may thereby characterize the subject-matter. We may say, for instance: a material object is something that is describable in language of such-and-such structure; a sense impression is something which can be described in such-and-such a language; a dream is——, a memory picture is ——, and so on."[29] That is, we may study ontology by way of grammar, not just for a particular concept but for whole regions of discourse and of the world.

Waismann argues that, once the subdivisions of language are well described, it should be possible to classify their subject matter systematically and thereby to "formalize" our concepts. "The analogy with science," he says, "is obvious."[30] That suggestion, clearly, is very different from anything Wittgenstein would undertake, not to say diametrically opposed to his orientation. Indeed, Waisman himself later expressed reservations about some of these ideas, just as Ryle warns that the idea of language categories is merely an idiom, harmful if pressed too far.[31] The idea of regions or strata or categories in our language is likely to foster the illusion of systematic rules, of sharply distinct, fixed subdivisions whose boundaries may not be violated. We are likely to want to list the regions, catalogue them, and thereby classify the world. We are, one might say, in danger of wanting to treat the center of our ancient city as if it consisted of nothing but suburbs. But any subdivisions we distinguish within the main body of our language will be only questionably distinct; the categories will be categories *we* set up because we happen to have concepts available for them: "science," "morality," "religion," and so on. They will always be to some extent arbitrary and *ad hoc*. One may treat mathematics as a language region, but one may also see it as a whole collection of different language regions with different rules. And how much more will this be true in "regions" like "historical discourse," "music-criticism discourse," "accounting discourse," and so on. How

[28] Stanley Cavell, *Must We Mean What We Say?* (New York: Charles Scribner's Sons, 1969), p. 93.
[29] Waismann, "Language Strata," p. 246.
[30] *Ibid.*
[31] *Ibid.*, p. 226 (editor's note); Ryle, *Dilemmas*, p. 9.

many categories are there? And does every possible utterance fit into just one of them? And is each of them internally consistent, or can they have conflicting subdivisions? Here, as elsewhere in the study of language, the borderlines will often depend on what we decide to take as a borderline for particular purposes.

Similar questions can, of course, be raised about Wittgenstein's concepts of "language games" and "forms of life." There, too, it seems arbitrary and difficult to demarcate one from another, or specify how many there might be, or list them. But Wittgenstein would never undertake to list extensively or to number our language games or our forms of life. (Indeed, he invents new language games.) He uses "language game" as more or less synonymous with "way of operating with language in action," and no one would be tempted to catalogue all the ways that we might do that. He uses "form of life" as more or less synonymous with "coherent pattern of human activity or reaction," and no one would be tempted to classify such patterns exhaustively. For Wittgenstein, the point is that language games and forms of life *exist*, and that they are tremendously *varied*, and that whenever we become particularly interested in a particular one we can describe and explore it.

To put the criticism one other way, any category that we label with an English word will depend for its coherence as a category partly on the meaning and use of that word. And if the meaning and use of that word are composites of families of paradigms, have mutually inconsistent implications, then any attempt to describe and classify the category "to which it refers" will reflect those complexities. Thus, a discussion of *the* nature or *the* essence of, say, religious discourse, will be successful only to the extent that religious discourse *has* a nature or an essence. And that depends both on what we mean by "religious" discourse (which may or may not be unambiguous), and whether the way people use language in "that" kind of discourse really shows a fair amount of internal consistency, really differs in uniform, recognizable ways from how they use language in, say, "scientific" discourse. So such an investigation will always be at least partially itself a grammatical investigation of whatever word we use to name the language category we are exploring.

Furthermore, it is by no means obvious whether the different regions of language are, as it were, mutually translatable, whether the terms of one region can be reduced to those of another: whether, for example, concepts used in relation to animate life can be translated into the language used in relation to inanimate objects, or whether a concept used in relation to individual human action or political phenomena can be translated into the language used in relation to the behavior of lower life-forms or inanimate objects. Waismann, who introduces the idea of language strata, clearly thinks that they are mutually translatable, being just different ways of looking at the same thing. "An action may be viewed as a series of movements caused by some physiological stimuli . . . or as something that has a purpose or a meaning irrespective of the way its single links are produced. . . . I mean that there are two different ways of looking at the thing; just as there are two different ways of looking at a sentence: as a series of noises produced by a human agent; or as a vehicle for thought."[32]

But others, like Winch, Polanyi, and Oakeshott, maintain that the regions are not mutually reducible, that the terms of one cannot be exhaustively characterized by or translated into the terms of another. $H_2O$ is not just another name for water, and promising is not just another name for physical movements. Winch says that the behavior of animals is not merely much more complex than the behavior of plants, but different in kind. For "the concepts which we apply to the more complex behaviour are logically different from those we apply to the less complex. . . . The reaction of a cat which is seriously hurt is 'very much more complex' than that of a tree which is being chopped down. But is it really intelligible to say it is only a difference in degree? We say that the cat 'writhes' about. Suppose I describe his very complex movements in purely mechanical terms, using a set of space-time coordinates. This is, in a sense, a description of what is going on as much as is the statement that the cat is writhing in pain. But the one statement could not be substituted for the other. . . . The concept of writhing belongs to a quite different framework from that of the concept of movement in terms of space-time coordinates; and it is the former rather than the latter which is appropriate to the conception of the cat as an animate creature."[33]

From this perspective there appears to be an irreducible gap between the concepts of one language region and those of another, between the idea of writhing and the mere succession of physical positions of the cat's limbs. Accordingly, some writers have taken up combat against what they consider mistaken efforts to reduce phenomena of one region to those of another—notably to explain human action in causal terms, or to explain or challenge religious ideas in a scientific mode. W. D. Hudson, for instance, criticizes attempts to "reduce theology" to "human psychology" as a "paradigm case of the kind of logical frontier-violation" which he takes Wittgenstein to "condemn."[34] But other writers point out that divisions among language regions are not that sharp; and that the different regions do, after all, form a single language. It may be foolish to suppose that the distance between the earth and the sun is the kind of thing which could, in principle, be measured by a ruler; but there is also some reason for that supposition. Our concepts of length and distance, after all, are compounded from all their normal uses. As Winch himself observes,

[32] Waismann, "Language Strata," p. 247.
[33] Peter Winch, *The Idea of a Social Science*, ed. by R. F. Holland (New York: Humanities Press, 1965), pp. 72–73.
[34] Donald Hudson, *Ludwig Wittgenstein* (Richmond: John Knox Press, 1968), p. 62.

"What can be said in one context by the use of a certain expression depends for its sense on the uses of that expression in other contexts (different language games).[35] Thus, the idea of language regions is a difficult and perhaps seductive one, the nature, identification, and distinctness of such regions being theoretically troublesome. We must consequently take special care never to use the conception as a pseudo-explanation, as an excuse for our failure to think or our failure to look and see how language is actually used.

## MORAL DISCOURSE

Having issued that warning, we can nevertheless proceed to examine in greater detail one region of language that has received special attention from several Wittgensteinian and ordinary-language philosophers. We might call it the region of moral discourse, though they do not speak of it that way. They simply share a distinctive way of approaching questions of morality and moral philosophy. Instead of studying moral rules or principles or traditional systems of morality, the teachings of religious leaders or philosophers, they are interested in the way moral discourse functions in everyday life, how we ordinarily talk about moral matters. For it is in ordinary use that our concepts of morality and action are learned and shaped; in that sense, speculative or didactic principles are dependent on ordinary usage for their concepts. Clearly this approach from ordinary usage is not the only way to think about morality or the language of morals, but it is a powerful and instructive way, and we shall be able to use it to illuminate certain features of the nature of action.

From the perspective of our ordinary employment of language in the region of morality, moral discourse particularly centers on actions, and on action gone wrong. It has to do with the assessment and repair of human relationships when these have been strained or damaged by the unforeseen results of some action. Part of the human condition, as Cavell says, is that "the realization of intention requires action, that action requires movement, that movement involves consequences we had not intended."[36] One might say, following Arendt, that human beings have developed two great modes of lessening the costs of this condition, the one prospective and the other retrospective.[37] Prospectively, we use commitment, promises, to reduce the risk and uncertainty associated with action to be performed. Retrospectively, we use forgiveness and what Austin calls "excuses," Cavell "elaboratives"—those pleas, explanations, justifications, and other modifiers that allow us to defend "conduct which comes to grief." Cavell

[35] Peter Winch, "Understanding a Primitive Society," *American Philosophical Quarterly*, I (October 1964), 321.

[36] Stanley Cavell, "The Claim to Rationality" (unpublished dissertation, Harvard University), p. 97.

[37] Hannah Arendt, *The Human Condition* (Garden City: Doubleday, 1958), pp. 213–216.

says that these concepts "make up the bulk of moral criticism," and their use constitutes the heart of moral discourse.[38] That is the reason, also, why Austin equates the study of excuses with ethics itself, and claims Aristotle's *Ethics* as a direct ancestor of his own work.[39]

From this perspective, the characteristic setting for moral discourse is one of dialogue among persons who are actually involved in what has happened; such discourse is very much contextual. No doubt we can contemplate moral principles in the abstract or hold public discourse about them, but the center of gravity of moral discourse falls in personal conversation between an actor and someone affected adversely by what he did. Moral discourse is personal, though not merely subjective or private; it is interpersonal but not really general or public. Moreover, it arises only where someone is moved to speak. As we saw, actions are discussed only when there is something special about them; and then the discussion is not about categories of action in the abstract, but about particular actions in which the participants are involved. Typically, Austin says, "the situation is one where someone is *accused* of having done something, or (if that will keep it any cleaner) where someone is *said* to have done something which is bad, wrong, inept, unwelcome, or in some other of the numerous possible ways untoward." Then someone injured or offended, or another speaking on his behalf, will accuse, blame, or remonstrate; and the actor, or another speaking on his behalf, will "try to defend his conduct or to get him out of it."[40] There are various ways of doing so, of course. He may admit the action and try to justify it, deny that it was bad. Or he may admit that it was bad, but deny full responsibility for it, pleading mitigating circumstances or otherwise qualifying the account of what was done. But in any case, "to examine excuses is to examine cases where there has been some abnormality or failure"; and what needs to be explained is not the performance of the action but its miscarriage.[41]

A further implication of taking "excuses" as central to moral discourse is that morality emerges as both conventionally traditional and pragmatically mundane, and consequently as having very definite limitations. For the vocabulary of action and morality—the concepts in terms of which we accuse, excuse, characterize our conduct—is essentially an inherited, relatively fixed vocabulary. It forms a relatively systematic body of categories, allowing us, as Oakeshott says, to appeal "from contemporary incoherence to the coherence of a whole moral tradition."[42] It embodies a system of morality, evolved in a language and a culture over generations. Thus, Kant asks, "who would think of introducing a new

[38] Cavell, "Claim to Rationality," p. 395.
[39] J. L. Austin, *Philosophical Papers* (Oxford: Clarendon Press, 1961), p. 128.
[40] *Ibid.*, pp. 123–124.
[41] *Ibid.*, p. 127; compare Cavell, *Must We Mean What We Say?*, p. 7.
[42] Oakeshott, *op. cit.*, p. 106.

principle of all morality, and making himself as it were the first discoverer of it, just as if all the world before him were ignorant what duty was or had been in thoroughgoing error?"[43] Of course, the tradition does evolve and it can be changed; there are moral teachers who are also innovators. Yet not just anything we do will be introducing a new morality, or even a new principle of morality. And normal moral discourse, our ordinary exchanges about conduct, do not involve the altering or innovating of moral concepts, but their application. Moral discourse is normally not legislative but adjudicative; it assesses conduct by fitting it into a traditional systematic vocabulary.

That feature may be taken as providing morality's wisdom and security, as when Austin observes, specifically with respect to excuses: "Our common stock of words embodies all the distinctions men have found worth drawing, and the connexions they have found worth marking, in the lifetimes of many generations."[44] But the traditional conventionality of our moral vocabulary also clearly means that moral discourse has very definite limitations. It is a relatively mundane and pragmatic tool, suitable for ordinary cases by its very familiarity but incommensurate with the extraordinary and the unique. Not every question about human conduct is a moral one. And, as Cavell argues, the competence of morality "as the judge of conduct and character is limited. This is what Kierkegaard meant by the 'teleological suspension of the ethical,' and what Nietzsche meant by defining a position 'beyond good and evil.' What they meant is that there is a position whose excellence we cannot deny, taken by persons we are not willing or able to dismiss, but which, *morally*, would have to be called wrong. And this has provided a major theme of modern literature: the salvation of the self through the repudiation of morality."[45]

Cavell argues that morality necessarily must leave itself open to this kind of repudiation. "It provides *one* possibility of settling conflict, a way of encompassing conflict which allows the continuance of personal relationships against the hard and apparently inevitable fact of misunderstanding, mutually incompatible wishes, commitments, loyalties, interests and needs, a way of healing tears in the fabric of relationship and of maintaining the self in opposition to itself or others. Other ways of settling or encompassing conflict are provided by politics, religion, love and forgiveness, rebellion, and withdrawal. Morality is a valuable way because the others are so often inaccessible or brutal; but it is not everything; it provides a door through which someone, alienated or in danger of aliena-

---

[43] Cited in Cavell, "Claim to Rationality," p. 321.

[44] Austin, *Philosophical Papers*, p. 130.

[45] Cavell, "Claim to Rationality," p. 352. Note that on this point Arendt disagrees sharply, arguing that "behavior" can be judged by conventional moral standards, but "action" must be judged in terms of its greatness, its uniqueness (*Human Condition*, p. 184); yet it is she who relates action (not behavior) to promises and forgiveness (*ibid.*, pp. 212–213).

tion from another through his action, can return by the offering and the acceptance of explanation, excuses and justifications, or by the respect one human being will show another who sees and can accept the responsibility for a position which he himself would not adopt. . . . But although morality is open to repudiation, either by the prophet or the raging and suffering self, or by the delinquent or the oldest and newest evil, and though it cannot assure us that we will have no enemies nor that our actions are beyond reproach even when they pass all *moral* tests; not just anybody, in *any way*, can repudiate it."[46]

Morality must leave itself open to repudiation in one sense because as a realm of discourse it is limited by the traditional concepts men have developed for assessing and accusing and excusing action. But it must be open to repudiation also in a different sense, one that has to do less with its concepts than with what Waisman would call its "logic"—the kinds of truth, evidence, principles of reasoning, standards of rationality, appropriate to it. These concern not the limitations of morality as a whole, but the limitations—the openness to repudiation—of particular moral claims and positions. Those positivistically inclined, including the early Wittgenstein, will doubt that moral discourse can have a logic or a rationality at all, since it seems to them "normative" and resting ultimately on personal preference or taste or feeling, beyond the reach of reason. In morality, unlike science for example, disputes often "cannot be resolved," do not culminate in agreement, do not result in conclusions everyone must accept.

Against this view, Waismann and Cavell and Oakeshott argue that moral discourse has its own standards of rationality; it does not lack logic, but its logic is of a different kind and structure than the logic of science. Oakeshott maintains, at least with respect to conduct, that each kind of human activity has an "idiom" of its own, with its own distinct rationality. Rationality is not one single thing, the same in all areas of human conduct or thought, but has its own particular, distinctive embodiments in various realms of human life. It consists essentially of faithfulness to the particular idiom in which one happens to be operating; it is a kind of consistency. Thus, for example, the activity of a scientist "may properly be called 'rational' in respect of its faithfulness to the tradition of scientific inquiry."[47] Winch says science is one mode of social life and religion is another, "and each has criteria of intelligibility peculiar to itself. So within science or religion actions can be logical or illogical: in science, for example, it would be illogical to refuse to be bound by the results of a properly carried out experiment; in religion it would be illogical to suppose that one could pit one's own strength against God's; and so on."[48]

[46] Cavell, "Claim to Rationality," pp. 353–354.
[47] Oakeshott, *op. cit.*, p. 103.
[48] Winch, *Idea of a Social Science*, pp. 100–101.

Looking for experimental proof in the realm of religion is as irrational as looking for revelation in the realm of science. In science or mathematics, the rationality of an argument depends upon its leading from premises all parties accept, in steps all can follow, to an agreement upon a conclusion which all must accept.[49] And, of course, "all must accept" does not mean that no human creature could conceivably refuse or fail to accept the conclusion. It means, rather, that anyone who fails to accept the conclusion is regarded as either incompetent in that mode of reasoning, or irrational.

But the criteria of rationality in scientific argument need not be taken as the only ones in the world, as equally defining rationality in esthetics or morals or politics. Cavell suggests: "Suppose that it is just characteristic of moral arguments that the rationality of the antagonists is not dependent on an agreement's emerging between them, that there is such a thing as *rational disagreement* about a conclusion. Why assume that 'There is one right thing to be done in every case and that that can be found out'? Surely the existence of incompatible and equally legitimate claims, responsibilities and wishes indicate otherwise?"[50] After all, we do not merely differ with others on such questions; often we are at odds with ourselves.[51] Perhaps the familiar lack of conclusiveness in moral and esthetic argument, "rather than showing up an irrationality, shows the kind of rationality it has, and needs."[52] But what kind is that; how is rationality in such realms of discourse to be determined? Cavell says, "By the argument, no doubt; and perhaps the argument is such that it could establish rationality in the absence of agreement—though agreement *may*, and hopefully will, supervene. Without the hope of agreement, argument would be pointless; but it doesn't follow that without agreement—and in particular, without agreement arrived at in particular ways, e.g., without anger, and without agreement about a conclusion concerning what ought to be done—the argument was pointless."[53]

The point of moral argument is not agreement on a conclusion, but successful clarification of two people's positions vis-à-vis each other. Its function is to make the positions of the various protagonists clear—to themselves and to the others. Moral discourse is about what was done,

[49] Cavell, "Claim to Rationality," p. 331.

[50] *Ibid.*, p. 332; compare Alexander Sesonske, *Value and Obligation* (New York: Oxford University Press, 1964), pp. 33–34.

[51] Compare Plato, *Phaedrus*, 263: "*Socrates*: Every one is aware that about some things we are agreed, whereas about other things we differ. . . . When any one speaks of iron and silver, is not the same thing present in the minds of all? . . . But when any one speaks of justice and goodness we part company and are at odds with one another *and with ourselves*." (My italics).

[52] Cavell, *Must We Mean What We Say?*, p. 86. For a similar and useful discussion of rational disagreement in ethics, see Bernard Mayo, *Ethics and the Moral Life* (London: Macmillan, 1958), pp. 63, 99, 113–114.

[53] Cavell, "Claim to Rationality," p. 332.

how it is to be understood and assessed, what position each is taking toward it and thereby toward the other, and hence what each is like and what their future relations will be like. The hope, of course, is for reconciliation, but the test of validity in moral discourse will not be reconciliation but truthful revelation of self. "The direct point" of moral discourse, Cavell says, is "to determine the positions we are assuming or are able or willing to assume responsibility for." Consequently, again, "what makes moral argument rational is not the assumption that we can always come to agreement about what ought to be done on the basis of rational methods. Its rationality lies in following the methods which lead to a knowledge of our position, of where we stand."[54]

Moral discourse is useful, is necessary, because the truths it can reveal are by no means obvious. Our responsibilities, the "extensions of our cares and commitments, and the implications of our conduct, are not obvious . . . the self is not obvious to the self."[55] That means both that we do not always see the implications of our own position, who we are; and that we do not always see the reality of our own action, what we have done. In the elaboration of our conduct through speech, we disclose and discover, as Arendt says, "the agent together with the act."[56] In action and its subsequent elaboration in speech, "one discloses one's self without ever either knowing himself or being able to calculate beforehand whom he reveals."[57] Hence the "revelatory quality of speech and action": moral discourse concerns self-definition and self-knowledge.[58]

In a way, what claims we enter and what positions we take in a moral discussion is up to each of us, a matter of individual choice; yet in a way it is not subjective at all. You can take any position you want, but at the same time there are standards, and your position defines you just as surely as your action itself. As Austin points out, given almost any excuse there will be cases of such a nature or of such gravity that in those cases that excuse is unacceptable. Some ways of elaborating our conduct only make things worse; our elaboration must be appropriate to the nature and gravity of the offense. "We may plead that we trod on the snail inadvertently: but not on a baby—you ought to look where you are putting your great feet. Of course it *was (really)*, if you like, inadvertence:

[54] *Ibid.*, p. 417.
[55] *Ibid.*
[56] Arendt, *Human Condition*, p. 160; compare Kenneth Minogue, *The Liberal Mind* (New York: Random House, 1968), p. 73, who argues that whereas traditional moral philosophy seems "concerned either to discover or to analyze reasons why we ought to do the right thing," the real "moral significance" of discourse about action "is found in the discoveries we make about ourselves in the course of our deliberations, the kind of temptations we encounter, and the moral character which is implied by the act when it is done."
[57] Arendt, *Human Condition*, p. 171; compare p. 159.
[58] *Ibid.*, p. 160; compare Oakeshott, *Rationalism in Politics*, p. 211; and Robert Denoon Cumming, ed., *The Philosophy of Jean-Paul Sartre* (New York: Modern Library, 1966), p. 416.

but that word constitutes a plea, which is not going to be allowed, because of standards. And if you try it on, you will be subscribing to such dreadful standards that your last state will be worse than your first."[59]

To put it another way, validity in moral discourse is not just a question of what will succeed in restoring relationship, getting the offender off the hook, persuading or hoodwinking the offended into giving up his claim. That would not be moral discourse but a caricature and perversion of morality; not just any conversation about action is a moral one. For moral discourse is supposed to result in truthful revelation of self; it must be conducted in a certain manner or style. And here the language philosophers merely join in a tradition transmitted but not initiated by Kant, specifying that discourse or conduct is moral only if it treats and addresses each person as a person, as an end in himself, rather than as an object or a means to some other end. "One property that makes a reason a moral one," Cavell says, "is that it is conceived in terms of what will benefit the person the speaker adduces his reasons *to*."[60] However morality is to be understood, "*what* must be understood is a concept concerning the treatment of *persons*," and that means creatures with cares and commitments and feelings and intentions and the capacity for moral responsibility.[61] Moral discourse, then, is precisely the kind of exchange which Martin Buber calls an "I-Thou" relationship, in which the other is addressed and conceived of as a human being, a person basically *like oneself*. It is a relationship that requires mutual identification and empathy. Thus, one can say, following Arendt, that moral discourse is a mode "in which human beings appear to each other, not indeed as physical objects, but *qua* men."[62] I take this feature of moral discourse to be directly related to the way moral discussion involves its participants, involves their feelings, helps to define who they are, the way that relationships are at stake in it. A moral argument must be addressed to the other man's cares and commitments or else it will not bear on, will not help to illuminate, his position truthfully.

In discussions about ordinary, empirical facts, we all know our shared standards of validity and proof—when a claim is in doubt and when a doubt has been refuted. If you say, "There is a goldfinch at the bottom of the garden," and are asked "How do you know?" You may, for instance, answer, "From its red head." If the response is then, "But gold-crests also have red heads," your claim is and remains in doubt unless you can make another competent response (like "But it's a different shade of

---

[59] Austin, *Philosophical Papers*, pp. 142–143; but of course there is a problem about whether "it was (really) inadvertence" in a situation where that term is inappropriate.

[60] Cavell, "Claim to Rationality," p. 372.

[61] *Ibid.*, p. 375; the passage actually is about justice, not morality.

[62] Arendt, *Human Condition*, p. 156; compare Oakeshott, *Rationalism in Politics*, p. 210.

red," or "But they have different eye markings."). Every competent speaker of the language knows the nature of doubt and proof here (though he may not know anything about bird markings, of course).

But moral discussions do not have the same kind of standardization. In the case of empirical knowledge, as Cavell says, "It is not up to the protagonists to assign their own significance to bases and grounds for doubt; what will count as an adequate basis and sufficient ground for doubt is *determined by the pattern of the assessment itself.* When I counter a basis by saying 'but that's not enough,' there is no room for you to say, 'For me it is enough.' But in the moral case *what* is 'enough' is itself part of the content of the argument. What is enough to counter my claim to be right or justified in taking 'a certain' action is up to me. I don't care that he is an enemy of the state; it's too bad that he took what I said as a promise; I know that others will be scornful, nevertheless . . . ; suppose I *have* done more or less what he did, my case was different. I can *refuse to accept* a 'ground for doubt' without impugning it as false, and without supplying a new basis, and yet not automatically be dismissed as irrational or morally incompetent. What I *cannot* do, and yet maintain my position as morally competent, is to deny the *relevance* of your doubts ('What difference does it make that I promised, that he's an enemy of the state, that I will hurt my friends')."[63]

In sum, the pattern of moral discussion is different from that of a discussion on empirical fact, because what is at stake in it is not factual knowledge of the physical world but self-knowledge and the knowledge of actions, and what constitutes rationality does not depend on ultimate agreement but on truthful clarification of positions. "Questioning a claim to moral rightness (whether of any action or of any judgment) takes the form of asking 'Why are you doing that?', 'How can you do that?', What *are* you doing?', 'Have you really considered what you're saying?', 'Do you know what this means?'; and assessing the claim is, as we might now say, to determine *what* your position is, and to challenge the position itself, to question whether the position you *take* is adequate to the claim you have entered. The point of the assessment is not to determine *whether* it is adequate, where *what* will be adequate is itself given by the form of the assessment itself; the point is to determine *what* position you are taking, that is to say, *what position you are taking responsibility for*—and whether it is one I can respect."[64]

Thus, disagreement in a moral discussion need not imply any failure in morality or any lack of rationality in the protagonists. Of course, our moral confrontation of another person may not "take." "We may mistake his cares and commitments, or he may suddenly *deny* us. But what then breaks down is not moral argument, but moral relationship. . . .

[63] Cavell, "Claim to Rationality," p. 350.
[64] *Ibid.*, p. 351.

What is required in confronting another person is not your liking him, but your being willing, from whatever cause, to take his position into account."[65]

ACTION

If Waismann is right, that the investigation of some region of discourse can help us to understand the grammar and therefore the nature of things talked about in that region, then an understanding of moral discourse might help to clarify a topic quite central to social and political study: the nature of action. That topic has received considerable theoretical and philosophical attention in recent years, both within and outside ordinary-language philosophy; but even a hasty survey of the literature reveals a number of inconsistencies, confusions, and difficulties. It may be that some of these difficulties can be resolved if the topic is approached indirectly by way of our discourse about action. But let us begin by reviewing the sort of thing that has recently been written on the nature of action.

One of the most striking features of the recent literature in this area is the diversity and inconsistency of its terminology. All of the writers want to distinguish something that is special in the conduct of human beings. Many of them call this special something "action," but there is the greatest variety in how they define this term, what they contrast it with, and how they distinguish actions from other phenomena. Probably the oldest and perhaps the most familiar way of drawing the distinction is by contrasting human beings with the rest of nature. Natural phenomena, we are told, are governed by causal laws and have no choice about the events in which they are involved; what befalls them is causally determined. But human beings are capable of choice, so that it makes sense to hold them responsible for what they do; they have, as the older tradition would put it, immortal souls; they have, as we continue to say, free will. Of course, human beings are also sometimes subject to events which they cannot control or influence; but sometimes they are able to take action and thereby change the course of events. In short, the capacity for action is what distinguishes man from the rest of nature. Only human beings can act.

Another, somewhat broader, but also very familiar way of drawing the distinction is between animate beings, including man, and inanimate objects. Objects, clearly, cannot do anything on their own initiative, but merely undergo the course of events. What characterizes living creatures is precisely their capacity to do things, to initiate change, to take action. Or, again, the distinguishing line may be drawn between animate creatures endowed with consciousness, with mind, on the one hand, and all other creatures and objects, on the other. Then what seems essential to the idea

[65] *Ibid.*, p. 436.

of action is having a mind, a will, the capacity to want or choose or decide on an action. Many writers acknowledge that human beings are *also* physical objects and animals, so that only some of their conduct is action. In a few writers, notably Arendt, action is accordingly defined in a quite restricted way, most human conduct being classified instead as "behavior." (Consequently, some of what we shall say about action will not fit the Arendtian concept. For example, she insists that action must be public and political, which would make morality and moral discourse quite irrelevant to it. Yet she herself introduces categories like promising and forgiveness into the discussion, which would fit better with action at the level of morality than at the public level.)

Indeed, the whole question of how to distinguish action is complicated in the literature by great terminological variety, sometimes even within the work of a single writer. Most commonly, "action" is contrasted with "behavior": while only human beings (or only animate beings, or only conscious beings) can be said to act, the rest of the world engages in behavior. (Or else human action is to be contrasted with human behavior, the capacity for which men share with animals and perhaps with things.) Sometimes action is regarded as one kind or subdivision of behavior (for example, "meaningful" or "significant" behavior). And sometimes a writer claims to be contrasting one kind of action ("free" action or "meaningful" action) with other kinds, with action in general. Further, as we shall see, many writers contrast two kinds of *explanations*—necessary, causal explanations characteristic of physical science, and contingent explanations in terms of purpose, motive, or intention, characteristic of human morality. They then associate the latter kind of explanation with "action," the former with "behavior" or "events."

We may feel that the particular terms don't matter, and indeed they don't, once we are clear what in the world we are talking about. But until that is clear, our terminology is likely to control the outcome of our investigations. The fact is that the many different distinctions these writers pursue are not identical; the demarcations between them do not coincide. The difference between human beings and inanimate objects is not the same as that between human beings and animals, which in turn is not the same as that between (the meaning of) "action" and (the meaning of) "behavior," or that between causal and purposive explanation. So the conclusions a particular writer draws depend very much on the particular terminology, the particular distinction, he investigates. But none of these writers is completely and singly wedded to a particular contrast or example; they all move about in this general terrain with greater or lesser degrees of constraint. Sometimes they investigate the meaning of the term "action," sometimes the nature of purposive explanation, sometimes a few of the many verbs for which "action" is a rough, general stand-in. The real problem is not the existence of all this ambiguity and complexity; that is not the writers' fault, but lies in the nature of our language. The real problem is that these writers sometimes seem to be oblivious of the complexity, insensitive to the difficulties it creates, and therefore unaware of the uncontrolled ways in which it dominates their own investigations.

Many of the recent writers on action are troubled about the rigidity of the borderlines they distinguish—whether action is really, fundamentally different from behavior or events, or whether these are just different ways of looking at the same thing. Waismann, as we saw, takes the latter position, that what human beings do "may be viewed as a series of movements caused by some physiological stimuli," like behavior of rats; "or as something that has a purpose or a meaning irrespective of the way its single links are produced," irrespective of physiological processes.[66] But other writers, like A. I. Melden, find an irreducible "gap between bodily movements and actions." He argues that "I raise my arm" means something different from "My arm rises," and cannot be reduced to the latter. The two expressions are by no means "alternative ways of saying the same thing," nor even "alternative descriptions of the same event. . . . No further description of the bodily movement in respect of its properties as a bodily movement could possibly disclose that additional feature that makes it a case of action."[67] Sometimes my arm rises because I raised it, and at other times it rises though I did not raise it—because someone else moves it, or a machine, or because I have an involuntary muscle-spasm. But behaviorally, in terms of observable phenomena, the two kinds of event might look exactly alike.

Proceeding ontologically, trying to investigate the nature of action itself, the recent writers in this area have suggested a number of essential features by which action may be distinguished from behavior or events. Probably the most common and surely the least controversial of the suggestions is that the idea of action is essentially linked to that of an agent. For every action, there must be an agent *whose* action it is. Events which merely happen to you are not actions; an action is something an agent does, rather than merely experiences. The agent is what makes the action happen, causes it, brings it about. He is the "causal factor," the source and origin of the action; he initiates it.[68] Yet if actions are different from events, how is an agent as causal factor different from the natural causation of physical events? Hannah Arendt says that the concept of action is linked with that of initiation, of beginning something new and unex-

[66] Waismann, "Language Strata," p. 247.

[67] A. I. Melden, *Free Action* (New York: Humanities Press, 1961), pp. 85–86; compare Richard Taylor, *Action and Purpose* (Englewood Cliffs: Prentice-Hall, 1966), p. 63.

[68] Roderick M. Chisholm, "Freedom and Action," in Keith Lehrer, ed., *Freedom and Determinism* (New York: Random House, 1966), p. 29; compare Charles Taylor, *The Explanation of Behaviour* (New York: Humanities Press, 1967), pp. 57, 61; and Richard Taylor, *Action and Purpose*, p. 109: "In describing anything as an act there must be an essential reference to an agent as the performer cr author of that act, not merely in order to know whose act it is, but in order even to know that it is an act."

pected. "To act, in its most general sense, means to take an initiative, to begin (as the Greek word *archein*, 'to begin,' 'to lead,' and eventually 'to rule,' indicates), to set something into motion (which is the original meaning of the Latin *agere*)."[69] But cannot physical events set something into motion?

Arendt argues that the agent initiating an action must necessarily be a human one, that action is a distinctively human capacity. Men are to some extent physical objects and to some extent animals, obeying natural causal laws; but only human beings, unlike objects and animals, can also act. "Action cannot even be imagined outside the society of men," she says, and "neither a beast nor a god is capable of it."[70] Yet we do sometimes speak of animals or objects as "acting." We talk about the effects of a certain chemical "agent," of the "actions" of water on sandstone cliffs, and the like. No doubt, there are many verbs that we predicate only of human beings (or of what strikes us as like a human being); "act" does not happen to be one of them. But we can decide to use "act" as a general designation, as a stand-in for such verbs. Another way to make the same point would be to say, with Richard Taylor, that actions can be brought about or modified or prevented by speaking to the agent. Actions are the sort of "things which can without any incongruity be commanded, requested or forbidden."[71] Then only creatures which understand language can act.

Two corollaries are drawn from this feature of action by various writers: first, actions differ from events in that they have a purposive character, an intentionality. Action involves "endeavor or purpose"; it involves " 'direction' to a goal or end."[72] Though men sometimes merely behave automatically or act on impulse without any reason, Peters argues "the paradigm case of a human action is when something is done in order to bring about an end."[73] At the same time, secondly, actions differ from events by being conventional, or rule-governed; they "conform to social standards and conventions."[74] An action is a performance, and there are right and wrong ways of performing which have to be learned; the action is imbedded in conventions and norms which define it, tell us how it is to be performed.

For both these reasons, we are told, actions characteristically have the potential of going wrong. "Only an activity can go wrong," says Polanyi, "and all activity incurs the risk of failure."[75] Because action is purposive,

[69] Arendt, *Human Condition*, p. 157.
[70] *Ibid.*, pp. 23–24.
[71] Richard Taylor, *Action and Purpose*, p. 104.
[72] Chisholm, "Freedom and Action," p. 29; Charles Taylor, *The Explanation of Behaviour*, p. 27; compare pp. 29, 32–34.
[73] R. S. Peters, *The Concept of Motivation* (New York: Humanities Press, 1958), p. 4; compare Richard Taylor, *Action and Purpose*, p. 186.
[74] Peters, *The Concept of Motivation*, pp. 5, 14.
[75] Michael Polanyi, *Personal Knowledge* (New York and Evanston: Harper & Row, 1964), p. 313.

involves intentions, it can succeed or fail in achieving its purpose or goal. Because action is governed by conventions and rules, it can be done well or badly, performed successfully or unsuccessfully. Thus, both as performances and as means, Louch says, actions can "be done well or ill, and appraised as achievements or failures."[76] And Winch tells us that all action "is *ipso facto* rule-governed," and the "notion of following a rule is logically inseparable from the notion of *making a mistake*. If it is possible to say of someone that he is following a rule that means that one can ask whether he is doing what he does correctly or not."[77] Physical objects behaving in accord with necessary, causal, natural laws cannot make mistakes. But of a human being, we can say that he "is doing something efficiently, intelligently, correctly. . . . It only makes sense to talk of actions in this way, not of cases where something happens to a man. . . . Movements *qua* movements are neither intelligent, efficient, nor correct."[78] But we do, after all, call animals "intelligent," and sometimes appraise what they do as "efficient" or "inefficient." Even machines can be judged on efficiency, and so can "mere" physical movements. Moreover, actions certainly will not contrast with behavior on the score of being rule-governed, for we admonish each other to "behave yourself," we speak of behaving well or badly, we even have a word for this specific purpose: "misbehaving." Why is there no corresponding word: "misacting"?

Arendt stresses that actions can go wrong not because they are rule-governed or purposive, but because they initiate something new, because of their potential for unforeseen, undesirable consequences. She says that action is by its very nature "boundless" in its consequences and "unpredictable" in its ultimate results, because man "acts into a medium where every reaction becomes a chain reaction."[79] Namely, man acts on and among other human beings, themselves capable of action and initiative, which he cannot foresee or control. In making things, manufacturing, working on inanimate matter, men can have full control over what they do, given only that they are sufficiently skillful. But this is never true with action, because it "goes on directly between men without the intermediary of things."[80] Yet physical events also often initiate something we

[76] A. R. Louch, *Explanation and Human Action* (Berkeley and Los Angeles: University of California Press, 1966), p. 58; compare Cavell, *Must We Mean What We Say?*, p. 22.

[77] Winch, *Idea of a Social Science*, pp. 52, 32. Winch actually says that "all behaviour which is meaningful (therefore all specifically human behaviour) is *ipso facto* rule-governed," but it seems clear that he means what we have been calling "action." Compare John Searle, *Speech Acts* (Cambridge: Cambridge University Press, 1969), p. 42: "Sometimes in order to explain adequately a piece of human behavior we have to suppose that it was done in accordance with a rule, . . . Two of the marks of rule-governed as opposed to merely regular behavior are that we generally recognize deviations from the pattern as somehow wrong or defective and that the rule unlike the past regularity automatically covers new cases. Confronted with a case he has never seen before, the agent knows what to do."

[78] Peters, *The Concept of Motivation*, p. 14.

[79] Arendt, *Human Condition*, pp. 169, 171.

[80] *Ibid.*, p. 9; compare p. 197.

did not expect. Both physical events and human actions have histories—are preceded and followed by other events and actions which may be related to them. The physical causal chain is surely "boundless" too, except insofar as we draw boundaries in conceptualizing it. Indeed, the expression "chain reaction" that Arendt uses has its home in nuclear physics.

The writers on action also tell us that it may be distinguished by a separate kind of explanation appropriate to it, different from the kind of explanation appropriate to behavior or physical events. For behavior and events governed by necessary physical laws, scientific, causal explanations are in order. But actions are to be explained in terms of the actor's purpose, motive, intention, his reasons for doing what he does, and in terms of the conventions governing the action he intends to perform. That is what explanation *means* in the context of action.[81] "The concept of action logically entails reference to . . . such mentalistic concepts as purpose, intention and motive," John Gunnell says, so that explanations referring to such concepts "provide the paradigm case of explanations of human action."[82] Peters agrees: "If we are in fact confronted with a case of genuine action (i.e. an act of doing something as opposed to suffering something), then causal explanations are *ipso facto* inappropriate."[83] Yet we do sometimes ask about, and explain, what "caused" a man to do what he did, and we say that he acted "because of" this or that. Wittgenstein even suggests that we fall back on causal explanations of our actions when we have exhausted explanations in terms of reasons or motives.[84]

The kind of explanations appropriate to actions, a number of writers argue further, differ from causal explanations also in that they help to define what is explained, rather than merely to clarify how it was brought about. A causal explanation, as Melden says, tells us how "an event whose characteristics are already known is brought to pass," but an explanation by purpose and motive "tells us what in fact the person was doing"; it gives a "fuller characterization of the action."[85] Yet we sometimes also

[81] Peters, *The Concept of Motivation*, p. 4; Winch, *Idea of a Social Science*, pp. 78, 115.

[82] John Gunnell, "Social Science and Political Reality: The Problem of Explanation," *Social Research*, 35 (Spring 1968), 188, 193. Compare also Waismann, "Language Strata," p. 247; Richard Taylor, *Action and Purpose*, p. 206; Charles Taylor, *The Explanation of Behaviour*, pp. 35–36; A. R. Louch, *Explanation and Human Action*, pp. 51–52.

[83] Peters, *The Concept of Motivation*, p. 12; compare p. 8.

[84] Wittgenstein, *Blue and Brown Books*, p. 15.

[85] A. I. Melden, *Free Action* (New York: Humanities Press, 1961), p. 88; compare p. 102; Charles Taylor, *The Explanation of Behaviour*, p. 36; Philippa Foote, "Free Will as Involving Determinism," in Sidney Morgenbesser and James Walsh, eds., *Free Will* (Englewood Cliffs: Prentice-Hall, 1962), p. 77: "Assigning a motive to an action is not bringing it under any law; it is rather saying something about the kind of action it was, the direction in which it was tending, or what it was done *as*."

explain a puzzling physical event by clarifying what it actually was (it wasn't merely a sphere of fire; it was ball lightning).

Lastly the writers on action argue that since the explanation of an action clarifies what action was done, and since the explanation involves intentions, motives, purposes, strictly speaking only the actor himself can tell us what he was doing or explain his action. Physical objects and animals have no intentional inner life and cannot speak. They simply do what we see them do; and when we describe and explain their behavior, they never have or offer rival accounts of what they were up to. Thus, where causal explanation is appropriate, the observer can describe and define what he has seen. But with respect to actions, where purposive explanations are involved, the observed actor has a rival account or definition of his action. And the writers on action typically conclude that the actor's account, the actor's definition, is privileged and decisive. Only the actor knows what he is doing.

When these points are made ontologically, as bald assertions about the nature of action, they share an annoyingly arbitrary quality that is even more troublesome than the particular inconsistencies or counterexamples we may find. Each assertion seems plausible, yet most of them also seem wrong in some way; and all of them leave us at a loss as to how to proceed with an investigation. We want to ask: What exactly is it about man that is supposed to be so special? Why can't animals or even objects act? Do they never surprise us? Is a certain level of brain development prerequisite? Is that because action is more difficult than behavior? Can intelligent animals, say porpoises or chimpanzees or pigs, act? Almost? What would count as an action on their part? Surely all sorts of animals make choices (which trail to follow, where to sleep); if we say that these are causally determined events unlike our free actions, how do we know that? Certainly a man choosing a banana looks a great deal like a chimpanzee choosing a banana. How do we know that the phenomena are different, and how shall we go about investigating the difference? One familiar impulse at this point is to say that we experience choice, responsibility, free will *in ourselves*, and merely project them onto other human beings, but have learned not to project them onto animals and objects. But this impulse is not very satisfactory. First, it makes the projection seem rather arbitrary: Why project onto other people but not onto animals? And, even more important, it goes counter to all we have learned in previous chapters about the nature of such concepts. For we found that understanding is not merely or particularly what I feel when I understand, expecting is not merely or particularly what I feel when I expect someone, even pain is not merely or particularly what I feel when I am hurt. If freedom and choice were merely private, "inner" experiences, we could never learn the words.

A Wittgensteinian approach suggests at least two avenues for coping with the mare's nest of puzzles and contradictions surrounding the concept of action. One might engage in a careful, Austinian analysis of the normal uses of terms like "action," "behavior," "cause," "explanation," and so on. That is far beyond the scope of our effort here. Alternatively, one might be able to achieve a clearer, ordering perspective by focusing on the language of action, rather than ontologically on action itself. Instead of asking what action is, or is like, one might ask how, in what ways, under what circumstances, for what reasons, human beings need to talk to each other about their conduct. What language games are played with the concepts in this region of language? Then we will see that language plays a wholly different role with respect to human actions than it does with respect to animal behavior or physical events. Any of these phenomena can be discussed, described, explained, in language. But language is also *used in the course of* human action, by the actors themselves, as it is not used by animals in their behavior or physical objects in the events that befall them. We use language not merely to talk about action, but to act—to carry on actions, to teach actions, to plan or produce actions, to assess actions done and redress any ways in which they have gone wrong. We do not talk with the animals we observe, nor with (or normally even to) the material objects on which we work; but we do talk to and with each other.

If we place this fact in relation to Wittgenstein's shift from words as labels to words as tools or signals, then we will see that the vocabulary of human action is likely to be systematically different in grammar and meaning from that of other language regions. For this vocabulary, as Charner Perry says, is "formed in relation to and for the guidance of practice. Its distinctions and terms reflect the purposes, needs and exigencies of action."[86] The vocabulary of human action, perhaps more than any other language region, is used in a multiple variety of signaling language games, not just for labeling. As Oakeshott says, "the character and purport of this speech is appropriate to the needs of the practical self. It is the means by which we engage the attention of other selves"; we use it "to explain, argue, instruct and negotiate; to advise, exhort, threaten and command; to pacify, encourage, comfort and console. By means of this language we communicate our desires, aversions, preferences, choices, requests, approvals and disapprovals; we make promises and acknowledge duties; we confess hopes and fears; we signify forgiveness and penitence."[87]

Much that was said earlier about the nature of action makes sense in a new way, makes clearer sense in the light of how we talk about actions, use language in connection with them. We said that action presupposes an agent, and that agent must be human or like a human being. Now we can see why that is so: we ascribe actions only to what is like a human being

[86] Charner Perry, "The Semantics of Political Science," *American Political Science Review*, XLIV (June 1950), 397.
[87] Oakeshott, *Rationalism in Politics*, p. 211.

because the meaning and use of our vocabulary of action derive from language games played in the course of action. Only someone who can talk and understand language can play those games; so only someone who can talk and understand language can act. Action, we might say, is primarily a first- and second-person phenomenon, and only derivatively a third-person phenomenon. As Arendt puts it, "Speechless action would no longer be action, because there would no longer be an actor, and the actor, the doer of deeds, is possible only if he is at the same time the speaker of words."[88] More guardedly, the doer of deeds is possible only if he is at the same time *capable of* speaking and understanding words. Our vocabulary of action is primarily applicable to human beings because its primary use is among human beings speaking to each other about what they are doing; that is why its concepts make sense only of beings capable of speech.

Action presupposes an agent, and an agent differs from the cause of an event because he makes a choice, is responsible, initiates something new rather than just continuing the causal chain. This again makes new sense if the contexts in which we talk about action are usually ones in which someone is being asked to act or to refrain from action, praised or blamed for what he has done. Men are responsible for their actions because we hold them responsible; we do not hold physical causes responsible because we do not talk with objects. An action is the sort of thing that can be commanded, forbidden, praised, and so on, because we command, forbid, praise actors. Physical events often have unexpected results, often surprise, disappoint, or harm us; but neither they nor their causes then offer excuses or plead for forgiveness. That is the sense in which part of our concept of action is that an action can "go wrong"; we do not so construe physical events when they cause unexpected damage.

The identification of actions, knowledge of actions, are significantly different from the identification and knowledge of events; again the role of language in action makes clearer how and why this is so. It is not that actions are by nature difficult to identify, like species of butterfly; but that a great deal more goes on in saying "what was done" than a mere descriptive identification. The identification of actions is problematic because action concepts are not merely labels for referring, but are compounded out of a variety of complex signaling language games in a variety of circumstances. Or, putting the same point another way, the identification of actions is problematic because the grammar of action words is significantly shaped in moral discourse, and in moral discourse we must take the other participant's views into account, since our relationship is what is at stake.

A fair proportion of our moral discourse has to do precisely with establishing what action was performed; and that involves attention not merely to externally observable behavior, but also to circumstances, intentions,

88 Arendt, *Human Condition*, p. 158.

motives, purposes, and reasons. Indeed, one important way of elaborating conduct gone wrong is by making clear that our intention was other than the results indicate, that therefore we did not really do what we appear to have done. "Justifying what was done (saying whether what was done was right or sensible or necessary . . .)," as Cavell reminds us, "always presupposes a *particular description* of what was done; under one description it may have been (called) dishonest, under another, courageous."[89] Austin says much the same: "It is in principle always open to us, along various lines, to describe or refer to 'what I did' in so many different ways. . . . Should we say, are we saying, that he took her money, or that he robbed her? That he knocked a ball into a hole, or that he sank a putt? That he said 'Done', or that he accepted an offer? How far, that is, are motives, intentions and conventions to be part of the description of actions?"[90] As Cavell puts it, "Apparently, *what* the 'case' in question is *forms part of the content of the moral argument itself.* Actions, unlike envelopes and goldfinches, do not come named for assessment, nor, like apples, ripe for grading."[91]

In some contexts, for example if we are talking about the assessment of moves or plays in a game, though a kind of action is at issue, elaboratives, excuses, intentions, have no place. Within the context of the game "what you did" depends on your (relevant) movements, and how it is to be assessed is specified by the rules. But human conduct in general, like our ordinary language, is rule-governed in a different way. If we are tempted to think of, say, promising, a kind of move in a game with learned rules, then we need Cavell's reminder: "imagine someone arguing that he shouldn't be called out because though he swung at the ball (made the promise) it was an inconvenient pitch; or because although he swung (cp. said 'I promise') he hadn't realized what the situation was, and meant only to bunt, or did it as a joke. Then there is some question whether he is competent, not merely at baseball, but at the form of life called 'playing a (competitive) game.' But comparable 'defenses' *are*, *sometimes*, competently entered in justifying your not keeping a promise, and *never* are, as part of the concept of playing baseball."[92]

It is part of what we call "moral" that rules and umpires cannot settle questions in that definitive way; it is part of what we call "competitive games" that apologies and excuses and other such elaboratives cannot affect the description or the evaluation of what was done. "If you swung at three pitches and failed to touch the ball on the third swing, then you *struck out*. To *know* you struck out all you need to know are the rules of the game and to have seen what you did. There is no gap between intention and action which *counts*. But outside the arena of defined practices, in

---

[89] Cavell, "Claim to Rationality," p. 410.
[90] Austin, *Philosophical Papers*, pp. 148–149.
[91] Cavell, "Claim to Rationality," p. 347.
[92] *Ibid.*, p. 393.

the moral world, what we are doing has no such defined descriptions, and our intentions often fail, one way or another, in execution. There, knowing what you are doing and what you are going to do and what you have not done, cannot fully be told by looking at what in fact, in the world, you do. To know what you are doing is to be able to elaborate the action: say why you are doing it, if that is competently asked; or excuse or justify it if that becomes necessary."[93] Knowing what you are doing involves being able to "elaborate" it, in somewhat the same way that knowing what you meant by something you said involves being able to elaborate that—put it in other words, explain why you said it, justify it. What you said may differ, depending on how you elaborate it ("I can walk; I mean, I have the time." "I can walk; I mean, my legs are well now."); and what you did will depend partly on how you meant it, how you explain and excuse it.

Of course we can speak objectively about actions, observe them neutrally, refer to them and describe them; but *what* we are then observing and referring to is complex, shaped as much by signaling language games and circumstances and intentions as by labeling and physical movements. We can simply and objectively refer to a promise, but what we then refer to includes the obligations and relationships of the institution of promising, not just the behaviorally observable mumbling of some words. We can simply and objectively describe something as knowledge, but what we are then saying about it includes the potential puzzlement about infallibility we discussed earlier. That is why action concepts are not "translatable" into concepts from another region of language, such as those for describing the physical movements of a body. With the same physical movement, with the stroke of a pen or the shake of his head, a man can break a promise or make one, renounce his birthright, insult a friend, obey a command, or commit treason. The same movement can, in various circumstances and with various intentions, constitute any of these actions; so in itself it constitutes none of them.

But what do we observe when we look at that man making the movement? We do not merely observe the physical movement and then somehow add or ascribe or impute intentions and circumstances leading to the hypothesis that he is making a promise. We observe a man making a promise. In speculating about this, we are misled by the fact that, in countless particular cases, when what we say is challenged we back off to the "brute facts" of what we saw ("He was furious." "Are you sure? He said later that he didn't mind." "Well, he certainly *looked* furious.") So we suppose that in general there must be basic, physical brute facts to observe, beyond which all is hypothesis. But that is not so. The observation that a man is angry or that he has promised need not be any less factual or "brute" than the observation that he is fuming or has mumbled some words. About any of these we can turn out, on particular occasions, to be

[93] *Ibid.*, pp. 416–417.

wrong; but they are equally real, equally observable, and equally dependent on concepts and conventions. Questions like "how can *that* be his anger?" or "how can mumbling some words *be* promising?" arise, Cavell suggests, from a "prior (philosophical) conviction or picture of what 'consisting in' must be like, a notion that what a thing consists of must be determined by physics and/or geometry (*rather* than by our conceptualization of it)."[94]

The nature of actions, the identification of actions, knowledge of actions, then, depend on the grammar of our language in the region of action, including but not limited to moral discourse. Consequently, actions are very different from physical events, and their study is bound to be different too from the study of physical nature. It can be objective and detached, but objectivity will have a different character in it than in the study of planets and molecules. We shall look at the peculiarities of action concepts, and their significance, further in discussing problems of social science. We shall also return to the political significance of action, in particular, when we discuss the nature of membership, and what is distinctive about political membership, political discourse, and the political.

[94] *Ibid.*, p. 87.

# VIII

## *Justice: Socrates and Thrasymachus*

WE HAVE now passed the continental divide of this book and entered its further slope; from here on it's all downhill. We have completed most of the explication of Wittgenstein's ideas, and of certain ideas of ordinary-language philosophers, and we turn now to their possible applications in the work of political and social science, political and social theory. Accordingly, the structure and style of our argument must change. Until now, the effort has been to provide a coherent and continuous discourse, each chapter building upon the one before it, ideas developing sequentially. From here, the chapters do not depend upon each other in orderly sequence, but rather radiate from a common center. If, to pursue a different metaphor, this book is a tree, then we have been climbing its trunk and have now arrived at the branches, which must be explored individually. That means, first, that the reader will be expected to return to the trunk at the outset of each new chapter (or, sometimes, pair of chapters), as we start along a different branch. It also means that each chapter will end in the void, diminishing into various small branches and leaves that point outward, where further growth could begin. We deal now with suggestions for applications, not completed studies; they are intended not to display achievement, but to invite it.

Let us begin by considering, in this chapter, the quarrel that Plato chronicles in the first book of the *Republic* between Socrates and the sophist Thrasymachus, about the central question of the whole dialogue: What is justice? Thrasymachus responds readily with the notorious contention that "justice is the interest of the stronger," which he then elaborates to mean that in every society the norms and standards defining what is just and what unjust are set by the ruling elite, the strongest group in society, acting in its own interest.[1] Socrates does not proffer his own answer until much later; when he does, he formulates it in several different,

---

[1] Plato, *Republic*, I, 338c–339a.

but related, ways. For our purposes, they might roughly be summarized as: "Justice is everyone having and doing what is appropriate to him."[2] Socrates and Thrasymachus disagree fundamentally. Yet further reflection reveals that they disagree *so* fundamentally that they do not really *disagree* at all. Rather, they seem to be addressing and answering different questions, and their arguments never really meet.

Socrates and Thrasymachus understand the question "What is justice?" in different ways. Each of them would insist that his understanding has to do with what "justice" itself really is, as distinct from mere verbal conventions or people's ordinary, thoughtless assumptions. Yet one could accurately characterize the difference between them this way: Socrates answers the question as if it were about the meaning of the word "justice"; or at least, we can recognize his answer as a plausible definition. This is not true of Thrasymachus' answer. He is not formulating a phrase more or less synonymous with the word "justice," but making a kind of sociological observation about the things which people call "just" or "unjust." The word "justice" does not *mean* "in the interest of the stronger," and Thrasymachus is not suggesting that it might. Thrasymachus is trying to tell us something about the things or situations people *say* are "just." Socrates, by contrast, is trying to tell us *what people are saying* about a thing *when* they call it "just," what they are saying *by* calling it "just."

Of course, either Socrates or Thrasymachus might be wrong, even on his own level. The word "justice" might not mean anything like "each having and doing what is appropriate to him," and people's norms and standards of justice might not in fact be defined by any elite. But it is also possible, one feels, that they might both be right. That would be the case if people had been so brought up that they considered only those things to exemplify "each having and doing what is appropriate to him," which were in fact in the interest of the stronger, the ruling elite in society. But is that an intelligible supposition? If people used the words "just" and "unjust" as Thrasymachus would, *can* those words then mean what Socrates says they do?

These questions are not trivial, nor is their significance limited to ancient Greece. The dispute between Thrasymachus and Socrates has modern parallels central to political and social concerns. The modern versions, too, generate the feeling that both sides might have something important to say, but that their arguments do not fully meet. The most obvious modern successor to Thrasymachus is the Marxist doctrine of ideology as false consciousness. According to this doctrine, human culture is only a reflection, a superstructure on the economic base of a society; the accepted standards and values and meanings embodied in the culture are in fact a reflection of class interest. So what things people call "just" or "beautiful" or "good" is really determined by what is in the interest of the ruling

[2] *Ibid.*, IV, 433a–434c. Actually, Socrates gives several slightly different formulations here, but he seems to consider them equivalent.

class in any society. "The ruling ideas of each age have been the ideas of its ruling class."³ Every ruling class suffers from a "selfish misconception" which "induces" it to "transform into eternal laws of nature and of reason, the social forms springing from" the modes of production and forms of property of that time.⁴ Like Thrasymachus, the Marxist teaches that what people call "just" is really only in the interest of the ruling class.

But Socrates, too, reappears, for instance in the guise of Karl Barth, who maintains that no such debunking argument can destroy the *ideas* of justice, truth, beauty, or goodness—the ideas that people mean to talk about when they call things just, true, beautiful, or good. For "Whatever is meant by the idea of justice or of truth cannot be shaken by proving that what was taken for justice or truth in concrete cases was merely the precipitate of the political or economic advantage of some social class. Even if it can be shown that interests—those determined by personal relationships and those determined by class relationships—exercise an undeniable influence over what people consider as the measure of justice or truth; still, this dependence does not vitiate the fact that what the order considered just, was taken to be, was precisely a *just* order."⁵ In other words, even if everything they consider just is really in the interest of the stronger, by calling it "just" they did not mean to say that it is in the interest of the stronger. Rather, they meant to invoke the (Socratic) idea of justice.

Still another way to think of the quarrel between Socrates and Thrasymachus would be in relation to the dispute in jurisprudence between legal idealism and legal realism. The legal idealist maintains that the law is an ideal set of deductively systematic norms, together with decisions correctly derived from them. No unconstitutional "law" or inconsistent "judgment" can be part of it. The law, from this perspective, is what guides a judge in making correct decisions—a conception roughly parallel to the Socratic understanding of justice. The legal realist responds that this is a meaningless abstraction; the law is really whatever the judges say and decide—right or wrong, consistent or inconsistent. It is found by studying the behavior of judges; it is what guides their actual decisions. From this perspective, the law is what litigants and attorneys actually encounter in court—a conception roughly parallel to the Thrasymachean view of justice.

The dispute is also reminiscent of certain basic methodological issues in social science. The Thrasymachean social scientist will argue, with Marx and Durkheim, that men's ideas about themselves are not to be taken at face value. "Just as our opinion of an individual is not based on

³ Karl Marx and Friedrich Engels, "Manifesto of the Communist Party," in Lewis S. Feuer, ed., *Marx and Engels: Basic Writings on Politics and Philosophy* (Garden City: Doubleday, 1959), p. 26.
⁴ *Ibid.*, p. 24.
⁵ Karl Barth, *Wahrheit und Ideologie* (Zürich: Manese Verlag, 1945), p. 154; my translation.

what he thinks of himself," the science of society cannot understand a society "by its own consciousness; on the contrary, this consciouness must rather be explained" itself.[6] Social life is explained scientifically if it is explained "not by the notions of those who participate in it, but by more profound causes which are unperceived by consciousness."[7] The Socratic response is likely to be that human actions are understood only through the intentions and motives of the actors, in terms of the actors' concepts and norms. This orientation will stress empathy and *Verstehen* as instruments in the study of man, a phenomenological rather than a behavioral approach. Each side is convinced it is right. Thus, for example, Ludwig Feuerbach argued that gods are really only human inventions, projections of our deepest values, hopes, and needs.[8] A modern theologian is likely to respond that gods are nothing of the sort; "God" means something wholly different from that. "It is just muddle-headed to suppose that, when you say something about God what you 'really mean' is something about men."[9]

So the quarrel between Socrates and Thrasymachus seems to exemplify a pervasive and significant issue, and we would like to understand its nature.[10] What are they disagreeing about? Words? Facts? Values? If indeed it is possible for them both to be right, why do they seem to be in conflict? How could one formulate a single, unified doctrine that would embrace both their truths simultaneously? I have found the questions here to be multiple and interrelated, and have been unable to treat them in as clear and orderly a fashion as I should have liked.

[6] Karl Marx, "Excerpt from A Contribution to the Critique of Political Economy," in Feuer, ed., *Marx and Engels*, p. 44.

[7] Emile Durkheim, review of A. Labriola, "Essais sur la conception matérialiste de l'histoire," *Revue Philosophique* (December 1897) quoted in Peter Winch, *The Idea of a Social Science*, ed. by R. F. Holland (New York: Humanities Press, 1965), pp. 23–24.

[8] Ludwig Feuerbach, *The Essence of Christianity* (New York: Harper & Brothers, 1957).

[9] Donald Hudson, *Ludwig Wittgenstein* (Richmond: John Knox Press, 1968), p. 62.

[10] Any number of other parallels suggest themselves, but not all of them turn out to have the same structure and be amenable to the same treatment as the quarrel between Socrates and Thrasymachus. Consider Hobbes saying tyranny is merely monarchy "misliked": *Leviathan*, ch. 19. Or Burke's way of characterizing the thinkers of the French Revolution: "On this scheme of things, a king is but a man, a queen is but a woman; a woman is but an animal, and an animal not of the highest order. . . . The murder of a king, or a queen, or a bishop, or a father are only common homicide": *Reflections on the Revolution in France* (Indianapolis: Bobbs-Merrill Company, 1955), p. 87. Or David Hume's critique of our notion of causality: that really what we call causation is "derived from nothing but custom," from repeated experience that certain phenomena "have been *always conjoined* together": quoted in Bertrand Russell, *A History of Western Philosophy* (New York: Simon and Schuster, 1945), pp. 671, 665. Compare Ludwig Wittgenstein, *Lectures and Conversations on Aesthetics, Psychology and Religious Belief*, ed. by Cyril Barrett (Berkeley and Los Angeles: University of California Press, 1967), p. 24: "The attraction of certain kinds of explanation is overwhelming. . . . In particular, explanations of the kind 'This is really only this.' "

Someone fascinated with language might at first assume, as I once did, that Socrates and Thrasymachus disagree about the meaning of "justice," so that their dispute could be authoritatively settled by a study of ancient Greek ordinary usage (and the modern parallel disputes, by English ordinary-language philosophy). Then the reason for their disagreement might be that they are using two different kinds of definitions. That idea finds support in Aristotle, who speaks in *De Anima* of two ways of defining terms, which sound very much like the two positions on justice. He distinguishes between physical definitions, used by natural scientists, and dialectical definitions, used by philosophers. "Take the question, what is anger? The latter will say, a desire for retaliation, or something similar; the former, an effervescence of blood and heat about the heart. Of these, the natural scientist designates the matter, the dialectician the form or idea."[11] Similarly, Aristotle says, if the question is, "what is a house?" the philosopher will answer, "a covering to prevent destruction from wind and rain and excessive heat," while the natural scientist will say "stones and bricks and timber."

But Socrates and Thrasymachus are not proposing two rival definitions of "justice." As we already observed, the word "justice" does not *mean* "in the interest of the stronger," and Thrasymachus never suggests that it might. Nor, for that matter, would anyone define the word "house" as meaning "stones and bricks and timber," not even a natural scientist (no more than a biologist would define "cell" as meaning "carbon and oxygen and hydrogen and nitrogen"). Houses do consist of stones and timber, but that is not what the word "house" means. And although Thrasymachus is telling us something (true or false) about justice, he is not defining the word. The meaning of a word, we have said, is what one finds in a good dictionary—a word or phrase that can be substituted for it. The meaning of "justice" has to do with what people intend to convey in saying it, not with the features of the phenomena they say it about. Concerning the

---

[11] Aristotle, *De Anima*, tr. by Kenelm Foster and Silvester Humphries (London: Routledge and Kegan Paul, 1951), p. 52. Aristotle himself, being half philosopher and half scientist in an age that did not draw such a distinction, at first seems to opt for the dialectical definition, but then suggests a third, combinatorial compromise definition: "the form; in those materials; for those reasons." Philip Rieff, who calls attention to Aristotle's distinction, maintains that only the dialectical definition "makes possible a moral science," while the physical or natural scientific "style of definition excludes the moral—that is, human—questions altogether": *Freud* (New York: Viking Press, 1959), p. 16. In this he takes his stand with phenomenologists and other action theorists. But it is important to notice that the coexistence of two kinds of definitions is by no means confined to human, psychological, moral, or abstract concepts. Aristotle's own second example after "anger" is "house." So the problem is a general epistemological or semantic one, not merely one about how to study human or moral questions.

meaning of "justice," Socrates is at least roughly right. But then what might Thrasymachus be right about?

From the modern philosophical literature, one might here draw the distinction between "connotation" and "denotation," and argue that Socrates is interested in the former, Thrasymachus in the latter.[12] But that distinction is likely to be misleading and will not really help us here. For while one might argue that Thrasymachus is not interested in the connotation—that is, the meaning—of "justice," one cannot argue that Socrates is uninterested in its denotation. If Socrates is right about what the word means, he is right both about connotation and about denotation; the word cannot then denote what Thrasymachus says it does.

Perhaps, then, Thrasymachus is telling us something new about the phenomena we consider just, something which we had not noticed and which therefore is not part of our definition of "justice," not part of what we mean when we call those phenomena just. That would make good sense if we consider examples of scientific discovery, where something genuinely new (or at least new to a particular culture) is learned about some class of phenomena. We discover that the earth is not flat but spherical, and in the process of assimilating this discovery our concept of "the earth" changes; the meaning of "the earth" changes. Wittgenstein calls our attention to "the fluctuation of scientific definitions: what to-day counts as an observed concomitant of a phenomenon will to-morrow be used to define it."[13] Thus it may seem that Thrasymachus has observed a hitherto unnoticed concomitant of the phenomena we call "just": namely, that they are always in the interest of the ruling elite. He is proposing, as one commentator has put it, "an important generalization" based on "supposed facts of psychology and politics," facts about the phenomena other people call "just."[14] Again one is tempted to say that, while Socrates is talking about the meaning of the word, Thrasymachus is talking about its application, how people apply it to the world, how they use it.

But a Wittgensteinian perspective does not seem to permit the kind of

[12] The literature on this and related distinctions is vast, and virtually every philosopher has his own way of drawing, and labeling, the distinction. Besides connotation/denotation, we find intension/extension, sense/reference, sense/nominatum, signification/denotation, and *Sinn/Bedeutung*. Major works to look at would include Gottlob Frege, "On Sense and Reference," in Peter Geach and Max Black, eds., *Translations from the Philosophical Writings of Gottlob Frege* (Oxford: Basil Blackwell, 1952); Rudolf Carnap, *Meaning and Necessity* (Chicago: University of Chicago Press, 1956); John Stuart Mill, *A System of Logic* (London: J. W. Parker, 1843); Charles Morris, *Signs, Language and Behavior* (New York: George Braziller, 1955); and Gilbert Ryle, "The Theory of Meaning," in Charles E. Caton, ed., *Philosophy and Ordinary Language* (Urbana: University of Illinois Press, 1963). This last discusses some ways in which the connotation/denotation distinction is likely to be misleading.

[13] Ludwig Wittgenstein, *Philosophical Investigations*, tr. by G. E. M. Anscombe (New York: Macmillan, 1968), par. 79.

[14] George F. Hourani, "Thrasymachus' Definition of Justice in Plato's *Republic*," *Phronesis*, VII (1962), 111; Hourani also cites N. R. Murphy, *The Interpretation of Plato's Republic* (Oxford: Clarendon Press, 1951), p. 2.

dichotomy we have arrived at, between a word's (Socratic) meaning and the (Thrasymachean) facts of its application or use. Wittgenstein teaches that for most purposes the meaning of a word is its use; that if we are conceptually puzzled about its meaning we should look at its use; that the meaning is learned from the use, is abstracted from it. If Wittgenstein is right about that, then surely Thrasymachus and Socrates must be addressing the same question after all, and they cannot both be ultimately right.

We can think about the problem in terms of language-learning. Suppose that there were a society in which Thrasymachus' thesis is actually true: those and only those situations are considered just which in fact serve the interest of the ruling elite. Could a child growing up in that society ever learn the (Socratic) meaning of the word "justice," or would it end up thinking that "justice" is synonymous with "in the interest of the ruling elite"? And if it could learn the (Socratic) meaning, how would that learning take place, how can it be explained? If Thrasymachus is right about the use of the word, how could Socrates ever discover a conflicting meaning?

This question was centrally troubling to Plato himself, and one could even argue that he invented an entire metaphysics to take care of it. For if Socrates is right about meaning, but Thrasymachus has a valid sociological point about how the word is used, how do we ever find out what "justice" means (Socratic meaning)? All we ever encounter is the "corrupted," Thrasymachean usage. More generally, it seemed to Plato that all our concepts are only imperfectly embodied in the objects or situations we use them to talk about. No beautiful thing is ever perfectly beautiful, no triangle is perfectly triangular, no pair of like things ever perfectly alike; no bed ever has all bedlike characteristics without any irrelevant ones, and so on. So how do we ever learn what "bed" or "beautiful" mean, when all we have to go on is our flawed, mixed, fallible experience? Plato's answer relied on the realm of forms, together with the doctrines of reincarnation and recollection.

Who finds that metaphysic hard to accept might be more satisfied by a Wittgensteinian approach, the basic elements for which we have by now available and need only to muster. As so often, our sense of a problem or difficulty here arises from the assumption that "justice" is a label for a certain class of phenomena, and that Thrasymachus and Socrates must therefore disagree about what this class of phenomena is (like). Then, indeed, they could not both be right. But "justice" is much more than a label, functions in many other language games, is not learned ostensively from an adult who points and says to the child, "That's justice." The meaning of "justice" is not—or not primarily—learned by observing the shared characteristics of those phenomena called "just," but by observing the shared features of the speech situations in which the family of words is used, their verbal and worldly contexts. On the verbal side, this implies that the meaning of "justice" is learned not merely in contexts where something is being called just or unjust, but also in contexts that involve doing someone an injustice, doing justice to a delicious meal, getting your just deserts, justifying a decision or an action, acting in a just cause, and so on. On the worldly side, it implies that the meaning of "justice" is learned from observing the kinds of situations in which the various members of the family of words occur, the kinds of changes in action or affect or relationship that they produce, in short, their signaling functions. Like the meaning of "rain," the meaning of "justice" can be learned as much from what we do about "it" as from how "it" looks. Like the meaning of "God," it can be learned even if the phenomenon is never experienced or is experienced only partially or imperfectly.

The same problem we have just analyzed in terms of the learning of language arises also in radical translation, in encountering a foreign language without the help of a translator or a dictionary. Suppose that an anthropologist were to come upon a society in which Thrasymachus' thesis is actually true: those and only those things are considered just which are in the interest of the ruling elite. Would he translate the relevant native word as "justice" or as "in the interest of the ruling elite"? And if he came to translate it as "justice," how did he discover that to be the correct meaning? Here, too, the answer lies in the larger pattern of the natives' language and life. As Wittgenstein says, "whether a word of the language of our tribe is rightly translated into a word of the English language depends upon the role this word plays in the whole life of the tribe; the occasions on which it is used, the expressions of emotion by which it is generally accompanied, the ideas which it generally awakens or which prompt its saying, etc., etc. As an exercise ask yourself: in which cases would you say that a certain word uttered by the people of the tribe was a greeting?"[15]

We learn the meaning and find the translation from the entire pattern of the word's use, both the verbal and the worldly contexts in which it, and related words, appear. It is Socrates, therefore, who is right not merely about the meaning of "justice" but also about its overall patterns of use; meaning and use do go together. But that again leaves us with the question of what Thrasymachus might be right about. It now seems as though he is right only about a small part of the word's use or grammar—about certain shared characteristics of the phenomena labelled "just," when that word is used for labeling. But then he is surely showing us a *discrepancy* within the word's grammar, between the meaning of "justice" and our standards for applying it in a labeling way. If Thrasymachus is right, the things we call "just" are *not* just, or at least there is good reason to doubt whether they are. We really have not begun to solve the problem until we

15 Ludwig Wittgenstein, *Blue and Brown Books* (New York and Evanston: Harper & Row, 1964), p. 103; compare Paul Ziff, *Semantic Analysis* (Ithaca: Cornell University Press, 1960), pp. 74–75; and Willard Van Orman Quine, *Word and Object* (Cambridge: M.I.T. Press, 1960), pp. 26–27.

can account for this kind of discrepancy, and explain why Thrasymachus' position is so powerful if indeed he is wrong about both the meaning and the use of "justice."

## THE "IS" AND THE "OUGHT"

The conventional wisdom of contemporary political science offers us a loud, clear answer as to the nature of Socrates and Thrasymachus' quarrel: the latter is concerned with what is, the former with what ought to be. Robert Dahl, for example, interprets the first book of the *Republic* in precisely that way: the two Greeks "are talking right past one another" because "Socrates was making a *normative* argument, Thrasymachus an *empirical* one."[16] Now that assertion might mean that Socrates is concerned with what justice ought to be, Thrasymachus with what it is in fact. But both men claim to be addressing the question of what justice *is*. If Socrates really intended to reform the concept, to revise what justice now is into something else that it ought to be, we would be entitled to ask him by what standards his proposed idea of justice is better than our present one. Why call *that* "justice"? But clearly this is not what is going on in the *Republic*. Socrates is not trying to change a concept; he believes that concepts are absolute and unchangable, corresponding to timeless forms. He commends his definition as telling us correctly what justice really is, what the word already means.

But in any case, Dahl did not intend to argue that Socrates addresses what justice ought to be; he intended to characterize the differing ways in which Socrates and Thrasymachus address the question of what justice is. In that shared inquiry about what is, Dahl says, "Socrates met Thrasymachus' attempt to describe how rulers generally *do* act by indicating how good rulers *ought* to act."[17] Certainly it is true that the imaginary state Socrates constructs in the *Republic* is not a descriptive account of some actual state, and that Socrates considers it a desirable ideal. Certainly it is true that Thrasymachus tries to describe the way rulers actually behave in all societies. Moreover, Socrates would probably agree with Thrasymachus' description; and if Thrasymachus is wise and honest, he will agree that Socrates' ideal exemplifies what most people mean by the word "justice." So it seems that they can both be right, and even agree, because one is talking about how things are, and the other about an ideal. Then why are they arguing?

We imagine them agreeing about the meaning of a word and about the facts of political conduct. But now, which of them is right about what justice is? Does that answer depend on the meaning of the word or on the facts of political life? Must we not say: both? But they seem to be incom-

[16] Robert Dahl, *Modern Political Analysis* (Englewood Cliffs: Prentice-Hall, 1963), p. 65.
[17] *Ibid.*

patible. Dahl says that Thrasymachus is concerned with the facts of how rulers do act. But if Thrasymachus concludes from his observations that justice is the interest of the stronger, saying, "Everywhere I see men pursuing power and self-interest in the name of justice," Socrates will respond, "You have been studying examples of *in*justice, hypocrisy, and corruption, carried on in the name of justice. To learn what justice is, you must ask what it is, in whose name these activities are carried on."

Empirical facts will be relevant to the question of what justice is only if they are, indeed, facts about *justice*; empirical investigation presupposes conceptual definition. Thrasymachus can discover a new fact about the things called "just" only if he can first identify those things. And doesn't their identification depend on the meaning of "justice"? Sometimes such identification is easy and relatively independent of meaning. To borrow an example from Frege: we say, "The evening star is really the planet Venus," a factual discovery. It would be absurd for a Socrates to respond that this is false because "star" obviously does not mean "planet." The point of the discovery is precisely that the meaning of "star" has turned out to be inappropriate to that thing, there, in the sky, which is in fact a planet. But such an example depends on a clear identification of "that thing, there," independent of the meaning of the old concept. Whether Thrasymachus' facts about how rulers act are relevant to the question of justice depends on what justice means. Similarly with Socrates. Dahl says that he is concerned with the way rulers ought to act. And so he is, since rulers ought to act justly. But we could equally well say that Socrates is telling us how rulers do in fact act *when* they act justly. That is a question of fact, of what is, not (merely) of what ought to be. Moreover, Thrasymachus' views are also about how good rulers ought to act.

Though there is a dispute here, it is not between what is and what ought to be, nor between facts and values. Both protagonists purport to tell us what justice is, and thereby what men in fact do when they act justly, which has clear implications about right conduct. One might say that Thrasymachus is talking about the facts of what people consider just, and Socrates about what they ought to consider just in the light of the meaning of "justice." But the meaning of "justice" depends on the facts of its grammar, so this is a dispute about facts, over the implications of two different kinds of facts. It depends on there being an inconsistency in the grammar of "justice," between what people consider just and what the word "justice" means. What is characteristic about a word like "justice" is that it allows of precisely this kind of inconsistency. Neither pole of the contrast need be subjective or idealistic, and both truly are based on the observation of usage.

### INSIDE AND OUTSIDE VIEWS

Another way to talk about the dispute between Thrasymachus and Socrates would be in terms of inside and outside. Thrasymachus' position strikes us as being in some sense outside of the accepted premises, questioning and debunking accepted assumptions, looking on at what other people say like someone from a different world. Socrates, by contrast, is within the traditional premises and assumptions, accepting and affirming them. But it is not easy to specify what this sense we have of inside and outside is really about, what the two men are inside and outside *of*. One possibility would be that their position relates to their culture and society, the assumptions and values of ancient Greece. Thrasymachus stands back from that culture, sets aside the false consciousness it takes for granted, and looks on detachedly at what the "natives" in fact do. He notices that they in fact use the word "justice" for a certain class of phenomena which happen always to be in the interest of the ruling elite. But clearly a man cannot literally get outside his own culture; Thrasymachus speaks and sees as a fifth-century Greek. We might say that he is trying to escape his culture, but that will not suffice for explaining why he seems to have something important to tell us. It doesn't explain why his discovery, if such it be, is meaningful to us in our very different culture, why his position is still viable today. Of course, Thrasymachus means his discovery to apply to all cultures and societies, but he can hardly have stepped outside of human society altogether.

Moreover, Socrates also seems to have stepped outside the traditional conventions, though in a different way. He refuses to accept the conventional standards of what kinds of phenomena or societies are to be called "just." Even if most people around him consider those things just which in fact serve the interests of the ruling elite, Socrates refuses to accept their standards. He clings to the meaning of "justice" and insists on judging for himself whether the conventional norms are in accord with it.

A different but related way of analyzing our sense of inside and outside here would be in relation to the concept of justice itself, its meaning, implications, and presuppositions. Socrates speaks from within the framework of what is supposed to be true of phenomena called "just," namely that they must involve each having and doing what is appropriate to him. He accepts the intention, the conventions, of the word at face value, and reaffirms them. Thrasymachus rejects these, or ignores them, and looks independently on his own at the common features of phenomena other people call "just." It is rather like trying to do ordinary-language philosophy by taking a public opinion survey; and the difficulties of Thrasymachus' position are related to the difficulties of that enterprise we discussed earlier. Thrasymachus, as it were, stands outside the word and observes how others use it, while Socrates uses it himself. But of course that can't be literally true. They both use the word. We might say that Socrates speaks from within the word's signaling or quasi-performative functions; his definition is derived from the claim made in calling something "just," the guarantee given by a speaker who makes that claim. He himself makes the claim, gives the guarantee, takes on the responsibility.

Thrasymachus somehow uses the word without making that claim or taking on that responsibility; it is as if he confines himself to the word's labeling functions.[18]

We might say that Thrasymachus uses the word "justice" in quotation marks, to mean "so-called justice," or "what other people call 'justice.' " When Thrasymachus says that justice is the interest of the stronger, it seems to me, he is using the word "justice" in this kind of quotation marks, but giving the rest of the words in the sentence their full, normal claiming weight. He is saying that so-called (what other people call) "justice" is in fact the real (what I, Thrasymachus, call) interest of the stronger. For it would be patently false to say that what is truly just, in the full Socratic sense of the word, is always in the interest of the ruling elite. And the other alternative, saying that so-called (what other people call) "justice" is equivalent to the so-called (what other people call) interest of the stronger, is not Thrasymachus' intention. Part of his point is that other people are not aware of the cultural hypocrisy, as he is, and that they therefore would not say what he says. Thrasymachus, then, refuses to step inside the concept of justice and take on the burden, the weight, of what is normally guaranteed or claimed in uttering it. He wants to question precisely those conventions.

### SOME ALTERNATIVE EXAMPLES

We all know that values, standards, and tastes differ from culture to culture, so that what serves as an example of beauty in one culture might be considered ugly in another, and what serves as an example of justice in one culture might be considered unjust in another. But then, do children growing up in radically divergent cultures learn the *same* concept of beauty or justice, or different concepts? If we answer that from systematically different examples they are bound to learn different concepts, then we ought not to translate the other culture's terms by our "beauty" or "justice." And then our initial statement of what "we all know" is wrong; those other cultures do not disagree about what is just, but simply do not have a concept of justice at all. If, on the other hand, we insist that children in different cultures can learn the same concept of beauty or justice, from divergent examples, we must explain how this is possible. Earlier in this chapter we suggested such an explanation: Meaning is not learned merely from labeling examples, from looking at the phenomena people call just, but from the word's entire grammar, from looking at the occasions when people say "just." So the same concept may be learned in two different cultures if its over-all grammar is the same, if it is used in

[18] Compare Austin Duncan-Jones, "Authority," *Aristotelian Society Supplementary Volume* 32 (1958), 243; Bernard Mayo, *Ethics and the Moral Life* (London: Macmillan, 1958), pp. 194–195; and Michael Polanyi, *Personal Knowledge* (New York and Evanston: Harper & Row, 1964), pp. 249–250.

the same kinds of language games, even if the examples of what is just and unjust are very different.

But now we must go on to notice that the answers we are inclined to give to such questions depend very much on the particular examples we examine. The answers will be different for a concept like "delicious" than for a concept like "green." That should, in the first place, warn us to be cautious about "justice," and in the second place, may allow us a clearer sense of what is special about it and concepts like it. Suppose that we inquire whether children in radically different cultures can grow up learning the same meaning for the concept "delicious" (granted, of course, that they will learn different words, different sounds, for the concept), even though they learn it from very different examples. We know, for instance, that Eskimos eat substances that are nauseating to us, and eat them with great gusto and relish. When an Eskimo finds his maggoty, rotten whale blubber "delicious," is he saying the same thing about it that an American child says about his ice-cream cone? The example of a term like "delicious" very strongly suggests an affirmative answer. The meaning of the term depends almost entirely on our relationship to the food—that we want more, that the hostess is pleased, that we offer it to our friends but not our enemies, and so on—and hardly at all on the characteristics of the food. "Delicious" is not the name of a certain set of foods, but a way of saying something about food, namely, that it tastes good. To find out the natives' word for "delicious," an anthropologist would not taste their foods, but observe their behavior about food. The meaning of the word seems quite independent of a particular culture's gustatory preferences. So if we construe "justice" on analogy with "delicious," we will conclude that children can indeed learn the concept even in a culture whose taste in what is just or unjust differs radically from ours.

But now we might ask the same question about a word like "green." After all, we know that different cultures divide up the color spectrum differently. Could children from different cultures learn essentially the same meaning of "green," though they learn it from quite different examples, so that what exemplifies "green" in one culture would be called some other color in the other culture? Here the answer seems clearly negative. If the term "green" is learned exclusively from examples of blue color, then the meaning that is learned is "blue," no matter what word is used for that meaning. And if the term "green" is learned from both green and blue examples, then the meaning learned is equivalent neither to the meaning of "green" nor to the meaning of "blue." In translating that term, we could not simply substitute our word "green" for it. So if we construe "justice" on the model of "green," we will conclude that it makes no sense to suppose that the word could have the same meaning in two cultures with radically different standards of what is just.

The two examples thus suggest conflicting conclusions about justice. "Delicious" suggests that taste is entirely independent of the word's meaning, so that the kind of observation Thrasymachus makes (noting common features of the things people call just) would simply have no bearing on the kind of observation Socrates makes (the meaning of "justice"). The example of "green" suggests that, wherever standards differ, meaning must differ accordingly, so that Socrates and Thrasymachus could not both be right. We may feel intuitively that "justice" must "lie somewhere in between" words like "delicious" and words like "green," being more objective than the former and more subjective or quasi-performative than the latter. But that intuitive response neglects a feature of justice that is lacking in both the other examples: the significance of standards.

Given any edible substance, we are prepared to believe that some culture considers it delicious if we see that those people want more of it, offer it to their friends, and so on. But such is not the case with examples of justice and injustice. We can allow a certain latitude for differing standards and differing cultures; but not merely *any* standards will qualify as standards of justice, not merely any example will be an example of justice. If a speaker considers a certain situation just, he must in principle be prepared to show us *how* it is just, what is just about it. We have no corresponding expectation about "delicious" or "green." Unlike "delicious," justice is not merely a matter of cultural habit or personal taste, but implies standards of justification. Unlike "green," it allows for a kind of disagreement that is neither merely verbal (different definitions) nor merely factual (different perceptions). Though some of our quarrels about justice may result from disagreements about what the word means, and some from disagreements about the facts of a situation, many concern differences in our standards of what is just. Thus, with respect to a concept like justice it makes sense to suppose that there might be a gap, a discrepancy, a conflict, between (Socratic) meaning based on grammar and (Thrasymachean) application based on people's standards. This makes no sense with respect to "delicious," because the gap is too wide to be a conflict; and it makes no sense with respect to "green" because there can be no gap between meaning and standards.

It seems that a concept like "justice" grows out of different sorts of language games, even out of different language regions than either "delicious" or "green," so that the solution to conceptual puzzles about it will take a different form. Wittgenstein once suggested that one might do well to divide a book on philosophy into sections on different "kinds of words" (language regions?). "You would talk for hours and hours on the verbs 'seeing', 'feeling', etc., verbs describing personal experience. We get a peculiar kind of confusion or confusions which comes up with all these words. You would have another chapter on numerals—here there would be another kind of confusion: a chapter on 'all', 'any', 'some', etc.— another kind of confusion: a chapter on 'you', 'I', etc.—another kind: a chapter on 'beautiful', 'good'—another kind. We get into a new group of confusions; language plays us entirely new tricks."[19]

Justice, then, is not in the middle of a continuum between subjective matters of taste and objective matters of fact; it is a different kind of concept altogether, one that involves standards and the possibility of judgment and justification (as the etymology would suggest). Our standards of what is just and unjust are obviously partly learned, but also subject to alteration by our own choice. Insofar as they are learned, they are learned in the same way, in the same process, as we learn the meanings of words and the nature of the world. To learn a concept like justice, apparently the child must master not merely two but three variables, or dimensions of variation: the meaning of the word, the facts of the world, and the standards for what is considered just.

Correspondingly, the radical translation of a term like "justice" presents problems along not merely two but three dimensions. Consider an example adduced by Weldon, bizarre because it is so difficult to imagine occurring naturally, but instructive in its bizarreness. Weldon invites us to "suppose that in Nazi Germany you had set out to discover the German equivalents of English words of appraisal, 'good,' 'honest,' 'praiseworthy,' 'treacherous,' and so on. You would have learnt that the correct usage was '*schön*,' '*ehrlich*,' '*ehrenwert*,' '*unehrlich*,' and so on. Further you would have found that the German words had the same inference licenses attached to them as the English ones. If you were *ehrlich* you were likely to get a decoration, if you were *unehrlich* you were likely to go to a concentration camp. So far, so good. But then you might have seen a S. A. man (or a lot of them) beating up a Jew and you might have said '*Das ist verbrecherisch*.' Your teacher would have said '*Durchaus nicht verbrecherisch. Eine ehrenwerte Tat*.' And what could you say then? You might accept the correction in the same way as that in which in the United States you accept the correction 'We don't call them braces, we call them suspenders, and what you call suspenders, we call garters.' But if you did your friends would not have said 'You have learnt German very well.' They would have said 'You are a liar and a hypocrite. You know it is wicked to behave like that, yet you are saying that it is praiseworthy. You are pretending in order to avoid trouble.' "[20]

In short, the German teacher is not correcting his pupil's grasp of what *ehrenwert* means, nor his perception of the event they both witnessed. Rather, the teacher simply considers something praiseworthy (*ehrenwert*)

[19] Wittgenstein, *Lectures and Conversations*, p. 1.
[20] T. D. Weldon, *The Vocabulary of Politics* (Harmondsworth: Penguin, 1955), pp. 42–43.

which his pupil considers criminal. They disagree about standards. But Weldon's example is bizarre among other things because it is rigged by the very language in which he describes it. We are given the authoritative facts by Weldon's account of what the men see, in which the protagonists are identified and the nature of their actions defined. Would the Nazi have called the action "beating up," or the equivalent German term? We are told that the various translations the student has learned are really correct, so we know the instructor cannot be correcting his German.

In actual life, in situations of radical translation, standards are no more absolutely separable from meaning on the one hand and facts on the other than meaning and facts are from each other. We have only to imagine Weldon's example as happening to an anthropologist visiting some primitive tribe, and immediately all aspects of the situation become problematic. Has the anthropologist learned the translations correctly? Maybe his language *is* being corrected. What exactly has he seen? Perhaps it was not a beating, but an official punishment for a crime, or a religious ceremony, or a game. Do the native terms he thinks of as meaning "criminal" and "honorable" really mean quite that, or are they different concepts altogether? And, what are the natives' standards of criminality and honorableness; what are this particular native's standards?

Similar difficulties can occur without any problem of radical translation; and in practice ambiguous situations must often be left forever unresolved. Consider this true example: An adolescent immigrant German girl in the United States finds herself alone with a middle-aged lady, also a German immigrant and an acquaintance of the girl's parents. They are making polite conversation when the lady says, apparently with admiration, "My, you are such a self-conscious young lady!" The girl is, of course, puzzled. The lady seemed to be paying a compliment, but self-consciousness is hardly a virtue. Perhaps she meant "self-possessed," and made a mistake in English? The girl is well aware of being both awkwardly self-conscious and maturely self-possessed. Hesitatingly, because it seems like fishing for a (further?) compliment, the girl asks, "Self-conscious? You don't by any chance mean 'self-possessed,' do you? The two are different in English, you know." But the lady says firmly, "Oh, very self-conscious." And there the matter rests. Later the girl consults a dictionary and discovers that indeed the German word for self-possessed (*selbst-bewusst*) is a compound whose parts separately would translate as "self" and "conscious," and that there is a different word for self-conscious altogether (*selbst-befangen*). So the girl concludes that her diagnosis was probably correct, but she will never know for sure. The lady may just have considered self-consciousness as a great virtue, to be politely praised.

Ziff suggests that "there is, as it were, a certain principle of exegesis employed" by the speakers of any natural language in coping with ambiguous or odd or deviant utterances. "Roughly speaking, the principle is this: construe what is said in such a way that, with a minimum of interpretation, it is significant."[21] Thus, if I say, "Look, there's a man!" and someone responds, "No, it's a scarecrow," chances are that he is correcting my perception of the facts, not my use of language. If I say, "Look, there's a shovel," and he responds, "No, it's a spade," chances are much better that he wants to correct the niceties of my English. If I say, "Look, that's a crying shame!" and someone responds, "No, it's just wonderful," the possibilities seem wide open; and clearly one possibility that must be considered is that what I *regard as* a shame, he *regards as* wonderful. If I regard as a spade what you regard as a shovel, or if I regard as a man what you regard as a scarecrow, one or both of us *must* either misperceive facts or be mistaken about the meaning of some word involved. But with terms like "shame," "wonderful," or "justice," that implication need not follow; instead, we might differ on standards.

The idea that concepts like "justice" imply standards of judgment can also be expressed by saying: Where someone considers a situation unjust, we expect him to be able to tell us how it is unjust, what's unjust about it. In the same way, if someone considers self-consciousness a virtue, we expect him to be able to tell us how it is a virtue, what's virtuous about it. Recall again the example of the anthropologist disagreeing with his native guide about the event they just witnessed; how might their discussion be likely to proceed, given time and good will? The anthropologist would begin to ask questions as best he might, to find out just what (the native thinks) happened, just what the words he thought he knew really mean. And if it continues to seem that the difference is one of standards, then he will ask the native, "*Why* do you consider *that* to be *honorable*?" And everything will then depend on the explanation the native can give, whether he can connect what he says he saw with something the anthropologist can recognize as a principle of honorableness. It will not be necessary that he convince the anthropologist to agree with his judgment, only that he enable him to see how someone could make such a judgment about honorableness.

Much the same thing goes on in the absence of translation problems. Suppose that you have spent the afternoon together with a friend, working in the library, and on the way home he says, "That was most unjust." You ask, "What was?" and he says, "The afternoon in the library. It was so unjust." You ask him what he means, and perhaps he says, "Well, there are so many books there." You say, "So?" and he says, "They're all different colors." "But why is that *unjust*?" you insist. The conversation can continue as long as both your patience lasts; but unless sooner or later he can connect up something about the afternoon in the library with something you can recognize as at least relevant to justice, you will not know what to conclude. You will not, for example, conclude that he simply has

[21] Ziff, *Semantic Analysis*, p. 132.

standards of justice different from yours; not just *any* standards will be standards of *justice*.

Our concepts are part of a more-or-less consistent, interrelated system of concepts, so that for us to recognize a situation as an instance of, say, justice, it must be related in appropriate ways to persons, to fairness, or to deserts, or to punishment and reward, in short, to other concepts grammatically related to justice. In this way, the explanation and justification of our judgments, for instance in realms like ethics or esthetics or politics, is very similar to the explanation and justification of meaning when we speak; it is related to the way we show what we meant, and to the way we learn new meanings in learning language, and to the way the meanings of words are gradually extended in language itself. In all of these cases, it is a matter of making or finding or showing connections, building bridges, "showing *how* A is (or could be considered) B." In all of these cases, not just *any* explanation or justification will be acceptable. And in all of these cases, that means simultaneously: not just any attempt at making connections will actually work with the particular person addressed, be causally, psychologically adequate to persuading him; and not just anything you say will, in general and objectively, *be* an explanation, a justification, a connection.

Wittgenstein says that giving a reason, an explanation, a justification is like tracing a path to the point where one is. "Giving a reason for something one did or said means showing a *way* which leads to this action. In some cases it means telling the way which one has gone oneself; in others it means describing a way which leads there and is in accordance with certain accepted rules."[22] In just this way, explaining what you meant by something you said, when you are questioned about it, means showing paths that lead from your words to other words in the language. They may be paths you yourself took before or while you spoke, but they may equally well be paths which you did not use, though you could have. Thus, "the question, 'On what grounds do you believe this?' might mean: 'From what are you now deducing it (have you just deduced it)?' But it might also mean: 'What grounds can you produce for this assumption on thinking it over?' "[23]

### FORM AND SUBSTANCE

Socrates and Thrasymachus, then, really do present us with yet another case of a dispute based on extrapolation from different aspects of a word's grammar. But the case is different in kind from any we examined earlier.

[22] Wittgenstein, *Blue and Brown Books*, p. 14; compare p. 145; *Philosophical Investigations*, pars. 525, 536–537, 539, and pp. 196–197; and *Zettel*, tr. by G. E. M. Anscombe, ed. by G. E. M. Anscombe and G. H. von Wright (Berkeley and Los Angeles: University of California Press, 1967), par. 506.

[23] Wittgenstein, *Philosophical Investigations*, par. 479; compare *Lectures and Conversations*, p. 22.

Instead of saying that both protagonists are right in that they start from a grammatical truth, but wrong in extrapolating from it to infinity, ignoring other grammatical truths inconsistent with their extrapolation, we must say something more complex. Socrates is not merely right about part of the meaning of "justice"; he is entirely right about the whole of its meaning. *Nevertheless* Thrasymachus might be right about justice in some particular society, and that would be an important insight about that society. We are, indeed, in a different region of language here, where grammar "plays us different tricks." Where with respect to a concept like "anger," the conceptual puzzle concerns grammatical links among the occasions, expression, and feeling of anger; where with respect to a concept like "knowledge," the conceptual puzzle concerns grammatical links between the occasions for invoking and those for revoking the concept, between the guarantee given and the evidence available; with respect to a concept like "justice," the conceptual puzzle has a different sort of grammatical root.

The concept of justice shares with many other concepts in the region of human action and social institutions what I have elsewhere called a tension between purpose and institutionalization, between substance and form.[24] That tension is essential to their function in language, and is the grammatical source for certain characteristic conceptual puzzles about them. The tension may arise through either of two possible historical sequences. Perhaps men conceive some ideal or goal or purpose, and develop an institution or a set of procedures for achieving and perpetuating that goal through time and in the activities of many men. They draw up a set of laws, or institute a school, or create a new agency. But rules require interpretation, and institutions have a way of developing purposes and directions of their own. After a time, men may find themselves torn between their commitment to the original purpose, and their commitment to the institutions that were supposed to bring it about. Or, conversely, a society may gradually and without any deliberate intent develop certain institutionalized or ritual ways of proceeding, and from these it may eventually abstract rules or principles or ideals. At first these rules or ideals may be merely descriptive abstractions of how the institution works, but after a time they become critical standards in accord with which the institution can be evaluated and reformed. Again the result is a tension between the "ideal substance" and the "practical form" in which it is embodied. This tension, whatever the pattern of its origin, is often embodied and reflected in the concepts associated with the particular practice or institution.

The first kind of causal sequence and its associated tension can be

24 See my *The Concept of Representation* (Berkeley and Los Angeles: University of California Press, 1967), pp. 235–240; and Joseph Tussman, *Obligation and the Body Politic* (New York: Oxford University Press, 1960), p. 86.

seen, for example, in an idea and practice like that of punishment.[25] Punishment is philosophically troubling in much the same way as justice. For on the one hand, punishment means (roughly) harm done to someone in retribution, because he has broken a law or violated a norm. That is what "punishment" means, its Socratic definition. And by that definition it is impossible—grammatically impossible—to punish a man unless he is in fact guilty, has in fact violated the norm. But we have also developed particular institutions for public punishment, and particular formulae and practices for punishing, say, our children; and we have come to call the working of those institutions and practices "punishing." But those institutions and practices sometimes inflict harm on the innocent; and in such cases it makes perfect sense to say "they have punished an innocent man." Indeed, in some contexts the term has come to be almost synonymous with inflicted harm, quite apart from any guilt, as when we say that a football player can take, or actually took, "a lot of punishment." (In much the same way, as Austin points out, the term "deliberately," which originally meant "with or after deliberation," has come often to mean merely the corresponding outward form: "slowly and unhurriedly, *as if* with deliberation.")[26]

The second kind of causal sequence and its associated tension is beautifully illustrated by Piaget's study of the development of the ideas of fairness or justice, and of rules, among children.[27] Piaget maintains that a child's conception of fairness or justice grows largely out of his relations with his peers, as one among equals; and to study the development of such a conception Piaget examines the way in which Swiss boys play and learn the game of marbles. They characteristically learn the game from other children, not from adults, and they play it with other children. And in the course of learning the game itself—the particular rules and the necessary motor skills and strategic devices—the children also learn, develop ideas about, what a game is, what a rule is, where rules come from, that rules can but may not be broken, that and how they can be changed. At the same time, Piaget's study shows that the children also acquire some concepts by which they are eventually able to judge the rules themselves and proposed innovations in the rules. These notions include the idea of justice or fairness, and the idea of what Piaget calls "the spirit of the game."[28] The latter would presumably govern only rules and innovations in the game of marbles (or other games with the same

[25] Compare John Rawls, "Two Concepts of Rules," *Philosophical Review*, LXIV (January 1955); J. B. Mabbott, "Punishment," *Mind*, XLVIII (1939), 152–167; Anthony Quinton, "On Punishment," in Peter Laslett, ed., *Philosophy, Politics and Society* (New York: Macmillan, 1956).

[26] J. L. Austin, *Philosophical Papers* (Oxford: Clarendon Press, 1961), p. 147.

[27] Jean Piaget, *The Moral Judgment of the Child*, tr. by Marjorie Gabain (New York: Collier Books, 1962).

[28] *Ibid.*, pp. 42, 65–76, 98. Piaget's own findings thus cast doubt on his categorical assertion (p. 71) that "procedure alone is obligatory" among the older children.

"spirit"); the former would apply in any game among peers, and probably in many other areas of life as well.

One might suppose that a concept of the spirit of the game or of fairness learned exclusively from and during the playing of marbles would necessarily be conservative with respect to the rules of that game. Those particular rules and ways of playing from which "fairness" is learned, one might suppose, will define what fairness is. (The meaning and content of "justice" in any society will always be in accord with the institutions in which that particular society embodies justice.) But Piaget shows that such is not the case. The children are able to innovate and to accept innovations, sometimes finding the new ways of playing more fair or more in accord with the spirit of the game than the older ways. That this is possible will seem puzzling only if we think of words as labels, as names. For then it will seem strange that a child who has learned to call all the members of a particular family "Smith" would one day somehow decide that one of them is not really a Smith at all, or that some newcomer is more of a Smith than they. But a term like "fairness" or "justice" participates in much more complex language games than mere labeling and is learned from them all. From the entire context of its use, its verbal and worldly relationships, a child can learn not merely what things are considered just by the speakers who use the word, but also what they are *saying* about those things by calling them "just." And that message—the meaning of justice—can then be predicated of other phenomena, or even denied of the phenomena in connection with which the word was first learned. More generally, though we learn the meaning of terms like "justice" and acquire some standards of what is just in connection with existing institutions and practices, we can and do use them to criticize and change those institutions and practices.

Thus, there really can arise tensions between purpose, substance, meaning, on the one hand, and institutionalization, form, conventionalized practice, on the other. This kind of tension can arise only with concepts where meaning is linked to application by way of standards; it cannot arise with a concept like "green," but equally not with a concept like "delicious." I would suggest that it arises with respect to concepts of action and social institutions because an important feature of the function of such concepts in our language and in our lives hinges on the duality of purpose and institutionalization. If our purposes and ideals could not be institutionalized, taught, put into practice in regularized ways, they would remain empty and idle, mysterious blessings which occasionally and inexplicably appear among us, but which we have no power to produce or to prolong. Therefore, their embodiment in social practice or individual action truly is their realization, truly deserves (almost) the same commitment from us as the initial purpose or ideal, is rightly called by the same name. Yet actions fall short of intention, and institutional practice develops a momentum of its own. We need, always, to hold our concepts partly aloof from the practices and institutions in which they are (supposedly) realized, in order to continue to be able to criticize, to renovate and to revise.[29]

Thrasymachus and Socrates debated in a time when, as in our own, a considerable disparity had developed between the meanings of concepts like justice and the standards by which people judged justness, the institutional forms and practices in which it was supposed to be embodied. That is how both Socrates and Thrasymachus stand "outside" the accepted conventions of their grammar. Each has chosen a different branch of the bifurcation. They both agree that the term "justice" is a sham when used in connection with contemporary standards and institutions. But Socrates opts for the meaning of the term, against those standards and institutions; while Thrasymachus opts for the *Realpolitik* of those institutions, against the traditional meaning of the term. Each position has its concomitant dangers: hypocrisy and ineffectiveness in the one, immorality and a different sort of ineffectiveness in the other.

We have said that Thrasymachus might be right about some particular society, where standards of what is just and unjust have become sufficiently corrupted, or social perception sufficiently distorted. But Thrasymachus himself proposed his thesis not about some particular corrupted society, but about all human society whatsoever. And if he is right about *that*, then what we have said about form and substance, about using the concept of justice to criticize existing practice, is nonsense. If he is right about that, then Socrates' being right about the meaning of "justice" makes no dent in Thrasymachus' argument at all; for then that meaning, and the word's signaling functions, are a colossal fraud, a socially shared and perpetuated illusion. Which is, indeed, what Thrasymachus thought.

But we need to look more closely at that alleged possibility, that seeming sociological generalization of Thrasymachus'. It has all the earmarks of being a typical conceptual "insight," an extrapolation to infinity like the "insight" that "all is flux" because nothing ever remains absolutely fixed or permanent. Such theses, as we have seen, are not false; we cannot really deny the possibilities they allege. Nor are they nonsensical. Yet they do not fully make sense, either. They need to be treated with Wittgensteinian questions that gradually return the relevant concepts to their home grounds, where their sense is fully clear. Thus we ask when con-

---

[29] But Albert Ehrenzweig warns against saying that form without substance, positive law without natural law, "is purely arbitrary," while substance without form, natural law without positive law, "is ineffective." That formulation, he argues, obscures the truth that positive and natural law, and correspondingly form and substance, "are not only supplementary but identical," because law is intentional, quasi-performative, or as he says, "justice-directed": "Psychoanalytic Jurisprudence: A Common Language for Babylon," *Columbia Law Review*, 65:2 (1965), pp. 1336, 1342. I thank Professor Walter Weyrauch for calling my attention to this article.

cepts like "flux," "change," "permanence," "fixity," are used; and find that they are fully meaningful only in particular mutual contrasts.

So, too, with Thrasymachus, though the characteristic philosophical fear of or desire for what is hidden, is different here. Here the problem is not in our relationship to physical reality—that we might always be mistaken, or that men might always lie in what they say to us; here the characteristic danger or hope is not lies but hypocrisy or bias—that men might be incapable of objective judgment. That difference in philosophical concerns, I think, tells us some important things about the grammatical functions of a word like "justice," and how they differ from those of a word like "knowledge" or like "see." But we must ask how its possible for Thrasymachus, or for us in following his argument, to step entirely outside all human societies and cultures, and see through their universal illusion? If all human societies in all times have corrupted or biased standards of what is just, standards which serve the interest of the ruling elite only, how is Thrasymachus able to determine this fact? By what standards does he judge or measure those other social standards to be biased? What can the term "biased" mean in the absence of any standards by which bias is to be measured, apart from any contrast with what is straight or fair? The answer would seem to be that Thrasymachus himself implicitly makes reference to the Socratic meaning of "justice," and that his standards for detecting bias are learned from the *claim* his fellow-citizens make in judging something just or unjust. In exactly the same way, Marx had a clear and fully articulated idea of true justice by which he judged his own society's institutions and found them woefully wanting.[30] If we ask how he came by that idea in such a corrupt society, the answer would seem to be that he learned from the meanings of words, not just from their apparent reference.

The point is that a concept like "justice" includes, in all of us, both form and substance, both conventionalized, traditional social practices and an idea that is an ideal by which to measure them. That idea and ideal are not simply the products, the captives, of the examples from which they are taught, for they are not merely labels and are not taught merely from examples. We are always potentially able to pry the idea loose from some particular example, and reassess its applicability. That, I think, is a major function of political discourse in our lives. It is, of course, a lifelong work, never completed. Thrasymachus can be right about particular societies at particular times to a remarkable degree; it is amazing how blind we can be to the social facts around us, how much habituated to the traditional or accepted ways of thinking, how reluctant to think critically on our own, because critical thought, once begun, is likely to require of us remedial action. But the possibility for critical thought and remedial

[30] Compare Ralf Dahrendorf, *Marx in Perspektive* (Hanover: J. H. W. Dietz, 1953).

action is always there, and it is kept alive precisely by the meaning of concepts like "justice," the "ideal" meaning that Socrates insists on preserving. In a society where standards of justice have become corrupted or biased, unrelated to the meaning of "justice" except by the force of habit and inertia, Thrasymachus is right to refuse to accept words at their face value, right to challenge the hypocrisy of corrupted speech. But Socrates is right to refuse to accept, to insist on challenging, corrupted action and corrupted lives. Thrasymachus' kind of detachment and standing outside of the conventional hypocrisy can help to restore health and coherence inside. But it can do so only in combination with the Socratic definition and its kind of standing outside of corrupted standards. If all societies are necessarily and equally corrupt, if the idea of justice is a sham, then reform, revolt, or maintenance of the *status quo* are all equally pointless.

Clearly, we have not achieved a satisfactory understanding of the nature of Socrates' quarrel with Thrasymachus, or of other disputes cast in the same form, or of justice and concepts like it. But perhaps some progress has been made. We have eliminated a few of the more tempting wrong approaches, and have tried a few that seem more promising. We still need a much clearer account of how Thrasymachus' kind of "discovery" differs on the one hand from the discoveries of science ("The evening star is really the planet Venus"), and on the other hand from the purely conceptual "insights" discussed earlier ("Strictly speaking, we can never really know what someone else is feeling"). We have spoken repeatedly about standards and bias and justification in connection with justice; but such ways of talking run diametrically counter to the conventional contemporary assumptions about "normative" or "value" judgments. They require an accounting, some attempt at which will be made in the discussion of judgment. We have made some progress on the topic of human action and institutions, and their characteristic complementarity of description and rule, of form and substance. This topic, too, will recur in the discussion of judgment, but needs much fuller exploration. Both it and the whole matter of the tension between inside and outside views will also come up again when we turn to social science. But first of all we shall have to take up a seemingly quite separate topic: the nature of membership and of the political.

# IX

## Membership, the Social, and
## the Political

AMONG THE CENTRAL concerns of political theory and social science
has always been the problem of membership: that whole cluster of
questions, issues, and difficulties having to do with how the individual is
a part of a larger collectivity, or how we are to think of individual and
collectivity in relation to each other. These problems include such familiar
concerns of social science as the nature of culture, how an individual is
shaped into a member of a particular society, how creativity and change
take place, how personality and culture interact, the roles of choice and
causality in historical change, and so on. They include also such familiar
concerns of political theory as the relationship between public and private,
the problem of political obligation, the nature of citizenship and of authority. In addition, both social scientists and political theorists have been
occupied with distinguishing among different kinds of membership; for
example, with what distinguishes political phenomena from other aspects
of human collective life, whether political membership is distinctive, which
phenomena are political, whether all peoples have political institutions.

To these issues, we shall attempt to apply a Wittgensteinian perspective
in this chapter. But we shall find that Wittgenstein and ordinary-language
philosophy allow of more than one approach here; it will not be enough
to follow the first lead that comes to mind, but necessary, as usual, to
investigate. Perhaps the most obvious approach is a simple exploitation
of the phenomenon of language itself, as a model of membership. Such
an approach is not, of course, uniquely drawn from Wittgenstein, but
rather from the general contemporary interest in language. We shall find
it an instructive source of insights, but specifically misleading about politics. Therefore we shall supplement it with an investigation of political
discourse, modelled on our earlier discussion of moral discourse; and with
some examination of the concept of the political itself.

Our explication of the Wittgensteinian vision of language earlier attempted to hold in balance two seemingly conflicting themes about the relationship of an individual speaker and his language, or his language group. On the one hand, Wittgenstein seems to stress nominalistic, individualistic, even relativistic themes: each child learns and interprets language regularities for himself; any rule or principle needs to be interpreted; words must always be capable of projection into new and unexpected contexts; concepts are fragmented and often their grammar has inconsistent implications; and since what is "in the world" depends very much on our concepts, the world itself shares these qualities. Yet, on the other hand, Wittgenstein and Austin also stress that there are mistakes in using language; that words do have meanings that can be looked up in a good dictionary; that not just any new projection of a concept will be acceptable; that not just any excuse will be appropriate; that we can't say just anything at any time and in any context; that it is not merely up to each individual what his words mean; and that in a significant sense we all live in the same, continuing, objective world, and our real activity in that world is what underlies and shapes our concepts.

This difficult dual perspective, I would suggest, is Wittgenstein's attempt to do justice to the manifest realities of how it is with human beings and our language. A natural language is obviously a social product. It exists before any particular individual speaker is born; he is initiated into it; the changes he makes in it during his lifetime are likely to be infinitesimal; and it remains after his death. Clearly, he is the product of his language much more completely than it is his product. A baby growing up in France becomes a French speaker, one growing up in Japan becomes a Japanese speaker; our native language is not a matter of choice but is absorbed from our society. The society shapes the individual speaker in accord with its own image. We master our native language with sufficient uniformity so that we can speak to and be understood by the other speakers of that language, so that it makes sense to say there is *a* language called English and another called Japanese. And these languages can be described as objective entities, apart from any particular single speaker of them; it is possible to write dictionaries and grammars. Moreover, when languages change, as they do, that change occurs in systematic, patterned ways, whose principles can be studied and described. Thus, language is a patterned unity greater than any of the individuals who participate in it and independent of any one of them.

At the same time, our language is one of the most intimate and significant constitutive features of our selves. We not only speak in that language, but we think in it as well. Its categories are what each of us has available for conceptualizing and understanding the world; its framework is the basis for all but the most basic and inarticulate of our thoughts. What we can say and think is very largely determined by the language we have available. If we are American we can think in terms of "fairness," as a German cannot, but we cannot think in terms of *"Gemütlichkeit."* We become the particular persons we become as we grow up because of the language community in which we grow up. The same is, of course, true of most cultural patterns; we become a certain person, with certain language, table manners, carriage, style of humor, taste in food, and so on indefinitely, all by being shaped by one culture rather than another. The culture, like the language that carries it, is first imposed on (or at least offered to) the individual from the outside, but eventually it becomes a part of his very self. We do not normally experience the categories of our language as constraints on our ability to think or to express ourselves; on the contrary, they are the very means that enable us to think articulately and to express ourselves.

One insight that the model of language membership suggests, then, is that our customary distinctions between individual and society, between the self and some larger whole to which it belongs, are not fixed, mutually exclusive dichotomies. Rather, they concern different aspects of, different perspectives on, a single reality. Society is not just "outside" the individual, confronting him, but inside him as well, part of who he is. All of the individuals in their relationships, including relationships with the past, constitute the society. Who an individual is both distinguishes him from all others and relates him to them. And language both exemplifies that duality and is its instrument. As Arendt says, it "has the twofold character of equality and distinction. If men were not equal, they could neither understand each other and those who came before them nor plan for the future and foresee the needs of those who will come after them. If men were not distinct, each human being distinguished from any other who is, was, or will ever be, they would need neither speech nor action to make themselves understood."[1]

In Wittgensteinian terms one might say "individual," "society," "culture," "state," are, first of all, concepts; they are words in our language. That does not mean that society is not real but a mere concept, any more than it means that the individual is not real but a mere concept. Individuals are real and so is society, but they are not separate entities of the same kind, and both are dependent on our conceptualization. We are tempted to suppose that society is a mere concept while individuals are really real because individual persons have tangible, visible physical bodies. But deeper reflection easily reveals that our concept of the individual person is by no means equivalent to that of his physical body; rather, it is every bit as complex, as abstract, as *conceptual*, as our concepts of society or culture. What an individual is depends as much on the grammar of "individual" as what a society is depends on the grammar of "society." Once that fact has penetrated into our habits of thought, new ways of investigating old issues about individuals and social wholes become accessible.

[1] Hannah Arendt, *The Human Condition* (Garden City: Doubleday, 1958), pp. 155–156.

Consider, more specifically, how language changes over time. Languages, after all, do not remain fixed; they are in constant, gradual change. And that change is not autonomous growth in a living organism, the language, independent of the individual human beings who speak it. Language change simply reflects the systematic, widespread changes in the way individuals speak. Language consists of the speech patterns of many individuals over time, and each of those individuals speaks as he pleases. No one forces him to adopt the existing language patterns or to innovate or change them. What changes take place occur freely and naturally in the speech of individuals. Yet these changes nevertheless are not random; they are systematic and have a direction; and they are in accord with patterns already observable in the language. Whorf has said it is almost "as if the personal mind, which selects words but is largely oblivious to pattern, were in the grip of a higher, far more intellectual mind which has very little notion of houses and beds and soup kettles, but can systematize and mathematize on a scale and scope that no mathematician of the schools ever remotely approached."[2] What happens, clearly, is that the millions of small and random changes made once or repeatedly by individuals become changes in *the* language only if they occur widely, or are widely adopted by many individuals. And that will happen only if they fill a need, are in accord with patterns already widely shared. For example, one of the best known "laws" of linguistic change is the tendency to assimilate irregular forms of expression to the regularities found in the rest of a language—to conjugate irregular verbs like regular ones, for instance. Often a number of different language regularities will bear on particular changes—reinforcing each other, or sometimes conflicting. Thus, Sapir lists four separate "reasons" of this kind for the increasing tendency among English speakers to say "Who did you see?" rather than "Whom did you see?"[3] The pressure to conform to existing patterns, to assimilate deviant cases, apparently is at work in all of us; as it produces some particular change in many of us the language changes.

One is tempted to speak of a kind of "natural selection" among changes in individual speech patterns: only the shared ones survive. The particular variations and innovations individuals introduce in language, Sapir says, "are random phenomena, like the waves of the sea, moving backward and forward in purposeless flux." But language as a whole changes systematically; it has a "drift," and that drift has "direction. In other words, only those individual variations embody it or carry it which move in a certain direction, just as only certain wave movements in the bay outline the tide. The drift of a language is constituted by the unconscious selection

[2] Benjamin Lee Whorf, *Language, Thought, and Reality*, ed. by John B. Carroll (Cambridge: M. I. T. Press, 1967), p. 257; compare Sapir, *Language* (New York: Harcourt, Brace & World, 1949), p. 150: "Language is not merely something that is spread out in space, as it were—a series of reflections in individual minds of one and the same timeless picture. Language moves down time in a current of its own making. It has a drift."

[3] Sapir, *op. cit.*, pp. 156–157.

on the part of its speakers of those individual variations that are cumulative in some special direction."[4]

Thus, language change seems to present us with an illuminating, perhaps even with a seductive, model of how individual choice and innovation can be combined with necessary causal laws at the social level, how individual freedom can be compatible with membership. "In the act of speaking," as Merleau-Ponty has seen, "the subject, in his tone and in his style, bears witness to his autonomy, since nothing is more proper to him, and yet at the same moment, and without a contradiction, he is turned toward the linguistic community and is dependent on his language. The will to speak is one and the same as the will to be understood. The presence of the individual in the institution, and of the institution in the individual is evident in the case of linguistic change. It is often the wearing down of a form which suggests to us a new way of using the means of discrimination which are present in the language at a given time. The constant need for communication leads us to invent and to accept a new usage which is not deliberate and yet which is systematic."[5]

Now consider, for example, how this sort of account of change in language parallels and illuminates the attempts of Marx and particularly Engels to explain how individual choice results in patterned historical social change. Arendt points out that like all historians and social theorists writing since the French Revolution, Marx and Engels were "confronted with the double riddle" that human history is the product of individual actions, of "many wills operating in different directions," as Engels said, and that at the same time "the sum of recorded actions which we call history nevertheless seems to make sense."[6] Engels is not merely aware of individual choice, but takes it as crucial to the distinction between human history and events in inanimate nature; yet the pattern is there, and the causal laws seem evident. He says that in human history "the actors are all endowed with consciousness, are men acting with deliberation or passion, working toward definite goals; nothing happens without a conscious purpose, without an intended aim. But this distinction, important as it is for historical investigation, . . . cannot alter the fact that the course of history is governed by inner general laws."[7]

When he tries to make clear how this duality is possible, Engels adduces very much the same kinds of arguments that linguists articulate about innovation and change in language. First, though change results from individual choice and action, the forces moving men to choose and act may

[4] Ibid., p. 155.
[5] Maurice Merleau-Ponty, In Praise of Philosophy, tr. by John Wild and James M. Edie (Evanston: Northwestern University Press, 1963), pp. 54–55.
[6] Hannah Arendt, "Religion and Politics," Confluence, II (September 1953), p. 115.
[7] Friedrich Engels, "Ludwig Feuerbach and the End of Classical German Philosophy," in Lewis S. Feuer, ed., Marx and Engels (Garden City: Doubleday, 1959), p. 230.

be widely uniform, so that many separate, similar choices are made at more or less the same time. As in language drift, so in history: the overall pattern of change is uniform because it reflects uniformity in "the driving forces" behind men's motives, the "historical causes which transform themselves into motives in the brains of the actors."[8] Secondly, though individual choices may be random and at cross-purposes, their interaction in given circumstances may nevertheless produce unintended, patterned consequences. As in language drift, so in history: some innovations catch hold and spread and become a lasting part of the language because conditions are ripe for them. "It is precisely the resultant of these many wills operating in different directions and of their manifold effects upon the outer world that constitutes history."[9]

Or consider the classical problem addressed by a whole series of major political theorists: the social contract. Though each theorist develops a distinctive line of argument, the basic problem is always the same: how to create or understand unity in multitude. The social-contract theorists always take for granted that men are by nature separate, autonomous, self-contained individuals, without relationship, membership, affiliation, or obligation; their problem then is to create such ties. The separate individual, they assume, is natural; relationship and authority are human conventions which must be created by men. Yet their task is always difficult, for there seems to be no way to create obligation or authority from scratch, without presupposing some conventions from which to build. The theorists find that they must make use of some device like a contract or covenant or mutual promises, so some such device must precede society; and they find that they must provide men a motive for using this device—usually in terms of rational self-interest. Often they provide these necessities by means of a law of nature that precedes social conventions.

But the transition to civil society is nevertheless always problematic in contract theory. Self-interest just does not seem to get translated into an obligation to the public interest. For, while it is true that an individual benefits from the existence of society and civility, and that they could not exist if most people did not behave civilly; nevertheless it is also true that any particular individual could reap the benefits without paying the price. This difficulty can, in effect, be overcome by building increasing amounts of disguised public obligation into the law of nature, but that has other disadvantages. The contract begins to seem less central, political obligation begins to seem natural, or the obligatory quality of contracts is called into question.[10]

[8] *Ibid.*, p. 231.

[9] *Ibid.*

[10] Compare David Hume, "Of the Original Contract," in Sir Ernest Barker, ed., *The Social Contract* (New York: Oxford University Press, 1960), p. 161: "We are bound to obey our sovereign, it is said, because we have given a tacit promise to that purpose. But why are we bound to observe our promise? . . . If the reason be asked of that obedience, which we are bound to pay to government, . . . Your

One need not be interested in language to suggest that some of these theoretical difficulties might derive from the initial assumption that people are by nature separate, self-contained, unrelated beings, somehow sprung into the world fully adult and independent. But a concern with language can stimulate or support such a suggestion; and I myself pursued that line of criticism on just such a basis at one time.[11] In reality, contrary to the assumptions of contract theory, we are born into society as virtual nonpersons. We become persons, become who we are, only by internalizing (some of) the norms, standards, and patterns of our society. We do not agree contractually to do so; we grow into them. Thus our concepts of promises and contracts are learned, not chosen. And even individual self-interest is very much a social product, taking quite different forms in different times and places.

Language seems to provide a model of membership showing how norms can be learned, acquired without choice and without a real alternative, and yet end up being obligatory. For, after all, there are mistakes in language, unacceptable projections. The rules of grammar seem to bind individual speakers even though they were never contractually adopted; we obey them because they have become part of our selves. They are not obstacles to our freedom, but our very means of free self-expression. As Joseph Tussman has said, "our habits are our powers; they are bonds only when we try to break them."[12] Evidently these considerations are related to that complementarity of rule and statement we have mentioned before, the fact that the same proposition may be sometimes a rule to be followed or enforced, sometimes a factual description of what is (to be) done, of "what we do." The rule may be acquired by the child from the behavior of adults around him, whom he imitates because he wants to be like them; or it may be deliberately taught and enforced with rewards and punishments. When it is successfully internalized, it becomes again description rather than rule: a fact of what the person does, who he is.[13]

---

answer is, *Because we should keep our word.* But . . . you find yourself embarrassed when it is asked, *Why are we bound to keep our word?* Nor can you give any answer but what would, immediately, without any circuit, have accounted for our obligation to allegiance."

[11] Hanna Pitkin, "Obligation and Consent," *American Political Science Review*, LIX (December 1965), 990–999, and LX (March 1966), 39–52.

[12] Joseph Tussman, *Obligation and the Body Politic* (New York: Oxford University Press, 1960), p. 7.

[13] Compare Torgny T. Segersedt, *Die Macht des Wortes* (Zürich: Pan-Verlag, 1947), pp. 116–117: "Das Ich aber, das in einer Gemeinschaft geboren wird, wird nicht umgeformt, sondern aufgebaut. . . . Das Ich wird durch den gesellschaftlichen Kontakt geschaffen, es wächst aus ihm hervor; das Ich kann nicht bereits existieren und dann erst den Kontakt mit anderen suchen, sondern es wird durch den Kontakt mit anderen geformt." Or, see Kenneth Minogue, *The Liberal Mind* (New York: Random House, 1968), p. 77: "To an eager young military volunteer, an account of his duties as a soldier has a purely descriptive force; it tells him what is involved in an activity for which he already has a great deal of enthusiasm. Should this enthusiasm wane with experience, then tasks like cleaning his rifle and polishing his buttons will become duties in a far more prescriptive sense; they become things

Evidently such a model of obligation and self is what informed Rousseau's vision of a free society—the product of a social contract, but not really a contractual association at all. Rousseau uses the conventional language of contract to express very different ideas, for he sees that society transforms the very self of "natural" man, changing not merely his obligations but also his desires and interests and needs. In becoming a member of a healthy society, natural man's "faculties will develop, his ideas take on a wider scope, his sentiments become ennobled, and his whole soul be so elevated" that he is in reality transformed "from a limited and stupid animal into an intelligent being and a Man."[14] Thus the acquisition of cultural norms in general, and of language in particular, seems to offer the ideal model of what Rousseau sought: a form of membership in which each individual is truly a member, truly "united to his fellows" and bound by the norms of the group, and yet is subject to no compulsion from outside but merely "renders obedience to his own will, and remains as free as he was before."[15] His freedom lies in obeying the norms; they are his powers, not constraints on him. Of course, he *can* do otherwise, as we can deviate from language regularities and moral norms. Yet normally we have no impulse to deviate from language regularities; and when we violate our own moral code, we recognize that the conflict lies within ourselves, that we have acted immorally.

Others have gone beyond Rousseau, to take language membership as a model not just of a free society, but of politics in general. Oakeshott, for instance, speaks of political activity as the "exploration of the intimations" of traditional patterns in a political community, continuing their development in directions to which they already trend.[16] Political life, he says, should emerge naturally and incrementally out of existing patterns, without ever coming to the point of large-scale, deliberate changes or discontinuities. Individual choice is involved, of course, but on the model of individual speech in language: "The politics of a community are not less individual (and not more so) than its language, and they are learned and practiced in the same manner."[17] That is, the political patterns or rules antedate any particular individual; he assimilates them into himself as he grows; he deviates from them when he has the impulse to do so, but that impulse will itself be governed by the patterns he has internalized,

---

which he has to do as a condition of being something else. . . . It also appears to be a common experience that duties begin as things which 'ought' to be done, and end by becoming part of the structure of a person's life, so that he feels lost without the doing of them."

[14] Jean-Jacques Rousseau, *The Social Contract*, in Barker, ed., *The Social Contract*, p. 185.

[15] *Ibid.*, p. 180.

[16] Michael Oakeshott, *Rationalism in Politics* (New York: Basic Books, 1962), pp. 124, 133–136.

[17] *Ibid.*, p. 129.

and it will become widespread, become a change in the system, only when others share it. From such a perspective, politics is "the activity of attending to the general arrangement of a set of people." Oakeshott says "attending to" rather than "making" arrangements, because in political states "the activity is never offered the blank sheet of infinite possibility. In any generation, even the most revolutionary, the arrangements which are enjoyed always far exceed those which are recognized to stand in need of attention."[18]

The analogy is suggestive, Oakeshott's argument is plausible, and seems in accord with Wittgenstein's stress on the complexity of language and the plurality of particular cases, how individual innovations are deeply controlled. Small wonder then if despite Wittgenstein's silence on the subject of politics, many commentators are convinced the implications of his doctrine for political thought must be conservative. I do not find them so. We need not blindly apply to politics the first image that Wittgensteinian vision of language brings to mind; he himself would urge us to investigate its implications and to look around for alternatives. And when we do that, we notice important ways in which political membership is not like membership in a language group, or a culture, or even a society. It is true, of course, that part of the culture we internalize—the behavior patterns, manners, values, standards, and language—is relevant to political life, forms our "political culture." And clearly the political culture we have acquired, the political selves we have become, undergird everything we subsequently do in politics: what we will want to do, how we will perceive political events, what political means will be possible for us, and so on. But they are not the whole of politics, and they do not characterize what is distinctive about it. Let us look briefly at only three areas of significant difference.

It is possible in political life, and does happen from time to time, for men to choose, deliberately and consciously, to initiate major changes: create new modes of political action, carry through a revolution, band together into a new political association, invent a new constitutional form, and so on. No doubt each such innovation has roots in the past, and the way new institutions will work in practice depends much on the habits, the traditional political culture, of the individuals who live under them. And no doubt there is change and innovation in language, too. But the role and character of political action is quite different: it is collective, public, rather than individual, and it is at least partly deliberate and intentional. People simply do not stage linguistic revolutions, draft new linguistic patterns, or band together into a new language group. It is possible to legislate some linguistic change, and that has on occasion been done in the service of cultural nationalism. But that is hardly typical of innovation in language.

[18] *Ibid.*, p. 112; compare p. 126.

A second way in which the analogy of language membership is misleading when directly applied to politics, is that it neglects the roles played by conflict, power, and interest. It is misleading about what is at stake in politics. Rarely if ever does some individual or group have a serious stake in the maintenance or alteration of linguistic patterns. Rarely if ever is change in language effected or prevented by the exercise of power. Again, it can happen, but such cases are themselves instructive, for they are examples of language politicized. Where two or more language and culture groups coexist in a single political association, questions of what shall be the official language, what language taught in schools, can be highly political and charged with interest and power. Where a single nation is polarized into distinctive subcultures—classes, regions, generations—they may develop distinctive ways of using their shared language to the point where communication between the subcultures becomes difficult. Such subdivisions of language, too, may have great political significance, play a role in power relationships. But these are special cases, cases where language is politicized. And precisely in such cases the analogy with language will *not* suggest free, uncoerced, automatically harmonious change.

A third way in which the analogy between language and politics misleads us involves the mechanisms of enforcement. The regularities of cultural patterns and language are internalized; they do not need to be enforced. But the laws and regulations of a political order are quite different. Though some of them may well be internalized, on the whole laws govern precisely the sort of conduct we *do* have an impulse to engage in, or an interest in engaging in. That is why laws carry sanctions; they must sometimes be enforced because they are sometimes violated. With language rules it is not a matter of "obedience" or "enforcement."

But again, closer scrutiny of the model of language can do more than merely show that the analogy with politics is false; it can teach us how politics is different and, thus, what politics is like. How is it that "society" goes about "imposing" the rules or regularities of culture, of language, on its members? Certain things are obvious: no single individual or group of persons consciously invents or imposes these norms. There is no "government" to act for society in this realm—neither to legislate nor to enforce. If uniformity results, if the individual becomes in fact a standard speaker of the shared language, it is simply because he has acquired the uniform patterns already shared by other individuals around him, with whom he comes in contact. The child learns its language not from "society" as a whole, nor from an official rule book, but from a relatively small number of persons it encounters, supplemented later by communications media, books, and the like. To the extent that these sources are already uniform, the child becomes part of that uniformity. If they are uniformly deviant from a larger social pattern—as in a particular dialect-area or subculture—the child will become deviant in the same way. If they are not uniform but diverse, the child may acquire mixed or inconsistent patterns, or may eventually become partly or wholly bilingual.[19] With respect to such cultural norms, the wholeness or uniformity of a society consists of nothing more mysterious than the acquisition of like patterns by children exposed to like patterns. That is how and why language can constitute a unity beyond individuals, and a group of people be truly said to speak *one* language.[20]

Politics, by contrast, is characterized by the active enforcement of norms, typically through a specialized agency, and by the possibility of deliberate, active, collective innovation or imposition of patterns. The effect of the analogy with language will therefore be to mislead us into imagining a politics that has become totally noncoercive on the one hand, and totally passive at the collective level on the other. A theorist like Rousseau accordingly leads us to confuse political life with cultural education; and that is why his political vision, so clearly aimed at perfect freedom, comes in the end to resemble perfect tyranny.

There are spheres of human life, like language, where all norms are internalized so that they become our way of self-expression. There are other spheres where norms are internalized, but inner conflict is also possible, as impulse or interest run counter to the dictates of those norms; morality, I think, is such a sphere. Political life has underpinning of both these kinds, but crucial and distinctive aspects of it are different from either, involving not internalized, implicit norms, but explicit ones, consciously adopted and externally enforced. To interpret political life entirely on the model of language, culture patterns, morality, or education is to obscure this crucial difference, and thereby to endanger both politics itself and political freedom. For it means assigning to external, political authority the power to enforce norms against individuals as if those norms had in fact been internalized by them, as if no enforcement were taking place. Conflict is disguised and denied.

It is one thing, then, to comprehend the way in which a "society" perpetuates itself by producing individuals who share in its uniformities. It is quite another to think of a particular agency of society as creating, imposing, and enforcing norms on the members. Confusing the two results in special, rather than general visions of politics: the enforced freedom of Rousseau, the incremental conservatism of Oakeshott. About political life in general it is misleading. But that would suggest that there may, after all, be good reason for the contract theorist's impulse to picture men as separate, self-contained adults, to stress their capacity for choice and innovation rather than their development through the internalization of

---

[19] See, for example, Werner Leopold, *The Speech Development of a Bilingual Child* (Evanston and Chicago: Northwestern University Press, 1939–1949).

[20] Tullio de Mauro, *Ludwig Wittgenstein* (Dordrecht: D. Reidel, 1967), p. 53.

social patterns. As political actors, they are or must be seen as adults. Yet the contract theorists are surely wrong to construe that as implying that those men have no obligations. What would be useful here is a new, critical account of political obligation that visualizes the independence and responsibility of active citizenship against a background of sociological insight into the nature of political culture.

POLITICAL DISCOURSE

An alternative way to inquire into the nature of politics and political membership, also from a Wittgensteinian perspective, would be to investigate political discourse as a language region, as Cavell and Austin and others discuss moral discourse. Clearly, political discourse, like moral discourse, concerns human action, and that action is not merely described by disinterested observers. Political discourse is itself a part of, is used in the course of, political activity by the participants. Accordingly, one would expect it to reflect, as moral discourse does, the dangerous unpredictability of action, its potential for going wrong or producing unexpected consequences. And one would expect it to face the same difficulties about the identification of actions; in politics, too, merely establishing the facts, what the situation is, is likely to have definitive consequences and therefore to be a central part of the discussion.

But there are other respects in which the parallel with moral discourse clearly will not hold. We spoke of moral discourse as characteristically dialogue, personal conversation about an action that has gone wrong or done damage, an attempt to restore the fabric of relationship. No one would be tempted to construe political discourse along such lines. In the first place, however one might construe it, political discourse is surely not personal dialogue among two or a very few persons directly affected by an action that one of them took. By contrast with such an image, political questions strike one as being of larger scope and scale, addressed to a larger audience, cast in a more general and impersonal mode. Unlike moral dialogue, political discourse is characteristically public speech, both with respect to its participants and with respect to its subject matter. Of course one can have personal conversations about politics, and some personal conversations can have absolutely crucial effects on political events. Just so, we said, one can also speak publicly about moral issues. But public sermons are not what moral discourse is for, what it is primarily about; and personal relationships are not the point of political discourse. There is no such thing as private politics, intimate politics.

There is a corresponding difference also in subject matter. Where moral discourse centers on the action of an individual, for which he bears personal responsibility and which has affected one or a few others he confronts directly, the topic of political discourse is likely to be public

204

action—the actions of groups of people, particularly of institutionally organized groups, or the publicly authoritative or publicly significant actions of individuals. Further, we suggested that moral discourse is primarily retrospective, helping to restore relationship after an action gone wrong; although of course it also plays a role in commitments and decisions about future actions. In political discourse, the balance is likely to tip the other way: though the assessment of past actions is not excluded, the central concern is communication about future collective action. Political discourse is about what is jointly to be done, and how it is to be done. If the central question of moral discourse might be characterized as "what was done?" the central question in politics would have to be, as Tussman suggests, "what shall we do?"[21] Only, that formulation tends to gloss over both the problematic identification of various courses of action (*what*, exactly, will we be *doing* if we pursue this course of action?), and the problematic membership that is always at stake (who are *we*; and who will we be if we pursue this course of action?).

So far the parallels and contrasts between moral and political discourse are fairly straightforward and accessible. But answers become more equivocal when we turn to questions of rationality, validity, and truth. Earlier, we contrasted moral with scientific discourse, saying that in science rationality consists in moving from premises all can accept in steps all can follow to conclusions all must accept. But the "all" means "all competent in science"; scientific discourse is the province of a special elite with shared training in what constitutes scientific procedure, evidence, and modes of resolution. We said that in morality, by contrast, no such elite exists; all men can participate in moral discourse. And rationality does not depend on reaching agreement—in particular, not on reaching agreement about the right thing to have been done, not on reaching agreement without changed relationship. We said that the criteria of validity in scientific argument, of what is enough to call a claim into question or to refute a doubt, are interpersonally standardized; but in moral discourse what is enough forms part of the argument. Here, each protagonist elaborates his own position, and rationality requires not so much accepting the other's position as being willing to take it into account, to address the other's cares and commitments. The ultimate purpose, and the hope, is for the restoration of relationship; but rationality and validity depend not on that but on the truthful revelation of one's position, of one's self.

What shall we say of political discourse in these regards? Is there, for example, an elite of professional experts? It seems that any answer to that question would be tendentious, already implying a particular type of political system. If one says there are no generally recognized experts, that, as in morality, each man must ultimately "do his politics for himself,"

[21] Tussman, *op. cit.*, p. 16.

one seems to be presupposing a democratic, participatory model. If one proclaims instead the universality of political elites, the significance of authority and hierarchy in political life, one seems to be presupposing an elitist model. Political discourse seems to imply both a plurality of legitimate views, and a kind of authority or organization absent from moral discourse. Certainly political elites are different from scientific ones, play a different role with respect to political discourse. The nature of elite education, the process of selection, the manner of assessing competence, are clearly very different. More significantly, the selection of the elite often forms an important part of politics, their qualifications an important topic of political discourse. Even the extent to which an elite should monopolize the field can itself be a significant political question; parallel questions about science are not an important part of scientific investigation. No doubt these differences have to do with the differing kinds of questions at issue in the two realms. Political discourse is concerned not primarily with how things work or what things are like, but with what we are to do. Again, the topic is action. So interest plays a role here that is relatively absent from scientific discourse.

If there is any elite in political discourse, is it, like the elite of science, agreed primarily on methods for resolving disputes—what will count as evidence, what constitutes a conclusive argument? There does not seem to be a recongizable kind of "political proof" or "political method" to correspond to scientific proof and method; in this respect, politics seems more like morality. Yet one might argue that the methods for resolving political disputes are not canons of proof or validity, but simply established *institutions*, that the resolving of disputes is precisely what political institutions are for. But in science, rationality and competence depend on acceptance of the standardized methods; shall we say then that competence and rationality in political discourse depend on acceptance of the established institutions? That is a familiar position, but again a tendentious one: that no rational man would question established political procedures and arrangements, but only seek his interests through and within them. But that is not merely to deny that revolution can be a political act; it is also to ignore the extent to which the methods and institutions of politics are in flux, are themselves consciously and deliberately revised in the course of political life, are assessed and disputed in political discourse. Thus, in a way, the methods for resolving disputes in politics must themselves be part of the dispute.

Here political apparently contrasts with both moral and scientific discourse. Disputes over the methods and canons for settling scientific issues are not themselves scientific; but disputes over political institutions are political. Moral discourse involves the elaboration of a personal position within a framework of inherited, traditional concepts; it is, we said, adjudicative rather than legislative. Political discourse, by contrast, strikes us as legislative, or rather as centered on political action, which is legislative.[22] There are traditional concepts, principles, institutions in politics, but reviewing and revising them is a familiar and frequent part of political life and thus a significant function of political discourse.

We said that, in science, everyone competent knows what constitutes a valid challenge to, or substantiation of, a claim that has been made. In morality, by contrast, one participant may competently and rationally reject the valid, rational position taken by another. What he cannot do, we said, is to reject the relevance of the other's concern; and we related this to the requirement that the other be treated as a person, with attention to his cares and commitments. Here again conflicting answers seem possible about political discourse. Certainly politics is often contrasted with morality, as being a realm where there is no right and wrong except what works, so that political discourse may seem the natural home of rhetoric, propaganda, and manipulation. Yet one may feel that even if these are common, they are not the essence but a perversion of political discourse. Again, either conclusion about political discourse seems to imply, or to presuppose, a particular style of political life.

We encounter similar difficulties in trying to say whether rationality in political discourse does or does not depend on reaching agreement. It is surely evident that intelligent, rational men often continue to hold incompatible political positions all their lives long. One might well say about political, what Cavell said about moral discourse: Why should we assume that there is one right thing to be done in every situation, and that it can be found out? Surely the existence of incompatible and equally legitimate claims, responsibilities, and wishes indicates otherwise. Yet if the principal point of political discourse is facilitating collective action, deciding what we are to do, then agreement seems quite essential. It will help here to recall that Cavell distinguished between the point of moral discourse, and its criteria for rationality. Without hope of agreement, or restoring relationship, he said, moral discourse would lose its point; but the measure of rationality was not agreement, but the revelation of moral truth, of self-knowledge. So perhaps one should say about political discourse that its point is the facilitating of collective action, and that without hope of agreement it would lose its point; but its rationality has to do not with agreement, but with the revelation of its characteristic kind of truth, the acquisition of its characteristic kind of knowledge. But what kind of truth and knowledge might be characteristic for political discourse?

We said that in moral discourse one acquires knowledge both of actions,

[22] Compare Alexis de Tocqueville, *Democracy in America*, tr. by Henry Reeve (New York: Schocken Books, 1961), I, 33: "In the moral world, everything is classed, adapted, decided, and foreseen; in the political world everything is agitated, uncertain, and disputed: in the one is a passive, though a voluntary, obedience; in the other an independence, scornful of experience and jealous of authority."

of what one has done, and of persons, of who one is. It would seem that a similar duality exists, at a different level, in political discourse. It too yields knowledge of actions, though not so much of what particular action has been done, as, one might say, of what the present position with respect to action is—what courses of action are open, how they are to be characterized, where they would lead. The second kind of question at stake in political discourse, the second kind of knowledge it yields, is: *Who* is in this position, who is "we"? In political discourse's problem of "what shall we do?" the "we" is always called into question. Part of the issue becomes, if we pursue this or that course of action open to us, who could affirm it, who could regard it as done in his name? Who will still be with "us" if "we" take this course of action?

In political discourse we do not (purport to) speak merely for our individual selves; we speak first person plural rather than singular. But saying "we" is entering a claim—a specific and particular claim different from that entered, for example, in saying "I." That is what Arendt means by arguing that "conscience is unpolitical. . . . It does not say, with Jefferson, 'I tremble for *my country* when I reflect that God is just; that His justice cannot sleep forever,' because it trembles for the individual self and its integrity."[23] The counsels of conscience are initially unpolitical because they are always expressed in purely individual, subjective form. But someone in a position of isolated dissent, who can speak only for himself, is not yet in a position—logically, grammatically, not yet in a position—to speak politically. And part of the knowledge revealed in political discourse is the scope and validity of the claim entered in saying "we": i.e., who turns out to be willing and able to endorse that claim. This is not at all the same as reaching agreement on conclusions. In political discourse there is, characteristically, disagreement before, during, and after deliberation on what is to be done. What one hopes for is not the absence or the eradication of dissent, but its containment within the political association, the avoidance of dissent so severe that it leads to dissociation. What one hopes for is that, at the end of political deliberation, the polis will be affirmed by its membership, despite continuing dissent.

### THE CONCEPT OF THE POLITICAL

The ambiguities we encounter in trying to characterize political discourse seem to display a certain systematic quality. On the one side, there begins to emerge a picture of politics that is participatory and democratic, equalitarian rather than hierarchical; a politics that is public-spirited and treats others as persons, in terms of their concerns and commitments; a politics that centers on action, and does not hesitate to call traditional

[23] Hannah Arendt, "Civil Disobedience," *The New Yorker*, XLVI (September 12, 1970), 72.

institutions into question. On the other side, there emerges a different picture: a stress on the role of hierarchy, organization, and elites in politics; a linkage between political rationality and the support of traditional institutions; a stress on power and the conflict of interests rather than on public-spiritedness; a politics in which men relate by bargaining, propaganda, and manipulation. Is there no way of characterizing political discourse that is free of tendentious implications in one or the other direction? What is the significance of such systematic ambiguity in our ideas about the political?

In the contemporary literature, the former image tends to appear in the writings of certain political theorists like Arendt, Wolin, Voegelin, and Strauss. Their conceptions are often rejected as "idealistic," and countered by the latter, more "realistic" image of politics by empirically oriented political scientists like Dahl and Easton.[24] Perhaps, then it will be helpful if we examine this dispute in the light of a Wittgensteinian understanding of concepts. The group of political theorists are agreed that what characterizes the political is, first of all, its public nature, its transcendence of private and personal concerns. "The words 'public,' 'common,' and 'general,' " Wolin maintains, "have a long tradition of usage which has made them synonyms for what is political. . . . From its very beginnings in Greece, the Western political tradition has looked upon the political order as a common order created to deal with those concerns in which all of the members of the society have some interest."[25] The etymological origin of "political" is, of course, the Greek term *"polis"* itself—the small, self-governing city-state; the political originally was simply what pertained to the *polis*. But this meant not merely what pertained to a compact set of people living in a single geographical area; not every collection of men was a *polis*. A *polis*, as distinct from other human collectivities and organizations, was a freely self-governing community, whose members participated in its public concerns. "In short, the association was political because it dealt with subjects of common concern, and because all of the members were implicated in a common life."[26]

Arendt argues, similarly, that the political life of the ancient Greeks, the life of the *polis*, took place in a "public space" created by men among

[24] Hannah Arendt, *The Human Condition* (Garden City: Doubleday, 1958); Sheldon S. Wolin, *Politics and Vision* (Boston and Toronto: Little, Brown, 1960); Eric Voegelin, *The New Science of Politics* (Chicago: University of Chicago Press, 1952); Leo Strauss, *Natural Right and History* (Chicago: University of Chicago Press, 1959), and "An Epilogue," in Herbert J. Storing, ed., *Essays on the Scientific Study of Politics* (New York: Holt, Rinehart and Winston, 1962); Robert Dahl, *Modern Political Analysis* (Englewood Cliffs, N. J.: Prentice-Hall, 1963); David Easton, *The Political System* (New York: A. A. Knopf, 1963), *A Systems Analysis of Political Life* (New York: John Wiley and Sons, 1965), and *A Framework for Political Analysis* (Englewood Cliffs, N. J.: Prentice-Hall, 1965).

[25] Wolin, *Politics and Vision*, p. 9; compare p. 429.

[26] *Ibid.*, p. 70.

men, and relating them to the ongoing enterprise of which they were a part, their community.[27] The political was a realm of action, rising "directly out of acting together"; and action is not in the least like the making of physical objects by a craftsman.[28] It results not in objects, but in the formation of events, relationships, and institutions. It is possible only among human beings. The rise of the city-state and its special form of government out of tribal and despotic systems meant that man received "besides his private life a sort of second life, his *bios politikos*. Now every citizen belongs to two orders of existence; and there is a sharp distinction in his life between what is his own (*idion*) and what is communal (*koinon*)."[29] All considerations of biological necessity, of what had to be done in the way of production and organization to keep human bodies alive—clothe and feed and house them—belonged to the former order, the life of "the household." Political life was a sphere of freedom, made possible because the constraints of physical necessity were taken care of in the other sphere. Political action presupposed leisure; political life presupposed slaves, who were not citizens but made it possible for other men to cultivate citizenship.

The Greeks considered that human freedom is "exclusively located in the political realm, that necessity is primarily a prepolitical phenomenon, characteristic of the private household organization, and that force and violence are justified in this sphere because they are the only means to master necessity—for instance, by ruling over slaves—and to become free. Because all human beings are subject to necessity, they are entitled to violence toward others; violence is the prepolitical act of liberating oneself from the necessity of life for the freedom of the world. . . . The whole concept of rule and being ruled, of government and power in the sense in which we understand them as well as the regulated order attending them, was felt to be prepolitical and to belong in the private rather than the public sphere."[30] So the *polis* was "a very special and freely chosen form" of human organization, sharply distinct from other power structures and societies, and characterized by the participation of its member-citizens as equals; it was a self-governing community of equal citizens, all involved in their shared public life.[31]

Moreover, the idea of the political involved from its inception a fundamental notion of participation and equality, of participation on the basis of the essential equality of political membership, of citizenship. If a man owns a herd of cattle, he may take care of them well or badly; he may give them what they need or what they want, or he may not. But his relationship to them will never be a political one, for though he may have

[27] Arendt, *Human Condition*, p. 50.
[28] *Ibid.*, p. 177.
[29] Werner Jaeger, *Paideia* (1945) I, 111, quoted *ibid.*, p. 25.
[30] Arendt, *Human Condition*, p. 29.
[31] *Ibid.*, p. 14.

to take their needs and reactions into account, he need not take *them* into account as persons, as persons like himself with claims of their own and the power to articulate and judge for themselves. Thus Aristotle distinguishes political authority from slavery, a household, or oriental despotism precisely on the basis that the latter are like ownership and imply a natural hierarchy, while the former occurs among essentially equal men. "The authority of the statesman is exercised over men who are naturally free"; it is "an authority over freemen and equals."[32] As Arendt says, "the *polis* was distinguished from the household in that it knew only 'equals,' whereas the household was the center of the strictest inequality. To be free meant both not to be subject to the necessity of life or to the command of another *and* not to be in command oneself. It meant neither to rule nor to be ruled."[33] That is why for Aristotle the virtue of a citizen depends on participation, a sharing in office, so that one is by turns governor and governed, and the community is self-governing.

This vision of the nature of political life clearly parallels some of what we had earlier said about morality. Both stress the element of action, with its implications of unpredictability and innovation, and consequently of freedom as well as responsibility. Both imply the uniquely human focus of the two realms: that they involve discourse not just about human beings as objects, but addressed to human persons—taking their interests and position into account. But to the modern political scientist such a view of political life is likely to seem hopelessly unrealistic, an ideal of public-spiritedness that is perhaps worth striving for (though many would question that, citing the crimes of horror that have been committed in the name of ideals), but certainly not an accurate picture of what political life is actually like today, or perhaps ever has been. If one looks frankly at the realities of politics, they might argue, one does not see a joint striving after the public good among men morally and rationally concerned for each other's welfare or the welfare of their shared enterprise. Instead one sees either a tale of dominance and power, in which political institutions serve to protect the interests and property of some men against the rest; or a tale of mutual accommodation among essentially separate, private individuals or groups, each with its own needs and interests, its own claims against the others. From the first of these closely related perspectives, participation and equality are antithetical to the very idea of political life; even the Greek ideal presupposed that the slaves simply be left out of account in viewing the political system. From the second perspective, participation is beside the point; it is only a means by which one might hope to facilitate one's own private claims and interests, but other means might well be more effective. People participate when they want something for themselves; and an efficient representative or a beneficent admin-

[32] Aristotle, *Politics*, ed. by Sir Ernest Barker (New York: Oxford University Press, 1958), p. 17; compare also p. 13.

[33] Arendt, *Human Condition*, p. 30; compare Aristotle, *Politics*, pp. 93, 103.

istrator may well be able to procure more from the system for the individual than the individual could extract for himself. From both of these latter perspectives, concepts like the public good or the public interest are at best rhetorical devices.

These writers do recognize an element of generality in the political, but they see it as confined to the effect or impact or legitimate range of political outcomes. Thus, David Easton, for example, defines politics as "the authoritative allocation of values for a society."[34] The allocation is general in the sense that it is binding, authoritative for the whole society. Political decisions are made by governments, and they result in law, which is binding on all. All, or many, are affected by the outcome; but the decision itself may or may not have been made by many, or from a general, public perspective. More likely it was made by a few, in terms of expedience. Thus, one can study politics wherever some men have power over others, make decisions that are generally binding for whole groups of men. Robert Dahl, for instance, defines a political system as "any persistent pattern of human relationships that involves, to a significant extent, power, rule or authority."[35]

Proponents of such power-oriented or interest-oriented views of politics will point out that nothing visible in modern political life remotely resembles the seemingly idealized picture ascribed to the Greeks by commentators like Wolin and Arendt. We see around us not public spirit but the pursuit of private interest, not rational and responsible action but ignorance and prejudice, not participation but apathy, not equality but elite dominance. And, indeed, both Wolin and Arendt speak of the political as having "declined" or been "sublimated" in modern times. They say that we have lost or forgotten or destroyed the political. "Few would contest," Wolin says, "the proposition that today Western societies exhibit little in the way of a widespread political consciousness among its members and fewer still would doubt that political things are mostly held in disrepute by the members of these societies."[36]

What has replaced the political, they argue, is "society" and the "social." The social also concerns men in large groups, and the unification of separate individuals into a single whole, but it differs in crucial ways from the political. Where the political deals with public, shared, common concerns, in which the whole is not merely a summation of separate parts, society is a realm of the unplanned, spontaneous, laissez-faire interaction of separate individuals who remain separate, each pursuing his own private goals and producing, unintentionallly, results which affect others. Thus, the political involves the conscious, deliberate exercise of power among men for public ends; the "power" of society over its members, by contrast, is indirect, unconscious, and unplanned. Where the political is the realm of free, au-

[34] Easton, *Political System*, p. 129.
[35] Dahl, *Modern Political Analysis*, p. 6.
[36] Wolin, *Politics and Vision*, p. 290; compare p. 353.

tonomous action, society is a pattern of human behavior subject to causal laws. The Greeks kept their politics pure by excluding causal necessity, economics, and coercive power from it; in modern times, these realms have intruded upon and largely destroyed the political, and it has become "sublimated" into bureaucracy, economics, administration, religion, or society.[37] Arendt says that society "on all its levels, excludes the possibility of action, which formerly was excluded from the household. Instead, society expects from each of its members a certain kind of behavior, imposing innumerable and various rules, all of which tend to 'normalize' its members, to make them behave, to exclude spontaneous action or outstanding achievement."[38]

But the scientifically oriented political scientist is likely to question by what standards one might regard contemporary political life as having declined, or as having been sublimated into nonpolitical relationships. He is likely to ask what is supposed to have changed: the conception of political life or its practice. If political practice, then he will argue that Wolin and Arendt are comparing contemporary practice with a Greek ideal, that Greek political practice was as ridden with conflict and the pursuit of selfish interests as ours, besides which whole categories of human beings were excluded altogether. If what is supposed to have declined is the conception of politics, so that the standard of comparison is properly Greek thought rather than Greek practice, then the question is why the ancient conception should be taken as the true one, so that change from it becomes a degeneration. Could one not argue equally well that when a concept changes it grows and develops, becomes enriched?

However, the standard to which Wolin and Arendt refer is not really the Greek conception of politics, but our own. Etymology and Greek conceptions are helpful only as didactic devices, for stressing aspects of our own concept which we have neglected or forgotten. Wolin and Arendt are talking about what *is* political, about the meaning of "political"; and they are trying to tell us that an important part of the meaning applies less and less well to the reality of the practice and institutions we still call, from habit, "political." They are trying to recall us from the habitual forms to the substance of the political, of our own concept of the political.

Thus the debate over the nature of the political begins to look like that between Socrates and Thrasymachus, like a matter of form versus substance. The Socratic substance of what is political, the meaning of "political," involves the idea of action, as Wolin and Arendt suggest, rather than mere passive subjection to events. It involves collective action, action by "we" rather than "I." In our substantive conception of the political are the idea of publicness, of collectivity, and the idea of action, of active intervention. But we also embody the conception, the purpose, in institutions, and we normally call those institutions political, too. In them,

[37] *Ibid.*, p. 288, and chapters 9 and 10, *passim.*
[38] Arendt, *Human Condition*, pp. 37–38.

political collectivity, the making of decisions and the taking of measures by the *polis*, may sometimes be collective in only a formal way. We can speak of the state as having acted in a quite formal sense, meaning only that some individual action or even unplanned event is formally ascribed to the collectivity. Or we can mean substantive participation by the members, or a large proportion of them, in a genuinely public decision leading to genuinely joint action.

Moreover, the difference between form and substance here moves along more than one dimension. It may, for instance, depend on the degree or extent of participation (democracy versus oligarchy or dictatorship, the exclusion of women or slaves), or it may depend on the kind or quality of participation (deliberation consciously directed to the public, collective good, or self-interested bargaining among groups, or imposed administrative decrees). It is thus possible for the political institutions of a society to deviate greatly from the conception of what is political. Like Socrates and Thrasymachus, if one lives in such a society one must in effect choose whether to adapt the concept to the new realities, or to retain the concept and stop applying it to existing institutions, or to retain it and change those institutions. Despite appearances, none of these courses of action is likely to be easy.

In these terms, it may seem that the dispute over the meaning of "political" is between the perspective of reform and that of detached description. It may seem that, like Socrates, Wolin and Arendt try to make us aware of discrepancies in our lives so that we may choose to change them, while the scientifically inclined political scientists are concerned to give an accurate account of how things are. But an accurate account of how things are is often an essential requisite for change. And Arendt and Wolin, too, are trying to give an accurate account of how things are.

Further, if we construe the dispute this way, suggesting a choice between the two positions, we may still miss how central this very dispute is to the nature of the political itself. For the rival definitions are both very much bound to the grammar of the word, and both illuminate it. "Political" is, of course, just one in a whole family of words from the same root, and an Austinian analysis of these terms easily shows that some of them lend themselves much more to an Arendtian conception of political things, some to a political-scientific one. Obviously we cannot carry out such an analysis here, but some preliminary guesses might be useful. Such an investigation is likely to reveal that the noun "politics" and particularly the adjective "politic" lend themselves best to the social-scientific, power or interest, interpretation of the political. When we ask "Is that a politic thing to do?" we really do mean something like "Will it get you what you want? Is it expedient? Will it pay off?" A word like "policy," by contrast, has no such implications, and lends itself much more readily to the stress on public interest; but it, in turn, need not imply plurality, conflict, or participation. The adjective "political" seems to be relatively neutral on this dimension, which I think is why Arendt and Wolin use it a great deal; why, in particular, they make it into a substantive ("the political), instead of using the noun already available, "politics." Indeed, Wolin says explicitly that there is plenty of politics in modern American life, even if "the political" has all but disappeared.[39]

Why should different members of the same family of words have divergent implications along just this central dimension? It is tempting to conclude that duality is itself central to the conceptual area in which these words function, that it is built into the grammar and therefore into the essence of what is political. That conclusion gains a certain plausibility when we notice that the ambiguity appears within the writings on each side of the controversy, and within ancient Greek political thought as well. Consider the puzzling discussion in the third book of Aristotle's *Politics* about the nature of political membership. Aristotle defines a citizen as a "man who shares in the administration of justice and in the holding of office," which is perfectly consistent with his characterization of a political association as being composed of freemen and equals.[40]

Citizens are peers who both govern and are governed; citizenship is participation. But then Aristotle's honesty and intelligence drive him on to admit a difficulty about the definition: it seems to imply that only a democracy is a political association, which was not what Aristotle intended. Alternatively, one might try to argue that in an aristocracy only the aristocrats, who participate in the government, are really citizens; and, presumably, that in a monarchy only the king is a citizen. But that is absurd, and would eliminate all distinctions among democracy, aristocracy, and monarchy. Aristotle attempts to get out of the apparent contradiction between what he knows to be crucial about political life, what distinguishes political power from slave-owning, and what he knows to be a commonplace about political life, that a *polis* may be a democracy, an aristocracy, a monarchy, or a mixture of forms. But his argument is not convincing.[41] Perhaps Aristotle's difficulties, like ours, originate in the complexities of the grammar of our shared concept of the political.

Perhaps what characterizes political life is precisely the problem of continually *creating* unity, a public, in a context of diversity, rival claims, unequal power, and conflicting interests. In the absence of rival claims and conflicting interests, a topic never enters the political realm; no political decision needs to be made. But for the political collectivity, the "we," to act, those conflicting claims and interests must be resolved in a way that continues to preserve the collectivity. "Expediency," as Wolin

[39] For instance at p. 353 (Wolin, *Politics and Vision*); compare also Jacques Ellul, *The Political Illusion*, tr. by Konrad Kellen (New York: A. A. Knopf, 1967), in which the very conditions Wolin and Arendt consider a decline of the political are described in terms of a total politicization of every aspect of life.
[40] Aristotle, *Politics*, p. 93.
[41] *Ibid.*, p. 95.

says, "is largely the result of the old problem of trying to establish a uniform rule amidst a context of differences. It is this that frequently leads to concessions and modifications in a policy. The reason is not simply that it is a good thing to formulate policies that will reflect a sensitivity to variations and differences throughout the society, but rather that a political society is *simultaneously trying to act and remain a community*."[42] Both the initial problem and the resolution are essential parts of our conception of the political; it concerns the process of transition from the one to the other. That is why Wolin himself criticizes Plato's *Republic* as not being truly political, because it eliminates conflict once and for all, so that "the art of ruling becomes the art of imposition." For political "order is not a set pattern, but something akin to a precarious equilibrium," a "continuing task."[43] And, on the other side, even Easton acknowledges that the political concerns not merely what is politic or expedient, but also "policy for the whole society"; indeed, he says that the former conception is tributary to the latter.[44]

That might suggest, further, that political discourse is neither just manipulative propaganda, nor just a moral concern with the cares and commitments of another person, but something like an addressing of diverse others in terms which relate their separate, plural interests to their common enterprise, to a shared, public interest. It would then be characteristic of political discourse that the meaning and content of the public interest themselves form part of the debate, that they are seen differently from the different perspectives of the participants. Arendt argues that this kind of plurality of perspectives is precisely what characterizes the political world: "the reality of the public realm relies on the simultaneous presence of innumerable perspectives and aspects in which the common world presents itself and for which no common measurement or denominator can ever be devised. For though the common world is the common meeting ground of all, those who are present have different locations in it, and the location of one can no more coincide with the location of another than the location of two objects. Being seen and being heard by others derive their significance from the fact that everybody sees and hears from a different position."[45]

It is no surprise that such things could not be said about science; but it may come as a surprise that—in a different way—such things could not be said about morality, either. In morality, too, each individual has his own, unique position; but one would not say that morality requires the simultaneous presence of innumerable perspectives. Moral discourse is personal dialogue; political discourse concerns a public, a community, and

[42] Wolin, *Politics and Vision*, p. 62; my italics. Compare Arendt, *Human Condition*, pp. 19, 38, 52.
[43] Wolin, *Politics and Vision*, p. 43.
[44] Easton, *The Political System*, pp. 126–128.
[45] Arendt, *Human Condition*, p. 52.

takes place among the members generally. Thus, it requires a plurality of viewpoints from which to begin; and the interaction of these varied perspectives, their reconciliation into a single public policy, though that reconciliation will always be temporary, partial, and provisional.

Arendt says that we form political opinions "by considering a given issue from different viewpoints," by taking into account "the standpoints of those who are absent." She says that "this is a question neither of empathy, as though I tried to be or feel like somebody else, nor of counting noses and joining a majority but of being and thinking in my own identity where actually I am not. The more people's standpoints I have present in my mind while pondering a given issue and the better I can imagine how I would feel and think if I were in their place, the stronger will be my capacity for representative thinking and the more valid my final conclusions, my opinion. . . . To be sure, I can refuse to do this and form an opinion that takes only my own interest, or the interests of the group to which I belong, into account; nothing indeed is more common, even among highly sophisticated people, than this blind obstinacy which becomes manifest in lack of imagination and failure to judge. But the very quality of an opinion as of a judgment depends upon its degree of impartiality."[46]

That would be in accord with at least one way of understanding Aristotle's doctrine that man is a political animal, a *polis* animal. Obviously Aristotle did not mean that every man always lives in a *polis*, but that men can become fully developed, truly human, exemplified to perfection *qua* men, only in a *polis*. But what is it that *polis* life contributes to the full flowering of man's humanity that could not be contributed by any lesser association—the household, the family, friendship—nor by other forms of large-scale organization? I believe that the answer to this question is to be found in the kind of simultaneous awareness of innumerable perspectives on a shared public enterprise we have been discussing, and in the experience of participating in reconciling these perspectives for common action. The family can teach men morality— respect for other persons, the mutuality of personal concern. But only a *polis*—an association of freemen and equals, of citizens—can teach men about *im*personal, large-scale, public sharing. The family can develop in men the capacity to think beyond selfishness, in terms of the needs of another; but only the *polis* can teach them to relate their own needs and interests to a shared, ongoing public good of which they are only a part. What is learned that way Aristotle called "justice," and he did, indeed, consider it an essential element in any fully developed, truly human man.

We have seen, then, how language can serve as a model of membership and freedom within order; but a model that must be investigated rather

[46] Hannah Arendt, "Truth and Politics," in Peter Laslett and W. G. Runciman, eds., *Philosophy, Politics and Society* (Oxford: Basil Blackwell, 1967), p. 115; compare Strauss, "An Epilogue," p. 310.

than accepted blindly as typical of all membership. We have briefly indicated some ways in which political membership may be distinctive— ways having to do with the special features of action, particularly of collective, public action. All this is, of course, far too sketchy. We need careful, detailed Austinian and Wittgensteinian analysis here, and we need to put it to work productively, to use it for thinking through anew some of the outstanding problems in political science and political theory.

# X

## *Judgment*

THE DOMINANT TRENDS in contemporary social and political science
share the axiom, inherited from positivism and largely unexamined,
that all the world may be divided into two categories: facts and values;
and that all statements may similarly be divided into descriptive and
normative. The former, the axiom says, concern what is, the latter what
ought to be; and since Hume it has been known that you cannot derive
the latter from the former. In our discussion of the quarrel between Socrates and Thrasymachus, we made a number of assertions and assumptions
which run counter to this axiom. We argued that both men were concerned about what justice *is*; we claimed that Socrates was giving an account of what rulers in fact do when they act justly; we argued that
"justice," unlike "delicious," is linked with rational standards and justification. It is time now to confront the problem of justification more directly, and to examine the axiomatic dichotomy between "the is" and "the
ought" critically from a Wittgensteinian perspective.

In my judgment, the alleged dichotomy cannot survive such an examination (though, of course, Wittgenstein's is not the only perspective from
which it can be criticized). That does not mean that Wittgenstein shows
facts and values to be the same, or shows that wishing something makes
it so, or shows that biased reports are no different from objective ones, or
teaches that it makes no difference whether we propagandize one another.
What a Wittgensteinian approach can show is that the distinction is not
an accurate or useful way to dichotomize either our utterances or the
world; in reality, each contains a rich plurality of elements among which
facts and values are only two. The distinction between facts and values,
one might say, is as valid and as useful as that between herrings and fruit.
*Of course* they are different, but hardly anyone ever doubted that. They
are so different that they are not even really comparable. But that is no
reason for trying to classify everything in the world as either (more or
less) a herring or (more or less) a fruit. That can be done, for instance

as a parlor game, especially if one postpones difficult cases until some later time; but enlightening it is not.

The dichotomy has been so widely accepted that its proponents now tend to take it for granted unexamined, while its critics have become ineffective and unnecessarily defensive. As a result, neither side is at all clear any more as to just what is meant by the distinction. Writers label it in a number of different ways which they apparently consider equivalent, but which obviously are not. Some speak of "the is" and "the ought," or of "what is" and "what ought to be," others of "facts" and "values," or of "assertions of fact" and "judgments of value," others of "descriptive" and "normative" utterances or theory, or of "empirical" and "normative," or of "descriptive" and "prescriptive."[1] But as we have learned to expect by now, each of these expressions has its own characteristic role in language, its distinctive meaning and implications; so that the dividing line between, say, facts and values, is not at all the same as that between description and prescription. Indeed, "dividing line" is a misleading expression here; what is "the dividing line" between herrings and fruit? Austin's work on terms like "voluntary" and "involuntary" suggests that even pairs of opposites may turn out not to be opposites at all, but merely different. Some writers further introduce a third, separate category, of definitions or tautologies. Again, definitions surely are different from facts and values, but not even these three categories exhaust the world or our utterances; and we merely torture our own minds by trying to force all there is into these boxes.

In particular, advocates of the dichotomy between, say, "the is" and "the ought" usually have a fairly clear, if narrow, notion of what will count as "the is," but "the ought" usually functions as a merely residual category to which everything else under the sun is assigned. Thus, they classify general scientific theories together with specific observations about particular events as part of "the is," but tend to ignore the status of personal facts—say, that I am angry or in pain. And "the ought" is made to include not merely values properly so called, but obligations, commands, wishes, judgments, and so on, which have nothing in common except that they are not part of "what is" as the dichotomists define it. It is interesting that out of the famous triumvirate of "the good, the true, and the beautiful," the dichotomists always select the true as obviously a matter of observable or demonstrable fact, leaving the other two terms as obviously matters of subjective value. But is this really obvious?

A further consequence of the wide acceptance of the dichotomy axiom is that those who should be its powerful critics have become unnecessarily defensive, conceding the axiom's major premise. Within political science, for example, advocates of the dichotomy have come to distinguish between

[1] On the dangers of these verbal confusions, see Alexander Sesonske, "Cognitive and Normative," *Philosophy and Phenomenological Research*, XVII (September 1956), 20.

what they call "empirical" or "systematic" or "scientific" theorizing which produces scientific theories of the political world; and what they call "normative" theory, which apparently embraces all, or most, of what used to be called political theory. But too often those familiar with political theory as a tradition have responded defensively: "Normative work is important too," they say; or "Students should consider values as well as facts"; or "Advocating how things ought to be is very useful to society." No doubt all that is true, but it concedes a distinction of doubtful validity or relevance, and accepts a wholly misleading categorization of what political theory is all about. Even with reference to those relatively rare works of political theory, like the *Republic*, which explicitly describe an ideal society, this categorization deflects instead of promoting understanding. For the *Republic* is very much about what is—for instance, as we have already suggested, about what justice is. But let us proceed from summary advocacy to investigation.

Suppose we start by trying simply to classify utterances under one of the two headings of "what is" and "what ought to be." We will find a certain number of utterances that contain these expressions and are therefore easy to classify, and many others which do not. But even the utterances which contain the word "is" or the word "ought" do not in fact correspond at all to what the advocates of the dichotomy apparently expect. For any number of statements of ethics, esthetics, politics, any number of evaluations, assessments, judgments, commands, suggestions, can be expressed in declarative form. If someone says, "That is a lovely painting," or "He was a brave man," or "It is imperative that you be there," or "That is manifestly unjust," shall we classify those utterances as being about what is the case, or what ought to be the case? And if the latter, why? Conversely, if someone looks at the sky and says, "It ought to rain tomorrow," or "It should rain tomorrow," is he not making a factual prediction? Evidently, the words "is" and "ought" cannot be used as literal touchstones for classifying utterances at all.

A second familiar alternative is to classify utterances by the presence or absence of other characteristic "value words." "That is an unjust law" may use the verb "is," but it can be recognized as an "ought" statement by the presence of the word "unjust." "Unjust," like "good" or "beautiful" or "delicious," is an emotive or value word, used to express the individual speaker's feelings and preferences. These are "hurrah words" and "boo words," conventionalized refinements of those laughs, tears, and grunts of pleasure that naturally indicate our emotive reactions to what we encounter. Such words are inherently vague and subjective as to content; they simply express the speaker's feelings. This was the position, for instance, of A. J. Ayer, in the influential *Language, Truth and Logic*.[2] It is evidently quite close to Wittgenstein's early views in the *Tractatus*, that "higher" concerns like beauty, goodness, or justice "make themselves

[2] A. J. Ayer, *Language, Truth and Logic* (London: Victor Gollancz, 1936).

manifest" but cannot be rationally, meaningfully, be talked about. *De gustibus non disputandum.*

A more complex and subtle position is elaborated in Charles L. Stevenson's *Ethics and Language*, where judgments of value or obligation are translated as being composed of two elements: an expression of the speaker's attitude, and an imperative appeal to the hearer to share that attitude.[3] Thus, "That is good," or "You ought to do that," are translated as "I approve of that; do so as well." From such a perspective, as from Ayer's, there can be no rational or objectively valid basis for the attitudes a man holds; they necessarily contain an element of arbitrary subjectivity. One can move rationally and objectively from some value propositions to others, by way of relevant facts and logic. But our values form a hierarchical system, so that ultimately at the apex there must be an ungrounded fundamental value which the individual merely postulates subjectively; lesser values may be deduced rationally from it, but it itself is irrational. Thus, there can be no ultimate standard of validity or rationality in discussions about value, other than the standard of causal efficacy in persuasion; whatever induces others to share your attitude is a valid argument.

Now, one difficulty at least of this position is evident on its face. These so-called value terms are part of our language and governed by grammar exactly like other words. That means that we learn words like "justice," "beautiful," and "good" in the same ways in which we learn words like "length," "run," or "magenta"—from hearing them used and eventually using them ourselves. It is no more up to us, as individuals, what the former words mean and how they are grammatically used, than what the latter mean and how they are used. That is to say, it is in a sense and to some extent up to each of us; we can deviate from regularities in certain ways, and we can extend and change meanings in certain ways. But not just any new or deviant utterance will be a metaphor, a redefinition, an extension of meaning, rather than a mistake or an oddity. So the meanings of these terms are no more and no less subjective than the meanings of other words, if by "subjective" we intend that their meanings are simply up to each individual.

Moreover, these words clearly differ from each other in meaning, and differ in ways which are neither vague nor subjective. Far from all being reducible to cries of pleasure or displeasure, to "hurrah" and "boo," they have quite definite and restricted spheres of meaning, governed by grammar as the rest of our language is. "Good" differs in meaning not merely from "bad" and "evil," but equally from "fine," "superb," "excellent," "satisfactory," "nice," and so on. Of course, if we must explain what "excellent" means briefly to a foreigner, we will say that it means "good" (rather than, say, "bad"). But that is only a first approximation, and these terms are by no means interchangeable; nor are their regions of use

[3] Charles L. Stevenson, *Ethics and Language* (New Haven: Yale University Press, 1960), p. 24 and *passim*.

defined subjectively by each speaker. For example, as Ziff points out, the fact that our language contains words like "excellent," "magnificent," and "superb" makes "good" into a relatively mild and dispassionate term by comparison. Thus, calling a painting good may well be damning it with faint praise. "I would not say '*Guernica* is a good painting.': it is a magnificent painting. Neither would I say 'Fouquet's picture of Agnes Sorel as the Madonna is a good painting.': it is an exquisite painting."[4] The sense of what is said depends on what else might have been said but wasn't. Ziff maintains that calling *Guernica* "good" is an understatement, but he adds, "whether I am wrong in so maintaining is irrelevant here: given that I feel as I do about *Guernica*, it would be somewhat odd for me to utter ['*Guernica* is a good painting.']."[5]

Ziff adds an even stronger observation: " 'magnificent,' 'grand,' 'superb,' all make sense in connection with *Guernica*: but it would be odd for me to use 'good' here, and odd for anyone to use 'lovely,' 'elegant'."[6] Ziff says it would be odd for him to use "good" here because of the way he feels about *Guernica*; "good" would not be an accurate rendering of his judgment. Presumably the reason it would be odd for anyone to call *Guernica* "lovely" or "elegant" is that it would be odd for anyone to *find* *Guernica* lovely or elegant; we would feel some reluctance to accept such a person's standards of loveliness *as standards of loveliness*, or to believe that he had really looked at *Guernica*. Such deviations are matters of degree, and we have various options in interpreting them.

Is the question of whether *Guernica* is a lovely painting a question of subjective value or of objective fact? Apparently the dividing line is not as clear as one might suppose. It may seem obvious that "good" and "bad," or "beautiful" and "ugly," are subjective expressions, value words. But most of our vocabulary simply defies classification in these categories. If I call a painting "beautiful," I may be making a value judgment expressing my subjective feelings about that painting. But what if I say that it is "dainty" or "decorative" or "stylized" or "symbolist" or that the painter "has a somber palette"? If I call an action "good," I may be making a value judgment expressing subjective feelings about that action. But what if I say that it was "accidental" or "inadvertent" or "voluntary" or "deliberate"? Is the choice among "killing," "murder," "assassination," and "execution" a matter of objective fact or of subjective value?

The truth is, I think, that no word is by nature "expressive" or "evaluative," or "factual" or "objective." What matters is not the character or meaning of a particular word, but how that word is used in particular utterances, whether to express emotion, assert fact, command, recommend, describe, explain, or in other ways. Certain words may be more likely to be used in certain kinds of speech, because their meaning is as-

4 Paul Ziff, *Semantic Analysis* (Ithaca: Cornell University Press, 1960), p. 147.
5 *Ibid.*, p. 221.
6 *Ibid.*

sociated with an area of human life where that sort of speech is frequent. But they need not be used that way, nor are they essential to that kind of speech. Very few English words correlate closely with specific speech acts, as "hello" is primarily but not exclusively used for greeting.[7] Clearly words like "good," "beautiful," and "just" can be used for commending, praising, or approving something. But so can "true," "flat," or "seldom." And even words like "good" or "just" need not be used for commending or approving. If one says, "Be sure to do a good job!" or "Is that a good example?" or "That account of 'good' is not good enough," or "No news is good news," one is not commending or approving anything.[8]

As Wittgenstein says, what makes a word an expression of approval is not the meaning of the particular word, nor the form of an utterance but "the game it appears in." Thus to study esthetic judgment, one must concentrate "not on the words 'good' or 'beautiful', . . . but on the occasions on which they are said—on the enormously complicated situation in which the aesthetic experience has a place, in which the expression itself has almost a negligible place. If you came to a foreign tribe, whose language you didn't know at all and you wished to know what words corresponded to 'good', 'fine', etc., what would you look for? You would look for smiles, gestures, food, toys."[9] To study evaluation or commendation, "we don't start from certain words, but from certain occasions or activities." And in the actual making of, say, esthetic judgments, words like "beautiful" or "lovely" play "hardly any role at all. Are aesthetic adjectives used in a musical criticism? You say: 'Look at this transition', or 'The passage here is incoherent'. Or you say, in a poetical criticism: 'His use of images is precise'. The words you use are more akin to 'right' and 'correct' (as these words are used in ordinary speech) than to 'beautiful' and 'lovely'."[10] Similarly, "What does a person who knows a good suit say when trying on a suit at the tailor's? 'That's the right length', 'That's too short', 'That's too narrow'. . . . Instead of 'That's too short' I might say 'Look!' or instead of 'Right' I might say 'Leave it as it is'. A good cutter may not use any words at all, but just make a chalk mark and later alter it."[11]

In sum, to say that a word like "justice" is a value word used to express our approval of something and invite the approval of others is not very helpful. No doubt the word can be used that way, but so can just about any other word. And even if "justice" conveyed a kind of approval, this explanation would still fail to account for the differences in kind and content of approval among "just," "beautiful," "good," "delicious," and so

[7] *Ibid.*, p. 228.

[8] *Ibid.*, pp. 229–230.

[9] Ludwig Wittgenstein, *Lectures and Conversations on Aesthetics, Psychology and Religious Belief*, ed. by Cyril Barrett (Berkeley and Los Angeles: University of California Press, 1967), p. 2.

[10] *Ibid.*, p. 3; compare Alexander Sesonske, *Value and Obligation* (New York: Oxford University Press, 1964), p. 8.

[11] Wittgenstein, *Lectures and Conversations*, p. 5.

on. To say that a decision was just is not to say that it was delicious, and to say that a painting is beautiful is not to say that it is just. Which term is appropriate depends not on how the speaker feels, but on the situations in and about which he speaks, and on the meanings these words have in English. We may or may not value, desire, or commend something that we are persuaded is just, good, or delicious. But that is not because we have been caused to have pleasurable associations with those words through some sort of psychological conditioning. We value a just judgment or a just society *because* we know what justice is. Accordingly, there will be other instances where we do not value something, even though we recognize that it is just, because what we happen to want or need at that point is injustice, or some other quality altogether.

An individual's values are one thing; the conceptual system of his language, complete with its implications for judgment and commitment, is quite another. And in neither case need values or commitments be hierarchically arranged, resting for ultimate justification on some highest, unquestioned, and arbitrary irrational commitment. What deceives us here, as so often in philosophy, is that in particular arguments we sometimes trace back one judgment to another, more basic one. But that does not mean that there exists one final, correct, hierarchical analysis of the values in our language, or of any particular person's values.[12] Our "values" are no more arranged in a general hierarchy than our beliefs or our knowledge; they are multiply and flexibly interrelated, and they are all partly but flexibly imbedded in our concepts. Whether a painting is lovely or somber, whether a musical passage is incoherent, whether an action was done by mistake, are questions that defy classification in the fact-value dichotomy. We must either conclude that they are sometimes one, sometimes the other, or that they are both at once, and there is something wrong with the dichotomization.

### DERIVING "OUGHT" FROM "IS"

Those who dichotomize the world into facts and values usually also cite the famous doctrine they usually attribute to Hume, that "one cannot derive an 'ought' from an 'is.' " But if in reality words and utterances cannot be unambiguously classified into the one category or the other, then it is not a matter of derivation at all; no derivation is necessary. Several Wittgensteinian and ordinary-language philosophers have developed examples on this topic in recent years. G. E. M. Anscombe, for instance, has undertaken to show that the simple "brute fact" that you have ordered and received groceries from the store and have not yet paid for them normally is enough to show that you owe the grocer money,

[12] Compare Sesonske, *Value and Obligation*, p. 53; Ludwig Wittgenstein, *Philosophical Investigations*, tr. by G. E. M. Anscombe (New York: Macmillan, 1968), par. 91.

have an obligation to pay.[13] (Of course in special circumstances you might not: the groceries are a gift, the grocer owed you money, and so on. But those circumstances are also factual.) If you have "bought" but not yet "paid," then you "owe a debt"; that is what those words mean. The idea of debt is, indeed, a mere social convention, but so are the brute facts of the case. Or at least, while some of the facts may strike us as more "brute" than others, it is very difficult to say where facts leave off and obligations begin, or whether there is any such point.

Similarly, John Searle has undertaken to show that the fact of someone's having said "I promise" under appropriate factual circumstances (he is not quoting, joking, reciting, and so on) already is enough to show that he has an obligation to perform.[14] If he has promised, he has an obligation; that is what "promise" means. Of course, the facts in such examples are what Searle calls "institutional facts"; they are in the realm of human institutions and actions, and we have seen that this means their identification is a different sort of matter from discovering the specific gravity of a metal or the height of a mountain.[15] But it is difficult to deny that they are facts, or to classify them as values.

Such a brief summary does not do justice to Searle's and Anscombe's arguments, but even at their best I think that arguments on this pattern are bound to be unsatisfactory to someone who believes in the axiom of dichotomy. For he is likely to feel that Anscombe and Searle have engaged in the familiar vulgarization, have at most proved a connection *in language* between words like "promise" or "debt" and words like "obligation." What needs to be shown, however, is a connection between the facts, in the real world, and real, binding obligation. But that demand cannot be accepted at face value, for Wittgenstein has taught us to be cautious about how separable such facts and obligations are from the concepts in which we conceive them. Someone who believes in the dichotomy between facts and values will object: "But how can the mere fact of his making certain noises in certain circumstances give rise to an obligation? Surely there is a hidden value-premise suppressed here, that promises oblige, that one ought to keep one's promises. Searle makes it look as if it were impossible to question the obligatory power of promises, but it isn't. We can question it, and sometimes questioning social institutions

[13] G. E. M. Anscombe, "On Brute Facts," *Analysis*, 18 (January 1958), 69–72; compare Stanley Cavell, *Must We Mean What We Say?* (New York: Charles Scribner's Sons, 1969), p. 28 n, who points out that this is why Kant maintained that "a deposit of money must be handed back because if the recipient appropriated it, it would no longer be a deposit."

[14] John Searle, "How to Derive 'Ought' from 'Is,' " *Philosophical Review*, LXXIII (January 1964), 43–58. Searle points out (p. 44) that his derivations are not strictly "entailed," but not just contingent, either.

[15] *Ibid.*, p. 54; compare Anscombe, "On Brute Facts," p. 70: "A set of events is the ordering and supplying of potatoes, and something is a bill, only in the context of our institutions."

is of the utmost importance." We need, however, to look carefully at that argument and its assumptions.

When someone undertakes to question whether promise oblige, *what* is he questioning? How would he define "promises" in his own question? He may choose to define it as (roughly) self-assumed obligations, a social practice compounded out of what is said and what is subsequently to be done, giving the word its full (Socratic) meaning. But then he should not be surprised if promises oblige. Then it is his question that seems puzzling. More likely he will define it as (so-called) "promise," as the empirical fact of speaking certain words in certain circumstances, conventionally said to (so-called) "oblige." Then his question is understandable, but the answer is negative: so-called "promises" do *not* necessarily oblige, though they are normally said to, though they (so-called) "oblige." A (so-called) "promise" may turn out not to have been a real promise, in which case it does not oblige. A word like "promise," having to do with action, has both formal and substantive aspects of meaning, as we suggested earlier. It has both signaling and labeling functions. It can be used sometimes with its full, signaling weight, which includes its obligatory consequences for commitment; but at other times it is used as if between quotation marks, for speaking about a so-called promise, what looked formally like a promise. Both the "fact" and the "obligation" are part of the grammar of "promise," being linked to varying degrees with various forms of the word (verb or noun, first or third person, and so on). *If* something is a promise in substance and not just in form, with the full weight of meaning of the term, *then* it must give rise to obligation.

But that need not mean, as Searle's argument does seem to suggest, that it is impossible to question conventional obligations or institutions. We can, under certain circumstances, competently and meaningfully question what is conventionally taken to be obligatory. But when we do, we are questioning the concept and the institution as a whole, not merely its "value component." We are asking not whether promises must oblige, but whether there must be such an institution as promising. We cannot even imagine a tribe among whom promises do not oblige, because we don't know what to imagine as a "promise" among them; if "it" doesn't give rise to any obligation, why call it a promise? But perhaps we can imagine a tribe among whom the institution of promising does not exist; that will depend on whether promising is a cultural convention like suttee or slavery, or whether instead it is part of necessary, natural human forms of life. We can imagine a tribe which recognizes no formal or special way of promising, of giving one's word; but if one construes promising more broadly, to include all the ordinary, implicit ways of giving one's word, then the institution and its obligatory power seem essential to human social life itself, so that they have to be accepted.

To the argument that the fact of someone's having promised cannot give rise to an obligation without the implicit value premise that promises oblige, one must respond that no such premise is necessary because it is already contained in the concept of what a promise is, and thus in the statement of fact. The apparent gap between the facts and the obligation is our familiar gap between the labeling and the signaling aspects of the word's grammar (for instance, between what is claimed in saying "I know" and what is ours to give). That is to say, no gap exists. Or, alternatively, the gap is bridged by the act of speaking, the commitment made in calling what he did "promising." So the problem is not how one can derive values from facts. No derivation is necessary. The values are already in the facts; or rather, there is something radically wrong with the supposition that everything must be either a fact or a value.

The same point can be made at a different level if we look at so-called "normative" and "descriptive" propositions, at rules and descriptions. Wittgenstein observed quite early that "every regulation (*Vorschrift*) can be understood as a description, every description as a regulation."[16] Cavell points out that if we actually look at rules, look in books about games or grammar or parliamentary procedure, we find the great bulk of rules formulated in the indicative mode. "In *Hoyle's Rules of Games* we find statements like, 'The opponent at declarer's left makes the opening lead. . . . Declarer's partner then lays his whole hand face up on the table, with his trumps if any on the right. The hand so exposed is the *dummy*. . . . The object of play is solely to win tricks, in order to fulfill or defeat the contract'; in *Robert's Rules of Order*, the rules take the form, 'The privileged motion to adjourn takes precedence of all others, except the privileged motion "to fix the time to which to adjourn," to which it yields' . . . ; taking a grammar at random we find, 'Mute stems form the nominative singular by the addition of -s in the case of masculines and feminines . . . Before -s of the nominative singular, a labial mute (p, b) remains unchanged.' "[17]

In one light, these rules seem to be commands, telling us what we must or should or ought to do; but in another they are what their indicative form suggests: descriptive statements of *how one does* certain things, like playing bridge or speaking English. Cavell argues that the explanation of this complementarity "has to do with the fact that its topic is actions. When we say how an action is done (how to act) what we say may report or describe the way we *in fact* do it . . . but it may also lay out a way of doing or saying something which is to be *followed*." If such expressions "are taken to state facts and are supposed to be believed, they are statements; if they are taken as guides and supposed to be followed, they are rules. Such expressions are no more 'in themselves' rules or (synthetic) statements than other expressions are, in themselves, postulates or con-

16 Ludwig Wittgenstein, *Philosophische Bemerkungen*, ed. by Rush Rhees (Oxford: Basil Blackwell, 1964), p. 59; my translation.
17 Cavell, *Must We Mean What We Say?*, p. 15.

clusions or definitions or replies."[18] That is why Socrates' observations on justice are as much about what is as what ought to be, why he tells us not merely what men ought to do but what they in fact do when they act justly.

Of course, rules sometimes sort with imperatives, but not always. "In the Britannica article (11th edition) on chess, only one paragraph of the twenty or so which describe the game is headed 'Rules', and only here are we told what we *must* do. This paragraph deals with such matters as the convention of saying 'j'adoube' when you touch a piece to straighten it." Perhaps matters of this kind differ from matters of how the pieces move, as penalties imposed for misplay differ from moves which determine whether we are playing at all, "so that we would cheerfully say that we can play (are playing) chess without the 'j'adoube' convention, but less cheerfully that we can play without following the rule that 'the Queen moves in any direction, square or diagonal, whether forward or backward'."[19] The difference would seem to be between doing a thing badly, wrongly, strangely, ineptly, partially, and not doing it at all. This would suggest that the declarative form is for those actions which are easy, natural, normal for us; the imperative for those which we have to be made, or admonished, or reminded to do. If before the introduction of chess our culture had played another, quite similar game in which the "queen" moved like a chess knight, we might need an admonitory "you must move the queen in straight paths."[20]

Thus, the same rule can be quite variously formulated, depending on the situations of the person speaking and the person addressed. Expressions like "You must (are supposed to, obliged to, required to) move the queen in straight paths" say and assert no more than the imperative "Move the queen in straight paths (you do, in fact, always move the queen in straight paths)." As Cavell puts it, "Which of them you say on a given occasion depends not on any special motive or design of yours, nor upon any special mode of argument. There is no question of *going from* 'is' to 'must', but only of appreciating which of them should be said when, i.e., of appreciating the position and circumstances of the person to whom you are speaking. Whatever makes one of the statements true makes them all true, though not all appropriate."[21]

Their appropriateness depends on the circumstances in which someone chooses to say them to someone else; and of course the forms do differ in this respect, in ways which are not in the least arbitrary or subjective but governed by grammar. Each of the different forms has its own distinctive background and, therefore, implications. There are a number of different forms to choose from, of what Cavell calls "modal imper-

18 *Ibid.*
19 *Ibid.*, p. 25.
20 *Ibid.*, p. 26 n.
21 *Ibid.*, p. 27.

atives," like "shall," "will," "must," "should," "ought to," "might," "may," "are to," and so on. Each of them is different in assumptions, implications, and appropriate context, in ways that their grammar regulates. "To tell me what I must do is not the same as to tell me what I ought to do."[22] The queen moves in straight paths; or, if admonition is needed, you must move it in straight paths. But "what would it mean to tell me that I *ought* to move the Queen in straight paths? 'Ought', unlike 'must', implies that there is an alternative; 'ought' implies that you can, if you choose, do otherwise. This does *not* mean merely that there is something else to do which is in your *power* ('I *can* move the Queen like the Knight; just watch!') but that there is one within your *rights*. But if I say truly and appropriately 'You must . . .' then in a perfectly good sense nothing you then do can prove me wrong. *You* CAN *push the little object called the Queen* in many ways, as you can *lift* it or *throw* it across the room; not all of these will be *moving the Queen.* . . . Again, if I have borrowed money then I *must* (under normal circumstances) pay it back (even though it is rather painful). It makes sense to tell me I *ought* to pay it back only if there is a specific reason to suppose, say, that the person from whom I got the money *meant to give* it to me rather than merely *lend* it (nevertheless he needs it badly, worse than I know), or if there is a reason to pay it back tomorrow instead of next week, when the debt falls due (I'll save interest; I'll only spend it and have to make another loan)."[23]

Similarly, if you have made a promise you have a *prima facie* obligation to keep it. If you are tempted not to, I may admonish you that you must; this is not at all the same as saying that you "should" or that you "ought to." The latter only makes sense when (and therefore implies that) you have a reason for breaking the promise strong enough to allow you to do so without blame, so that you have a real alternative, but where I am urging you to make a special effort or sacrifice. This is one reason why the formulation common in philosophy, of what is taken to be a typical moral precept, "You ought to keep your promises," is so queer and produces such queer discussions. Both "ought" and "must" here suggest that we "always want badly to get out of fulfilling promises." In addition, "ought" further suggests "that we always have some good (anyway, *prima facie*) reason for not keeping them (perhaps our own severe discomfort) and that therefore we are acting *well* when we do fulfill. But we aren't, normally; neither well nor ill."[24]

All of the modal imperatives have point only in the context of, against the background of, knowledge of what the person addressed is doing, or the position he is in—that he is doing a certain thing, but in danger of

[22] *Ibid.*, pp. 27–28.
[23] *Ibid.*, p. 28.
[24] *Ibid.*, p. 30.

doing it badly, inappropriately, self-defeatingly, and so on. What we may, should, must, are allowed, are supposed, ought to do depends on who we are and what we are engaged in doing, what we are in a position or able to do. The modal imperatives, unlike a pure imperative or command, "require the recognition of a background action or position into which the relevant action is placed. . . . Whether I can command depends only upon whether I have power or authority, and the only characteristics I must recognize in the object of the command are those which tell me that the object is subject to my power or authority. Employing a modal 'imperative,' however, requires that I recognize the object as a person (someone doing something or in a certain position) to whose reasonableness (reason) I appeal in using the second person. (Compare 'Open, Sesame!' with 'You must open, Sesame.')"[25] Thus commands, pure imperatives, are in no way the paradigm of moral utterance, any more than of factual utterance; they constitute an alternative to it.

### VERIFICATION AND THE IMPERSONAL MODE

Still another way of attempting to distinguish "the is" from "the ought" frequently invoked by advocates of the dichotomy and derived from logical positivism, is the criterion of falsifiability. We are told that an utterance concerns fact, or what "is," if it can *in principle* be falsfied by some empirical evidence encountered in experience.[26] But what sorts of utterances actually are in principle falsifiable by experience or observation? Surely when we judge a painting to be lovely or somber, a man to be courageous or cruel, an action to be accidental or mistaken, we do so on the basis of observation and experience. Of course, others may disagree, but that is true about our "factual" observations of physical events as well. In both kinds of assertions, it seems we can be right or wrong, evidence and arguments can be mustered to suport what we say. The dichotomist will answer that, in statements of fact, we are agreed as to what evidence would in principle falsify the statement decisively. But is that really always true of scientific propositions or common-sense observations about physical events? And is it really always false of our judgments about actions or works of art?

The fact is that, within a realm of discourse like ethics or esthetics, we distinguish mere propaganda, personal preference, and the like from genuine judgment based on knowledge.[27] As Ziff points out, the initial

[25] *Ibid.*, pp. 30–31.
[26] See for example, Sesonske, "Cognitive and Normative," p. 2; Arthur Pap, *Elements of Analytic Philosophy* (New York: Macmillan, 1949), p. 124.
[27] Compare Sesonske, *Value and Obligation*, p. 13: "Nothing in this common sense usage indicates ethical statements are regarded as being true or false in any different sense than are non-ethical statements. Our verbal responses are, in general, quite similar and our behavior follows the same pattern in either instance. If we

implausibility of equating "that is good" with "I approve of that; do so as well!" results from the fact that the first expression, but not the second, "has the form of an impersonal remark."[28] It is a remark about the object, not about the speaker or the person addressed. In saying that a certain painting is good, one is "presumably talking about the painting, whereas in saying 'I approve of that painting.' one is clearly telling someone something about oneself." Moreover, one can stress the impersonal aspect of "That is a good painting" in various ways. For example, we say, "That is a good painting but I don't like it." And certainly there is nothing odd about "That is a good potato but I detest potatoes," or "That is a good screwdriver but I have no interest in screwdrivers."[29] On the other hand, even the impersonal remark about the painting has some personal implications. Thus, while "That is a good painting but I don't like it" sounds quite natural, one could hardly say "That is a good painting and I don't like it"—except, as Ziff points out, in a "fairly special context, e.g., one in which someone has been telling me that I do in fact like all good paintings."[30]

What Ziff calls the "impersonal form" of an utterance like "That is good," which separates it from a statement of personal approval or preference, is what Kant calls "speaking in a universal voice."[31] Kant distinguishes two kinds of "aesthetical judgments" or judgments of taste: the "taste of sense" and the "taste of reflection."[32] Cavell describes the distinction this way: "The former concerns merely what we find pleasant, the latter must—logically must, some of us would say—concern and claim more than that. And it is only the second whose topic is the beautiful, whose role, that is, would be aesthetic in its more familiar sense. The something more these judgments must do is to 'demand' or 'impute' or 'claim' general validity, universal agreement . . . ; and when we make such judgments we go on claiming this agreement even though we know from experience that they will not receive it."[33] Kant says that who calls a

---

accept a statement as true, we adjust our behavior to accord with it; if we doubt it, we seek justification and if satisfactory reasons are given, we then admit the assertion to be true." Or compare Bernard Mayo, *Ethics and the Moral Life* (London: Macmillan, 1958), pp. 86–88, who cites, of all people, David Hume, on objectivity in judgment as parallel to objectivity in physical perception.

[28] Ziff, *Semantic Analysis*, p. 233; compare John Searle, *Speech Acts* (Cambridge: Cambridge University Press, 1969), p. 139: " 'If this is good, then we ought to buy it', is not equivalent to 'If I commend this, then we ought to buy it'. 'This used to be good', is not equivalent to 'I used to commend this'. 'I wonder whether this is good' is not equivalent to 'I wonder whether I commend this', etc."

[29] Ziff, *Semantic Analysis*, p. 233.

[30] *Ibid.*, p. 235.

[31] Immanuel Kant, *Critique of Judgment*, sections 7 and 8, cited in Cavell, *Must We Mean What We Say?*, p. 89. Compare Michael Polanyi, *Personal Knowledge* (New York and Evanston: Harper & Row, 1964), pp. 300–311; and Sesonske, *Value and Obligation*, p. 16: "Ethical statements make claims upon us, but claims advanced as impersonal and rationally justifiable."

[32] Cavell, *Must We Mean What We Say?*, p. 88.

[33] *Ibid.*, pp. 88–89.

painting beautiful or good speaks as if he judges "not merely for himself, but for all men"; he demands "the assent of everyone."[34]

Kant also expresses this idea by saying that we speak "of beauty as if it were a property of things." Cavell explains: "Only 'as if' because it cannot be an ordinary property of things: its presence or absence cannot be established in the way ordinary properties are; that is, they cannot be established publicly, and we don't know (there aren't any) causal conditions, or usable rules, for producing, or altering, or erasing, or increasing this 'property'. They why not just say it *isn't* a property of an object? I suppose there would be no reason not to say this, if we could find another way of recording our conviction that it is one, anyway that what we are pointing to is *there*, in the object; and our knowledge that men make objects that create this response in us, and make them exactly with the idea that they will create it; and the fact that, while we know not everyone will agree with us when we say it is present, we think they are *missing something* if they don't."[35]

To borrow Kant's illustration, someone "is quite contented that if he says, 'Canary wine is pleasant', another man may correct his expression and remind him that he ought to say, 'It is pleasant *to me*'. And this is the case not only as regards the taste of the tongue, the palate, and the throat, but for whatever is pleasant to anyone's eyes and ears. . . . To strive here with the design of reproving as incorrect another man's judgement which is different from our own, as if the judgements were logically opposed, would be folly. . . . The case is quite different with the beautiful. It would (on the contrary) be laughable if a man who imagined anything to his own taste thought to justify himself by saying: 'This object (the house we see, the coat that person wears, the concert we hear, the poem submitted to our judgement) is beautiful *for me*.' For he must not call it *beautiful* if it merely pleases him. . . ."[36]

He must not call it beautiful if it merely pleases him; what sort of a "must" is that? what authority speaks? Kant calls this kind of rightness and wrongness transcendental. Wittgenstein would call it a matter of grammar. The grammar of taste is different from that of beauty, which is different from that of approval, and so on. He says "there is a realm of utterance of delight, when you taste pleasant food or smell a pleasant smell, etc., then there is the realm of Art, which is quite different."[37] In the latter realm, "when we make an aesthetic judgment about a thing, we do not just gape at it and say: 'Oh! How marvellous!' We distinguish between a person who knows what he is talking about and a person who doesn't."[38]

Esthetic judgments are most likely to coincide with mere expressions of

[34] *Ibid.*, p. 89 and n.
[35] *Ibid.*
[36] Quoted *ibid.*, p. 90.
[37] Wittgenstein, *Lectures and Conversations*, p. 11.
[38] *Ibid.*, p. 6.

personal pleasure or displeasure where the speaker does not know what he is talking about, where he is technically ignorant about the kind of thing he is judging. If a man who knows nothing about roses says "That rose over there, with two colors, is a good one," then, as Ziff points out, "the inference that he rather likes the rose is fairly safe." By contrast, someone who says "The Contessa de Sastago is a very good hybrid tea rose, "is much more likely to be making an impersonal remark. The ignorant man who calls a rose good simply because he likes it "is in a difficult position. One could look at the case in the following way: he wants to talk impersonally, to keep himself out of the picture, to say something about the rose; but since he knows nothing about roses, he can find no fact about the rose to take hold of to lift himself out of himself. Consequently he lifts himself by his own bootstraps."[39]

The point is that if he says it's good and cannot provide competent support for his judgment, falls back on his liking the rose, he has made a *retreat*. That, I think, is what Kant means by saying we "mustn't" speak in the universal voice, in the impersonal mode, if we are merely expressing personal preference. Cavell reformulates Kant's example:

A: Canary wine is pleasant.
B: How can you say that? It tastes like canary droppings.
A: Well, I like it.[40]

Here personal taste is perfectly apropos, not a retreat. Now compare this exchange with either of the following:

A: He plays beautifully, doesn't he?
B: Yes, too beautifully. Beethoven is not Chopin.

A: He plays beautifully, doesn't he?
B: How can you say that? There was no line, no structure, no idea what the music was about. He's simply an impressive colorist.

In the latter examples, A can no longer simply retort "Well, I liked it." Or rather, as Cavell says, "Of course he *can*; but don't we feel that here that would be a feeble rejoinder, a *retreat* to personal taste? Because B's reasons are obviously relevant to the evaluation of performance, and because they are arguable, in ways that anyone who knows about such things will know how to pursue. A *doesn't have* to pursue them; but if he doesn't, there is a price he will have to pay in our estimate of him."[41] Cavell's point here is much like Austin's point about excuses in moral discourse, that there are "standards of the unacceptable" in these realms every bit as much as in realms like science or mathematics. Words are governed by grammar in all these realms, and what you say has implications which you may or may not be able to support competently.

[39] Ziff, *Semantic Analysis*, p. 234.
[40] Cavell, *Must We Mean What We Say?*, p. 91.
[41] *Ibid.*, pp. 91–92.

Of course, the appeal to standards can be abused, but that is true in any realm; it does not make the abuse *typical* of ethical or esthetic discourse any more than of scientific discourse. "That is a lovely figurine" is no more equivalent to "I approve of that figurine; do so as well!" than "There is a goldfinch at the bottom of the garden" is equivalent to "I believe (imagine?) there is a goldfinch at the bottom of the garden; do so as well!" As Cavell says, "It is true that we sometimes appeal to standards which our interlocutor does not accept; but this does not in the least show that we are . . . (merely) expressing our own opinion or feeling on the matter. We of course *may* express our private opinion or feeling—we normally do so where it is not clear what (or that any) rule or standard fits the case at hand and where we are therefore not willing or able to appeal to any."[42] We do so, in short, when we know nothing about (say) roses, or when we encounter an unprecedented case.

"The practice of appealing to a norm," Cavell continues, "can be abused, as can any other of our practices. Sometimes people appeal to a rule when we deserve more intimate attention from them. Just as sometimes people tell us what we ought to do when all they mean is that they want us to. But this is as much an abuse where the context is moral as it is where the context is musical ('You ought to accent the appoggiatura'), or scientific ('You ought to use a control group here'), or athletic ('You ought to save your wind on the first two laps'). Private persuasion (or personal appeal) is not the paradigm of ethical [or esthetic, or political] utterance, but represents the breakdown or transcending" of these modes of interaction.[43] Though we can often say "It meets those standards, but is it good?" that fact is by no means confined to ethics or esthetics or politics, to so-called value judgments. It sometimes makes equally good sense to say, "It is true enough that the thing weighs fifty pounds, but is it heavy?", "It is true enough that the thing looks red to an ordinary person under white light but is it red?"[44]

Moreover, standards can be challenged and sometimes changed. But, of course, that is as true of the standards of science as it is of the standards of esthetics.[45] And in both cases, though in different ways, not just anything you do will be challenging standards, not just any challenge will be a proposal for new standards. We already have, as it were, some implicit notions of what will *count as* a new principle of esthetics or morality, a new scientific method or a new type of proof in mathematics, a new application of a familiar concept. All of these enterprises, like language, have rules, but are not everywhere circumscribed by rules. Innovation is possible, yet not just any new move will be an innovation.

Someone who believes in the dichotomy between facts and values is

[42] *Ibid.*, p. 23.
[43] *Ibid.*
[44] Ziff, *Semantic Analysis*, p. 235.
[45] Sesonske, *Value and Obligation*, p. 27; Cavell, "The Claim to Rationality" (unpublished dissertation, Harvard University), pp. 343–344.

likely to feel, however, that such arguments at most demonstrate something about linguistic *forms*, not about reality. For example, we have distinguished between personal and impersonal form in esthetic utterances, between claims "demanding universal assent" and those content to express personal preferences. But, of course, the dichotomist never argued that "this is a lovely painting" literally *means the same* as "I like this painting; do so as well"; he argued only that they are *functionally equivalent*. He recognizes that the form and sense of "this is a lovely painting" imply the existence of standards and evidence. What he wants to question is whether what is implied here is really *true*, whether any such objective standards *exist* in a realm like esthetics, whether we are *entitled* to speak in an impersonal form here.[46] He believes that the forms of our language here make us seem to offer what in fact is not ours to give, make us speak as if there were standards and objectivity where none exist.

But one must ask what is the measure of "standards" or of "objectivity" here. By what measure is science or mathematics found to be "objective" while ethics or esthetics or politics is "subjective" or "normative"? Standards, objectivity, rationality, work differently in different realms of discourse. The fact that we speak differently about art than about physical events is not proof that esthetic discourse is less objective than scientific discourse. On the contrary, we need to look and see how objectivity functions, what it is like, in different realms. Only then will we understand what rationality in ethics looks like, and how it differs from rationality in science.

For example, we have said that establishing facts about actions is not like establishing facts about physical events, because our talk about action (which shapes the grammar of our action concepts and thus our notion of what counts as a fact here) serves different purposes, has different functions. We use language in different ways here. Specifically in moral discourse, the point is not so much establishing an objective general truth, independent of time and person, as making one's own position clear with respect to a specific situation. For that function, moral discourse must be sufficiently flexible to allow each speaker to choose a position true of him, to find his personal position; this would not be possible if moral facts were established in the same impersonal way as facts about physical objects, so that what is truth for one is truth for all. At the same time, the language of moral discourse must be stable enough so that what a man says really does constitute taking *a position*, really tells us something about him. In this sense, what is true *of* a particular individual is not merely true *for* him personally, but is objectively true *of* him *for* everyone. It is not up to him alone to assess the significance or even the truth of the position he chooses to take; it is not up to him alone to decide whether he has adequately supported and elaborated the initial claim he has entered. The stability is supplied by our concepts and their connections in grammar,

46 Compare Mayo, *op. cit.*, p. 89.

which we did not choose and can only change in restricted ways. The flexibility is supplied by the way we operate with these concepts, by the way we use them in action, relate them to the world. The identification of actions is significantly different from the identification of objects, but the difference has to do not so much with subjectivity or values as with commitment. As we said earlier, talking about actions requires the speaker to take a position with consequences for commitment and responsibility, quite apart from what he may feel or want or value.

There are standards, mistakes, good and bad reasons, valid and invalid arguments in ethics (and esthetics and politics) just as in science or mathematics. Of course, ethical standards are not absolute or beyond all challenge. There is no Master Ethical Umpire in the Sky to decide our disputes about actions once and for all. All we ever have is a collection of fallible human beings confronting each other, each with his own standards and values, each trapped in his own subjectivity. But why should we suppose that absolute, unchallengeable standards or a Master Umpire are necessary? Their absence is just as characteristic of mathematics and science as it is of ethics and esthetics. None of these realms has access to any transcendent or superhuman standards or judges. We merely *use* standards differently there. Some human forms of life have umpires, some have explicit standards, some have right and wrong answers, some have rule books. But the umpires are always human and fallible, the standards always in the minds of individual men, the answers worked out by men, the rule books written by men.

What happens when we feel that realms like ethics or esthetics are arbitrary and subjective is that we compare our actual use of standards and judgment in these realms with an incorrect idealization of what goes on in science or mathematics—an ideal of standards free of any convention, absolute, capable of being invoked without the possibility of contradiction and therefore without responsibility or commitment. But that ideal does not exist in reality. Even in science and mathematics there are assumptions and conventions guaranteed only by our commitment to them, the way we use them. Science and mathematics do not have access to any transcendental guarantees, nor do they achieve universal agreement. People get varying results even to problems in arithmetic; from time to time someone questions even the law of gravity. What characterizes mathematics or science is not that deviant positions are literally impossible, but that they are not acceptable as positions in mathematics or science. The fact that someone gets a different answer in arithmetic does not shake our faith in the existence of "right answers" in that field, even for an instant. If someone tells us that, for his part, he regards three times twenty as equaling seventy, we do not say that he is entitled to his opinion, nor do we anxiously review the validity of mathematics. In mathematics, we can prove the validity of propositions deductively. But what that means is not that no human being could conceivably doubt them, but only that

237

we will not accept doubts about such proofs as relevant or competent. In mathematics and science, there are experts who teach us laymen the right answers and how to derive them. But what that means is simply that we fallible human beings are prepared, in these fields, to regard some among us with special training *as* experts.

Wittgenstein discusses the role of axioms and of proof in mathematics at length in the *Foundations of Mathematics*, asking what makes a proposition into an axiom, and what makes a proof binding. The answer to both questions is, essentially: what we do; which rests in turn on our forms of life. "Something is an axiom, *not* because we accept it as extremely probable, nay certain, but because we assign it a particular function, and one that conflicts with that of an empirical proposition. . . . An axiom, I should like to say, is a different part of speech."[47] It is how we use it, not a transcendent message from another world, that makes a proposition into an axiom. So too with proof and its binding power, or, as Wittgenstein calls it, "the hardness of the logical *must*."[48] We say to someone, " 'You admit *this*—then you must admit *this* too.' —He *must* admit it—and all the time it is possible that he does not admit it!"[49] The "must" is not a prediction that no one could possibly fail to accept a proof or a logical conclusion; rather, it announces what attitude we are prepared to take toward anyone who does fail to accept it. It depends on what we do. "I *go through* the proof and then accept its result. —I mean: this is simply what we *do*. This is use and custom among us, a fact of our natural history."[50]

Of course, the proof must be such that we can use it in this way, must be capable of convincing, must show us not merely that something is so (as an experiment might) but how it is so. It is not "that the rule compels me to act like this; but that it makes it possible for me to hold on to it and let myself be compelled by it."[51] A proof is not like a scientific experiment: "We do not accept the result of a proof because it results once, or because it often results. Rather, we see in the proof the reason for saying that this *must* be the result."[52] Unlike an experiment, a mathematical proof "does not merely shew *that* it is like this, but: *how* it is like this. It shows *how* 13 + 14 yield 27. 'A proof must be capable of being taken in [*übersehbar*, perspicuous]' means: we must be prepared to use it as our guide-line in judging."[53] A proof is not just something that most people will agree on, though unless most people could agree on it it could not be a proof. But what makes it a proof is the game we play with it; and

[47] Ludwig Wittgenstein, *Remarks on the Foundations of Mathematics*, tr. by G. E. M. Anscombe, ed. by G. H. von Wright, R. Rhees, and G. E. M. Anscombe (Oxford: Basil Blackwell, 1964), p. 114.

[48] *Ibid.*, p. 37.

[49] *Ibid.*, p. 18.

[50] *Ibid.*, p. 20.

[51] *Ibid.*, p. 193; my translation.

[52] *Ibid.*, p. 81; my translation.

[53] *Ibid.*, p. 75.

that game is not majority rule, but that everyone must agree or be judged incompetent or irrational. "We say, not: 'So *that's* how we go!', but: 'So *that's* how it goes!' "[54]

These observations about mathematical proof and "the hardness of the logical *must*" can, I think, help us to see what certainty and standards and rationality and proof are like among human beings. When we speak impersonally, in a way that claims universal validity, in an objective mode, it is never because we have transcendent, superhuman guarantees, nor because we are absolutely certain that no one will disagree with us. Instead we, as it were, announce what attitude we are prepared to take toward those who disagree with us, what kind of support we would be able to muster for our assertion if challenged, how we regard that assertion and intend to use it, how it is to be used and considered by others. And we are responsible for what we thus take on; if we cannot support our position in the appropriate way, we pay a price.

That price is different in each realm of discourse, but in each realm, as Cavell says, the particular price is "necessary, and specific to the sorts of judgments we call aesthetic," or moral, or scientific, or mathematical, or historical.[55] If a man pleads inadvertence when he has stepped on the baby, we may conclude that he is callous and will certainly keep the baby off the floor when he is around. If he retreats to "Well, I liked it," after someone else has maintained that a musical performance lacked line and structure and the performer was just an impressive colorist, we may draw certain conclusions about his knowledge of music, and they will affect whether we accept his reports on musical performances in the future.

The price is different with respect to questions of physical fact. Consider, for example, this sequence:

A: There is a goldfinch in the garden.
B: How do you know?
A: From the color of its head.
B: But goldcrests also have heads that color.
A: Well, *I* think it's a goldfinch (it's a goldfinch to me).

As Cavell says, "This is no longer a feeble rejoinder, a retreat to personal opinion," nor is it the invoking of dreadful standards. And we will not conclude that the man is ignorant about goldfinches, or not very articulate, or a callous boor. "The price here is that he is either mad, or doesn't know what the word 'know' means, or is in some other way unintelligible to us. That is, *we rule him out* as a competent interlocutor in matters of knowledge (about birds?): whatever is going on, he *doesn't* know there is a goldfinch in the garden, whatever (else) he thinks he 'knows'. But we do not, at least not with the same flatness and good conscience, and not with the same consequences, rule out the person who liked the performance of Beethoven [or who stepped on the baby]: he still has a claim upon us,

[54] *Ibid.*, p. 96.
[55] Cavell, *Must We Mean What We Say?*, p. 92.

however attenuated; he *may* even have reasons for his judgment, or counters to your objections, which for some reason he can't give (perhaps because you've browbeaten him into amnesia)."[56]

There are important differences among realms of discourse, and they sometimes make us want to say that mathematics and science are objective and rational in a way that ethics and esthetics are not. But three important modifications must be kept in mind in understanding that proposition. First, the differences are not dichotomous but plural; the differences between objectivity in mathematics and in science, or in science and in everyday common sense, or in ethics and esthetics, are every bit as interesting and important as those between objectivity in science and in esthetics. Lumping all of these different realms of discourse into two great classes really obscures instead of clarifying. Second, the differences which exist result from how *we act*, how we operate with language in these various realms. They do not result from any transcendental guarantee accessible in certain realms but not others. All utterances, all truth, all judgments, all assertions, are in fact made, assessed, accepted, or rejected by fallible human beings. Third, there are also important differences *within* each realm of discourse between rational and irrational, between self-referential and impersonal, between competent and incompetent, between well-supported and unsupportable ways of talking. There are always standards for distinguishing, though the standards work differently in different realms, depending on the way language functions there.

[56] *Ibid.*

# XI

## Action and the
## Problem of Social Science

IF THE GRAMMAR of human action really forms a distinctive region of language whose concepts cannot be translated into those of other regions, if actions are really irreducibly different from physical events, then serious consequences evidently follow for the study of politics and society. In recent years, a growing body of literature has criticized the attempt to make this study scientific, to develop a science of politics or of society. The literature draws from a wide variety of roots; its authors include defenders of traditional political theory like Voegelin and Wolin, Natural Law theorists like Strauss, philosophers influenced by existentialism and phenomenology like Arendt, Schutz, Natanson; philosophers influenced by ordinary-language analysis like Louch, and Charles and Richard Taylor; Winch, who explicitly claims to derive his views from Wittgenstein; and many others.[1] Yet, despite their divergent perspectives and some important differences among them, their basic arguments are remarkably parallel, so that joint treatment is feasible. Much of what they have to say closely resembles Wittgensteinian views, some of them specifically invoke his

[1] Eric Voegelin, *The New Science of Politics* (Chicago: University of Chicago Press, 1952); Sheldon S. Wolin, *Politics and Vision* (Boston and Toronto: Little, Brown, 1960), and "Political Theory as a Vocation," *American Political Science Review*, LXIII (December 1969), 1062–1082; Leo Strauss, *Natural Right and History* (Chicago: University of Chicago Press, 1959), and "An Epilogue," in Herbert J. Storing, ed., *Essays on the Scientific Study of Politics* (New York: Holt, Rinehart and Winston, 1962); Hannah Arendt, *The Human Condition* (Garden City: Doubleday, 1958); Alfred Schutz, *Phenomenology of the Social World*, tr. by George Walsh and Frederick Lehnert (Evanston: Northwestern University Press, 1967), and *Collected Papers*, ed. by Maurice Natanson (The Hague: M. Nijhoff, 1962–1966); Maurice Natanson, ed., *Philosophy of the Social Sciences* (New York: Random House, 1963); A. R. Louch, *Explanation and Human Action* (Berkeley and Los Angeles: University of California Press, 1966); Charles Taylor, *The Explanation of Behaviour* (New York: Humanities Press, 1967); Richard Taylor, *Action and Purpose* (Englewood Cliffs, N. J.: Prentice-Hall, 1966); Peter Winch, *The Idea of a Social Science and its Relation to Philosophy* (New York: Humanities Press, 1965), and "Understanding a Primitive Society," *American Philosophical Quarterly*, I (October 1964), 307–324.

work, and they are, indeed, trying to tell us something true and important about social science. But their actual arguments are too often inaccurate, oversimplified, absurd, or simply false; and they conflict with Wittgenstein's teachings just where he might be most useful for them. In this chapter and the next, we shall first examine what they say, and then subject it to an attempt at a Wittgensteinian critique, in hopes of separating the valuable point from the unsatisfactory arguments which cannot sustain it.

In brief summary, the common structure of their arguments runs something like this: The subject matter of social and political study is actions—something unique to human beings, involving freedom, choice, and responsibility, meaning and sense, conventions, norms, and rules. Though other, animal aspects of human conduct can perhaps be studied scientifically, actions cannot. This is because, the language of actions being used and shaped in the course of action by the actors, actions can only be identified in the actors' concepts and according to the actors' norms. This means, first, that detached, objective, scientific observation of actions is impossible; and second, that the explanation of actions must necessarily be in terms of the actors' intentions, motives, reasons, purposes—never in scientific, causal terms.

There are of course significant variations from this basic pattern of argument. Some result from the great variety of ways of distinguishing and defining "action"—a topic whose difficulties we considered earlier. Thus, as we mentioned, Arendt defines action narrowly, confining it to the public, political realm. As a result, she attacks the possibility of a scientific political science, but thinks a scientific social science perfectly feasible. Indeed, she argues that social phenomena are entirely constituted of human behavior, not action, so that they are predictable and caused and quite amenable to scientific study. But action, and therefore true political life, are not; they are creative, unpredictable, free of causal necessity. The birth of scientific social science "coincided with the rise of society," the gradual eclipse of the political by the social. Both society and social science share "the same conformism, the assumption that men behave and do not act with respect to each other."[2] Thus social science is not only feasible, but becomes increasingly successful as men become increasingly social, behaving, predictable creatures of the mass, and lose their capacity for action.

From this perspective, the attempt to make the study of political life scientific is not just hopeless, but directly undermines the uniqueness of action, the autonomy of the political realm. Arendt, Wolin, and Strauss all develop arguments along this line, attacking the causal explanation of political phenomena in nonpolitical terms. Social science assumes "that political phenomena are best explained as the resultant of social factors, and hence political institutions and beliefs are best understood by a

[2] Arendt, *Human Condition*, pp. 38–39.

method which gets 'behind' them to the 'underlying' social processes which dictate the shape of things political," Wolin says.[3] This assumption "is not solely methodological, nor even primarily ethical in character, but substantive; that is, it concerns the status of politics and the political. When modern social science asserts that political phenomena are to be explained by resolving them into sociological, psychological, or economic components, it is saying that there are no distinctively political phenomena."[4] Arendt agrees; modern social science assumes "that politics is nothing but a function of society, that action, speech and thought are primarily superstructures upon social interest." This assumption, which she calls the "functionalization" of the political, "makes it impossible to perceive any serious gulf between" the political and the social realm, and hence to understand the true nature of political action.[5] Its true nature, as Strauss says, "is *sui generis* and cannot be understood as derivative from the sub-political."[6]

More commonly, however, the attack is directed against all social science, against attempts to study any uniquely human activities in a scientific manner. Indeed, even Arendt sometimes conceives of action more broadly than her definition would allow; and even Strauss' explanation of why a political science is impossible would apply equally well to any social science. Like many of these writers, Strauss explicitly acknowledges that some aspects of human behavior can be scientifically studied: "we can observe, if we try hard enough, the overt behavior of humans as we observe the overt behavior of rats."[7] But with rats, this is all we can do, whereas with human beings we have an alternative because of language. "In the case of rats we are limited to observing their overt behavior because they do not talk, and they do not talk because they have nothing to say or because they have no inwardness."

Strauss thus gives two reasons for man's unique resistance to scientific explanation—one quite traditional, and one much more modern. He says that men are distinguished by "having inwardness," or more explicitly by having "souls" which cannot be observed. "The soul's actions, passions, or states can never become sense data."[8] But Strauss also says that what distinguishes men is their use of language, and here he is supported by almost all the other writers in this group. Unlike rats or inanimate objects, men use language in the course of their activity, and that makes the subject matter of political science fundamentally different from that of physical science.

As Winch says, both physical and social scientists bring a system of concepts to their subject matter, but what the physical scientist studies

[3] Wolin, *Politics and Vision*, p. 287.
[4] *Ibid.*, p. 288.
[5] Arendt, *Human Condition*, p. 31.
[6] Strauss, "An Epilogue," p. 311.
[7] *Ibid.*, p. 320.
[8] *Ibid.*, p. 316.

also has "an existence independent of those concepts. There existed electrical storms and thunder long before there were human beings to form concepts of them. . . . But it does not make sense to suppose that human beings might have been issuing commands and obeying them before they came to form the concept of command and obedience. For their performance of such acts is itself the chief manifestation of their possession of those concepts. An act of obedience itself contains, as an essential element, a recognition of what went before as an order. But it would of course be senseless to suppose that a clap of thunder contained any recognition of what went before as an electrical storm."[9] The distinctive thing about social science, then, is that "*what the sociologist is studying*, as well as his study of it, is a human activity," and therefore governed by rules, intentional, conceptual.[10] The people studied by a sociologist have their own conceptions of what they are doing. Thus, "the conceptions according to which we normally think of social events . . . enter into social life itself and not merely into the observer's description of it."[11] Similar passages occur in Gunnell, Schutz, and Voegelin.

But whether the crucial difficulty is the human soul or the human use of language, it would seem to extend beyond the political life of man into almost all areas of human activity. We use language, and our concepts structure and interpret what we do, not merely in politics but in social, economic, scientific, esthetic, moral, and religious activity as well. So the attack on scientific study should really extend to all these realms, and a social science is problematic in the same way as a political science. Any field of human endeavor that involves language will present the observer with a pre-articulated interpretation of what is being done, an articulation in terms of which the endeavor is being carried on.

From this fact, most of these critics of social science derive the major thesis that the identification of actions necessarily must be in the actors' terms, in the actors' norms and concepts. Noting that action is conventional and purposive, they argue that it can be identified only in accord with the conventions governing it and the purposes informing it. Many of them are struck, as Winch is, by the difficulties of identifying actions,

---

[9] Winch, *Idea of a Social Science*, p. 125.

[10] *Ibid.*, p. 87.

[11] *Ibid.*, p. 95; compare John Gunnell, "Social Science and Political Reality," *Social Research*, 35 (Spring 1968), p. 180; Alfred Schutz, "Concept and Theory Formation in the Social Sciences," in Natanson, ed., *Philosophy of the Social Sciences*, pp. 242, 246; and Voegelin, *New Science of Politics*, p. 27: "Political science is suffering from a difficulty that originates in its very nature as a science of man in historical existence. For man does not wait for science to have his life explained to him, and when the theorist approaches social reality he finds the field pre-empted by what may be called the self-interpretation of society. Human society is not merely a fact, or an event, in the external world to be studied by an observer like a natural phenomenon. Though it has externality as one of its important components, it is as a whole little world, a cosmion, illuminated with meaning from within by the human beings who continuously create and bear it as the mode and condition of their self-realization."

specifying what was done, saying whether two actions were the same, differentiating an action from mere movements. Winch examines the example of a man voting for the Labour Party; what the man does "is not *simply* to make a mark on a piece of paper; he is *casting a vote*. And what I want to ask is, what gives his action *this* sense, rather than, say, that of being a move in a game or part of a religious ritual." Considered in terms of physical movements, all these actions might look (smell, sound, and so on) exactly alike, so how are they distinct from each other, and from the equivalent physical movements made by a machine? "More generally, by what criteria do we distinguish acts which have a sense from those which do not?"[12] The problem is familiar, and Winch is quite explicit in deriving his argument from Wittgenstein. But where Wittgenstein's solution is multiple, involving the social context and the quasi-performative quality of attributing an action, and rejecting the idea that some particular inner feeling or thought (regularly) characterizes an action, Winch's solution is quite otherwise.

At one point he appears to be moving toward a Wittgensteinian emphasis on the social context, the surrounding circumstances of an action. He says that for the man's mark on the paper to be a vote, he "must live in a society which has certain specific political institutions" and "his act must be a participation in the political life of the country."[13] But Winch then goes on to develop a different position with respect to the voter, a position he adopts generally in the rest of his book, apparently without the realization that it constitutes any sort of break with Wittgenstein. For the action to be an act of voting, Winch goes on, the voter "must himself have a certain familiarity with" the political institutions in which he acts, "must be aware of the symbolic relation between what he is doing now and the government which comes into power after the election."[14] Similarily, if a man "places a slip of paper between the leaves of a book he can be said to be 'using a bookmark' only if he acts with the idea of using the slip to determine where he shall start rereading."[15] In general, an action is to be defined and identified by the actor's intention, awareness, and conception of what he is doing. The notion of action is tied to those of intention, motive, purpose; and the identification of action is thus dependent on the actor's understanding. As Schutz says, "strictly speaking, the actor and he alone knows what he does, why he does it, and when and where his action starts and ends."[16]

[12] Winch, *Idea of a Social Science*, p. 49; compare p. 35. Note that Winch defines the subject matter of social science not as "action," but, following Max Weber, as human activity "if and in so far as the agent or agents associate a subjective *sense* (*Sinn*) with it," thus as *meaningful* behavior, which Winch says is "all specifically human behaviour." Max Weber, *Wirtschaft und Gesellschaft* (Tübingen: Mohr, 1956), Ch. I, quoted at p. 45. The quotations from Winch himself are from p. 52.
[13] *Ibid.*, p. 51.
[14] *Ibid.*
[15] *Ibid.*, p. 50.
[16] Schutz, "Concept and Theory Formation," p. 243.

Winch concludes that the student of society and politics can identify his subject matter only by the concepts of the actors he is studying. For "two things may be called 'the same' or 'different' only with reference to a set of criteria which lay down what is to be regarded as a relevant difference. When the 'things' in question are purely physical the criteria appealed to will of course be those of the observer. But when one is dealing with intellectual (or, indeed, any kind of social) 'things', that is not so. For their *being* intellectual or social, as opposed to physical, in character depends entirely on their belonging in a certain way to a system of ideas or mode of living. It is only by reference to the criteria governing that system of ideas or mode of life that they have any existence as intellectual or social events. It follows that if the sociological investigator wants to regard them *as* social events (as, *ex hypothesi*, he must), he has to take seriously the criteria which are applied for distinguishing 'different' kinds of actions and identifying the 'same' kinds of actions within the way of life he is studying. It is not open to him arbitrarily to impose his own standards from without. In so far as he does so, the events he is studying lose altogether their character as *social* events."[17] Thus, for example, one cannot understand the behavior of Chaucer's Troilus toward Cressida, or even identify it, except in relation to the conceptions and conventions of courtly love, for they define his action and give it meaning.[18]

Strauss makes very much the same argument in relation to the study of politics. Its conceptualizations must be drawn from "the language of political man," of "the market place," and its truths depend on "the prescientific awareness of political things."[19] Only this prescientific awareness of the political participants can define and identify political phenomena; thus, a political science which rejects it lacks "orientation regarding political things." It has no "criteria of relevance," and thus "no protection whatever, except by surreptitious recourse to common sense, against losing itself in the study of irrelevancies."[20]

Moreover, Winch argues that not merely the identification of actions, but also what will count as evidence, as proof, as reality, with respect to them, depend on the concepts and norms of the actors and their particular enterprise. His idea here is much like the notion of language regions. He argues, for example, that in theology and religious discourse God is real, though He is not to be discovered through scientific experiment. What kind of reality He has, in what sense He is real, "can only be seen from the religious tradition in which the concept of God is used . . . The point is that it is *within* the religious use of language that the conception of God's reality has its place."[21] Winch is quick to point out that this does not mean that God's reality is "subjective" or "at the mercy of what anyone

[17] Winch, *Idea of a Social Science*, p. 108.
[18] *Ibid.*, p. 82.
[19] Strauss, "An Epilogue," pp. 315, 310, 311.
[20] *Ibid.*, p. 318.
[21] Winch, "Understanding a Primitive Society," p. 309.

cares to say; if this were so, God would have no reality." Reality, rationality, proof, are independent of particular individuals' views, but they are dependent on the kind of human activity going on, which must be defined by the participants. We have trouble seeing this, Winch argues, only because "the fascination science has for us makes it easy for us to adopt its scientific form as a paradigm against which to measure the intellectual respectability of other modes of discourse."[22]

The thesis becomes most powerful and poignant when Winch and Schutz draw examples not from within a single culture and language, but from anthropological research "where the object of study is a society which is culturally remote from that of the investigator."[23] For there the apparent gap between the movements the anthropologist can observe from the outside, and their significance within the culture, for the actors, is most striking. As Schutz points out, two sets of movements that look totally alike may have "entirely different meanings to the performers" in two different cultures. The social scientist must derive his interpretation from the actors, because what interests him is precisely the difference—whether that pattern of movement "is a war dance, a barter trade, the reception of a friendly ambassador, or something else," and only the actors themselves can tell him.[24]

Winch considers the example of a people who believe in and practice magic. The system of magic has its own rules, its own consistency, which is independent of any particular individual; individuals can sometimes make mistakes in magic, just as they can make mistakes in science. Winch quotes Collingwood's view that "savages," just like us, sometimes mistakenly suppose that they "can do what in fact cannot be done. But this error is not the essence of magic; it is a perversion of magic. And we should be careful how we attribute it to people we call savages, who will one day rise up and testify against us."[25] In other words, what magic means in a primitive culture that truly believes in and practices it is nothing like what "magic" means to us, with our traditions of medieval black magic, modern science, theater magicians, and the rest.

As an example, Winch takes a study of the Azande, an African people, done by E. E. Evans-Pritchard.[26] To a Zande, witchcraft is not "illusory," "superstitious," or "irrational." It is "a commonplace happening and he

[22] *Ibid.*, p. 308.

[23] Winch, *Idea of a Social Science*, p. 90.

[24] Schutz, "Concept and Theory Formation," p. 237.

[25] R. G. Collingwood, *Principles of Art*, p. 67, quoted in Winch, "Understanding a Primitive Society," pp. 309–310.

[26] E. E. Evans-Pritchard, *Witchcraft, Oracles and Magic Among the Azande* (Oxford: Clarendon Press, 1965). The same study is used for similar philosophical purposes by Michael Polanyi, *Personal Knowledge* (New York and Evanston: Harper & Row, 1964), pp. 287–294. See also Ernest Gellner's extraordinary article, "The Entry of the Philosophers," *Times Literary Supplement* (April 4, 1968), 347–349, in which Winch is misquoted as saying many foolish things about the Azande which he does not in fact say.

seldom passes a day without mentioning it. . . . He would be just as surprised if he were not brought into daily contact with it as we would be if confronted by its appearance. To him there is nothing miraculous about it."[27] The Azande in fact conduct their ordinary affairs to their own satisfaction in terms of witchcraft and magic, and are at a loss and bewildered when deprived of it—for instance, when they fall into the hands of European courts. Indeed, when Evans-Pritchard lived among them, he ran his own household in the Zande way, and says "I found this as satisfactory a way of running my home and affairs as any other I know of."[28]

Zande magic, witchcraft, and oracles are an internally consistent system on the basis of which it is possible to conduct a satisfactory human life and a satisfactory human culture. Deviations and errors are possible within that system, as they are in our science, but the system itself defines what counts as a deviation or an error. Like us, the Azande are even sometimes skeptical about parts of their own system of thought, but "such skepticism does not begin to overturn the mystical way of thinking, since it is necessarily expressed in terms belonging to that way of thinking."[29] In terms of our system of thought, our scientific orientation, we would like to say that their system as a whole is an error, that it mistakes the true nature of reality. But does such an assertion even make sense? The problem is clearly one version of the dilemma of cultural relativism: Can one judge an entire culture or system of thought by the standards of another?

The Zande witchcraft system includes the use of a poison oracle, in which a ritually prepared poison is administered to a chicken; what results is an oracular power that answers questions positively or negatively. If the oracle answers a particular question both positively and negatively in immediate succession, the Azande are not dismayed, but have a number of explanations for the oracle's behavior: a breach of taboo, improper preparation of the poison, and the like. They see no contradiction. Further, witchcraft is supposed to be a hereditary, organic condition whose presence or absence can be established posthumously by examining the person's entrails. But the Azande are aware of their blood relationships beyond the immediate family, recognizing a set of relatively few clans. So, in our terms, a relatively small number of autopsies should soon prove that all Azande are witches, and also that none is a witch. Evans-Pritchard says, "Azande see the sense of this argument but they do not accept its conclusions, and it would involve the whole notion of witchraft in contra-

---

[27] Evans-Pritchard, *Witchcraft, Oracles and Magic Among the Azande*, p. 64, quoted in Winch, "Understanding a Primitive Society," p. 310; compare Schutz, "Concept and Theory Formation," p. 238: "To the inhabitants of Salem in the seventeenth century, witchcraft was not a delusion but an element of their social reality."

[28] Winch, "Understanding a Primitive Society," p. 311.

[29] *Ibid.*, p. 313.

dictions were they to do so."[30] Again, this does not bother them. Evans-Pritchard says, "Azande do not perceive the contradiction as we perceive it because they have no theoretical interest in the subject, and those situations in which they express their belief in witchcraft do not force the problem upon them."[31]

Winch argues that this is because "Zande notions of witchcraft do not constitute a theoretical system in terms of which Azande try to gain a quasi-scientific understanding of the world." He says that the European who presses Zande thought "where it would not naturally go—to a contradiction" is committing a "category-mistake," like treating concepts from one language region as if they belonged to another.[32] Specifically, "the spirit in which" the Azande consult oracles or otherwise engage in witchcraft "is very unlike that in which a scientist makes experiments. Oracular revelations are not treated as hypotheses and, since their sense derives from the way they are treated in their context, they therefore *are not* hypotheses. They are not a matter of intellectual interest but the main way in which Azande decide how they should act."[33] And a visiting anthropologist finds that he can run his household by them, as well as any other way he knows. No doubt a scientific Westerner would want to argue that, in the long run and over-all, science and scientific technology work better than witchcraft; but even that may still be too much within our own technological perspective. Zande standards of what matters in life and what counts as "working well" may also be different.

The Azande have no science like ours, so in their terms the system of witchcraft is neither "scientific" nor "unscientific." But Winch points out that, as a matter of fact, the Azande do have "a fairly clear working distinction between the technical and the magical."[34] They do apply something very like what we would call primitive technology in the course of their agriculture, but "their attitude to and thought about their magical rites are quite different from those concerning their technological measures." Consequently, "there is every reason to think that their concept of magical 'influence' is quite different."[35] Winch suggests that instead of assimilating Zande witchcraft to a kind of primitive science or even technology, we try to understand it through our concept of religion. Then the

[30] Evans-Pritchard, p. 24, quoted in Winch, "Understanding a Primitive Society," p. 314.
[31] *Ibid.*, p. 25, quoted *ibid.*
[32] Winch, "Understanding a Primitive Society," p. 315.
[33] *Ibid.*, p. 312.
[34] *Ibid.*, p. 319.
[35] *Ibid.*, p. 320; compare Ludwig Wittgenstein, "Bemerkungen über Frazers *The Golden Bough*," *Synthese*, 17 (1961), p. 237: "Der selbe Wilde, der, anscheinend um seinen Feind zu töten, dessen Bild durchsticht, baut seine Hütte aus Holz wirklich und schnitzt seinen Pfeil kungstgerecht und nicht in Effigie. . . . Ein Irrtum entsteht erst, wenn die Magie wissenschaftlich ausgelegt wird." The important thing to notice about a native rain dance, Wittgenstein points out, is that it is conducted *at the onset of the rainy season* (pp. 243-244).

Zande consulting his oracle no longer looks like someone trying to cause a physical event he desires to happen. He looks much more like a Christian praying for what he desires, whose prayer surely is not a causal mechanism to make God perform as programmed. When a Christian prays, "if it be Thy will," Winch says, though that prayer is an expression of the desire that a certain event should take place, it must also be regarded "as freeing the believer from dependence on what he is supplicating for. Prayers cannot play this role if they are regarded as a means of influencing the outcome for in that case the one who prays is still dependent on the outcome. He frees himself from this by acknowledging his complete dependence on God; and this is totally unlike any dependence on the outcome precisely because God is eternal and the outcome contingent."[36]

Winch is careful to say that Zande magic rites differ in many ways from Christian prayer, but he suggests that they are alike in the desire to "come to terms with" the fact that the important things in life are contingent. One way of doing that, the way most common in our society, is to use scientific technology to control or master contingency. But a man might want to come to terms with the contingency of important events "in quite a different way: to contemplate it, to gain some sense of his life in relation to it," and thereby to become inwardly free of it. Then it is not a matter of making sure of the right outcome, for whatever we do the outcome may be wrong. "The important thing is" understanding *that* and coming to terms with it. So Zande magic, like a certain aspect of Christian prayer, may be seen as a recognition of, a coming to terms with, the fact "that one's life is subject to contingencies, rather than an attempt to control these."[37]

The example of a primitive society culturally different from our own makes clear, then, what Winch considers true within even a single society: each realm of discourse has its own logic and consistency and must be understood from within its own conventions. The realm of human action, in particular, can only be understood in terms of the concepts and conventions of action, and that means the concepts and conventions of the actors. Explanation must be founded in the actor's own understanding, just as explanation of another society must be founded in that society's understanding. Sometimes Winch seems merely to want to say that explanations and understanding are better, deeper, more successful if framed in the actor's terms than if framed in the terms of an external, detached observer. Thus, "a monk has certain characteristic social relations with his fellow monks and with people outside the monastery; but it would be impossible to give more than a superficial account of those relations without taking into account the religious ideas around which the monk's life revolves."[38] Or again, "would it be intelligent to try to explain how

[36] Winch, "Understanding a Primitive Society," p. 320.
[37] *Ibid.*, pp. 320–321.
[38] Winch, *Idea of a Social Science*, p. 23.

Romeo's love for Juliet enters into his behaviour in the same terms as we might want to apply to the rat whose sexual excitement makes him run across an electrically charged grid to reach his mate? Does not Shakespeare do this much better?"[39]

But at other times Winch seems to want to say that explanation not framed in the actor's own terms is not an explanation at all, cannot yield any understanding of human action, does not even make sense. Take again the case of the man, N, who votes for the Labour Party, and suppose that an observer, O, says of him that he did so because he thought that party was the most likely to preserve industrial peace. "The force of O's explanation rests on the fact that the concepts which appear in it must be grasped not merely by O and his hearers, but also *by N himself*. N must have some idea of what it is to 'preserve industrial peace' and of a connection between this and the kind of government which he expects to be in power if Labour is elected." N may not have clearly formulated his own reason for voting as he does, and the observer may formulate it for him; but even then, "the acceptability of such an explanation is contingent on N's grasp of the concepts contained in it. If N does not grasp the concept of industrial peace it must be senseless to say that his reason for doing anything is a desire to see industrial peace promoted."[40]

Winch encounters some difficulties about Freudian psychoanalytic explanations of action, which often cite unconscious motives or reasons of which the actor is not aware. At first Winch says that even such explanations, "if they are to be acceptable, must be in terms of concepts which are familiar to the agent as well as to the observer. It would make no sense to" explain an everyday slip on the basis that the actor resented another man's obtaining promotion over his head, unless the actor himself understood "what was meant by 'obtaining promotion over somebody's head'."[41] But later he maintains that "a psychoanalyst may explain a patient's neurotic behavior in terms of factors unknown to the patient and of concepts which would be unintelligible to him."[42]

The latter view is, I think, a part of the more moderate position Winch ultimately wants to assume: that actions can be explained in terms unintelligible to the actors, but only if those terms are translatable into the actors' own. The social scientist does not need to "stop at the unreflective kind of understanding" which the participants in a social institution have of what they are doing; but "any more reflective understanding must necessarily presuppose, if it is to count as genuine understanding at all, the participant's unreflective understanding. . . . For example, liquidity preference is a technical concept of economics: it is not generally used by business men in the conduct of their affairs but by the economist who

39 *Ibid.*, p. 77.
40 *Ibid.*, pp. 46–47.
41 *Ibid.*, p. 48.
42 *Ibid.*, pp. 89–90.

wishes to *explain* the nature and consequences of certain kinds of business behaviour. But it is logically tied to concepts which do enter into business activity, for its use by the economist presupposes his understanding of what it is to conduct a business, which in turn involves an understanding of such business concepts as money, profit, cost, risk, etc. It is only the relation between his account and these concepts which makes it an account of economic activity as opposed, say, to a piece of theology."[43] So, like Voegelin, Strauss, Gunnell, and Schutz, Winch allows for reflective refinement of the vocabulary of the market place, but requires that the refined vocabulary start from and remain tied grammatically to the market vocabulary.[44]

But that requirement, finally, is what they regard as making a scientific social science impossible, because the vocabulary actualy used in human social life, in the course of action by the actors, is logically incompatible with causal, scientific explanation. Human action may be more complex than animal behavior or physical events, but it is not merely more complex. Winch says, "what is, from one point of view, a change in degree of complexity is, from another point of view, a difference in kind: the concepts which we apply to the more complex behavior are logically different from those we apply to the less complex." Human action "involves a scheme of concepts which is logically incompatible with the kinds of explanation offered in the natural sciences," so that attempting to talk about action in terms of causal laws inevitably creates "logical difficulties."[45] Louch says much the same thing: "The idea of a science of man or society is untenable" because its method and its conception of science are "borrowed from physics," while its conception of its subject matter is "borrowed from moral action."[46] Accordingly, Winch argues about the scientific prediction of actions much as Wittgenstein does about conceptual paradox and "insight": "The central concepts which belong to our understanding of social life are incompatible with concepts central to the activity of scientific prediction. When we speak of the possibility of scientific prediction of social developments of this sort, we literally do not understand what we are saying. We cannot understand it, because it has no sense."[47]

Our concepts of action require explanation in terms of motives and reasons rather than causes; with respect to them, understanding means,

---

[43] *Ibid.*, p. 89.

[44] Compare Voegelin, *The New Science of Politics*, p. 28; Strauss, "An Epilogue," p. 310; Gunnell, "Social Science and Political Reality," p. 186; Schutz, "Concept and Theory Formation," pp. 242, 246. Compare also Karl-Otto Apel, *Analytic Philosophy of Language and the Geisteswissenschaften*, tr. by Harald Holstelilie (Dordrecht: D. Reidel, 1967), p. 29.

[45] Winch, *Idea of a Social Science*, pp. 72, 117.

[46] Louch, *Explanation and Human Action*, pp. viii, 235. Compare also Richard Taylor, *Action and Purpose*, pp. 140, 242, but also pp. 112–116, 133, 206; Gunnell, "Social Science and Political Reality," pp. 178, 188, 193, 195; Charles Taylor, *The Explanation of Behaviour*, pp. 35–36; Apel, *Analytic Philosophy*, p. 20.

[47] Winch, *Idea of a Social Science*, p. 94.

consists in, "grasping the *point* or *meaning* of what is being done or said. This is a notion far removed from the world of statistics and causal laws: it is closer to the realm of discourse and to the internal relations that link the parts of a realm of discourse."[48] This parallel between understanding human action and understanding human speech is the ultimate basis of Winch's main thesis, that the study of society must be philosophical rather than scientific. Here, too, the exact content of Winch's thesis is not easy to make out. Sometimes he seems to be saying that a scientific study of society is impossible, that any study of society is bound to be philosophical. Sometimes he says merely that "any *worthwhile* study of society must be philosophical in character," that it is "disastrous" to be nonphilosophical and unselfconscious about concepts in the investigation of a human society.[49] He then regards nonphilosophical accounts as feasible, but "superficial," "puzzling," and less "intelligent" than philosophical ones.[50] At still other times, he says merely that "many of the more important theoretical issues which have been raised" in social science really "belong to philosophy rather than to science."[51] For instance, "the central problem of sociology, that of giving an account of the nature of social phenomena in general, itself belongs to philosophy."[52] In any case, other writers in this group make a similar point: rather than scientific, the study of society must be philosophical. Louch says "ethics and the study of human action are one."[53]

A final corollary drawn by several writers is that social study can never be value-free, because of the very concepts it is bound to employ. As Strauss says, any political science which uses "the perspective of the citizen" also "necessarily evaluates political things; the knowledge in which it culminates has the character of categorical advice and of exhortation."[54] Others say that a study of action, using the vocabulary of action is "inescapably normative."[55] The language of action itself contains "values" and "appraisal," Louch says, and lacking this language, "we are no longer in a position to identify performances." The processes of identifying and appraising an action are not separable; we "identify and describe" it "by means of terms of appraisal."[56] Consequently, "there are not two stages, an identification of properties and qualities in nature and then an assessment of them, stages which then could become the business of different

[48] *Ibid.*, p. 115; compare R. S. Peters, *The Concept of Motivation* (New York: Humanities Press, 1958), p. 7; Gunnell, "Social Science and Political Reality," p. 193.
[49] Winch, *Idea of a Social Science*, pp. 3, 103.
[50] *Ibid.*, pp. 23, 88, 77.
[51] *Ibid.*, p. 17.
[52] *Ibid.*, p. 43.
[53] Louch, *Explanation and Human Action*, p. 235; compare Strauss, "An Epilogue," pp. 308–309; Gunnell, "Social Science and Political Reality," p. 183.
[54] Strauss, "An Epilogue," p. 316.
[55] Geoffrey Madell, "Action and Causal Explanation," *Mind*, LXXVI (1967), 39.
[56] Louch, *Explanation and Human Action*, pp. 58–59.

experts. There is only one stage, the delineation and description of occurrences in value terms."[57]

From the initial premise that the subject matter of social science is fundamentally different from that of natural science, Winch and others reach the conclusion that scientific study of social and political things is inadequate or impossible. The two most important links in their chain of argument are the thesis that actions must necessarily be identified in the actors' concepts, and the thesis that action concepts are logically incompatible with causal explanation. Both these theses deserve further attention; for they are both literally false, yet each points to a genuine difficulty that social science faces. We shall devote the rest of this chapter to a more careful consideration to the first of these theses, saving the problem of causal explanation for the next chapter. The first thesis, about the identification of actions, is particularly slippery because it is often argued on several different levels simultaneously: that an individual actor's own conception defines what he is doing; that the concepts and norms of (all the actors in) a given language region or human enterprise define actions in that region; and cross-culturally, that the norms and concepts of (the actors in) a given culture define their actions. The thesis is false at each of these levels.

The argument that really, strictly speaking, only the individual actor knows what he is doing is so patently false that only someone in the grip of conceptual puzzlement might persuade himself of its truth. Of course it is *sometimes* the case that only the actor knows what he is doing, that despite all appearances and the opinions of all observers, he was doing only what he says he meant to do. But there are also other occasions when, as we say, the actor did not know what he was doing, did not realize what he was doing. He might, for example, be acting-out neurotically, so that his real intentions and the real significance of his action are not accessible to his own consciousness. Or he might be callous or obtuse, so that he is simply unable to see what he has really done; though his simple-minded intentions were good, his actual deed was something else again, even if he fails to comprehend it. Or his action might have consequences and significance of a large-scale, historical kind of which he is ignorant and which he never intended. He would deny having "done" those things, but an objective observer would have to affirm that the man did do them, though perhaps the blame is lessened. ("Father, forgive them; for they know not what they do.") All of these are commonplaces of our understanding and assessment of actions.

Moreover, the matter depends to a considerable extent on what sort

[57] *Ibid.*, p. 56.

of action we take as an example; some (of what we ordinarily call) actions are much more dependent on the actor's intentions and concepts than others. Thus, we might agree that one cannot promise without intending to promise (though we could argue even this point), but who would want to maintain that one cannot offend without intending to offend? That one cannot disappoint without intending to disappoint? One may have to intend to lie in order to lie, but one need not intend to deceive in order to deceive. With actions as with crimes in our legal system: some are contingent on the relevant intention, while others hinge on the objective consequences.

It is tempting to say that the more an action approximates physical movements, can be done by animals or even objects, the less it hinges on intention, awareness, or concepts in the actor. Such actions do not require that the actor have a concept of the action. The more, conversely, an action is complex, abstract, governed by social conventions, compounded perhaps out of a variety of not entirely consistent language games, the less we can ascribe it to someone lacking the relevant concept, awareness, intention. Many activities of human beings can quite readily be ascribed to, performed by, children and animals. Thus, one can eat without having a concept of eating (and without the intention?), kill without either the concept or the intention of killing (but murder?), escape without the concept or intention or even awareness of escaping (but flee?), and so on through "want," "need," "notice," "fear," "help," and hundreds of other verbs. Often things are complicated even with respect to a single verb; recall Wittgenstein's point that a dog can "be afraid his master will beat him," but not "be afraid his master will beat him tomorrow."

Winch argues, for example, that obeying "contains, as an essential element, a recognition of what went before as an order."[58] Obeying means doing something *because* you are ordered to, so it involves a conceptual awareness of something as an order, an element of intention to obey. Yet nothing is more common than for us to speak of animals as obeying (or disobeying) us. Do they have a concept of obedience? We can immediately generate the usual philosophical "gap" between meaning and application here: obeying seems to mean, to imply, that the action is taken *because of* the command, in recognition of the command. Yet "all we ever know" of animals, and indeed of other people, is that they act after the command is issued; we cannot "see into their minds" to tell whether they intended to obey or not. So we are tempted to say, with Thrasymachean reductionism, that obedience is a mere hypothesis which we impose on observed behavior (the command issued, the movements that follow). Then we might be tempted to respond with the refutation that this very observed behavior is what we have all learned to call "obedience," hence what "obedience"

---

[58] Winch, *Idea of a Social Science*, p. 125; compare Gilbert Ryle, *The Concept of Mind* (New York: Barnes and Noble, 1949), p. 144; and my "Obligation and Consent," *American Political Science Review*, LX (March 1966), 50.

means. But by now we can recognize these temptations and the conceptual puzzlement in which they originate. Obeying, like expecting, understanding, and the like, is defined neither simply by "outward performance" or behavior, nor by "inner experience" or intention, but by either or both of these against the background of an appropriate context, a social setting. Many different combinations of these elements can be "obeying," even though not everything that looks like obedience is. Thus, we will sometimes conclude that a man was not really obeying an order, but only happened to do what the order had said. At other times we will conclude that he did obey even though he insists that was not his intention; we will say "actions speak louder than words." It all depends on the circumstances and on our reason for being concerned.[59] When animals are trained to obey, we are not philosophically troubled about whether they "really" have the requisite "intention." When human beings obey, the ambiguities of interpretation become possible and therefore relevant, because human beings are able to *express* their intentions, to argue with our version of what they are doing.

Such exchanges about what action was performed constitute, we have argued, a large proportion of our talk about actions and an essential element in moral discourse. But in such discussions the views of both participants are at least relevant; we are not bound to take either the actor's or the observer's word for it in every case, as to just what was done. Sometimes we will conclude that, despite the actor's intentions, he did obey; sometimes we will conclude that, lacking the requisite intention, he did not obey; sometimes we will be ourselves uncertain about what to conclude. Neither intentions nor observed results are a priori definitive of action. Their relative roles depend very much on the situation, our interest in it, and the particular action at issue. The real point about action and intentionality is not that action can be identified only according to intention, and therefore by the actor himself; but that with respect to human action, intention and therefore the actor's views are always potentially relevant and must be taken into account.

Of course, Winch might still want to maintain, or we might decide, that only those actions to which intention and awareness are essential are truly "actions", or that social science is (or should be?) concerned only with those actions and contexts where the actor's intention is relevant (or definitive?). But we are in a better position to see now just what would be the costs and difficulties of that decision. The nonintentional category is just far wider than Winch and the others suppose; and the dividing line between occasions where intention is relevant or definitive and occasions where it is not is far more ambiguous and difficult than they suppose. Do

[59] Compare Wittgenstein's contrast between "I am leaving the room because you tell me to" and "I am leaving the room, but not because you tell me to." Under what circumstances do we believe, or doubt, such statements? *Philosophical Investigations*, tr. by G. E. M. Anscombe (New York: Macmillan, 1968), par. 487.

they really mean to argue that social science is not concerned with, say, obedience? Noticing? Helping? Offending? No, the truth is that these writers just have not considered the plurality of possible examples.

Let us turn now to the second level: the alleged self-containedness of fields of human endeavor and language regions. Each, we are told, has its own characteristic rules, norms, and concepts, its own definition of what will count as any particular action. The identification of any action must be made in terms of the region to which it belongs. Winch examines prayer as an example: "Was the Pharisee who said 'God, I thank Thee that I am not as other men are' doing the same kind of thing as the Publican who prayed 'God be merciful unto me a sinner'? To answer this one would have to start by considering what is involved in the idea of prayer; and that is a *religious* question."[60] Presumably both men think that they are praying; so, in the first place, if only the actor himself can tell, then they are praying. But Winch does see a further question here, which he says can be answered only in religious discourse. Presumably the issue he anticipates is this: One might claim that any discourse addressed to a god is prayer, or one might argue that a selfish or hypocritical communication is not really a prayer, not really addressed to God. Settling that issue seems to be what Winch considers the religious question. But in that dispute, both sides are in the same realm of discourse; its conflict is not between language regions, but between form and substance, or application and meaning, or behavior and intention—all of those difficult qualities we have encountered before.

One *can* imagine other disciplines or language regions addressing the question of whether the Publican and the Pharisee are doing the same thing, but then the outcome will be different than Winch anticipates. For example, psychology might inquire about the significance each man's action has in his own psychic economy. Or law might inquire, say, in order to settle a dispute about prayer in public schools. Does Winch really mean to say that such investigations are impossible? Improper? Such accounts of what the men are doing, from rival disciplines or language regions, need not be mutually incompatible; they can coexist. Suppose that a religious figure argues that embellishing his church with precious stones is a way of honoring and worshipping God. An economist looks on and says, no, it is an investment of funds in nonproductive goods. An anthropologist adds, "It looks just like an art form to me; I say it's an art form." But that example makes it quite clear that the choice is not exclusive. A man's way of worshipping may well also be a form of art and an act of economic exchange or saving. The economist or anthropologist is wrong only in stating his views as exclusive alternatives to the man's own. Of course, we do not ask the economist what constitutes prayer; but then, economics doesn't purport to tell us what constitutes prayer, either. Conflicts and problems over what counts as prayer do take place only in

[60] Winch, *Idea of a Social Science*, p. 87.

certain realms of discourse; but "prayer" is not the only truthful way of characterizing the man's action. And even if a nonreligious discipline, like law, undertakes to decide what constitutes prayer, we cannot conclude with Winch that it must accept a religious definition of the activity. Here, too, it is simply not true that the actors' norms and concepts are necessarily definitive.

The Winch thesis is most powerful at the cross-cultural level, obviously, because we are most likely to go wrong about describing the actions of people from a very different culture on the strength of nothing more than observation—without knowing their language, and customs, and institutions. Here, if they do not tell us what they are doing, we seem to lack information not merely about intentions (as may be the case with an individual actor in our own society), but also about the conventions and rules that define the action and how it is to be done. Even here, however, one cannot say flatly: "Only the actors can really tell what they are doing."

As before in discussing action, the choice of examples plays a major role. When Schutz says the anthropologist's problem is to tell whether the observed movements of the natives add up to "a war dance, a barter trade, the reception of a friendly ambassador, or something else," he conjures up the image of an anthropologist who maintains he is witnessing a war dance, when the natives keep telling him it is barter. That example does make the anthropologist's position sound peculiar. How can he possibly insist that what they consider barter is "in reality" a war dance? But such examples predetermine the outcome and mislead in several ways. First, they neglect other kinds of actions which the anthropologist can safely ascribe and describe without any knowledge of the native language or culture. Suppose that the anthropologist says, "I don't know what they mean to be doing, but I can see that in fact their movement scatters those seeds in fertile spots, and later they harvest the fruit. It may be a game or a religious ceremony or something else, but in fact they are *planting*." Similarly, he may identify hunting, eating, making clothing, and many other activities.

Indeed, sometimes the anthropologist *must* diverge from the natives' account of what they are doing, in order not to deceive his readers, because of the commitment entailed in *his* act of speaking or writing. Suppose the natives engage in certain procedures they tell him are "making rain." How will he truthfully report what they are doing? If he says simply "they are making rain," he is implying that their magic really can causally produce precipitation; such is the nature of our language. If he says "they are engaged in a magic ritual designed to make rain," he is at least strongly suggesting that their actions cannot produce rain; in that case, he is true to knowledge, but in a significant way false to their world, their way of perceiving and acting. As in our discussion of "the world," and the difference between corpses and cadavers, it begins to seem as if there may be nothing completely neutral for the anthropologist *to* say; anything he says has implications. Our language contains various expressions ("making rain," "trying to make rain," "engaging in a ritual," and so on) each of which has its characteristic uses and implications. What to say will depend on whether we are interested in their intentions and perceptions, or in (as we say) "the objective results of what they are doing."

But the most common situation is one where the anthropologist's account is not a rival to the native's own account but coexists quite peacefully with it. Here the anthropologist says not "although they claim it's A, it's really B they're doing," but rather "in doing A, I can see that they are at the same time doing B, though they may deny or ignore it." The anthropologist may be able to see social, political, economic consequences and configurations of which the natives are not aware. It may seem obvious that the tribe could not be engaged in a war dance without knowing it, without intending to engage in a war dance and conceiving of what they are doing as a war dance. But would we feel that as decisively if the example were different? Suppose that the anthropologist said that they are "reaffirming tribal norms" or "reintegrating alienated members into the tribe" or "permitting discharge of hostility in controlled and socially harmless ways" or "demonstrating respect for the authority of tribal elders." It seems to me that they might well be doing any of these things without knowing or saying that they are doing them. In such cases, of course, they are not doing what the anthropologist claims *instead of* what they say they are doing, but rather are doing both, doing the one *by way of* the other.

This, I think, is what Winch and the others try to get at by saying that the social scientist can use concepts unknown to the actors so long as those concepts are defined in terms of the actors' own. He means that the anthropologist *can* discover that the natives are "reintegrating an alienated member," but of course he must *show* that that is what they're doing—that there is someone alienated, that after the action he is reintegrated, and so on. And showing those things will presuppose his understanding some native norms and concepts. But Winch's way of expressing this requirement is too stringent. It's not that "reaffirming tribal norms" must be translatable into "Spring Dance" or any other native term, nor that, as Winch says, there must be a "logical tie" between the expressions. Rather, the anthropologist must be able to know, able to show, that they *are* reaffirming tribal norms by that dance, and for that he may have to relate it to *some* native concepts and customs. Whether "reaffirming tribal norms" and "Spring Dance" are one and the same action is one of those by now familiar questions to be answered both yes and no. The expressions do not in general mean the same; but *that*, there, what the natives are doing, can truthfully be spoken of in either way.

Our initial image, of an anthropologist insisting that he witnessed a war dance though the natives say it is barter, is misleading also in its omission of any awareness of translation problems. If the anthropologist is convinced their action is a war dance, why does he translate their word for it as "barter"? We argued earlier that such a question may be answered in terms of the entire system of native words and practices. Perhaps the anthropologist feels forced to translate the native word as "barter" because of its ties to other expressions and occasions. He may even have found a *different* native word that seems to mean "war dance." Yet the action is also part of a larger context, and it may continue to look like a war dance—may seem to be preceded by an incident of provocation, followed by acts of war, and so on. It may not have any of the configurations we associate with an act of barter, may not be preceded by preparation of goods or followed by acts of exchange.

If this sort of conflict of interpretation persists, we are essentially helpless. What we will *not* do is to conclude, with Winch, that the natives must be right (that our translation of the natives' word must be right). What is most likely here, of course, is that the natives have a different distribution of concepts altogether, a different conceptual system than ours, so that neither "war dance" nor "barter" is an adequate translation. Perhaps they have one word for both, somehow thinking of bargaining as a prelude to hostilities, or threats and boasting as a prelude to exchange. Everything then depends, as Winch himself says, on selecting the correct one among our concepts from which to extrapolate, and extending it correctly toward theirs, as Winch himself connects Zande witchcraft with Christian prayer.

As a matter of fact, I think that Winch's own discussion of witchcraft among the Azande disproves his major thesis about cross-cultural views of action. For he does give us an account of what the Azande do and how it is to be understood, and that account is in English, based partly on anthropological observation of what they do and partly on translations of what they say. And Winch ends up explaining Zande witchcraft in relation to one of our institutions—a certain form of Christian prayer. What he shows is not that translation is impossible, nor that action cannot be described by an observer outside the culture, nor that only the natives can define what they do, nor that action must be explained in terms of their concepts and institutions rather than ours. What he shows is merely that certain anthropologists did their work badly; observed superficially, drew unwarranted conclusions, were misled by assumptions, used the *wrong* English words and the *wrong* analogical western institutions. Winch himself gives an "outsider's" account of Azande witchcraft; what else could he possibly give?

Selecting the appropriate English concept or institution and "extending" it or modifying it until it fits the native concept or institution is obviously another instance of the kind of innovation within constraints we have discussed repeatedly before. As before, it depends very much on seeing or showing *"how* the new concept is (can be seen as)" an instance of the old. We will not, as Cavell says, call just "anything they do 'sacrificing,' 'atoning,' 'placating,' etc. unless we understand *how* what they do could count as (grammatically, be) such actions." The tribe we study may be culturally very different from us; they may "hope for a different future, fear a different region, question in different forms than we do; but hope will still be grammatically related to satisfaction and disappointment, expressed in obvious ways; fear will still be grammatically related to some reason for fear which, though it may not be one we in fact are affected by, we can understand as such a reason."[61]

Their telling us that they are "atoning" or "bartering" will not by itself be enough to decide the matter, for it is always open to us to question the translation of what they say. Here again, as within a single culture or society, action is ultimately dual, consisting *both* of what the outside observer can see *and* of the actors' understanding of what they are doing. The duality, not the latter feature alone, is what distinguishes action. The duality, and not intentionality alone, sets the problem for social science. That problem is not, as Winch and the others argue, our inability to observe actions objectively or to identify them without consulting the actors. Instead, the problem is twofold: conceptual puzzlement when social science attempts to generalize about actions, and the necessity of commitment and judgment.

Action concepts, developed largely in the course of action, are significantly shaped by signaling or quasi-performative language games, so that their grammar is rich in potentially contradictory implications. They work well in context, in particular cases; but anyone attempting to articulate broad, general, abstract principles about the nature of promises, obedience, voting, and the like will encounter conceptual puzzlement and paradox. Anyone attempting to study such phenomena scientifically, through empirical observation, will be troubled by the problem of just what phenomena count as instances of promises, obedience, voting, roughly in the way that Thrasymachus and Socrates are at odds over what counts as an instance of justice.

The same grammatical complexity of action concepts also means that the identification of actions, and discussion of them, though it can be objective and detached, is never like the identification and discussion of physical events. It always carries implications about commitments and responsibilities; it always involves, in that sense, taking a position. The vocabulary of action can be used to label, to refer, to describe, even to explain causally. But the referring, describing, explaining, will be in terms of the over-all meaning of the concepts used, and that meaning is partly shaped by their roles in other kinds of language games. Thus, as Geoffrey Madell points out, "to remember is not merely to make a memory claim, but to make a *correct* one; to perceive is to be right about what is in front of one's eyes; to infer is to state *correctly* what follows from certain premisses."[62]

---

[61] Stanley Cavell, "The Claim to Rationality" (unpublished dissertation, Harvard University), p. 98.

[62] Madell, "Action and Causal Explanation," p. 39.

This is evidently the basis for Madell's and Louch's and Strauss's view which we examined earlier, that social study must necessarily be "normative," engage in "exhortation" and "appraisal," and express even its descriptions and explanations in "value terms." But such ways of putting the matter are grievously misleading because they are still in the grip of the dichotomization between fact and value. If talking about an action is not factual in the way that talking about a physical event is, they assume that it must then be normative or evaluative or even exhortatory—as if that were the only alternative. But there are not just two alternatives here; action concepts are neither purely labels nor purely performatives.

Richard Taylor at one point is tempted by the possibility that the distinction between actions and events might be not a "real or natural" distinction at all, but merely a "relative distinction men draw for practical purposes—like the distinction between things which are and are not tools, for instance, or things which are and are not food, and so on. In asserting that a given object is a tool, one is not strictly *describing* the object, but rather imputing something to it—namely, utility as an instrument for fabrication and the like. Similarly, in asserting of a given specimen of human behavior that it is someone's act, it may be that one is not describing anything at all, but is rather imputing something to that person, namely responsibility for the behavior in question."[63] Sometimes an action will look exactly like an involuntary movement, so it is tempting to say that the difference is merely one we ascribe. "We do not find something in him which we then label his responsibility for his behavior, but rather, *impute* the responsibility to him, and thereby *invest* his behavior with the status of an act."

But Taylor ultimately rejects this interpretation, on the grounds that "it is quite possible and even quite common to be *mistaken* in holding a man responsible for some act, whether morally, legally, or otherwise, whereas this would be logically impossible if his being responsible consisted merely in his having this imputed to him. The ascription of responsibility is in this respect like the ascription of any common predicate—not like the ascription of those predicates sometimes embodied in so-called 'performatory utterances.' "[64] But then, the same argument applies to Taylor's own examples: our calling something a tool does not make it a tool, and our calling something food does not make it food.

We have suggested that such concepts are neither labels nor strictly performatives but quasi-performatives. You can be wrong about whether you "understand," and yet saying that you do understand is more than a description; it is a commitment. So, too, with the identification and description of various actions. An action, as Chisholm says, "is both imputative and descriptive. When we say of a man that he *did* something, we may be declaring, by way of imputation, that the man is to be held re-

[63] Richard Taylor, *Action and Purpose*, p. 100.
[64] *Ibid.*, p. 101.

sponsible for making a certain thing happen; that is to say, we may be pronouncing a verdict, notifying our hearers that forthwith we are holding this man responsible. But we are also making a descriptive statement; we are saying that the man was a causal factor in making something happen, or in keeping something from happening."[65] And of course the two are inextricably interrelated: we ascribe responsibility *because* he *did* the action, and part of what it means for him to have done the action is that he is responsible for it. Our saying that he acted goes beyond the labeling of observed motions into imputation, but not arbitrarily so.

So the point about actions is not that even in referring to or describing them objectively we must necessarily evaluate, assess, or exhort. Rather, it is that we must necessarily make claims or judgments which have implications. The issue is not evaluation but responsibility. It is not that whenever we say that someone promised we are thereby evaluating him or what he did; but we are implying something about his subsequent obligations and commitments. Similarly, it is not that, whenever we speak of "knowledge" or say that someone "knows" something, we are evaluating him or his knowledge; but we are implying that the "knowledge" is true, we are committing ourselves to that implication. These implications are part of the concepts because of the language games in which these concepts originate, and no social science which uses our ordinary action concepts or others based on them will be free of such implications. We shall look shortly at attempts to escape this necessity through redefinition, but first we must turn to a critique of the second main thesis developed by Winch and the others: the problem of explanation.

[65] Chisholm, "Freedom and Action," in Keith Lehrer, ed., *Freedom and Determinism* (New York: Random House, 1966), p. 28.

# XII

## Explanation, Freedom, and the
## Concepts of Social Science

WINCH AND THE OTHER critics of social science argue that action concepts are logically incompatible with causal necessity and thus with
scientific, causal explanation. We have suggested that this contention is
false, but nevertheless points toward a genuine difficulty about explanation
in social science. In this chapter we shall first examine the issue of explanation in social science, and then turn to one major way in which social
science has attempted to escape both the difficulties of explaining actions
and the difficulties about identifying them which we discussed in the last
chapter: the attempt to create a new vocabulary or new definitions.

It is clearly true, as Winch and the others maintain, that when we are
asked to explain one of our actions we often answer in terms of our intentions, motives, purposes, or reasons for doing what we did. We never
give such explanations for events, unless we are construing an event as an
action—for instance, as an action of God's, and speculating about his
motives or purposes. In this way actions surely are different from events.
But the perhaps uncomfortable fact is that we *also* sometimes talk, in
quite ordinary and familiar ways, about the causes of an action; we also
give causal explanations of actions. One of the critics of social science
does note this fact, but dismisses it as a careless habit of speech, a "convention of language whereby in supplying a reason for an action one employs the term 'because.' "[1] But in such matters the conventions of language are not often a mere distraction, but usually important pieces of
evidence. Are we really sure that when a man explains his action using
the word "because" he is always "supplying a reason" and never a cause?
Winch himself says that our concept of "causal influence" is not "mono-
lithic: when we speak, for example, of 'what made Jones get married,'
we are not saying the same kind of thing as when we speak of 'what

[1] John Gunnell, "Social Science and Political Reality," *Social Research*, 35 (Spring
1968), 193.

made the aeroplane crash'."[2] Yet he does not draw the appropriate conclusion from his own example: that if getting married is an action, then causation *is* sometimes relevant to actions.

Let us consider an example. Suppose that we are observing a chess game, and after a particular move you ask me, "Why did he do that?" An Austinian catalogue of possible answers might include at least these:

"He's trying Petroff's defense."
"He wants to let the kid win for a change."
"He made a mistake."
"He's terribly tired."
"He's an idiot."
"The knight was threatening his rook."
"That's called 'castling.' "

Which of these explanations could be preceded by "because"? Are they all explanations in terms of purposes, reasons, motives, or intentions? Are some of them causal? Do the causal ones imply that the move was not an action? Are some of them difficult to classify as either purposive or causal explanations?

Gunnell says "To refer to the cause of an action is to refer to an agent who brings it about."[3] But that is wrong; a man is not normally the cause of his own actions, he simply acts. What Gunnell is trying to say is that if what we observe has a cause, rather than an agent, it is not an action at all. As we saw earlier, the concept of an action requires an agent. But at least some actions can nevertheless also be explained causally. This happens, as Richard Taylor points out, when we give a causal explanation for the actor's will, motives, reasons, and so forth. The cause acts on the mind of the agent, not on the event directly. The causal explanation of an action does not explain "what caused it to happen" but "what caused him to do it." Taylor concludes that, so long as this one rule is observed, the concept of action is "perfectly compatible with the thesis of universal causal determinism to which one might at first want to oppose it."[4]

But matters are not that simple. For if the agent's will is causally determined, there no longer seems to be any difference between an agent and an inanimate cause, an event causing another event. Like many action theorists, Taylor says that what distinguishes an agent is that he "originates things, produces them, or brings them about."[5] But if his will is causally determined, that formula applies to him no more and no less than to an inanimate physical cause. Either can be said to originate things *in a sense,*

[2] Peter Winch, "Understanding a Primitive Society," *American Philosophical Quarterly*, I (October 1964), 320.

[3] Gunnell, "Social Science and Political Reality," p. 195.

[4] Richard Taylor, *Action and Purpose* (Englewood Cliffs: Prentice-Hall, 1966), p. 115.

[5] *Ibid.*, p. 112; compare pp. 115, 140.

but both are mere links in a causal chain. Unfortunately, at such crucial points Taylor backs off, arguing that the concepts of action and agency are at bottom "logically unanalyzable," so that there is nothing more to be said.[6]

What is problematic about action and causation here is precisely parallel to an ancient, traditional philosophical problem; indeed, it is *the* modern version of that problem: the problem of free will. In its origins, in patristic thought, the issue was the apparent incompatibility between action (free will) and the omniscience and omnipotence of God (determinism). It seemed that men were to be saved or damned on the basis of what they did and thought; yet God made men and the world as they are (so that He, and not they, should be blamed for their faults), and God already knew what they would do (so that their apparent free choice must be predetermined). Science and causality have replaced God in more recent versions of the problem, as in other spheres, and we have lost the hope of salvation; but the philosophical issue remains the same. We all know that men are not to blame for what is not their doing, what merely befalls them. But we do praise and blame men and hold them responsible for at least some of their actions, so those actions must be their doing, must be the result of free choice. Moreover we have all had the experience of choosing, of making up our minds, of acting freely.

Yet we can also all follow the logic of a determinist argument. A man's choices and actions can be explained in retrospect (and sometimes predicted). He chooses what he does, acts as he does, because of who he is, what he is like, and because of the situation in which he finds himself. But he did not choose that situation; and who he is, is the result of earlier events, experiences, and choices. He himself made those earlier choices, but always in a given situation, and always as a result of who he then was, which in turn was the product of still earlier events, experiences, and choices. And so we trace the man back to his infancy, until we reach a point where he plainly was not yet capable of choice but merely the victim of events. Thus, it seems that the feeling of choosing, and our ways of talking about action, are deceptive.

To someone who has felt the force of these conflicting positions, the facts of ordinary usage by themselves are of no use, will seem irrelevant. He is not impressed by the alleged fact that we do not talk about the causes of actions but only about motives and the like, or the causes of the agent's will. Despite Taylor's assurances, he will feel that there is a conflict here, and that the concept of action is not compatible with that of causal determinism even if we do sometimes couple them in ordinary speech. To be of use here, the appeal to ordinary language must be applied more subtly, must not attempt to deny or refute the conflict, but to account for it.

By now we know fairly well how a Wittgensteinian approach goes about

6 *Ibid.*, pp. 112, 91ff.

doing that. Our sense of conflict, our conviction that an action must be free of determinism, and that causation implies determinism, has its roots in the grammar of concepts like "action," "freedom," "causation," just as surely as the alleged proof that no problem exists. It is the facts of our grammar that have contradictory implications when we try to generalize about action and causation in the abstract. And the discrepancy is not, as the critics of social science suggest, between the concept of action and that of causation, but *within* the grammar of action, *within* the grammar of causation. A word like "causation," as Wittgenstein says, is used in a variety of "very different ways." He invites us to compare a question like "What is the cause of unemployment?" (to which the answer might be something like "A decline in durable-goods investment") with one like "What caused you to jump like that?" (to which an answer might be "Your shadow startled me") or one like "What causes that wheel to go round?" (which one might answer by drawing a mechanism).[7] If it helps, one can say that these questions occur in different language regions, but they are all about causation and generalizations about causation must take them all into account.

Similar things can be said about prediction. Winch maintains that the concept of prediction is logically incompatible with that of action. Yet, of course, we can and do predict other people's actions sometimes, and sometimes with great accuracy. We have no difficulty is using and understanding statements like "George will come to the meeting tomorrow" or "Daddy will be furious" or "General Custer will lead the cavalry himself." Sometimes we even predict our own actions, which is not to be confused with deciding what to do. Of course, we sometimes are wrong in our predictions, and some people are difficult to predict, and some kinds of actions and situations even more so. But it is by no means obvious what that proves. The real confusions arise in generalization, in theorizing. The problem is not that we cannot predict actions, or that we cannot predict them with certainty, but that "predicting what he will do" or "knowing with certainty, what he will do" has a different grammar from "predicting the position of Mars" or "knowing with certainty the structure of a certain kind of molecule." We cannot consistently treat them as the same, for their implications are different; yet we cannot settle for treating them as entirely different, either, for our idea of "prediction" (or "certainty" or "causation") is constructed out of cases like these.

The language of action, we said, is characteristically shaped by being used in the course of action by the actors; but those are not its only uses, or the only influences on its grammar. Sometimes we do (what is called) describe an action objectively; sometimes we do (what is called) predict an action; sometimes we do (what is called) give a causal explanation of

[7] Wittgenstein, *Lectures and Conversations on Aesthetics, Psychology and Religious Belief*, ed. by Cyril Barrett (Berkeley and Los Angeles: University of California Press, 1967), p. 13.

an action. So the problem for social science is not that prediction and causation do not apply to actions, or that objectivity is impossible, but that these concepts apply to actions in distinctive ways, ways which give rise to conceptual difficulties when we try to generalize about them.

While it could not remove this problem, a careful Austinian analysis of our ways of explaining actions would surely be of great utility for social and political study. It would help us to become clear about the differences among such concepts as "purpose," "motive," "reason," "intention," and it would show just how causation does and does not function in the realm of actions.[8] We have already noted one feature of causation in this realm: that it affects the agent's will or mind or intentions, rather than causes the event (action) directly. Peters calls our attention to other features: for instance, that the separation between action and event is not as fixed as one might suppose, and that reference to causation sometimes draws us toward that dividing line. He points out that there is a difference between asking "What was *his reason for* doing it?" and asking "What was *the reason why* he did it?"[9] The former is always an intentional question, concerned with what goes on in the man's mind. But the latter, though also about "reasons," can sometimes correctly elicit causal answers. But, Peters maintains, in such cases some doubt is raised about the status of the action as (being fully) an action. We are particularly likely to give "the reason why he did it" a causal interpretation in cases where something has gone seriously wrong. In our ordinary usage, as distinct from social science, talking about what caused a man to take a certain action

[8] Some useful efforts toward such a study will be found in Austin's own uncompleted "Some Ways of Spilling Ink," in Carl J. Friedrich, ed., *Responsibility* (*Nomos* III) (New York: Liberal Arts Press, 1960), pp. 305–308; Wittgenstein, *Blue and Brown Books* (New York and Evanston: Harper & Row, 1964), pp. 15, 88, 143; Alfred Schutz, "Concept and Theory Formation," in Maurice Natanson, ed., *Philosophy of the Social Sciences* (New York: Random House, 1963), and the writings of Kenneth Burke. Other useful materials would be found in: R. B. Braithewaite, *Scientific Explanation* (Cambridge: Cambridge University Press, 1964); R. Brown, *Explanation in Social Science* (Chicago: Aldine Press, 1963); Douglas Gasking, "Causation and Recipes," *Mind*, 64 (1955), 479–487; N. R. Hanson, "On the Symmetry between Explanation and Prediction," *Philosophical Review*, 68 (1959), 349–358; John Hospers, "What is Explanation?" in Antony Flew, ed., *Essays in Conceptual Analysis* (London: Macmillan, 1956); Daniel Lerner, ed., *Evidence and Inference* (Glencoe, Ill.: Free Press, 1959); Daniel Lerner, ed., *Cause and Effect* (New York: Free Press, 1965); Arnold Levinson, "Knowledge and Society," *Inquiry*, 9 (Summer 1966), 132–146; A. M. MacIver, "Historical Explanation," and G. J. Warnock, " 'Every Event has a Cause,' " in Flew, *Logic and Language*; Alasdair MacIntyre, "A Mistake About Causality in Social Science," in Peter Laslett and W. G. Runciman, eds., *Philosophy, Politics and Society* (Second Series) (New York: Barnes and Noble, 1962); John Passmore, "Explanation in Everyday Life, in Science, and in History," *History and Theory*, II (1962), 105–123; and of course the works of Ernest Nagel and Carl G. Hempel, as well as the various useful books of readings in the philosophy of science edited by Herbert Feigl.

[9] R. S. Peters, *The Concept of Motivation* (New York: Humanities Press, 1958), p. 9.

is like asking "what made, drove or possessed him to do it. These are usually cases of lapses from action or failure to act—when there is some kind of *deviation* from the purposive rule-following model, when people, as it were, get it wrong. . . . In such cases it is as if the man suffers something rather than does something," and they resemble the kinds of cases in which the Homeric Greeks "suggested that the gods intervene and take possession of the individual's mind."[10] When we ask "What made you do it?" we as it were imply (courteously) that the man must have been possessed or compelled from the outside to do so untoward a thing. It almost seems as if the action is only half action and half (unexpected) event which has intruded; and the event is what needs to be explained causally. Yet we continue to speak of it as his action, what he did; we do not switch to "What made it happen?" or "Who *did* do it?"

But it seems to me that our use of causal explanation in connection with action is still wider than Peters suggests. We ask and give causal explanations of particular actions in a whole variety of contexts where the actor's choice and responsibility either are at a minimum or *do not interest us*. For instance, when we discuss how to get someone else—some third party—to do what we want, we talk about what will or might cause him to do it. Here causes are not incompatible with motives, reasons, or intentions; one of the best ways to cause someone to do a thing is to give him a good reason or at least a motive for doing it. Or again, causal explanations figure in accounting for actions where the context is not moral dialogue but third-person and removed in time from the action, where we are less interested in the credit or blame due to the actor than in why he had the intentions he had, what brought them about. This is often the case in historical explanation. Here we do not deny that the man acted, nor even that he bears responsibility for what he did; we simply deflect interest (or presuppose an interest already deflected) from those aspects of action.

Such an Austinian study of the explanation of actions would also have to attend carefully to the differences between explaining particular actions and explaining whole categories of action; for that difference is likely to be one of the crucial ones separating our ordinary discourse about action for social scientific explanation. Outside of social science, one suspects, explanation of actions is usually the explanation of particular actions, notably of actions that have in some way gone wrong or been peculiar. Social science, by contrast, is often concerned with explaining the normal functioning of whole classes of actions. Philosophers of social science have sometimes argued that our ordinary explanations of particular actions must presuppose implicit general explanatory principles, which can be made explicit and systematic. But the whole thrust of Wittgenstein's work

[10] *Ibid.*, p. 10; compare E. R. Dodds, *The Greeks and the Irrational* (Berkeley and Los Angeles: University of California Press, 1951).

should be a warning against such assumptions. What functions smoothly in particular cases may not lend itself to consistent generalization in the abstract; and we should be cautious about assuming that implicit general principles "must" be there.

Again, this is because our concepts of action, causation, explanation, are not merely unchanging labels with a meaning that remains fixed independent of the context in which they are used, and of the claim made in uttering them. For example, one familiar feature of what distinguishes a free action from a caused event is that the actor had a choice, could have done otherwise. But what we can and cannot do is not merely a matter of impersonal fact, independent of context and speaker. Suppose you ask a friend, "Please go with me tonight," and he responds that he "can't," that he "isn't free to." He might, of course, mean, "I am physically paralyzed (or imprisoned) so that I would be unable to go with you no matter what I wanted or decided or did," though it is difficult to imagine a set of circumstances in which you need to be told that and he tells it to you in those words. But he might also say, "I can't; I mean, I have another engagement," or "I can't; I mean, I am waiting for a telephone call," or "I can't; I mean I'd miss the late late show." Noticing this variety, we might next be inclined to say that "I can't" is purely a signal, a performative expression equivalent to saying "I won't; but don't blame me." (The parallels to Stevenson's treatment of "value judgments" as meaning "I approve of this; do so as well," discussed in Chapter X, should be evident.) It is as if "I can't" was an invitation (or a demand?) that we *treat* the situation as if I were crippled or imprisoned, though we both know that I am not.

But that interpretation cannot be fully right either. For it is not proper to say "I can't" if all we mean is "I won't; but don't blame me." The other person would be right to upbraid us if we said "I can't" in such circumstances. It is always possible to challenge the claim made by "I can't" by saying "You can, too; you just don't *want* to." And then we must decide whether I really can't or just don't want to. And everything hinges on what will count as a good reason for not going, *in our particular relationship and circumstances*, including the importance of your request and the degree of your need. That, I would suggest, is what "I can't" is all about. By saying it, I take a position with respect to you, our situation, and what is preventing me from going; and by that position I will be judged. The late late show may be a perfectly adequate reason for refusing if you asked for a minor favor, but hardly if you asked me to save your dying baby. "I can't" is neither a strict performative, the uttering of which *creates* the condition it names, as "I won't" sometimes does; nor is it a mere detached observation of neutral fact, though it may sound like one. It is a combination of signal and label.

Whether I "can" or "cannot" do something, whether I "have a choice," whether I did something "freely," are questions partly dependent on the position adopted by the speaker and the particular situation at issue. We decided such questions about particular actions in particular contexts. That does not mean that any decision is a good as any other, that calling an action "freely chosen" makes it so. But it does mean that the generalized extrapolation to infinity, the question of whether any action is ever really free, does not fully make sense. We do not really know what we are supposing when we suppose that "man has free will" or that "all actions are causally determined." And we do not know it, for at least two reasons both of which are by now familiar. First, a very few terms, like "free" and "determined," are here used as stand-ins for entire conceptual categories. What is a free action? "Well, *you* know," we say, "one that is chosen, where we could have chosen otherwise, one that is done of our own free will, voluntarily, not involuntarily, one for which we are rightly held responsible, one done deliberately, one that isn't determined or caused, and so on." But each of these expressions has its own particular functions and implications; they are not equivalent, and the conclusions to be drawn about "free actions" will depend on the examples from which we start. The second, related, reason why we do not fully know what we mean by freedom of the will or determinism is that expressions like "free" or "cause" are ordinarily used in particular contexts, for assessing some particular action taken or contemplated. The terms are fully defined only in the contexts in which they are ordinarily used; and there they appear always by contrast with something else. An action is free rather than constrained, say; and we know in practical cases how to tell whether that action, in that context, was done "of his own free will." We have no such way of telling in the general case. The criteria by which we ordinarily distinguish cannot be the ones by which *all* actions are seen as causally determined, since these ordinary criteria differentiate some actions from others. So our determinist supposition, though it obviously makes some sense, does not fully make sense. We do not fully know ourselves what it is we are supposing.

It is impossible really to imagine how one might "discover" that all our actions are causally determined, so that one "finds out" that even so-called free actions and choices are not free. For the freedom or causal determination of actions are not empirical facts of our world like the boiling point of alcohol. They are deeply embedded in our conceptual system, and if we try to imagine them changed we must imagine our conceptual system altered in fundamental ways. That is why additional empirical facts about, say, brain physiology, do not change the problem; the facts we find are already structured by the conceptual system we bring to them. Charles Taylor suggests that enough new and different, anomalous facts might eventually force a major reconceptualization toward determinism, somewhat in the way that Kuhn describes scientific revolutions.[11] But *these* concepts are used in our lives and our interactions, as the concepts of

[11] Charles Taylor, *The Explanation of Behaviour* (New York: Humanities Press, 1967), pp. 99–102.

physical science are not. Changing these concepts would require changing fundamental aspects not just of how we see the world but of how we interact and relate to each other.

Consider, for example, what happens to so seemingly distant a concept as that of the "self," of a "person," in the development of the determinist thesis. So long as we are concerned only with external impediments to one's freedom of action, there is no conceptual problem; the way they interfere with the action of the self or person is clear. But when we follow the determinist argument about the way a man's choices are shaped by his character and ideas, and these by his previous experiences and choices, and these by his still earlier character and ideas, and so on back to helpless infancy—something peculiar happens to the notion of the person. We see that men are compelled by their character to do what they do, prevented from doing otherwise. But who is this "person" who is compelled by his "character"? How can a man's character, his personality, his mind, his will, have become something external to "him," that compels "him" causally? There is, one wants to say, no "him" left at that point to be compelled; for a man *is* his character, personality, or will. As Polanyi says, "As we identify ourselves in turn with one level of our person or another, we feel passively subjected to the activities of the one which we do not acknowledge for the time being."[12] Our normal concept of the person breaks down here, for it is a concept we use in our language games, in our lives, in ways that tie it grammatically to notions of choice and responsibility.

Our concepts are conventional, but the conventions on which these concepts rest are not arbitrary; they are shaped by our human condition and conduct, by our forms of life. The determinist says that our distinctions here result from our ignorance, that we call some events actions, or some actions free, because we are ignorant of their causes. But that is not true. We do not call an event a free action just because we happen to be ignorant of its causes. What distinguishes actions from events is not our knowledge or ignorance but the different forms of life that surround them.

The fact is that we have here two different perspectives—that of the actor engaged in action, and that of the observer—two different kinds of language games. Both kinds of games are played with one and the same set of concepts, though they are combined in various ways and to various degrees in the grammar of different particular concepts. There are many different language games involved, even if we can group them according to the two basic perspectives. Both these perspectives are old and familiar, and neither was invented by social science. And we need both of them in our lives, cannot dispense with either.

Perhaps there have been or can be cultures and societies in which this

12 Michael Polanyi, *Personal Knowledge* (New York and Evanston: Harper & Row, 1964), p. 320.

duality is at a minimum. We are told that among the ancient Greeks the word *dike*, which came to mean "justice" and to measure the rightness of human action, originally meant simply "the way": a descriptive account of how things in fact were, or were done. Similarly the Greek words that came to mean "goodness" and "virtue," originally meant something closer to "profitability," "efficiency," "vigor," "usefulness." Such usage suggests, as it did to Nietzsche, a society which still knows a perfect unity between duty and desire, in which norms are flawlessly internalized. Kant thought of this condition as characterizing a perfectly rational being; Nietzsche tried to recreate it.

Lacking the kind of changes in our lives and selves that Nietzsche envisaged, we continue to need both detachment and engagement as separate perspectives. We need to predict and explain other people's actions, and sometimes our own, in relation to the circumstances that brought them about. If we had to regard all actions as arbitrary choices, all men as having purposes which cannot be causally influenced, we would be helpless to bring about even small alterations in each other's conduct, let alone large-scale social change. But we also need to make commitments, hold each responsible, and decide for ourselves what to do. Neither of the two perspectives is in general more true or more valid than the other. Indeed, as Leon Goldstein has said, they are "complementary and, in fact, mutually require one another."[13] Both Kierkegaard and Freud tell us true and important things about anxiety.[14] Though we are accustomed in some circumstances to say that the scientific explanation tells us the "real truth" about anxiety, we are accustomed in other circumstances to say that the phenomenological, experiential account tells us the "real truth" about it. And that strongly suggests that neither is the real truth in any exclusive, absolute sense.

One wants to say that these are different perspectives on a single reality. But they have logically incompatible implications, and reality is not supposed to be logically contradictory. The man who is troubled about free will, or about action and social science, does not want to hear about our contradictory concepts. He wants to know whether men's actions are in reality, in fact, free or causally determined. What Wittgenstein tries to show is that not merely the possible answers to that question, but the question itself is necessarily framed in language, and that, therefore, no matter how insistently it tries to get beyond words to the reality of facts, it remains dependent on the meanings of its concepts. What the questioner wants to know is not unambiguous, even if it feels perfectly clear to him.

[13] Leon J. Goldstein, "The Phenomenological and Naturalistic Approaches to the Social," in Natanson, ed., *Philosophy of the Social Sciences*, p. 291; compare p. 286; and Gunnell, "Social Science and Political Reality," p. 182 (but contrast the argument in the rest of Gunnell's article).

[14] Rollo May, quoted in Goldstein, "Phenomenological and Naturalistic Approaches," pp. 289–290.

Even the critics of social science usually concede that it is possible to observe the behavior of men as we observe the behavior of rats, amoebas, and molecules. We will be distracted and biased by our conceptual system in these observations, but that is as true in physics or biology as in social science. The question is: If we observe human conduct in this way, *what* will we be observing? In what language will we express it? Whatever a hypothetical, concept-free observer of mankind might see, he would surely not see promises or decisions or power or interests or organization or war or worship; for none of these phenomena strike the naked, concept-free eye (although they are perfectly "observable" to someone with concepts). All of these concepts are significantly shaped by quasi-performative language games. So the concept-free observer's science would not be about such phenomena. It would, as Schutz has said, "not tell us anything about social reality as experienced by men in everyday life." It would be "abstract," and its concepts "remote from the obvious and familiar traits in any society."[15]

One way of trying to imagine what sorts of things such a science could see is to consider what can and cannot be accomplished by skilled observers of animal behavior. They can see much and they can develop a science. But the *kind* of thing they see, the *kinds* of questions that occur to them to ask, the *kinds* of things that seem to require explanation, and the *kind* of observation that counts as an explanation are just very different from any account of human social or political life. The transformation of our existing ways of observing and explaining mankind into that sort of science, as Charner Perry has said, "involves much more than the superficial application of scientific method to a given subject matter. It involves a transformation of the subject matter, a substitution of one point of view and set of terms for another."[16] In other words, a "purely observational" social science independent of our existing conceptual system in the realm of action might or might not be possible, might or might not be interesting or useful; but it could not tell us the things we now want to know about society and politics. It could not answer the questions we now can formulate, for they are formulated in the concepts we have.

In practice, what social scientists do is not, of course, any concept-free observation of events among human beings, but an attempt to fiddle with the concepts we already have in such a way as to make them scientifically usable. This has meant the invention of new, technical concepts, the attempt to confine work to those concepts which seem "realistic" or

[15] Schutz, "Concept and Theory Formation," p. 241.
[16] Charner Perry, "The Semantics of Political Science," *American Political Science Review*, XLIV (June 1950), 398.

"factual," the use of "operational definitions," and the attempt to redefine familiar concepts in such a way as to make them realistic, factual, or scientific. The effort has not been spectacularly successful (which is not to say that there are no spectacular achievements in the realm of social science). Technical terms still reflect our conceptual system, in relation to which they must be defined. Terms that appear realistic or factual turn out to be grammatically as complex as any "value word." Operational definitions ultimately are useful only if they come close to real definition; if our operational definition of "power" is not related to the meaning of "power" then the results of any study we conduct with it will not yield information about power. And the attempt to redefine familiar terms to make them scientific is subject to vicissitudes of its own.

Because of the widely shared assumption of a dichotomy between "facts" and "values," social scientists tend to assume that they will be safe from conceptual confusion if they confine their work to "value-free," realistic terms. They suppose that except for "value" terms, other words can be assumed to function as labels. Thus, for example, political scientists tend to assume that if they stick with a hard-headed, realistic, nasty concept like "power," avoiding idealistic and evaluative ones like "justice," then they should have no serious problems about identifying what in the world it is they are studying. But "power" is every bit as much a part of our action vocabulary as "justice," every bit as much used in complex language games which can give rise to seeming grammatical contradictions.

Of course, a Wittgensteinian perspective and Austinian tools of analysis are not absolute prerequisites for the kind of perspicuous overview of plural grammar that is needed here. Various writers in the social sciences do sometimes make significant "Wittgensteinian" discoveries about a concept like "power" without benefit of ordinary-language philosophy. But the examples of this kind of insight I have come across tend to be quite limited in scope. The discovery is more or less accidental, and it often covers only a fraction of what needs to be said about a word's grammar. Further, the writer is often unable to characterize what he has discovered with full accuracy, being limited by the usual label-and-object assumptions about the nature of meaning. So he often cannot follow through on his discovery, or put it to anything like its full potential of use.[17]

Instead of developing these themes further at the general level, let us examine two case studies of troublesome concepts: "power" and "legiti-

---

[17] Examples of this kind of partial conceptual insight that remains incomplete, with respect to the concept of power, may be found in Peter Bachrach and Morton S. Baratz, "Decisions and Nondecisions: An Analytical Framework," *American Political Science Review*, LVII (September 1963), 632–642; Donald J. Kreitzer, "An Analysis of the Nature of Power," *Southwest Social Science Quarterly*, 45 (March 1965), 375–383; William H. Riker, "Some Ambiguities in the Notion of Power," *American Political Science Review*, LVIII (June 1964), 341–349.

macy." In the course of examining them, we shall incidentally also indicate one kind of utility Austinian analysis can have as a technical aid for the clarification of concepts in social science.

The concept of power has been an extremely troubling one in political science research, to the point where some commentators have suggested it be abandoned.[18] A Wittgensteinian approach will suggest that we begin by asking not what power is, but how the word "power" is used. Etymologically, it is related to the French *pouvoir*, to be able, from the Latin *potere*, to be able. That suggests, in turn, that power is a something—anything—which makes or renders somebody able to do, capable of doing something. Power is capacity, potential, ability, or wherewithal. It is much better thought of as a "capacity" word than as a "thing" word "which is uniquely referential," as Dorothy Emmet puts it.[19] Now, some social scientists studying power have argued that, though this is so, the only practical way to observe power is in its exercise, so that an operational definition of the word might still look to actual achievements or successes. But in the first place, that operational definition is so far from the normal meaning of "power" as to be seriously deceptive unless it is used with the utmost care; and in the second place, the assumption on which it rests is false. We have any number of more or less reliable ways of assessing the power of individuals, groups, offices, nations, which are quite independent of the exercise of that power (though of course observing its exercise is one way of assessing power).

Next, we are often told in the social science literature that power is a relation, is relational.[20] But ordinary usage suggests that this is not true. "Power" is something which one may "have" or "not have," "exercise" or "not exercise." One may also "have" a "relationship," but always "with" someone else; one does not usually "have power with" someone else. And one does not "exercise" a "relationship" at all. What the social scientists mean by calling power relational, if I understand them, is that the phenomena of power go on among people, that they involve one man's having power over another but not over a third. But that need not be so.

It is important to distinguish here between the expressions "power to" and "power over." If "power" were a label for certain phenomena, such a distinction could not be of great importance, since the two expressions would necessarily involve the same idea of power simply set in different verbal contexts. But if the concept of power is built up out of, abstracted from, its various characteristic expressions and occasions of use, then the idea of power in "power to" may be significantly different from the idea

[18] For instance, in James G. March, "The Power of Power," in David Easton, ed., *Varieties of Political Theory* (Englewood Cliffs: Prentice-Hall, 1966), pp. 68–70.
[19] Dorothy Emmet, "The Concept of Power," *Aristotelian Society Proceedings*, LIV (1953–1954), 19–20.
[20] See for example, Robert Dahl, "The Concept of Power," in S. Sidney Ulmer, ed., *Introductory Readings in Political Behavior* (Chicago: Rand McNally, 1961), p. 344.

of power in "power over." That is, indeed, the case. One man may have power over another or others, and that sort of power is indeed relational, though it is not a relationship. But he may have power to do or accomplish something all by himself, and that power is not relational at all; it may involve other people if what he has power to do is a social or political action, but it need not. That a man has the power to do something may be proved by the actual doing, though he may well have the power without exercising it, without doing the thing. That a man has power over another may be proved by his getting the other to do something, but also by his doing something to the other (though this verges on having him *in* one's power); and again the power may exist without being exercised.[21]

A remarkable number of social scientific studies on power begin by announcing that they will not attempt to distinguish power from influence, control, or other closely related phenomena, because such fine distinctions do not really matter. Even if these terms were labels, that would be a questionable scientific assumption; but given that they are not, the results can be disastrous. Social scientists are as liable as philosophers to think in terms of broad dichotomies and avoid the seemingly trivial chore of fine distinctions. That is all very well where our object of study can be clearly identified apart from the words in which we speak of it ("study that thing, there, whatever it is"); but if its identification depends on concepts, then confusion about terms will result, as Arendt has said, "in a kind of blindness with respect to the realities."[22] If you use distinct terms interchangeably or ignore fine differences, then as Cavell puts it, there is likely to be "something you aren't noticing about the world."[23]

But more commonly we do not really succeed in eliminating the distinctions marked in our language, but only allow them to direct our thinking in unexamined and therefore uncontrolled ways. The "blindness with respect to realities" that results is not random, but reflects and perpetuates certain unexamined assumptions about the world. In the case of the vocabulary of power, influence, and authority, Arendt says, "Behind the apparent confusion lies a firm conviction that the most crucial political issue is, and always has been, the question of Who rules Whom? Only after one eliminates this disastrous reduction of public affairs to the business of dominion will the original data concerning human affairs appear or rather reappear in their authentic diversity." In other words, the social scientist who purports to use "power" and "influence" *interchangeably* does not really do so. He has simply abdicated from the task of noticing the pat-

[21] The distinction is noticed by Riker as he contrasts two other writers' definitions of power: "Some Ambiguities in the Notion of Power," p. 343. But Riker cannot accept such ambiguity because "however desirable in poetry," it "has no place in science or philosophy"!

[22] Hannah Arendt, "Reflections on Violence," *New York Review of Books*, XII (February 27, 1969), 24; compare her *Between Past and Future* (Cleveland and New York: World Publishing, 1961), p. 95.

[23] Stanley Cavell, *Must We Mean What We Say?* (New York: Charles Scribner's Sons, 1969), p. 36.

terns in accord with which he uses now one term, now the other; and thereby he leaves his own assumptions and implications in this region unexamined and uncontrolled by his own critical intelligence.

In his article on power, for example, Dahl announces that he is seeking to explicate the "primitive notion" underlying "all" of the concepts related to power, including influence, control, and authority.[24] He requests the reader's permission to use the terms "interchangeably," though he thinks that some readers might "prefer" for him to use the word "influence" and others the word "control." When he proceeds to explicate the basic, primitive notion underlying all the power-related terms, Dahl contrasts a man standing on a street and saying to himself, "I command all cars to drive on the right side of the street," with a policeman directing traffic. And he concludes "A has power over B to the extent that he can get B to do something that B would not otherwise do." Now, A's getting B to do something could indeed result, in varying situations, from his power or his authority or his control or his influence. So what harm does Dahl do by calling this "power" and taking it as the primitive notion that underlies influence, authority, and the rest?

As we have suggested, the potential harm is twofold, depending on whether he actually uses the two words completely interchangeably, or whether he merely switches back and forth between them for reasons he himself has not examined. In the former instance, he is blurring an important distinction, importing the assumptions and implications that go with our concept of power into talk about influence, and vice versa. To say accurately what these differing assumptions and implications are, one would have to conduct an Austinian study of the two word families; and here again I am only suggesting a possible line of inquiry, not demonstrating it. I suspect that such a study would draw important conclusions from such facts as these: that we speak of "indirect influence" but not "indirect power"; that there is such a thing as "physical power" but no such thing as "physical influence"; that one can have "the power of (attorney, the sword, the purse)" but not "the influence of (anything)"; that one can be "in power" but not "in influence." Some differences of course arise from the fact that "influence," unlike "power," has a verb form in English. But "to power" has come into our vocabulary in recent years through advertising and engineering jargon, and one could probably formulate interesting hypotheses about the difference in meaning between the two nouns from examining the difference in meaning and implications between "to power" and "to influence."

The meanings of "power" and "influence," then, differ in important ways, and power is not much like influence, even though in many situations both power and influence are involved. But while Dahl apparently thinks that he is using the two words interchangeably, in fact he often uses them quite selectively in accord with their respective ordinary meanings.

[24] Dahl, "The Concept of Power," p. 344.

278

The question we should ask ourselves is this: Why does Dahl need to bring in the word "influence" at all? why does he not confine his article to the term "power"? So we examine the instances where "influence" appears and find that Dahl uses it where the word "power" would sound distinctly odd. For example, Dahl writes:

Some of the possible bases of a President's power over a Senator are his patronage, his constitutional veto, the possibility of calling White House conferences, his *influence* with the national electorate, his charisma, his charm, and the like.[25]

All of the other times when he uses the word "influence," except where it is one among a list of synonyms for "power," have to do with the relationship between an individual Senator favoring or opposing a bill, and the rest of the Senate membership.[26] Here Dahl almost never speaks of the Senator's "power" over the Senate, but of his "influence." And rightly so; for while some Senators do have power over some of their colleagues, the great bulk of their activities for or against legislation involve the exercise of influence over others, not power over them. Of course, one cannot say flatly that power is not involved, for every successful exercise of influence demonstrates that someone had at least the *power to* influence another. But that need not mean power *over* him.

The trouble clearly is that terms like "power" and "influence" are not labels for mutually exclusive categories of phenomena, like "gorillas" and "elephants." The grammar of each of these terms is internally complex, allowing contradictory inferences; and at the same time the concepts are not strictly comparable. They are of different kinds, or move in different dimensions. The social science literature is full of attempts either to distinguish them in simple ways, or to make one of them into a sub-category of the other. But the terms do not have neat boundaries, and do not fit together like pieces in a jigsaw puzzle. This becomes much easier to see once we switch from "What is power?" to "What are we saying when we call something 'power'?" or even better to "When and how do we use 'power' and related words?"

The trouble with those latter questions, and the answers to them we are likely to find, is that they will not produce a consistent whole, free of internal ambiguity: the "phenomenon" to which the word "power" refers. And that suggests that a term like "power" may not be capable of serving for formulating the kind of unambiguous, general hypotheses or laws the social scientist seeks to formulate. If "power" were an exceptional word in this respect, one could simply advise social scientists to abandon it and turn to other concepts instead. But if its complexities are fairly characteristic of our entire vocabulary of action and socio-political phenomena, then the problem is more grave. Besides, *what* phenomena shall we study instead, when what we persistently want to know more about, to understand, is *power*?

[25] *Ibid.*, p. 345; my italics.
[26] *Ibid.*, pp. 349, 355, 356, 358, 361.

Besides the selection of "realistic," "factual" words and the use of operational definitions, social scientists have also attempted to forge a conceptual system suitable for scientific work by redefining available concepts. They have often done so in a certain characteristic way, designed to remove those aspects of a term's meaning that seem to carry implications of judgment or commitment, and thus to strip the term down to its labeling or formal component. Yet typically they have assumed at the same time that no real, substantive change has been made in the term's meaning. We have already suggested some of the difficulties inherent in such an effort, for instance in the attempt to imagine a concept of "promising" that includes no obligation to perform. But the point is probably better, more subtly, and more convincingly made if we look at an actual rather than a hypothetical example and see exactly what is and is not possible in the way of "neutral" redefinition, and what consequences redefinition is likely to have. One of the clearest and also most significant examples is presented by the social-science career of the concept of legitimacy. The notion of legitimacy was, so far as I know, first "cleansed of subjectivity" and redefined for social scientific use by Max Weber, though, as usual in such a process, Weber did not intend any substantive redefinition. By now, Weber's definition of "legitimacy" has become common currency in most of the social sciences, so its vicissitudes form a story of considerable general significance.

Etymologically, the *Oxford English Dictionary* tells us, the word "legitimate" "expresses a status which has been conferred or ratified by some authority," though in English it does not carry the original participial sense. A legitimate child is a child "having the status of one lawfully begotten." A legitimate sovereign is one whose title rests "on the strict principle of hereditary right," and with respect to any government legitimacy means "the condition of being in accordance with law or principle." In general, then, what is legitimate is "conformable to law or rule, sanctioned or authorized by law or right," and hence sometimes "normal, regular, conformable to standard type," or "sanctioned by the laws of reasoning, logically admissible or inferrible." Now obviously these meanings involve the signaling or quasi-performative functions which the term "legitimacy" serves. To call something legitimate is at least normally to imply something about its authoritativeness, bindingness; to call something legitimate is to take a position toward it—a position that may have consequences with respect to one's own or other people's obligations and responsibilities. (There are grammatical ties, we can also say, between the term "legitimacy" and terms like "authority," "obedience," "obligation," but also, of course, terms like "illegitimate," "resistance," "rebellion.")

Yet the word is by no means a pure performative, nor an expression of

280

personal preference or individual taste. As John Schaar has pointed out, the dictionary definitions "all revolve around the element of law or right, and rest the force of a claim upon foundations external to and independent of the mere assertion or opinion of the claimant."[27] Like "justice," the term "legitimacy" invokes standards, and thus resembles neither "green" nor "delicious."

But Weber sought a term that would be a pure label, neutral with respect to the speaker's position and commitment. So he saw the term "legitimacy" very differently. Specifically, he argued that such terms have both a "normative" and an "empirical" meaning, and that the sociologist must use only the latter.[28] How might one formulate the "normative" and "empirical" meanings of the term? Weber does not tell us about the "normative" meaning explicitly, but the definition he urges for social scientific use is that "legitimacy" means "the prestige of being considered exemplary or binding."[29] Weber argues that a sociologist will regard a law as valid or a political system as legitimate precisely to the extent that people's actions or behavior are "oriented toward" that law or that system. This orientation commonly takes the form of obedience, but disobedience carried out secretively or guiltily is equally a recognition of the law. Either way, "the legitimacy of a system of authority may be treated sociologically only as the probability that to a relevant degree the appropriate attitudes [toward the system] will exist, and the corresponding practical conduct ensue."[30]

Presumably, if the "empirical" definition of "legitimate" is "the prestige of being considered exemplary or binding," then its "normative" definition would have to be something like "deserving to be ought to be? must be?) considered exemplary or binding." I would suggest, however, that neither of these is at all a satisfactory definition of "legitimacy." For Weber's definition is essentially equivalent to defining "legitimate" as "the condition of being considered legitimate," and the corresponding "normative" definition comes out as "deserving to be considered legitimate." If one must choose, the latter comes closer, for whatever is legitimate deserves to be considered legitimate; but one can imagine cases in which something deserves to be considered legitimate for other reasons, even though in fact it is not. The truth is that "legitimate" means something like "lawful, exemplary, binding"—not "what *is commonly considered* lawful, exem-

[27] John H. Schaar, "Reflections on Authority," *New American Review*, 8 (1970), 48; compare Hannah Arendt, "What Was Authority?" in Carl J. Friedrich, ed., *Authority (Nomos* I) (Cambridge: Harvard University Press, 1958), p. 83.

[28] Max Weber, *Basic Concepts in Sociology*, tr. by H. P. Secher (New York: Citadel Press, 1962), p. 73. Anyone criticizing Weber in the way that I do here must also acknowledge Weber's profound awareness, in other contexts, of the costs and dangers of scientific rationality, the "iron cage."

[29] *Ibid.*, p. 72; compare Max Weber, *The Theory of Social and Economic Organization*, tr. by A. R. Henderson and Talcott Parsons, ed. by Talcott Parsons (London: William Hodge, 1947), p. 114.

[30] Weber, *Theory of Social and Economic Organization*, p. 299.

plary, binding," nor "what *ought to be considered* lawful, exemplary, binding."

As so often in such cases, Weber's own use of the term is inconsistent, since he did not realize he was engaged in a major substantive redefinition. Thus, he sometimes uses it in accord with his definition and sometimes in the normal, ordinary way. For example, he repeatedly speaks of people's "belief in the legitimacy of" their government, and says that governments try to "foster this belief" in various ways.[31] But in terms of his definition, this would mean "belief in the people's *belief* that the government's acts are exemplary or binding," which clearly is not what Weber means. He means belief in the government's legitimacy, in the full, normal meaning of that word—the very belief that elsewhere he has defined as equivalent to legitimacy itself.

Clearly what Weber has done is much like the reductionism of Thrasymachus, and it has some of the same roots and consequences. He has taken the stance of the visiting anthropologist, the outside observer looking on, and defined "legitimacy" to mean so-called legitimacy or "what they (the natives) call 'legitimacy.' " He has refused to take on the commitment and responsibility implied in the word's signaling functions, trying to take himself as speaker entirely out of the picture. It is as if he had defined "red" to mean "having the status of being considered red," or "false" to mean "having the liability of being considered contrary to truth." In at least one passage, Weber explicitly makes the equation himself, apparently without feeling any incongruity. He says that the state "is a relation of men dominating men, a relation supported by means of legitimate violence (i.e. violence considered to be legitimate) [*auf das Mittel der legitimen (das heisst: als legitim angesehnen) Gewaltsamkeit gestützt*]."[32]

Let us examine a few implications and consequences of adopting Weber's definition. In the first place, defining legitimacy as "being considered binding" invites the question "By whom?" Weber never poses that question or sees it as problematic. He takes it for granted that the relevant belief is to be held by those subject to a law or system and to be reflected in their conduct. That assumption clearly presupposes the one context with which Weber is in fact concerned—political legitimacy; if we are concerned with legitimate birth or legitimate inference, then the question "*Who* must believe the birth or the inference to be exemplary or lawful?" has no such seemingly obvious answer. Further, the answer Weber takes for granted manages neatly to combine his own democratic predilections (a government is legitimate only to the extent that it has the consent of the governed) with a familiar basic principle of international

[31] For example, *ibid.*, p. 298.

[32] Max Weber, "Politics as a Vocation," in H. H. Gerth and C. Wright Mills, trs. and eds., *From Max Weber* (New York: Galaxy, Oxford University Press, 1958), p. 78; "Politik als Beruf," in Johannes Winckelmann, ed., *Gesammelte Politische Schriften* (Tübingen; J. C. B. Mohr [Paul Siebeck], 1958), p. 493.

law: that *de jure* legitimacy is ultimately dependent on *de facto* legitimacy, on the capacity to govern successfully over time. One can see why Weber's definition seemed obviously right to him; it was, as the psychoanalysts like to say, "overdetermined." But international law does distinguish between *de facto* and *de jure* here, and specifies under what circumstances (for instance, after how much time) the one becomes (equivalent to) the other. And the seemingly democratic impulse to identify legitimacy with majority consent confuses majority rule with the other–directed personality. Democracy requires that the individual accept the majority decision after a vote is taken, not that he try to guess the outcome of the vote and cast his own vote in accord with the anticipated majority.

Ironically, Weber's definition is, in a way, more in accord with phenomenological than with positivistic social study; it makes the social scientist passively responsive to whatever is in the mind of the observed subjects, rather than an active seeker after independent, objective social reality. Or perhaps one should say that Weber's definition is phenomenological toward others, the observed subjects, and positivistic toward himself. The one judgment of legitimacy he will not accept at face value, or indeed accept at all, is his own. As Schaar points out, the normal meaning of "legitimacy" implies some standards external to the claimant, but Weber's definition dissolves legitimacy "into belief or opinion. . . . By a surgical procedure, the older concept has been trimmed of its cumbersome 'normative' and 'philosophical' parts," so that the sociological "investigator can examine nothing outside popular opinion in order to decide whether a given regime or institution or command is legitimate or illegitimate. To borrow the language of the law, there can be no independent inquiry into the title."[33] In seeking to insulate the sociologist from the context of judging and taking a position, Weber in effect made it incomprehensible that anyone might judge legitimacy and illegitimacy according to rational, objective standards. For by what criteria do the subjects whom the social scientist observes make their decision about legitimacy? Weber's definition gives them no criterion. The necessary counterpart to the "objectivity" of Weber's social scientist is the total subjectivity and irrationality imputed to the subjects he studies. The positivistic conviction that people's decisions about what is legitimate must be irrational expressions of personal preference is a perfect correlate to Weberian "objectivity."

Indeed, in terms of Weber's definition, the subjects whom the sociologist studies need make no *decision* about legitimacy at all. Weber removes the sociologist from the ordinary concept of legitimacy not just by one step, but by two. For the notion of "what they [the observed subjects] consider legitimate," he soon substitutes a further "operationalization." They are taken to consider a government or a law legitimate if they *act as if* they do. As a result, as Schaar points out, the "analysis dissolves legitimacy into

[33] Schaar, "Reflections on Authority," 48.

acceptance or acquiescence" on the part of those subject to power.[34] But there can be many reasons for obeying, or for disobeying in a furtive manner, besides the reason Weber builds into his definition—that one considers the law or the government legitimate. The Weberian definition blocks our intellectual access to such issues.

By now, Weber's definition has become more or less standard jargon in social and political science. Schaar has collected three representative contemporary definitions, to which we may add a fourth:

Legitimacy involves the capacity of the system to engender and maintain the belief that the existing political institutions are the most appropriate ones for the society.

In the tradition of Weber, legitimacy has been defined as the degree to which institutions are valued for themselves and considered right and proper.

We may define political legitimacy as the quality of "oughtness" that is perceived by the public to inhere in a political regime. That government is legitimate which is viewed as morally proper for a society.

Belief that the structure, procedures, acts, decisions, policies, officials or leaders of government possess the quality of "rightness," propriety, or moral goodness and should be accepted because of this quality—irrespective of the specific content of the particular act in question—is what we mean by "legitimacy."[35]

Thus, an uninitiated student dropping in on the middle of a modern political science course may be startled to hear such propositions as that a government may become increasingly legitimate by the judicious and efficient use of secret police and propaganda. Which seems about as accurate as that one can increase the validity of an argument by threatening to shoot anyone who disagrees.

The shift in its definition initiated by Weber is typical of a whole series of similar shifts in social science—sometimes explicit and sometimes implicit, but never so far as I can see with awareness of the significance we have been discussing here. The shift is always away from the signaling or quasi-performative parts of a concept's grammar toward the labeling or referring parts, from its substantive toward its formal meaning. So the question becomes: What happens if a whole region of human intellectual enterprise attempts a systematic shift in definitions of a whole range of vocabulary, away from the vocabulary's signaling and toward its labeling functions? The answer seems to be, first, confusion. The shift is never completely made; the signaling functions cannot really be abandoned, yet their use can be minimized. The social scientist tries to use words one

[34] *Ibid.*
[35] Seymour Martin Lipset, *Political Man* (Garden City: Doubleday, 1960), p. 77; Robert Bierstadt, "Legitimacy," in *Dictionary of the Social Sciences* (New York: U.N.E.S.C.O., 1964), p. 386; Richard M. Merelman, "Learning and Legitimacy," *American Political Science Review*, LX (September 1966), 548; Robert Dahl, *Modern Political Analysis* (Englewood Cliffs: Prentice-Hall, 1963), p. 19.

way in his life and another way in his work, but usually without any awareness that this involves a significant difference in the words' meanings, or what that difference is like. As a result, each realm is "infected" by the other. And, second, it is no wonder if, as a further consequence, the uninitiated develop a vague but persistent feeling about social science and social scientists: that they are somehow destructive or cynical, that they are somehow cowardly or reluctant to make commitments and judgments, that they are somehow intrinsically conservative and supportive of the *status quo*.

Is there, perhaps, also a danger that the new definitions and the conceptions they imply might spread from social science into other realms of activity, for instance, into the processes of government and political life itself? That surely is close to the heart of the danger the critics of social science seem to anticipate. Theorists like Arendt, Wolin, and Strauss are not really concerned about the danger that political phenomena might be explained by nonpolitical, social, economic, psychological ones, as if what is at stake were the independent prestige of the concept of the political. They are concerned that we do not lose, abandon, forget, or undermine our capacity for political action—not for blind, reactive response (like the subjects of Weber's sociology), but for rational action, action that is tied to judgment and to responsibility.

It is perfectly possible, and most desirable, to study man objectively, to know ourselves objectively. That enterprise was not born with modern social science, though it may not have existed in tribal, traditional society. But we have argued that modern social science pursues that enterprise in new ways, some of which give rise to both theoretical problems (like the nature of causal explanation in human affairs) and practical ones (like those anticipated by Wolin, Arendt, and Strauss). We have suggested that action is confined neither to what is behaviorally observable nor to what is phenomenologically given in experience; which suggests that our need is for forms of social and political study that can do justice to the full complexity of action, that are not rigidly doctrinaire on such questions, but open, inventive, observant, flexible.

That need seems very close to C. Wright Mills' plea for what he called "the sociological imagination," the ability to perceive and understand social phenomena at more than one level of analysis at a time. Mills was primarily concerned with one particular duality: the distinction between "the personal troubles of milieu" and "the public issues of social structure." Troubles occur and are properly resolved within the sphere of "the individual as a biographical entity and within the scope of his immediate milieu—the social setting that is directly open to his personal experience and to some extent his willful activity." Issues, by contrast, "have to do with matters that transcend these local environments of the individual and the range of his inner life. They have to do with the organization of many such milieux into the institutions of an historical society as a whole, with the ways in which various milieux overlap and inter-penetrate to form the larger structure of social and historical life. An issue is a public matter."[36]

Too often the philosopher or social theorist feels it imperative to choose between these two perspectives, assuming that there must be a single, consistent reality—either that of the individual and his experiences or that of the society in which they take place. The former perspective is then supported by examples like "the reality of war is what is experienced by the individual soldier at the front." The latter is supported by examples like "you cannot solve mass unemployment by encouraging the individual to try harder to find a job." But it is a mistake to choose between these perspectives at all. We need to see at both levels, to be both hedgehogs and foxes simultaneously. In the same way, we need the "sociological, or political, imagination" to see action from both the perspective of choice and the perspective of causation. Only thus will we truly comprehend the nature of action.

In short, I am suggesting the urgent need for modes of social and political study that do not demean and diminish man; that are objective without ignoring the reality of the investigating self, without anesthetizing compassion and anger, and without reducing knowledge to impotence. As one pioneering social scientist put it, in discussing human affairs we by no means need "to choose between the vivid, intuitive description of an artist and the detached abstractness of a scientist thinking only quantitatively. It is not necessary and not permissible to lose feeling when feeling is investigated scientifically."[37] Something more will be said in the last chapter about the contemporary significance of that problem.

[36] C. Wright Mills, *The Sociological Imagination* (New York: Oxford University Press, 1959), pp. 8–9.

[37] Otto Fenichel, *The Psychoanalytic Theory of Neurosis* (New York: W. W. Norton, 1945), p. 9.

# XIII

## Philosophy and the Study
## of Political Theory

IT IS TIME to return to the topic we have long postponed: the relationship between conceptual puzzlement and philosophy, and the nature of philosophy itself. Where we have spoken throughout of "conceptual" puzzlement, paradox, and insight, Wittgenstein speaks of "philosophical" confusion or puzzlement; and he calls the man who is concerned with such problems "the philosopher." As we mentioned at the outset, our altered terminology was introduced for several reasons: to stress the ubiquity of such problems in realms other than philosophy, such as political and social theory; to prevent a premature rejection of Wittgenstein's ideas under the misapprehension that he denigrates traditional philosophy; and to allow postponement of his complex views on philosophy until after his other ideas had been introduced. In the first half of this chapter we shall examine those views, so that we may begin, in the second half, to assess their significance for political theory.

Let us begin by reviewing Wittgenstein's two major diagnoses of conceptual or philosophical puzzlement, as we discussed them earlier. The one diagnosis emphasized the paradoxical quality of conceptual "insights," the way they simultaneously conflict with and yet depend on ordinary usage. Wittgenstein ascribed this quality, and the puzzlement itself, to our "craving for generality," our attempt to derive general, consistent rules from the grammar of our language, when in reality that grammar has inconsistent implications. The second diagnosis emphasized the origin of such puzzlement and "insight" in contemplation, in the absence of any genuine speech situation where one person would actually use the puzzling word to tell another something. Wittgenstein ascribed this quality, and the puzzlement itself, to the fact that when "language is idling," it is deprived of those elements of meaning or sense normally supplied by the context of speech and the act of speaking.

A third diagnosis, or element of the over-all Wittgensteinian diagnosis, which has not yet been discussed, grows out of the notion of forms of life. Wittgenstein maintains that conceptual or philosophical problems arise because we want to escape or reject aspects of our own grammar which cannot be escaped or rejected because they arise from our forms of life. When we are puzzled in this way, we think we are asking an empirical question about "a fact of the world," but it really concerns "a matter of expression."[1] Thus, we "predicate of the thing what lies in the method of representing it."[2] And that prevents us from seeing that our real objection is to the seeming arbitrariness of our grammar, the limitations it seems to impose on thought and the world. When we are conceptually or philosophically puzzled, our "notation dissatisfies us. . . . Our ordinary language, which of all possible notations is the one which pervades all our life, holds our mind rigidly in one position, as it were, and in this position sometimes it feels cramped, having a desire for other positions as well."[3] Feeling cramped, we rebel against "the use of *this* expression in connection with *these* criteria."[4] But our grammar is not merely arbitrary; it is founded in what we do, in our forms of life. And these are "what is given," what simply "has to be accepted." In trying to escape or rebel against them, the philosopher is trying to do the impossible, and traditional philosophy is a record of the "bumps that the understanding has got by running its head up against the limits of language."[5]

That is likely to sound like a catastrophic critique of traditional philosophy, and we should not be surprised if Wittgenstein is often misunderstood as dismissing philosophical problems as pseudo-problems, and philosophical doctrines as errors about or violations of ordinary usage. Moreover, as our talk of diagnoses suggests, Wittgenstein often speaks of philosophical puzzlement as a disease, for which he has developed "therapies."[6] He says "the philosopher treats a question; like the treatment of an illness."[7] In both cases, the sign of a successful treatment is that the illness disappears. Philosophical problems are not so much solved but dissolved; given a perspicuous view of our grammar, we cease to be puzzled. "For the clarity that we are aiming at is indeed *complete* clarity. But this simply means that the philosophical problems should *completely* disappear."[8]

Of course, the prime patient in the analogy, as well as the physician, is

<hr/>

[1] Ludwig Wittgenstein, "The Yellow Book" (unpublished), quoted in Alice Ambrose and Morris Lazerowitz, "Ludwig Wittgenstein: Philosophy, Experiment and Proof," in C. A. Mace, ed., *British Philosophy in the Mid-Century* (London: George Allen and Unwin, 1966), p. 169; compare Ludwig Wittgenstein, *Blue and Brown Books* (New York and Evanston: Harper & Row, 1964), p. 57.

[2] Ludwig Wittgenstein, *Philosophical Investigations,* tr. by G. E. M. Anscombe (New York: Macmillan, 1968), par. 104.

[3] Wittgenstein, *Blue and Brown Books,* p. 59.

[4] *Ibid.,* p. 57.

[5] Wittgenstein, *Philosophical Investigations,* par. 119.

[6] *Ibid.,* par. 133.

[7] *Ibid.,* par. 255; my translation, following Erich Heller in *The Artist's Journey into the Interior* (New York: Random House, 1959), p. 204.

[8] *Ibid.,* par. 133.

Wittgenstein himself, who knew from bitter experience the power of conceptual doubts and paradoxes, of "pictures" that hold the mind captive. Thus, it is clearly himself he means in the famous line, "What is your aim in philosophy? —To shew the fly the way out of the fly-bottle."[9] And that is why he insists that the real philosophical discovery is "the one that gives philosophy peace, so that it is no longer tormented by questions which bring *itself* in question."[10] In a way, it is precisely in passages like these, where Wittgenstein diagnoses his own earlier "illness," that he still seems closest to the views that emerged from that "illness" and appear in the *Tractatus*. For it was the *Tractatus* that concluded that language—what can meaningfully be said—has definite limits, and that most of traditional philosophy lies beyond those limits. It was the *Tractatus* that concluded with a ukase of philosophical limitation: "What we cannot speak about we must consign to silence."

The whole orientation of Wittgenstein's later philosophy, we have argued, is otherwise. It does not legislate; it describes. The fact is that philosophers do write, and are read; and one would suppose that the later Wittgenstein's attitude would be that we should "look and see" what they are up to, how they use language, what sort of meaning and sense their utterances have. Moreover, as early as 1930, the man who thought of philosophers as running their heads up against the limits of language also mocked and questioned his own metaphor: "Run up against the limit of language? But language is not a cage."[11] And he is reported to have said, "Don't think that I despise metaphysics or ridicule it. On the contrary, I regard the great metaphysical writings of the past as among the noblest productions of the human mind."[12] Several of Wittgenstein's followers have also stressed the value of philosophy, "what philosophy might positively accomplish and the kind of importance it might have"; and Waismann, in particular, undertakes a passionate defense of metaphysics as "one of the great liberating forces."[13] Is such a view compatible with the notion of philosophy as disease, as the desire to escape what must be accepted?

I would suggest that when Wittgenstein seems critical of traditional philosophy, speaks of it as a disease to be cured or a flight from what must be accepted, he has in mind primarily one aspect of philosophy, what we

[9] *Ibid.*, par. 309; compare Ludwig Wittgenstein, *Remarks on the Foundations of Mathematics*, tr. by G. E. M. Anscombe, ed. by G. H. von Wright, R. Rhees, and G. E. M. Anscombe (Oxford: Basil Blackwell, 1964), p. 17; and Heller, *The Artist's Journey into the Interior*, p. 226.

[10] Wittgenstein, *Philosophical Investigations*, par. 133.

[11] Friedrich Waismann, *Wittgenstein und der Wiener Kreis*, ed. by B. F. McGuinness (London: Basil Blackwell, 1967), p. 117; my translation.

[12] M. O'C. Drury, "A Symposium on Wittgenstein," in K. T. Fann, *Ludwig Wittgenstein* (New York: Dell, 1967), p. 68; compare Waismann, *Wittgenstein*, p. 118.

[13] Stanley Cavell, *Must We Mean What We Say?* (New York: Charles Scribner's Sons, 1969), p. 46; Friedrich Waismann, "How I See Philosophy," in H. D. Lewis, ed., *Contemporary British Philosophy* (New York: Macmillan, 1956), p. 461.

have called conceptual puzzlement, insight, paradox. He has in mind not the great philosophical systems of the past, but the initial puzzles or doubts or questions from which these arise; and secondarily the brief, aphoristic, initial "insights" or "discoveries" with which we counter these doubts. Sometimes such puzzlement and "insight" remain sterile, or even continue to haunt us obsessively and to interfere with the pursuit of other topics. ("But this isn't *seeing!*" —"But this is seeing!" "A *picture* held us captive. And we could not get outside it, for it lay in our language and language seemed to repeat it to us inexorably.")[14] They do not give us what we need. Then they are a disease. But sometimes they result in, become the focus of, a great work of philosophy. What characterizes such a work? What does it provide that might be of value? How does it differ from the disease of philosophy? Answering these questions entails no smaller topic than the nature of philosophy itself; and what can be said here must be taken as a very tentative attempt.

PROGRESS THROUGH QUESTIONING CONCEPTS

Wittgenstein accuses the philosopher of becoming dissatisfied with, and rebelling against, our notational system, which has to be accepted as given. Yet in other contexts, dissatisfaction with an inherited notation, rebellion against accepted assumptions, reexamination of fundamental concepts, can be highly productive and conducive to intellectual progress. In science, for example, questioning unexamined assumptions can sometimes, as Cavell puts it, "produce such discoveries as that the earth may revolve around the sun rather than vice versa, or that the problem about motion is not what keeps an object moving but what makes it stop."[15] Upon such shifts of assumptions there may follow a whole new era of scientific progress. Obviously, the first man to suppose that the earth might revolve around the sun was rebelling against the previously accepted concept of "the earth." In science, as Wisdom says, "some of the most preposterous statements ever made have turned out to convey the most tremendous discoveries."[16] If the impulse to rebel against accepted concepts is so productive in science, why should it be a disorder in philosophy?

Kuhn says that the self-conscious reexamination of concepts and assumptions occurs in science only at times of crisis. When science is progressing normally, scientists work successfully from shared paradigms from which they have learned; rules are left largely implicit, and concepts are taken for granted. Kuhn argues that established paradigms and theory make it difficult for anomalous cases to emerge and be recognized as such. "Novelty emerges only with difficulty, manifested by resistance,

[14] Wittgenstein, *Philosophical Investigations*, p. 203, par. 115.
[15] Stanley Cavell, "The Claim to Rationality" (unpublished dissertation, Harvard University), p. 184.
[16] John Wisdom, *Paradox and Discovery* (Oxford: Basil Blackwell, 1965), p. 124.

against a background provided by expectation."[17] But it does emerge; and if it emerges persistently and with increasing frequency, if the "puzzles" of normal science no longer come out in accord with the predictions of accepted theory, then a scientific crisis may result. What happens is not, of course, that the accumulated anomalies falsify existing theory, since no theory can be abandoned until there is "an alternative candidate . . . available to take its place."[18] What happens, rather, is a "blurring" of the accepted paradigm, a "proliferation" of different versions of the paradigm, and consequently a "loosening" of the (largely implicit) rules for normal research.[19]

It is only at such times, Kuhn argues, that scientists feel the need to examine and make explicit the assumptions and implications of their previously accepted paradigms. "Rules" become important only when paradigms "are felt to be insecure. . . . Deep debates over legitimate methods, problems, and standards of solution . . . recur regularly just before and during scientific revolutions, the periods when paradigms are first under attack and then subject to change."[20] In normal science, these debates are not necessary; the fundamentals can be taken for granted. "So long as the tools a paradigm supplies continue to prove capable of solving the problems it defines, science moves fastest and penetrates most deeply through confident employment of those tools. The reason is clear. As in manufacture so in science—retooling is an extravagance to be reserved for the occasion that demands it."[21]

Kuhn explicitly calls the questioning of fundamental assumptions, of the conventions previously taken for granted, "philosophical," and says that scientists turn to it "particularly in periods of acknowledged crisis. . . . Scientists have not generally needed or wanted to be philosophers. Indeed, normal science usually holds creative philosophy at arm's length, and probably for good reasons. To the extent that normal research work can be conducted by using the paradigm as a model, rules and assumptions need not be made explicit. But that is not to say that the search for assumptions (even for non-existent ones) cannot be an effective way to weaken the grip of a tradition upon the mind and to suggest the basis for a new one. It is no accident that the emergence of Newtonian physics in the seventeenth century and of relativity and quantum mechanics in the twentieth should have been both preceded and accompanied by fundamental philosophical analyses of the contemporary research tradition."[22]

The example of science thus suggests a hypothesis about when, under what circumstances, we are moved to reexamine and question our concepts

[17] Thomas S. Kuhn, *The Structure of Scientific Revolutions* in *International Encyclopedia of Unified Science* (Chicago: University of Chicago Press, 1970), p. 64.
[18] *Ibid.*, p. 77.
[19] *Ibid.*, pp. 80, 84.
[20] *Ibid.*, pp. 47–48.
[21] *Ibid.*, p. 76.
[22] *Ibid.*, p. 88.

and our fundamental assumptions. The times "when you need to do philosophy," as Cavell puts it, are "when you have more facts than you know what to make of, or when you do not know what new facts would show. When, that is, you need a clear view of what you already know."[23] There are times when we feel that we know everything empirical we need to know about a situation, and the meanings of all the relevant words, that "everything is in front of our eyes. And yet we feel we don't know something, don't understand something." Here we might have the impulse to ask a question like "What is *X?*" and yet feel at the same time that we already know the answer. "One might say we have all the *elements* of an answer," but lack the proper arrangement, the perspicuity.[24] Wittgenstein says that philosophical investigation "takes its rise not from an interest in the facts of nature, nor from a need to grasp causal connexions: but from an urge to understand the basis, or essence, of everything empirical. Not, however, as if to this end we had to hunt out new facts; it is, rather, of the essence of our investigation that we do not seek to learn anything *new* by it. We want to *understand* something that is already in plain view. For *this* is what we seem in some sense not to understand."[25] For example, when Augustine contemplates the nature of time, he says that though he knows what time is when no one asks him, as soon as he is asked to *say*, he does not know. Wittgenstein comments: "Something that we know when no one asks us, but no longer know when we are supposed to give an account of it, is something that we need to *remind* ourselves of. (And it is obviously something of which for some reason it is difficult to remind oneself.)"[26] Just such considerations led Plato to a doctrine of recollection.

Both the scientist and the philosopher seem to lack a clear view of the facts before them. But the scientist feels that lack when his normal ways of proceeding have broken down, when his enterprise is in crisis. The philosopher, by contrast, characteristically becomes dissatisfied with his notational system when it is not in use. In ordinary use, the concepts work just fine; it is only when they are contemplated abstractly that they give rise to philosophical perplexity. Moreover, a conceptual "discovery" in philosophy is not really *new* in the way that a new scientific conceptualization is. Rather, it is one half, or a prominent aspect, of our old, preexisting conceptual system, our grammar. The philosopher becomes captivated by that aspect, that particular example or picture, and extrapolates a general rule or insight from it, only to find himself in conflict with the familiar remainder of the concept's grammar. Because of the conflict, he concludes that he has made a new discovery. Yet unlike the philosophizing scientist, he is unable really to abandon the remaining part

---

[23] Cavell, *Must We Mean What We Say?* p. 21.
[24] *Ibid.*, p. 20.
[25] Wittgenstein, *Philosophical Investigations*, par. 89.
[26] *Ibid.*

of grammar and leave it behind. The scientist is enabled to do what the traditional philosopher cannot, at least partly because he finds ways to use the new conceptualization in his work. The new conceptualization suggests new scientific language games, as it were, and he is free to explore their consequences without first having to change his own or other people's ordinary language games. The concept he reexamines may already be a technical one, used only in scientific discourse. But even if it is a quite ordinary concept, like those of "time" or "simultaneity" which are deeply imbedded in various ordinary language games and in our ordinary lives, still, when the scientist revises them, he can pursue his new conceptualization quite apart from our ordinary ways of talking or acting in regard to time or simultaneity. He simply makes the new concept technical, then and there. That is how Einstein's philosophizing about time produces radically different consequences from Augustine's. (Of course, one could also argue that we *regard* conceptual insights as scientific only if they are productive of new work in science; otherwise, they remain in the realm of philosophy.)

In philosophy, we characteristically question or rebel against concepts whose foundations run very deep in our lives and in our selves; and we have no further, pragmatic use to which to put our "discoveries." Sometimes a philosopher questions conventions shaped by language games that are truly forms of life, truly natural to human beings in all times and places, and which therefore literally cannot be changed. In this respect, philosophy, as Cavell says, "concerns those necessities we cannot, being human, fail to know. Except that nothing is more human than to deny them."[27] At other times, the philosopher may object to a convention that is in fact cultural, and therefore could conceivably be changed. But it could be changed in the slow and complex ways in which implicit culture patterns change, and not by intellectual insight. Mere philosophizing cannot change it, nor is such change a simple matter of decision or choice. Take philosophical concern over seeming contradictions in the grammar of "knowledge"; under what circumstances could it fruitfully lead to a changed concept of knowledge, free of those seeming contradictions? To change such a concept, the philosopher would have to change not merely our words, but the language games we play. For the concept of "knowledge" is as it is because of how we use it; no concept free of those "contradictions" could function as it does in our lives.

That, I think, is why Wittgenstein's presentation seems to blur the line between natural and cultural conventions. With respect to any given adult individual, the line *is* blurred; many of the conventions of his culture are as much a part of him, as natural *to him*, as those conventions truly natural to all human beings. Our culture becomes part of our nature. Consequently, for any particular philosopher, it is almost as difficult to change or escape from those parts of his conceptual system based on

[27] Cavell, *Must We Mean What We Say?* p. 96.

cultural conventions as from those based on univeral forms of life. No doubt, basic features of our nature, like what catches our attention, how we express our feelings, how we move about in the world, are to some extent cultural rather than natural; but that does not make them easily changeable. We can escape them at most by becoming deeply initiated into a different culture, and even then we escape only into its conventions. "Compare a concept with a style of painting," Wittgenstein suggests at the end of the *Investigations.* "For is even our style of painting arbitrary? Can we choose one at pleasure? (The Egyptian, for instance.) Is it a mere question of pleasing and ugly?"[28] We may be able to learn to paint (but to see?) like an Egyptian, but *what* must we do to learn it? And would it have so much as occurred to us if we had no knowledge of Egyptian painting?

### SUCCESSFUL PHILOSOPHY

What Wittgenstein is saying, I think, is something like this: philosophizing is the attempt to get clear about the most significant and fundamental and inescapable features of the world and ourselves, not by gathering new facts but by reinvestigating the facts we already have. But that necessarily means getting clear about our concepts, their limits, and their implications. Though in philosophizing we are not interested in our language but in reality, nevertheless our investigation is as truly about the one as about the other—is about the one by way of the other. In philosophizing we look at the world and at language simultaneously.[29] Our impulse is to get away from, get outside of, get free of, what seems arbitrary and merely conventional in our language; we would like to escape the limits of our conceptual system and acquire perspective on the implicit presuppositions it imposes on our thought. Cavell says that in philosophizing we are "led to speak as if beyond the limits of human language, as it were, looking back at it."[30] And, of course, our conceptual system *is* conventional, and it *does* contain contradictory implications, and it *does* tend to structure and limit our thought. That is why what Wisdom calls the philosopher's "strange pronouncements which purport to throw doubt upon all statements of some familiar sort, for instance statements about good and evil or statements about the past and the future," really do have a foundation in "some real idiosyncrasy" of the grammar of these statements.[31]

In this sense, the impulse to philosophy is the impulse to become self-conscious about our own concepts and assumptions, and thereby to penetrate beyond conventionality to the true necessities of self and world. And what Wittgenstein says about that impulse is not that its aim is

[28] Wittgenstein, *Philosophical Investigations,* p. 230.
[29] Cavell, *Must We Mean What We Say?* p. 99.
[30] Stanley Cavell, "Existentialism and Analytic Philosophy," *Daedalus,* 93 (Summer 1964), 969.
[31] Wisdom, *Paradox and Discovery,* p. 119.

impossible, but that where the aim fails the continuing impulse becomes like a disease. Where the aim succeeds for some particular individual thinker, it is because he has become accurately aware of (some part of) his assumptions and (simultaneously) his world, about which he was previously unaware but puzzled. Where that individual's assumptions and world and confusion are those of an entire society or an entire age, the result may be truly great philosophy. It is about such achievements that one might say, with Cavell, that philosophy is "the world of a particular culture brought to consciousness of itself."[32] Obviously, this is a task that is never finished, never accomplished once and for all, both because the world changes and is different for different individuals, cultures, and times, and because what we need to be told or shown always depends on what we are failing to see. The hidden, the repressed, the distorted, the content of "false consciousness," also varies with person, culture, and time. Indeed, what is a liberating philosophical insight for one generation can become the encrusted and misleading conventional wisdom of the next. Successful philosophy allows the inquiring mind to discover what it needs to know about itself or the world; great philosophy performs this service for us all.

At one point, Wittgenstein says that the philosopher *has* made a new discovery, but not of a new fact so much as of "a new way of looking at things. As if you had invented a new way of painting; or, again, a new metre, or a new kind of song."[33] He says that the notion of such a new way of seeing is reminiscent of what happens when a picture puzzle which first struck us in one way is suddenly seen in a different way as well. We see nothing we did not see before, yet we see it differently. "Before there were branches there; now there is a human shape. My visual impression has changed and now I recognize that it has not only shape and colour but also a quite particular 'organization'. —My visual impression has changed; —what was it like before and what is it like now? —If I represent it by means of an exact copy—and isn't that a good representation of it? —no change is shewn."[34]

If that is taken as an analogue to traditional philosophy, then, I think, it is an analogue not so much to conceptual puzzlement and "insight"— what Wittgenstein considers a "disease"—but to those great philosophical systems which truly transform our ways of seeing by reorganizing them, so that nothing, and everything, is changed. A philosophical system, in this sense, as Waismann says, "is not content to establish just one isolated point of truth, but effects a change in our whole mental outlook so that, as a result of that, myriads of such little points are brought into view or turned out of sight, as the case may be." Consequently, what is central to a philosophical system is "vision," and "what is decisive is a new

[32] Cavell, *Must We Mean What We Say?* p. 313.
[33] Wittgenstein, *Philosophical Investigations*, par. 401; compare pars. 144, 610.
[34] *Ibid.*, p. 196.

way of seeing."[35] Out of his initial puzzlement or sense of insight, the great traditional philosopher develops an elaborate structure of vision, exploring its systematic implications, and redeploying various aspects of reality and of our lives into a new, coherent whole. Such a system has an internal coherence making it relatively immune to challenge from individual anomalous "facts" or isolated counterarguments, much as scientific theories are resistant to challenge by empirical counterevidence. In such a developed philosophical system, one might say, we are offered a purportedly new, coherent, systematic account of the nature of the world or of some major subregion of the world (human action, mental states, art, perception).

From this perspective, Wittgenstein himself both is and is not a successful philosopher. Of course, he has experienced both the philosophical impulse and its frustration in the disease of conceptual puzzlement. But where he succeeds, he gives us perspicuity over some part of our grammar and world *without* constructing any philosophical system. He gives us, as it were, the instruments and insights for doing philosophy ourselves, when and where we need it. One might say that in our time philosophical systems have become an impossibility; the world is too fragmented, and our self-consciousness has progressed too far. Then Wittgenstein provides a kind of substitute for philosophy suitable to our age, a kind of do-it-yourself philosophy that yields only partial, *ad hoc* clarity, not a systematic doctrine. Wittgenstein himself said that there had been a "kink" in the "development of human thought," so that what he was doing was a kind of successor to traditional philosophy, a "new subject," and not merely a stage in a "continuous development."[36]

Insofar as philosophy attempts to provide coherence and order where our actual conceptual system has inconsistent implications, it may yield a satisfying sense of new vision, but it will deceive. But insofar as it accurately teaches us the unity and coherence our conceptual system has— together with its limitations and presuppositions—philosophy will perform a most vital service. Thus, when Wittgenstein appears to condemn the traditional philosopher for "predicating of the thing what lies in the method of representing it," we might read him as speaking not of philosophy as such, but of philosophical disorder. We might read him not as describing all philosophy as a disease, but as describing philosophy in a diseased condition. For Wittgenstein, after all, also said that "grammar tells us what kind of thing anything is," which surely suggests that sometimes "predicating of reality what lies in our method of representation" is perfectly healthy and informative.

As Cavell says, such predication "causes disorder only when we *mistake*

[35] Waismann, "How I See Philosophy," pp. 483–484.

[36] G. E. Moore, "Wittgenstein's Lectures in 1930–1933," in Robert R. Ammerman, ed., *Classics of Analytic Philosophy* (New York: McGraw-Hill, 1965), p. 283; compare p. 271.

our method of representation, or fail to appreciate its real functioning."[37] For only through a method of representation are we able to conceive the world coherently at all. "The analogy with painting would be this: Looking at a landscape with one near and one distant figure in it, someone unfamiliar with our conventions of representation may take one figure's being smaller than another *on the canvas* to mean (represent) that that figure is, in reality, smaller than the other. It makes sense there to say: He has predicated of the persons what lies in the method of representing them. But how, then, do *we* know that one person is (being represented as) *further away and approximately the same size* as the other? Can't we also say: Because we predicate of the persons what lies in the method of representation? Only *we* have got the method *right*. For 'the method' *now* means 'the method for making one figure more distant' and it consists not merely in 'painting one figure smaller than another' (for that, in itself, *might* represent one person's being smaller than another) but also in 'placing the figures in different planes.' Reading the method accurately, we accurately read the world."[38]

But though philosophy in this sense is an attempt at a meta-view of one's own conceptual system, the only tools it has available for formulating or answering its questions are the parts of that same conceptual system. One can look critically at a particular concept, or even a region of language, but one will do so with the conceptual system one already has: what else could one possible use? As Wittgenstein says very early, even a game played with the rules of some other game as its "pieces," is still just one more game, not really a meta-game.[39] There is no external archimedean point where we can stand to look back critically on our language as a whole. It is as Otto Neurath said about science: "we are like sailors who must rebuild their ship on the high seas, without ever being able to take it apart in dry-dock and construct it anew out of the best components."[40]

That is why the philosopher's statement of what puzzles him, or of his "insight," is characteristically paradoxical, both dependent on and in conflict with "what we all ordinarily say." Sometimes philosophers themselves recognize and acknowledge that paradoxicality, as when Hume marvels that, however clear and decisive his skeptical insights are in his study, he cannot live by them when he goes out into the practical world.[41] For other philosophers, the paradoxical quality of their findings remains unacknowledged and is revealed only over time, in the work of their successors. Over time, we see that philosophical problems are characteristically not really *solved* by the philosophers who discuss them; their dis-

[37] Cavell, "Claim to Rationality," p. 88.
[38] *Ibid.*, p. 89.
[39] Waismann, *Wittgenstein*, pp. 120–121, 134.
[40] Quoted as the epigraph in Willard van Orman Quine, *Word and Object* (Cambridge: M.I.T. Press, 1960); my translation.
[41] Cavell, *Must We Mean What We Say?* pp. 59–61.

cussion continues over generations, opponents in a controversy seem to talk past each other, one man's position is rarely conclusive for another, and the questions of philosophy never seem to get settled.

What philosophy can, positively, accomplish is to teach us that our language is conventional, that any language is conventional, and what the conventions of our language are. If philosophy is taken to mean dissatisfaction with a conventional system that cannot be changed, then it will seem like a disease to be cured. But it can also be taken, more broadly, to mean the quest for perspective on our own assumptions, the attempt to stand back from, or get outside of, what we normally take for granted, the desire to escape our limitations and achieve a universal point of view. Taken that way, philosophy has the capacity for making us aware of our own method of representation, our conceptual system—both *that* it is a conventional, conceptual system, and *how* it represents, how it is to be "read." To do so, philosophy need only make fully clear for us the assumptions and conventions we already have. That is why Wittgenstein so often stresses the purely descriptive, nonreformational character of philosophy; it "may in no way interfere with the actual use of language; it can in the end only describe it." Philosophy "leaves everything as it is."[42]

If, as Waismann says, philosophy is "one of the great liberating forces," that is not because it liberates us from conventionality as such, for that is inescapable. Inevitably, "to speak is to speak a language," and every language, "every particular notation stresses some particular point of view."[43] Nor is philosophy liberating in the sense that it liberates us from the particular conventions and presuppositions of our own conceptual system. Rather, philosophy liberates us from illusions about that conceptual system, from fragments of earlier philosophies become empty slogans of interpretation, from evasions and hypocrisies, from distortions and misunderstandings. That kind of liberation does "leave everything as it is," except, of course, the mind that is liberated.[44] It is not that nothing can change our concepts or our grammar. The scientist changes them in one way, the poet in another, the incremental drift of our ordinary speech in still another. But though there are any number of ways of changing language, philosophizing is not one of them.[45] Where philosophy succeeds, it reveals our conceptual system as it now exists, not its trivial and evanescent details, but its deep necessities. For philosophy is concerned with precisely those concepts that reflect our most central forms of life. To change these concepts, our forms of life would have to change; and that is not accomplished through philosophizing.

[42] Wittgenstein, *Philosophical Investigations*, par. 124.

[43] Cavell, "Claim to Rationality," p. 88; Wittgenstein, *Blue and Brown Books*, p. 28.

[44] K. T. Fann, *Wittgenstein's Conception of Philosophy* (Berkeley and Los Angeles: University of California Press, 1969), p. 105.

[45] Cavell, *Must We Mean What We Say?* pp. 57–58.

But what might be the implications of such an understanding of philosophy for political theory? First, it clearly means that there is a difference between political philosophy and political theory. Political philosophy is, presumably, philosophy occupied with the political realm, with central political concepts. But if by political theory we mean that long and varied tradition of discourse including at least Plato and Aristotle, Cicero and Machiavelli, Hobbes, Locke, Rousseau, and Burke, Bentham, and Marx, then political theory is not merely, is not identical with, political philosophy. If philosophy means self-consciousness about one's own concepts, the simultaneous investigation of fundamental features of the world and language, then some political theorists have been much more philosophical than others. Compare, for example, Hobbes in his lengthy and explicit examination of the nature of freedom, or contract, or representation, with a writer like Machiavelli who takes his own conceptual system almost completely for granted. (Of course *we* can learn much from attending carefully to Machiavelli's concepts of virtue, of fortune, of the state; but he himself does not examine them.) Even in Plato, who clearly was both philosopher and political theorist, there are important differences in style and structure between the political dialogues and those which are purely philosophical.

Like philosophy, political theory is concerned with examining and questioning fundamentals, with disclosing connections and relationships that normally remain hidden, with providing perspective and overview on what is normally perceived only piecemeal, in fragmented forms. But where philosophy is concerned with those fundamental concepts that grow out of the human condition itself, or out of those cultural patterns that change only slowly and inadvertently, without deliberate planning, political theory is often concerned with features of our lives which might be different if we chose to change them. It is concerned with precisely those patterns and institutions which are, or could become, political— subject to our collective, public, deliberate choice and action. Political theory is not concerned merely with discrepancy and order in our conceptual system, but with discrepancy and order in the relationship between our concepts and our institutional practices. The concepts it utilizes are often those allowing of that tension between form and substance which we discussed in relation to justice, punishment, and the political itself. And its interest is not merely in the internal tensions of the concept and what they tell us about the world, but in the tensions between the concept and our practice, between what we say and what we do. Similarly, its concepts are those, like "justice," which involve what we have called "standards," which are to some extent separable from both conceptual meaning and worldly facts. Thus, political theory is also concerned with discrepancy and order in our institutions and public practices, which may not be reflected in conceptual problems at all but may lodge in the gap between form and substance, or between meaning and standards.

But what is perhaps most strikingly distinctive about political theory is its intention, both in the sense of aim or purpose, and in the sense of style or structure. In philosophy, the primary impulse is contemplative; there is a desire for order, but order is to be achieved in the mind, through understanding. If there is an (as Wittgenstein argues, misguided) impulse toward change or renovation, the intended change is at most one in thought and speech. But political theory, particularly great and successful political theory, has almost always aimed at effecting change in the world. It need not intend radically progressive transformations; indeed, the great bulk of traditional political theory has looked backward rather than forward, has chosen order over innovation. Yet great political theory has also always had an element of the heroic, an admixture of prophecy—including the prophet's summons to return to the true tradition of a people, his sense of absolute urgency and mission, his apocalyptic vision, and his call to action.[46] Philosophy is contemplative; political theory, though it has always had an admixture of the detached, judicious contemplation of the original *theoros*, has also known the prophet's demanding vision of alternatives within reach.[47] Philosophy speaks to a mind or a culture out of joint; political theory to a polity in crisis. Of course, political theory, too, is just words and can directly change nothing but our consciousness. But, in the political realm, consciousness is the foundation of action, and a changed view of the world can lead us to change the world. The political theorist never loses sight of that fact.

These differences between philosophy and political theory are neither fixed nor obvious, nor should we expect them to be. It is not obvious in advance which of our concepts are founded in forms of life that must be accepted as given, either because they are inevitable for humans or because they can change only through cultural drift; it is not obvious in advance which might be altered through collective choice, just as it is not obvious what alternative courses of action are actually open to men at a given time. Nor is the demarcation between concepts and institutions fixed or obvious; though standards are separable from meaning, they are not wholly separate, their flexibility is limited. So the relationship between political theory and philosophy is bound to be both intimate and complex. Sometimes the two enterprises will be useful to each other or even over-

[46] See particularly Sheldon S. Wolin, *Hobbes* (Los Angeles: William Andrews Clark Memorial Library, University of California, 1970), and "Political Theory as a Vocation," *American Political Science Review*, LXIII (December 1969) 1062–1082.

[47] On the *theoros*, see Sheldon S. Wolin, "Political Theory: II. Trends and Goals," *International Encyclopedia of the Social Sciences* (1968), vol. 12, pp. 318–329.

lap; sometimes they will be far apart, and conceptual or philosophical problems may get in the way of work in political theory.

In an earlier study, I tried to disentangle conceptual from political-theoretical questions with respect to one traditional problem: that of political obligation and the theory of the social contract.[48] Almost the first thing that struck me in that attempt was that "the" problem of political obligation was in fact a whole cluster of questions, some of which are clearly philosophical-conceptual and some of which are clearly not. The problem may be formulated in relation to alternative courses of action in a situation where political disobedience is contemplated. Then it concerns the limits of obligation—when, under what circumstances, obligation ends, and resistance or revolution is justified. Or under slightly different circumstances, when an organized revolutionary movement already exists, the same relatively practical problem may take the form of questioning the locus of sovereignty: Whom is one obligated to obey? But as the theorist attempts to formulate general principles in response to these problems, more abstract questions emerge which are equally involved in political obligation. The theorist then seeks the general difference between legitimate authority which has the right to command, and mere coercive power without legitimacy. And here the philosophical puzzles begin, for the theorist is soon asking whether there really is any difference between governments and highway robbers, whether there is really any such thing as "legitimate authority," and ultimately why even legitimate authority should be obeyed. It is not difficult to show that different theories of political obligation address themselves primarily to some rather than others of these questions, and that even a single theorist seems to be answering now one question, now another. Moreover, it often seems as though the theorist gets distracted or seduced by the conceptual-philosophical issues, abandoning the initial quest for general but practical theory. Sometimes a theorist seems to be led by his own conceptual speculations to adopt a position that is wholly unsatisfactory in terms of his own concrete initial problem and goals. Thus, contract theorists, seeking to delineate a rational doctrine about when and why resistance or rebellion is justified, often end up with a theory justifying unlimited obedience.

One relatively obvious way in which Wittgensteinian philosophy can be useful in political theory, then, is for the resolution of conceptual puzzlement, when it arises as an extraneous intrusion, diverting us from the problem under investigation. Wittgenstein can help us to disentangle conceptual or grammatical issues from the rest of a complex theoretical argument. But this is a relatively trivial and trivializing function, making use of techniques of conceptual analysis but not of Wittgenstein's new per-

[48] Hanna Pitkin, "Obligation and Consent," *American Political Science Review*, LIX (December 1965), 990–999, and LX (March 1966), 39–52.

spectives. We must not stop here but must proceed to look for Wittgenstein's deeper significance for political theory. It may usefully be examined first in relation to the study of political theory, the critical assessment and understanding of what political theorists of the past have said; and second in relation to the actual substance, the enterprise of political theory itself. We shall consider the first of these topics in the remainder of this chapter; the second, in the next.

WITTGENSTEIN AND THE STUDY OF POLITICAL THEORY

The most important Wittgensteinian contribution to the study of past political theories is simply an awareness of concepts, a sensitivity to a theorist's use of language. Wittgenstein is obviously not the the only source from whom one might learn such an awareness, but he does give it a particular style and orientation. He teaches us that language is not just a neutral vehicle for the transmission of thoughts arrived at independently of it; the thought is not neatly separable from the language in which it is expressed. And he teaches us something about the way our conception of the world is structured by language. Applied to theorists from other times and cultures, careful attention to concepts is thus a guide to the understanding of a different political world; we learn not to take translations for granted. Applied to theorists from our own culture, attention to concepts yields important clues to the full meaning of a theory. And a Wittgensteinian awareness of the significance of conceptual plurality and inconsistency helps in the analysis of continuing theoretical controversies.

We may start from the fact that some works of political theory are so heavily philosophical that they can usefully be interpreted in their entirety as conceptual inquiries. Such an interpretation should not, of course, be taken as exclusive. Like all criticism, it can be a useful supplement to other perspectives on a work, in proportion as it enriches our access to the work's complexities and implications. Take Plato's *Republic* again. Most contemporary political scientists, in the grip of the fact-value dichotomy, will aver that the *Republic* is obviously a utopia, a sketch of Plato's ideal society. Perhaps they will add that it also contains a number of primitive empirical observations and explanatory generalizations about actual political life, or an early comprehension of functional interdependence in society. Other, more traditional interpretations include the suggestion that the *Republic* concerns the well-ordered soul, a vision of what we would now call psychic health of a unified personality, or that it is primarily a book about education.

Many of these interpretations seem useful. But they can also usefully be supplemented by a conceptual view, which is in a way naive, because it takes the *Republic* to be about exactly what the participants say it is about: the nature or meaning of justice. That view would stress its connection with earlier dialogues pursuing the nature of other significant concepts like friendship or courage. And it would suggest an alternative understanding of the political society sketched by Socrates. Perhaps that society is not, or not exclusively, Plato's ideal of the good society, but rather specifically designed to illustrate the meaning of a particular concept. Perhaps at least some of its important features are as they are because the idea of justice requires them, rather than because Plato happened to like them.

Suppose that we accept the ultimate Socratic definition of justice as roughly satisfactory: "justice" means something like each member of a system getting and having and doing what is appropriate to him (be the allocation distributive or retributive or of some other kind). Now, consider in this light the criticism commonly leveled against Plato, that the *Republic* is undemocratic and inegalitarian, merely a crystallization of Plato's aristocratic predilections. If the state Socrates envisions is in fact designed to illustrate the idea of justice, then the inegalitarian features may be quite essential, or at least serve an important heuristic purpose. Of course, an egalitarian state, composed of equals who get, and do, and have, like things, could be considered just; it is not unjust. But in a way the justice achieved in such a state is too obvious. As an illustration, such a state is what the mathematicians call a limiting or degenerate case of what justice means. For anyone can cut up a pie into as many equal pieces as there are persons present and give one piece to each person. That's easy. The real problems and subtleties of justice only begin, and therefore its real nature can only be studied or displayed, where we find unequal, different people, with different needs and abilities, different claims and deserts, so that the problem is assigning different, but precisely appropriate, things to each. In other words, one can really illustrate justice in all its complexity only in a situation where there is a *problem* about precisely what will *be* appropriate to each.

Consider further the elaborate educational machinery of the *Republic* which Plato develops with such loving care. That, too, can be seen as contributing to the illustration and understanding of justice. For if the system has a number of different kinds of members, and the problem is to assign appropriate roles and rewards to each, then the essential requirement will be some absolutely accurate and reliable mechanism for classifying the members and ascertaining what is appropriate to each kind. The system will be just only to the extent that it can make such classifications and such attribution and distribution unerringly, without equivocation or ambiguity. Surely this is one reason for the elaborate control of breeding in the *Republic*, and the detailed educational procedures—indeed, for the general intolerance of ambiguity in the Platonic system.

Thus, one might defend the *Republic*, whatever its defects as a political ideal, as being nevertheless a good illustration of the meaning of justice. But I think that many of us will continue to feel profoundly uncomfortable with that suggestion. A cynic might conclude that we are reluctant to believe that a society which does not correspond to our ideal could be the most just; or, alternatively, one could reject the argument developed here and insist that only a democratic society is truly just. But I think that even within the framework of the argument developed, our feeling of discomfort can be understood and accommodated. Perhaps there are other structural features of Plato's imaginary society which, because of the meaning of "justice" and not merely because of our personal preferences, strike us as profoundly *un*just.

The justness of the *Republic* hinges in crucially significant ways on whether the system as a whole *finds* men or *makes* them into members of the various classes. It hinges on whether the educational system is engaged essentially in testing and developing the inborn natural capacities of the citizens, separating natural artisans from natural soldiers, or whether it is engaged in shaping men so that some become artisans, others soldiers, others philosophers. The textual evidence on this point is really remarkably ambiguous. Sometimes Plato seems clearly to say that men are made into members of one class or another, often than their natural talents are merely discovered, and sometimes that both processes go on simultaneously.[49] The resolution also depends on whether we include the breeding system as part of "the system" which does the distributing and assigning, the system which is just or unjust. For if the breeding system is included, then men surely are made into what they become.

Insofar as men are made into members of one class or another by the state in the *Republic*, the system is, in Plato's own terms, unjust. This is because the members of some classes are clearly better off than the members of others, as is most obvious with respect to the philosopher-kings. Though they are not richer than artisans or soldiers, and though their power and status are not regarded by them or the other citizens as a blessing, they are profoundly better off than the rest. For, consider what happens to the *souls* of the lower classes. A just, balanced, healthy soul is one in which reason rules over passion and appetite; each part performs its function, and the function of reason is to rule the rest. But the soul of the artisan is ruled by appetite, and that of the soldier by passionate anger. Only the philosopher-king has, himself, a just soul; only the philosopher-king is able to enjoy the blissful contemplation of the Forms. This advantage is even more clearly revealed in the afterlife. In the Myth of Er, as the human souls choose new lives to live in their next incarnations, we meet an unfortunate fellow who chooses hastily and chooses to be a despot, under the illusion that this will provide him a happy life. Plato tells us the reason for the man's faulty choice: "He was one of those who . . . [had] spent his former life in a well-ordered commonwealth and become virtuous from habit without pursuing wisdom."[50]

Now, if men are by nature different, so that only a few are capable of

---

[49] See for example, *Republic*, II, 337; III, 413–414; IV, 429.
[50] *Ibid.*, X, 619.

wisdom, self-control, and a just soul, then the *Republic* may well be a just society. For a man who by nature lacks the capacity for self-control or inner virtue, the next best thing is surely some form of benevolent external control, forcing or training him into virtuous habits he does not really understand and has not really made his own. It is sad that he can advance no further, but such is his nature. But if the system *makes* some men into philosophers with balanced souls, and others into artisans or soldiers needing external control, then it is profoundly *un*just to the latter. And this will be true no matter how accurately and reliably it ultimately gives an artisan's life to the men it has made into artisans, a soldier's life to the men it has made into soldiers.

That may well be one major function of the Platonic Myth of the Metals. If the ultimate role in breeding is left to the gods, or if breeding is denied altogether, then men's differing capacities are indeed natural and not part of the operation of "society," and they can be left out of account in the computation of society's justness. The whole issue has its practical and poignant counterparts, of course, in contemporary questions of social justice, in the conflicting claims of various criteria for attribution or distribution. Shall we assume men by nature equal and assure them only just deserts for achievement or delict? Shall we take note of socially imposed inequalities, and make our distribution on a compensatory basis, seeking to bring everyone up to a level of equality?

There is still a further, different way in which one might call into question not the general desirability, but the specific justness, of Plato's *Republic*. One might distinguish between substantive and procedural aspects of the idea of justice, and argue that even if the *Republic* achieves substantive justice (setting aside the doubts we have been discussing) it ignores the concept's procedural side. For the *Republic* is at most an ideal, static picture of justice achieved, once and for all. In the city envisioned by Socrates we see, not justice at work, but justice accomplished: an illustration of how the world would look after justice had done its work. But insofar as justice is a procedural conception, having to do with the resolution of conflicting claims, with the creation of fair solutions out of initially ambiguous situations, the *Republic* misses the point. For the imaginary society is constructed in such a way that genuinely conflicting claims, genuinely multivalued, ambiguous situations cannot arise. There is, one wants to say, no need for justice in the life of that society, because it is already just, once and for all, by definition. The argument is not unlike Wolin's point that Plato's political ideal lacks a crucial element of politics, misses the central problem of politics, the continual re-creation of order in a living, plural society where ever new claims arise.[51]

To say all this in yet a different way, justice is a concept human beings have developed in their dealings with each other; it applies to persons and

[51] Sheldon S. Wolin, *Politics and Vision* (Boston and Toronto: Little, Brown, 1960), p. 43.

their institutions. One cannot be just or unjust to an inanimate object. That is, we are not at all clear on what might count as, might be, an injustice to an object. As Cavell says, "however justice is to be understood —whether in terms of rendering to each his due, or in terms of equality, or of impartiality or of fairness—*what* must be understood is a concept concerning the treatment of *persons*; and that is a concept, in turn, of a creature with commitments and cares. But for these, and the ways in which they conflict with one another and with those of other persons, there would be no problem, and no concept of justice."[52] From this perspective, the *Republic* is not so much unjust (since one cannot be unjust to inanimate objects, any more than one can be just to them) as irrelevant to justice. For it treats its citizens as objects, as inanimate materials, not as men. A distribution imposed by fiat from above, on creatures with no claim of their own, programmed to accept as their own what the system assigns, cannot really illustrate the problems of justice but only avoid them.

But until now we have been ignoring another crucial aspect of studying the *Republic* in relation to the concept of justice, another aspect for which a Wittgensteinian perspective is illuminating. We have not yet discussed the problem of translation. Plato was not, in fact, writing about the nature of justice at all. He was writing about the nature of *dike* or *dikaiosyne*, Greek concepts we usually translate by our word "justice." But that is not a very good translation, even if it is the best we have. So it may be that a number of the odd or peculiar things Plato seems to say about justice are not really peculiar views about justice at all, but perfectly ordinary, familiar Greek ideas about *dike*. Having learned that words are not labels, we will not be surprised that a Greek concept in the same general area as ours can be fundamentally different in structure, quite apart from the question of whether Greek "standards of justice" differed from ours. The Greeks had no standards of justice, but only standards of *dike*.

Ernest Barker tells us, as any good translator should, that "justice" is not an entirely accurate translation of *dike*.[53] He says that the Greek term "has a broader sweep than our word 'justice'; is something more than legal; and includes the ethical notions (or some of the ethical notions) which belong to our word 'righteousness'." He argues that an accurate translation of the title of Plato's dialogue, *politeia e peri dikaiosynes* would be "polity, or concerning righteousness," that using the word "justice" here would in fact "fail to convey Plato's meaning." And he points out that in the Greek of Saint Paul *dikaiosyne* is regularly translated as

---

[52] Cavell, "Claim to Rationality," p. 375; compare Giorgio Del Vecchio, *Justice*, tr. by Lady Guthrie, ed. by A. H. Campbell (Chicago: Aldine Press, 1952), esp. Chs. 7–8. But note that one can "do justice" to inanimate objects, for instance, to a meal.

[53] Aristotle, *Politics*, tr. by Sir Ernest Barker (New York: Oxford University Press, 1958), p. 362.

"righteousness." I think that these examples can help us to understand a number of puzzling features of Plato's argument. For instance, they help us to understand why Plato, like his fellow Greeks, considers that justice is the "master virtue," encompassing all others and ordering them. This doctrine, which we are taught to accept arbitrarily as simply something the Greeks believed, but which continues to strike us as odd, is hardly odd at all if predicated of righteousness instead. If someone maintains that righteousness is the master virtue containing all others, we might find the locution stilted, but we could see why he would think so. Righteousness means something like doing what is right, performing virtuous actions and being virtuous, so of course it contains all virtues. (A slight new oddness arises, I think, from the fact that in English righteousness is not really "*a* virtue" at all.)

Again, the connection to our righteousness helps us to understand why Plato often treats justice as a *personal* virtue, a virtue of individual men, why he speaks of "the just man." We do also call men just or unjust sometimes in English, but the expression obviously has a quite different, much broader impact for Plato. We are likely to call a man just or unjust only in quite specific, narrow contexts—primarily when the quality of his *judgments* is at stake, in contexts involving his decisions on the relative merits or deserts of two or more persons or groups. For Plato it has a much broader meaning, closer to our "righteousness." Thus, we would never spontaneously say in English, as Cephalus does in the translated *Republic*, that a man is just if he tells the truth and pays his debts. Not that such a man is *unjust*, of course. He is a good man, perhaps, or a dutiful one, or a moral one, or perhaps righteous (though that really sounds much too grandiose for such simple virtues; righteousness for us goes with wrath and glory). So when we read in the *Republic* of just men, we are always torn between the implications of the English words, which point one way, and the implications of context and argument, which point another (not opposite, but different) way.

The difference in meaning between "justice" and *dike* may also help us to understand why Plato lays so much stress not merely on the system giving to each what is appropriate to him, but on each citizen's accepting and performing his assigned function. This stress centers in the conjunction of what are to us two quite separate notions, which were not separate for the Greeks but part of a single, untranslatable concept: the notion of a system that gives to each what is truly his, and the notion of a man who is virtuous and fulfills his appointed duties. Plato is, as it were, demonstrating, and at the same time trading on, the connection between justness-righteousness and justness as in a just society. A just man is one who fulfills his justly assigned duties.

The concept of justice and the differences in meaning between "justice" and *dike* stand, then, at the very center of some major features of Plato's argument in the *Republic*. The same turns out to be true of a number of other, less crucial but still significant concepts, equally hard to render into English. Thus, one can learn much about Plato and the *Republic* by studying the various Greek words for knowledge; they lead, for example, to a much better comprehension of the famous but mysterious Socratic doctrine that "virtue is knowledge." Similar insights can be gained from the study of Greek concepts we translate as "virtue," "art," or "love." At first, one feels that Greek works should perhaps be translated with these crucial words left in the original Greek. But then one begins to suspect that the lesser adjectives and prepositions and conjunctions, the very structure of syntax and rhetoric, play as much of a role as the central nouns. No doubt it would be best to read all works in their original language; but that advice is not very useful.

### CONCEPTS IN MACHIAVELLI

It seems that the study of ambiguities of translation can lead us quite directly into the heart of what is troubling or difficult to understand in a political theorist's views. Consider the case of Machiavelli, on whom such excellent and painstaking literary scholarship is available. What is most striking about Machiavelli as a political theorist is surely his break with medieval Christian thought, the extent of his modernity, his concern with the technics of power rather than the advocacy of moral virtue. This aspect of his thought lies behind the fascinating subsequent history of the reception and misinterpretation of his ideas—the entire controversy about whether Machiavelli was or was not "machiavellian." And it lies behind the exegetic controversy about the relationship between the seemingly machiavellian *Prince*, and the *Discourses*, which seem cast in a different mold. A study of Machiavelli's language can hardly settle these matters, but it can shed some new light on them in rather surprising ways. We will consider only two concepts here, as illustrative of the possibilities: virtue, and the state.

At the heart of Machiavelli's morality, or seeming immorality, lies his concept of *virtù*, which apparently leads or allows him to express what strike us as bizarre or paradoxical or utterly immoral views. For example, Machiavelli attributes Hannibal's success in commanding his army to "his *inhuman cruelty*, which together with his infinite *other virtues*, made him always venerated and terrible in the sight of his soldiers, and without it his *other virtues* would not have sufficed to produce that effect."[54] Now, what sort of man would consider inhuman cruelty among the great virtues? Surely only a perverse and immoral lover of cruelty, a true machiavellian.

But, of course, the passage is a translation, and we need to ask, as we did with Plato, whether Machiavelli is saying something bizarre about virtue or something quite conventional about *virtù*. For the Italian term

[54] Niccolò Machiavelli, *The Prince and The Discourses*, tr. by Luigi Ricci (New York: Random House, 1940), p. 62; my italics.

does not merely mean virtue, in the sense of goodness or morality.[55] In the Renaissance, it was often used, for instance, to mean something like power or motive force. It appears in Leonardo's notes on dynamics as more or less equivalent to physical motive power. The Italian term derives etymologically from the Latin *virtus*, on the root *vir*, meaning "man." *Virtus* thus meant something like manliness, energetic strength, and was one of the traditionally admired Roman virtues along with *dignitas* and *gravitas* and the others. But, as J. H. Whitfield points out, there was already in Latin "a gap between *virtus* and *virtutes*," the singular and the plural. Only the former, the singular, could be used in the sense of "energy of the will or bravery"; the second already was "concerned with good qualities."[56] (Of course, the Roman idea of what constitutes good qualities, good behavior, virtue, was different from ours, and was intimately connected with qualities of manliness, dignity, and a serious, courageous continuation of the authoritative work of the Founders.) These earlier uses of the concept of virtue remain only in occasional English forms like "by virtue of," which clearly implies not morality but force, or "virtuosity," which is a matter of skillfulness and achievement, not of good motives or good behavior.

Machiavelli's *Prince* is but one in a series of late medieval works advising princes on their duties and the skills of their trade. Earlier works in that tradition were intensely Christian and moralistic in tone, using *virtù* primarily in the plural and entirely as equivalent to Christian virtue—humility, charity, piety, and so on. Machiavelli hardly ever uses the word that way. He rarely uses the plural form at all; Whitfield cites one passage in the *Discourses* where Machiavelli appears to have replaced a Latin plural by a singular with the sense of "virtue" or goodness." He uses *virtù* to mean "virtue" or "goodness" only rarely, but employs a number of other terms when he wants to talk about goodness in the sense of Christian morality.[57] J. H. Hexter maintains that the term is used that way only three times in *The Prince*, and they are passages where the Prince is warned against the dangers of virtuousness. Much of the time in *The Prince*, *virtù* is a quality not of princes but of soldiers, and "refers unmistakably to their fighting quality, their valor."[58] It is particularly useful

[55] The works primarily used in the following discussion are: J. H. Whitfield, *Machiavelli* (New York: Russell and Russell, 1965); J. H. Hexter, "*Il principe* and *lo stato*," *Studies in the Renaissance*, IV (1957), 113–138, and "The Loom of Language," *American Historical Review*, LXIX (July 1964), 945–968; Felix Gilbert, "On Machiavelli's Idea of Virtu," *Renaissance News*, IV (1951), 53–55, and V (1952), 21–23; Allan Gilbert, tr., *Machiavelli, The Chief Works and Others* (Durham: Duke University Press, 1965). Other relevant works include Fredi Chiapelli, *Studi Sul Linguaggio del Machiavelli* (Florence, 1952); Francesco Ercole, *La Politica di Machiavelli* (Rome, 1926); and H. de Vries, *Essai sur la Terminologie Constitutionelle chez Machiavel "Il Principe"* (s'Gravenhage: Excelsior, 1957).
[56] Whitfield, *Machiavelli*, p. 98.
[57] *Ibid.*, pp. 95, 96, 98.
[58] Hexter, "Loom of Language," 955–956.

for keeping a state, once the prince has somehow obtained one; though he can sometimes obtain one by *virtù*, as well as by use of an army, or craft, or villainy, or fortune.

In short, some of the time Machiavelli uses *virtù* to mean "virtue," but most of the time he uses it for "a union of force and ability, something that can be summed up in force alone, if by force one means human, not mechanical, force: will, and therefore force of ability."[59] This complexity of usage is completely obscured, not to say obliterated, in translation, for of course a good translator will use "virtue" in the former cases but only rarely in the latter. When he does, the result is a bizarre passage like the one about Hannibal; much of the time *virtù* has to be translated "force" or "energy" or "strength of will." But for Machiavelli, as for the Romans, this manly force is a kind of—is *the* central kind of—virtue. That is only to say that Machiavelli is thoroughly a man of the Renaissance. Like the Romans, he admires manliness and the virtues of soldiers, and he is skeptical, to say the least, of the Christian virtues, humility and gentleness, that have intervened to undermine the manliness of his people.

Quite similar ambiguities are to be found in another of Machiavelli's central concepts, *lo stato*. As Hexter points out, "it seems fairly clear that" the term was never used in the modern sense of "state" in any European language in the fifteenth century, yet by the seventeenth century it was used that way in all of them.[60] That in itself is hardly surprising; the modern concept of the state and the modern nation-state itself emerged together in this period. Machiavelli is often cited as the first theorist to use the term in its modern sense. Etymologically, the word derives from the Latin *status*, which comes from *stare*, to stand. It means something that has been "set up," standing, fixed, established, permanent, particularly a fixed or established condition. Related contemporary English expressions would be ones like "man's estate," "solid state," "state of mind," "state of war," "state of matrimony." In medieval thought, the term was commonly used to mean social condition or order of society. Thus medieval writers would speak of the "states of the realm" as one spoke later in English of the "estates of the realm," meaning the major class divisions of society: temporal lords, clergy, commoners; and king. A man's "state" in this sense is a combination of what we would call "status" and what we would call "estate," except of course that in medieval thought both status and estate are fixed and permanent, having to do with the station in life to which one is born.[61]

Thus, when the Middle Ages speak of *lo stato* in connection with a prince, they might mean either of two ideas. They might mean something like the over-all state or condition of the prince's realm, somewhat as we speak today of the president's "state of the nation" address, but again

---

[59] Whitfield, *Machiavelli*, p. 94, quoting Gentile, quoting Burckhardt.
[60] Hexter, "*Il principe*," 115.
[61] *Ibid.*, p. 117; and "Loom of Language," 952.

with the suggestion of permanence or fixity: the fixed condition or order of the realm, its constitution (another term of related etymology). Or, second, they might mean the princely estate, which differs from that of clergy or commoner—his estate both in the sense of his permanent possession and in the sense of his established position in society, complete with its fixed rights and duties, including the authority to govern (as the Middle Ages saw that authority).[62]

Now, when Machiavelli uses *lo stato* in *The Prince*, as Whitfield says, it has "a whole gamut of meanings ranging from the Latin one of *state, condition,* to something very near the modern conception of the *State*; but with a general tendency to convey something less than this last, *power, those that hold it, government,* rather than territory—though this last is not absent."[63] A few pasages in which the term appears are clearly and fully medieval, and a few seem strikingly modern, but the great bulk are (for us) ambiguous. Hexter points out that the term is almost never the subject of an active verb. Three-quarters of the time it is the subject of a passive verb or the object of an active one. Further, *lo stato* is never worked for, helped, served, revered, admired, feared, loved; it is added to, asaulted, possessed, occupied, seized, taken, acquired, kept, or lost. In short, in *The Prince*, "*lo stato* is what is politically up for grabs." It is not the body politic, organized for action, but "an inert lump."[64]

Much that seems immoral in Machiavelli, that seems machiavellian, is urged upon the Prince to "maintain the state," "save his state," avoid "losing *lo stato*." But once we are aware of the medieval meaning of the term we can see that the entire interpretation of this advice hinges on whether Machiavelli is recommending evil actions for the Prince's personal aggrandizement (to keep or gain his princely estate) or for the welfare of his nation (to maintain the state he rules). There is, for example, a passage at the end of Chapter XV of *The Prince* where, in the Ricci translation, Machiavelli says the Prince must "avoid the scandal of those vices which would lose him the state . . . yet he must not mind incurring the scandal of those vices, without which it would be difficult to save the state."[65] Allan Gilbert translates the same passage without using the word "state" at all, but speaks only of "his [the Prince's] position."[66] Is the danger to be avoided the dethroning of a prince or the collapse of a state? If the former, the advice sounds much more "machiavellian" than if the latter is intended.

It might seem that our whole discussion dissolves into nothing more interesting than a problem of translation, of no special concern to the

[62] Hexter, "*Il principe*," 118.

[63] Whitfield, *Machiavelli*, p. 93, from Ercole, *La Politica*, p. 65. Hexter notes one passage in which "the state" is said "not to rebel"; "*Il Principe*," 122.

[64] Hexter, "Loom of Language," 953–954; and "*Il principe*," 119ff.

[65] Machiavelli, *The Prince and the Discourses*, tr. Ricci, p. 57.

[66] Allan Gilbert, *Machiavelli, The Chief Works*, I, 58. A similar contrast can be seen between pp. 71–72 of the Ricci translation and I, 72, of Gilbert's.

philosopher or political theorist. Certain passages in bad translations sound as if the author had bizarre views, but in a good translation the bizarreness disappears. Thus, the original puzzling passage we quoted from the Ricci translation, about Hannibal's inhuman cruelty and other great virtues, is translated by Allan Gilbert "inhuman cruelty . . . together with his numberless abilities."[67] Virtues become abilities, "other" disappears, and nothing bizarre has been said. So we might conclude that what is required is a good translator, one who knows when *virtù* means "virtue" and when it doesn't, when *lo stato* means "the state" and when it means "his position." But that view, while in a way perfectly valid, obscures what is for our concerns the most important consideration.

We are likely to construe the question, "Is the danger the dethroning of the Prince or the collapse of the state?" a dichotomous choice, for a translator must write either "the state" or "his position," or else leave *lo stato* untranslated. But the point is precisely that what are for us two sharply different ideas are for Machiavelli encompassed in a single term, without any apparent sense of ambiguity. It is not enough to ask whether Machiavelli means the nation or the Prince's position; the point is that the two form a single concept for him. It is not enough to ask whether he means virtue or manliness; for him that distinction is not of significance. At the very heart of what is most controversial and difficult to interpret in Machiavelli, and most characteristic of his ideas, we find terms whose meaning is (to us) ambiguous, whose meaning is in transition in Machiavelli's time. He lived in a time emerging out of medieval thought and rediscovering the ancient classics. He himself spoke and wrote the language of his day in his diplomatic career, yet he worked intensively with the Latin classics when he came to write about politics. Anyone who has worked intensively with materials in a foreign language, or even in a different dialect or from a different social milieu than his own, knows that his own language and thought are to some extent affected, or infected, by them. No doubt the effect is stronger if the two languages are close, so that one does not really notice one's own style changing. This was the situation of the Florentine Machiavelli communing in his study with the Latin authors. Machiavelli is completely unselfconscious in his use of terms; so, as Whitfield suggests, he employs terms like *virtù* and *lo stato* as they come to him, to cover any of their (as we see it) several meanings, "begining with what he found in his Latin authors and ending with current meanings."[68] But that implies, finally, that Machiavelli's "doctrine of *virtù*" is not really a doctrine at all, but "a common (and . . . a common-sense) inheritance."[69] The bizarre views he seems to express about virtue or about the Prince's relationship to the state are, to

---

[67] Gilbert, *ibid.*, I, 63.
[68] Whitfield, *Machiavelli*, p. 95; compare p. 97.
[69] *Ibid.*, p. 99.

a considerable extent, not bizarre at all, but quite ordinary views common in his time about a set of concepts different from ours.

What is significant for the study of political theory here is not so much the information gained about some particular theorist, as the increased awareness that other cultures and times have seen the world in radically different ways. Such awareness—not the intellectual acknowledgment of the fact of relativity, but its genuine comprehension and assimilation—is of the greatest significance for social and political study in general and for intellectual history in particular. Of course, Wittgenstein is not the only source of such awareness, but he is one relatively effective source of it.

Even within our own culture and language, careful attention to a theorist's use of concepts can yield fundamental clues to his unstated assumptions and implications, to the full meaning of what he wanted to say. The concepts to be examined characteristically are not technical ones, but quite ordinary ones the theorist uses unselfconsciously; and they are most revealing when his way of using them is somehow odd or deviant from ordinary usage. Hobbes, for example, defines "representation" in a way that clearly is not adequate to our ordinary use of that word, or indeed to his own use of it. In itself, that piece of information is of little interest; one would hardly take a philosopher of Hobbes' stature and power to task for an occasional faulty definition. But if we ask whether the faults of his definition bear any relationship to his basic assumptions about man and society—assumptions that underlie his political theory and are never questioned—the answer is clearly, yes. His conception of representation is part of a systematic way of viewing the world, and therefore revelatory of much about Hobbes besides his ability at making definitions.[70] As we saw, Weber's definition of legitimacy, subsequently adopted by much of social science, differs noticeably from our ordinary ways of using the term. In itself, that is no crime; but neither he nor his followers seem aware that they have redefined the term, let alone the extent to which the nature of the redefinition reveals their fundamental, and unexamined, assumptions.

It pays, then, to attend to the odd things that political theorists are tempted to say, if one wants to understand the assumptions that shape their doctrines. The point of the enterprise is never refutation. The attempt to refute a philosophical position by evidence from ordinary usage is always a vulgarization and cannot succeed. The idea is not to refute but to understand the position that is reflected in an odd or deviant usage; and when we understand it, we may see that it does not merely conflict with or deviate from what we ordinarily say, but also conforms to (other parts of) what we ordinarily say. The point is only that our *verbal* deviations are symptomatic of our patterns of thought, both to others

[70] Compare Hanna Pitkin, *The Concept of Representation* (Berkeley and Los Angeles: University of California Press, 1967), chs. 1–2.

and potentially to ourselves. Who neglects these symptoms cuts himself off from an important source of insight about what is being said and why it is believed by the speaker.

A Wittgensteinian perspective suggests that there is almost always some valid, truthful basis for any theoretical position or philosophical doctrine, no matter how bizarre. Such positions always have a foundation in insight of some kind; they are extrapolated from an initial grain of truth. Thus, the critic's first task becomes the discovery of that valid foundation, that grain of truth; for without it, he cannot understand the doctrine. If a theoretical position strikes us as obviously false or absurd, perhaps that is because we have not understood what the theorist is trying to say. It is well, before rejecting the position, to ask ourselves "How *could* he have believed *that*?" "What could have ever given him such an idea?" Until we can answer such questions ("see *how* it is a . . . "), we are not ready to criticize or reject, because we do not yet know what is being proposed. Understanding must take precedence over criticism. Or rather, successful criticism depends on prior understanding. In the long run, the only successful kind of refutation of a theoretical position is one which gives the opponent his due. For he knows that his theory has a foundation in truth, and he clings to the theory with all the conviction that that foundation can yield. He will modify his position only if he can see a way of nevertheless retaining that true foundation, see how his theoretical extrapolation is not the only possible extrapolation from that starting point.

The Wittgensteinian orientation is particularly useful with respect to those characteristic, interminable controversies familiar in the history of political theory, which persist over generations, are taken up by one able theorist after another, and yet are never resolved, each writer merely choosing a position on one side or the other, the two sides talking past each other. "When such an obstinate problem makes its appearance," as Wittgenstein says, "it is never a question about facts of experience (such a problem is always much more tractable), but a logical, and hence properly a grammatical question."[71] Thus, such controversies cannot be resolved by abandoning the theoretical level and turning to historical or empirical research instead; for the very terms of the controversy assure that we will carry it with us into our historical or empirical studies and that their results will be equally ambiguous. If we approach such controversies from a Wittgensteinian perspective, we see that each side seems to have a point, that either one taken separately can persuade us. We are tempted to reject one side only because the other seems convincingly right, and we assume that they cannot both be right. But perhaps they can both be (partially) right, each extrapolated from a valid insight or

[71] Ludwig Wittgenstein, *Zettel*, tr. by G. E. M. Anscombe, ed. by G. E. M. Anscombe and G. H. von Wright (Berkeley and Los Angeles: University of California Press, 1967), par. 590.

example; and perhaps only the extrapolations are in conflict. Then a simultaneous contemplation of what is right in each view might produce a new synthesis, or at least a perspicuous overview of why we are torn between the two positions. And if the conceptual controversy has gotten in the way of substantive work on some theoretical or practical problem, such a perspicuous overview may release us from the controversy to concentrate our attention on the problem.

In an earlier work, I attempted this sort of analysis of what I called the mandate-independence controversy in the theory of political representation—the controversy about whether a representative is supposed to do what his constituents want or what he thinks best in terms of the public interest.[72] That controversy, I found, rested on the ambiguously dual implications of the concept of representation—the idea of making something present that is nevertheless not literally present. And a preoccupation with the abstract, conceptual problem, with resolving the irresoluble once and for all, has often prevented attention to the actual complex requirements of different kinds of representation in different situations.

Clearly, the Wittgensteinian capacity to see incompatible perspectives simultaneously, to see what is valid in a variety of conflicting positions, is subject to its own characteristic abuses. It must not be confused with some sort of policy of compromise, nor with the mindless acceptance of any and all views. To see why someone believes what he does, how he means the things he says, need not entail agreeing with him. Moreover, what is useful for the study of other people's political theories may not be what is needed for the production of new and important political theory. Most of the great political theory of the past has not been characterized by reasonableness and moderation, but by the bold, insistent claim made by its innovative vision. Does that mean that Wittgenstein's teaching, while useful for the study of political theory, is at bottom hostile to the innovative and synthesizing vision of great political theory? To that question we must turn in the next and final chapter.

[72] Pitkin, *Concept of Representation*, Ch. 7.

# XIV

## Political Theory and the
## Modern Predicament

WE TURN NOW to speculating about the significance that Wittgenstein might have for political theory itself—for its actual substance, as distinct from the study of its history—and for our troubled modern condition, which must be the focus of any contemporary political theorizing. The topic necessitates speculation, or at least extrapolation, since, as we have already said, Wittgenstein himself was not a political theorist. He did not write about society or history or revolution or alienation. Probably the closest thing to a political remark in his writings is the hope expressed in the preface to the *Investigations* that the work might have some small impact on "the darkness of this time."[1] Yet the topic is of great potential interest and importance, so speculation is worth-while. We shall approach it by three different roads: a general consideration of the modern condition and Wittgenstein's relationship to it, the question of what a Wittgensteinian political theory might look like, and some more specific implications of Wittgenstein's philosophy for speech and politics in our time.

Though he never addresses them explicitly, Wittgenstein's thought is continually centered on the problems of the contemporary human condition—is both expressive of them and designed to combat them. At the risk of a banal restatement of what we all know, one might characterize our condition, the growth of the modern consciousness, as a story of increasing knowledge and objectivity, increasing detached, scientific, rational awareness both of the world we live in and of our selves, increasing technological power to manipulate the world and each other; but all of this accompanied by, even purchased at the price of, a steadily de-

[1] Ludwig Wittgenstein, *Philosophical Investigations*, tr. by G. E. M. Anscombe (New York: Macmillan, 1968), p. x; compare also Wittgenstein's comment on the Soviet Union quoted in Friedrich Waismann, *Wittgenstein und der Wiener Kreis*, ed. by B. F. McGuinness (London: Basil Blackwell, 1967), p. 142: "Die Leidenschaft verspricht etwas. Unser Gerede dagegen ist kraftlos."

creasing sense of security, of stable foundations. We might say: once men thought as children—their ideas about the world around them were mixed with fantasy and projection, they considered their universe ordered, directed, and guarded by a great parent whom they called God, and they took it for granted that they—man—stood at the center of that universe, God's favorite, special child with a unique destiny. Well, the growth of secularism and science and technology have changed all that. We are no longer naive children; we have accepted the scientific facts. Copernicus taught us that the earth is not at the center of the universe—or even of the solar system. Einstein taught us that there is no center, that motion is relative to the observer, so that even science has to postulate its coordinate systems arbitrarily. Darwin taught us that we are the product of natural evolution, like other animals, not God's special creation. Marx and Freud taught us that our own seemingly most civilized and rational powers are not reliable, not to be accepted at face value; they are always liable to turn out to be mere ideology, mere rationalization of unconscious motives. And Hegel announced what more and more men had come to know for themselves—that God is dead.

At first it seemed obvious that these developments would make men freer, more powerful than man had ever been before, as the well-informed, competent, rational adult is more powerful than the naive, impulsive, dreamy child, and freer too, because he has more choices open to him. Marx still believed that his science would increase our power to act; Freud believed that about his. Yet somehow, with all our technological skill and achievement, what we have reaped is not power but a profound sense of our own powerlessness; not a capacity to act but an overwhelming awareness of the hopelessness of action; not freedom but an awareness of constraint; a sense not of competence but of anxiety; not of oneness with the universe of which we know (intellectually) we are a part, but of desperate alienation from it, each other, and ourselves.

All significant contemporary thought is, in one way or another, a response to this predicament or an attempt to escape it. So we should not be surprised to find that Wittgensteinian philosophy has much in common with the two great Continental philosophical movements of our time: existentialism and phenomenology (and, indeed, with earlier American pragmatism). It is not so much a matter of shared doctrine—since Wittgenstein really taught no doctrine—as of shared outlook, emphasis, orientation. All three philosophical movements start from the assumptions of the modern predicament, from a profound distrust of all religions, ideologies, metaphysics, and would-be absolute standards. If God is dead and men create what order or meaning the world holds, then all systems of thought and all standards of judgment are bound to be suspect. And so the three philosophical movements share a distrust of the philosophical tradition, of received doctrine and inherited generalization. They are all "by intention and in feeling, revolutionary departures from traditional philosophy."[2]

All three reject the traditional systems and generalities in favor of a stress on concrete particularity. As Camus says, quoting René Char, what we need is "obsession with the harvest and indifference to history."[3] More particularly, all three of these movements seek to restore the significance of subjectivity, or, rather, to restore our sense of our selves in a way that is not shackled to subjectivity. Phenomenology recalls us from the abstract systems of metaphysics and science to the reality of our experience, of pure consciousness, in which they are founded. Existentialism challenges us to acknowledge our individual capacity for choice and action, and the correlate responsibility; it demands authentic personal commitment. Kierkegaard diagnoses in the *Concluding Unscientific Postscript* that we have lost our capacity for inwardness, for subjectivity, and live in the universal rather than in our particularity.[4] Wittgenstein, too, is concerned with our "craving for generality," and draws us back to particular cases, to the limitations of our humanity. And when he recalls us to the ordinary examples of language use, that does not mean merely nonphilosophical examples; rather, as Cavell suggests, it is "meant to carry the force of 'authentic' examples authentically responded to in language." The various voices that speak in his writings argue no positions that are not genuinely felt; they never speak for the sake of argument. Their comments are ones which "come from conviction, which are made with passion and attention, and which, as one reads, seem always something one wants oneself to say, or feels the power of."[5]

Both phenomenology and existentialism diagnose our modern malaise along lines very reminiscent of Wittgenstein's main concerns, delineating three related complaints: our alienation from reality, our alienation from each other, and our loss of the capacity for action. The phenomenologists have been most interested in the first and second of these complaints, the existentialist in the second and third. All three together shape the particular configuration of our alienation from ourselves. The phenomenologist is particularly struck by the disparity, the apparent gap between our naive experience of the world and what we have been taught to believe it is really, objectively like. The villain here used to be metaphysics, with its claim to privileged insights demonstrating that things are not what they seem, but in our time the villain has come to be science. The tools and methods of our objective science have become so powerful that scientific knowledge of the world has long since left common sense and ordinary human understanding hopelessly behind. Science, as Galileo said,

[2] Stanley Cavell, "Existentialism and Analytic Philosophy," *Daedalus*, 93 (Summer 1964), 948.

[3] Albert Camus, *The Rebel*, tr. by Anthony Bower (New York: Random House, 1956), p. 302.

[4] Cavell, "Existentialism," 958–959.

[5] *Ibid.*, 957.

commits "a rape upon [the] senses."[6] At first it merely contradicts our common perceptions and understanding. Thus, anyone can "see" the sun rise and set, but science teaches us that it is the earth that turns; anyone can kick a solid object, but science teaches us that such objects actually consist of energy particles in motion. Later, as science advances still farther, it leaves our ordinary understanding behind altogether. "The 'truths' of the modern scientific world view, though they can be demonstrated in mathematical formulas and proved technologically, will no longer lend themselves to normal expression in speech and thought."[7] As a result, we are increasingly unable to trust our own experience, our own perceptions; we have learned that science shows their untrustworthiness. Thus, by a peculiar psychological irony, instead of making us feel powerful in our amazing capacity to discover the underlying nature of electrons and solar systems, science ends up making us doubt our capacity to know or perceive anything at all.

Though he was hardly a phenomenologist, Albert Camus expressed both the predicament and the impulse toward a phenomenological cure beautifully in *The Myth of Sisyphus*: "Here are trees and I know their gnarled surface, water and I feel its taste. These scents of grass and stars at night, certain evenings when the heart relaxes—how shall I negate this world whose power and strength I feel? Yet all the knowledge on earth will give me nothing to assure me that this world is mine. You describe it to me and you teach me to classify it. You enumerate its laws and in my thirst for knowledge I admit that they are true. You take apart its mechanism and my hope increases. At the final stage you teach me that this wondrous and multicolored universe can be reduced to the electron. All this is good and I wait for you to continue. But you tell me of an invisible planetary system in which electrons gravitate around a nucleus. You explain this world to me with an image. I realize then that you have been reduced to poetry: I shall never know. Have I the time to become indignant? You have already changed theories. So that science that was to teach me everything ends up in a hypothesis, that lucidity founders in metaphor, that uncertainty is resolved in a work of art. What need had I of so many efforts? The soft lines of these hills and the hand of evening on this troubled heart teach me much more. I have returned to my beginning. I realize that if through science I can seize phenomena and enumerate them, I cannot, for all that, apprehend the world. Were I to trace its entire relief with my finger, I should not know any more. And you give me the choice between a description that is sure but that teaches me nothing and hypotheses that claim to teach me but that are not sure."[8]

Confronted with the total doubt and the sense of unreality generated

[6] Quoted in C. C. Gillespie, *The Edge of Objectivity* (Princeton: Princeton University Press, 1960), pp. 19–20.

[7] Hannah Arendt, *The Human Condition* (Garden City: Doubleday, 1958), p. 3.

[8] Albert Camus, *The Myth of Sisyphus*, tr. by Justin O'Brien (New York: Vintage Books, Random House, 1959), p. 15.

by the power of modern science, the phenomenologist prescribes a return to our perceptions and experiences, without presuppositions. We must temporarily set aside ("bracket") the teachings of science and, indeed, all received conventional interpretation. We must set aside all questions of reality and existence, and seek the essence given in experience. We must learn to see and feel again naively, to trust in our own capacity to perceive objects and persons around us and feelings within us. To the man overcome by perpetual doubt as a result of having been told so often that the world is not as he perceives it, phenomenology says: Trust yourself! The world *is* as you perceive it. That advice corresponds, I think, to a certain kind of experience that can, indeed, be of great significance to particular persons at particular times. An adult who wants to become a landscape painter may have to learn all over again how to see colors—to discover that the "green" grass is not green at all, but an amazing combination of hues. Or the psychiatrist may say to his patient, "Don't tell me what you think you are supposed to feel, but look and see what you really do feel." And perhaps the patient, freed thereby to acknowledge that he hates where convention requires him to love, regains some of his contact with the reality of his feelings, and some confidence in his ability to know them.

There is good reason to regard such experiences as breakthroughs from received presumptions to true objectivity, to the true experienced reality. But they are not, of course, experiences in the absence of a conceptual system; and when they are subsequently expressed and refined in words, we are inevitably again within the grammar of the language. We have discovered that grass is not green, but it *is* other colors. We have discovered that we feel not love but hate, or perhaps we master the more complex concept of ambivalence. The phenomenological investigation of what is given in experience as such is always partly an investigation of what is given in grammar; this is only the converse of Austin's suggestion that his work was a kind of phenomenology. Like phenomenology, Wittgenstein seeks to restore to us the kind of secure stability that a conceptual system can give to the world, and that we lose in becoming estranged from parts of our conceptual system and our world.

The problem is most poignant, the sense of a discontinuity between perception and reality most haunting, in the realms of human, social, political concerns. No doubt this is both because the conventionality of our concepts is most striking here and because these concerns most directly affect the quality of our lives. It seems that with the increasing success of science, and our growing capacity for objectivity and detachment, we learn to see ourselves and other men as objects. We master scientific objectivity and detachment, and as a result we suddenly feel not merely detached but cut off, not merely objective but objectlike in a world of objects. We become increasingly sophisticated about the conventions and assumptions of our ordinary lives by which we relate to each other; we accept the scientific verdict that they are not objectively given but merely arranged by men, and suddenly we can no longer take them seriously, rely on them. We encounter what Camus has called "the chaos of an experience divested of its setting," that "state of the soul in which . . . the chain of daily gestures is broken, in which the heart vainly seeks the link that will connect it again."[9] We look at a human being and, with a sense of penetrating through convention to brute reality, see only an object moving in space-time coordinates. Even human beings, as Camus says, can "secrete the inhuman. At certain moments of lucidity, the mechanical aspect of their gestures, their meaningless pantomime makes silly everything that surrounds them. A man is talking on the telephone behind a glass partition; you cannot hear him, but you see his incomprehensible dumb show: you wonder why he is alive."[10] If, as Melden says, we regard a human action "in total abstraction from any of the background circumstances that operate in our normal understanding of actions and agents," we will no longer see a person at all, "but something which, if it irritates one might brush aside in just the sort of way in which one straightens out an annoying wrinkle in the rug on the floor."[11] We see human beings in "a totally dehumanized way," deprived of meaning, of sense.

The consequences of this kind of experience, the costs of coming to see men too often or too exclusively as inhuman objects, are multiple. First, and most obviously, the experience is likely to bear fruit in action; conceiving of men as objects, we are increasingly likely to treat them that way. This need not mean doing them harm, any more than we customarily damage the objects around us. But it does *allow* us to do harm with a minimum of guilt. It does not mean treating men immorally so much as treating them amorally, in a manner in which morality plays no role. As individuals, we become increasingly incapable of the moral attitude; or, to put it more psychologically, incapable of spontaneous identification, of genuine empathy. On the social and political level, we think in terms of "social engineering," manipulatively; we see the problem as one of channeling men by neutral, administrative measures. Feeling that we know the real, objective causes of others' actions and social condition, we no longer need to listen to their views; feeling that we can determine their needs scientifically, we become impatient with their wants. Both individually and socially, human relations are resolved into technical problems. Even without the advent of socialism (and in a sense ironically different from Marx's intention), the governing of men is replaced by the administration of things.

A second consequence of our increasing objectivity and detachment is in our relations to ourselves; we become unable, as it were, to treat even ourselves morally, to identify even with ourselves, to perceive even

9 *Ibid.*, pp. 20, 10.
10 *Ibid.*, p. 11.
11 A. I. Melden, *Free Action* (New York: Humanities Press, 1961), p. 192.

ourselves as persons. We become unable to experience integrally, with our whole selves, to be totally absorbed in experience. Always a part of ourselves seems to stand aside and observe, "objectively," what we are doing. Even as we say or think "I promise" or "That is unjust," or "I love you," we are aware of the conventionality of standards of justice, the likelihood of our being dominated by unconscious motives or ideological "false consciousness," the absence of any transcendent guarantee for our standards and commitments. "Such a man," as Nietzsche said, "no longer believes in himself or his own existence."[12] Thus, our objectivity about ourselves and other men has still a further consequence: we become increasingly unable to judge, to commit ourselves, to act. As our sophistication grows about the sociology of knowledge, about unconscious motivation, about propaganda techniques, in short, about the causal sources of our opinions and standards, it becomes more and more difficult for us to take a position. We mistrust and debunk our own judgments before they are even uttered, perhaps before they are even thought. We lose the capacity for sustained, purposeful action.

It has always been the conviction of social scientists, from the earliest beginnings of the idea of social science, that objective knowledge about the causes of what men do would increase human freedom and power. Engels argued the case as clearly as anyone: "Active social forces work exactly like natural forces: blindly, forcibly, destructively, so long as we do not understand, and reckon with, them. But when once we understand them, when once we grasp their action, their direction, their effects, it depends only upon ourselves to subject them more and more to our own will, and by means of them to reach our own ends. . . . [W]hen once their nature is understood, they can . . . be transformed from master demons into willing servants. The difference is as that between the destructive force of electricity in the lightning of the storm and electricity under command in the telegraph and the voltaic arc, the difference between a conflagration and fire working in the service of man."[13]

Yet physical science can increase man's power over nature, can show him how to *use* inevitable natural laws for his own purposes, "subject" them to his "will," precisely because that will is outside the kind of causal chains those sciences explore. His body, of course, is not outside those causal chains; it obeys the laws of chemistry and physics like any object. But his "will"—the sources of the "purposes" and "ends" which can be furthered by a knowledge of chemistry and physics—*that* is "outside the system," the unmoved mover. The same can be maintained about psychology and social science as well, so long as one thinks about their achievements piecemeal, or as applied only to certain people (the "sub-

[12] Friedrich Nietzsche, *The Use and Abuse of History* (Indianapolis and New York: Bobbs-Merrill, 1957), p. 6.

[13] Friedrich Engels, "Socialism: Utopian and Scientific," in Lewis S. Feuer, ed., *Marx and Engels: Basic Writings on Politics and Philosophy* (Garden City: Doubleday, 1959), pp. 104–105.

jects" being studied). For then one can still say: The juvenile delinquent's behavior is caused in these-and-these ways. I, being outside that "system" (not being a juvenile delinquent), can use what we know about the causes of delinquency to change conditions so that delinquency is eliminated, or to change this particular individual so that he is no longer delinquent. But that line of argument holds only so long as we confine our image of social science to (say) the causes of delinquency rather than to the causes of *all* human behavior. For once we think of social science as explaining the causes of all human behavior, it explains the causes of the scientist's behavior as well, the causes of his "will," so that he no longer stands outside with unexamined purposes as an unmoved mover. He, too, can only have those purposes and apply his science in those ways that are open to him, given his character and his circumstances; and these, in turn, have causes, too.

Neither particular causal explanations of our own past actions nor general causal "laws" about human behavior can ultimately tell us what to do. Of course, such information can be a partial help. Insofar as it tells me what others are likely to do or how I can influence them, it may help my decision. And insofar as it gives me insight into some unconscious motives of my own that have hitherto dominated and determined my actions, it can free me from those motives, and thus affect my decision. But ultimately, information about what I will inevitably do and the causes that impel me to do it is no help to me when I am trying to decide what to do. The point is both grammatical and practical. Grammatically, the notion of "deciding what to do" is logically incompatible with the notion of my will or my action being causally inevitably determined. As soon as I *know* what I will do, no decision remains to be made. And practically, faced with a real decision, it is no help for a knowing friend to predict my choice and explain its causes to me. What he says may well influence me, but it might influence me either way: to fulfill or to resist his prediction. And what I really need is not his prediction but his advice; not the causes for why I am about to do one thing rather than another, but the reasons why I should do it. In short, the perspectives of causal explanation and of action or choice really are different perspectives. And to the extent that we have become preoccupied with the perspective of causal explanation exclusively, we have lost contact with the point of view, the conceptual tools, the orientation, that enables man to choose rationally and responsibly, to combine action and thought (speech), to use his mind in the service of his actions.

Both existentialism and phenomenology address this problem, reminding us of our capacity for empathic understanding, identification, and personal relationship, for seeing and treating others as persons like ourselves. We saw earlier how some writers claiming phenomenological roots and others claiming Wittgensteinian ones have attacked social science for the dehumanizing effect of its detached objectivity; and have argued that only empathy, *Verstehen,* and phenomenology can help us to understand human affairs. We have argued, by contrast, that Wittgenstein suggests a dualistic or even dialectical view, that what characterizes human action is not the impossibility of external observation but the coexistence of observation and intentionality. Thus, from a Wittgensteinian perspective, both "behavioral" and "phenomenological" approaches to action may strike us as wrong, because partial. Anger, we have said, is neither merely what I feel when I am angry nor what he does when he is angry. But one might also conclude, alternatively, that both behavioral and phenomenological approaches can be right, and that they need not conflict. For what is "given in experience," phenomenologically, is not merely my inner feelings but also my experience of other people's actions. And what is perceptible to an objective observer, behaviorally, is not merely the physical movements of others, but everything that we perceive, including our own feelings and the actions and feelings of others (in the way that we perceive the actions and feelings of others—how else?) As Wittgenstein put it, "When one says 'Still, an inner process does take place here' —one wants to go on: 'After all, you *see* it.' "[14]

The very sense of alienation from the world and from other people, the sense of a discontinuity between thought and reality, arises only because of man's dual nature—because we are both animals and persons who act, ascribing meaning and making commitments. Only man, as Sartre says, is capable of self-definition and therefore of self-deception. Though we live in the world as animals do, we also talk and think conceptually about it and ourselves, as animals do not; and that gives rise to our discomfort. "If I were a tree among trees, a cat among animals," Camus says, the "problem would not arise, for I should belong to this world. I should *be* this world to which I am now opposed with my whole consciousness. . . ." If the world in which we live with our bodies and act is our "existence" or "being," and our thought about it, our conceptualizations of various things are their "essence," then the existentialist position can be summed up in Sartre's formulation, that human "*existence* comes before *essence.*" That is, concepts are thought by human beings, who must live in order to think, who first live and then think; in particular, they first live and act and only then conceive of who they are and what they have done (their own "essence"). This theme is, of course, a very widely articulated one in modern thought, from Marx's "Consciousness does not determine life, but life determines consciousness," through Camus' "We get into the habit of living before acquiring the habit of thinking," to Wittgenstein's doctrine of "forms of life."[15] Wittgenstein's contribution

[14] Wittgenstein, *Philosophical Investigations,* par. 305.

[15] Jean-Paul Sartre, "Existentialism is a Humanism," in Walter Kaufmann, ed., *Existentialism from Dostoevsky to Sartre* (New York: Meridian, 1956), p. 289; Marx, "Excerpts from the German Ideology," in Feuer, *Marx and Engels,* p. 247; Camus, *Myth,* p. 7.

here is of some new and fruitful ways of conceiving, and investigating, the problem.

### THE POSSIBILITY OF A WITTGENSTEINIAN POLITICAL THEORY

Could there be such a thing as a Wittgensteinian political theory? What might it look like? It is tempting to say no to the first question and dismiss the second; but serious investigation produces some intriguing possibilities. Presumably, if a Wittgensteinian political theory were possible at all, it would be as different from traditional political theory as Wittgenstein's philosophizing is from traditional philosophy, which is to say: radically different and yet recognizably related. Presumably it would mark in political theory what Wittgenstein felt he marked in philosophy, a sharp discontinuity, a "kink," a difference not just of degree but of kind. But then, great philosophers and political theorists have always felt their own work to be a radical innovation, to mark a "kink" in the discipline, if not to found a new discipline altogether. The significance of that feeling would have to be investigated, and its specific content in Wittgenstein's case assessed.

Presumably the main dimensions along which a Wittgensteinian political theory would differ from the tradition are the same as those along which his philosophizing differs from the tradition. It would presumably share his suspicion of broad, systematic generalization, his therapeutic stress on the particular case, on the investigating and speaking self, and on the acceptance of plurality and contradiction. But at least in terms of the tradition, such an orientation seems positively antitheoretical, not so much a new form of theory as a hostility to theorizing. And that is why one must take seriously the possibility that there could be no Wittgensteinian political theory at all.

However, we saw that Wittgenstein is often read as being hostile to traditional philosophy, too, and to metaphysics, and we argued that this is a misunderstanding. Perhaps the same is true when we extrapolate his ideas into political theory. What we said about Wittgensteinian philosophy was that it is not one more system in the tradition but a new way of philosophizing that produces no system. It stresses the activity of philosophizing, as Wittgenstein stresses the activity of speaking rather than the finished system of our language, and as writers like Kuhn and Oakeshott emphasize a continuing practice over the body of propositions it produces. Perhaps, then, when we try to imagine a Wittgensteinian political theory, we should instead think about a Wittgensteinian way of theorizing about the political.

What sort of a way of theorizing might that be? Presumably it would be fully aware of, and make full use of, the plurality of particular cases and their conflicting implications (whether they be components of a concept, of the self, of the law, of a social institution, or of a political system). Presumably, like Wittgenstein's philosophizing, it would substitute partial overviews, developed *ad hoc* where they are needed, for the older vision of a single, dominating politico-theoretical system. While that specification is still distressingly vague, it does suggest some interesting possibilities, for it hints at a way of theorizing that might be peculiarly suited to its political subject matter. In the past, political theory has always wrestled with the difficult problem of trying to generalize about an inherently disjunct subject matter; all too often, the subject matter has been distorted in the process, has been sacrificed to the exigencies of theorizing.

We have suggested in the course of our discussion several respects in which the political is necessarily and characteristically plural and inconsistent. We spoke of the convergence in the political realm of the fundamentally incompatible perspectives of action, choice, and responsibility on the one hand, and causal explanation, objective observation, and historical necessity on the other. We spoke of the similar convergence, both in the realm of politics and in the realm of political thought, between the particular position and experience of each individual and the overview appropriate to a polity, a public, a collectivity articulated for action. And we spoke, more generally, of the way that political questions always involve a plurality of valid, rival claims, a plurality of conflicting needs and interests, a plurality of perspectives and positions. These very pluralities and potential inconsistencies in the political realm have helped to make order the central problem for most traditional political theorizing. But often the result has been theoretical structures that ultimately defeat their purpose by distorting their own subject matter.

We have already noted Plato's *Republic* as a case in point, as an attempt to theorize about the problem of order in the polity, that ultimately fails to address the political problem by eliminating politics; an attempt to theorize about justice that fails by eliminating the need for, and thus the real nature of, justice. It is easy to attack Plato as a totalitarian and a bad political theorist on such grounds, but that would be to miss the significant point. The point is that what happens in Plato's theorizing is no isolated phenomenon in the history of political theory, but a common failing among libertarian as well as conservative theorists, among "realistic" as well as "utopian" ones; there seems to be something in the enterprise of theorizing itself that makes the resulting system seem totalitarian and in that sense nonpolitical. The theorist stands outside the political system about which he speculates and writes; of necessity he deploys and manipulates its citizens without consulting their wishes or opinions. Thus, even Rousseau, so evidently committed to individual liberation, envisions a polity in which each member is totally subject to collective decisions; and this coercion is defined as freedom. Even a theorist like Marx, committed not merely to liberation but also to the prevalence of conflict and the significance of revolutionary action in history, still seems forced by his enterprise to undermine these commitments. He wants and needs to see on the large scale, whether in explaining history or in envisioning a classless society; and somehow the intellectual order he imposes on his subject matter simultaneously emerges as a political or natural order imposed on the individual men about whom he writes. Apparently it is not easy to see men in their large-scale, long-range relationships, to have an overview of political life, without also seeing in a totalitarian, manipulative, and basically nonpolitical way—without seeing other men as objects and oneself as the only person.

Must political theory suffer from this defect? Are there ways of theorizing that overcome it? The answer is not at all obvious to me, nor is it clear whether a Wittgensteinian approach could make a difference. It may be helpful to note that, in a way, Wittgenstein faced a similar dilemma within philosophy, in the realm of ethics. The problem in ethics that one might construe as parallel to the problem of coercive or totalitarian theorizing about politics is that of "moralism." It concerns the tendency of some philosophers of ethics to sound as if they were talking down to, or preaching at, their audience; as if they imagined themselves as the source of all ethical wisdom and their audience as its passive recipients; as if they imagined themselves to be free of, or even exempt from, the faults they see around them.[16]

Wittgenstein and some of the ordinary-language philosophers respond to this problem of moralism in ethical theory in ways that may be instructive for political theory. They stress the importance of speech, and of particular contexts in which someone is moved to speak, for completing meaning. The tendency to moralism in ethics results, they suggest, partly from the general philosophical impulse to abstract from any particular speech situation. Ethical discourse becomes moralistic instead of moral when it deals with concepts like responsibility, choice, guilt, in abstraction from any occasion for their use; when it deals with action in general, including perfectly normal actions where nothing has gone wrong. Another way of saying this would be: Ethical discourse becomes moralistic instead of moral when the philosopher leaves himself out of the picture ("living in the universal" to the exclusion of the particular). Such moralism is thus related in complex ways to the Weberian kind of striving for objectivity in social science, as reflected in Weberian definitions like that of "legitimacy." While the moralistic philosopher seems to want to impose his standards on others, and Weber wants only to keep his personal standards out of the picture, at a deeper level both are exempting themselves from humanity in ways which fundamentally distort their teachings. But we cannot develop the parallel here.

[16] Compare Stanley Cavell, "The Claim to Rationality" (unpublished dissertation, Harvard University), p. 212: "Wittgenstein's originality lies in having developed modes of criticism, which are not moralistic, that is, which do not leave the critic imagining himself free of the faults he sees around him."

It seems possible, then, that a Wittgensteinian return to specificity, to particular cases and to the self, might somehow help with the problem of coerciveness in political theorizing. But the matter is difficult. For political questions, unlike moral ones, are not primarily about the self or the particular individual; they concern precisely our more distant, indirect, and impersonal relations, our collective lives. That, we have argued, is why Aristotle maintained that life in the polis can teach a man justice, as life in the family or other small groups cannot. But in that case, leaving oneself out of the picture, or abstracting from particular cases, should have an entirely different significance in political than it has in ethical theory.

Perhaps one could say that a Wittgensteinian political theory would be addressed from one citizen to others—not necessarily his equals in intellect or insight, but still addressed as fellow members, as fellow human beings. Such a theorist would speak neither (in Plato's favorite analogy) as physician to the body politic, a professional making his skills available to the ignorant layman, nor (in the familiar tradition) as a prophet, who claims our attention in the name of higher powers. Such a theorist would speak about the political situation of "we," not "you" or "they." And saying "we" here is an invitation, not a command; the theorist's is not the royal "we." Of course, that has always in fact been true of theory, but theorists have not generally conceived of themselves in these terms, or written or thought in a style appropriate to that fact. The possibility we have been exploring is that such a new style of theorizing might have become necessary in our time, and that Wittgenstein may offer some ways of going about it.

There remains the question raised at the end of the last chapter and again at the beginning of this section, whether such a new style, with its stress on piecemeal overviews of particular pluralities, can ever constitute a real theory—whether, in particular, it can constitute a theory suitable for providing the sense of coherence and mastery men need for political action. Even if reality and truth are in fact plural and inconsistent, it may nevertheless be true that what men need to give guidance and meaning to their political lives is a consistent and general view, an illusion of order and mastery. Much of Sorel's argument about the nature of myth would support such a view. But it is not obvious that this must be so; and the painful fact is undeniable that in our time such theories are no longer forthcoming, and what theories of this kind are available no longer function. It thus seems possible that a different form of theorizing might be effective in a new way. Certainly Wittgenstein need not be read as a conservative influence, adding to our sense of fragmentation and helplessness. He can be seen as seeking precisely to liberate us from the paralyzing weight of our alienation. But that argument is better made from a slightly different, separate approach.

Wittgenstein's teaching about the importance of language and about the responsibility entailed in speaking may also be applied more directly to our modern problems of alienation. One might put the matter this way: We live in a time in which people perceive each other and themselves as objects, and this is reflected, among other places, in our use of language. We use language as an instrument for manipulating objects, as a propaganda device, not to establish the truth but to get others to believe what we want them to believe. As Camus says, "dialogue and personal relations have been replaced by propaganda or polemic."[17] Children growing up in such a world learn from experience that language is primarily for lying, that hypocrisy is its mode. As a result, they—we—no longer recognize even as a serious possibility what Arendt calls the truth-revealing function of language. And so we are cut off from its power to reveal our true selves and the reality around us, its power to establish genuine relationships, and its power to create what Arendt has called a "public space"—an institutional arena in which shared public deliberation and free political action are possible.

Quite simply, without some foundation in stable truth, men are unable to orient themselves toward the world or toward each other, and hence lack a stable sense of self.[18] Among the many functions of language, perhaps the most central is that of reality-testing, of comparing private perception of the world and action with other perspectives in order to get one's bearings. "To be deprived of it means to be deprived of reality, which, humanly and politically speaking, . . . is guaranteed by the presence of others, by its appearing to all; 'for what appears to all, this we call Being,' and whatever lacks this appearance comes and passes away like a dream, intimately and exclusively our own but without reality."[19] That does not mean that wordless experience is unimportant, any more than our dreams are unimportant; but it does mean that a breakdown in the functioning of the language that normally secures our reality results in alienation. "It has frequently been noticed that the surest result of brainwashing in the long run is a peculiar kind of cynicism, the absolute refusal to believe in the truth of anything, no matter how well it may be established. In other words, the result of a consistent and total substitution of lies for factual truth is not that the lie now will be accepted as

---

[17] Camus, *Rebel*, pp. 239–240. Compare Clamence's remark that "for the dialogue we have substituted the communiqué"; in *The Fall*, tr. by Justin O'Brien (New York: A. A. Knopf, 1966), p. 45.

[18] Hannah Arendt, "Truth and Politics," in Peter Laslett and W. G. Runciman, eds., *Philosophy, Politics and Society* (Oxford: Basil Blackwell, 1967), p. 129.

[19] Arendt, *Human Condition*, p. 178; the quotation within the quotation is from Aristotle's *Nicomachean Ethics*, 1172b36 ff.

truth, and truth be defamed as lie, but that the sense by which we take our bearings in the real world—and the category of truth versus falsehood is among the mental means to this end—is being destroyed."[20] When we no longer strive to articulate what we really believe, but only what we would like others to believe, we increasingly lose contact with our own selves. We become unsure of what we do believe and can no longer distinguish between truth and our own deception. Wordless, personal experience may be intense sometimes and of the greatest value, but by itself it yields neither reality nor meaning. It can occur as readily in dreams as in our waking lives, and it fails to distinguish between the two. A life founded exclusively upon it is neither intense nor valuable, but every bit as impoverished as one founded only on the idols of externality and hypocrisy.

Moreover, when we find that those who speak to us speak not truth but only what they want us to believe, we can trust no one; every act of speech addressed to us becomes an assault, against which we must defend our already fragile sense of self. Who undermines our sense of reality and of our selves is an enemy. As Arendt has seen, in our time it is hypocrisy that transforms "engages" into "enrages"; "to provoke action even at the risk of annihilation so that the truth may come out—these are still among the strongest motives in today's violence. And this violence again is not irrational. Since men live in a world of appearances, hence depend upon manifestation, hypocrisy's conceits—as distinguished from temporary ruses, followed by disclosure in due time—cannot be met with what is recognized as reasonable behavior. Words can be relied upon only so long as one is sure that their function is to reveal and not to conceal. It is the semblance of rationality, rather than the interests behind it, that provokes rage. To respond with reason when reason is used as a trap is not 'rational.' "[21]

All this is clearly of the greatest political significance, for while private, wordless experience may still be of value for the isolated individual, it is disastrous for public life. "There may be truths," as Arendt says, "beyond speech, and they may be of great relevance to man . . . in so far as he is not a political being, whatever else he may be. Men in the plural, that is, men in so far as they live and move and act in this world, can experience meaningfulness only because they can talk with and make sense to each other and to themselves." Following Aristotle, Arendt sees an intimate link between the human capacities for speech and political life. "Speech is what makes man a political being," and "wherever the relevance of

[20] Arendt, "Truth and Politics," p. 128; compare Frantz Fanon, *Black Skin, White Masks*, tr. by Charles Lam Markmann (New York: Grove Press, 1967), pp. 231–235; and Harold Lasswell, "Propaganda and Mass Insecurity," in A. H. Stanton and S. E. Perry, eds., *Personality and Political Crisis* (Glencoe: Free Press, 1951), pp. 15–43.

[21] Hannah Arendt, "Reflections on Violence," *New York Review of Books*, XII (February 27, 1969), 28.

speech is at stake, matters become political by definition."[22] That is, "political action, in so far as it remains outside the sphere of violence, is ... transacted in words," and speech is itself political action. "Only sheer violence is mute." The connection begins with the Greeks, for whom being political "meant that everything was decided through words and persuasion and not through force and violence." The *polis* was "a way of life in which speech and only speech made sense and where the central concern of all citizens was to talk with each other."[23]

But within the realm of politics and speech, Arendt draws a further significant distinction in terms of the manner in which speech is used. She distinguishes speech in the service of truth, or at least of the quest for truth, and speech as a means of persuasion, as a manipulative tool for moving others in desired directions, quite apart from the truth or validity of what is said. The distinction is first "elaborated by Plato (especially in the *Gorgias*) as the antagonism between communicating in the form of 'dialogue', which is the adequate speech for philosophic truth, and in the form of 'rhetoric' by which the demagogue, as we would say today, persuades the multitude."[24] In modern thought, Arendt argues, that distinction between rational truth and eloquence has completely disappeared, or at least the philosopher's rational truth is no longer considered in any way relevant to political life. But much the same distinction or conflict is reenacted today, between factual truth and political rhetoric, as nations rewrite past history on a grandiose scale, or even dissimulate about existing current states of affairs. The deliberate political lie is, of course, very old; what is new, Arendt argues, is the massive scale of dissimulation, and the fact that the lie is to be believed not merely by some enemy, but by the nation itself, including the people who initiate the deception. Modern political mass deception is not about state secrets but about facts generally and publicly known, "and yet the same public that knows them can successfully and often spontaneously prohibit their public discussion and treat them as though they were what they are not, namely, secrets."[25]

Now, one might suppose that the distinction between truthful public speech and manipulative, deceitful rhetoric corresponds to the two views of political life we discussed earlier, so that truth-telling corresponds to the public-spirited common pursuit of the public interest, and rhetoric corresponds to the selfish conflict of individual or group interests. In that case, it would seem that Arendt, in her obvious disdain for deception and rhetoric, is harking back to a golden age that probably never existed and cannot be realized, in which all men were unselfish and public-minded. But that is not the case, and really misses the point she seeks to make. Rhetoric and manipulation and even deception can be most effective and

[22] Arendt, *Human Condition*, p. 4.
[23] *Ibid.*, pp. 25–27.
[24] Arendt, "Truth and Politics," p. 109.
[25] *Ibid.*, p. 111.

useful, perhaps are even necessary to political life; the point is that political life itself is only possible on a more fundamental basis of shared
truth. When rhetoric and deception come to be regarded and used as the
only possible modes of speech, public communication becomes meaningless and politics impossible. Deprived of a stable sense of reality, of truth,
of the past, of themselves, man becomes incapable of political action,
incapable of the kind of public speech that it presupposes. "Not the past,
and all factual truth concerns of course the past, and the present insofar
as it is the outcome of the past, but the future is open to action; if this
past and present are treated as parts of the future—that is, changed back
into their former potentiality—the political realm is deprived not only
of its main stabilizing force but of the starting-point from which to change
and begin something new."[26] Political life is, as Wilhelm Hennis has said,
"determined by the possibility and necessity of collective deliberation,"
and if that capacity declines, politics and the specifically human of our
common life, our freedom, are endangered at their heart.[27]

In our time, it seems to me, the retreat from authentic personal dialogue
and from truthful, rational public debate has turned into a full-scale,
headlong rout; we flee in utter panic in all directions, before any encounter
has even taken place. Some flee into cynicism and psychologism and become inside-dopesters, propagandists, manipulators; they become the
public relations men whose only awareness of themselves comes from the
reflection of the "image" they "project." Others flee into some version of
positivism and (misperceived) science, seeking security in sterility, and
order in the withdrawal from engagement to "mere" description. They
become the petty functionaries in the scientific establishment, the intellectual bureaucrats. Still others flee into silence: some into the aggressive,
explosive silence of violence, of blind activity unmediated by concept or
reason; others into the privatized, passive silence of the dream, the drug
experience, and the wordless life.

Existentialism, one might say, directs its attack primarily against the
propagandists and the bureaucrats; it challenges them, in the name of
authenticity, to face up to the isolation and anxiety they are seeking to
escape. The existentialist maintains that since man has no essence but
chooses and makes himself through his actions, he who cites his role or
his character to justify the necessity of what he does is a hypocrite. As
Kaufmann says, paraphrasing Sartre, a man is not a waiter or a homo-
sexual or a coward in the same way in which he is six feet tall or has
a weak heart. His being a waiter or a coward constantly depends on
his conduct, his explicit or implicit decisions. "I may say: I must leave
now—or, I am that way—because I am a waiter, or a coward, as if

26 *Ibid.*, p. 129.
27 Wilhelm Hennis, "Topik und Politik," in Robert H. Schmidt, ed., *Methoden der
Politologie* (*Wege der Forschung*, vol. LXXXVI) (Darmstadt: Wissenschaftliche
Buchgesellschaft, 1967), p. 515.

being a waiter or a coward were a brute fact. Actually, this apparent statement of fact veils a decision."[28]

There is thus in existentialism an intense stress on the freedom to choose and to change, on the need for action, commitment, responsibility. In a sense, this is a liberation; there are no absolutes to govern what the individual does, and he is free to do as he pleases. But the existentialists acknowledge and even stress that this freedom is not, on the whole, pleasurable. They acknowledge our yearning for order, for authority, for God or parents; and they speak eloquently of the anguish, anxiety, care, and loneliness that characterize the human condition when it is seen without illusion, in all its stark nakedness. Moreover, they stress the responsibility entailed in action; they demand authenticity. Not only is each man entirely responsible for all the consequences of what he does, or omits to do, but he is also responsible for what he is, and in that sense for mankind.[29] In action, man makes himself; and in choosing, he chooses for all men. That is why Camus says, "I rebel—therefore we exist."[30]

But for that very reason, existentialism speaks less effectively to those who have fled not into manipulativeness or bureaucratic positivism, but into silence, privatization, violence. These, who seem increasingly to include the best of our young, lack not authenticity but responsibility, not honesty but hope. Their failures stem less from cowardice and moral obtuseness than from an overly sophisticated awareness of causal infinitude and human fallibility. When, as Cavell says about our time, "consequences became fully unlimited and untraceable," the burden of responsible action is too great to bear.[31] Such persons shun responsibilities not out of selfishness but because they no longer know where responsibilities end, "what is and is not news, what is and is not a significant fact in present history, what is and is not relevant to one's life." Here, too, we live in the universal instead of our particularity, and the burden is paralyzing. "The newspaper tells me that everything is relevant, but I cannot really accept that because it would mean that I do not have one life, to which some things are relevant and some not. I cannot really deny it either because I do not know why things happen as they do and why I am not responsible for any or all of it. And so to the extent that I still have feeling to contend with, it is a generalized guilt, which only confirms my paralysis."[32] And the counterpart to paralysis, when the strain becomes too great, is explosion.

To someone in this situation, the call to authenticity and responsibility

[28] Walter Kaufmann, ed., *Existentialism from Dostoevsky to Sartre* (New York: Meridian Books, 1956), p. 44.

[29] Existentialism "places the entire responsibility for [man's] existence squarely upon his own shoulders," *ibid.*, p. 291.

[30] Camus, *Rebel*, p. 22.

[31] Stanley Cavell, *Must We Mean What We Say?* (New York: Charles Scribner's Sons, 1969), p. 343.

[32] *Ibid.*, p. 348; compare pp. 346–347.

issued by existentialism is likely to seem both arbitrarily moralistic and excessively burdensome. Infinite responsibility is too great; in the absence of gods or absolute standards, why should anyone accept it? Or, even if one accepts it, how can it become the basis for meaningful action? Who can foresee infinite consequences before he acts? So either action is avoided or it becomes disconnected from thought. Here, it seems to me, Wittgenstein offers an alternative approach, suggesting a responsibility it is humanly possible to take on. For Wittgenstein reminds us that notions like responsibility, action, consequences, are made to be used in actual cases where we converse with one another about particular actions in our lives. In assigning responsibility for action, we speak always against the background of particular circumstances, as particular individuals. There, our concepts of responsibility and consequences are at home; there they make sense. But there they are also finite. They do not fully make sense applied to our entire lives in the abstract and in general. We are not constantly acting and choosing; the consequences of an action are not *everything* that follows it forever after (any more than the cause of a physical event is *everything* that went before).

Wittgenstein allows us to see how, when it comes to choosing (an action, a position, a standard, but also a book, a friend, an example) we *already are* somebody; we never have to start from scratch, because we never *can* start from scratch. Values, and order, and meaning are indeed created by men, by men's choices. But that does not mean that they are created in their entirety by each man at each point in time; it does not mean that they are created in just *any* way at all, arbitrarily. For all of us, they have their foundation in human nature; and for each of us they have a further foundation in the life he has already lived, the growing-up he has already done, the language he has already learned, the person he has become. Wittgenstein teaches us that, by the time we are old enough for the problem to arise, we already *have* values and standards and meanings and a conception of the world, just as we already have a language in which they are largely embodied. In this sense, we really are part of an ongoing human community, whether we like it or not, whether we know it or not.[33]

Wittgenstein is as concerned as any phenomenologist with our sense of alienation, with our sense of a gap between world and mind, between facts and meanings, between objects and the human. He sees our sense of a gap clearly related to our progressively increasing self-knowledge and self-awareness, which makes us more pervasively conscious of the role of convention in human life than men have ever been before. We feel the burden of maintaining those conventions more heavily because we are more fully aware of how much is conventional. It is as if we have come to realize that the ground on which we walk is not solid earth at all, but a

[33] This point is surely one reason for Camus' quarrels with existentialism, and his conclusion that there is a "human nature" after all; *Rebel*, p. 16.

mere fragile network of convention stretched over an abyss; we look down through the net and are dizzied by the view of empty space yawning below us. But Wittgenstein suggests that that may be because we are looking for the wrong sort of foundations. The conventions of our language and thought rest in the language games that we play. And that means that the seeming gap between thought and reality is bridged on the one hand by human forms of life, and on the other hand by human action, by the responsibility we assume when we speak. Forms of life are what bridge the apparent gap—what explains why there is no gap—between the subjective feelings characteristic of expectation, the occasions when something is to be expected, and the various (verbal and nonverbal) expressions of expectation. The act of speaking is what bridges the apparent gap—shows why there is no gap—between the subjective feeling characteristic of sudden understanding, and the guarantee of future ability to proceed correctly contained in the declaration "I understand," between the criteria of understanding and the meaning of "understand." Wanting to escape our forms of life, we construe the responsibilities of speech so broadly that they seem unattainable; our sense of a gap between mind and world rests on a misunderstanding of the nature of the conventions involved.

Wittgenstein's notion of grammar, Cavell argues, "is meant to explain both the kind of security our general knowledge of the world has . . . and the way in which that security depends upon the ability to make claims which 'may' be overturned although we cannot protect our intellect and indeed we crucify it—in trying to anticipate every place it may fail. This is no new Quest for Certainty—that Quest was never really for that, but was a quest for a dream of certainty, a fantasy of the *total* grasp of object, situation and consequence, a wish for God's knowledge—but, I wish to say, a quest for responsibility. For entering a claim is making an assertion, something human beings *do*; and like everything else they do, something they are responsible, answerable for. Saying anything involves risks; countless things can happen which we 'can't' have known; but it was *said*, and what must be said if it fails depends upon *what* was said and when, and upon what happened. . . . The risks do not deprive us of certainty; the acceptance and competent handling of risks is what makes the claim to human certainty responsible."[34]

What bridges the gap between mind and world for Wittgenstein, Cavell says, "is the appreciation and acceptance of human forms of life, human 'convention.' This implies that the *sense* of gap originates in an attempt, or wish, to escape (to remain a 'stranger' to, 'alienated' from) those shared forms of life, to give up the *responsibility* of their maintenance. (Is this always a fault? Is there no way of becoming responsible for *that*? What does a moral or intellectual hero *do*?) Traditional philosophy, so far as this enters the Anglo-American academic tradition, has never taken

[34] Cavell, "Claim to Rationality," pp. 108–109.

this gap seriously as a *real, practical* problem. It has either filled it with God or bridged it with universals which *insure* the mind's collusion with the world; or else it has denied, on theoretical grounds, that it *could* be filled or bridged at all. I think that is what Nietzsche meant when he ridiculed philosophers for regarding life 'as a riddle, as a problem of knowledge' implying that we question what we cannot fail to know in order not to seek what it would be painful to find out. This, of course, does not suggest that skepticism is trivial; on the contrary it shows how profound a position of the mind it is. Nothing is more human than the wish to deny one's humanity."[35]

Clearly, then, what Wittgenstein offers us is basically much like what was offered by Marx or Nietzsche or Freud: a further increase in human self-knowledge, a further increase in our rational perspective on ourselves. But if that is so, he seems to be just one more in the long series of teachers who have helped to cast man out of Eden by feeding him from the tree of knowledge, who have brought on our modern predicament. He, too, removes illusions which gave a false sense of stability and order. For he teaches us that even our concepts, the very apparatus with which we think, are but the product of human convention. Like Nietzsche and Marx, Wittgenstein teaches that our thought is a reflection of our activity; like Freud, he is concerned to liberate us from illusion, from mental "pictures" which "hold us captive"; like Einstein, he teaches that there is no absolute but only relative position. Despite our craving for order and transcendent meaning, the fact is that words have no absolute, God-given meaning; and the order in our language is fragmentary. Meanings are simply the product of our various uses of words; and since they nevertheless determine our world in important ways, our world itself is dependent upon human practice and convention. There is no Master Umpire to judge the meaning or the truth of what we say; there is only a collection of fallible human beings, interacting.

In a way, Wittgenstein does say these things and is one of these teachers. But there is also a significant evolution in his thought, from the *Tractatus* to the later writings. Confronted with the modern predicament, with a universe in flux, lacking center or meaning or stability, the *Tractatus* is essentially a failure of nerve, a retreat to what seems the only remaining solid ground, the one fortress that still seems defensible, ruthlessly abandoning whatever is outside the walls. If language defines our world, then for that world to retain any kind of stability language *must* be a system of fixed, exhaustive, systematic rules. If we stay within those rules, we will be safe, will save meaning and sense and reality. Of course, much will have to be given up. For all of art and esthetics, all of religion and ethics, all really of judgment, sensibility, and affect will have to be abandoned outside the fortress. Those things cannot be talked about, and if men continue to experience them they must do so in silence and therefore in

[35] *Ibid.*, pp. 129–130.

isolation, in the wordless private world of dreams. Our language and our common life must be confined to the lucid, ordered crystal palace of mathematics, logic, science, a world secured against all ambiguity. That, I think, is the spirit of the *Tractatus*.

Wittgenstein himself clearly experienced the insights of his later philosophy as a liberation from that earlier spirit, a release from the rigid and frantic commitment to unambiguous order. Instead of retreating to a last island of certainty, Wittgenstein's later philosophy examines the craving for certainty itself, and concludes that we are, after all, able to live on the sea. It is an attempt to accept and to live with the illusionless human condition—relativity, doubt, and the absence of God. Like the other great teachers of modernity, then, Wittgenstein seems both to contribute to the maladies of perspective, and to insist on more perspective, more self-knowledge, as the cure for that malady. Like them, he responds to alienation by the attempt to move deeper into and *through* it, and out the other side to whatever lies beyond.

Whether the attempt strikes us as promising will depend on whether we regard our modern condition as the result of series of successful destructive revolutions (industrial, social, political, religious, educational, and so on), or whether, with Paul Goodman, we believe that most of our revolutions have been incomplete and their constructive power therefore diverted or poisoned.[36] If Wittgenstein has something new and important to add to our objective self-knowledge, then that may be because Freud and Marx and the other teachers who preceded him had not completed the task of teaching us who we are. And in that case, the seeming harmful consequences of their teachings may be the fault, not of those teachings, but of those teachings misunderstood, distorted by our defenses against them, whether those be the socio-political defenses of established interests and institutions or the inner psychological defenses erected by our fear. Wittgenstein felt his achievement to be, like Freud's, the discovery of a systematic method for preventing the quest for rational self-awareness from becoming self-defeating, from being defeated by the self.[37]

Self-knowledge, perspective on ourselves, acceptance of the truth of human limitations, is alienating, one might suggest, only so long as it is confined to the intellectual realm, is kept out of contact with—and, indeed, is used as a defense against contact with—our real, inner selves and our real, outer lives. Like Freudian doctrine, it can be distorted into a new, supersophisticated weapon of propaganda and manipulation; but like Freudian doctrine it can be a humanizing and liberating force where it takes the form of genuine insight rather than merely superficial, intellectual mastery. Wittgenstein teaches that philosophy is purely descrip-

[36] Paul Goodman, *Growing Up Absurd* (New York: Random House, 1962), pp. 216–217.
[37] K. T. Fann, *Ludwig Wittgenstein: The Man and his Philosophy* (New York: Dell, 1967), p. 44; compare Cavell, *Must We Mean What We Say?* pp. 66–67, 72.

tive, that it "may in no way interfere with the actual use of language," that it results ultimately in the discovery of our "forms of life" which have to "be accepted as given." That can be experienced, and has sometimes been experienced by contemporary philosophers, as a confining doctrine, as if Wittgenstein were forbidding us to do something that might otherwise be possible if we tried hard enough. But it can also be perceived, as it was by Wittgenstein himself, as facilitating rather than blocking movement. Recognizing what we say, what we do, what we feel, who we are, can mean giving up some dreams of change as impossible; but it can also be a foundation—perhaps the only effective foundation—for genuine change. It is, as Cavell suggests, "like the recognition of our present commitments and their implications; to one person a sense of freedom will demand an escape from them, to another it will require their more total acceptance. Is it obvious that one of those positions must, in a given case, be right?"[38]

We might say, where our forms of life are cultural in the sense that they could well be otherwise among human beings—perhaps have been otherwise in other times and cultures—the discovery of our conventions can be achieved by Wittgensteinian analysis, or by genuinely deep anthropological acquaintance with radically different existing cultures, or by genuinely deep historical acquaintance with radically different times. Here freedom begins, as it were, in an awareness of plurality, of alternatives. But even here mere awareness does not yet constitute freedom, any more than we can "see" the world as an Egyptian saw it merely by becoming acquainted with Egyptian art. Where our forms of life are more than cultural, are natural in the sense that human beings or our world would have to be radically different for the forms to change, it may truly and fully be the case that what is must be accepted. But even here the perspicuous awareness of convention—of human nature—can be of the utmost value. Here freedom lies not in plurality or in changed patterns of life, but in acceptance of the inevitable, or our real selves and our situation.

This is not an easy idea to express without paradox (because, of course, of the grammar of the words we have available for expressing it). Hegel tried to say it about all of history, past and future; Nietzsche sought to confine it to the past. It obviously is in constant danger of being misexpressed or misunderstood into a quietistic doctrine, advising men to accept what in fact could be changed, or to pretend (to themselves as well as others) to accept what in fact remains unacceptable. But that is not the idea. The idea is, rather, that where something truly cannot be changed the continuing desire for change itself becomes suspect. That does not mean that the desire should be denied or repressed or disguised; it does mean that the desire should be further examined. *What* is it that we have a desire *for* when we want to escape our human condition? What so

[38] Cavell, *Must We Mean What We Say?* p. 57n.

much as makes us suppose that there are alternatives? Where do we get what notions we have of what those alternatives might be like (immortality, infinity, omniscience, omnipotence, God)? Wittgenstein suggests, as Feuerbach did about gods, that these ideas and expectations that seem to transcend our human condition are in fact drawn from our human condition—not from its facts but from its enterprises. The philosopher's dream of Godlike knowledge arises out of (part of) the ordinary, human grammar of "to know": namely, out of that part having to do with the guarantee we give when we claim to know, the promise we offer, the responsibility we take.

Second, saying that freedom lies in accepting what truly cannot be changed means that the acceptance of reality is the only possible basis for genuine change, as the recognition of who we are and what we value, of where we are and what we face, of "our present commitments and responsibilities," is the only genuinely solid foundation for successful action and meaningful change. If you want to move purposefully, knowing where you are may seem to limit your alternatives, but it is also a prerequisite. Such knowledge is like friction. As Wittgenstein says, in our desire for absoluteness, for transcending the human condition, "we have got on to slippery ice where there is no friction and so in a certain sense the conditions are ideal, but also, just because of that, we are unable to walk. We want to walk: so we need *friction*. Back to the rough ground!"[39] The desire to escape our human condition does come to each of us at times. It is a real desire, but not a desire for something real. It is a vain desire.

To be sure, theorists like Marx and Freud offered fairly concrete proposals for remedial action along with their diagnoses of social ills. Their contributions to our self-knowledge include a vision of alternative possibilities and some instructions as to how it might be achieved. Wittgenstein, by contrast, has no plan, no program, no alternative course of action to propose. He is truly not a political theorist but a philosopher, giving us a clear vision of the current state of affairs. Nor, evidently, is his teaching of a form readily accessible to large numbers of people.

We shall have to find and formulate our own course of action if we wish to accept the Wittgensteinian challenge and make the self-knowledge he offers our own. But there can be no doubt that Wittgenstein intended just that, intended to summon us back to reality, to ourselves, to action, to our responsibilities. He realized that knowledge demands acknowledgement, that it is not neutral with respect to action. A Wittgensteinian approach makes possible, but also requires of us, that we take other people, and other cultures, *seriously*, that we really listen, that we become able to see from the perspective of another. But it also makes possible, and requires of us, that we take ourselves seriously, that we be serious, that we accept our own perspective as our own, that we say what we really

[39] Wittgenstein, *Philosophical Investigations*, par. 107.

mean and live by what we say. It teaches that words are not by nature vague or unreliable, not by nature shaped for hypocrisy and betrayal. It teaches us to see when *we* speak vaguely, unreliably, hypocritically, and that we need not do so. It shows, to borrow Arendt's words, that "even if there is not truth, man can be truthful, and even if there is no reliable certainty, man can be reliable."[40]

Thus, when Wittgenstein says that our forms of life must be accepted, that is not the same as saying that our lives as we lead them must be accepted, that our ways of theorizing about them must be accepted. Rather, it suggests, as Cavell says, "that criticism of our lives is not to be prosecuted in philosophical theory, but continued in the confrontation of our lives with their own necessities."[41] It is not that we cannot change our concepts or our habits or our institutions; but that not every change is possible, and philosophizing will not change them. If they are to change, we must change them in our actions, in our lives; and ultimately that means that we cannot change them in isolation. Here Wittgenstein is very close to Marx. The famous thesis on Feuerbach, that "philosophers have only *interpreted* the world, in various ways; the point, however, is to *change* it," need not be read either as an invitation to change the world by philosophizing or as a condemnation of philosophy as useless. It can, instead, be read as parallel to Wittgenstein's observation, that "the sickness of a time" is cured only "by an alteration in the mode of life of human beings," through alternative modes of "thought and life, not through a medicine invented by an individual."[42]

[40] Arendt, *Human Condition*, p. 254.
[41] Cavell, "Existentialism," p. 963.
[42] Ludwig Wittgenstein, *Remarks on the Foundations of Mathematics*, tr. by G. E. M. Anscombe, ed. by G. H. von Wright, R. Rhees, and G. E. M. Anscombe (Oxford: Basil Blackwell, 1964), p. 57.

# BIBLIOGRAPHY

Ambrose, Alice, and Morris Lazerowitz. "Ludwig Wittgenstein: Philosophy, Experiment and Proof," in C. A. Mace, ed., *British Philosophy in the Mid-Century*. London: George Allen and Unwin, 1966.

Anscombe, G. E. M. *An Introduction to Wittgenstein's Tractatus*. Second edition. New York: Harper & Row, 1965.

———. "On Brute Facts," *Analysis*, 18 (January 1958), 69–72.

Apel, Karl-Otto. *Analytic Philosophy of Language and the Geisteswissenschaften*, tr. by Harald Holstelilie. Dordrecht: D. Reidel, 1967.

Arendt, Hannah. *Between Past and Future*. Cleveland and New York: World Publishing, 1961.

———. "Civil Disobedience," *The New Yorker*, XLVI (September 12, 1970), 70–105.

———. *The Human Condition*. Garden City: Doubleday, 1958.

———. "Reflections on Violence," *New York Review of Books*, XII (February 27, 1969), 19–31.

———. "Religion and Politics," *Confluence*, II (September 1953), 105–126.

———. "Truth and Politics," in Peter Laslett and W. G. Runciman, eds., *Philosophy, Politics and Society* (Third Series). Oxford: Basil Blackwell, 1967.

———. "What Was Authority?" in Carl J. Friedrich, ed., *Authority* (*Nomos* I). Cambridge: Harvard University Press, 1958.

Aristotle. *De Anima*, tr. by Kenelm Foster and Silvester Humphries. London: Routledge and Kegan Paul, 1951.

———. *Politics*, tr. by Sir Ernest Barker. New York: Oxford University Press, 1958.

Austin, J. L. *How to Do Things with Words*, ed. by J. O. Urmson. New York: Oxford University Press, 1965.

———. *Philosophical Papers*. Oxford: Clarendon Press, 1961.

———. *Sense and Sensibilia*, ed. by G. J. Warnock. Oxford: Clarendon Press, 1962.

———. "Some Ways of Spilling Ink," in Carl J. Friedrich, ed., *Responsibility* (*Nomos* III). New York: Liberal Arts Press, 1960.

Ayer, A. J. *Language, Truth and Logic*. London: Victor Gollancz, 1936.

Bachrach, Peter, and Morton S. Baratz. "Decisions and Nondecisions: An

Analytical Framework," *American Political Science Review*, LVII (September 1963), 632–642.

Bambrough, Renford. "Universals and Family Resemblances," in Pitcher.

Barker, Sir Ernest, ed. *The Social Contract*. New York: Oxford University Press, 1960.

Barth, Karl. *Wahrheit und Ideologie*. Zürich: Manese Verlag, 1945.

Bellugi, Ursula, and Roger Brown, eds. *The Acquisition of Language*. Monograph of the Society for Research in Child Development, vol. 29, no. 1, serial no. 92 (1964).

Berlin, Brent, and Paul Kay. *Basic Color Terms*. Berkeley and Los Angeles: University of California Press, 1969.

Berlin, Sir Isaiah. *Two Concepts of Liberty*. Oxford: Clarendon Press, 1958.

Bierstadt, Robert. "Legitimacy," in *Dictionary of the Social Sciences*. New York: U.N.E.S.C.O., 1964.

Bodenheimer, Edgar. "A Neglected Theory of Legal Reasoning," *Journal of Legal Education*, 21 (1969), 373–402.

Bourne, Lyle E., Jr. *Human Conceptual Behavior*. Boston: Allyn and Bacon, 1966.

Braithewaite, R. B. *Scientific Explanation*. Cambridge: Cambridge University Press, 1964.

Brower, Reuben A., ed. *On Translation*. Cambridge, Mass.: Harvard University Press, 1959.

Brown, R. *Explanation in Social Science*. Chicago: Aldine Press, 1963.

Burke, Edmund. *Reflections on the Revolution in France*. Indianapolis: Bobbs-Merrill Company, 1955.

Camus, Albert. *The Fall*, tr. by Justin O'Brien. New York: A. A. Knopf, 1966.

———. *The Myth of Sisyphus*, tr. by Justin O'Brien. New York: Random House, 1959.

———. *The Rebel*, tr. by Anthony Bower. New York: Random House, 1956.

Carnap, Rudolf. *Meaning and Necessity*. Chicago: University of Chicago Press, 1956.

Carroll, John B. *Language and Thought*. Englewood Cliffs, N. J.: Prentice-Hall, 1964.

———. *The Study of Language*. Cambridge, Mass.: Harvard University Press, 1959.

Cassirer, Ernst. *An Essay on Man*. Garden City: Doubleday, 1953.

———. *Philosophie der symbolischen Formen*. Berlin: B. Cassirer, 1923–1931.

Caton, Charles E., ed. *Philosophy and Ordinary Language*. Urbana: University of Illinois Press, 1963.

Cavell, Stanley. "The Claim to Rationality: Knowledge and the Basis of Morality." Unpublished doctoral dissertation, Harvard University, 1961–1962.

———. "Existentialism and Analytic Philosophy," *Daedalus*, 93 (Summer 1964), 946–974.

———. *Must We Mean What We Say?* New York: Charles Scribner's Sons, 1969.

Chambers, Will Grant. "How Words Get Meanings," *Pedagogical Seminary*, 11 (1904), 30–49.

Chappell, V. C., ed. *Ordinary Language*. Englewood Cliffs, N. J.: Prentice-Hall, 1964.

Charlesworth, Maxwell John. *Philosophy and Linguistic Analysis*. Louvain: Editions E. Nauwelaerts, 1959.

Chihara, C. S., and J. A. Fodor. "Operationalism and Ordinary Language: A Critique of Wittgenstein," in Pitcher.

Chisholm, Roderick M. "Freedom and Action," in Keith Lehrer, ed., *Freedom and Determinism*. New York: Random House, 1966.

————. *Perceiving*. Ithaca, N.Y.: Cornell University Press, 1957.

Chomsky, Noam. *Cartesian Linguistics*. New York and London: Harper & Row, 1966.

————. "Current Issues in Linguistic Theory," in Fodor and Katz, eds., *The Structure of Language*.

————. *Language and Mind*. New York: Harcourt, Brace & World, 1968.

Church, Joseph. *Language and the Discovery of Reality*. New York: Random House, 1961.

Cumming, Robert Denoon, ed. *The Philosophy of Jean-Paul Sartre*. New York: Modern Library, 1966.

Dahl, Robert. "The Concept of Power," in S. Sidney Ulmer, ed., *Introductory Readings in Political Behavior*. Chicago: Rand McNally, 1961.

————.*Modern Political Analysis*. Englewood Cliffs, N. J.: Prentice-Hall, 1963.

Dahrendorf, Ralf. *Marx in Perspektive*. Hanover: J. H. W. Dietz, 1953.

Del Vecchio, Giorgio. *Justice*, tr. by Lady Guthrie, ed. by A. H. Campbell. Chicago: Aldine Press, 1952.

de Mauro, Tullio. *Ludwig Wittgenstein, His Place in the Development of Semantics*. Dordrecht: D. Reidel, 1967.

Dienes, Z. P. *Concept Formation and Personality*. Leicester: Leicester University Press, 1959.

Dodds, E. R. *The Greeks and the Irrational*. Berkeley and Los Angeles: University of California Press, 1951.

Drury, M. O'C. "A Symposium on Wittgenstein," in Fann, *Ludwig Wittgenstein*.

Duncan-Jones, Austin E. "Authority," *Aristotelian Society Supplementary Volume* 32 (1958), 241–260.

Easton, David. *A Framework for Political Analysis*. Englewood Cliffs, N. J.: Prentice-Hall, 1965.

————. *The Political System*. New York: A. A. Knopf, 1963.

————. *A Systems Analysis of Political Life*. New York: John Wiley and Sons, 1965.

Ehrenzweig, Albert. "Psychoanalytic Jurisprudence: A Common Language for Babylon," *Columbia Law Review*, 65:2 (1965), 1331–1360.

Elam, Claude B. *Inductive Concept Formation in Normal and Retarded Subjects*. Fort Worth: Texas Christian University Press, 1962.

Ellul, Jacques. *The Political Illusion*, tr. by Konrad Kellen. New York: A. A. Knopf, 1967.

Emmet, Dorothy. "The Concept of Power," *Aristotelian Society Proceedings*, LIV (1953–1954), 1–26.

Engelmann, Paul. *Letters from Ludwig Wittgenstein, with a Memoir*, tr. by L. Furtmüller, ed. by B. F. McGuinness. New York: Horizon Press, 1968.

Evans-Pritchard, E. E. *Witchcraft, Oracles and Magic Among the Azande*. Oxford: Clarendon Press, 1965.

Fann, K. T. *Wittgenstein's Conception of Philosophy*. Berkeley and Los Angeles: University of California Press, 1969.

————, ed. *Ludwig Wittgenstein:The Man and his Philosophy*. New York: Dell, 1967.

Fanon, Frantz. *Black Skin, White Masks*, tr. by Charles Lam Markmann. New York: Grove Press, 1967.

Fenichel, Otto. *The Psychoanalytic Theory of Neurosis*. New York: W. W. Norton, 1945.

Feuer, Lewis S., ed. *Marx and Engels: Basic Writings on Politics and Philosophy*. Garden City: Doubleday, 1959.

Feuerbach, Ludwig. *The Essence of Christianity*. New York: Harper & Brothers, 1957.

Flew, Antony, ed. *Essays in Conceptual Analysis*. London: Macmillan, 1956.

———, ed. *Logic and Language* (First and Second Series). Garden City: Doubleday, 1965.

Fodor, Jerry A., and Jerrold J. Katz. "The Availability of What We Say," *Philosophical Review*, LXXII (January 1963), 57–71.

———, eds. *The Structure of Language*, Englewood Cliffs, N. J.: Prentice-Hall, 1964.

Foote, Philippa. "Free Will as Involving Determinism," in Sidney Morgenbesser and James Walsh, eds., *Free Will*. Englewood Cliffs, N. J.: Prentice-Hall, 1962.

Freud, Sigmund. *The Interpretation of Dreams*, tr. by James Strachey. New York: Basic Books, 1961.

Gardner, Riley W., and Robert A. Schoen. "Differentiation and Abstraction in Concept Formation," *Psychological Monographs*, 76 (1962), no. 41.

Gasking, Douglas. "Causation and Recipes," *Mind*, 64 (1955), 479–487.

Gasking, D. A. T., and A. C. Jackson. "Wittgenstein as a Teacher," in Fann, *Ludwig Wittgenstein*.

Geach, Peter, and Max Black, eds. *Translations from the Philosophical Writings of Gottlob Frege*. Oxford: Basil Blackwell, 1952.

Gellner, Ernest. "The Entry of the Philosophers," *Times Literary Supplement*, (April 4, 1968), 347–349.

———. *Words and Things*. London: Victor Gollancz, 1959.

Gilbert, Allan, tr. *Machiavelli, The Chief Works and Others*. 3 vols. Durham: Duke University Press, 1965.

Gilbert, Felix. "On Machiavelli's Idea of Virtu," *Renaissance News*, IV (1951), 53–55, and V (1952), 21–23.

Gillispie, C. C. *The Edge of Objectivity*. Princeton: Princeton University Press, 1960.

Goldstein, Kurt. "The Problem of the Meaning of Words Based Upon Observation of Aphasic Patients," *Journal of Psychology*, 2 (1936), 301–316.

Goldstein, Leon J. "The Phenomenological and Naturalistic Approaches to the Social," in Natanson.

Goodman, Paul. *Growing Up Absurd*. New York: Random House, 1962.

Gunnell, John. "Social Science and Political Reality: The Problem of Explanation," *Social Research*, 35 (Spring 1968), 159–201.

Gusdorf, Georges. *Speaking*, tr. by Paul T. Brockelman. Evanston, Ill.: Northwestern University Press, 1965.

Hall, Roland. "Excluders," in Caton.

Hallett, Garth, S. J. *Wittgenstein's Definition of Meaning as Use*. New York: Fordham University Press, 1967.

Hanson, N. R. "On the Symmetry Between Explanation and Prediction," *Philosophical Review*, 68 (1959), 349–358.

Hare, R. M., *et al.* "Symposium on the Nature of Analysis," *Journal of Philosophy*, 54 (November 1957), 741–766.

Hart, H. L. A. "The Ascription of Responsibility and Rights," in Flew, *Logic and Language*.

Hartnack, Justus. *Wittgenstein and Modern Philosophy*, tr. by Maurice Cranston. Garden City: Doubleday, 1965.

Harvey, O. J., David E. Hunt, and Harold M. Schroder. *Conceptual Systems and Personality Organization.* New York: John Wiley and Sons, 1961.

Haufmann, Eugenia, and Jacob Kasanin. "A Method for the Study of Concept Formation," *Journal of Psychology*, 3 (1937), 521–540.

Heidegger, Martin. *Existence and Being.* Chicago: Henry Regnery, 1968.

Heller, Erich. *The Artist's Journey into the Interior.* New York: Random House, 1959.

Henle, Paul, ed. *Language, Thought and Culture.* Ann Arbor: University of Michigan Press, 1965.

Hennis, Wilhelm. "Topik und Politik," in Robert H. Schmidt, ed., *Methoden der Politologie.* Darmstadt: Wissenschaftliche Buchgesellschaft, 1967.

Hester, Marcus B. *The Meaning of Poetic Metaphor.* The Hague and Paris: Mouton, 1967.

Hexter, J. H. "*Il Principe* and *lo Stato*," *Studies in the Renaissance*, IV (1957), 113–138.

———. "The Loom of Language," *American Historical Review*, LXIX (July 1964), 945–968.

Hobbes, Thomas. *Elements of Law*, ed. by Ferdinand Tönnies. Cambridge: Cambridge University Press, 1928.

———. *Leviathan*, ed. by Michael Oakeshott. Oxford: Basil Blackwell, 1957.

Hospers, John. "What is Explanation?" in Flew, *Essays.*

Hourani, George F. "Thrasymachus' Definition of Justice in Plato's *Republic*," *Phronesis*, VII (1962), 110–120.

Hudson, Donald. *Ludwig Wittgenstein.* Richmond, Va.: John Knox Press, 1968.

Humboldt, Wilhelm von. *Über die Verschiedenheit des menschlichen Sprachbaues*, ed. by A. F. Pott. Second edition. Berlin: S. Calvary, 1880.

Hume, David. "Of the Original Contract," in Barker.

Hunt, Earl B. *Concept Learning.* New York and London: John Wiley and Sons, 1962.

Kantor, Jacob Robert. *An Objective Psychology of Grammar.* Bloomington, Ind., and Evanston, Ill.: Principia Press, 1952.

Kasanin, J. S., ed. *Language and Thought in Schizophrenia.* New York: W. W. Norton, 1964.

Kaufmann, Walter, ed. *Existentialism from Dostoevsky to Sartre.* New York: Meridian Books, 1956.

Klausmeier, Herbert John, and Chester W. Harris, eds. *Analyses of Concept Learning.* New York: Academic Press, 1966.

Kreitzer, Donald J. "An Analysis of the Nature of Power," *Southwestern Social Science Quarterly*, 45 (March 1965), 375–383.

Kuhn, Thomas S. *The Structure of Scientific Revolutions. International Encyclopedia of Unified Science*, II, 2. Second edition. Chicago: University of Chicago Press, 1970.

Laffal, Julius. *Pathological and Normal Language.* New York: Atherton Press, 1965.

Lasswell, Harold. "Propaganda and Mass Insecurity," in A. H. Stanton and S. E. Perry, eds., *Personality and Political Crisis.* Glencoe, Ill.: Free Press, 1951.

Lazerowitz, Morris. *Structure of Metaphysics.* London: Routledge and Kegan Paul, 1955.

Lenneberg, Eric. "The Capacity for Language Acquisition," in Fodor and Katz, eds., *The Structure of Language.*

———, ed. *New Directions in the Study of Language.* Cambridge, Mass.: M.I.T. Press, 1966.

Leopold, Werner. "Semantic Learning in Infant Language," *Word*, IV (1948), 173–180.

————. *The Speech Development of a Bilingual Child*. Evanston and Chicago: Northwestern University Press, 1939–1949.

Lerner, Daniel, ed. *Cause and Effect*. New York: Free Press, 1965.

Levinson, Arnold. "Knowledge and Society," *Inquiry*, 9 (Summer 1966), 132–146.

Lewis, Morris Michael. *Infant Speech*. New York: Harcourt, Brace, 1936.

Linsky, Leonard, ed. *Semantics and the Philosophy of Language*. Urbana: University of Illinois Press, 1952.

Lipset, Seymour Martin. *Political Man*. Garden City: Doubleday, 1960.

Louch, A. R. *Explanation and Human Action*. Berkeley and Los Angeles: University of California Press, 1966.

Mabbott, J. B. "Punishment," *Mind*, XLVIII (1939), 152–167.

MacDougall, Robert. "The Child's Speech. IV. Word and Meaning," *Journal of Educational Psychology*, 4 (1913), 29–38.

Machiavelli, Niccolò. *The Prince and The Discourses*, tr. by Luigi Ricci. New York: Random House, 1940.

MacIntyre, Alasdair. "A Mistake about Causality in Social Science," in Peter Laslett and W. G. Runciman, eds., *Philosophy, Politics and Society* (Second Series). New York: Barnes and Noble, 1962.

MacIver, A. M. "Historical Explanation," in Flew, *Logic and Language*.

Madell, Geoffrey. "Action and Causal Explanation," *Mind*, LXXVI (1967), 38–48.

Malcolm, Norman. *Knowledge and Certainty*. Englewood Cliffs, N. J.: Prentice-Hall, 1963.

————. *Ludwig Wittgenstein: A Memoir*. London: Oxford University Press, 1962.

Mannheim, Karl. *Ideology and Utopia*, tr. by Louis Wirth and Edward Shils. New York: Harcourt, Brace, 1936.

March, James G. "The Power of Power," in David Easton, ed. *Varieties of Political Theory*. Englewood Cliffs, N. J.: Prentice-Hall, 1966.

Marcuse, Herbert. *One-Dimensional Man*. Boston: Beacon Press, 1968.

Mates, Benson. "On the Verification of Statements about Ordinary Language," in Chappell.

Mayo, Bernard. *Ethics and the Moral Life*. London: Macmillan, 1958.

Melden, A. I. *Free Action*. New York: Humanities Press, 1961.

Merelman, Richard M. "Learning and Legitimacy," *American Political Science Review*, LX (September 1966), 548–561.

Merleau-Ponty, Maurice. *In Praise of Philosophy*, tr. by John Wild and James M. Edie. Evanston, Ill.: Northwestern University Press, 1963.

Mill, John Stuart. *A System of Logic*. London: J. W. Parker, 1843.

Mills, C. Wright. *The Sociological Imagination*. New York: Oxford University Press, 1959.

Minogue, Kenneth. *The Liberal Mind*. New York: Random House, 1968.

Moore, G. E. "Wittgenstein's Lectures in 1930–1933," in Robert R. Ammerman, ed., *Classics of Analytic Philosophy*. New York: McGraw-Hill, 1965.

Morick, Harold, ed. *Wittgenstein and the Problem of Other Minds*. New York: McGraw-Hill, 1967.

Morris, Charles. *Signs, Language and Behavior*. New York: George Braziller, 1955.

Nadelman, Lorraine. "The Influence of Concreteness and Accessibility on

Concept-Thinking," *Psychological Reports Monograph Supplement*, 4 (1957).

Natanson, Maurice, ed. *Philosophy of the Social Sciences*. New York: Random House, 1963.

Nida, Eugene A. "Principles of Translation as Exemplified by Bible Translating," in Brower.

Nietzsche, Friedrich. *The Use and Abuse of History*. Indianapolis and New York: Bobbs-Merrill, 1957.

Oakeshott, Michael. *Rationalism in Politics and Other Essays*. New York: Basic Books, 1962.

Öhman, Susanne. *Wortinhalt und Weltbild*. Stockholm: Kungl. Boktryckeriet P. A. Norstedt & Söner, 1951.

Pap, Arthur. *Elements of Analytic Philosophy*. New York: Macmillan, 1949.

Passmore, John. "Explanation in Everyday Life, in Science, and in History," *History and Theory*, II (1962), 105–123.

Perry, Charner. "The Semantics of Political Science," *American Political Science Review*, XLIV (June 1950), 394–406.

Peters, R. S. *The Concept of Motivation*. New York: Humanities Press, 1958.

Piaget, Jean. *The Moral Judgment of the Child*, tr. by Marjorie Gabain. New York: Collier Books, 1962.

Pitcher, George, ed. *Wittgenstein: The Philosophical Investigations*. Garden City: Doubleday, 1966.

Pitkin, Hanna Fenichel. *The Concept of Representation*. Berkeley and Los Angeles: University of California Press, 1967.

―――. "Obligation and Consent," *American Political Science Review*, LIX (December 1965), 990–999, and LX (March 1966), 39–52.

Plato, *The Dialogues of Plato*, tr. by B. Jowett. Two volumes. New York: Random House, 1937.

Podell, Harriett Amster. "Two Processes of Concept Formation," *Psychological Monographs*, 72 (1958), No. 15.

Polanyi, Michael. *Personal Knowledge*. New York and Evanston: Harper & Row, 1964.

Pole, David. *The Later Philosophy of Wittgenstein*. London: University of London, The Athlone Press, 1963.

Quine, Willard van Orman. *Word and Object*. Cambridge, Mass.: M.I.T. Press, 1960.

Quinton, Anthony. "On Punishment," in Peter Laslett, ed., *Philosophy, Politics and Society*. New York: Macmillan, 1956.

Rabin, L. "Linguistics of Translation," in *Aspects of Translation* (Studies in Communication No. 2). London: University College Communications Research Center, 1958.

Rawls, John. "Two Concepts of Rules," *Philosophical Review*, LXIV (January 1955), 3–32.

Reed, Homer B. "Factors Influencing the Learning and Retention of Concepts," *Journal of Experimental Psychology*, 36 (1946), 71–87, 166–179, 252–261.

Rieff, Philip. *Freud, the Mind of the Moralist*. New York: Viking Press, 1959.

Riker, William H. "Some Ambiguities in the Notion of Power," *American Political Science Review*, LVIII (June 1964), 341–349.

Rousseau, Jean-Jacques. *The Social Contract*, in Barker.

Russell, Bertrand. *A History of Western Philosophy*. New York: Simon and Schuster, 1945.

Ryle, Gilbert. "Categories," in Flew, *Logic and Language*.

————. *The Concept of Mind*. New York: Barnes and Noble, 1949.

————. *Dilemmas*. Cambridge: Cambridge University Press, 1966.

————. "Ordinary Language," in Chappell.

————. "The Theory of Meaning," in Caton.

Sapir, Edward. *Language*. New York: Harcourt, Brace & World, 1949.

Sartre, Jean-Paul. "Existentialism is a Humanism," in Kaufmann.

————. "An Explication of *The Stranger*," in Germaine Brée, ed., *Camus*. Englewood Cliffs, N. J.: Prentice-Hall, 1962.

Schaar, John H. "Reflections on Authority," *New American Review*, 8 (1970), 44–80.

Schulz, Walter. *Wittgenstein. Die Negation der Philosophie*. Stuttgart: Günter Neske Pfullingen, 1967.

Schutz, Alfred. *Collected Papers*, ed. by Maurice Natanson. The Hague: M. Nijhoff, 1962–1966.

————. "Concept and Theory Formation in the Social Sciences," in Natanson.

————. *The Phenomenology of the Social World*, tr. by George Walsh and Frederick Lehnert. Evanston: Northwestern University Press, 1967.

Searle, John. "How to Derive 'Ought' from 'Is,' " *Philosophical Review*, LXXIII (January 1964), 43–58.

————. *Speech Acts*. Cambridge: Cambridge University Press, 1969.

Segerstedt, Torgny T. *Die Macht des Wortes*. Zürich: Pan-Verlag, 1947.

Sesonske, Alexander. " 'Cognitive' and 'Normative,' " *Philosophy and Phenomenological Research*, XVII (September 1956), 1–21.

————. *Value and Obligation*. New York: Oxford University Press, 1964.

Shibles, Warren. *Wittgenstein, Language and Philosophy*. Dubuque: William C. Brown, 1969.

Shipstone, Eva I. "Some Variables Affecting Pattern Conception," *Psychological Monographs: General and Applied*, 74 (1960) No. 17, Whole No. 504.

Smith, Norman Kemp, ed. and tr., *Descartes Philosophical Writings*. New York: Random House, 1958.

Smoke, Kenneth. "Negative Instances in Concept Learning," *Journal of Experimental Psychology*, 16 (1933), 583–588.

————. "An Objective Study of Concept Formation," *Psychological Monographs*, XLII (1932), Whole No. 191.

Specht, Ernst Konrad. *Sprache und Sein*. Berlin: Walter de Gruyter, 1967.

————. "Die sprachphilosophischen und ontologischen Grundlagen im Spätwerk Ludwig Wittgensteins," *Kantstudien Ergänzungshefte*, 84 (1963).

Stern, Clara and William. *Kindersprache*. Darmstadt: Wissenschaftliche Buchgesellschaft, 1965.

Stevenson, Charles L. *Ethics and Language*. New Haven: Yale University Press, 1960.

Strauss, Leo. "An Epilogue," in Herbert J. Storing, ed. *Essays on the Scientific Study of Politics*. New York: Holt, Rinehart and Winston, 1962.

————. *Natural Right and History*. Chicago: University of Chicago Press, 1959.

Strawson, P. F. "Review of Wittgenstein's *Philosophical Investigations*," in Pitcher.

Taylor, Charles. *The Explanation of Behaviour*. New York: Humanities Press, 1967.

Taylor, Richard. *Action and Purpose*. Englewood Cliffs, N. J.: Prentice-Hall, 1966.

Tocqueville, Alexis de. *Democracy in America*, tr. by Henry Reeve. New York: Schocken Books, 1961.

Toulmin, Stephen. "Ludwig Wittgenstein," *Encounter*, XXXII (January 1969), 58–71.

———. *The Uses of Argument*. London and New York: Cambridge University Press, 1958.

Turbayne, Colin Murray. *The Myth of Metaphor*. New Haven: Yale University Press, 1962.

Tussman, Joseph. *Obligation and the Body Politic*. New York: Oxford University Press, 1960.

Ullmann, Stephen. *Semantics*. Oxford: Basil Blackwell, 1962.

Van Peursen, C. A. "Edmund Husserl and Ludwig Wittgenstein," *Philosophy and Phenomenological Research*, XX (December 1959), 181–197.

Voegelin, Eric. *The New Science of Politics*. Chicago: University of Chicago Press, 1952.

Vygotsky, Lev Semenovich. *Thought and Language*, ed. and tr. by Eugenia Haufmann and Gertrude Vakar. Cambridge, Mass.: M.I.T. Press, 1966.

Waismann, Friedrich. "How I See Philosophy," in H. D. Lewis, ed., *Contemporary British Philosophy* (Third Series). New York: Macmillan, 1956.

———. "Language Strata," in Flew, *Logic and Language*.

———. *Principles of Linguistic Philosophy*, ed. by R. Harré. New York: St. Martin's Press, 1965.

———. "Verifiability," in Flew, *Logic and Language*.

———. *Wittgenstein und der Wiener Kreis*, ed. by B. F. McGuinness. London: Basil Blackwell, 1967.

Wallace, J. G. *Concept Growth and the Education of the Child*. National Foundation for Educational Research in England and Wales, Occasional Publication Series No. 12 (1965).

Warnock, G. J. " 'Every Event Has a Cause,' " in Flew, *Logic and Language*.

Weber, Max. *Basic Concepts in Sociology*, tr. by H. P. Secher. New York: Citadel Press, 1962.

———. "Politics as a Vocation," in H. H. Gerth and C. Wright Mills, trs. and eds., *From Max Weber*. New York: Galaxy, Oxford University Press, 1958.

———. "Politik als Beruf," in Johannes Winckelmann, ed., *Gesammelte Politische Schriften*. Tübingen: J. C. B. Mohr (Paul Siebeck), 1958.

———. *The Theory of Social and Economic Organization*, tr. by A. R. Henderson and Talcott Parsons, ed. by Talcott Parsons. London: William Hodge, 1947.

Weisgerber, Leo. *Vom Weltbild der Deutschen Sprache*. Düsseldorf: Pädagogischer Verlag Schwann, 1950.

Weldon, T. D. *The Vocabulary of Politics*. Harmondsworth: Penguin Books, 1955.

Wheelwright, Philip. *Metaphor and Reality*. Bloomington: Indiana University Press, 1962.

Whitfield, J. H. *Machiavelli*. New York: Russell and Russell, 1965.

Whorf, Benjamin Lee. *Language, Thought, and Reality*, ed. by John B. Carroll. Cambridge, Mass.: M.I.T. Press, 1967.

Winch, Peter. *The Idea of a Social Science and Its Relation to Philosophy*, ed. by R. F. Holland. New York: Humanities Press, 1965.

———. "Understanding a Primitive Society," *American Philosophical Quarterly*, I (October 1964), 307–324.

Wisdom, John. "Ludwig Wittgenstein, 1934–1937," in Fann, *Ludwig Wittgenstein*.

———. *Other Minds*. Berkeley and Los Angeles: University of California Press, 1968.

———. *Paradox and Discovery*. Oxford: Basil Blackwell, 1965.

————. *Philosophy and Psycho-Analysis.* New York: Philosophical Library, 1953.

————. *Problems of Mind and Matter.* Cambridge: Cambridge University Press, 1963.

Wittgenstein, Ludwig. "Bemerkungen über Frazers *The Golden Bough,*" *Synthese,* 17 (1967), 233–253.

————. *Lectures and Conversations on Aesthetics, Psychology and Religious Belief,* ed. by Cyril Barrett, compiled from notes taken by Yorick Smythies, Rush Rhees and James Taylor. Berkeley and Los Angeles: University of California Press, 1967.

————. *Notebooks 1914–1916,* tr. by G. E. M. Anscombe. Oxford: Basil Blackwell, 1961.

————. *On Certainty,* tr. by Denis Paul and G. E. M. Anscombe, ed. by G. E. M. Anscombe and G. H. von Wright. New York and Evanston: Harper & Row, 1969.

————. *Philosophical Investigations,* tr. by G. E. M. Anscombe. Third edition. New York: Macmillan, 1968.

————. *Philosophische Bemerkungen,* ed. by Rush Rhees. Oxford: Basil Blackwell, 1964.

————. *Preliminary Studies for the 'Philosophical Investigations,' Generally Known as The Blue and Brown Books.* New York and Evanston: Harper & Row, 1964.

————. *Remarks on the Foundations of Mathematics,* tr. by G. E. M. Anscombe, ed. by G. H. von Wright, R. Rhees, and G. E. M. Anscombe. Oxford: Basil Blackwell, 1964.

————. *Tractatus Logico-Philosophicus,* tr. by D. F. Pears and B. F. McGuinness. New York: Humanities Press, 1961.

————. "Wittgenstein's Notes for Lectures on Private Experience and 'Sense Data,' " with notes by Rush Rhees, *Philosophical Review,* 77 (July 1968), 271-320.

————. *Zettel,* tr. by G. E. M. Anscombe, ed. by G. E. M. Anscombe and G. H. von Wright. Berkeley and Los Angeles: University of California Press, 1967.

Wolin, Sheldon S. *Hobbes.* Los Angeles: William Andrews Clark Memorial Library, University of California, 1970.

————. "Political Theory: II. Trends and Goals," *International Encyclopedia of the Social Sciences,* 1968, vol. 12, pp. 318-329.

————. "Political Theory as a Vocation," *American Political Science Review,* LXIII (December 1969), 1062-1082.

————. *Politics and Vision.* Boston and Toronto: Little, Brown, 1960.

Ziff, Paul. *Semantic Analysis.* Ithaca, N. Y.: Cornell University Press, 1960.

# INDEX

Action: speech as, 3–4, 13, 24, 34–45,
48, 82, 88, 95–96, 113, 132, 138–139,
196, 201, 224, 228–229, 287, 325,
330, 335; "normal," 13–14, 327; capacity for, 22–23, 191–192, 317–318,
322, 328–329, 333–334, 339–340;
mental, **65–76**, 140, 296; concept of,
69, 88–89, 149, 151n, **157–168**, 189,
192, 228–229; knowledge of, 115,
154–155, 184, 223, 225, 231, 236–
237, 321, 324; as language region,
147–148, 150, **157–168**, 326; and politics, 158, 204–214, 217–218, 285–286,
300–301, 311, 328–332; and social
science, **241–274**, 277, 279
Actor: perspective of, 148, 273, 286,
323; as agent in action, 154, 159, 164–
165, 265–266, 268, 272; as knowing
own action, 163, 172, 242–261 *passim*
Alienation, 151, 317–318, 324, 328–329,
334–335, 337
"All of it," 76–79, 82
Analysis, logical, 28–29, 42, 225, 266
Anger: concept of, 109–110, 125–126,
129, 131, 133–134, 167–168, 187,
220, 324; and rationality, 153, 286,
330; in Aristotle, 173
Anscombe, G. E. M., 5, 225–226
Anxiety, 108, 273, 332–333
Approval, 222–225, 232–233, 235
Aquinas, St. Thomas, viii
Arendt, Hannah: on world, 113; on
facts, 144, 329, 331; on action, 149,
154–155, 158–161, 165, 197; on language membership, 195; on the political, 208–217, 285, 329–330; on social
science, 241–243; on power, 277; on
truth, 340

Aristotle: as philosopher, viii, 299; on
language, 30, 173; on physics, 107–
108, 111–112; on logic, 142; on
action, 150; on politics, 211, 215, 217,
328, 330
Art. *See* Beauty; Esthetics.
Assertion. *See* Proposition
Augustine, St.: as philosopher, viii; on
language, 31–33, 35–36, 39, 42–43;
on time, 292–293
Austin, J. L.: as philosopher, vii, ix, 5,
18, 94, 120, 194, 204, 320; analytic
technique, 9, 14–17, 164, 214, 218,
265, 268–269, 275–276, 278; on language, 10, 13–14, 82, 135, 188, 220;
on performatives, 37–39, 88, 94–95;
and phenomenology, 120, 320; on
anger, 129, 134; on excuses, 149–151,
154, 166, 234
Authenticity, xi, 23, 318, 332–333
Authority: and power, 9, 231, 277–278,
301; in speech, 58, 88; identification
of in world, 108, 110, 259; political,
193, 198, 203–206, 211–212, 259,
281, 311; and legitimacy, 280–281;
yearning for, 333
Ayer, A. J., 221–222
Azande, 247–250, 260

Barker, Sir Ernest, 306
Barth, Karl, 171
Beauty: and ugliness, 12–13; in *Tractatus*, 29–30; learning about, 108–109,
175; judgment of, 170–171, 180, 220–
225, 232–234; and philosophy, 183
Bentham, Jeremy, 299
*Blue and Brown Books, The* (Wittgenstein), 18, 26, 89, 126, 132

Buber, Martin, 155
Burke, Edmund, 8, 299

Camus, Albert, 318–319, 321, 324, 329, 333
Cassirer, Ernst, 34
Causation: and causal laws, 3, 161–162, 193, 197–198, 213, 333; concept of, 6, 264, 267–273; and freedom, 13, 321–323; and explanation, 148, 158–165, 242–243, 252–254, 261, 264–274, 285–286, 326; by an actor, 159, 165, 263, 265–266; and religion, 250, 258
Cavell, Stanley: as philosopher, vii–ix, xiii, 318; on Wittgenstein, xi, 2, 5, 62, 116, 118–119, 318, 335; on knowledge, 16, 62, 96, 98, 113, 116, 277, 335, 340; on action, rules, 19, 133, 228–229, 333, 338, 340; on language-learning, 33–36, 39, 43, 49, 58, 108–110, 112; on grammar, 61–64, 83, 97, 118–119, 133, 260; on mental activities, 72, 74–75; on making sense, 76–79; on ethics, rationality, 146, 149, 151–156, 166, 168, 204, 207, 239, 306; on esthetics, 232–235; on science, 290, 292–296
Cephalus, 307
"Chair," 62, 117–119, 133, 135–136
Change. See Innovation
Char, René, 318
Chisholm, Roderick M., 262
Chomsky, Noam, 5, 44, 58
Cicero, 292
Circumstances. See Context
City, language as a, viii, x–xi, 140, 146
Collingwood, R. G., 247
Color: system, 11, 103, 123–125, 134; pointing to, 31–32, 43, 75–76, 80, 101, 122; seeing, 111, 128, 320; concept of, 111, 121, 145, 181–182, 189, 235, 281
Commitment: and rationality, 23, 225, 285, 322; entailed in speaking, 39, 67, 72, 88, 98, 179–180, 225, 227–228, 237, 261, 280–282, 329, 339; and morality, 151, 155, 205–207, 209, 216, 306; and action, 205, 273, 318, 324, 333–335
Common law, 50–51, 53, 55, 60
Common sense: and philosophy, 8, 19–20, 93; and science, 231, 240, 318–319; in Machiavelli, 312
Composition, principle of, 58–60
Conceptual puzzlement, insight: nature of, 4–21, 85–98, 116–117, 125–126, 129, 134, 190, 256, 261, 287–302,

314; and language regions, 182, 187, 192
Connotation and denotation, 174
Conservatism, political, 138, 201, 203, 285, 300, 326, 328
Contemplation: in philosophy, 6, 8, 93–98, 287, 292, 300; in science, 107, 111; in poetry, 142
Context: completes meaning, 38, 66, 69–70, 71–98, 100–101, 119, 149, 260, 270–271, 287, 327; projection into new, 49, 58, 61–63, 65, 78, 80, 135–136, 194; of language-learning, 56–58, 60, 120, 175–176; and circumstances of action, feelings, 71–76, 130–132, 134, 137–138, 165, 245, 256; for modal imperatives, 229–230
Contradiction: and conceptual puzzlement, 6, 19–20, 61, 85, 90–93, 129–130, 261, 287, 289–290, 297, 302; in grammar of concepts, 85, 87–93, 98–99, 275, 294, 338; in "knowledge," 87–93; in "permanence," 95; in "world," 100, 111–113, 328; in "anger," "pain," 129–130; in Azande witchcraft, 248–249; in action, 261, 266, 273; in "representation," 314–315; in politics, 325–326, 328
Convention: in language, 122–125, 127–128, 132–138, 168, 293, 320–321, 334–338; and action, 160–161, 320–321; and society, 198–199, 204. See also Forms of life
Copernicus, Nicolaus, 317
"Corpse" and "cadaver," 99–101, 114, 258
Criteria, 116, **126–132**, 136–137

Dahl, Robert: on justice, 177–178; on politics, 209, 212; on power, 278–279
Darwin, Charles, 317
Definition: and philosophy, 9, 19, 87, 89–90, 92, 98, 173, 313; and redefinition for social science, 20, 264, **274–286**, 327; and truth, 28–29, 99–139 passim, 182, 220; ostensive, 31–35, 40, 43, 47; in language-learning, 45, 47–48, 55, 60, 62, 136; dependence on how we use, 54, 69, 136, 141, 229; as meaning, 80; Socratic, 170, 174; physical and dialectical, 173; of actions, 242, 244–247, 253–254, 256–259; operational 275–276, 280, 283; of man, 324
"Delicious," 181–182, 189, 219, 221, 224–225, 233, 281
Democracy, 206, 208, 211–212, 214–215, 282–283, 303–304
Descartes, René, viii, 93–94, 96

Descriptive. *See* Dichotomization; Normative

Determinism. *See* Necessity

Deviant. *See* Odd

Diagnoses, Wittgenstein's, 89, 93, 116, 287–288

Dialectic: Socratic, xi, 23, 173, 331; Wittgensteinian, 22–23, 114, 116, 313–315, 324; and physical definition, 173

Dichotomization: between normative, descriptive, 13, 22, 177, 219–221, 228–231, 236, 262, 281, 283; tendency toward, 13–14, 277; between fact, value, 22, 219–221, 225, 228–231, 235–236, 240, 262, 302

Disease, philosophy as, xii, 91, 288–290, 295–296, 298

Duck-rabbit. *See* Picture puzzle

Durkheim, Émile, 171

Easton, David, 209, 212, 216

Einstein, Albert, 293, 317, 336

Elite: of experts, 144, 205–206, 238; ruling, in society, 169–171, 174–176, 179–180, 191, 206, 209, 212

Emmet, Dorothy, 276

Engels, Friedrich, 197, 322

Essence: in language-learning, 36, 45, 47, 49, 58; of language, 42, 63; of games, 63–64; in conceptual puzzlement, 84, 91, 117; expressed by grammar, 117; of language region, 147; and existence, 320, 324

Esthetics: in *Tractatus*, 29–30, 120, 336; as language region, 144, 146, 186; judgment in, 146, 186, 221, 223–225, 231–240 *passim*; of conceptualization, 294, 297, 338. *See also* Beauty

Ethics: in *Tractatus*, 29–30, 120, 336; as language region, 143, 186; and excuses, 150; limitations of, 151; judgment in, 186, 221, 231, 235–237, 240; and social science, 253; element in *dikaiosyne*, 306; moralism in, 327–328. *See also* Morality

Etymology, 10–11, 209, 276, 280, 309–310

Evans-Pritchard, E. E., 247–249

Excuses, 17, 149–152, 154, 165–167, 194

Existentialism, 22, 317–318, 323, 332–334

Expecting, 65–66, 72, 74, 80, 126, 131–132, 163, 256, 335

Explanation: and training, 35, 43–45, 48–49, 80; of meaning, sense, 35, 41, 60, 77–78, 186; must come to an end,

40, 138; and knowledge, 85; causal and purposive, 158, 162–164, 167, 242–243, 250–252, 254, 261–263, **264–273**, 274, 285, 323, 326; in Azande witchcraft, 248

Extrapolation. *See* Generalization

Facts: and values, 22, 172, 182–185, 199, 219–240 *passim*, 262, 275, 302; and actions, 37–38, 156, 270–271; in common law, 51; structured by language, 87, 101–103, 105, 111, 177–178, 273, 280, 288, 296, 317, 334; and historical knowledge, 144–145, 329, 331–332; brute, 167, 225–226, 321, 333; institutional, 226; and philosophy, 292, 294, 296; and theory, 300

Falsification, 28–29, 97, 231

Family resemblance, 61, 64–65

Fanon, Frantz, 106

Fear: concept of, 109–110, 122, 135, 164, 255, 261; in Machiavelli, 311; of self-knowledge, 337

Feeling: knowledge of, 6, 115, 125–132, 134, 137–138, 192, 320, 324, 330, 338; and reason, judgment, 22, 88, 221, 223, 225, 235, 237, 286; expression of, 45, 129–132, 134–135, 137–138, 261; in speech context, 49, 56–57, 81, 95, 153, 155; and mental activities, 66, 68, 72, 74–75, 129–132, 134, 137–138, 140, 245, 324, 335; grammar of, 145, 182; in *Tractatus*, 336

Feuerbach, Ludwig, 172, 339–340

Fodor, Jerry A., 5

Form and substance, **186–192**, 213–214, 227, 257, 284, 299–300

Forms of life: and language, 36, 42, 49, **132–139**, 272; Wittgenstein's conception of, 49, **132–139**, 140, 147, 272, 324, 335, 338, 340; individual variations in, 78, 109, 293–294; and mathematics, 145, 238; and philosophy, 227, 287–288, 293–294, 298, 335

Freedom: and rules, 3, 194, 197, 199–204, 217; concept of, 7, 10–11, 138, 299; and causation, 13, 23, 83, 157, 163, 242, 266–267, 270–273, 333; political, 53, 200–204, 210–211, 212, 215, 217, 326, 329, 332; philosophy as aid to, 250, 289, 298, 337–339; in modern condition, 317, 322, 337–339. *See also* Causation; Necessity

Frege, Gottlob, 178

Freud, Sigmund: and Wittgenstein, xi–xii, 317, 336–337, 339; on dreams,

28n; on psychoanalytic explanation, 251; on anxiety, 273
Function: concept of, 57–58, 60, 109; in *Republic*, 302, 307

Galileo Galilei, 107–108, 111–112, 318
Game: concept of, 9, 63–65, 70, 75, 95, 297; as analogue to language, 36–37, 63–64; and rules, 46, 52, 81, 90, 166, 188–189, 228–229. *See also* Language games
Generalization: language and capacity for, 43–49 *passim*, 56–63 *passim*, 78, 89, 92; and conceptual puzzlement, 89–93, 95, 132, 187, 190, 270–271, 287, 314, 318, 325–326
Gilbert, Allan, 311–312
Goldstein, Leon J., 273
"Good": grammar of, 11–13, 183, 223; meaning of, 11–12, 17, 222–223; in dichotomization, 12–13, 294; in *Tractatus*, 29–30; as subjective "value term," 170, 221; as objective judgment, 171, 220–224, 232–235
Goodman, Paul, 337
Grammar: as taught in school, 18, 53, 104, 141; contradictions in, 69, 78, 87–89, 91–92, 94–98, 99, 112, 194, 214–215, 222, 227–230, 267, 275, 284, 292–294, 339; and world, 80, 83, 96–97, **116–139**, 146, 157, 195, 199, 287–288, 296, 298, 314, 320, 335; of "knowledge," 87–89, 94–98, 339; connections in, 119, 208, 260–261, 280, 323; and language regions, 140–141, 146–147, 157, 164–165, 168, 222, 227–230, 233–234, 236, 241, 272; of "justice," 176, 178, 180, 186–188, 191
Gunnell, John G., 162, 244, 252, 265

Hannibal, 308, 310, 312
Heidegger, Martin, vii, 2–3
Hegel, Georg Wilhelm Friedrich, vii, 109, 317, 338
Heller, Erich, vii–viii, x, xi
Henle, Paul, 103
Hennis, Wilhelm, 332
Hertz, Heinrich, 90n
Hexter, J. H., 309–310
Hobbes, Thomas, 299, 313
Hudson, W. Donald, 148
Humboldt, Wilhelm von, 102
Hume, David, 219, 225, 297

Idealism: philosophical, 120; legal, 171; political, 209, 211
Imperatives, 222, 229–231
Inconsistency. *See* Contradiction

Individuality, 3, **193–218**, 285–286, 328, 330. *See also* Membership; Person
Induction, 33–34, 49, 56, 58
Influence: and power, authority, 9, 277–279; magical, 249
Innovation: in language, 3, 44–45, 49, 58, 61–63, 65, 78, 80, 113, 121, 134–138, 141, 194, 196–198, 201–202, 222, 271–272, 293, 298; in science, 54, 290–293, 298; in morality, 150–152, 206, 335; in culture, 188–189, 193; in politics, 202–203, 207, 211, 299–300, 337–340; in philosophy, theory, 292–300 *passim*, 325, 337–340
Instrument. *See* Tool
Intention: in promising, 38, 88; as mental activity, 47–49, 65, 67, 69–70, 73–74; and point of speech, 77–79, 82–85, 93–98 *passim*; in action, 149, 158, 160–168 *passim*, 172, 189, 197, 242, 244–245, 254–259, 261, 264–265, 268–269, 324; in "justice," 179; in politics, 201; in political theory, 300
"Is." *See* "Ought"

Justice: and fairness, 11, 103–104; concept of, 153n, **169–192**, 219, 229, 261, 273, 281, 299, 322; in *Republic*, **169–192**, 219, 229, 261, 302–307, 326; divine, 208; learned in politics, 215, 217, 328; as "value word," 221–222, 224–225, 275

Kant, Immanuel: as philosopher, viii, 7; on transcendental knowledge, 120; on morality, 150, 155, 273; on esthetics, 232–234
Katz, Jerrold J., 5
Kaufmann, Walter, 332
Kierkegaard, Søren, viii, 151, 273, 318
Kluckhohn, Clyde, 104
Knowledge: of persons, self, xi, 154–156, 208, 236, 267, 286, 334, 336–337, 339; of feelings, 6, 115, 125–132, 134, 137–138, 192, 320, 324, 330, 338; of language, 7–9, 14–16, 33–34, 48, 56–57, 80, 109–110; concept of, 11, 13, 19, 70, **85–89**, 93–98, 117–118, 126, 138, 155, 167, 187, 191, 225, 228, 239, 258, 263, 293, 308, 339; philosophy not from new, 20, 92, 292, 294–295; of world and language, 32–36, 106–115, 117, 119–120, 135–136, 319, 335–336; of actions, 154–156, 165–168, 207, 245, 254, 256, 258–259, 267, 272, 286, 323; political, 208; and judgment, 231,

233–234; modern scientific, 316, 318–320, 322

Kuhn, Thomas S.: on science as activity, 50, 53–54, 144, 290–291, 325; on paradigms, 53–54, 107, 111, 290–291; on world of scientist, 106–108, 111–112, 271; on philosophizing in science, 290–291

Labels. *See* Reference

Language: and philosophy, xii, 6–9, 85–98 *passim*, 287–298 *passim*; contemporary interest in, 2–3, 5, 193; as activity, 3–4, 24, 34–45, 48, 132, 138–139, 196, 200; innovation in, 3, 44–45, 49, 58, 61–63, 65, 78, 80, 113, 121, 134–138, 141, 194, 196–198, 201–202, 222, 271–272, 293, 298; Wittgenstein's two visions of, 3–4, **24–49**; regions, 4, **140–149**, 157, 164–165, 168, 182, 187, 239–240, 241, 246–247, 249, 252, 254, 257, 267, 297; knowledge of, 7–9, 14–16, 33–34, 48, 56–57, 80, 109–110; as system, 11–12, 14–16, 58–60; as analogue of games, 36–37, 63–64; primitive, 39–40, 42

Language games: in language learning, 35, 39–49, 50, 80; concept of, **39–49**; and mental activities, 66–73; as context in which word is at home, 76, 93, 98; as shaping meaning, 84, 91, 103, 112, 114, 122; and "knowledge," 88–89; and colors, 124–125; and forms of life, 132–139 *passim*, 147, 335; and language regions, 140, 142, 149; and action, 164–165, 167, 255, 261, 263, 272, 274; and "justice," 181–182, 189; and esthetics, 224

Language-learning, 3, 31–70 *passim*, 80–83, 108–111, 120, 137, 175–176, 186, 200, 203

Lavoisier, Antoine Laurent, 108

Legitimacy, 275–276, **280–284**, 301, 313, 327

Leighton, Dorothea, 104

Length, 60–61, 97, 123–124, 149, 222

Limits: of language, 29–30, 121, 288–289, 294, 296, 298; of a concept, 61, 89, 141; of morality, 150–152; of our humanity, 227, 288, 293–294, 298, 318, 335, 337; of political obligation, 301

Linguistics, 2, 4, 5, 7, 8, 11, 14, 102–109, 196–197

Locke, John, viii, 299

Logic: in *Tractatus*, 5, 28–30, 42, 89–90, 121, 337; and pragmatics, 82–83, 266; and paradox, 87; constraints of,

120–122, 208, 252, 254, 262, 280, 314, 323; and language regions, 141–143, 146, 148, 152, 162

Logical Positivism. *See* Positivism

Louch, A. R., 161, 241, 252–253, 262

Love: concept of, 70n, 108–110; and commitment, 108–110, 320, 322; and morality, 151; in other cultures, 246, 251, 308, 311

Machiavelli, Niccolò, 299, 308–312

Madell, Geoffrey, 261–262

Malcolm, Norman, 5

Mannheim, Karl, 21

Marx, Karl: and Wittgenstein, 22, 122, 317, 324, 336–337, 339–340; Marxism, 170–171; on justice, 171, 191; on history, 197; as political theorist, 299, 321, 326

Mates, Benson, 81, 83, 85

Mathematics: as ideal calculus, vii, 61, 90, 337; *Remarks on the Foundations of* (Wittgenstein), 26, 238–240; as language region, 29, 141, 143–146, 153, 235, 237–239, 303; and forms of life, 42, 74, 145, 235, 237–239; series games, 45–49, 66–67, 72–74, 89

Meaning: and reference, 3–4, 27, 31, 39–41, 45, 111; knowledge of, 7, 16, 35–36, 45–47; in ordinary-language philosophy, 9–13, 100, 278; and sense, **12n**, 28–29, **79–80**, 93, 289, 321, 336; and language-learning, 35–47 *passim*, 50–70 *passim*; and use, 36, 39–43, 47–49, 56, 66, 70–72, 76, **80–85**, 92, 98, 173–177, 179–191, 213, 222, 261, 299–300, 336; and context, 38, 66, 69–70, **71–98**, 100–101, 119, 149, 260, 270–271, 287, 327; as mental activity, 49, 65, 67–70, 71, 73, 75–76, 117–119, 167; and translation, 104, 176, 181–185, 259–261; and language regions, 164–165; and meaningfulness, 324, 328, 330, 334, 336. *See also* Definition

Measurement, 61, 123–124, 134, 148–149

Melden, A. I., 159, 162, 321

Membership, 3, 168, 192, **193–218**

Mental Activities. *See* Action, mental

Merleau-Ponty, Maurice, 197

Metaphysics: Wittgenstein on, 19, 29–30, 289, 317–318, 325; our implicit, 21–22, 219; and knowledge, 86, 175

Method. *See* Technique

Mills, C. Wright, 285

Misuse, 18–19, 46

Modal imperatives. *See* Imperatives

Moore, G. E., 26

Moral Discourse, **149–157**; rationality in, 146, 152–157, 230–231, 234–236, 239; and action, 158, 165–168, 211; and knowledge, 166–168, 256, 269; and political discourse, 204–208, 216–217

Morality: Oakeshott on, 50, 52–53, 55, 60; principles of, 50, 52–53, 149–151, 155, 230–231, 284; internalization of, 52–53, 201–203; and responsibility, 149, 157, 252, 262, 269, 333, 335; innovation in, 150–152, 207, 335; not public, 150, 158, 205–206, 208, 217, 307; limits of, 151–152; and persons, 207–208, 211, 216–217, 321; Machiavelli on, 308–310, 312; and moralism, 327–328, 334. *See also* Ethics

Motives: and grammar, 81, 141, 229; and explanation of action, 158, 162–163, 166, 172, 198, 242, 245, 251–252, 264–266, 268–269; unconscious, 251, 254, 322–323

"Must," 228–231, 233, 238–239. *See also* Imperatives

Names. *See* Reference

Natanson, Maurice, 241

Nature: human, 1, 102, 119, 122, 124–125, 133, 138, 227, 292–294, 334, 336, 338; concept of, 9–10; and capacity for language, 32, 48–49, 58; and action, 115, 155–161, 168, 197, 210–211, 213, 226, 253, 262, 322; and expression of feeling, 131, 134–135, 137–138, 261; natural law, 171, 198, 322, 327; natural selection in language, 196; and social contract, 198–200

Necessity: and forms of life, 133–139 *passim*, 272, 288, 293–294, 298, 335–340 *passim*; causal, and action, 210–211, 213, 264, 266–267, 270–272, 322–323, 327

Neurath, Otto, 297

Nida, Eugene A., 103

Nietzsche, Friedrich: and Wittgenstein, viii, 22, 122, 336, 338; on morality, 151; on rationality, 273; on self-alienation, 322

Normative, 152, 192, 253; and descriptive, 13, 22, 177, 219–221, 228–231, 236, 262, 281, 283. *See also* Dichotomization

Numbers: and language-learning, 31–33, 40–41; grammar of, 40–41, 182; in mathematical series games, 45–49, 66–67, 72–74; system of, 123–124. *See also* Mathematics

Oakeshott, Michael: on morality, 50, 51–54, 150, 152, 164, 325; on politics, 52, 201, 203; on language regions, 141–142, 152, 164

Obedience: and rules, 95–96, 202; and intention, 167, 244, 255–257, 261; political, 200, 280–283, 301

Objectivity: and commitment, 23, 93, 321–323; of the world, 101–103, 106–107, **109–115**, 320; and study of man, 167–168, 242, 254–263 *passim*, 268, 285–286, 320–329 *passim*; and language, 182–183, 194; and judgment, 191, 222–223, 236, 283; and language regions, 236, 240. *See also* Subjectivity

Obligation, 220, 222, 225–228, 230, 263, 280; political, 193, 198–200, 204, 301

Odd expression, 11, 14, 19, 184, 222–223, 307, 313

Ordinary-language philosophy, ix, xiii, 4–21, 81, 157, 169, 173, 179, 275, 301; and Wittgenstein, 5, 19–22, 122; vulgarization of, 19, 87, 90, 125, 226, 313; on morality, 149 ff, 327; on membership, 193 ff; on obligation, 225 ff

Ostensive definition. *See* Definition

"Ought," 177–178, 219–222, **225–231**, 235, 284. *See also* Imperatives

Overview. *See* Perspicuity

Oxford philosophy. *See* Ordinary-language philosophy

Pain, 110, 118, 121–138 *passim*, 148, 163, 219

Paradigm: in science, 53–54, 107, 111, 291; in language, 58n, 62, 87, 118, 147; and language regions, 148, 231, 235, 247; and action, 160, 162

Paradox. *See* Contradiction; Conceptual puzzlement

Pascal, Blaise, viii

Paul, St., 306

Performative, **37–39**, 71, 84, 88, 131, 262, 270. *See also* Quasi-performative

Permanence, 89, 95, 190–191

Perry, Charner, 164, 274

Person: treating as, 155, 186, 207, 208, 211, 216–217, 231, 272, 305–307, 322–324, 327; becoming a, 195, 199–200, 334; personal and public, 204–205, 285–286, 328; and determinism, 272; perceiving as, 320–322, 339

Perspective: in philosophy, 1, 21, 295–299; of action and explanation, 148, 273, 286; and objectivity, 195, 323, 337, 339; in politics, 206, 216–217, 326, 329. *See also* Seeing

Perspicuity, 92–93, 117, 238, 275, 292, 296, 299, 314–315, 326–328
Peters, R. S., 160, 162, 268–269
Phenomenology: and positivism in study of man, 4, 172, 273, 283, 285, 323–324; and Wittgenstein, 22, 317–318, 323–324, 334; and experience, 101, 111, 273, 285, 318–320, 323–324; and Austin, 120, 320
*Philosophical Investigations* (Wittgenstein), 26–27, 31, 63, 65, 90, 100, 294, 316
Piaget, Jean, 188–189
Picture: "holds us captive," xi, 91–92, 97, 168, 289–290, 336; language as, 3, 27, 30, 63, 116, 288, 296–298; of language, 31; puzzle, 100–101, 111, 295
Plato, 7, 143, 299; on language, 30; on knowledge, 85, 175, 292, 328, 331; on justice, 169, 302–307, 326; *Republic*, 169, 177, 216, 221, 302–307, 326; on politics, 216, 303, 305, 326, 328; on dialectic, 331
Poetry, viii, 76, 141–144, 224, 233, 298, 319
Pointing, 32–33, 39–40, 46, 72, 75–76, 80, 100–101, 122–123
Polanyi, Michael, 160, 272
Political science: and Wittgenstein, ordinary-language philosophy, ix, 20–23, 169, 218, 268; conception of political in, 20, 209, 211, 213–214; and positivism, 22, 219–220, 302; and science, 241–246, 253; definition in, 275–286. *See also* Social science
Political theory: and Wittgenstein, ordinary-language philosophy, 5, 169, 193, 218, **299–340**; conceptual problems in, 6, 20, 287; on social contract, 198 ff; conception of political in, 209 ff
Politics, the political: study of, ix, xiii, 4, 21–23, 99, 157, 221, 241–246, 254, 259, 274, 279, 284–285, 302, 313, 325–328; Wittgenstein on, 1, 201, 316; nature of, 4, 20, 115, 151, 168, 192–193, **198–218**, 242–243, 303, 305, 320, 328; as language region, 4, 144, 147, 153, 168, 186, 191, 193, **204–208**, 209, 216–217, 221, 235–237; Oakeshott on, 52, 201, 203; and rationality, 153, 186, 205–208, 235–237, 283, 285, 330–332; and action, 158, 204–214, 217–218, 242, 245, 277, 285–286, 300–301, 311, 328–332; elites, 169–171, 174–176, 179–180, 191, 206, 209, 212; membership, obligation, legitimacy, 193, 198–204, 280–

284, 301; culture, 201–204; plurality in, 206, 216–217, 303, 305, 326, 329; and contemporary problems, 316, 321–322, 328–334, 337–340
Positivism, 22, 25–26, 30, 97, 99, 152, 219, 231, 283, 332–333
Pragmatics, 80–81, 83–85
Pragmatism, 317
Power: concept of, 9–10, 21, **274–279**, 301; ". . . over," 10, 231, 276–279, 283, 301, 304, 308; ". . . to," 10, 230, 276–279, 309; as central to politics, 178, 209–212, 215–216; of society, 202, 213; and knowledge, 317, 319, 322
Prediction, 161, 252, 266–268, 273, 323
Principles. *See* Rules
Projection. *See* Innovation
Promise: as performative, 37, 72, 84, 88, 227; and knowledge, 88; and trust, risk, 108, 110, 149, 158, 164, 322; identification of, 148, 156, 166–168, 261, 274; and obligation to perform, 156, 166, 226–228, 230, 280; and political obligation, 198–199; and intention, 255
Proposition: as (not) model of all utterances, 3, 27–30, 37–39, 42–43, 49, 97, 141; and statement, assertion, 13; descriptive and normative, 22, 231, 238; elementary, 28–29; and rules, 228–229; as an action, 335
Psychoanalysis, xi, xii, 251, 283
Public: and private, 150, 158, 193, 205; interest, 198, 211–213; and political, 201, 204–205, 208–218, 277, 326, 329–332; issues, 285–286
Punishment, 40, 49, 186, **188**, 199, 299
Purpose: and action, 158, 160–163, 166, 242, 244–245, 264–265, 268–269; and institutionalization, 186–192. *See also* Intention; Motives

Quasi-performative, 39, 70, 262; and mental activities, 68, 71–72; and knowledge, 88, 96; and justice, 179, 182; and actions, 245, 261–262, 274; and social science, 274, 284; and legitimacy, 280
Quine, Willard van Orman, 106

Rabin, L., 104
Rationality: and objective judgment, 22–23, 219, 222, 236, 239–240, 283, 285, 316–317, 323, 336–337; and morality, 52, 153–154, 205–207, 211; in language regions, 52, 152–154, 222, 236, 239–240, 247, 331–332; in poli-

tics, 205–209, 211, 283, 285, 330–332
Rawls, John, 18
Reading, 65, 66, 72. *See also* Actions, mental
Realism. *See* Idealism; Objectivity
Reference, meaning as, 3–4, 24, 27–28, 30–35, 41–43, 45, 57, 59, 65–67, 69–70, 71, 73, 85, 87–88, 90, 93, 96, 99–100, 175–176, 180, 189, 191, 227–228, 261–263, 270, 275–277, 279, 281, 284
Regularities. *See* Rules
Religion: in *Tractatus*, 30, 120, 336; concepts in, 89, 109, 111, 176, 257–258, 266, 269; as language region, 146–148, 152–153, 244, 246–247, 252, 257–258; and skeptical criticism, 148, 153, 172, 317, 339; and morality, 149, 151, 266; and politics, 213, 244; and magic, 249–250, 260
*Remarks on the Foundations of Mathematics* (Wittgenstein), 26, 238–240
Representation: concept of, ix, 10, 20, 104, 299, 313, 315; language as a method of, 3, 116, 288, 296–298; political, 20, 217, 315
*Republic* (Plato), 169, 177, 216, 221, 302–307, 326
Responsibility, 109, 153, 204, 323; entailed by speech, 39, 67, 72, 88, 98, 179–180, 225, 227–228, 237, 261–263, 280–282, 329, 339; entailed by action, 89, 150, 157, 165, 204, 211–212, 242, 262–263, 266, 269, 271–273, 318, 323, 326–327, 333–335; entailed by position adopted, 152, 154, 156, 237
Revolution: scientific, 107, 112, 271; socio-political, 201–202, 206, 301, 316, 326, 337
Ricci, Luigi, 311–312
Rieff, Philip, xii
Rilke, Rainer Maria, 109
Roman law, 50–51, 53, 55
Rousseau, Jean-Jacques, 200, 203, 299, 326
Rules: and freedom, 3, 18, 195, 199–203, 213, 216; and regularities in language, 8, 15, 17–20, 29–30, **45–49**, 62, 80–81, 89–93, 117, 121, 135–136, 146, 194–196, 199–203, 222, 336; and statements, complementarity of, 18–19, 192, 199, 228–229; in games, **45–49**, 81, 135–136, 166, 188–189, 228–229, 237, 297; in mathematics, 45–49, 238–239; in philosophy, 45–49, 89–93, 117, 121; in common law, 51, 55–57, 60; in morality, 52–53, 55–57, 60, 149, 200; in science, 53–

54, 55–57, 60, 144, 291; and action, 160–161, 166, 213, 228–229, 242, 244, 258, 269; and judgment, 235, 237–238, 280
Russell, Bertrand, 8, 25, 143
Ryle, Gilbert, 5, 8, 140–141, 146

Sapir, Edward, 4, 102, 106, 112, 196
Sartre, Jean-Paul, 324, 332
Schaar, John H., xiii, 281, 283–284
Schutz, Alfred, 241, 244–245, 247, 252, 258, 274
Science: and common sense, 5, 20, 240, 318–320; and ordinary-language philosophy, 7–8, 11, 14–17, 179; and philosophy, 16–17, 20, 174, 192, 290–293, 297–298; and feeling, action, 22–23, 221, 242–246, 248–249, 252, 254, 261, 264, 266, 316–322; as language region, 41, 141–148, 152–153, 205–207, 216, 235–240, 247, 297; as activity, 50, 53–55, 60, 106–107, 111–112, 248–249, 271–272, 325; and world, 106–107, 111–112, 248–249, 319–320; and study of man, 221, 242–249, 252, 254, 261, 264, 266, 273–275, 280, ·316–322; explanation in 242–243, 252, 254, 264, 273
Searle, John, 226–227
Seeing: and philosophy, 1, 21, 182, 290, 294–298, 315, 319–320, 338; concept of, 101–102, 111–113, 115, 137, 182, 261, 290, 324; and the world, 107–108, 111–113, 115, 135, 140, 167, 191, 261, 319–320; and politics, 206, 216–217, 315, 326, 329
Self: and language, xi, 3, 44, 194–195, 199–200, 203; and philosophy, xi, 293–296, 299; and objectivity, 22–23, 286, 316, 321–322, 325–330, 336–339; and morality, 152, 154–156, 205, 208; knowledge of, 154–156, 206, 208, 294–296, 316, 326, 329–330, 332, 334, 336–339; consciousness of, 184, 294–296, 299, 316, 334; concept of, 194–195, 199–200, 203, 272; and alienation, 318, 321, 330, 332
Semantics, 80–81, 83–85
Sense: and meaning, **12n**, 28–29, **79–80**, 93, 289, 321, 336; making, **76–85**, 97–98, 190, 252, 271; action as having a, 242, 245
Signals, words as, 37, 57, 67, 69–70, 71–72, 84–85, 88, 93, 99, 131, 164–165, 167, 176, 179, 190, 227–228, 261, 270, 280, 282
Social Science: and language, 3–4, 7–8, 11, 14–17, 194–197, 275–286; and philosophy, 21–23, 169, 219, 253; and

action, 115, 157, 168, 171–172, **241–286**; and politics, 212, 214, 242–243; consequences of, 322–323, 339

Society, the social: philosophy and study of, xiii, 1, 4–5, 20–23, 99, 115, 157, 169, 287, 295, 313, 316, 326; imaginary, 40, 177, 302–305; inside and outside views, 179–180, 187, 190–192, 326–328; and individual, 193–195, 199–201, 203–204, 295; contractual, 198–200, 204, 299, 301; and political, 212–213; state of, in Machiavelli, 310–311; engineering, 321

Socrates: as philosopher, xi, 190–192; on knowledge, 85, 308; and Thrasymachus, **169–192**, 213–214, 219, 227, 261; on justice, **169–192**, 229, 302–308

Sorel, Georges, 328

Speech: ordinary, 5, 7, 92, 319, 325, 327; situation, 56–59, 71, 93, 95–96; with and without meaning, 67–69; elaboration of conduct through, 153–157, 165–167, 253; and politics, 300, 316, 323, 329–332, 335. *See also* Language as activity; Signals

Standards: of justice, 170, 176, 179–186, 189–192, 219; of judgment, 179–186, 189–192, 223, 234–240 *passim*, 283, 299–300, 327; socio-cultural, 189–192, 199, 202, 246, 283, 327; absolute, 237–240, 317, 334

State, the, 195, 201–202, 281–282, 303; in Machiavelli, 299, 308–312. *See also* Politics; Society

Statement. *See* Proposition

Stevenson, Charles L., 222

Strauss, Leo, 209, 241–243, 246, 252–253, 262, 285

Strawson, P. F., 136

Subjectivity: and pragmatics, 81–82; and world, 113, 335; and judgment, 150, 152, 178, 182–183, 220–223, 236–237; and politics, 208; and definition, 280; and self, 318. *See also* Objectivity; Self

Synonyms, 9–10, 12n, 13, 41, 73, 80, 99, 170, 175, 209

Syntactics, 80–81

Tautology, 29, 128

Taylor, Charles, 241

Taylor, Richard, 160, 241, 262, 265–266, 271

Technique: and philosophy, xiii, 5, 9, 14–21, 90, 301; of linguistic analysis, 9, 14–18, 301; speaking as, 36, 90; and scientific method, 53–54, 153,

205–207; and mathematics, 74, 145, 237–239; and measuring, 123; and social science, 243, 328; of power in Machiavelli, 308; and contemporary problems, 316–317, 319–320

Thrasymachus, **169–192**, 213–214, 219, 255, 261, 282

Time, 105–106, 108, 110, 292–294

Tools: words as, 36–37, 40, 42–43, 69, 91, 164; concept of, 262

*Tractatus Logico-Philosophicus* (Wittgenstein), 5, **25–30**, 42, 46, 63, 120, 221, 289, 336–337

Training, 39–49 *passim*, 50, 80

Translation: of Wittgenstein, difficulties in, vii, 84; analysis as, in *Tractatus*, 28–29, 42; language-learning as, 35; between language regions, 147–148, 159, 167, 241; radical, 176, 181–185, 224, 259–261; in study of political theory, 302, 306–313

Truth: and meaning in *Tractatus*, 28–30, 43, 97, 99, 120; and performatives, 37–39; and knowledge, 85–89, 98, 117; truthfulness and action, 88, 108, 149, 307, 322, 328–332, 355–337, 340; not reason for speaking, 96; and world, 101–102, 107, 124; and language regions, 141–143, 146, 152, 154, 205–206, 207, 236; concept of, 171, 220, 224; as basis for theory, 313–314. *See also* Falsification; Verification; World

Tussman, Joseph, 199, 205

Universals. *See* Essence

Understanding: a philosophy, theory, vii–viii, 314; as mental activity, 45–46, 49, 65–67, 70, 71–73, 131, 133, 163, 256, 262, 335; actions, persons, 245, 250–254, 261, 323–324; the world, 249, 292, 319. *See also* Explanation; Knowledge

Use. *See* Language games; Meaning; Signals

Value: and fact, 22, 29–30, 172, 178, **219–228**, 262, 302; judgments, 192, 219–222, 225, 231–235; in society, 201, 212, 334; and "value words," 221–224, 254, 262, 275; and commitment, 237, 253–254, 262–263, 334, 339; in social science, 253–254, 262–263, 274–286 *passim*

Verification, 142, 146, **231–240**. *See also* Falsification; Truth

Vienna Circle. *See* Positivism

Vinci, Leonardo da, 309

*Virtù*, 299, 308–312